Windows NT Server 4.0
for NetWare Administrators

Windows NT Server 4.0 for NetWare Administrators

Robert Bruce Thompson

O'REILLY™

Cambridge · Köln · Paris · Sebastopol · Tokyo

Windows NT Server 4.0 for NetWare Administrators
by Robert Bruce Thompson

Printed in the United States of America.

Editor: Robert Denn

Production Editor: Nancy Wolfe Kotary

Printing History:

October 1997: First Edition.

This book is printed on acid-free paper with 85% recycled content, 15% post-consumer waste. O'Reilly & Associates is committed to using paper with the highest recycled content available consistent with high quality.

ISBN: 1-56592-280-8

For my parents,

Lenore Fulkerson Thompson and William Ewing Thompson,

without whom I would not have been possible.

Table of Contents

Preface

You have a lot invested in Novell NetWare 3.1x—personally and professionally. You've read books, taken courses, attended seminars, subscribed to magazines—all of them devoted to increasing your knowledge of NetWare. You've spent nights and weekends solving problems and keeping your NetWare network humming. In the process, you've learned most of what there is to know about NetWare. You have your NetWare network tuned perfectly and running rock-solid. Maybe you've invested the time, effort, and money needed to pick up your CNE somewhere along the way. You can finally consider yourself a NetWare guru, or at least you're well on the way to becoming one.

Now, suddenly, all that seems to be threatened, and all because the new kid on the block—Microsoft Windows NT Server—is apparently all that anyone is talking about. Novell can't seem to market its way out of a paper bag, while Microsoft's marketing machine is in overdrive and seems to be doing everything right. Windows NT Server has "mind share" while the general industry perception seems to be that Novell is on a slippery downward slope.

For years, Microsoft struggled to create a network operating system that would be taken seriously as an alternative to NetWare. Their early attempt, LAN Manager, was a competent network operating system (NOS) for its time, but it sold in tiny numbers because of the overwhelming market dominance of NetWare. Microsoft's current effort, Windows NT Server, is likely to replace NetWare as the dominant PC LAN operating system, and Microsoft can thank Novell for this.

Don't get me wrong. In Windows NT Server 4.0, Microsoft has created a superb NOS. They have marketed it well, and taken all the other steps they could to ensure its success. But Windows NT Server still could not have become the runaway success that it is without the unwitting help of Novell. The success of

Windows NT Server really started with the ill-fated introduction of Novell NetWare 4.0. With NetWare 4.0, Novell made three major blunders.

First, in terms of product placement, Novell wanted NetWare 4.0 to be considered their "advanced" NOS. They introduced it at a significant price premium over NetWare 3.1x, which they continued to sell. Upgrades from 3.1x to 4.0 were expensive, and, accordingly, they sold in very small numbers. Even worse, because Novell failed to make a compelling case for NetWare 4.0, until recently most new NetWare sales continued to be NetWare 3.1x rather than the flagship NetWare 4.x product.

Second, Novell failed to understand the importance of the rapidly developing market for application servers and to capitalize upon that market. By integrating UnixWare for application services and NetWare 4.x for file and print services, Novell might have created an unbeatable one-two punch. Instead, they allowed UnixWare to slip away and continued to depend upon NetWare as an application server platform. Because NetWare was not (and is not) the best choice to run an application server, Novell ceded that important market to others—like Windows NT Server.

Third, and probably most important, although Novell presented NetWare 4.x as the logical follow-up to NetWare 3.1x, NetWare 4.x was not really just a simple upgrade. It was a completely new network operating system. Even expert NetWare 3.1x system administrators found NetWare 4.0 confusing. The conceptual framework differed from NetWare 3.1x, and few of their hard-won 3.1x skills transferred. Mistakes made in creating the NDS tree were difficult or impossible to correct without completely reinstalling the software.

Novell failed to sell the advantages—primarily NDS (originally NetWare Directory Services, now Novell Directory Services)—of NetWare 4.x over NetWare 3.1x. Many administrators came to believe that it would be just as easy to change to a different vendor's operating system as to upgrade to NetWare 4.0. As a result, a lot of evaluation copies of NetWare 4.0 were put on the shelf to gather dust, and most administrators decided just to stick with NetWare 3.1x. That's where many of them remain today.

Shops that have run NetWare exclusively for years now find Windows NT Server coming in the back door. If you aren't running at least one Windows NT Server box now, chances are you will be soon. Perhaps the Marketing folks want to bring up a web site with Internet Information Server running on Windows NT Server, or Sales wants Windows NT Server RAS to provide their traveling salespeople with dial-up networking. One way or another, there's a good chance you're going to have to cope with Windows NT Server, and it's likely to be sooner rather than later.

If you believe what some people say, the new-found dominance of Windows NT Server means that all of your hard-won NetWare skills will soon be obsolete. Wrong! Here's the truth. Most of what you know about NetWare can be applied directly to Windows NT Server. This book gives you a fast-start tool that will allow you to get up to speed with Windows NT Server based on what you already know about NetWare. Spend a week working with it—or even an intense weekend—and you're likely to become your company's Windows NT guru. The way things are heading, that's not a bad thing to be.

Scope of This Book

This book is divided into the following chapters.

Chapter 1, *Introduction to Windows NT Server*, provides a quick overview of the similarities and differences between Windows NT Server and Novell NetWare 3.1x. It focuses on the conceptual, architectural, and design similarities and differences between the two operating systems and on the network services provided by Windows NT Server that are not available or that are optional in NetWare. By providing a conceptual framework for understanding Windows NT Server, this chapter will help demystify Windows NT Server and eliminate its threatening "black box" aspect. After completing this chapter, you will be able to place Windows NT Server in context within your understanding of NetWare.

Chapter 2, *Introduction to Microsoft Networking*, examines fundamental Microsoft networking concepts and how they compare with similar concepts that form the basis of NetWare. It covers the basic Microsoft peer networking concepts which are central to understanding the Microsoft networking architecture. The chapter goes on to describe Microsoft server-based and enterprise networking concepts, including a detailed examination of Windows NT Server Domain Models and the place of domain controllers within each. After completing this chapter, you will understand fundamental Microsoft networking concepts in the context of your existing knowledge of Novell networking.

Chapter 3, *Configuring Windows NT Server Networking*, describes how to install and configure Windows NT Server. After completing this chapter, you will understand how to install and configure network adapters, protocols and services. At the conclusion of this chapter, if you are following each step on hardware of your own, you will see your system boot as a live Windows NT 4.0 server.

Chapter 4, *Managing Disk Storage with Windows NT*, begins by explaining the fundamentals of disk storage and the specifics of the file systems supported by Windows NT Server. It describes how to use Disk Administrator to configure and manage disk storage, prepare a raw hard disk drive, and create and format partitions. It then describes the concepts behind volume sets, mirror sets, and stripe sets, including their relation to traditional RAID levels, and provides detailed step-by-step instructions for creating and working with them. After completing this chapter, you will understand how to configure and manage disk storage in the Windows NT Server environment

Chapter 5, *Managing Users and Groups*, addresses all aspects of creating and maintaining user accounts and group accounts in a standalone server environment and in a domain-based enterprise environment. It describes the default users and groups that are created when you install Windows NT Server; explains how to use User Manager for Domains to create and maintain users and groups; examines user properties, profiles, and account restrictions; explains the concepts of local and global groups; covers using the User and Group Management Wizard; and concludes with a description of Windows NT Server policies and trust relationships. After completing this chapter, you will understand how to create, modify, delete, and otherwise manage user and group accounts.

Chapter 6, *Controlling Access to Volumes, Folders, and Files*, explores the tools provided by Windows NT Server for controlling user access to directories and files, contrasting them with those provided with NetWare. The chapter begins by explaining the concept of shares, and detailing how to create a share and control access to it. It touches on using the Managing File and Folder Access Wizard—a simplistic tool, but one you may nonetheless find useful. The chapter goes on to explain the concept of NTFS permissions at the file and directory level, and to detail how to create and modify them. It explores how permissions are inherited and contrasts this with the methods used by NetWare. The chapter closes with a discussion of replication, first explaining the concepts and then going on to detail how to set up a replication user, start the replication service, create and configure import and export directories, and so on. After finishing this chapter, you will understand everything needed to control which network disk resources can be accessed by each user or group.

Chapter 7, *Printing with Windows NT Server*, examines printing in the Windows NT Server environment. It begins with an overview of Windows NT printing concepts, describing the significant differences between the Windows NT printing environment and that of NetWare. It details how to plan the Windows NT Server printing environment, how to implement printing and how to manage it. It provides an overview of how Windows NT Server handles printing in a heterogeneous environment, including NetWare and UNIX, but defers some of the details on this subject to later chapters. After completing this chapter, you will understand how to set up and manage server-based and remote printing in the Windows NT Server environment.

Chapter 8, *Backing Up Windows NT Server*, explores backing up and restoring Windows NT Server. The chapter opens with an overview of some of the options in backup hardware for Windows NT Server, including QIC, Travan, DLT, and DAT/4mm/8mm tape drives. It then describes choosing network backup software. The chapter concludes with a description of how to develop and implement a network backup plan. After finishing this chapter, you will be prepared to establish and follow a plan for backing up your data.

Chapter 9, *Working with the Windows NT Registry*, explores the "black box" of the Windows NT Registry. The chapter begins with an overview of the Registry, describing what it is and how it is structured. It goes on to describe how to edit Registry values and how to backup the Registry. Next, it explains how to secure and audit the Registry. Finally, the chapter describes how to work with Registries on remote computers. After reading this chapter, you will have a basic understanding of what the Registry does, how to view and modify Registry entries, and how to use the tools available for the job.

Chapter 10, *Monitoring and Optimizing Server Performance*, provides an overview of the monitoring tools available with Windows NT Server. It begins by covering the use of Performance Monitor to detect hardware- and tuning-related performance bottlenecks, and advises you on how to cure the most common of these. It goes on to examine Windows NT events—what they are, how the recorded event data is structured, and how to view and archive logs. After reading this chapter, you will understand the monitoring tools supplied with Windows NT, and be able to use these tools to keep your server running smoothly.

Chapter 11, *Understanding TCP/IP*, introduces the essentials of TCP/IP for NetWare administrators who do not have a detailed understanding of TCP/IP. After completing this chapter, you will have a basic understanding of TCP/IP protocols and Internet addressing, and will have established a foundation for understanding the Microsoft TCP/IP products described in later chapters of this book.

Chapter 12, *Using Dynamic Host Configuration Protocol*, describes how to understand, install, configure, and use DHCP. Using DHCP allows you to automate many of the routine administrative tasks required to configure and manage a TCP/IP network. After completing this chapter, you will understand how to use Microsoft DHCP to configure and manage your TCP/IP network.

Chapter 13, *Using Windows Internet Naming Service*, describes how to understand, install, configure, and use WINS. WINS provides a centralized name resolution service in the Microsoft networking environment, and allows you to avoid using and maintaining individual configuration files for this purpose at each client. After completing this chapter, you will understand how to use Microsoft WINS to provide name resolution on your network.

Chapter 14, *Using Domain Name Service*, describes how to understand, install, configure, and use the Microsoft DNS service. Like WINS, DNS provides a centralized name resolution service, but for TCP/IP and the Internet. After completing this chapter, you will understand how to use Microsoft DNS to provide TCP/IP name resolution for your network, Intranet, and the Internet.

Chapter 15, *Using Remote Access Service*, covers installing and using Microsoft Remote Access Service (RAS). RAS provides your dial-up users with access to the same network services as those enjoyed by users connected to the LAN. RAS also provides a usable alternative for linking remote branch offices, using PPTP and the Internet to provide an inexpensive and secure connection. After finishing this chapter, you will understand the fundamentals of RAS, how to install and configure it, and how to use it.

Chapter 16, *Microsoft Tools for NetWare Integration*, provides an overview of the standard and optional tools available from Microsoft to ease integration of Windows NT Server into a Novell NetWare environment, and how these tools relate to each other. After finishing this chapter, you will understand which is the appropriate tool to use in each circumstance.

Chapter 17, *Building Clients for Mixed NetWare and Windows NT Server Environments*, focuses on client-side issues. Although Windows NT Server allows you to use your existing clients as is, you may well decide to update your client software to accommodate not only the mixed NetWare and Windows NT environment, but to provide TCP/IP connectivity for the Internet and intranets. After reading this chapter, you will understand how to configure Windows 95, Windows 3.11 for Workgroups, and Windows NT Workstation 4.0 as universal clients.

Chapter 18, *Using Gateway Service for NetWare*, explains how to understand, install, configure, and use the Gateway Service for NetWare (GSNW), a utility that is bundled with Windows NT Server 4.0. GSNW is installed on the system running Windows NT Server, and allows that machine to access shared disk and printer resources on NetWare servers. GSNW also allows the network administrator to create gateways that allow clients running only Microsoft networking client software to access these shared NetWare resources. After completing this chapter, you will understand when (and when not) to use GSNW, how to install and configure it, and how to build and manage gateways to shared NetWare file and print resources.

Chapter 19, *Using File and Print Services for NetWare*, describes the features of FPNW, how to install and configure it, and how to use it. FPNW is a Windows NT Server utility that is part of the optional Microsoft Services for NetWare. Installing FPNW on a Windows NT Server allows clients running only Novell client software to access shared file and printer resources on the Windows NT Server as though they were connecting to an actual NetWare 3.1x server. After completing this chapter, you will understand how to configure your Windows NT servers to be accessible by workstations that are running only NetWare client software.

Chapter 20, *Managing Servers in a Mixed NetWare and Windows NT Server Environment*, examines two aspects of managing servers in a multiple server environment. It first covers the features of Windows NT Server Manager and how to use it to manage computers and domains in a LAN with multiple Windows NT Servers. It then describes the optional utility Directory Service Manager for NetWare (DSMN). DSMN allows you to use Windows NT Directory Services to manage the binderies on multiple NetWare 3.12 servers. DSMN allows you to manage user accounts and similar information on Windows NT Server, and then proliferate the changes to your NetWare 3.12 servers. After completing this chapter, you will understand how to manage mixed servers, both on an ongoing basis and simply as a step in transitioning from NetWare to Windows NT.

Chapter 21, *Migrating to a Pure Windows NT Server Environment*, describes using the Migration Tool for NetWare (MTNW) to replicate data and account information from one or several NetWare servers to Windows NT Server. After completing this chapter, you will understand how to take the final step—moving everything to Windows NT Server and shutting down the old NetWare warhorses.

Appendix A, *Windows NT Server Resources*, lists my own favorite places to go when I need help with Windows NT Server. It's not an exhaustive list by any means, but it will at least get you started when you're ready to go beyond the material covered in this book.

Appendix B, *Using Norton Utilities 2.0 for Windows NT*, describes how to install, configure, and use Norton Utilities for Windows NT (NUNT). After Microsoft Services for NetWare, NUNT is probably the most important supplemental software you can add to your Windows NT servers. It fills a critical gap in Windows NT by providing the ability to retrieve files deleted by network users, and provides a disk defragmenting utility and other useful tools that aren't bundled with Windows NT Server. After reading this appendix, you will understand why installing NUNT is important and how to use it.

Conventions Used in This Book

The following conventions were used throughout this book to help you identify key concepts:

Italic
: Used for filenames, directory names, new terms, URLs, and hostnames

`Constant width`
: Used for NT commands and code examples

Boldface
: Used for GUI menu choices (**Start ➤ Admin Tools**)

Emailing Me

I get a lot of email in response to my books. Most of it is what you'd expect. The biggest category is the "how do I do such-and-such" questions. Some of these are very useful to me, because they point out areas that I should have covered better. Others are from people who are simply looking for free consulting. Still others—the most frustrating ones—are those that ask a question that was clearly answered in the book.

The next biggest category is general commentary—praise and criticism, factual corrections (everyone loves to catch an author with his pants down), explicit suggestions for additional coverage in areas I have glossed over or neglected entirely, and so on. I appreciate all of these comments. They help improve succeeding editions.

Time allowing, I try to respond meaningfully to every email message I receive from a reader. If you don't get an immediate response from me, please be patient. If I'm running on a tight deadline or otherwise fully occupied, I may respond with a boilerplate message to inform you that I received your message and will respond in more detail when I have time to do so.

Also, a standing joke among computer book authors is that readers think we've each written only one book. In the last year and a half, I've written or contributed material to half a dozen computer books. By the time you read this book, I'll probably have written at least one more. I constantly receive messages something like, "I don't understand what you mean in the third paragraph on page 237." Arrrgh. If you email me, please include the name of the book. You can reach me at: *thompson@oreilly.com*.

I recently heard an automated attendant message that foreshadows a real shift in the way things are being done, and not one for the better. "If you do not have a Touch-Tone® telephone, please hang up now and call back from a different telephone." Although I imagine that almost every reader of this book has Internet email, I didn't want to make the same mistake. If for some reason you don't have access to Internet email, you can write to me at the following address:

Robert Bruce Thompson
c/o O'Reilly & Associates, Inc.
101 Morris Street
Sebastopol, CA 95472-9902

You can send O'Reilly & Associates, Inc. email as well. To join the mailing list or request a catalog, send email to:

info@oreilly.com

To ask technical questions or comment on the book, send email to:

bookquestions@oreilly.com

Mistakes in This Book

There are mistakes in this book. I know it. I just don't know where they are. Some of them are here because I took someone else's word for something instead of verifying it personally. That's not sloppiness. That's just the reality of resolving complex issues in time to meet publishing deadlines. I think I make at least as much effort as any author—and more than most—to avoid this type of mistake.

Sometimes, arriving at a definitive answer to a seemingly simple question takes a lot of work. For example, I have read various books that comment on the default transport protocols that are installed when you install Windows NT Server. Some of them say that only IPX/SPX is installed. Others say only NetBEUI or only TCP/IP. Still others name various combinations. I've even seen statements in Microsoft publications that were at odds with each other.

Finally, I spent an entire day finding out the real answer. I tore down a server repeatedly and installed Windows NT Server to a freshly partitioned and formatted drive. I installed Windows NT Server with and without a NetWare server running on the network; with and without a TCP/IP host running on the network; and with and without a NetBEUI client active on the network. What I found was interesting. Windows NT Server installed the TCP/IP and NWLink (IPX/SPX) protocols no matter what. It also installed NetBEUI only if setup detected NetBEUI frames on the network.

Even after all this work, I can't be absolutely certain that I've arrived at a definitive answer. For example, each time I formatted the disk, I used NTFS. Perhaps if I'd used FAT instead, the protocols would have been different. Probably not, but I can't say for sure. For all I know, there may have been a few leftover TCP/IP packets lurking among the dust bunnies under my desk. I also can't be sure that the next update or Service Pack won't change this observed behavior. When you try to get definitive answers about something as complex as a network operating system, you're shooting at a moving target. Sometimes, you miss.

Another category of errors are those that occur because a fact that I "know" to be true turns out not to be. By definition, these are the hardest ones to catch. You can't question everything you think you know, at least not if you plan to ever finish the book.

This book has been checked exhaustively for errors. This process started while I was actually writing the book. If I even suspected that something I was stating as a fact was questionable, I took the time to verify it. The process continued during an informal technical edit pass. My friends and colleagues John Mikol and David Rowe, both of Walker and Associates, Inc., read many of the chapters, and each of them contributed valuable insights, comments, and corrections. Finally, O'Reilly and Associates, Inc. sent the manuscript to various industry experts for a formal technical review pass. Still, when all is said and done, it's inevitable that some errors remain, and each of them is solely my responsibility. If you find an error, or even what you think may be an error, please email me with the details. I'll make every attempt to verify it and let you know what I find. If appropriate, I'll include the fix in the next edition.

Of course, that doesn't do other readers any immediate good. Recognizing this problem, O'Reilly & Associates maintains an errata page for this book on their web site. As readers report errors to me, I'll do my best to resolve them, and post the results on the web site at *www.oreilly.com/catalog/netware/*.

Hardware and Software Used for This Book

When you're writing (or reading) a book like this, you don't do the work on a production network, at least not if you have any sense. Researching and writing such a book involves constantly installing and removing software—some of which may be in alpha or beta stages—and frequently tearing down and rebuilding the machines. Accordingly, I built a test-bed network to support my writing. The machines on this network are connected by 10Base2 (thin coax) Ethernet, and include:

Thoth
: A Gateway 2000 P5-133 Pentium tower with 64 MB of RAM, a 3 GB EIDE hard drive, and a Seagate TapeStor 8000 TR-4 tape drive. *Thoth* runs Windows NT Server 4.0 (Build 1381 with Service Pack 3 installed) as the Primary Domain Controller.

Kerby
: A Gateway 2000 P4D-66 tower with 48 MB of RAM and an 850 MB EIDE hard drive. *Kerby* runs Windows NT Server 4.0 (Build 1381 with Service Pack 3 installed) as a Backup Domain Controller and has the optional Microsoft Services for NetWare software installed.

Valentine
: A Gateway 2000 P4D-66 tower with 48 MB of RAM and an 850 MB EIDE hard drive. *Valentine* runs Windows NT Workstation 4.0 (Build 1381 with Service Pack 3 installed) as a network client.

Theodore

An old Gateway 386/33 with 16 MB of RAM and a 340 MB IDE hard drive. *Theodore* runs a free 2-user version of NetWare 3.12.

Mandy

A home-brew 486 DX2-80, with 32 MB RAM and a 1 GB EIDE hard drive. *Mandy* dual-boots the retail version of Windows 95 and Windows 3.11 for Workgroups.

Kiwi

A home-brew 486 DX2-66, with 8 MB of RAM and a 340 MB IDE hard drive. *Kiwi* runs BSD UNIX and Samba (an SMB service for UNIX), and serves both as a representative UNIX host for writing purposes and as a router for my Internet link.

NOTE I regularly receive queries about my machine names. All but one are named after members of my wife's collection of stuffed bears. In ancient Egypt, *Thoth* was the god of technical writing. I'm not making this up.

If you're smart, you'll take the same approach to learning Windows NT Server. You'll get much more out of this book if you actually do what it talks about, step-by-step, rather than just reading about it. A friend of mine, who is a developmental psychologist, tells me that play serves an essential purpose in children's learning and development. This is no less true in learning about a new network operating system. Spend some time playing with Windows NT Server. You'll learn a lot more, and you'll learn it a lot faster.

You need only four machines—and three will do in a pinch. They don't have to be high-end ones. Any old box capable of running NetWare 3.12 will do as your test NetWare server. You also need at least one computer running your typical client software. Finally, you need two computers to run Windows NT Server. These can be as little as a couple of 486's with 24 MB or 32 MB of RAM. You can get by with only one Windows NT server if absolutely necessary, but by doing so you give up some ability to work with domain-related issues.

Chances are you'll be able to scrounge these resources from stuff floating around the office. You may even have what you need at home. In fact, this may be just the excuse you need to buy that new computer you've been lusting after, but that your spouse keeps frowning at—"but, honey, I **need** this new computer for career development and job security ..."It works. I know. I do it. Fortunately, my wife never reads my books.

I'd also like to thank the production staff of O'Reilly & Associates. Nancy Wolfe Kotary was the production editor and project manager. Robert Romano somehow managed to turn my chicken scratches into attractive, information-rich graphics. Ellie Fountain Maden performed the quality control check. Production services, indexing, and typesetting were provided by PageMasters, Inc.

Most of all, I'd like to thank my editor. Robert Denn is the best editor an author could want. Robert actively participated in structuring and developing the content of this book. He patiently answered a lot of my questions, made valuable technical suggestions, caught potentially embarrassing mistakes, and kept things moving. His efforts made this book much better than it otherwise could have been.

Enough talk. Let's get started with Windows NT Server.

In this chapter:
- *Windows NT Server Versus NetWare*
- *Windows NT Server Specifics*
- *Windows NT Server NetWare Integration Tools*
- *Windows NT Server Extras*

1

Introduction to Windows NT Server

When I was 18 years old, I had 20/10 vision and the reflexes of a fighter pilot. I thought nothing of playing five sets of serve-and-volley tennis at high noon in August. Now that I'm forty-something, I need glasses to drive, have the reflexes of a three-toed sloth, and get tired just watching the Wimbledon finals on television. NetWare 3.12 is in a similar state of decline.

Unlike me, NetWare 3.12 has at least aged somewhat gracefully. It can still do everything it once did as well as ever. The problem is, the world moved on while NetWare 3.12 stood still. In its time, NetWare 3.12 was a superb network operating system (NOS). Unfortunately, that time is long passed. By today's standards, NetWare 3.12 just doesn't do very much. Although it still provides top-notch file and print services, various past decisions by Novell—architectural and marketing—make it a less than ideal choice in today's server environment.

Today, network administrators want their file servers to do double duty as application servers. NetWare 3.12 is one of the worst possible choices for this task. They also want an NOS that supports a broad variety of protocols, so that it can fit in easily with the heterogeneous internetworks that are becoming increasingly common. Again, NetWare 3.12 fails. It'll speak anything you want, as long as it's IPX. Full support for the Internet goes almost without saying. NetWare comes up short here, too. It offers only grudging support for TCP/IP—even that is optional—and provides no Internet applications. In short, NetWare 3.12 can no longer be taken seriously as an NOS for the enterprise.

As bad as NetWare 3.12 is at providing the essential components of a modern NOS, it's even worse when it comes to the "nice to have" features. Centralized administration of multiple servers using graphical utilities is taken almost for granted nowadays. NetWare 3.12 offers only character mode utilities and requires that you manage each server individually—thank you very much. Many administrators would like to relocate system service applications—DHCP servers, DNS servers, mail servers, and the like—from the UNIX boxes that have always run them to their main servers. NetWare 3.12 won't let you do that.

Let me hasten to say that none of this is Novell's fault. For years now, they have been marketing a perfectly fine, modern NOS called NetWare 4.x (latterly, IntraNetWare). NetWare 4.x addresses all but one of the failings of NetWare 3.12, that being that NetWare 4.x is still not the best choice as an application server platform. NetWare 4.x has so many strengths and so few weaknesses, in fact, that it's easy to make a strong case for NetWare 4.x as the best NOS now on the market.

The trouble is, NetWare 4.x isn't just a simple version upgrade of NetWare 3.12—it's really a whole new operating system. If you decide to upgrade from NetWare 3.12 to NetWare 4.1, many of your hard-won skills go for naught. The Supervisor isn't even called that anymore. The most fundamental concepts differ. An acquaintance of mine, a CNE of long standing, attempted to upgrade to NetWare 4.0 shortly after it was released. After several hours of fruitless thrashing, he pretty much summed up the problem when he asked me, "What the hell is a container, anyway, and why is it full of branches and leaves?" NetWare 4.x boggles most NetWare 3.x administrators. It's as simple as that.

By failing to provide an easy upgrade path from NetWare 3.1x to NetWare 4.x, Novell left the door ajar. Microsoft happened along with Windows NT Server and kicked it off the hinges. Microsoft decided that if an administrator had to learn a whole new operating system anyway, it might just as well be Windows NT Server as NetWare 4.x. Thousands of administrators apparently agree, as a look at the market share statistics quickly confirms.

Ironically, most NetWare 2.x and 3.x administrators I know that have made both transitions find that Windows NT Server is easier to grasp than NetWare 4.x. Simply stated, Microsoft makes it easier to upgrade from NetWare 3.12 to Windows NT Server than Novell makes it to upgrade from NetWare 3.12 to NetWare 4.x. If you know that it's time to make a change, but you're concerned about how your existing NetWare skills will transfer, then Windows NT Server is probably your best choice.

NOTE If you have hundreds of servers and thousands of workstations deployed in scores of locations in an enterprise environment, take this book back and get a refund. For an internetwork of this scale, you need NetWare 4.x. In particular, you need Novell Directory Services (NDS).

The sole weakness of Windows NT Server relative to NetWare 4.x is that Windows NT Server does not have a true directory service, but instead depends on a domain-based schema. Microsoft desperately wants decision makers to regard Windows NT Server as an enterprise NOS. They maintain that domains accomplish much the same thing as NDS. They're both right and wrong.

For medium-scale networks—up to perhaps 25 servers and a few hundred workstations at a dozen or so sites—a properly configured Windows NT Server domain structure will probably work about as well for you as NDS. If you go much beyond this scale, however, the proliferation of complex domain relationships may rapidly make your life miserable. Significantly, one of the major upgrades planned for Windows NT Server 5.0 is the implementation of a true directory service.

This chapter begins with a differential look at Windows NT Server versus NetWare 3.12. Later sections describe the fundamentals of Windows NT Server in more detail, followed by an overview of the NetWare integration options available for Windows NT Server. The chapter concludes with brief descriptions of the various network services provided by Windows NT Server that have no equivalent in NetWare 3.12.

Windows NT Server Versus NetWare

First things first. If you're like most NetWare administrators, the most important question you have about Windows NT Server is how it handles clients. Are you going to have to visit every single one of your NetWare clients and update its software to use Windows NT Server? The short answer is no. Windows NT Server can provide full access to NetWare clients using only their existing client software. Chapter 17, *Building Clients for Mixed NetWare and Windows NT Server Environments*, and Chapter 19, *Using File and Print Services for NetWare*, detail how this works.

That aside, one of the first things you probably want to find out is how Windows NT Server differs from NetWare. The following sections detail these differences.

Comparative Core Feature Sets and Capacities

A principle familiar to any architect or designer says that form follows function. That is, the appearance and other characteristics of an object are often determined largely by what that object was designed to do. If you examine two similar objects from different manufacturers, you almost always find that, although they may differ in minor details, their overall appearance and function is similar. This is true for objects as diverse as hammers, pistols, bulldozers, cars, umbrellas, or belts. The similarities are mandated by the job at hand—driving nails, propelling bullets, moving earth, transporting people, keeping the rain off, or holding up your pants. The differences take a back seat to the similarities.

Network operating systems are also subject to this principle. Much of what a network operating system does is fundamental. If it doesn't do at least a certain minimum—sharing files and printers, controlling access to resources, maintaining user accounts, and so forth—it isn't a network operating system. Just as some cars have more or better features than others, some network operating systems are more feature laden than others.

At first glance, it would be hard to imagine two network operating systems that were less similar than NetWare 3.12 and Windows NT Server 4.0. And, while there are significant differences both "under the hood" and in the user interfaces, when you dig a little deeper you find that the similarities are more profound. It's true that Windows NT Server does more than NetWare 3.12, but their core functions are remarkably similar at least in purpose, if not always in implementation. Just think of NetWare as the 1914 Model T, with everything manual, and Windows NT Server as the 1997 Rolls-Royce, with automatic everything.

Rather than focusing on what NetWare 3.12 and Windows NT Server have in common, the following sections focus on their differences. For brevity, I've used tables to highlight these differences, and, where necessary, included brief textual descriptions for further explanation. If you don't see a particular feature mentioned, it's safe to assume that both operating systems support that feature. There may be minor differences in the way the feature is implemented, but the real-world result is the same.

Interface

Let's get the most obvious difference out of the way first. NetWare uses character-mode graphics and command-line utilities for everything. As a quick flip through this book will show, Windows NT Server 4.0 uses graphic utilities that follow the familiar Windows 95 interface conventions. However, Windows NT Server doesn't limit you to using the GUI. Essentially, everything you can accomplish from a GUI utility can be done from the command line, and *vice versa*. I don't spend a lot of time on the command-line utilities, simply because it almost never makes sense to use them. Only in very specialized circumstances, e.g., adding a large number of users very quickly, does it make sense to go with the command-line option.

Architecture

At this point in most Windows NT books, you'd find a detailed description of the low-level architecture of Windows NT Server, with pretty graphics describing how all the pieces fit together. I am assuming that you probably don't care much about the nuts-and-bolts details of network operating system architecture. Frankly, I don't either, except to the extent that those details affect routine use of the operating system.

Of the differences shown in Table 1-1, the most important is that Windows NT Server uses preemptive multitasking, while NetWare 3.12 depends on cooperative multitasking similar to that used by Windows 3.1x. This means that a poorly written NetWare NLM can crash the entire server, while in Windows NT Server, an equivalent problem may cause the application to terminate, but leaves the server running and stable.

Another important difference is that NetWare 3.12 is limited to using a single processor, while Windows NT Server 4.0 has standard support for up to 4 processors, and optional support for up to 32 processors. Many servers today don't support more than four processors, and even those that do only provide rapidly diminishing returns as the number of processors grows beyond four. Windows NT Server 5.0 will supposedly scale efficiently to eight processors, but for now consider four processors as a realistic maximum. Even this minimal support for symmetric multiprocessing provides significant scalability advantages for Windows NT Server.

Microsoft initially trumpeted the availability of Windows NT Server on multiple platforms as an important step toward vendor independence. In fact, this advantage is largely illusory. Microsoft apparently recognizes this. They discontinued the MIPS version of Windows NT Server in late 1996, announcing that they sold only one copy for this platform. In early 1997, they announced that they would no longer support the PowerPC platform, leaving Intel and the Digital Equipment Corporation (DEC) Alpha as the only two supported processors.

Table 1-1. Architectural Differences Between Windows NT Server 4.0 and NetWare 3.12

	Windows NT Server 4.0	NetWare 3.12
Preemptive multitasking	■	❏
Processor types	Alpha, Intel, MIPS, PPC	Intel
Symmetric multiprocessing	■	❏

Table 1-1. Architectural Differences Between Windows NT Server 4.0 and NetWare 3.12 (continued)

	Windows NT Server 4.0	NetWare 3.12
Microkernel architecture	■	❑
Paged virtual memory	■	❑
Dynamic memory cache	■	❑
Memory protection for applications	■	❑
Structured exception handling	■	❑
Hardware abstraction layer	■	❑
Unicode support integral to operating system	■	❑

Capacities

One of the most noticeable differences between NetWare 3.12 and Windows NT Server is the great disparity in the various capacities of these two systems, shown in Table 1-2. At first glance, these differences may appear to be significant, but when you think about it, they usually aren't. Your Ferrari may have a top end of 250 MPH, but in the real-world of 55 MPH speed limits, a Ford Taurus gets you from Point A to Point B in about the same amount of time.

For example, NetWare 3.12 permits a maximum file size of "only" 4 GB, while Windows NT Server permits files of up to 17 billion GB, or about four billion times larger. Most people don't have files anywhere near the 4 GB NetWare limit. If you do have such files, the greater capacity of Windows NT Server may be significant. Otherwise, don't worry too much about the capacity differences between NetWare 3.12 and Windows NT Server.

One major capacity difference between the two operating systems has to do with the way NetWare 3.12 and Windows NT Server handle caching. On a NetWare 3.12 server, the amount of memory required is very tightly linked to the amount of disk space the server supports. If you don't have enough RAM, the disk simply won't mount. Windows NT Server has no such link between RAM and disk space. It can support essentially any amount of disk with any amount of RAM, although adding RAM will always increase disk performance.

What this means in the real world is that you may not be able to install a large amount of disk in your NetWare server, simply because it cannot accommodate enough RAM, or because you can't afford the amount of RAM that NetWare requires. In a world where 10 GB disks are commonplace, and 25 GB disks are available, Windows NT Server has a tangible advantage in supporting large disk farms.

NOTE Computers are gradually getting us involved with ever-increasing powers of ten. Since the names and abbreviations for some of these large powers of ten may be unfamiliar to some readers, we'll depart from the known point of a gigabyte (GB):

1 Terabyte (TB) equals 1,024 GB (or a million megabytes)

1 Petabyte (PB) equals 1,024 TB (or a million GB)

1 Exabyte (EB) equals 1,024 PB (or a million TB)

1 Zettabyte (ZB) equals 1,024 EB (or a million PB)

1 Yottabyte (YB) equals 1,024 ZB (or a million EB)

To put this in perspective, the largest current disk farms store something in the single-digit or low double-digit Terabyte range. A few TB would store the contents of a typical academic library. One PB would allow you to digitize and store every movie ever made and every piece of music ever recorded. The larger prefixes describe amounts of storage beyond human imagination.

Table 1-2. Comparative Capacities of Windows NT Server 4.0 and NetWare 3.12

	Windows NT Server 4.0	**NetWare 3.12**
Maximum concurrent users	No limit	250
RAM: minimum required/maximum supported	16 MB / 4 GB	4 MB / 4 GB
Total disk storage supported	408 EB	32 TB
Maximum file size	16 EB	4 GB
Maximum partition size	16 PB	Drive size
Maximum volume size	16 PB	32 TB
Volumes per server	25	64
Disk drives per server	Hardware limit	1,024
Maximum simultaneous file opens	No limit	100,000
Maximum simultaneous file locks	No limit	100,000

Filesystem

NetWare 3.12 uses a highly modified version of the ancient DOS FAT filesystem, which it designates the *Universal File System*. Windows NT Server uses a modern purpose-built filesystem called NTFS. NTFS is the hands-down winner. Table 1-3 shows some of the reasons why.

One of the most important advantages of NTFS relative to the NetWare filesystem is that NTFS is transaction-based. This means that, if a crash occurs, NTFS is able to roll back the state of the disk to what it was before the crash. NetWare can't.

Here's an example of the differences. I was writing another chapter during a thunderstorm. One of my Border Collies, who is terrified of thunder, forced his way under my desk and managed to pull all of the power cords out of the UPS, bringing my Windows NT Server, my NetWare 3.12 server, and my BSD UNIX box to abrupt halts.

The Windows NT server was very busy at the time, with several applications running, using about 300 active threads. The BSD UNIX box was busy processing mail. The NetWare server was just sitting there not doing much of anything. When I fired up the BSD UNIX box, it ran *fsck* and recovered without error. When I started Windows NT Server, I again found that nothing had been lost. When I started the NetWare server, the *SYS* volume refused to mount. I ran *VREPAIR*, which located 102,000 (!) errors. I ended up running *FDISK* on the *SYS* volume and reinstalling NetWare. NTFS is bullet-proof. In comparison, the NetWare filesystem is relatively fragile.

Another filesystem difference that may or may not be important to you is that Windows NT Server 4.0 supports dynamic compression of volumes, folders, and individual files, while NetWare 3.12 does not. Disk space is cheap, and using compression can reduce performance, so you may decide that the game isn't worth the candle. Even so, it's nice to have the option.

One filesystem aspect that affects anyone is the difference in how NetWare 3.12 and Windows NT Server allocate disk space to files. NetWare assigns disk space in clusters, which can vary in size from 4 KB to 64 KB, depending upon the size of the volume and other factors. Each file is assigned at least one cluster. Files larger than a single cluster are assigned additional clusters. Any space within a cluster that is not used by the file is wasted. This means that, on average, each file stored on your NetWare volume wastes half a cluster. On a big NetWare volume that uses large clusters, you can easily lose a gigabyte or more to slack. Windows NT Server can use fixed 512 byte clusters—or one sector per cluster—so you lose an average of only 256 bytes to slack per file. This means that a typical NTFS volume loses only a few megabytes to slack, even on a very large volume with many files.

One place where NetWare has an advantage is in its ability to restrict users to a particular amount of disk space on a volume, a feature for which Windows NT Server has no native equivalent. Disk quotas were an important feature to some administrators back when disk space cost $2.50 per megabyte. Now that disks costs ten or twenty cents per megabyte, restricting users usually makes little sense. If you need to enforce disk quotas under Windows NT Server, various third party utilities are available that allow you to do so. I have not used any of them myself, so I cannot recommend specific products. However, an AltaVista search for *+NT +"disk quota"* will quickly show you the available alternatives.

NetWare offers another advantage if your network requires NFS support. Although NFS is not a standard feature with NetWare 3.12, it is at least available from Novell at an extra cost. Microsoft offers no support in Windows NT Server for NFS, optional or otherwise. You can, however, purchase NFS for Windows NT Server 4.0 from third parties.

Table 1-3. Filesystem Characteristics of Windows NT Server 4.0 and NetWare 3.12

	Windows NT Server 4.0	NetWare 3.12
Transaction based filesystem	■	❑
File compression	■	❑
Disk quotas	❑	■
Asynchronous I/O	■	❑
Memory mapped file I/O	■	❑
Cluster size	512 bytes	4 KB–64 KB
Long filename support	■	Via OS2.NAM
DOS (FAT)/OS/2 (HPFS) support	■/■[a]	■/■
NFS/Macintosh support	❑/■	■[b]/■

[a] Previous versions of Windows NT server provided full HPFS support. Windows NT Server 4.0 can read HPFS volumes, but not write to them.
[b] NFS support for NetWare 3.12 is an extra-cost option.

Protocols

Shared protocols are the foundation of interoperability. Accordingly, I've made an exception in Table 1-4 by listing all of the major core, transport, and IPC protocols supported by both operating systems. From the standpoint of integrating Windows NT Server into a NetWare environment, the two most important of these are clearly the NetWare Core Protocol and the IPX/SPX transport protocol, both of which are fully supported by Windows NT Server. In essence, Windows NT Server supports every major protocol used by NetWare, and also supports its own native protocols, providing all of the low-level "plumbing" you need to integrate the two operating systems.

Table 1-4. Protocols Supported by Windows NT Server 4.0 and NetWare 3.12

	Windows NT Server 4.0	NetWare 3.12
Core Protocols		
NetWare Core Protocol (NCP)	■[a]	■
Server Message Block (SMB)	■	❑
Transport Protocols and Routing		
Appletalk	■	■[b]
DECNet	■	❑

Table 1-4. Protocols Supported by Windows NT Server 4.0 and NetWare 3.12 (continued)

	Windows NT Server 4.0	NetWare 3.12
DLC	■	■
IPX	■	■
IPX (dialup)	■	■
Large Internet Packet (LIP)	■	■
NetBEUI	■	❑
OSI	■	■
Packet burst	■	■
TCP/IP (native/tunneled)	■/❑	❑/■
Internal Routing (TCP/IP / IPX)	■/■	❑/■
IPC		
Asynchronous Procedure Calls	■	❑
DCE-compatible Remote Procedure Calls (RPC)	■	❑
Local Procedure Call	■	❑
LU 6.2, LU0, LU1, LU2, LU3	■[c]	■[d]
Mutexes	■	❑
Named Pipes—Client/Server	■/■	■/❑
Semaphores	■	❑
Timers	■	❑
Transport Library Interface (TLI)	■	❑

[a] Windows NT Server supports NCP via the bundled Gateway Service for NetWare (GSNW), and via the optional File and Print Services for NetWare (FPNW) component of Microsoft Services for NetWare.
[b] NetWare 3.12 bundles support for five Macintosh users. Full support for additional users requires purchasing optional software.
[c] Requires Microsoft SNA Server.
[d] Requires Novell NetWare SAA.

Fault tolerance

NetWare 3.12 and Windows NT Server 4.0 differ significantly in fault tolerance features. The truth is that for many administrators, NetWare will hold the perceived edge in fault tolerance.

At the low end, how many times in the last month have you used *SALVAGE* to recover a file that was accidentally deleted by a user? Imagine living without that capability. Windows NT Server allows you to undelete files from the Recycling Bin, but only if those files were deleted from the console. When a user connected across the network deletes a file, that file is gone forever. Various third-party utilities are available to improve this situation, but only one of them that I've seen holds a candle to the NetWare *SALVAGE* utility.

That exception is the Norton Utilities 2.0 for Windows NT (NUNT), which is described in Appendix B. The Norton Protection/Unerase feature allows an administrator working at the Windows NT Server console to retrieve any file that has been deleted from a local disk, whether that file was deleted locally or by a user connecting across the network. Unlike *SALVAGE*, however, NUNT does not allow users to retrieve their own files from client workstations. Still, NUNT fills a gaping hole, and should be installed on any computer running Windows NT Server.

At the high end, Windows NT Server 4.0 currently has nothing to compete with SFT III server mirroring, although third-party alternatives are available, notably Octopus. Again, I have not used any of these products myself, and cannot recommend a specific product. In any event, the long-term viability of this market niche is in doubt, with Microsoft having announced plans to implement native server mirroring in a future release.

Actually, SFT III isn't the panacea that many administrators believe it to be. It's true that SFT III protects you by failing over to the backup server if the main server experiences a hardware problem. If your power supply dies or your processor smokes, SFT III will keep the network up and running.

However, hardware problems are both less common and more easily protected against than software problems. Most modern servers have a UPS, ECC memory, RAID disk subsystems, and so forth, to protect against common hardware failures. Software problems are a much more common cause of NetWare server crashes, and are much more difficult to protect against. If your main server crashes because of an NLM conflict, the backup server is going to crash about a microsecond later. Using SFT III requires that you duplicate your main server in nearly every respect, which is not inexpensive. To add insult to injury, that expensive backup server just sits there contributing nothing to the cause unless the main server fails. That's a pretty expensive insurance policy, especially given the limited protection it confers. So much for SFT III.

Microsoft plans to trump Novell's SFT III ace in the near future, however, by implementing server clustering. Clustering goes a step further than mirroring, by allowing every server that participates in the cluster to provide services full time. For example, if you have five servers in a cluster, you can routinely use the resources of all five. If one server fails, all network services continue to be available, although performance will degrade proportionately.

One aspect of fault tolerance where Windows NT Server 4.0 holds a clear lead is in disk redundancy. Like NetWare 3.12, Windows NT Server supports disk mirroring and duplexing in software. Windows NT Server goes beyond this, however, to provide a software RAID 5 implementation, which Microsoft calls Disk Striping with Parity. Although it offers lower performance and less convenience than most hardware RAID 5 implementations, Disk Striping with Parity provides all of the security you'd expect from RAID 5. It is a perfectly adequate solution for small servers, most of which would otherwise have no RAID at all.

Table 1-5. Differences in Fault Tolerant Features Supported by Windows NT Server 4.0 and NetWare 3.12

	Windows NT Server 4.0	NetWare 3.12
Automatic file replication	■	❏
Filesystem recovery log	■	❏
Hot fix sector sparing (dynamic/static allocation)	■/❏	❏/■
RAID 5 Stripe Sets with Parity	■	❏
Salvage (undelete)	❏	■
Server job scheduling	■	❏
Server mirroring	❏	■

System security

Windows NT Server wins this one hands-down, as Table 1-6 shows. Although Microsoft is careful not to claim C2 certification for their product, they do rightly state that it was designed to be compliant with C2 requirements. The truth is, if you take care to configure them properly and physically protect the server from unauthorized access, either product offers about the same real-world level of security, which is reasonably high.

Conversely, someone who knows what he is doing, has the proper tools, and has physical access to the server can seriously compromise either operating system. With NetWare 3.12, the required tools can be as simple as a DOS boot floppy and a copy of the Norton Utilities. With only these tools, the cracker can read and alter files with a disk editor, or, if he's in a particularly destructive mood, he can destroy the entire volume.

NOTE A cracking NLM that used to be widely available on the Internet, but now seems to have largely disappeared, allows an intruder to gain Supervisor access to the server, make changes, and then disappear almost undetectably. Please don't bother asking me for a copy of this NLM. The only valid purpose it serves is to allow an administrator who has somehow lost the Supervisor password to gain access, and Novell can fix that problem if it happens to you. I won't discuss it further with anyone, let alone provide a copy.

With Windows NT Server, the situation is somewhat better. At least one utility that is readily available on the Internet allows an intruder read NTFS data freely. Writing data to an NTFS volume is a different story. I don't know how to do it, which is not to say that it cannot be done.

Table 1-6. Differences Between System Security Features Supported by Windows NT Server 4.0 and NetWare 3.12

	Windows NT Server 4.0	NetWare 3.12
Audit security policy changes	■	❑
Audit server shutdown/restart	■/■	❑/❑
C2 Security compliant design (Red/Orange)	■/■	❑/❑
C2 Certification	❑	❑
Limit concurrent connections	❑	■
Replaceable client logon	■	❑
Security event alerts/auditing	■/■	❑/❑
Single, secure logon to network/applications	■/■	❑/❑

Printing

NetWare 3.12 and Windows NT Server provide similar support for printing, although it is implemented differently. Table 1-7 lists the main differences in printing support for the two operating systems. In reality, on most networks, either product will probably do the job.

On the plus side of the ledger for NetWare is that it supports forms-based printing, which Windows NT Server does not. NetWare also allows you to specify a notify list for printer errors, a capability lacking in Windows NT Server. Windows NT Server, on the other hand, has the advantage of supporting UNIX printing at no extra cost, and of supporting peer-based print services.

Table 1-7. Differences Between Printing Features Supported by Windows NT Server 4.0 and NetWare 3.12

	Windows NT Server 4.0	NetWare 3.12
Forms support	❑	■
Peer print services	■	❑
Printers per server	No limit	16
Specify user to be notified on print error	❑	■
UNIX printing support	■	■[a]

[a] Extra cost option

Licensing Issues and Costs

In most networks, the cost of the network operating system software itself is a fairly minor component of the total cost. Still, it's nice to know that for most configurations Windows NT Server is less expensive than NetWare 3.12. For some network configurations—particularly those with many servers, each of which is accessed by many clients—Windows NT Server can be dramatically less expensive.

NetWare 3.12 has always been a cash cow for Novell. When NetWare 4.0 was first introduced, it was positioned as Novell's premium NOS, and was sold at a correspondingly higher price. Buyers stayed away in droves. Eventually, Novell decided that it was shooting itself in the foot by discouraging people from buying NetWare 4.0, so they began selling the two versions at the same price.

Lately, the screw has turned further. A quick check of the mail order places shows that NetWare 3.12 is now selling at a significantly higher price than NetWare 4.x. In addition, licensing changes that benefit the customer—like additive licensing—are offered only for NetWare 4.x. Novell really wants you to migrate to NetWare 4.x, although doing so is not inexpensive. If you insist on sticking with NetWare 3.12 for your current servers and installing it on your new servers, you'll pay a price for doing so.

If you are installing a new network, the costs of NetWare 3.12, NetWare 4.x, and Windows NT Server 4.0 are roughly comparable if the network is small—a single server and a few workstations. As the number of workstations increases—and particularly as you add multiple servers—Windows NT Server rapidly becomes the less expensive alternative. Table 1-8 shows the approximate licensing costs for networks of various typical configurations. These costs are based on a quick survey of mail order prices as of July 1997. I didn't go to any great lengths to find the absolute lowest prices for any of the products, but the prices in the table are representative.

Table 1-8. Approximate Licensing Costs for New Networks of Various Configurations

Configuration	NetWare 3.12	NetWare 4.x	Windows NT Server 4.0
1 Server + 5 clients	$650	$600	$650
1 Server + 25 clients	$2,350	$2,300	$1,250
1 Server + 50 clients	$3,250	$3,000	$2,000
1 Server + 100 clients	$4,500	$4,250	$3,500
3 Servers + 100 clients	$13,500	$12,750	$4,400
10 Servers + 250 clients	$90,000	$78,000	$12,500

If you are considering upgrading an existing NetWare 3.12 network to either NetWare 4.x or Windows NT Server 4.0, you will find that the costs are relatively similar, as long as there is only one server involved. If the existing network has multiple servers, Windows NT Server rapidly becomes the less expensive alternative, unless you can consolidate multiple NetWare 3.12 servers to a single NetWare 4.x server. Table 1-9 shows the approximate licensing costs for networks of various typical configurations. Again, these costs are quick-and-dirty real-world costs as of July 1997, but they are representative of the actual costs you will probably incur.

Table 1-9. Approximate Licensing Costs for Upgrading NetWare 3.12 Networks of Various Configurations to NetWare 4.x Versus Windows NT Server 4.0

Configuration	to NetWare 4.x	to Windows NT Server 4.0
1 Server + 5 clients	$325	$350
1 Server + 25 clients	$1,000	$650
1 Server + 50 clients	$1,300	$1,050
1 Server + 100 clients	$1,900	$1,850
3 Servers + 100 clients	$5,700	$2,350
10 Servers + 250 clients	$33,000	$6,500

Windows NT Server offers two client licensing options. For either option, you first purchase an individual server license for each computer that will run Windows NT Server. That takes care of licensing the actual server, but does not provide any client access licenses. For client licenses, you can select one of two choices:

- *Per-server licensing* works almost exactly like NetWare 3.12 licensing. You decide how many concurrent users you want the server to support, and buy that many licenses. Any client can access the server, as long as the number of concurrent users has not been exceeded. If, for example, you have 100 workstations and purchase only a 50 user per-server license, any 50 of those 100 workstations may be logged on concurrently. The fifty-first user who attempts to log on will be refused access. The administrator can always log on to resolve problems, even when the number of current users equals the license count. If you add a second Windows NT server, you must purchase additional per-server licenses, duplicating those you purchased for the first server.
- *Per-seat licensing* requires you to buy a client access license for each workstation that is connected to the network and able to access the server. If, for example, you have 100 workstations connected to the network, you must buy 100 client access licenses, even if no more than 50 of those workstations will ever be logged in to the server at the same time. Each workstation with a per-seat license can, however, access any number of Windows NT servers using that single license.

Per-server licensing is usually the best choice for small networks, when you are first getting started, or when you have a relatively large number of clients who will connect infrequently and for short periods of time to the Windows NT server. As long as you have only one Windows NT server, per-server licensing provides the flexibility of allowing any client to log onto the server, within the concurrent license limitation.

There is one significant difference between NetWare 3.12 concurrent user licensing and Windows NT Server per-server licensing. Although Novell has adopted the concept of additive licensing for NetWare 4.x—probably due to pressure from Windows NT Server—NetWare 3.12 still requires you to purchase licenses in large chunks. For example, if you are running a 100-user copy of NetWare 3.12 and need to add the just one more user, your only option is to upgrade the 100-user license to a 250-user license. If the same situation occurs on a Windows NT server, you can simply buy a single license (or a 5-user license pack) to expand your total to 101 or 105 concurrent users.

Per-seat licensing begins to come into its own when you have more than one Windows NT server, or when many clients will connect frequently and for long periods of time to the Windows NT server. Consider, for example, a LAN with 5 Windows NT servers and 100 workstations. If you choose per-server licensing in this environment, you will have to buy 5 server licenses and 500 client access licenses—100 for each server. If instead you use per-seat licensing, you will still have to buy 5 server licenses, but only 100 client access licenses. Each of the 100 clients can use its individual per-seat license to access all 5 servers.

NOTE This type of situation is where NetWare 3.12 concurrent licensing really operates to the detriment of the user, and Windows NT per-seat licensing pays off big time. With 5 servers and 101 users, all of whom require access to all 5 servers, you would have to buy 5 250-user NetWare licenses, at a street price of about $45,000—that's 1,250 user licenses to serve 101 workstations, at a cost of almost $450 per seat. In the same situation with Windows NT Server, you'd buy 5 server licenses and 100 per-seat client access licenses, at a total street price of perhaps $5,700, or less than $60 per seat.

Don't say that Microsoft never does anything for the little guy. Your choice of per-server or per-seat licensing is not cast in stone. You can start by licensing per-server to minimize costs. If and when your situation changes to the point where per-seat licensing makes more sense, you can convert your existing per-server licenses to per-seat licenses at no cost. Microsoft allows you to do this exactly once. You don't have to change any software, pay any upgrade fees, or even let

Microsoft know what you're doing. With one mouse click, you simply unmark "per-server" and mark "per-seat." That's all there is to it.I

Performance Issues

NetWare 3.1x has always had a deserved reputation for providing blazingly fast file and print services. When NetWare 4.0 first shipped, some observers were surprised to find that it was noticeably slower than NetWare 3.12 at providing these services. They shouldn't have been surprised, because NetWare 4.0 was doing a lot more behind the scenes than NetWare 3.1x. If NetWare 3.1x was a performance-tuned sports car, NetWare 4.0 was a land yacht.

In comparison to NetWare 3.1x, the first release of Windows NT—which was numbered 3.1 to correspond with the then-current version of Windows for the desktop—was even worse. It was so much slower than NetWare 3.1x that, during magazine comparative tests, it sometimes failed to complete the test when running a large number of clients.

The next release of both operating systems closed the gap considerably, although NetWare 3.12 was still the reigning speed champion by most measures. The reason that the newcomers were able to make such gains on NetWare 3.12 is obvious in retrospect—NetWare 3.12 was receiving essentially no development effort, while the flagship Novell and Microsoft products were receiving intensive tuning.

As things now stand, the current versions of both NetWare 4.x and Microsoft Windows NT Server are in general fully comparable to NetWare 3.12 in file and print performance when run on comparable servers. In the case of Windows NT Server, this is all the more surprising in view of the several advantages enjoyed by NetWare 3.12.

First, NetWare runs at Ring 0 of the Intel processor, which is the fastest and most privileged level. Running at Ring 0 offers many performance advantages, at the expense of additional risk. A misbehaved process running at Ring 0 can take down the server, as many NetWare administrators have found when running poorly written NLMs.

In the interest of safety, much of Windows NT Server runs instead in Ring 3, which offers slower performance, but protects the processor as a whole from misbehaved processes. Microsoft took a lot of heat when, with Windows NT 4.0, they moved certain video operations to Ring 0. Many observers noted that this made sense for Windows NT Workstation, where interactive responsiveness is an important issue, but did not make sense for Windows NT Server. Most Windows

NT Server 4.0 administrators take the sensible approach, and avoid problems by using only the video drivers provided by Microsoft. Loading the latest and greatest video driver on your server makes no sense at all, given the minimal benefits versus the potential risk.

The second major advantage that NetWare 3.12 has compared to Windows NT Server 4.0 is that NetWare drivers are written directly to the hardware, which increases performance at the expense of portability. Windows NT Server, on the other hand, places a Hardware Abstraction Layer (HAL) between the device drivers and the actual hardware. The device drivers sit on top of the HAL and make standard calls to it. HAL in turn translates these calls and places them to the hardware itself. Changes to the server hardware require changes to the HAL. The device drivers use the same calls they've always used, and aren't even aware of the changes to the hardware. This approach increases portability at the theoretical expense of reducing performance. That Windows NT Server 4.0 maintains high performance is a testimony to the quality of the programming that went into the HAL interface.

The third major advantage that NetWare 3.12 holds over Windows NT Server 4.0 is that the IPX/SPX protocol is an intrinsic part of NetWare, with roots very deep in the operating system itself. IPX/SPX and NetWare were designed from the ground up to work together to provide extremely high LAN performance, and they accomplish this goal very well. Windows NT Server, on the other hand, installs transport protocols as drop-in modules. As with the HAL, this method increases portability and flexibility at the potential cost of providing lower performance. With transport protocols, Microsoft has again done an excellent job of maintaining high performance while operating under a handicap.

The fourth major advantage that NetWare 3.12 holds over Windows NT Server 4.0—and probably the most important one—is that NetWare depends heavily on hand-coded and optimized assembly language, while Windows NT Server is written largely in C and its derivatives to maintain portability. Novell has spent the last decade optimizing their assembly language to squeeze the most out of every last processor tick. Microsoft instead depends on Pareto's Principle—otherwise known as the 80/20 Rule—by using hand-coded and tuned assembly language for only the most critical portions of the system.

The one performance advantage that Windows NT Server indisputably holds is its support for multiple processors. NetWare 3.12 and Windows NT Server are roughly comparable when each is running on a single processor server. Adding a second processor lets Windows NT Server blow the doors off of NetWare. As a matter of fact, here's an amazing true fact that Microsoft's marketing folks somehow forgot to mention. Because NetWare 3.12 supports only one processor, Windows NT Server running on a dual processor machine will outperform NetWare 3.12 running on a similar server with quad processors. It may not be playing fair, but in the real world you can always make a Windows NT server run faster than any NetWare server. Just add more processors. That's one trump card that NetWare can't match.

Windows NT Server Specifics

The preceding sections briefly described some of the significant differences between NetWare 3.12 and Windows NT Server. The following sections go into a little more detail about some of the important aspects of Windows NT Server.

Windows NT Services Versus NetWare Loadable Modules

A Windows NT Server *service* is almost exactly analogous to a NetWare Loadable Module (NLM). A service is a process that is owned by the system rather than by an individual user. Like an NLM, a service is ordinarily started when the server is booted. Also, like an NLM, a service may be dynamically loaded or unloaded without rebooting the server.

You can view and modify the status of installed services from the Services applet in Control Panel, which displays the name of each installed service, its status, and how it is configured to start—automatic, manual, or disabled. Installing Windows NT Server with the installation defaults installs a basic set of 25 individual services, as displayed in Table 1-10.

Table 1-10. The Default System Services Installed With Windows NT Server 4.0

Service Name	Purpose
Alerter	Supports notification of designated computers and users when a system event occurs. This service is used by other services, and requires that the Messenger service be loaded.
ClipBook Server	Supports the ClipBook viewer, a Network DDE service that allows pages to be viewed by remote computers. This service is configured by default for manual startup.
Computer Browser	Discovers and displays the Microsoft Networking resources available on the network.
DHCP Client	Allows the computer to request an IP address and other IP configuration information from the designated Dynamic Host Configuration Protocol (DHCP) server.
Directory Replicator	Supports automatic replication of folders and files from an export server to an import computer. This service is configured by default for manual startup.

Table 1-10. The Default System Services Installed With Windows NT Server 4.0 (continued)

Service Name	Purpose
EventLog	Supports recording of significant system, application, and security events to the corresponding event log.
FTP Publishing Service	An FTP server.
Gopher Publishing Service	A Gopher server.
License Logging Service	Dynamically tracks the number of licenses in use for Windows NT Server and other BackOffice components against the number licensed.
Messenger	Supports notification of designated logged on users when a significant system event occurs. Also supports other internal messaging functions, including broadcasts by the administrator.
NetLogon	Provides clients with a single access point to the primary domain controller and backup domain controllers. Authenticates logons and synchronizes the master PDC directory database to BDCs.
Network DDE	Supports Network Dynamic Data Exchange (NetDDE) data sharing by opening two opposing unidirectional pipes between applications to provide transport services and security. This service is not started automatically by default.
Network DDE DSDM	The DDE Share Database Manager manages shared DDE conversations. This service does not start automatically by default.
NT LM Security Support Provider	Supports Windows NT security between RPC programs. This service is not started automatically by default.
Plug and Play	Although Windows NT 4.0 does not implement full Plug and Play, it does install the Plug and Play service. (Note the difference in syntax. I was unable to locate any significant further details despite an exhaustive search of various Windows NT resources. If you know what this service actually does, please let me know.)
Remote Procedure Call (RPC) Locator	Manages the RPC name service database. Allows RPC servers to register and RPC clients to query for the location of the server.
Remote Procedure Call (RPC) Service	Supports standard client-server IPC mechanisms that are used to establish connections between computers on the network. This RPC service is compatible with the OSF DCE specification.
Schedule	Provides scheduling services to the AT command, which is similar to UNIX cron, and can be used to specify that a particular program will execute at a selected time.
Server	Provides connections requested by client redirectors to allow them to access network resources.
Spooler	The print spooler service.
TCP/IP NetBIOS Helper	Supports the Computer Browser service in a TCP/IP environment.
Telephony Service	Supports Telephony Application Program Interface (TAPI) applications. This service is not started automatically by default.

Table 1-10. The Default System Services Installed With Windows NT Server 4.0 (continued)

Service Name	Purpose
UPS	Allows the server and UPS to communicate when a problem occurs, so that the server can be shut down in an orderly fashion. This service is not started automatically by default.
Workstation	Receives user-mode requests and passes them to the kernel-mode redirector for processing. This service allows Windows NT Server to function as a client and as a server simultaneously.
World Wide Web Publishing Service	A web server.

Installing Windows NT Server with the installation defaults also installs the basic set of six network services shown in Table 1-11. You can view installed network services and modify their properties, if applicable, from the Network applet in Control Panel. This is really just a different view of the services previously described. The Computer Browser Service, the Server Service, and the Workstation Service are the same as those described in Table 1-10. The other network services are combinations of various individual services. For example, the Microsoft Internet Information Server 2.0 Service is a combination of the FTP Publishing Service, the Gopher Publishing Service, the World Wide Web Publishing Service, and other required supporting services.

Table 1-11. The Default Network Services Installed with Windows NT Server 4.0

Network Service Name	Purpose
Computer Browser	Uses a distributed protocol to discover and display the Microsoft Networking resources available on the network.
Microsoft Internet Information Server 2.0	Provides FTP, Gopher, and HTTP (web) servers.
NetBIOS Interface	Defines the interface and naming conventions that are used by Microsoft Networking.
RPC Configuration	Provides the support routines needed to allow RPC-aware applications to perform distributed processing across multiple computers.
Server	Installs server-side support for Server Message Block (SMB) protocol, the foundation of Microsoft Networking.
Workstation	Installs client-side support for SMB.

You may also elect to install some or all of the optional network services displayed in Table 1-12 when you install Windows NT Server. Those that you do not install when you first install Windows NT Server may also be installed at any time subsequently.

Table 1-12. Optional Services that May Be Installed with Windows NT Server 4.0

Network Service Name	Purpose
DHCP Relay Agent	Supports proxy DHCP services by relaying DHCP and BOOTP broadcast messages between the local DHCP server and a client that is located on another network segment connected by an IP router.
Gateway and Client Services for NetWare	Provides a local NetWare redirector for the server upon which it is running, as well as a proxy redirector for Microsoft Networking clients connected to that server.
Microsoft DHCP Server	Provides Dynamic Host Configuration Protocol (DHCP) services, including automatic assignment of IP addresses to DHCP clients and centralized management of those IP addresses.
Microsoft DNS Server	Provides Domain Name Service (DNS) IP name resolution services.
Microsoft TCP/IP Printing	Supports TCP/IP printing, e.g., to UNIX printers.
Network Monitor Agent	Available for both Windows NT Server and Workstation. Collects raw packet data from the network, which can subsequently be displayed by the Network Monitor.
Network Monitor Tools and Agent	Available for Windows NT Server only. Installs both the Agent and the Network Monitor application, which displays packet data collected by the Agent.
Remote Access Service	Installs the applications and supporting services for Microsoft RAS, a dial-up communications server that supports IP, IPX, and NetBEUI.
Remoteboot Service	Provides services to support remote boot of diskless workstations.
RIP for Internet Protocol	Provides the IP routing component of the Microsoft Multiprotocol Router service.
RIP for NWLink IPX/SPX Compatible Transport	Provides the IPX routing component of the Microsoft Multiprotocol Router service.
RPC Support for Banyan	Installs services needed to support Remote Procedure Call functions for interoperability with Banyan VINES servers.
SAP Agent	Provides supporting services for Novell Service Advertising Protocol.
Services for Macintosh	Provides supporting services for Apple Macintosh clients.
Simple TCP/IP Services	Installs a basic (and pretty useless) set of TCP/IP applications.
SNMP Service	Supports Simple Network Management Protocol for remote monitoring and configuration of supported devices.
Windows Internet Name Service	Provides dynamic name resolution services in a Microsoft Networking environment.

All of the services listed in Tables 1-10, 1-11, and 1-12 are bundled with Windows NT Server. Many Microsoft add-on software products are also implemented as services. Right now, for example, in addition to many of the standard services, my server is running half a dozen other services that support the optional Microsoft Services for NetWare and Microsoft Exchange Server products. Third-party software may also be implemented as services. My server, for example, is now running three services that support the Seagate Backup Exec package, and another that supports the Norton Utilities Speed Disk utility.

The Windows NT Filesystem

NetWare 3.12 uses a heavily modified version of the DOS FAT filesystem as its foundation. By adding caching, directory entry tables, and other enhancements, Novell was able to extend the functionality of the FAT filesystem to yield fast multiuser performance, high security, and other aspects of filesystem behavior that were not originally a part of FAT. Novell supports other filesystems, e.g., NFS, OS/2, and Macintosh, by adding additional directory entry tables to support the special requirements of those filesystems.

In each case, the underlying native filesystem remains DOS FAT. Novell depends on the brute force method—lots of RAM devoted to file and directory caching—to maintain high performance. On the one hand, this means that NetWare volumes provide extremely fast response and high throughput. On the other hand, this also means that the amount of RAM required by a NetWare server is very closely tied to the size and types of volumes that it supports. Neither is it a matter of your willingness to accept lower performance in return for smaller memory requirements. If you don't have the minimum amount of RAM that NetWare requires to support a given size and type of volume, it simply refuses to mount that volume.

The native Windows NT Server filesystem is called NTFS. Although Windows NT Server also provides full support for the DOS FAT filesystem, and read-only support for the OS/2 HPFS, most Windows NT servers run NTFS exclusively. This is because NTFS provides much better security and performance than FAT. Relative to FAT and NetWare, NTFS provides the following advantages:

Capacity
: NTFS supports much larger volume and file sizes than FAT. For example, NTFS supports individual file sizes as large as 16 EB (2^{64} bytes).

Recoverability
: NTFS tracks transactions against the filesystem, automatically logging all updates to folders and files. If a crash occurs, NTFS can use this log to roll back the state of the disk.

Hot Fixing

Like NetWare, NTFS supports hot fixing. However, with NetWare, you must allocate a hot fix area of predetermined size when preparing the disk. NTFS dynamically swaps out sectors as necessary.

Security Support

NTFS is tied intimately to the Windows NT security model. DOS allows only the most basic access restrictions.

For POSIX compliance, NTFS file and folder names preserve case, but they are not case-sensitive. You may, for example, save a file using either the name *AUTOEXEC.NT* or *AUTOexec.NT*, and subsequently see the filename displayed in a directory listing using the same case combination you saved it under. However, those two files could not coexist in the same folder, because NTFS regards them as having the same name. Accordingly, the commands *DEL AUTOEXEC.NT*, *DEL AUTOexec.NT*, and *DEL AuToExEc.Nt* have exactly the same effect, which is to delete any file named *autoexec.nt*, regardless of the case used to name the file.

NTFS does almost everything well. It does have two weaknesses, one minor and one major. First, it does not support dynamic file encryption, which would be a relatively easy addition to the existing dynamic compression algorithm. Second, and more startling, it does not make any provision for recovering deleted files. Windows NT Server administrators quickly learn to make frequent incremental or differential backups, and to archive those tapes for a reasonable time. Although this isn't a perfect replacement for the NetWare *SALVAGE* utility, it's the best you can do.

Workgroups and Domains

Windows NT Server networks are organized using the concepts of workgroups and domains. Workgroups are associated with small peer-to-peer networks, like those created with Windows NT Workstation, Windows 95, or Windows 3.11 for Workgroups. Windows NT Server can be a peer participant in a workgroup-based network. Domains are associated with larger client/server networks.

Workgroups

A *workgroup* is a named collection of computers that are grouped for a particular purpose. For example, you might create a workgroup named *SALES* and assign the ten computers in the sales department to this workgroup. Each member of the *SALES* workgroup can then both share its own resources—e.g., printers, hard drives, and CD-ROM drives—with other members of the *SALES* workgroup, and use resources shared by other members of the *SALES* workgroup.

What characterizes a workgroup is that security and access control is distributed rather than centralized. Each member of the workgroup may choose to share some or all of its resources with other members of the workgroup. Access control for each shared resource is done at the individual computer that owns that resource. Each member of the workgroup maintains its own local user account database, which stores information about the shared resources on that computer and which other workgroup users are permitted to access them.

For example, if the computers named *SUE* (used by Sue) and *BILL* (used by Bill) are both members of the *SALES* workgroup, and Sue wants to share her printer with Bill, then Bill must either have a user account on *SUE* that has the necessary privileges to access that printer, or must be a member of a local group on *SUE* that has such permissions. Similarly, if Sue needs to access a shared hard disk on *BILL*, Sue must either have an individual user account on *BILL*, or be a member of a local group on *BILL* that has such privileges.

Creating a workgroup is a quick and easy way to share resources, as long as the number of computers involved is relatively small. However, because the account structure must be duplicated on each member machine, it becomes increasingly difficult to administer the workgroup as the number of member computers assigned to that workgroup grows. In addition to such administrative problems, the lack of central authentication means that security in a workgroup environment is usually lacking.

Domains

A Windows NT Server *domain* is a named logical grouping of computers that share a common account database and security policy. In addition to client workstations, a domain includes at least one—and possibly several—servers running Windows NT Server. In a domain-based network, clients log on to the domain itself, rather than logging on to individual servers within that domain.

One Windows NT server within the domain is designated as the *Primary Domain Controller* (*PDC*). The PDC maintains the user account database and security policy, which are used to validate clients as they log on, and to control access to shared resources within the domain. To avoid loss and to distribute the workload of authenticating users and controlling access to shared resources, additional Windows NT servers may participate within the domain as *Backup Domain Controllers* (*BDC*). The user account database and security information maintained by the PDC is automatically replicated periodically to the BDCs. If the PDC fails, a BDC can be promoted to take its place.

What characterizes a domain, and differentiates it from a workgroup, is that the account database and security are stored, accessed, and maintained on the central domain controllers, rather than residing on the individual computers within the domain. Individual computers may still share resources with other domain users, but are no longer responsible for controlling access to them.

For example, the workgroup network described above might be converted to a domain-based network by adding a Windows NT server named *ROY*, which is configured as a PDC. The administrator might first configure the printer on *SUE* and the hard drive on *BILL* as shared network resources, which will appear to all domain users as shared resources of the server *ROY*. The administrator then creates user accounts on *ROY* for the users Sue and Bill, and grants each account the right to access the shared resource located on the other's computer. The user accounts, and their associated permissions, are maintained on *ROY* rather than on the client workstations. When, for example, Sue wants to perform a task or access a shared network resource, her rights and permissions are first checked on the domain controller *ROY* to verify that Sue has the necessary privileges to perform the task or access the resource.

Windows NT Server domains are treated in greater detail in Chapter 2, *Introduction to Microsoft Networking*.

NOTE Do not confuse Windows NT Server domains with Internet domains. The two are unrelated.

User and Group Accounts

Windows NT Server user accounts and group accounts are generally analogous to NetWare users and groups. They serve the same purpose and work in pretty much the same way. Windows NT Server, however, makes more extensive use of group memberships to control access to resources and to determine which actions a user is authorized to perform than NetWare. What NetWare accomplishes with user types and security equivalences, Windows NT Server uses group memberships to do.

A user account or a group account may be granted *rights*, which allow that account to perform certain activities, e.g., backing up files, restoring files, logging on from the console, or setting the server clock. A user account or a group account may also be granted *permissions*, which allow that account to access specified resources, e.g., a particular folder or file on a specified volume, or a network printer. Throughout this book, I use the term *privileges*—which is not defined within Windows NT Server—to mean some arbitrary combination of rights and permissions assigned to a user or group account. I also use the term *privileged* to refer to a user account that has rights and permissions greater than those enjoyed by an ordinary user account.

User accounts

A Windows NT Server user account defines all information that pertains to an individual user. This information includes the username and password that the user uses to log in, that user's rights and restrictions, and the groups to which that user is assigned membership. Like NetWare, Windows NT Server allows you to create multiple accounts for a single user, with each account having differing levels of permissions. For example, the system administrator may have a privileged account under one username that he uses to perform administrative tasks, and a second account with fewer privileges that he uses for routine day-to-day work.

When you install Windows NT Server, it automatically creates three built-in user accounts, as follows:

- *Administrator* is the equivalent of the NetWare user Supervisor, and has full system privileges. Although you cannot delete the user Administrator, you can rename it for security purposes.
- *Guest* is analogous to the NetWare user Guest, has very limited privileges, and is disabled by default. You cannot delete the user Guest, but you can rename it to something less obvious.
- *Initial User account* is created and named during the installation of Windows NT Server. This account is automatically assigned to the Windows NT Server group Administrators, and therefore has the privileges and rights of the user Administrator.

When you create a user account, Windows NT Server assigns it a *Security Identifier (SID)*, which is the true account identifier. You can subsequently rename an account without affecting its rights and permissions. If you delete an account, however, all rights and privileges associated with that account are deleted. Simply creating a new account with the same username as the original account does not automatically grant that new account the permissions and rights that were assigned to the old account of the same name, because the new account has a different SID.

Each user account may have an associated user environment profile, which stores configuration information, e.g., desktop settings specific to that user. This allows each user to maintain a customized environment regardless of where he logs on. As with NetWare, each user account may be assigned a home directory location and a logon script that is run each time that user logs on.

Windows NT Server also makes provision for *system accounts*, or *service accounts*, that are used by various system services. For example, your backup utility may have certain components that run as system services, and are started when the server boots. These services logon using a system account rather than an individual user account.

Windows NT Server includes a graphical utility named *User Manager for Domains*, which is used to create and maintain user accounts. Chapter 5, *Managing Users and Groups*, describes these functions in greater detail.

Group accounts

In Windows NT Server, a group account is basically a specialized type of user account. It differs from an ordinary user account in that it may contain other users, which are referred to as members of the group. A group account, like a user account, may be assigned rights to perform specified activities and permissions to access specified resources. A right or permission that is granted to a group account is automatically granted to all user accounts that are members of that group account.

Like NetWare, Windows NT Server uses group accounts to simplify administration. You may assign many user accounts to a single group account. By granting rights and permissions to the group account, you simultaneously grant those rights and permissions to group members. Also, like NetWare, Windows NT Server allows you to assign explicit rights and permissions to individual user accounts, which are then summed with the rights and permissions granted by that user's group memberships to arrive at the effective rights for that user.

Local and Global Groups. Windows NT Server allows you to create two kinds of group accounts, as follows:

- *Global groups* may contain user accounts only from the domain in which the group was created. A global group may be assigned privileges in another domain, allowing users assigned to the global group to access resources on another domain without having an account on that domain. Global groups cannot contain other groups.
- *Local groups* may contain both users and global groups. A local group may be assigned privileges only in the domain in which it is created. Privileges granted to a local group are inherited by users and global groups that are members of the local group. You can assign global groups from several domains to a single local group, and then manage this local group as a single entity, making it easier to control access to domain resources by users from other domains.

Default Group Accounts. Windows NT Server creates 11 default groups—called system groups—when you install it. You can change the rights and permissions assigned to a system group, but you cannot rename or delete it. Windows NT Server creates the following standard system groups when you install it:

- *Account Operators* can create and manage user accounts and groups in the domain, but can only grant rights by assigning users to one or more groups previously created by an Administrator. Membership in this group grants a user powers roughly equivalent to, but more extensive than, those of a NetWare Workgroup Manager.
- *Administrators* can access any system resource and perform any task. Membership in this group is equivalent to a NetWare supervisor equivalent user.
- *Backup Operators* can back up any file or directory on the server, regardless if their privileges otherwise give them access to the file or directory. Backup Operators do not automatically have the right to restore the server. There is no direct NetWare equivalent for membership in the Backup Operators group.
- *Domain Admins* are assigned Administrator privileges for the entire domain. The Domain Admins group is automatically assigned membership in the Administrators local group, which grants Domain Admins local administration privileges. NetWare doesn't use domains, so there is no direct NetWare equivalent for the Domain Admins group. In a multiserver NetWare environment, the closest equivalent would be assigning a user as a supervisor equivalent on every server.
- *Domain Guests* can exercise the limited privileges associated with a guest account throughout the domain.
- *Domain Users* are granted a standard set of privileges, valid throughout the domain, that are adequate for the typical user. Membership in this group confers privileges equivalent to those assigned to an ordinary NetWare user account.
- *Guests* can exercise the limited privileges associated with a guest account, but only on the local machine.
- *Print Operators* can create and manage print shares in the domain, log on to the server console, and shut down the server. There is no direct NetWare equivalent for the Print Operators group. Membership in this group grants the powers similar to, but more extensive than, those available to a NetWare Print Queue Operator and Print Server Operator.
- *Replicator* is a special group that confers the privileges needed to perform directory replication. "Real" users are never assigned to this group.
- *Server Operators* are assigned most of the privileges available to administrators. A server operator has all of the privileges needed to maintain and administer the server on a routine basis. Only rarely used functions that fundamentally affect the functioning of the server are prohibited to server operators.

- *Users* are granted a standard set of privileges, valid only on the local machine, that are adequate for the typical user. Membership in this group confers privileges equivalent to those assigned to an ordinary NetWare user account.

Windows NT Server Security Policies

Windows NT Server security policies allow the administrator to enforce an additional level of control over user behavior. Windows NT Server provides three types of security policies, which are described in the following sections.

Account policy

Account Policy allows you to control user access to the domain. You use Account Policy to control things like maximum and minimum password ages, minimum password length, password uniqueness, and account lockout. Settings made in Account Policy are enforced globally, and apply equally to any user that is a member of the domain. Any change you make to Account Policy affects each user the next time that user logs in.

User rights policy

The User Rights Policy determines which rights are available to each user account and group account. In order to perform an action, a user must have the right to do so.

Do not confuse rights with permissions. A Windows NT Server permission determines which users can access a particular system resource, and at what level. A permission is associated with a specific resource, like a file or a printer. In other words, Windows NT permissions correspond to NetWare trustee "rights." Windows NT "rights," on the other hand, determine what actions can be performed by the user. A right is associated with a specific action, like backing up a file or shutting down the server. A defined group of Windows NT rights corresponds roughly to a specific NetWare "user type," e.g., Supervisor, or Workgroup Manager.

Windows NT Server offers you much more flexibility than NetWare in this respect. With Windows NT Server, rights can be assigned individually and in any combination. With NetWare, you can only select among various user types that confer predefined sets of abilities. Each standard group in Windows NT Server has a predefined set of rights. Although you can modify these as needed, there is usually no need to do so. You can also assign rights to individual user accounts, although, again, there is usually no need. It's easier just to assign the user to a group that has the necessary right.

Audit policy

The final Windows NT Server security policy is the Audit Policy. By using Audit Policy, you can specify which system events will be recorded in the audit logs. You may specify that Success, Failure, or both be logged. You can select the following events:

- Logon and Logoff
- File and Object Access
- Use of User Rights
- User and Group Management
- Security Policy Changes
- Restart, Shutdown, and System
- Process Tracking

You can also configure auditing for individual folders and files, either globally or on a per-user or per-group basis.

Windows NT Server Resource Security

Windows NT Server is an object-oriented operating system. An *object* in Windows NT Server is defined as a combination of a data set and a group of actions than can be used to manipulate that data set. For example, a file object comprises both the data stored in the file and the system functions need to open, close, read from, and write to that file.

Windows NT Server treats everything as an object. Objects may be physical resources like disk drives, printers, memory, and communications ports. Objects may also be logical resources like volumes, folders, files, and shares. Finally, objects may be dynamic resources, like processes, threads, and windows.

Windows NT Server protects its resources by associating authorized users with system resources, keeping track of which users and system services are authorized to access each resource object. The functions used to manipulate an object are associated with the object itself, as are the users and groups that are authorized to use those functions. Functions that are associated with a particular object can be used to manipulate only that object, and not other similar objects.

Access control lists

Windows NT Server controls access to each object by using an Access Control List (ACL). The ACL contains a list of users and groups that have been granted access to an object, and the specific rights and permissions granted to each user and group. When a user attempts to access an object, Windows NT Server compares the Security Identifier (SID) of that user and the user's group memberships to the ACL for the object to decide whether to permit the user to access the object at the requested level.

An administrator modifies the ACL for an object by granting or denying access to that resource to a particular user or group. When a user or group is either granted or explicitly denied access to an object, that information is added to the ACL list for the object as an Access Control Entry (ACE). The ACE contains the user account along with the specific rights and permissions granted and the restrictions to be enforced. Restriction ACEs ("deny permission") appear first in the ACL.

Assume, for example, that you want to control the access of three users to the file *MAIN.MDB*. User *BETTY* is to be granted read, write, and delete access; user *JOHN* is to be granted read-only access; user *DIANE* is to be prevented from accessing the file at all. When the administrator assigns the necessary permissions to effect these changes, three ACEs are added to the ACL for *MAIN.DBF*. Each ACE contains a user account SID, along with the different level of access permission granted to that user.

Securing access to objects

Windows NT Server enforces a mandatory logon. Each user must log on by providing his username and password before he can access any resources. Access control begins when the user has successfully logged on to Windows NT Server. At this point, the Windows NT security subsystem creates an *access token* and issues it to the user. The access token contains various information about the user, including the username and the groups of which that user is a member. It identifies the user to the system, and remains in effect for that user until he logs off.

When a user spawns a process, that user's access token is attached to the process, permanently associating that user with that process. When a process attempts to access a resource, Windows NT compares the access token associated with that process to the ACL for the resource to decide whether or not to grant access to that process (and, therefore, to that user).

Security Identifiers. Windows NT Server actually stores a username as a *Security Identifier* (*SID*) and a group name as a *Group Security Identifier* (*Group SID*). An SID is a unique numeric handle for a user or a group. Access tokens and ACLs store SIDs instead of the actual username or group name. An SID takes the form of a long numeric string. For example, the SID for my account (with a few numbers changed, just in case...) is S-1-5-21-2020078333-1018241490-349765860-1001.

NOTE SIDs are buried deep in the internals of Windows NT Server. You don't ordinarily see an SID, let alone have to work with it. I had a hard time just finding one to look at to verify the syntax. I finally ended up running the *GETSID.EXE* utility from the Resource Kit.

In Windows NT Server, usernames and group names are really only aliases for the true name of the account—the SID. The implications of this can be confusing to new Windows NT administrators when they begin managing users and groups. Consider, for example, an existing user account named *JIM*. *JIM* has been explicitly granted access to the file *MAIN.MDB*. If you delete the user *JIM* and then create a new user, also named *JIM*, you might be surprised to find that the new user *JIM* does not have access to *MAIN.MDB*. After all, the ACL for *MAIN.MDB* lists *JIM* as an authorized user, right?

Not really. Here's what happened. When you deleted the original *JIM* account, you deleted not only the username (or alias) *JIM*, but also the SID associated with that username. When you created the new user account *JIM*, a new SID was assigned for the new account. The ACL for *MAIN.MDB* contains the SID for the original *JIM* account, but not the SID for the new *JIM* account. When Jim attempts to access *MAIN.MDB* with his new account, the new SID doesn't match the ACL, and *JIM* is denied access.

NOTE This characteristic of Windows NT Server security also applies to groups, so be **very** careful when deleting group accounts.

Permissions Checking. When a user attempts to access a system resource, the Windows NT security subsystem uses the following procedure to decide whether to grant access:

1. It extracts the SID from the access token of the user process to identify the user making the request.
2. It compares the SID against each ACE in the ACL for the object to determine if that ACE explicitly denies the type of access that is being requested for the SID or Group SID associated with the user process. If it encounters an explicit deny, it refuses the user request immediately.
3. If, after examining every ACE within the ACL, it was unable to locate an explicit deny, it begins again at the top of the ACL, looking for specific permissions that are explicitly granted to the SID or Group SID. It accumulates these permissions until they total those necessary to fulfill the user

request, and then grants the user request immediately. If instead it arrives at the last ACE without having accumulated sufficient permissions, it denies the user request.

NOTE Consider the implications of the process described above, because they may affect access control in unexpected ways. For example, a user who has been granted specific permissions for an object, but who is also a member of a group that has been explicitly denied access to that object, will not be able to access the object. Remember that denials are parsed first and take precedence.

From the above description, it might seem that Windows NT Server would be spending most of its time checking permissions. After all, a user who accesses a resource may access that resource many times and in several different ways in the course of a single session. The user might, for example, open a file, save changes to it repeatedly, and finally close the file. Verifying each individual access would add substantial overhead to server operations.

The Windows NT Server security subsystem addresses this by making the reasonable assumption that the permissions in effect when a user first accesses an object should remain in effect for the duration of that user's session with that object. When it first grants access to the object, it creates a handle for the object, which associates the object with the user process. It performs the permissions check described above, creates a list of the maximum permissions available to that user process for that object, and stores that list with the user process itself. When the user process subsequently accesses the object, permissions are verified against the permissions list stored in the process table of the user process, rather than being verified directly against the ACL for the object.

The Windows NT Registry

As any NetWare administrator knows, the heart and soul of a NetWare 3.12 server is its bindery, which is an object-oriented database that stores information about users and resources. The Windows NT Server *Registry* serves a similar purpose, but differs in several significant respects, as follows:

- The bindery maintains information about only some aspects of the NetWare server, while the Registry is intimately involved in every aspect of Windows NT Server operations.
- The bindery is relatively static. Most changes to it occur only as a result of explicit modifications made by a supervisor or other privileged user. The Registry is dynamic. It changes constantly from moment to moment, both from

explicit changes made by an administrator, and from implicit changes that occur due to routine user and system activities.

- The bindery is a local database. It maintains information only about the NetWare server upon which it resides. The registry is a distributed, global database. It maintains information about users and resources that are located both on the local and remote machines connected to the network.
- The bindery is maintained locally, on the server upon which it resides. The Registry is designed for distributed and remote administration.
- The Windows NT Registry is fully described in Chapter 9, *Working with the Windows NT Registry*.

Windows NT Server NetWare Integration Tools

The NWLink IPX/SPX Compatible Transport protocol bundled with Windows NT Server provides the foundation for interoperability with NetWare servers and clients. In addition, Microsoft bundles two services—the Gateway Service for NetWare and the Migration Tool for NetWare—that facilitate integration. Microsoft offers an optional $149 product, called Microsoft Services for NetWare, that includes two additional services—File and Print Services for NetWare and Directory Service Manager for NetWare—that extend interoperability features. These services provide the following functions:

Gateway Service for NetWare (GSNW)
: The bundled GSNW service lets Windows NT Server function as a gateway that allows clients with only Microsoft Networking client software installed to access shared resources on NetWare servers. Installing, configuring, and using GSNW is described fully in Chapter 18, *Using Gateway Service for NetWare*.

File and Print Services for NetWare (FPNW)
: FPNW is a component of the optional Microsoft Services for NetWare package. This service lets Windows NT Server emulate a NetWare 3.12 server, allowing clients with only NetWare client software installed to access shared resources on Windows NT servers. Installing, configuring, and using FPNW is described fully in Chapter 19, *Using File and Print Services for NetWare*.

Directory Service Manager for NetWare (DSMN)
: DSMN is another component of Microsoft Services for NetWare. This service allows bindery-based NetWare servers to be added to the Windows NT Server domain, where they can be managed with Windows NT Server utilities. Installing, configuring, and using DSMN is described fully in Chapter 20, *Managing Servers in a Mixed NetWare and Windows NT Server Environment*.

Migration Tool for NetWare (MTNW)
: This bundled MTNW service automatically transfers users, groups, scripts, directories, and files from NetWare servers to Windows NT Server, and largely preserves the security information associated with those resources. You can use this tool either to migrate completely from NetWare to Windows NT Server, or simply to quickly replicate the contents of a NetWare server to a new Windows NT server. Installing, configuring, and using MTNW is described fully in Chapter 21, *Migrating to a Pure Windows NT Server Environment.*

Windows NT Server Extras

I've mentioned several times in this chapter that Windows NT Server does much more than NetWare 3.12. Here are some examples of standard functions bundled with Windows NT Server that have no equivalent in NetWare 3.12:

DHCP Server
: TCP/IP is a wonderful transport protocol, but using it can be an administrative nightmare if you have to manage IP addresses and other TCP/IP configuration items manually. The DHCP Server service automates and centralizes many of these TCP/IP management functions. Installing, configuring, and using the Microsoft DHCP Server is described fully in Chapter 12, *Using Dynamic Host Configuration Protocol.*

DNS Server
: Domain Name Services (DNS) is one of the foundations of the Internet, and of corporate TCP/IP networks. DNS resolves host names from numeric IP addresses. Installing, configuring, and using the Microsoft DNS Server is described fully in Chapter 14, *Using Domain Name Service.*

Internet Information Server (IIS)
: IIS is a major application. It provides a full-blown web server that can form the foundation of an Internet web site or a corporate Intranet. It also provides an ftp server and a gopher server, along with various tools designed to help you build and maintain the server and develop content. Because a chapter-level summary treatment of IIS would be of little use, and a detailed treatment would require a book of its own, this book does not include coverage of IIS.

Remote Access Service
: This service allows a computer running Windows NT Server to function as a dial-up communications server, supporting as many as 256 concurrent users. The RAS Server supports both Microsoft clients running proprietary dial-up networking client software, and non-Microsoft clients running generic PPP client software. RAS allows clients to establish a network connection to the

server, using TCP/IP, IPX/SPX, or NetBEUI, and to access any resource on the network for which they are authorized. Installing, configuring, and using RAS is described fully in Chapter 15, *Using Remote Access Service.*

WINS Server

WINS provides services in the Microsoft Networking environment similar to those provided by a DNS Server in the TCP/IP environment. Installing, configuring, and using the Microsoft WINS Server is described fully in Chapter 13, *Using Windows Internet Naming Service.*

2

In this chapter:
- *Windows NT Networking Architecture Overview*
- *Browsing the Network*
- *Understanding Domains*

Introduction to Microsoft Networking

NetWare 3.12 is an essentially pure client/server network operating system. With very few exceptions—most of which are related to remote printing or backup—NetWare clients use network resources and services provided by NetWare servers, but do not in turn provide resources to other NetWare clients or to NetWare servers. Conversely, NetWare servers provide resources to clients, but do not use resources provided by clients.

Windows NT Server takes a different approach. Microsoft's initial attempt at a server-based network operating system, LAN Manager, was a failure in the marketplace, but established many of the fundamental concepts of Microsoft networking, e.g., Server Message Block as the core protocol. Later versions of Microsoft operating systems, including Windows 95, Windows NT Server, and Windows NT Workstation build on both LAN Manager and Microsoft peer networking to provide an integrated server OS environment with strong peer features. A Microsoft Networking client can easily share a printer, hard drive, CD-ROM drive, or other resource with other clients on the network. Some NetWare administrators will be concerned about this perceived lack of control with Windows NT Server. There really isn't any need to be. A Windows NT server can be secured at least as tightly as a NetWare server.

This chapter begins with a description of the Microsoft networking architecture, which differs significantly from the architecture of NetWare. It then continues to describe the Browsing Service, an essential component of Microsoft Networking, and concludes with an explanation of the Microsoft domain concept.

Windows NT Networking Architecture Overview

You don't have to understand much about Windows NT networking architecture to use it successfully. In fact, you don't need to understand it at all. Although a detailed description of the low-level network architecture of Windows NT Server is beyond the scope of this book—and beyond the interests of most readers—many administrators feel more comfortable if they have at least some idea of what's going on "under the hood." Accordingly, this section provides a brief overview of some of the basic concepts of Windows NT Server networking.

NOTE For a detailed description of the Windows NT networking architecture, see the Windows NT Server resource kit.

Windows NT was originally designed as the first PC client operating system to have built-in rather than added-on networking capabilities. A computer running Windows NT can by design function as either a client or a server—or both—in a distributed environment. It can also simultaneously participate in a peer-to-peer network arrangement.

The original release of Windows NT—called Windows NT 3.1 after the then-current version of the mainstream Microsoft Windows 3.1 desktop operating system—put in place most of the key networking elements used by the current version of Windows NT. Windows NT 3.1 was soon followed by a version optimized for providing network services, and named Windows NT Advanced Server. With the next release, Version 3.5, Microsoft dropped the Advanced Server designation, and simply began referring to the two versions as Windows NT Server and Windows NT Workstation.

With each succeeding release, Microsoft has extended the ability of Windows NT to interoperate in a heterogeneous environment. Although Microsoft now differentiates between the server and workstation versions of Windows NT, the underlying networking features of both are nearly identical. With the release of Version 4.0, Windows NT Server supports the following network environments:

Microsoft Networking
: Windows NT Server 4.0 is fully compatible with all other Microsoft network implementations, including earlier versions of Windows NT Server and Windows NT Workstation, Windows 95, Windows for Workgroups, and LAN Manager.

Novell NetWare

Windows NT Server 4.0 provides nearly complete support of NetWare 2.x and NetWare 3.x servers, and of bindery-mode NetWare 4.x servers. It also provides partial (but normally adequate) support for NDS-mode NetWare 4.x servers.

TCP/IP

Microsoft hasn't overlooked the growing importance of TCP/IP for Internet access, UNIX connectivity, and corporate internetworks. Windows NT Server 4.0 provides complete support for the TCP/IP environment, including various supporting utilities, e.g., DNS and DHCP, that formerly ran only on UNIX hosts.

Apple Macintosh

Although the Apple Macintosh never really made it as a major player in the corporate environment, and has since fallen on hard times, Windows NT Server 4.0 provides comprehensive support for Macintosh clients, Macintosh file structures, and AppleTalk. Unlike NetWare 3.12, which bundles only a five-user Macintosh license, a Windows NT server can support any number of Macintosh clients out of the box, although each still requires a client access license.

Dial-up Networking

The Remote Access Service, described in Chapter 15, *Using Remote Access Service*, allows dial-up clients to use TCP/IP, NWLink, or NetBEUI to access shared resources on the server.

Components

The key reason that Windows NT Server is able to provide such a high degree of interoperability is that it is built on a modular basis, using the OSI Reference Model as a framework. NetWare integrates the NetWare Core Protocol (NCP) and IPX/SPX transport deep into the internals of the operating system. Windows NT Server provides programming "hooks" that allow additional protocol support modules to be added (or upgraded) easily.

Windows NT Server networking components come in three varieties, as follows:

- *Network Adapter Drivers* function at the Physical and Data Link Layers of the OSI Reference Model, and define the interface between the actual network hardware and the remainder of the protocol stack. In order to be accessible to Windows NT, each installed physical network adapter must have its associated device driver loaded. Windows NT uses the Network Driver Interface Specification (NDIS), which is analogous to the Open Datalink Interface (ODI) specification used by NetWare. The NDIS driver operates at the upper half of the Data Link Layer, which is called the Logical Link Control (LLC) sublayer. The NDIS driver provides the interface between the network adapter card drivers operating at the Media Access Control (MAC) sublayer of the Data Link Layer below and the transport protocols above.

- *Transport Protocols* function at the Session, Transport, Network, and Data Link Layers of the OSI Reference Model. Transport protocols define the methods used to communicate data across the network. Windows NT 4.0 supports three general-purpose transport protocols—NWLink (IPX/SXP), TCP/IP, and NetBEUI—and the special-purpose Data Link Control (DLC) protocol. You can run these transport protocols in any combination.
- *File System Drivers* function at the Application and Presentation Layers of the OSI Reference Model, and allow user-mode applications to access system resources. For example, a request to open a file a local NTFS partition is processed by the NTFS FSD. In addition to FSD's that support local NTFS and FAT partitions, Windows NT Server includes various network FSDs that allow a computer to access resources on the network. Among these network FSDs are the Server service, the Workstation service, Named Pipes, and Mailslots, each of which is described in later sections.

Boundary Layers

Windows NT Server defines a boundary layer as a unified interface between each of the networking component types. Using boundary layers aids in maintaining modularity, and allows components to be added and updated discretely, because each component need only be written to the hooks in the appropriate boundary layers rather than addressing the entire OSI model space.

- *Network Driver Interface Specification (NDIS)* provides the interface between the network hardware and its associated drivers and the remainder of the stack. NDIS provides a standard interface between the transport protocols above it and the networking hardware below it. NDIS is similar in concept and functionality to the Link Support Layer (LSL) and Multiple Link Interface Driver (MLID) components of the Novell Open Datalink Interface (ODI) driver model. NDIS allows a computer to support an unlimited number of physical network adapters, each of which may support an unlimited number of protocols. NDIS is responsible for routing inbound packets to the appropriate transport above it.
- *Transport Driver Interface (TDI)* provides the interface between network File System Drivers—for example, the Server service or the Workstation Service—and transport protocols, allowing these upper layer services to function independently of the transport protocol that happens to be in use. Unlike NDIS,

there are no drivers associated with the TDI. It is simply a tightly defined standard interface between FSDs and transport protocols.

- *Programming Interfaces* provide the interface between applications and File System Drivers. Windows NT supports a variety of programming interfaces, including Windows Sockets, NetBIOS, Remote Procedure Calls, and Network Dynamic Data Exchange (NetDDE). Although Microsoft does not treat the programming interface as a true boundary layer, it is similar conceptually.

Network Layer and Transport Layer Protocols

In line with common casual usage, Microsoft often refers to the group of protocols that function at the Network and Transport Layers of the OSI Reference Model as transport protocols. Four standard transport protocols are included with Windows NT Server. The Windows NT network architecture makes it possible to run these transport protocols singly or in any combination. Windows NT Server includes the following transport protocols:

- *NWLink IPX/SPX Compatible Transport (NWLink) protocol* is the Microsoft NDIS implementation of the Novell IPX/SPX protocol. NWLink provides the Network and Transport Layer support necessary for Windows NT Server to interoperate with NetWare, and is also often used as the sole transport in homogeneous Windows networks. NWLink is fast and efficient, and requires little configuration and essentially no routine management. NWLink is also a routed protocol, which makes it at least marginally acceptable for internetworking. However, because it lacks support for subnetting, packet fragmentation, and other technical features useful in an internetworking environment, it is usually not the first choice of transport protocol for an internetwork.

  The NWNBLink component of NWLink is a Microsoft implementation of Novell NetBIOS. NWNBLink is used to process NetBIOS requests for transport by NWLink. NWNBLink is installed automatically with NWLink.

- *Transmission Control Protocol/Internet Protocol (TCP/IP)* provides the Network and Transport Layer support necessary for Windows NT Server to interoperate with UNIX hosts and the Internet. TCP/IP is usually the best choice for primary transport protocol, for homogeneous networks and heterogeneous networks, for local networks, and for internetworks. Like NWLink, TCP/IP is fast and efficient. Unlike NWLink, TCP/IP requires substantial effort to configure initially and to manage on an ongoing basis. TCP/IP is a routed protocol, and was designed with internetworking in mind.

- *NetBIOS Extended User Interface (NetBEUI)* was developed by IBM in the mid-1980s, and is now a relic. Intended for small local area networks that would not be connected to other networks, NetBEUI provides fast, efficient, and easy-to-configure transport at the expense of limited flexibility. NetBEUI frames contain only hardware addresses needed to deliver data locally, and not the software addresses needed to route packets across an internetwork. Microsoft continues to support NetBEUI to provide backward compatibility with Windows for Workgroups and other early Microsoft network products. The NetBEUI support in Windows NT Server is useful primarily for those who need to accommodate in-place legacy Microsoft peer networks.

- *Data Link Control (DLC) protocol* differs from the other supported transport protocols as it provides direct access to the Data Link Layer, hence the name. Because DLC does not use the Transport Driver Interface, it cannot be used by Windows NT File System Drivers, including the Server and Workstation services. Accordingly, DLC is not used as a general-purpose transport protocol to connect PCs.

  Instead, DLC is used in two specialized situations. First, and more commonly, DLC is used to support Hewlett-Packard direct-connect network printers. These printers connect directly to the network cable using a JetDirect card or equivalent interface, and do not require a workstation to process print jobs sent to them. For this purpose, only the computer functioning as a print server for the direct-connect network printer needs to have the DLC protocol installed. Clients who use the printer do not need DLC because they communicate with the print server using their primary transport protocol. Second, DLC is sometimes used with 3270 emulation software to access IBM mainframes. In this case, each computer that is running the 3270 emulation software must have the DLC protocol installed.

Distributed Processing Support

Distributed processing is a mechanism by which different portions of a single application program may execute on multiple computers that are members of the same network. For example, a typical client/server database application uses distributed processing to place the user interface elements of the application on client workstations, while using a central application server to store the database, execute the code necessary to perform searches, update the database, and so forth.

Windows NT Server 4.0 supports the Component Object Model (COM) introduced in previous versions to provide Inter-Process Communication (IPC) on the local machine. Windows NT Server 4.0 extends COM to support the Distributed Component Object Model (DCOM)—previously known as Network Object Linking and Embedding (Network OLE)—which provides similar functionality across the network. DCOM allows application processing to be distributed across the network transparently to the user. If the client and server portions of an application reside on the same computer, DCOM may also be used for local interprocess communication.

In addition to DCOM, Windows NT Server 4.0 provides several other IPC mechanisms. Two are implemented as File System Drivers, as follows:

- *Named Pipes* are defined areas of memory allocated to providing connection-oriented, reliable, bidirectional messaging between two processes. In essence, a Named Pipe can be thought of as a bulletin board where each involved process can both place messages and retrieve them. Named Pipes are a modified version of the API originally developed for OS/2.
- *Mailslots* provide a connectionless, unreliable, bidirectional mechanism for broadcast messages. Windows NT implements second-class Mailslots, which are useful for high-volume, noncritical broadcasts like those used by the Browser service, which is described later in this chapter. Mailslots are also commonly used for sending broadcast messages to computers and users, and to register computer, user, workgroup, and domain names on the network.

Named Pipes and Mailslots differ from other IPC mechanisms because they are implemented as Windows NT File System drivers. Named Pipes and Mailslots can be used for Inter-Process Communication on one computer or, via the redirector, for IPC between computers. Because Named Pipes and Mailslots are implemented as File System Drivers, they share the common characteristics of other FSDs, including security.

- *NetBIOS* was the first widely deployed IPC mechanism implemented as an application programming interface (API) to support client/server applications. NetBIOS was developed in the early 1980s, popularized by IBM, and is still commonly used. The NetBIOS interface provides a mapping layer between NetBIOS applications and the TDI.

  Windows NT Server supports NetBIOS for all three primary transport protocols. NetBEUI supports NetBIOS using the NetBEUI Frame protocol (NBF); NWLink uses the NWNBLink component; TCP/IP uses the Internet-standard NetBIOS over TCP/IP (NetBT) protocols, defined in RFC 1001 and RFC 1002. NetBIOS is an obsolescent IPC mechanism. More recent IPC implementations, e.g., Named Pipes and Remote Procedure calls, provide higher performance, more flexibility, and easier portability.
- *Mailslots* is an application programming interface that provides a standard Windows interface to transport protocols. Winsock is the Microsoft implementation of the Sockets interface developed at UC Berkeley in the early 1980s. With the growth of the Internet and applications designed to access it, the Winsock API has become ubiquitous. In addition to TCP/IP, Winsock supports NWLink.

- *Remote Procedure Calls (RPC)* were developed initially by Sun Microsystems, Inc., and subsequently adopted by the Open Software Foundation (OSF) as a component of the Distributed Computing Environment (DCE). Microsoft RPC is completely compatible with and interoperates with DCE RPCs.

  Microsoft RPC can use other IPC services to communicate information between the IPC client and IPC server. Windows NT RPC uses NetBIOS, Winsock and Named Pipes to communicate. Local Procedure Calls (LPCs) can be used to communicate data between processes and subsystems running on the same computer. RPC includes several components implemented as dynamic link libraries (DLL), as follows:

  — *RPC Stub* processes RPCs and passes them to the RPC Runtime.

  — *RPC Runtime* receives RPC packages from the RPC Stub and passes them to the RPC server.

  — *Application Stub* receives RPC requests from the RPC Runtime, processes them, and calls the remote procedure.

  — *Remote Procedure* is the actual called remote procedure.

  RPC-aware applications are compiled and linked using RPC Stub libraries, which appear to the application as local subroutines. When the application makes a call using the RPC routines, the call is redirected to the RPC Runtime module running on the RPC client. The RPC Runtime module locates the appropriate RPC server and sends the query to that server. The server processes the RPC call and executes the Remote Procedure. When the Remote Procedure completes, the RPC server transfers the results to its own RPC Runtime, which communicates those results to the RPC Runtime module running on the RPC client. The client RPC Runtime module returns the results to the application that generated the call.

- *Network Dynamic Data Exchange (NetDDE)* is an extended implementation of the Dynamic Data Exchange (DDE) protocol that was initially released in Windows 2.0, and is by now familiar to most Windows users. DDE allows applications to exchange data by establishing two unidirectional pipes to link the applications—one in each direction. DDE is limited to exchanging data between applications running on the same computer. NetDDE extends the DDE protocol, allowing applications running on different computers to exchange information.

  An application that initiates a DDE transfer does so by establishing a DDE conversation. The initiating application, called the DDE client, establishes a pipe to the target application. The target application, called the DDE server, in turn establishes a pipe to the DDE client. Any DDE-aware application can function as a DDE client, a DDE server, or as both simultaneously. NetDDE uses NetBIOS to make DDE functions available across the network. Because NetDDE is a simple extension of DDE rather than a separate product, any DDE-aware application can use NetDDE transparently. The NetDDE service examines each DDE conversation and redirects it as necessary across the network.

Server Message Block

The Server Message Block (SMB) protocol forms the foundation of Microsoft Networking, and is similar in function and purpose to the NetWare Core Protocol (NCP). SMB defines a set of commands that are used by the local redirector to package Network Control Block (NCB) queries for delivery to a remote computer on the network. The local redirector may also use SMB to communicate with the protocol stack on the local machine. SMB uses four message types to provide these functions, as follows:

- *Session Control Message* is used to build up or tear down a redirector session establishing a connection to shared resources on the remote server.
- *File Message* requests access to a file on the remote server.
- *Printer Message* places print jobs in a queue on the remote server, and to query the current status of such print jobs.
- *Message Message* exchanges messages between one workstation and another, between a workstation and a server, or between servers.

Accessing Network Resources

In NetWare, an application that needs to access a network resource does so by making a local call, which is intercepted by the NetWare redirector or requester, and routed to the appropriate network resource. Windows NT introduces another layer between the application and the redirector. This layer comprises two components, the Multiple Universal Naming Provider (MUP) and the Multi-Provider Router (MPR). These two components perform similar functions. Which is used depends on how an application makes a call. MUP and MPR are described in the following list.

- *MUP* provides the interface between the application and the redirector when the application makes an I/O call using a Universal Naming Convention (UNC) name. The UNC may be used to designate servers and resources on those servers. UNC names take the form of two backslashes followed by the server name, followed by a single backslash and the resource name. UNC names are hierarchical, and use additional single backslashes to separate child resources. For example, the file *document* in the folder *users* on volume *sysvol* on server *admin* is represented in UNC as *admin**sysvol**users**document*.

When an application makes a UNC I/O call, that call is received by the I/O Manager and passed to MUP, which forwards the call to the appropriate UNC provider, or redirector. If MUP has that UNC location cached, it forwards the call to the appropriate redirector immediately. If MUP has not seen that UNC recently, it polls the redirectors that are registered with it to determine which one can process the I/O request.

- *MPR* is similar in purpose and function to MUP, but works with the Win32 Network APIs instead of with UNC names. When MPR receives a WNet command from an application, it determines which redirector should handle the command, and passes it to that redirector.

Workstation Service

The Windows NT Workstation Service handles all user-mode requests. It allows the computer to function as a client on the network, by providing the ability to log on to the domain and to access share files and printers. The Workstation Service requires a TDI-compliant transport protocol and MUP. The Workstation Service has two components, which bridge user mode and kernel mode:

- *User Mode Interface* is contained in *Services.exe*. The User Mode Interface processes user mode requests and passes them to the kernel mode redirector.
- *Redirector* is contained in *Redir.sys*, a File System Driver which interfaces to the TDI. The Redirector allows the computer to access remote files and printers by redirecting local calls to the appropriate remote resource.

When a process attempts to open a file located on a remote computer, the process first calls I/O Manager to request the file open. When I/O Manager determines that the file is located on a remote computer, it passes the request to the redirector, which in turn passes it to the remote server to be processed.

Server Service

The Windows NT Server Service allows a server to create and protect shared resources, and to make those resources available to its clients. The Server Service is also implemented as an FSD, and works with other FSDs to fulfill client requests. Like the Workstation Service, the Server Service comprises two elements:

- *Server Service* is contained in *Services.exe*. The Server Service does not require MUP, since it is not a UNC provider. The Server Service only provides connections requested by other computers; it does not initiate connections to other computers.

- *Server FSD,* contained in *Srv.sys,* is a File System Driver that works with other FSDs as needed to satisfy client requests, and manages interactions with the lower layers that actually transport the requests to the remote machines.

Browsing the Network

If clients are to use a network service or resource, they must know that the service or resource exists and where it is located. With NetWare, the situation is relatively uncomplicated. NetWare uses an essentially pure client/server architecture. NetWare servers provide services and shared resources, and NetWare clients use them. NetWare 3.1x servers use Service Advertising Protocol (SAP) to announce the availability of the services they provide. There's not much problem locating network resources, either—they're all right there on the server. A NetWare client can simply look to the server to find what's available.

With Microsoft Networking, the situation is a bit different. Microsoft Networking combines aspects of both client/server architecture and peer-to-peer architecture, distributing services and resources across the network. Because any Microsoft Networking computer connected to the network can both provide and use services and shared resources, some means of keeping track of where these shared resources and services are located is necessary. There are several possible solutions which might be used, individually or in combination, to meet this requirement, as follows:

Broadcasts

A server might advertise the availability of its services and its shared resources by periodically sending broadcast messages to the entire network. This is the method Novell NetWare 3.12 uses, via SAP broadcasts, to advertise services. Broadcasts consume network bandwidth, and are a particularly poor choice on slow wide-area network links.

Local Lists

Each workstation might maintain its own local lists of services and shared resources available on the network, similar to the *HOSTS* and *LMHOSTS* files that may be used for IP name resolution and NetBIOS name resolution, respectively. If maintained manually, such lists have the disadvantage of requiring substantial manual effort to create and maintain, and of becoming outdated when the network environment changes. If maintained dynamically, e.g., by receiving periodic network service availability broadcasts and using this information to update the local file automatically, local lists are viable, but do nothing to reduce network loading. Most network operating systems use local lists only for relatively static information, such as network drive mappings.

Directory Service

A formally structured, centralized database might be used to maintain a current list of all available network services and shared resources. Clients that are attempting to locate such resources query the central database to determine which services and resources are currently available, and where they are located. This is the method used by NetWare 4.x, via Novell Directory Services (NDS).

Browser Service

A browsing methodology might be used to parse the network to discover available network resources, and list those resources on one or more central machines for subsequent lookups by clients.

Windows NT allows you to designate certain computers on the network to serve as *browsers*. Browsers, in addition to their other duties, run the Windows NT Computer Browser service. Browsers maintain a centralized list of network resources, called a *browse list*, which can be accessed by clients that are attempting to locate shared network resources. By maintaining the browse list and making it available to other computers, browsers eliminate the need for each workstation to maintain its own local list of network resources. By limiting the number of computers that participate in the discovery process, using browsers also allows you to minimize associated network traffic.

Browser Types

Allowing only one computer to provide browser services would introduce a single point of failure into the network and would also prevent you from optimizing throughput on slow network links. Accordingly, Windows NT allows multiple computers to serve as browsers on a single network. These browsers are of various types, as follows:

Master Browser

A computer that collects the information needed to build the network resource list, also called the browse list, maintains the primary copy of the browse list, and distributes it other browsers. Each domain or workgroup may have only one Master Browser. The Primary Domain Controller (PDC) automatically becomes the Master Browser for its domain.

Backup Browser

A computer that receives a copy of the browse list from the Master Browser and distributes the browse list to clients that request it. Backup Browsers can be used both to reduce the workload on the Master Browser and to reduce network traffic across slow links. Each domain or workgroup may have multiple Backup Browsers. Backup Domain Controllers (BDC) are automatically assigned as Backup Browsers for their domain.

Potential Browser

A computer that is capable of serving as a Backup Browser, but does not do so unless the Master Browser requests it.

Non-Browser

A computer configured not to maintain a browse list, typically a workstation. Non-Browsers may access the browse list maintained by browsers, but do not otherwise participate in the browsing process.

You may also designate a computer to be the *Preferred Master Browser (PMB)*. When this computer is started, it attempts to become the Master Browser for the domain or workgroup. If a Master Browser is already active on the network, the PMB forces an election. In a domain environment, the PDC will always win that election. In a workgroup environment, the PMB wins the election over another computer that had assumed the role of the Master Browser.

How Browsing Works

The browsing service works as follows:

1. When any Windows NT computer that runs the Server service is started, it registers its name and browser type with the Master Browser.
2. When a client is started, and first needs to access a browse list, it contacts the Master Browser for the domain or workgroup of which it is a member, receives a list of Backup Browsers for that domain or workgroup from the Master Browser, and contacts a Backup Browser to obtain a copy of the browse list.
3. The Backup Browser returns to the client a copy of the browse list, which includes a list of domains and workgroups and a list of the servers that are local to that client.
4. When the client accesses the browse list—for example, by double-clicking Network Neighborhood—Windows displays the browse list. The list of domains and workgroups is contained within the Entire Network item, and may be expanded by double-clicking it. Local servers are displayed and listed individually by name. The client can then expand the listing for individual servers to display the shared resources available on those servers.

Browser Elections

Exactly one Master Browser must exist for each domain or workgroup. To determine which computer will be the Master Browser, Windows Networking assigns each potential browser a priority ranking based upon the operating system and version it is running, and upon its current role in the browsing environment. This ranking is used when a new Master Browser must be determined, a process referred to as an *election*. An election occurs if a browser client or Backup Browser is unable to locate a Master Browser or if a computer that has been designated a Preferred Master Browser is started in a domain or workgroup that already has an active Master Browser.

When one of these situations occurs, the computer that identified the conflict begins the election by broadcasting an *election packet*. When a computer that is currently configured as a browser receives an election packet, it compares its own ranking to that contained in the packet. If its own ranking is the same or lower, it does nothing. If its ranking is higher than that received in the election packet, it broadcasts its own election packet. This process continues until one computer is identified as having the highest available ranking, and is assigned as the new Master Browser for the domain or workgroup.

Configuring Browsers

Ordinarily, there is no need to configure the browser environment manually. However, it is possible to specify that a particular computer not provide browser services, or to configure it as a Potential Browser by modifying the value of the Registry key

```
HKEY_LOCAL_MACHINE\SYSTEM\CurrentControlSet\Services\Browser
\Parameters\MaintainServerList
```

as follows:

- *TRUE*. This setting, which is the default value for Windows NT Server computers that are configured as domain controllers, indicates that the computer will participate as a browser. When it starts, it will contact the Master Browser to obtain a browse list. If it is unable to locate the Master Browser, it will initiate an election, and will become either the Master Browser or a Backup Browser.
- *FALSE*. This computer will not participate as a Browser of any sort under any circumstances.
- *AUTO*. This setting, which is the default value for Windows NT Workstation computers and for Windows NT Server computers that are configured as member servers, indicates that the computer will become a Potential Browser.

You can also designate a Windows NT Workstation or Windows NT Server member server computer as Preferred Master Browser by modifying:

```
HKEY_LOCAL_MACHINE\SYSTEM\CurrentControlSet\Services\Browser
\Parameters\IsDomainMaster
```

Possible values are:

- *Yes*. This value, which must be entered manually using the Registry Editor, specifies that this computer is configured as the Preferred Master Browser, and that it will always force an election when it is started. In a workgroup environment, this computer is given a very high ranking, and therefore will always become the Master Browser. However, in a domain environment, the Primary Domain Controller is always assigned the highest ranking, and therefore becomes the Master Browser whether or not a Preferred Master Browser is present.

- *No.* This setting is the default value for any Windows NT computer, whether or not it is currently the Master Browser.

Understanding Domains

As I described in Chapter 1, small Windows NT Server networks may be organized using the workgroup concept common to peer networks, while larger Windows NT Server networks use the concept of domains. The following sections first examine alternative methods that can be used to organize a network, and then describe the domain concept that forms the basis of Windows NT Server networks.

Network Organization

In broad terms, four methods can be used to organize a network. The simplest networks have only one server, which makes administering them relatively easy—until you add a second server. NetWare 3.1x is inherently a single-server network, and makes no provision for managing multiple servers on a single network. Networks that have more than one machine providing shared resources and services can be organized in several ways. The most complex and powerful of these methods is the directory services method used by NetWare 4.x. The simplest method in theory—although it often turns out to be very complex in practice—is the workgroup method used by peer networks. Between these two methods, in both complexity and power, is the domain method used by Windows NT Server. The following sections examine each of these methods.

Single server networks

The first PC local area networks usually had only one server, and it was almost always running NetWare 2.x or NetWare 3.x. All shared network resources were located on that one server. Laser printers, large hard disk drives, memory, server hardware, and the network operating system itself were all very expensive. Therefore it made sense to centralize everything and run it on one capable machine.

This arrangement made it easy for clients to locate and use shared network resources. There was no question about where a network printer or shared volume was located. It was always right there on the server. To make things even easier for clients (and themselves), most administrators set up all of their workstations with standard predefined printers, drive mappings, and so on. Access to shared network resources became so transparent to users that many weren't aware of when they were using local resources and when they were using network resources.

These single server networks were also easy to administer, again because everything was in one place. The NetWare bindery on that one server stored all information about every user authorized to access the network. The supervisor could use any workstation connected to the network to maintain user accounts and otherwise administer the server. An adventurous administrator could even dial in to the server and maintain it remotely.

Even the server names were standardized. Just as many newly installed Windows NT domains use the default domain name DOMAIN, and at least half the NetWare servers running used the default server name NS1. Everything was fine until the day NS2 showed up. The problem arose because there were now two servers on the network, each of which had to be maintained separately. Each server had resources under its own control, and each had its own bindery controlling access to those resources.

All of a sudden, users had to log on (or attach) to more than one server if they needed to access resources on different servers. They could no longer simply use resources—they had to know where a particular resource was located. Administrators had to maintain multiple binderies. Things were bad enough with two servers on the network. As the number of servers increased beyond that, the situation rapidly became unworkable.

Directory services

Novell's solution for this problem was NDS, which originally stood for NetWare Directory Services, and was later renamed as Novell Directory Services. A directory service is a formal, structured, hierarchical database that contains information about every object on the network. An object may represent a traditional shared resource, like a printer or a disk volume. An object may also represent a user account, a group, or a system service. A server itself is an object in the directory service database. In fact, any aspect of the network may be represented as a directory object.

In concept, a directory service resembles the Yellow Pages in your phone book. Related resources may be grouped, and a user can search the directory to locate objects of a particular type, or can browse the directory. A directory is also inherently scalable, and can be expanded to serve very large and complex networks.

The real attraction of using a directory services scheme is that it is network-centric rather than server-centric. Users log on to the network itself rather than to individual servers, and can access any shared resource on the network for which they are authorized without having to know where that resource is actually located. Similarly, administrators can maintain the network rather than individual servers. For example, updating a user account record modifies the directory services database itself, and that single change is subsequently reflected across the entire network.

The idea of a directory service is not new. The CCITT/ITU maintains the X.500 directory service specification as an international standard. X.500 is comprehensive, complicated, and powerful, and has never been released as an actual product. Other commercially available directory services, however, are based to a greater or lesser extent on the data structures and concepts of the X.500 standard.

For example, Banyan developed the StreetTalk directory service for their VINES network operating system, and it remains one of the great strengths of VINES. Recognizing this advantage, Banyan subsequently ported StreetTalk to other network operating systems, including NetWare 3.12, as the Banyan Enterprise Networking System (ENS). Unfortunately for Banyan, ENS for NetWare arrived on the scene about the same time that Novell released NetWare 4.0, which included its own directory service, called NDS.

Although it is not X.500-compliant, NDS is based closely on X.500. Like X.500, the initial implementation of NDS was clumsy and hard to use. For example, many inexperienced NetWare 4.0 administrators (including me) were surprised to find that they could not undo changes they had made to their NDS trees, requiring them to reinstall the operating system. Subsequent revisions of NDS have improved the situation dramatically, and NDS is now a viable means for organizing a network.

NDS is Novell's only real trump card in its ongoing struggle to prevent Windows NT Server from further eroding NetWare's market share. NDS allows Novell to present NetWare 4.x as a credible enterprise NOS, a positioning that Microsoft has so far been unable to establish for Windows NT Server, despite their persistent effort. Recognizing the strategic importance of NDS as standard directory services platform, Novell has announced plans to port NDS to Windows NT Server.

Although they don't talk about it much, Microsoft recognizes that the lack of a true directory service for Windows NT Server places it at an extreme disadvantage relative to NetWare 4.x in the competition for mind-share in the enterprise NOS segment. They have tried to present the Windows NT Server domain-based organizational schema as a directory service, which it is not, and have even gone so far as to use the term *directory service* in at least one product name—Directory

Service Manager for NetWare. Clearly, Microsoft wants to be a player in the directory service market.

Microsoft has announced that Windows NT Server 5.0 will include Active Directory Services (ADS), their first real directory service implementation. ADS is based on the industry-standard Lightweight Directory Access Protocol (LDAP)—which is a subset of X.500—and on the Internet standard Domain Name Service (DNS). No one, including Microsoft, is making any claims that ADS will be superior to NDS. However, NDS was developed before the Internet and TCP/IP became major factors, and is not as well integrated with these important enterprise networking components as it might have been. ADS, on the other hand, will be tightly integrated with TCP/IP and the Internet.

The decision to implement a directory services scheme is not a trivial one. Designing and implementing directory services impacts every department in the organization, and requires that a strong central leadership role be played by the MIS department. A successful deployment requires that many issues be resolved in detail, some of which are technical, some organizational, and others purely political. Deploying directory services properly requires technical design skills that many organizations do not have in-house. Actual organizational dynamics do not always, or even usually, follow the formal organization chart. Departments that have historically managed their own networks may look askance at plans to centralize network planning and management. While it may solve many existing problems, implementing directory services may also raise new problems of its own.

Today, a directory service scheme is an absolute requirement only for very large networks. Small- and mid-size networks can get along using older methods, at least for the time being. In the long run, all networks will use some form of directory services, but that day has not yet arrived.

Workgroups

Diametrically opposed to the directory services concept is the workgroup concept. Where directory services are formal, structured, and relatively rigid, workgroups are informal, unstructured, and flexible. Directory services place the onus of administering the network on a central administrator. Workgroups distribute that responsibility and power to the individual network users, along with the associated headaches.

A workgroup is a named logical grouping of computers that do not share a common account database or security policy. In a workgroup, each user decides for himself which of his computer's resources he will share with other members of the workgroup, which other workgroup members will be authorized to access those shared resources, and what level of access will be granted to each other user. Because resource sharing decisions are enforced at the individual workstation level, each computer must maintain its own list of shared resources. Access to these shared resources can be controlled in one of two ways, both of which are clumsy.

First, each resource may be protected by its own password. For example, if Mary wants to share her printer, she first assigns a password to it. If Ed wants to send a print job to Mary's printer, he must first supply the password that Mary previously assigned to the printer before the print job will be accepted. This method obviously results in the rapid proliferation of passwords, and is unmanageable in all but the smallest networks. In reality, what usually happens is that resources are shared with no passwords assigned, allowing anyone to access any resource. Although this may work well enough in a small office, it is the antithesis of a managed network.

Alternatively, each computer might maintain a local user account database that contains a record for each user who is authorized to access a shared resource on that computer, and a list of resources that that user is authorized to access. In this case, if Ed and Sarah are to share Mary's printer, Mary must create local accounts for each of them on her computer. If Sarah wants to share her CD-ROM drive with Mary and Ed, she must first create accounts for each of them on her computer, and so forth. Although this method offers considerably more security and flexibility than the method described in the preceding paragraph, it requires that each user take on some of the responsibilities of a network administrator. It also requires that each user have more knowledge of networks than is often the case.

Workgroups are inextricably linked to the idea of peer-to-peer networking, which for many NetWare administrators is a nasty concept. Despite the access control problems and complex administration issues that make workgroups inappropriate as the sole management mechanism for larger networks, the workgroup concept has a legitimate place in many network environments. Even in a large scale client/server network, using workgroups at the local level can provide users with the flexibility and responsiveness they need to address their immediate problems.

Workgroups have been a fundamental part of Microsoft Networking since its introduction. With the release of Windows 3.x for Workgroups, Microsoft brought the workgroup concept into common usage on the desktop. With Windows 95, they extended it considerably. Even Windows NT Workstation—and Windows NT Server 4.0 when it is configured as a member server—use workgroups to organize their resources and control access to them.

Domains

The domain concept incorporates aspects of both directory services and workgroups. Like directory services, domains centralize user authentication and security, and allow users to log on to the network rather than to individual servers. Like workgroups, domains provide the additional flexibility of peer resource sharing. For small- and medium-size networks, domains often provide the best mix of central control and flexibility. Only in very large and complex networks do domains become difficult to manage.

A Windows NT Server domain is a group of computers that share a common account database and security policy. In essence, a domain may be thought of as a formalized workgroup. A domain may comprise only a few computers, or several thousand. A single domain may encompass dozens of sites scattered throughout the world, or it may be limited to a single floor of an office building.

Domain Controllers and Servers

A Windows NT server can assume one of the following three roles (each of which is described more fully in the following sections):

Primary Domain Controller (PDC)
: The Windows NT Server computer that stores the master copies of the account and security databases for the domain.

Backup Domain Controller (BDC)
: A Windows NT Server computer that stores a backup copy of the account and security databases for the domain.

Server
: A Windows NT Server computer that is a member of the domain, and may provide shared resources for clients, but does not function as a domain controller.

You specify which of these three roles the computer is to play when you are installing Windows NT Server. Once the software is installed, these roles are sometimes not readily convertible, so deciding early which role you want the computer to play is important. If, for example, you initially install Windows NT Server configured as a server and later decide that you want that computer to be a domain controller, your only alternative is to reinstall Windows NT Server from scratch. Each of these roles is described more fully in the following sections.

Primary domain controller

Every Windows NT domain must have exactly one Primary Domain Controller (PDC). The PDC stores the master copy of the user account database and the security database for the domain. The PDC authenticates users, maintains Access

Control Lists (ACLs), and serves as the master browser for the domain. The administrator uses User Manager for Domains to modify the contents of these master databases.

Backup domain controller

One or more of the other Windows NT Server computers in the domain may be configured as a Backup Domain Controller (BDC). Each BDC stores a backup copy of the master administrative databases located on the PDC. Changes made to the master databases on the PDC are replicated periodically to each BDC, keeping it in synch. Like the PDC, a BDC may be used to authenticate users. In a distributed network, using a BDC located at a remote site to authenticate users at that site reduces the amount of traffic that must be carried by the slow WAN link. Also, if your network includes more than a few hundred users, you may use a local BDC to reduce the workload on the PDC.

Using a BDC also provides a degree of redundancy to improve network fault tolerance. If the PDC fails, a BDC may be promoted to PDC, thereby maintaining network availability. For this reason, all but the smallest Windows NT Server networks should include at least one BDC. On a single-server Windows NT network, the server is almost always configured as a PDC. When a second server is added to this domain, it should be configured as a BDC. When a third server is added, it should also be configured as a BDC. Only if your domain already includes several local servers configured as BDCs should you consider not making a new server another BDC.

All changes must be made to the master databases running on the PDC. This means that if the PDC fails or otherwise becomes unavailable, no changes to user or group accounts can occur until either a new PDC is installed or a BDC is promoted to PDC. However, on a network that is temporarily without a PDC, the BDC can continue to authenticate users and otherwise to participate in domain activities. If, for example, the WAN link fails that connects a BDC at a remote office to the PDC at the home office, the remote BDC can continue to support the network at the remote site. When the link is re-established, the BDC again synchronizes with the PDC, and any changes made in the interim to the PDC are replicated to the BDC.

Server

The third role that Windows NT Server may play is that of a server. A server may or may not be a member of a domain, as follows:

Member Server

If a Windows NT Server computer configured as a server is a member of a domain, it is referred to as a *member server*. Member servers do not function as domain controllers, but may use the databases maintained by the domain controllers to authenticate users and control access to resources. You use User Manager for Domains to maintain the account database on a member server.

Standalone Server

If a Windows NT Server computer configured as a server is not a member of a domain, it is referred to as a *standalone server.* A standalone server functions much like Windows NT Workstation. It maintains its own local account and security databases, which are administered using User Manager (rather than User Manager for Domains). By definition, a standalone server is used in a workgroup setting.

There are several reasons why you might decide to configure a computer as a member server, as follows:

- Functioning as a domain controller places an additional load on the computer, because it must validate logon requests and perform other administrative tasks. In small- and medium-size domains, this additional load is so small it is unnoticeable. In very large domains—those with thousands of users—a domain controller may spend most of its time performing these administrative duties. If your domain already includes several local Backup Domain Controllers to provide redundancy, configuring additional servers as member servers allows them to devote all of their resource to handling user requests.
- It is very difficult to move a computer that is configured as a domain controller to a different domain. If your network includes multiple domains and many servers, configuring a new server as a member server makes it much easier to relocate that server as needed.
- If you use dedicated application servers on your network, e.g., one server dedicated to running Exchange Server, another to running SQL Server, and so forth, configuring these servers as member servers makes it easy to assign a specific staff member as the server administrator for each of the servers.

Each of these reasons applies primarily to medium- and large-scale networks. In smaller networks, there is seldom a good reason to configure Windows NT Server as a standalone server. You might do so with the intention of creating a semiformal workgroup environment. Rather than sharing resources willy-nilly between workstations, you might provide one capable machine with a lot of memory and disk as the central server, with Windows NT Server installed on it and configured as a standalone server.

This is a good idea, as far as it goes, but you would be much better off installing that single server as a PDC to allow for network growth. If you install the original server as a PDC—and thereby create a domain—when it comes time to add a second server you can simply add it to the domain as a BDC.

If instead you install the original server as a standalone server, you've limited your choices for installing additional servers. You could configure the new server as the PDC, and make the original server a member server of the new domain, but that's not a desirable state of affairs. To convert the original server to a BDC, you must reinstall the software. You might also install the new server as a second standalone server, but that gives you two independent servers that must be managed separately. Basing a network on a standalone server limits you to the workgroup schema, and paints you into a corner. Configure your first server as a PDC instead.

Synchronizing Domain Controllers

All changes to the domain databases are made to the PDC, which then periodically replicates these changes automatically to each computer that is configured as a BDC. This replication process is called *synchronization*. There are two types of synchronization, as follows:

Partial Synchronization

Modifications made to the PDC databases—adds, changes, and deletions to user accounts and group accounts, user rights, and so forth—are recorded to a change log on the PDC. A partial synchronization occurs automatically at defined intervals, and transmits only the changed values from the PDC to the BDC.

Complete Synchronization

When you first install a BDC, you specify the domain to which that BDC belongs. Setup locates the PDC for that domain and replicates the entire contents of the PDC administrative databases to the BDC. Under normal circumstances, this is the only time that complete synchronization occurs. However, if the BDC is out of contact with the PDC for an extended period—perhaps because it is turned off or because the link between them is down—a complete synchronization will occur when the BDC comes back online.

A complete synchronization is required under these circumstances because the PDC change log is limited in how many changes it can record—by default to about 2,000 records. The change log uses a FIFO buffer, and discards the oldest changes first. This means that, if the BDC remains out of contact with the PDC for an extended period, there is no guarantee that all changes that occurred on the PDC will be available to replicate to the BDC. A complete synchronization therefore occurs automatically to resolve the problem.

TIP If you need to build a BDC that will subsequently be connected to the PDC via a slow WAN link, build the BDC while it is connected to the same LAN as the PDC. This allows synchronization to occur on the fast LAN rather than on the slower WAN. Once the BDC has synchronized, power it down and move it to the remote location.

The NetLogon Service provides users with a single unified network logon. It also is responsible for synchronizing domain controllers by replicating changes that occur on the PDC to all BDCs. The NetLogon service periodically sends notifications to the BDCs, prompting them to request updates from the PDC. When a BDC requests an update—by default every five minutes—it informs the PDC of the date and time of the latest update it received, allowing the PDC to determine which entries from the change log need to be replicated to the BDC.

Understanding Trust Relationships

A single domain can contain many servers. It is possible to build a very large network—once that comprises dozens of servers and hundreds or even thousands of workstations—using only a single domain. There are two good reasons, however, why an organization might want to implement a network that comprises multiple domains.

- Departments or remote offices may want to manage their own networks, which is more easily accomplished if each is assigned its own domain.
- Although you can assign many servers to a single domain, performance degrades if too many servers are included in one domain. In very large networks, it is sometimes necessary to create additional domains simply to limit the number of servers per domain. Also, the total size of the domain database may become a factor in a very large network. For best performance, it should be limited to about 40 MB. Although this is a soft limit, it effectively restricts the number of clients, user accounts, and group accounts that can be accommodated within one domain.

Multiple domains are commonly organized on a geographic basis, an organizational basis, or both. For example, if your organization has offices in Pittsburgh, Winston-Salem, and Chicago, and each of these offices has departments named Sales, Administration, and Accounting, you might use one of three methods, as follows:

- *Geographic domains* create three domains, one for each of the three offices. All computers that are physically located in the Pittsburgh office, for example, would be assigned to the Pittsburgh domain.

- *Distributed Organizational domains* create three domains, one for each of the three departments. All computers that belong to the Sales department, wherever they are physically located, are assigned to the Sales domain.
- *Local Organizational domains* create nine domains, one for each of the three departments at each of the three locations. Computers are assigned to individual domains based both upon their physical location and the department to which they are assigned. For example, only computers that belong to the Sales department in the Pittsburgh office are assigned to the Pittsburgh Sales domain.

As long as your entire network is contained within a single domain, administration is relatively straightforward. All user accounts reside on the single PDC, and are replicated to one or several BDCs. Any authorized user can access resources on any server within the domain. When you create multiple domains, you also create multiple PDCs, each of which maintains its own directory database, independent of other PDCs. This means that any user who needs to access resources in more than one domain must have an account in each domain. This takes us back to the bad old days of standalone servers and maintaining multiple accounts for each user.

Fortunately, Windows NT Server addresses this problem. It does so by allowing you to establish *trust relationships* between domains. Trust relationships allow a user from one domain to access the resources of a second domain without first logging on to that second domain.

For example, you might have two domains, named Domain A and Domain B. If you establish as a trust relationship that Domain A trusts Domain B, users who successfully log on to Domain B can also access resources on Domain A without first logging on to Domain A. In this case, Domain A is referred to as a *trusting domain*, and Domain B is referred to as a *trusted domain*.

Trust relationships are unidirectional. That is, if you want Domain A and Domain B to trust each other, you must establish two separate trust relationships, one that says A trusts B and one that says that B trusts A. Such an arrangement is called a *two-way trust relationship*.

Trust relationships are not transitive. That is, you might have three domains, named A, B, and C. If you establish a two-way trust relationship between domains A and B, and another two-way trust relationship between domains B and C, that does not create any trust relationship between domains A and C. Establishing a full trust relationship between all three domains requires that you create six different trust relationships—A to B, B to A, B to C, C to B, A to C, and C to A.

This nontransitive characteristic of domain trust relationships is one of the greatest weaknesses of the domain schema for large networks. As the number of domains increases, the number of required trust relationships increases even faster, because, if the number of domains is n, (n^2-n) trust relationships are required. For example, two domains require (2^2-2), or two trust relationships; three domains require (3^2-3), or six trust relationships; four domains require (4^2-4), or twelve trust relationships; and ten domains require (10^2-10), or 90 trust relationships! As the number of domains increases, the number of trust relationships that you must create and maintain rapidly becomes unmanageable.

In theory at least, you can avoid this proliferation of trust relationships by establishing a hierarchical model and using unidirectional trust relationships between each level and its parent. For example, you might create a top-level domain for the home office, second-level domains for each of the three branch offices, and third-level domains for the departments within each branch office.

Each of the branch office domains—Pittsburgh, Winston-Salem, and Chicago—would trust the home office domain, but would not be trusted by it. Each of the departmental domains would trust its own office domain, but not be trusted by it. For example, Chicago Sales would trust Chicago, and Pittsburgh Accounting would trust Pittsburgh. Setting up this type of tiered unidirectional trust relationship matrix theoretically provides many of the benefits of a directory service while avoiding numerous complex trust relationships.

In practice, this method seldom works very well. Inevitably, other "temporary" trust relationships are created to serve the needs of the moment. You end up with Pittsburgh Sales trusting and being trusted by Chicago Accounting, Winston-Salem trusting Chicago sales, and so forth. Before long, you have a complete mess. The lesson to be learned is that you should keep the number of domains as small as possible, and minimize your dependence on trust relationships.

Understanding Domain Models

Using trust relationships properly allows you to build an enterprise network that retains the single unified network logon characteristic of a single domain. Microsoft defines four types of domain models that are suited for different environments. One of these—the Single Domain Model—does not use trust relationships. The other three models use trust relationships in various ways. These models are examined in the following sections.

The single domain model

The *single domain model* is by far the simplest model to create and administer. A single domain network is the easiest type to manage because all administrative information resides on one PDC. By definition, trust relationships, which may require significant effort to create and maintain, are not required in the single domain model. Use the single domain model for your network if at all possible.

At some point—and Microsoft is notoriously unclear about how to determine just when this point occurs—the single domain model is no longer adequate to handle the demands of the network. There is no hard and fast rule that defines when you need to move to a multiple domain model. As the domain becomes larger and more complex, performance begins to degrade. As servers and workstations are added, browsing becomes increasingly inefficient.

In reality, however, few single domain networks are expanded to multiple domain networks because of performance problems. Usually, the motivation is to provide individual departments or sites with their own domains, or to locate specific resources within isolated domains. If, for whatever reason, you find that you need to expand your network to include multiple domains, one of the following multiple domain models may be right for you.

The master domain model

The *master domain model* uses one domain to handle all user accounts. User accounts within the master domain may be assigned to global groups, which are described in more detail in Chapter 5, *Managing Users and Groups*. Global groups defined in the master domain can be exported to subsidiary domains. Global groups can then be mapped to local groups within subsidiary domains, and local privileges assigned to each local group, relieving the subsidiary domains of the necessity of maintaining user accounts. When a user logs on to the network, he logs on to the master domain, and can then access resources in the domains that trust the master domain, according to his group memberships.

The master domain model has several advantages. Inherently, it centralizes security management, allowing it to be the responsibility of the MIS department rather than the individual user departments or sites. It distributes the browsing load among multiple domains. It allows departments or sites to manage their own local resources and to control their own permissions. By using global groups, it simplifies management at the department or site level.

Against these advantages, two disadvantages must be considered, both related to logon activity limited to the master domain. First, it introduces a single point of failure. Because only the master domain can validate user logons, failure of the master domain controller can be catastrophic, because no user anywhere on the network will be able to log on. In a master domain environment, it is essential that at least one BDC exist, and preferably several. It is also essential that reliable—and preferably redundant—communications links exist between the master domain and subsidiary domains. Second, because all logon activity is restricted to the master domain, in very large networks the amount of activity may exceed the capabilities of a single domain to handle. According to Microsoft, a master domain model allows about 40,000 users and computers. For any network larger than this, you will need to use the Multiple Master Domain Model described in the following section.

The multiple master domain model

For very large networks, the master domain model can be extended to use multiple master domains. This model is called, logically enough, the *multiple master domain model.* In a multiple master domain model network, the user accounts are divided roughly equally between two or more master domains to spread the logon activity between multiple domains. The master domains essentially have no purpose except to maintain user accounts and validate logons.

Under the multiple master domain model, each master domains trusts, and is trusted by, all other master domains. This makes it easier for administrators to maintain the domains. To maintain security, access to resources in master domains is normally restricted to administrators. Ordinary users are given permissions only for shared resources that are located in the subsidiary domains. Each subsidiary domain trusts all master domains, but does not trust other subsidiary domains.

Users gain most of their privileges based on their membership in global groups on a master domain, so users who need to access similar groups of resources are assigned accounts on the same master domain. Keeping users clustered in this fashion reduces the need to create similar groups on more than one master domain, which rapidly becomes unmanageable.

In theory, at least, the multiple master domain model has all of the advantages of the master domain model, and adds the ability to scale the network beyond 40,000 users. Against this advantage must be weighed the drawbacks of administrative complexity as the number of trust relationships grows and the segmenting of user accounts into separate locations proliferates.

The complete trust domain model

Although I mention the complete trust domain model for completeness, it's a bad idea that nobody talks much about any more. The *complete trust domain model* is just what the name describes—every domain trusts and is trusted by every other domain. Each user logs in to his own local domain, and can then access resources on remote domains via the trust relationships established between the domains. If this concept horrifies you, you're not alone.

Maintaining security with the complete trust domain model requires each domain administrator to maintain absolute air-tight security on his own domain. If just one domain administrator allows security holes to occur, the integrity of all the domains is compromised. It's an unusual organization in which every domain administrator can accept as a matter of faith that every other domain administrator will do his job properly every single time.

In earlier versions of Windows NT Server, Microsoft advocated using the complete trust domain model for its several putative advantages. These included the fact that the complete trust domain model does not require a central MIS department to manage it; that it allows individual domain administrators to retain control of their own users and resources; that users and resources are grouped logically by location or function; and that it is scalable to any size network.

Against these advantages are several disadvantages. The most compelling is the lack of security described earlier in this section. Beyond that, the complete trust domain model is subject to the $(n^2 - n)$ problem as domains proliferate, and places every user and domain administrator at the mercy of the perhaps bizarre practices of other domain administrators. With Windows NT Server 4.0, Microsoft has withdrawn their endorsement of this model. A description of it no longer appears in the Resource Kit or in other domain planning documents.

In this chapter:
- *A Word About Installing Windows NT Server*
- *Configuring Windows NT Server Networking*

3

Configuring Windows NT Server Networking

The process of configuring networking for Windows NT Server is very similar to that of doing the same for Novell NetWare 3.1x. It only looks completely different. As you install and configure Windows NT Server networking components, you realize that the similarities outweigh the differences.

Like Novell NetWare 3.1x, Windows NT Server 4.0 is a modular network operating system. Both use loadable programs that run in the background to provide essential network functions, although NetWare calls them NLMs and Windows NT Server calls them services. Both allow you to load multiple network adapter drivers and to bind multiple transport protocols to these drivers, although NetWare uses a command-line interface and Windows NT Server uses a graphical user interface (GUI) to accomplish the same task. The two network operating systems have much in common under the surface, at least with respect to network configuration.

The differences between configuring networking for NetWare 3.1x and doing so for Windows NT Server 4.0 are largely those of interface, generation, and scope. Interface differences exist because NetWare depends on DOS command-line utilities and text-mode graphics while Windows NT Server uses a modern GUI. Generation differences exist because NetWare uses text configuration files like *STARTUP.NCF* and *AUTOEXEC.NCF* and a local bindery database to store configuration information, while Windows NT Server instead uses a distributed object-oriented database called the Registry. Scope differences exist because the heart of NetWare, NCP, is inextricably bound to IPX/SPX transport, while Windows NT Server is designed from the ground up for interoperability with other networks. Windows NT Server simply gives you more options.

As a result, configuring networking for Windows NT Server is at once simpler and more complex than doing so for Novell NetWare 3.1x. It's simpler because the

Windows NT Server GUI isolates you from the *SET*, *LOAD*, and *BIND* statements used by NetWare, and more complex because Windows NT Server simply does more.

This chapter covers the installation and configuration of the components needed to support basic Windows NT Server networking. The procedures described in this chapter are initially performed when you install Windows NT Server, but you can return to them later as needed to make changes to your network configuration. More advanced aspects of Windows NT Server networking—the Remote Access Service, installing and configuring servers for WINS, DNS, DHCP, and so on—are covered in later chapters.

A Word About Installing Windows NT Server

Compared to NetWare 3.x, installing Windows NT Server is a stroll in the park. The setup program is well thought out, and almost always works without a hitch. Although Windows NT Server 4.0 is not Plug-N-Play compliant, its automatic hardware detection routines ordinarily find all but the most unusual hardware. Installing Windows NT Server is usually a simple matter of watching prompts, making a decision here and there, and otherwise accepting the recommended default choices.

Even a first-time user can usually install Windows NT Server without referring to instructions. How long it takes depends to some extent on your server hardware and the options you choose to install, but you can typically figure on about an hour for your first installation, and somewhat less for subsequent installs. If you need detailed instructions for installing Windows NT Server, refer to the Start Here booklet included with the software.

Configuring Windows NT Server Networking

All of the network configuration options covered in this section are accessed from the Network Property sheet. You can bring up the Network Property sheet in either of two ways:

- Right-click on the Network Neighborhood icon on your desktop and then click Properties.
- From Control Panel, double-click the Network applet.

- Taking either of these actions displays the Network Property sheet, shown in Figure 3-1.

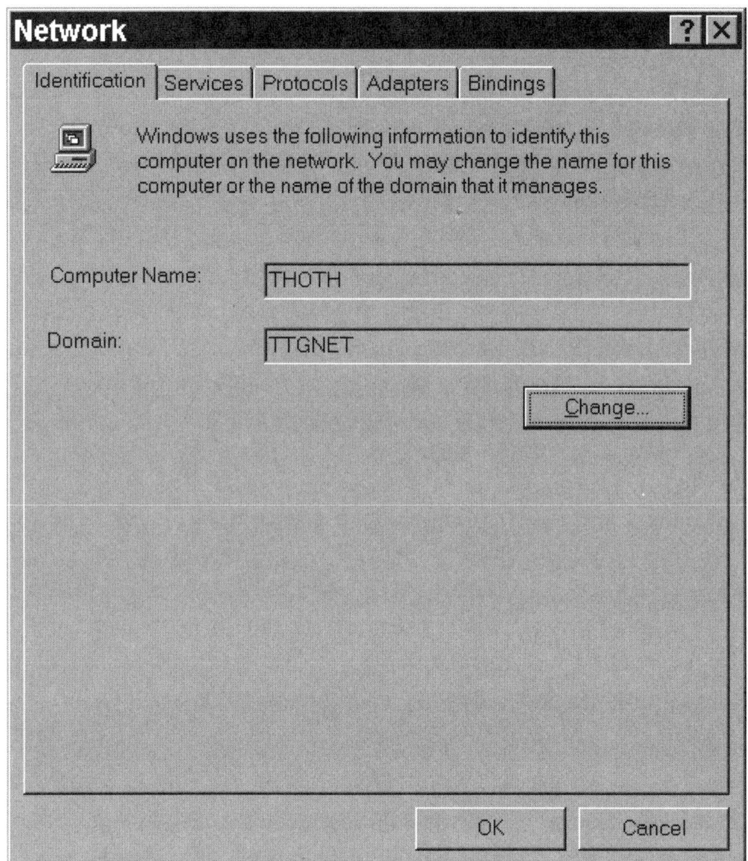

Figure 3-1. The Network Property sheet allows you to set Windows NT Server Network Options

Server Identification

The Identification page is shown initially when you display Network properties. The Identification page shows the name you assigned to this server when you installed Windows NT Server and the domain of which the computer is a member. This page is normally used only to display this information. Although you will seldom have reason to do so, you can change the Computer Name, the Domain, or both by clicking Change.

WARNING Do not change the Computer Name or the Domain unless you know exactly why you want to do so. Both the Computer Name and the Domain to which it belongs are fundamental characteristics of the computer. Changing either of these items significantly changes your entire network environment. You ordinarily make such changes only as a part of replacing or relocating a server. Treat changes to the Computer Name or Domain with the same level of caution that you would apply to formatting a disk drive or reinstalling the operating system.

When you attempt to change the name of the server, Windows NT Server warns you that changing the computer name without first having a Domain Administrator change the computer name on the domain will result in domain accounts not being able to log on to the computer. Confirm the change only if you are absolutely certain that you want to make it. You may assign any valid new computer name that does not already exist in the specified domain.

When you attempt to change the domain to which a server is assigned, Windows NT Server attempts to locate a domain controller for the new domain name. If no domain controller can be located, Windows NT Server notifies you of that fact and allows you to re-enter a new domain name. If a domain controller for the new domain is located, Windows NT Server displays a warning message to allow you to verify the change before it is made.

NOTE Windows NT Server can be installed as a Primary Domain Controller, as a Backup Domain Controller, or as a standalone server. Only standalone servers can be reassigned to a new domain. Relocating a Domain Controller to a new domain requires that Windows NT Server be reinstalled.

Network Services

Network Services are system level processes that continue to run in the background even when no one is logged on to the server, allowing these services to be available to network users as long as the server itself is running. The Windows NT Server distribution disk includes about two dozen services. A few of these are installed by default when you install Windows NT Server. Most are not installed by default, but may be chosen during the installation of Windows NT Server.

NOTE In the interest of conserving system resources on the server, you should install optional services only if you need the functions they provide. It is quick and easy to install most of the optional services on a running server, and few of the optional services even require that you reboot the server to activate them.

Most of the services provided with Windows NT Server require that you make few, if any, configuration choices when you install them. Once installed, those services that have user-configurable options, when selected, activate the Properties button in the Services page of the Network property sheet. Those services that do not have user-configurable options, when selected, leave the Properties button grayed out and inactive to indicate that they cannot be configured. Complex services, e.g., the Remote Access Service, the DHCP Server, and the DNS Server, are configured and managed elsewhere, typically with a dedicated management program.

By default, the following services are installed during Windows NT Server installation:

Computer Browser
: Maintains a current list of the resources available on the network for use by applications and system processes. The Browser Configuration dialog allows you to add and remove domains to specify which domains will be visible to the browser service.

NetBIOS Interface
: Defines a programming interface and naming convention for use by Microsoft Networking. The NetBIOS Configuration dialog allows you to edit the mapping of LANA numbers to network routes.

RPC Configuration
: Enables Remote Procedure Call (RPC) support. RPC-enabled applications can execute in distributed fashion, using the resources of multiple computers simultaneously. The RPC Configuration dialog allows you to modify the Name Service Provider, the Network Address, and the Security Service Provider. By default, Windows NT Server installs the Windows NT Locator as the name service provider. You may accept the default, or choose the alternative DCE Cell Directory Service. If you select the DCE Cell Directory Service, enter the network address for the provider in the Network Address field. Windows NT Server by default installs the Windows NT Security Service as the only option for the Security Service Provider. If you install the DCE Security Service, you may select it here.

Server

The SMB server software that allows the computer to share and secure its own resources, and to function as a server in a client/server application. The Server service is implemented as a File System Driver (FSD). FSDs also exist for each of the disk filesystems, i.e., FAT, NTFS, CDFS. The Server service FSD interacts with these other FSDs to fulfill user requests.

The Server dialog allows you to choose among four predefined Optimization levels:

— *Minimize Memory Used.* Configures the server service to function with minimal RAM. This selection is most appropriate for a server used by 10 or fewer client workstations.

— *Balance.* Configures the server service to use minimal RAM while providing support for 64 connections. This selection is the default for NetBEUI installations.

— *Maximize Throughput for File Sharing.* This setting is appropriate for a Windows NT Server that provides primarily file and printer sharing services on a large network. Choosing this setting devotes additional memory to caching files requested by network clients and otherwise optimizes the server for file and print sharing duties.

— *Maximize Throughput for Network Applications.* This setting is appropriate for a Windows NT Server that functions primarily as an application server on a large network for applications like Microsoft SQL Server that provide their own caching.

Mark the "*Make Browser Broadcasts to LAN Manager 2.x Clients*" check box if you have a server running LAN Manager on your network and you want resources on the Windows NT Server to be browsable by that server.

- *Workstation.* The SMB client software that allows the computer to access resources on the Microsoft network, including logging in to a domain and sharing files and printers, and to function as a client in a client/server application. Like the Server service, the Workstation service is implemented as an FSD. The Workstation service has no user-configurable Properties.

You may also install the following network services, which are supplied with the Windows NT Server distribution:

DHCP Relay Agent

Allows Windows NT Server to forward Dynamic Host Configuration Protocol (DHCP) broadcasts to another Windows NT Server across a Wide Area Network. The DHCP Relay Agent service has no user-configurable Properties. This service is covered fully in Chapter 12, *Using Dynamic Host Configuration Protocol.*

Gateway Service for NetWare

Allows other computers to access resources on Novell NetWare servers while running only Microsoft client software. The Gateway Service for NetWare service has no user-configurable Properties. This service is covered fully in Chapter 18, *Using Gateway Service for NetWare.*

Microsoft DHCP Server

Automatically assigns Internet Protocol (IP) addresses to workstations running DHCP client software, and allows you to manage these shared address pools. The Microsoft DHCP Server service has no user-configurable Properties. This service is covered fully in Chapter 12, *Using Dynamic Host Configuration Protocol.*

Microsoft DNS Server

The Microsoft Domain Name Service (DNS) Server maps Internet Domain Names to IP addresses, allowing an unknown IP address to be resolved from a known Internet host name. For example, the DNS Server resolves the known host name *thoth.ttgnet.com* to its associated IP address of 204.238.30.165. The Microsoft DNS Server service has no user-configurable Properties. This service is covered fully in Chapter 14, *Using Domain Name Service.*

Microsoft Internet Information Server 2.0

IIS is a full-function web server that provides HTTP, ftp, and gopher services. It provides an excellent foundation for a public web site or a private corporate Intranet. The Microsoft Internet Information Server 2.0 service includes an active Properties button. However, clicking Properties for this service simply yields a message that tells you to use the Internet Manager to configure the service. IIS is not covered in this book.

Microsoft TCP/IP Printing

Allows Windows NT Server to print to network printers that use only TCP/IP transport, including those connected to UNIX hosts. The Microsoft TCP/IP Printing service has no user-configurable Properties.

Network Monitor Agent

Provides the raw network transaction data needed by monitoring programs like the Performance Monitor and the Network Monitor. The Network Monitor Agent Service has no user-configurable Properties.

Network Monitor Tools and Agent

Installing this service installs the Network Monitor Agent as well as tools for monitoring and troubleshooting network problems. The Network Monitor Tools and Agent Service has no user-configurable Properties.

Remote Access Service

The Remote Access Service (RAS) supports dial-up network connections to Windows NT Server, allowing RAS clients to connect via modem to the server and to network resources as though they were locally connected. RAS provides services essentially similar to the inbound services provided by Novell NetWare Connect, and is a direct replacement for it. Installing the Remote Access Service invokes the Remote Access Setup procedure, which is covered fully in Chapter 15, *Using Remote Access Service*.

Remoteboot Service

This service allows diskless network client computers to boot MS-DOS and Microsoft Windows from the network server. Installing the Remoteboot service requires that the NetBEUI and DLC transport protocols first be installed. During installation, you will be prompted for the name of a directory where the remote boot files are to be stored, by default C:\WINNT\rpl. You are also given the opportunity to migrate the remote boot directory from a LAN Manager 2.2 server. The Remoteboot Service has no user-configurable Properties.

RIP for Internet Protocol

This service provides the Internet Protocol (IP) routing component of the software-based Multiprotocol Router which, in conjunction with the IPX/SPX routing component listed below, essentially duplicates the services provided by the Novell Multi-Protocol Router (MPR) add-on. The MPR service provides similar functionality to that provided by a hardware router, albeit more slowly, and may allow a small branch office or other remote site to avoid purchasing a router. The RIP for Internet Protocol service has no user-configurable Properties. This service is not covered in this book.

RIP for NwLink IPX/SPX compatible transport

This service provides the IPX routing component of the Microsoft MPR. In conjunction with the IP routing component listed above, this service duplicates the services provided by Novell MPR. The RIP for NwLink IPX/SPX compatible transport service has no user-configurable Properties. This service is not covered in this book.

RPC support for Banyan

Provides RPC support for networks that include one or more Banyan VINES servers. The RPC support for Banyan service has no user-configurable Properties.

SAP Agent

The Service Advertising Protocol (SAP) broadcasts (or advertises) the services available from each server on the network and their associated addresses. The SAP Agent service has no user-configurable Properties.

Services for Macintosh

Allows Windows NT Server to function as an AppleTalk router and enables Macintosh clients to participate in file and printer sharing. The Microsoft AppleTalk Protocol Properties dialog allows you to select the Default Adapter and the Default Zone, and to specify routing configuration parameters.

Simple TCP/IP Services

Provides several client programs for TCP/IP services like Daytime, Echo, and Quote of the Day. The Simple TCP/IP Services service has no user-configurable Properties.

SNMP Service

Provide Simple Network Management Protocol (SNMP) support, allowing the Windows NT Server computer to be managed remotely using an SNMP manager. Installing this service invokes the Microsoft SNMP Properties property sheet, which allows you to provide information about the Agent, Traps, and Security needed to configure the server for SNMP.

Windows Internet Name Service

The Windows Internet Name Service dynamically maps NetBIOS computer names to IP addresses. This service is covered fully in Chapter 13, *Using Windows Internet Naming Service*. The Windows Internet Name Service has no user-configurable Properties.

In addition to the services listed above, which are bundled with the Windows NT Server distribution, various add-on software that installs as a service is available from Microsoft and from third parties. These software packages are supplied on diskette or CD-ROM, and are installed using the Have Disk option described in the section immediately following.

Adding network services

To install a network service, choose the Services page of the Network property sheet. Select Add to display the Select Network Service dialog. Highlight one of the services listed in the Network Service pane, and click OK. You may instead choose Have Disk and follow the prompts to install a new or updated service from CD-ROM, diskette, or from a network volume. In either case, Windows NT prompts you for the location of the distribution files. Accept the default location, or enter a new location, as appropriate.

When all files have been copied, the Network property sheet is redisplayed showing the newly installed service as available. Click Close to complete the installation. Windows NT configures, stores, and reviews the bindings, and then prompts you to restart the server to make the new services available.

NOTE When installing most services, you return to the Network property sheet immediately after the files are copied. A few services bundled with Windows NT Server, and many third-party services, run an initial configuration procedure before returning to the Network property sheet.

Removing network services

On occasion you may want to remove an installed network service. There are two common reasons for removing an installed service. First, you may remove a service and reclaim the resources used by that service because the need for the service no longer exists. Second, installing an updated version of a service may require that you remove the older version before installing the newer one. In either case, to remove the service, simply highlight the name of the service in the Network property sheet Services page and click Remove. You must reboot Windows NT Server after you remove a service in order to completely clear all remnants of that service from memory, particularly if you are going to install a newer version of that same service.

NOTE In order to function, some services require that one or more other services be present. If you attempt to remove a service that is required by another installed service, Windows NT Server informs you of the dependency and allows you to cancel the removal. If you remove the service anyway, you should also remove the services that depend on the removed service to avoid startup error messages each time you boot the server.

Setting network access order

Windows NT Server allows you to specify the order in which network service providers are searched for resources. Once the required server or other resource is located on one network, the search concludes without searching other branches lower in the tree. Ordinarily, you will not need to change the Network Access Order. If you want to do so, choose the Network Access Order button on the Services page of the Network property sheet to display the Network Access Order dialog. Highlight a provider in the Network Providers pane and use the Move Up and Move Down buttons to relocate the provider as needed.

NOTE The Network Access Order button appears only if the server is connected to multiple networks.

Adding and Configuring Network Protocols

Windows NT Server provides standard support for six transport protocols. These include:

- *DLC Protocol.* The Data Link Control (DLC) protocol is an IBM mainframe transport protocol. DLC is useful in the Windows NT Server environment in only two specialized situations:
  - — When the network includes remote print servers, e.g., the HP JetDirect, that use DLC transport. DLC print servers allow printers to be connected directly to the network cable instead of requiring that a PC be used to drive the printer.
  - — When the Windows NT Server machine is a part of a network with IBM host connectivity requirements.
- *NetBEUI Protocol.* The NetBIOS Extended User Interface (NetBEUI) transport protocol provides connectivity for clients running Windows 3.11 for Workgroups and other NetBEUI-based peer networks. NetBEUI as provided with Windows NT Server is not truly NetBIOS. However, because it conforms to the Transport Driver Interface (TDI) and uses the NetBIOS Frame Format (NBF), it appears to the network as NetBEUI and is fully interoperable with earlier NetBEUI versions.
- *NWLink IPX/SPX Compatible Transport.* The NWLink transport protocol is the Microsoft implementation of IPX/SPX. It is fully interoperable with Novell IPX/SPX, and is commonly used in mixed environments to support integration of NetWare resources. Some Windows NT Server administrators elect to run NWLink transport in pure Microsoft networks to avoid the complexity and maintenance requirements of TCP/IP.
- *Point-to-Point Tunneling Protocol.* The Point-to-Point Tunneling Protocol (PPTP) is supported by Windows NT Server for the first time in Version 4. PPTP provides packet-level encryption, allowing secure end-to-end communications to take place via an insecure path like the Internet. PPTP is supported by RAS, covered fully in Chapter 15, *Using Remote Access Service.* PPTP may soon be superseded by the Layer 2 Tunneling Protocol (L2TP). L2TP is being jointly developed by Cisco and Microsoft as a replacement for the earlier Cisco L2F and Microsoft PPTP protocols, and is now designated RFC1661 by the IETF.
- *Streams Environment.* Streams originated in AT&T UNIX System V, and provides a standardized method for exchanging messages between protocol layers. Streams is supported in the Windows NT Server environment primarily for the benefit of programmers who are developing software to integrate UNIX and Windows NT.

- *TCP/IP Protocol.* The TCP/IP protocol is the foundation of the Internet and, increasingly, of corporate Wide Area Networks. The Windows NT Server implementation of TCP/IP provides full interoperability with UNIX systems and the Internet, and is the transport protocol of choice for any large or multi-site Windows NT Server network.

Windows NT Server setup always installs the NWLink and TCP/IP protocols by default. Setup installs NetBEUI only if it detects the presence of NetBEUI frames on the wire during installation. The other protocols are never installed automatically by setup. You must specify them manually.

Adding the DLC protocol

On most networks, the DLC protocol is a solution in search of a problem. The most common reason for installing the DLC protocol is to support the Hewlett-Packard JetDirect card, which connects a printer directly to the network. This allows that printer to be located conveniently for network users without requiring that a PC be installed to drive the printer. The DLC protocol need be installed on only one server if DLC printing is to be implemented. All other servers and workstations on the network can use the services provided by the single server upon which DLC is installed. Installing the DLC protocol on a Windows NT Server machine also installs the HP JetDirect driver, which is supplied by Hewlett-Packard and bundled with Windows NT Server.

NOTE If your network is running TCP/IP transport, as it probably should be, there is even less reason to install the DLC protocol. The JetDirect card can be configured to provide a direct network printer connection using IP and *lpd* (line printer daemon). If your network is part of an internetwork, using TCP/IP has one further big advantage: DLC is not a routed protocol, meaning that shared printing services using DLC can only be provided by a server that resides on the same network as the DLC printer. TCP/IP, on the other hand, is a routed protocol, which means that any user on any network that is a part of the internetwork can use shared printing services under TCP/IP.

To install the DLC protocol, choose the Protocols page of the Network property sheet. Select Add to display the Select Network Protocol dialog. Highlight DLC Protocol and click OK. Windows NT prompts you for the location of the distribution files. Accept the default location, or enter a new location, as appropriate.

When all files have been copied, the Network property sheet is redisplayed showing the DLC Protocol as available. Click Close to complete the installation. Windows NT Server configures, stores, and reviews the bindings. After the bindings review process is complete, Windows NT Server displays the Network Settings Change dialog to inform you that you must restart the server before the changes will take effect. Click Yes to restart the server immediately. Click No to defer availability of the DLC protocol until the next time the server is restarted routinely.

NOTE The DLC Protocol has no user-configurable properties, as is indicated by the grayed out Properties button when the DLC Protocol is highlighted in the Protocols page of the Network property sheet.

Adding the NetBEUI protocol

The NetBIOS Extended User Interface (NetBEUI) Protocol was originally designed for peer-to-peer networks like those running Windows 3.11 for Workgroups. NetBEUI is fast and requires essentially zero configuration, making it an ideal transport for very small networks, particularly those managed by nontechnical people. On the downside, NetBEUI packets do not contain network layer addresses, which makes it impossible to route NetBEUI. That NetBEUI may be bridged but not routed makes it essentially unusable on a Wide Area Network, and inappropriate in the enterprise. Microsoft includes NetBEUI support in Windows NT Server to support legacy peer networks.

NetBEUI is installed automatically with NT Server if Setup detects NetBEUI on the wire, but many system administrators remove it as a matter of course. If you find that you need to reinstall NetBEUI, perhaps to connect a previously standalone peer network to your main network, use the same steps as described in the section immediately preceding, simply substituting NetBEUI for DLC. Like DLC, NetBEUI offers no user-configurable Properties.

Configuring NWLink IPX/SPX compatible transport

The NWLink IPX/SPX compatible transport protocol is the Microsoft implementation of the IPX/SPX transport originally developed by Novell for NetWare. NWLink is fully interoperable with the Novell IPX/SPX protocol, and is installed automatically with Windows NT Server.

NOTE If for some reason you have removed the NWLink IPX/SPX compatible transport and need to reinstall it, simply follow the steps described in the preceding section for installing the DLC Protocol, substituting NWLink for DLC, and then configure the NWLink protocol as described in this section.

To configure the NWLink IPX/SPX compatible transport protocol, display the Protocols page of the Network property sheet. Highlight NWLink IPX/SPX compatible transport and then choose Properties to display the General page of the NWLink IPX/SPX Properties property sheet, shown in Figure 3-2.

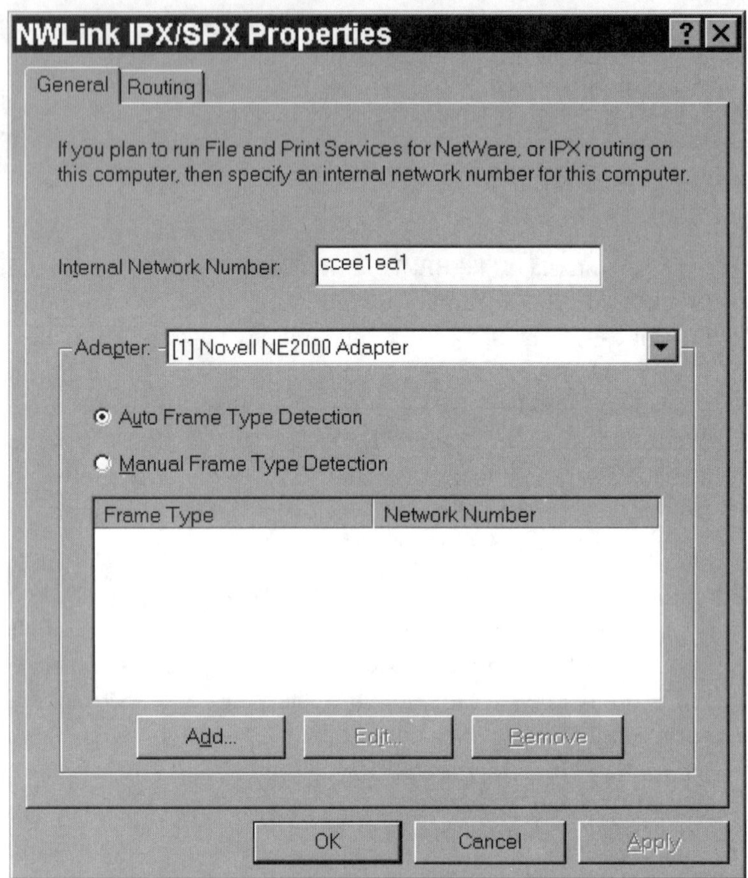

Figure 3-2. The General page of the NWLink IPX/SPX Properties property sheet allows you to specify an Internal Network Number and, for each installed adapter, the frame type(s) to be used

If this server will provide IPX routing services using the Microsoft Multiprotocol Router, or if the server will run File and Print Services for NetWare, enter a valid value in the Internal Network Number field. If you are running TCP/IP transport, one of the best ways to generate a guaranteed-unique Internal Network Number for a server, is to convert the dotted decimal IP address of that server to hexadecimal and assign the hexadecimal form as the Internal Network Number. For example, the server *kerby.ttgnet.com* is assigned the IP address 204.238.30.161.

Converted to hexadecimal, this IP address yields the Internet Network Number CCEE1EA1.

Even if you run a DHCP server to assign IP addresses to workstations automatically, servers are nearly always assigned a static IP address so that they can always be located. This ensures that any server will always have a specific IP address, and therefore will also have the corresponding hexadecimal version of this number as a unique Internet Network Number. You can use the Windows NT calculator applet in Scientific mode to perform quick conversions from decimal notation to hexadecimal notation. Simply enter the decimal value with the Dec option button selected, and then click the Hex button to redisplay the decimal number in hexadecimal format.

By default, Windows NT Server sets the frame type to Auto Frame Type Detection for each installed adapter. If you have only one network adapter installed in this server, that adapter is displayed in the Adapter list box. If you have more than one network adapter installed, and you want to use Manual Frame Type Detection, use the Adapter drop-down list to select the adapter to be modified. With the proper adapter displayed in the Adapter list box, click the Manual Frame Type Detection option button and then click Add to display the Manual Frame Detection dialog.

Use the Frame Type drop-down list to select a frame type, enter an appropriate value for Network Number, and choose Add to configure the selected adapter to use the specified frame type. The General page of the NWLink IPX/SPX Properties property sheet is redisplayed, with the newly assigned Frame Type and Network Number visible. Repeat this step as needed to add support for other frame types. You may modify or delete an installed manual frame type by highlighting it and clicking Edit or Remove respectively.

If you want Windows NT Server to function as an IPX router, click the Routing tab to display the Routing page of the NWLink IPX/SPX Properties property sheet. Mark the Enable RIP Routing check box to turn on IPX routing. This check box is grayed out and cannot be selected unless the RIP for NWLink IPX routing component of the Multiprotocol Router has been installed as a service.

Ethernet Frame Type Mismatches

If client workstations are having problems seeing the server, or if servers aren't communicating with each other, chances are that a frame type mismatch is the cause of the problem. You can avoid problems like these by ensuring that Windows NT Server is configured to support all of the Ethernet frame types in use on your network by using Manual Frame Type Detection to specify each active frame type. If you haven't already, make sure that each of your NetWare servers is configured to support all Ethernet frame types active on your network.

Novell NetWare and Microsoft Windows NT Server support the same four Ethernet frame types. Although Novell and Microsoft use slightly different names to refer to each particular frame type, the corresponding frames themselves are fully compatible and interoperable. The Microsoft Ethernet frame types, with the corresponding Novell name in parentheses, are as follows:

Ethernet 802.2 (Ethernet_802.2). Ethernet 802.2 is the current standards-based Ethernet frame definition, and uses the OSI 802.2 Logical Link Control (LLC) specification. Novell introduced Ethernet_802.2 as the default Ethernet frame type when NetWare 4.0 shipped. When Novell released NetWare 3.12 shortly thereafter, they also made Ethernet_802.2 the default Ethernet frame type for it.

Ethernet 802.3 (Ethernet_802.3). Ethernet 802.3 is a proprietary Novell frame type, referred to colloquially as "802.Novell" or "Novell Ethernet." Novell adopted this frame type when standards were pending in the hope that it would be adopted as a standard. Subsequently, few vendors other than Novell supported this frame type. Ethernet 802.3 is the default Ethernet frame type for NetWare 3.11 and earlier versions.

Ethernet II (Ethernet_II). Ethernet II is the second implementation of the Ethernet frame type definition originally specified by the DIX (Digital Equipment Corporation/Intel/Xerox) standard.

Ethernet SNAP (Ethernet_SNAP). Ethernet SNAP was originally conceived as an interim solution during the transition to standards-based Ethernet frames. Ethernet SNAP today is largely obsolescent.

So, with this plethora of Ethernet frame types to choose from, which will best serve your network? Novell recommends using Ethernet_802.2, the current standard. Microsoft suggests that you set Ethernet frame type to Autodetect to ensure that Windows NT Server will automatically use the correct frame type. Both of them have a point, but there is a downside to following either course. Using Ethernet_802.2 may cause problems on a network that incorporates older active network components that handle 802.2 frames incorrectly. Setting Windows NT Server to automatically detect the Ethernet frame type works most of the time, but has been known to fail. A better choice is to standardize your network on Ethernet II frames.

—Continued—

—Continued—

Ethernet II is old, and therefore might easily (and mistakenly) be considered obsolete. The reality is that the majority of Ethernet traffic is still carried on Ethernet II frames. Any active network component, no matter how old, obscure or obsolete, can handle Ethernet II frames. This cannot be said for the other Ethernet frame types. Using Ethernet II frames guarantees, at least for the present time, compatibility with anything out there.

NOTE If you use the IPX component of the Microsoft Multiprotocol Routing service to allow this server to perform IPX routing, you must also enable NetBIOS Broadcast Propagation (Type 20 packets) if any Windows clients connect to this server using NWLink IPX/SPX Compatible Transport. Broadcasting of Type 20 packets is disabled by default. Enabling it degrades WAN performance, particularly when using a slow link. You are notified of this issue when installing the IPX routing service, and you may elect then to enable Type 20 packet broadcasting or to leave it disabled.

When you finish configuring the NWLink IPX/SPX Properties, click OK to return to the Network property sheet. Click Close to complete the process. Windows NT Server configures, stores, and reviews the bindings, and then displays the Network Settings Change message to inform you that you must restart the server before the changes you have made take effect. Click Yes to restart the server immediately, or click No if you prefer to wait until the next routine server restart for these changes to take effect.

You can also edit the configuration parameters for NWLink directly using the Registry editor. These values are in the following Registry locations:

```
HKEY_LOCAL_MACHINE\SYSTEM\CurrentControlSet\Services\NwlnkIpx
HKEY_LOCAL_MACHINE\SYSTEM\CurrentControlSet\Services\NwlnkNb
HKEY_LOCAL_MACHINE\SYSTEM\CurrentControlSet\Services\NwlnkSpx
```

Adding and configuring the Point-to-Point Tunneling Protocol

Support for the Point-to-Point Tunneling Protocol (PPTP) is new with Windows NT Server 4.0. PPTP provides packet-level encryption, allowing insecure public data networks like the Internet to be used for transport between PPTP servers without compromising the security of the data being transported. Using PPTP, you can create a *Virtual Private Network* (VPN) to link corporate sites securely while avoiding the cost of dedicated connections between the secure sites. Because PPTP encrypts the data flowing between the secure sites, an eavesdropper may intercept the data from the public data network, but is unlikely to be able to decrypt or otherwise use it. The 40-bit RC4 algorithm used by international versions of Windows NT Server can no longer be considered completely secure. The 128-bit encryption available to U.S. and Canadian users remains secure from all but national intelligence organizations.

NOTE Implementing a Virtual Private Network using PPTP may involve more than simply installing PPTP at each of your sites. PPTP can operate in two environments.

If every client workstation (including notebooks) that needs to use secure PPTP connections is running Windows NT 4.0 Workstation, a secure PPTP link can be established end-to-end directly, from the workstation to the remote PPTP server. This method does not require that the ISPs involved explicitly support PPTP.

If instead some of your client workstations are running earlier operating systems, another method of making a PPTP connection can be used. With this method, the non-Windows NT 4.0 client first establishes a standard (insecure) PPP connection with his local ISP, which must explicitly support PPTP on his server. With this method, the connection is insecure from the local workstation to the local ISP, but secure from the local ISP, through the remote ISP, and to the remote PPTP server.

Microsoft is making inroads at ISPs with Windows NT Server and its various Internet server products, so chances are good that your current ISP supports PPTP, or has plans to do so. If you think that PPTP and VPNs might be a useful tool for your environment now or in the future, pick up the phone and call your ISP to find out if they offer PPTP support. If they don't, you probably won't be the first person who has called them to request that they add PPTP support. Every such request helps get things moving.

PPTP is a dial-up networking (DUN) protocol. To use PPTP, you first make an ordinary IP network connection to your Internet Service Provider. Once this connection is established, you create one or more PPTP DUN sessions to specific destination hosts that are also running PPTP. The only real difference between making an ordinary DUN connection and a PPTP DUN connection is that you enter a telephone number for the former and an IP address for the latter. Each PPTP DUN session creates a virtual private network between your server and the remote PPTP host whose IP address was used to establish the session.

To install PPTP, display the protocols page of the Network property sheet. Choose Add to display the Select Network Protocol dialog. Highlight Point-to-Point Tunneling Protocol and then click OK. Windows NT Server prompts you for the location of the distribution files. Accept the default location, or type another location where the files can be found. Choose Continue to begin installing the protocol.

After the distribution files have been copied, Windows NT displays the PPTP Configuration dialog. Use the Number of Virtual Private Networks drop-down list to specify how many VPN connections you want to make provisions for. Each VPN connection represents the ability to connect one remote network server using PPTP. You may specify a number of VPN connections ranging from the default value of 1, to the maximum 256 connections supported by RAS. After you have set the desired number of VPN connections, click OK to continue.

NOTE If Remote Access Service (RAS) is not already installed, a Setup Message is displayed to inform you that RAS will now be installed. After the RAS files are copied, RAS Setup is invoked, allowing you to configure the PPTP ports so that you can use RAS over PPTP. For more information about installing and configuring Remote Access Service, see Chapter 15, *Using Remote Access Service.*

Windows NT Server returns you to the Network property sheet, showing the PPTP protocol as installed. Click Close to complete the installation. Windows NT Server configures, stores, and reviews the bindings, and then displays the Network Settings Change dialog to inform you that the server must be restarted for the changes to take effect. Click Yes to restart the server immediately, or click No to wait until the next routine server restart for PPTP is available.

Reconfiguring the Point-to-Point Tunneling Protocol

The PPTP protocol has only one user-configurable property, Number of Virtual Private Networks. To modify this setting, highlight the PPTP protocol in the Protocols page of the Network property sheet and click Properties to display the PPTP Configuration dialog. Use the drop-down list to specify a new Number of Virtual Private Networks and then click OK. Windows NT Server again invokes the Remote Access Setup dialog to allow you to configure PPTP ports for use with RAS.

When you have completed configuring ports, click Continue to return to the Protocols page of the Network property sheet. Click Close to complete the procedure. Windows NT Server configures, stores, and reviews the bindings, and then displays the Network Settings Change dialog to inform you that the system must be restarted for the changes to take effect. Click Yes to restart immediately, or click No to defer the restart until later.

You can also view and edit the configuration parameters for PPTP directly using the registry editor. These values are stored in many registry locations, including the following:

```
HKEY_LOCAL_MACHINE\SOFTWARE\Microsoft\RAS\TAPI DEVICES\RASPPTPM
HKEY_LOCAL_MACHINE\SOFTWARE\Microsoft\RASPPTP
HKEY_LOCAL_MACHINE\SOFTWARE\Microsoft\RASPPTPE
HKEY_LOCAL_MACHINE\SOFTWARE\Microsoft\RASPPTPM
HKEY_LOCAL_MACHINE\SOFTWARE\Microsoft\Windows NT
```

Adding the Streams Environment

The Streams Environment was originally developed for AT&T UNIX System V as a means to allow bidirectional messaging between layers of a protocol stack. Microsoft Windows NT Server includes support for the Streams Environment primarily as an aid to programmers and software developers who are porting UNIX Streams-based drivers to Windows NT.

Few servers will need the Streams Environment installed. If yours does, display the Protocols page of the Network property sheet. Select Add to display the Select Network Protocol dialog. Highlight Streams Environment, and then click OK to begin the installation. Windows NT Server installs Streams and related services.

Select Close to complete the installation. Windows NT Server configures, stores, and reviews the bindings, and then displays the Network Settings Change dialog to inform you that the server must be restarted for the changes to take effect. As usual, click Yes to restart the server immediately, or click No to defer the restart. The Streams Environment has no user-configurable properties.

Adding and configuring the TCP/IP protocol

Windows NT Server support three major transport protocols. The NetBEUI protocol and the NWLink IPX/SPX Compatible Transport protocol were both designed with Local Area Networks in mind. On the upside, both offer fast, efficient, and reliable local transport, and neither requires much effort from the network administrator to configure or manage. On the downside, neither NetBEUI nor IPX/SPX is a good choice for a Wide Area Network. NetBEUI makes no provision for the Network Layer addresses used by routers, and accordingly can only be bridged. IPX/SPX is a routable protocol, but lacks some features desirable in an internetworking transport protocol, including its lack of provision for subnetting.

If your environment includes a router-based internetwork, if your network includes UNIX hosts, or if your users need access to the Internet, then Transmission Control Protocol/Internet Protocol (TCP/IP) is the transport protocol of choice. TCP/IP is the foundation of the Internet, and has also become by default the standard for corporate internetworking. On the upside, TCP/IP is fast, efficient, and reliable, and includes all of the functionality you need to build an internetwork. The downside of TCP/IP is twofold:

Security
: TCP/IP was not designed as a secure protocol, and this lack of security is becoming an increasingly important issue as companies continue to standardize on TCP/IP transport for their internetworks. The shift from the use of dedicated private data lines to use of the Internet as a public data network has exacerbated this problem. The implementation of the forthcoming Internet Protocol V6 (also called IPv6 or IPng) will ultimately address this problem. In the interim, add-on solutions like firewalls, encrypting routers, and the PPTP protocol provide adequate security for most corporate needs, at the expense of added cost, demands on staff, and complexity.

Complexity
: More important to most administrators than even these security concerns is the complexity of managing TCP/IP. An F-15 fighter plane is a more capable weapon than a rock, but almost anyone can throw a rock. Using the F-15 efficiently and effectively requires a substantial investment in initial training and ongoing effort. Similarly, TCP/IP is a much more capable protocol than the alternatives, but deploying and managing TCP/IP requires a significant investment in staff time to acquire the expertise required. Very few companies employ a staff member who specializes in NetBEUI or IPX/SPX. Many companies employ entire groups of people who spend all day, every day, managing TCP/IP and the corporate internetwork.

TCP/IP isn't simple to install and manage, and it isn't cheap to support. It is, however, the only viable choice of transport upon which to base your corporate internetwork. Fortunately, as TCP/IP has migrated from universities and government agencies to the corporate environment, it has also acquired numerous tools designed to make it easier to deploy and manage. For example, Dynamic Host Configuration Protocol (DHCP) automates the process of assigning and managing IP addresses to clients. Before DHCP, addresses had to be assigned and managed manually, which was horribly time-consuming and error-prone.

Windows NT Server provides a reasonably complete complement of the tools needed to manage TCP/IP efficiently. The major TCP/IP management tools bundled with Windows NT Server are described in Chapter 12, *Using Dynamic Host Configuration Protocol*, Chapter 13, *Using Windows Internet Naming Service*, and Chapter 14, *Using Domain Name Service*.

Windows NT Server setup installs TCP/IP by default. If for some reason you have removed TCP/IP, you can reinstall it using the procedures described in the preceding sections. Whether it is installed automatically by setup or manually by an administrator, the TCP/IP installation routine invokes a series of detailed configuration dialogs, which are described in the remainder of this section.

Windows NT Server first displays a TCP/IP Setup message. If another server on your network is configured to provide DHCP Server services, and you wish to use these services, click Yes. If you do not have a DHCP Server on your network, or if this machine will itself be configured to provide DHCP Server services, click No. Any Windows NT Server which runs the DHCP Server service must have a static IP address specified. A DHCP Server cannot obtain its IP address from another DHCP Server.

TIP The Microsoft TCP/IP Properties property sheet has three buttons at the bottom. Two of these buttons (OK and Cancel) are global to the property sheet, and the third (Apply) is local to the page currently displayed. As you configure TCP/IP Properties, you will make changes to several of these pages. Do not click OK until you have completed all pages. Clicking OK completes the TCP/IP configuration process and exits, perhaps before you have finished your changes to all of the pages. Similarly, clicking Cancel discards the changes not just to the page currently displayed, but to all pages. As you complete each page, click the Apply button to save the changes for that page.

The Windows NT Setup dialog prompts you for the location of the distribution files needed to install TCP/IP, defaulting to the drive and directory from which you originally installed Windows NT Server. Accept the default location, or enter a new location where the files can be found. After all files have been copied, Windows NT Server returns you to the Network property sheet, with the TCP/IP Protocol installed and visible. Click Close. Windows NT Server configures, stores, and reviews the bindings, and then displays the Microsoft TCP/IP Properties property sheet, as shown in Figure 3-3.

NOTE Apparently, Microsoft thinks big, at least if the default subnet mask is any indication. The default subnet mask of 255.255.0.0 indicates an Internet Class B network.

If you have only one network adapter installed in your server, it will be selected in the Adapter list box. If you have more than one adapter installed, use the drop-down list to specify the adapter to be configured. If you chose to use a DHCP Server, the "*Obtain an IP address from a DHCP server*" option button will be selected, and the individual IP Address fields will be grayed out. If you chose not

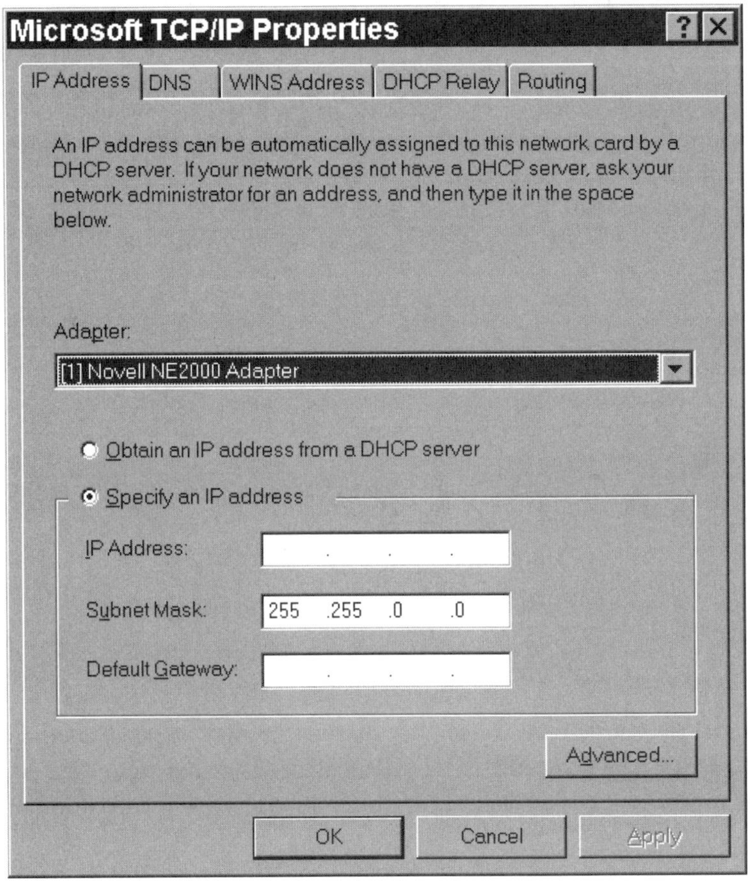

Figure 3-3. The IP Address page of the Microsoft TCP/IP Properties property sheet allows you to select the adapter to be configured, to determine whether IP parameters will be assigned manually or by a DHCP Server, and to set Advanced IP Address properties

to use a DHCP Server, the *Specify an IP address* option button will be selected, and the individual IP Address fields will be active. Complete these fields as follows:

IP Address
: Enter a valid IP address for this computer, using dotted decimal format. In the example, we assign 204.238.30.161 as the IP address for this machine.

Subnet Mask
: If your TCP/IP network is subnetted, enter the appropriate subnet mask, using dotted decimal format. In the example, we have subnetted the Internet Class C network address 204.238.30.0 into six subnets, each with 30 hosts, by using a 3-bit subnet mask. For this subnet configuration, the appropriate

subnet mask is 255.255.255.224. If your Internet Class C TCP/IP network is not subnetted, enter the default subnet mask of 255.255.255.0.

Default Gateway
Microsoft uses the term *gateway* in the same sense that it is used by the Internet community (as a synonym for "router") rather than in the OSI sense of a device used to translate incompatible protocols. The Default Gateway is the default router to which this system will look to resolve IP addresses. Enter the IP address for that router in dotted decimal format.

WARNING Use extreme care when entering these IP addresses. A simple typographical error here can cause real problems. If you're lucky, those problems might be a simple, easily resolved address conflict. If you're unlucky, you can crash the network. If you don't understand one or more of these fields, or if you are unsure about what to enter, contact your TCP/IP administrator for assistance. If you *are* the TCP/IP administrator and you are still confused, learn more before you attempt to continue. See *TCP/IP Network Administration* by Craig Hunt (second edition to be published in late 1997, O'Reilly & Associates, Inc.). You can often get help from your Internet Service Provider.

Choose Advanced to display the Advanced IP Addressing dialog, as shown in Figure 3-4. If your server has more than one physical network adapter installed, use the Adapter drop-down list to specify the adapter for which you want to configure properties.

Windows NT Server allows you to assign multiple IP addresses to a single physical network adapter. This can be useful, for example, if you want to run an FTP server and a web server on the same machine, but have each of these services individually addressable as a unique IP host. To add more IP addresses to your network adapter, click Add to display the TCP/IP Address dialog. Enter the address to be added for that adapter in the IP Address field.

Windows NT Server fills in the Subnet Mask field with a value appropriate for the network address class of the IP address you entered, but it assumes that your network address is not subnetted. For example, Windows NT Server assigned the subnet mask of 255.255.255.0, which would be correct for the Class C IP address shown, were it not subnetted. Because the IP address is a member of a subnet that uses a 3-bit subnet mask, the correct value is 255.255.255.224. Always verify that the subnet mask is correct to avoid connectivity problems that can be very difficult to resolve. After you have entered proper values for the IP Address and

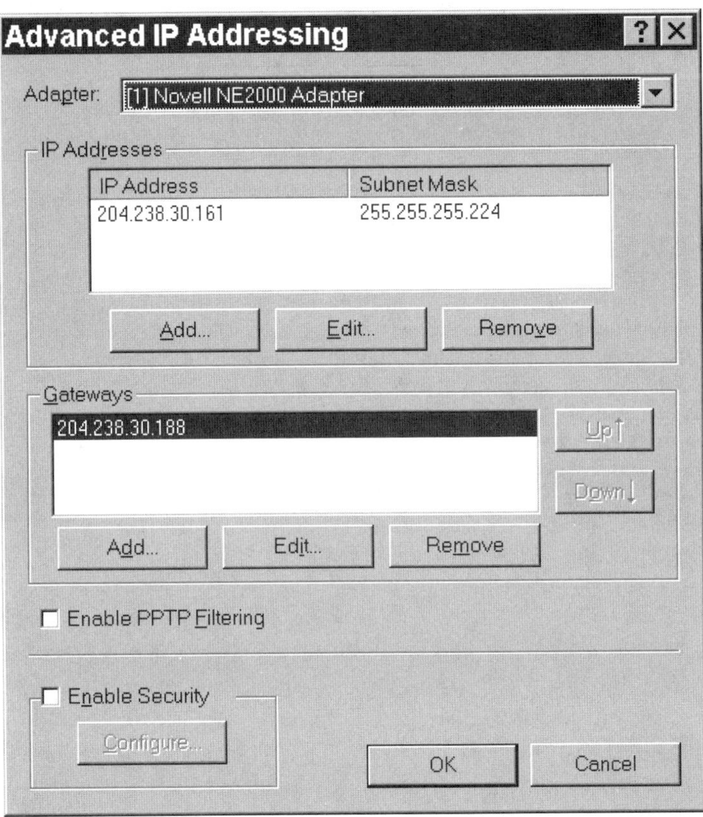

Figure 3-4. The Advanced IP Addressing dialog allows you to assign multiple IP addresses to a single physical adapter, to maintain a list of alternative gateways, and to configure PPTP and security options

Subnet Mask, click Add to complete the procedure. Windows NT Server returns you to the Advanced IP Addressing dialog and displays the newly added IP address.

You can click Edit to modify the IP Address and Subnet Mask values for an installed IP address. Doing so displays a dialog nearly identical to the TCP/IP Address dialog. The only difference will be that the Add button is instead labeled OK. As you might expect, you can remove an IP address by highlighting it in the *IP Addresses* pane and clicking Remove.

NOTE Previous versions of Windows NT Server allowed as many as 16 IP addresses to be assigned to a single physical network adapter. Version 4 supposedly removes this limit and allows an unlimited number of IP addresses to be assigned to one adapter. In our consulting practice, my partner and I found by experience that this is not the case. One of our clients, who runs a commercial web site hosting service, found that he was able to enter and use 27 IP addresses without any problem. When he attempted to enter the twenty-eighth address, Windows NT Server refused to accept it. When contacted, Microsoft tech support staff acknowledged the problem, but were unable to explain the reason why it occurred. The problem does not appear to be related to the amount of RAM on the server or to available system resources. We have since confirmed that the problem is not specific to that particular server by building a test-bed server from scratch and finding that the problem is manifested on that server as well. Unless you need a truly extraordinary number of IP addresses on a server, the problem is easy enough to resolve. Simply add another physical network adapter to your server and continue assigning additional IP addresses to it.

Windows NT Server also allows you to define multiple Gateways, using a procedure similar to that described in the preceding step. To add a gateway, click Add to display the TCP/IP Gateway Address dialog. Enter the IP address for an additional gateway, and click Add to add it to the list of Gateways displayed in the Gateways pane. Click Edit to modify the IP address for an installed gateway, or click Remove to remove an installed gateway. At least one gateway must be installed and available at all times for TCP/IP to function across a WAN. If all computers are on the same logical IP network (have the same network address and subnet mask), they can communicate with each other even if a gateway is not defined.

Note that specifying multiple gateways differs from specifying multiple IP addresses for a single network adapter, because only one default gateway can be active at any one time. Windows NT Server always uses the first gateway shown. Only if that gateway is down or otherwise not accessible, does it attempt to use additional gateways. If you do enter additional gateways, use the Up and Down arrow keys to arrange the order of the gateways so that the primary gateway is listed first. You can specify as many as five additional default gateways.

Mark the Enable PPTP Filtering check box if you want the selected adapter to handle only PPTP traffic. Marking this check box causes the adapter to filter (and discard) non-PPTP packets. The most common use for this setting is in a multi-homed server that has one physical network adapter connected via router to the Internet and another physical network adapter connected to the internal network.

Enabling PPTP filtering on the adapter that connects to the Internet allows remote callers to establish a secure PPTP session and access resources on that server. Marking this check box by mistake on a production server with only one adapter causes the server to become unavailable to local network users.

Windows NT Server allows you to closely control which TCP ports, UDP ports, and IP Protocols are available to network users. If you are comfortable working with low-level IP port and protocol issues, and would like to specify which of these are or are not available to users, mark the Enable Security check box and then click Configure to display the TCP/IP Security dialog shown in Figure 3-5.

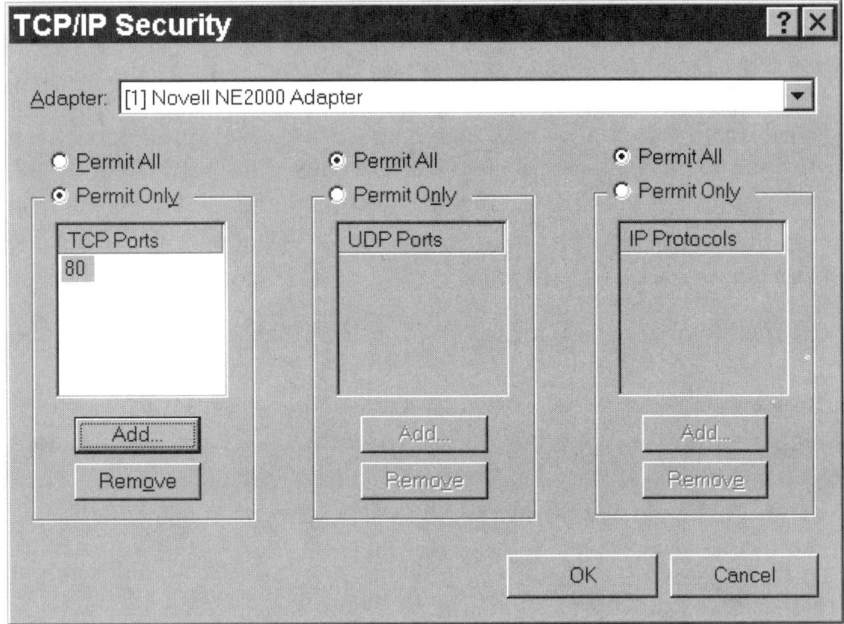

Figure 3-5. The TCP/IP Security dialog allows you to control finely which IP ports and protocols are available on this adapter

---

NOTE Although this port filtering ability of Windows NT Server can be useful in some situations, it is very limited when compared with, say, access lists on a Cisco router. If you need more capability—for example, the ability to filter port ranges or the ability to allow outbound but deny inbound traffic for a particular port—consider installing the Microsoft Routing and RAS upgrade (formerly known as Steelhead). RRAS expands the limited IP routing capabilities of Windows NT Server to include most of the features of a dedicated router. You can download this free upgrade from the Windows NT Server home page at *www.microsoft.com/ntserver*.

Use the Adapter drop-down list to select the adapter for which you want to set *TCP/IP Security* properties. By default, Windows NT Server sets Permit All for all three categories. This means that any network user can access any TCP Port, any UDP Port, or any IP Protocol available on the server. If you want to restrict one or more of these elements, click the Permit Only option button for that pane. Use the Add and Remove buttons for that pane to list only those ports or protocols that users will be permitted to access. Marking the Permit Only option button for a pane and leaving the associated list blank prohibits users from accessing any resources in that category.

Once you have configured permissions for Ports and Protocols, click OK to return to the Advanced IP Addressing dialog. Click OK once more to return to the Microsoft TCP/IP Properties property sheet. Click the DNS tab to display the DNS page, as shown in Figure 3-6.

Type the Internet name of this machine into the Host Name field. By default, Windows NT Server fills in the Windows machine name for this field. Although you *can* assign an Internet host name different from the Windows machine name, that way lies madness.

Type the Internet domain name into the Domain field. Windows NT Server does not enter a default value for this field. Note that this field refers to the Internet domain name, e.g., *ttgnet.com* rather than to the Windows domain to which this server belongs, which happens in this case to be *TTGNET.* In many organizations, the Internet domain name and the Windows domain often have very similar names. Don't make the mistake of entering the Windows domain name here.

The DNS Service Search O*rder* pane has no default entries. Use the Add button to enter the IP address of at least one server available on the network that is configured to provide DNS Server services. This will usually be either a UNIX box or a Windows NT Server configured to provide DNS. You may (and should) enter the IP address for one or more additional DNS Servers. If you have a medium or large organization, it may maintain two or more local DNS Servers. Small organizations typically provide one local DNS Server and depend on a DNS Server located at their ISP for secondary DNS services. Use the Add, Edit, and Remove buttons as needed to configure your DNS Service Search Order list appropriately. Then use the Up and Down buttons to rearrange the list, placing the primary DNS Server first and subsidiary DNS Servers in the order that you want to search them.

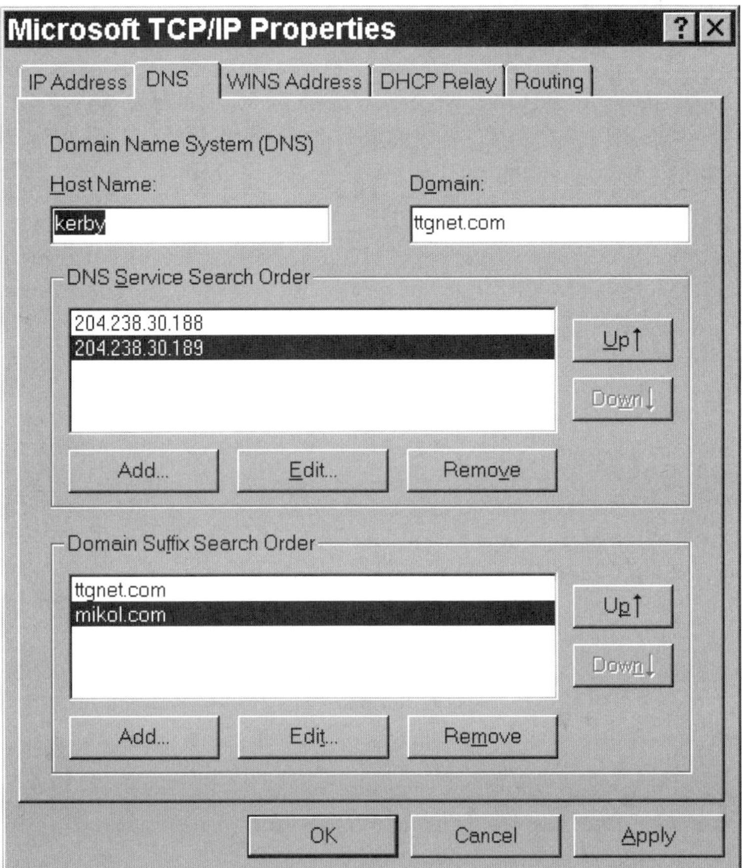

Figure 3-6. The DNS page of the Microsoft TCP/IP Properties property sheet allows you to designate primary and secondary DNS Servers and to specify the domain suffix search order for commonly used domains

---

NOTE When Windows NT Server needs to resolve an IP address, it always attempts to use the primary DNS Server first. If that server is unavailable, Windows NT Server then attempts to resolve the IP address using the secondary DNS Server. If the secondary DNS Server fails to respond, Windows NT continues to try DNS Servers in the order they are listed until it is either able to resolve the address or it runs out of DNS Servers to try.

The Domain Suffix Search Order pane also has no default entries. Unlike the DNS Service Search Order pane, for which entries are mandatory, the Domain Suffix Search Order is simply a convenience to users. If this pane is left blank, users are required to enter a Fully Qualified Domain Name (FQDN) to do a DNS lookup.

For example, with this pane left blank, resolving the IP address for the computer *kerby.ttgnet.com* would require that you enter the full host name and domain name, i.e., *kerby.ttgnet.com.* If there is an entry for *ttgnet.com* in this pane, the user could resolve the IP address for *kerby.ttgnet.com* simply by entering *kerby.* When Windows NT is asked to do a DNS lookup with a partially qualified name, it attempts the lookup by concatenating the partial name supplied by the user with each of the entries in the Domain Suffix Search Order pane.

You should always enter your local Internet domain name in this list. If you or your users frequently access systems located on other Internet domains, enter those domain names as well. Use the Add, Edit, and Remove buttons to manage the entries on this list. Once you have done so, use the Up and Down buttons to arrange the order in which the domain suffixes will be attempted.

Click the WINS Address tab to display the WINS Address page, as shown in Figure 3-7.

If your server has more than one network adapter installed, use the Adapter drop-down list to select the adapter to be configured. Enter the IP address for the Primary WINS Server and, optionally, for the Secondary WINS Server. If you do not enter an address for at least one WINS Server, Windows NT resolves IP addresses from computer names by using name query broadcasts in conjunction with the local *LMHOSTS* file. This method works only on the local network. Complete WINS Address configuration by specifying the following items:

Enable DNS for Windows Resolution

Mark this check box if you want to use DNS name resolution on the Windows Network. Marking this box also provides *DNS support in UNC names.* This support allows you to use an Internet FQDN or an IP address as part of a UNC name. For example, when this box is marked, the names *\\kerby.ttgnet.com\WINNT* and *\\204.238.30.161\WINNT* are both valid UNC names. If the check box is unmarked, neither name is a valid UNC name. If this check box is marked, Windows NT uses the DNS Server addresses entered on the DNS page.

Enable LMHOSTS Lookup

Mark this check box if you want to use the *LMHOSTS* file for NetBIOS name resolution. By default, Windows NT Server uses the *LMHOSTS* file located in the *\System32\Drivers\Etc* subfolder of the Windows NT root folder. You can use any text editor to create an *LMHOSTS* file manually based on the sample file *Lmhosts.SAM* installed by Windows NT in this folder. You can also import an existing *LMHOSTS* file by clicking Import *LMHOSTS* and browsing for the file.

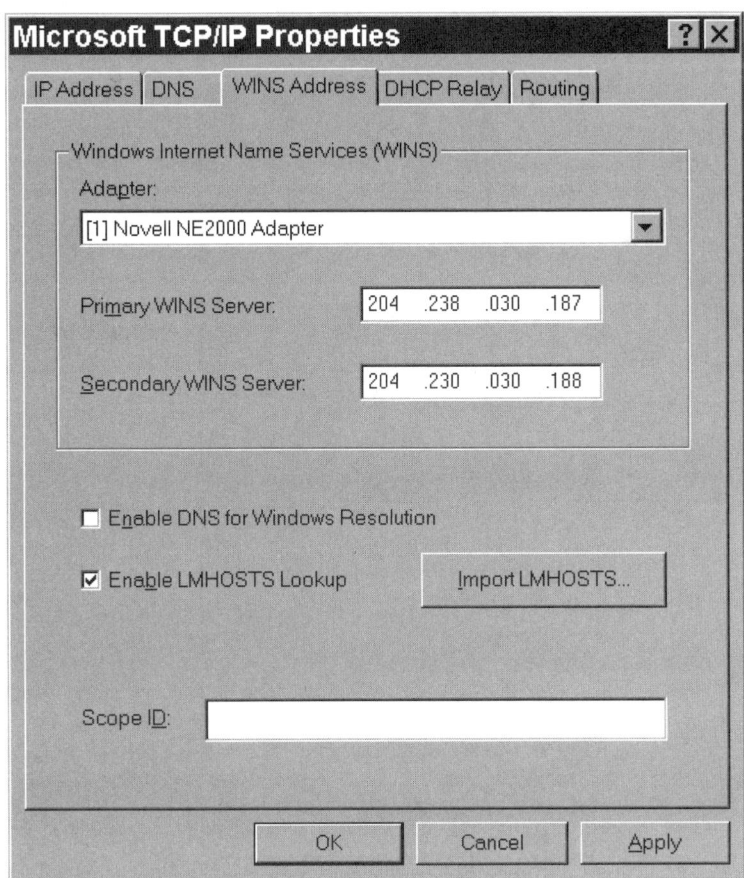

Figure 3-7. The WINS Address page of the Microsoft TCP/IP Properties property sheet allows you to specify the addresses for WINS Servers and to configure how Windows NT handles Windows name resolution

Scope ID

This field should usually be left blank. However, if you are running NetBIOS over TCP/IP (NBT) on an internetwork, enter a value here for the Scope ID. All machines on an internetwork running NBT must have an identical value for Scope ID if they are to be able to communicate with each other.

Click the DHCP Relay tab to display the DHCP Relay page, as shown in Figure 3-8.

DHCP is a broadcast protocol. Many routers cannot forward DHCP broadcast messages across an internetwork. If your internetwork uses such routers, a DHCP client on one subnet cannot directly use the services of a DHCP server on another subnet. There are three possible solutions to this problem:

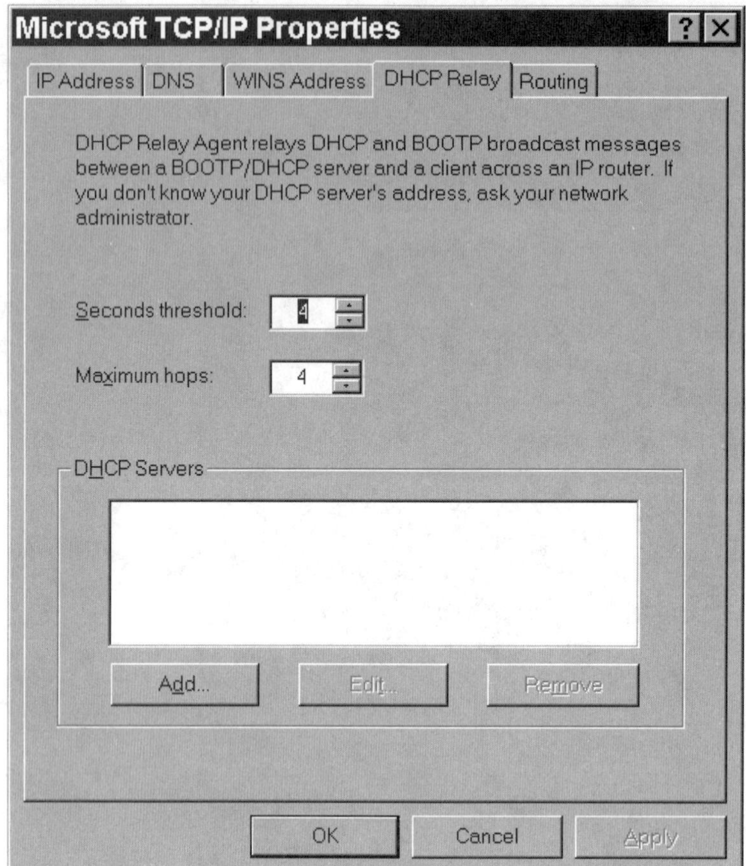

Figure 3-8. The DHCP Relay page of the Microsoft TCP/IP Properties property sheet allows you to configure DHCP Relay Agent properties and to specify the IP addresses of DHCP Servers located on remote subnets

Install a DHCP server on each subnet

If each of your subnets has a Windows NT server installed, this may appear to be a viable solution. After all, the DHCP server software comes free with Windows NT Server. Why not install it? Because using many independent DHCP servers largely defeats the purpose of using DHCP at all. Doing so balkanizes your IP addresses and increases the management effort needed to maintain your TCP/IP internetwork.

Install RFC-1542 compliant routers

If you are building a new internetwork or upgrading your routers, by all means specify that the new routers be RFC-1542 compliant. Such routers are capable of forwarding DHCP broadcast messages across the internetwork, allowing one DHCP server to serve DHCP clients anywhere on the internetwork. If your current routers are not RFC-1542 compliant and cannot be upgraded, this solution will probably be ruled out on the basis of cost alone.

Install the DHCP Relay Service

If your internetwork uses noncompliant routers, there is still hope. The DHCP Relay service can substitute for RFC-1542 compliant routers. Install this service on each Windows NT Server on a subnet that does not have a local DHCP Server. The DCHP Relay service intercepts calls from DHCP clients on that subnet and relays them to a designated DHCP Server on a remote subnet for processing. The result is that a single DHCP server can process requests from DHCP clients anywhere on the internetwork.

Accept the default values for Seconds threshold and Maximum hops, or use the arrow keys to set new values. The default values work well for most networks. Click Add to display the DHCP Relay Agent dialog. Enter the IP Address of a DHCP Server located on a remote subnet, and click Add to add this server to the DHCP Servers pane. Repeat this process if you want to add more DHCP Servers. Use the Edit and Remove buttons to modify the contents of the DHCP Servers list until you have it arranged correctly.

Click the Routing tab to display the Routing page. If you want Windows NT Server to function as an IP router, mark the Enable IP Forwarding check box. If you have installed the RIP for Internet Protocol service component of the Multiprotocol Routing service, Windows NT Server will route IP packets using the dynamic routing tables built and maintained by RIP. If you have not installed the RIP for Internet Protocol service, Windows NT Server will route IP packets using the static routes that you have entered with the *route –p add* command.

When you have completed all pages of the Microsoft TCP/IP Properties property sheet, click OK and return to the Network property sheet. Click Close to complete the configuration process. Windows NT Server displays the Network Settings Change dialog. Click Yes to restart the server immediately, or click No to defer the changes you made taking effect until the next routine server restart.

Adding and Configuring Network Adapters

When it comes to detecting installed network adapters and loading the correct drivers for them, Windows NT Server does a good imitation of Plug-N-Play (PnP). Unfortunately, it's only an imitation.

Real PnP requires that the computer BIOS, the adapter card, and the operating system itself all be PnP compliant. In a true PnP environment, the BIOS, the adapter, and the OS all take an active role in determining what is installed in the system and how best to configure it. A PnP adapter, for example, not only tells the rest of the system what exactly it is, but also provides information about how it is currently configured and what alternative configurations might be acceptable. If the current settings conflict with those of another installed device, the PnP adapter settings can actually change on-the-fly, without human intervention.

TIP If, when adding a network adapter card, you think you may have a conflict, run **Programs ➤ Administrative Tools (Common) ➤ Windows NT Diagnostics**. The Resources page displays the IRQs, DMA channels, I/O ports, and memory that are already in use.

Although Windows NT Server doesn't provide PnP, it does the next best thing. During installation, Windows NT Server scans the memory space of the computer, looking for ROM-based copyright notices, version numbers, and so forth. It compares what it finds with a large database that includes information about hundreds of common network adapter cards and their default settings. Windows NT Server uses nearly all of the information available to it during autodetection. For example, if you install Windows NT on a computer that is currently running Novell client software, Windows NT uses information in the *NET.CFG* file to determine more about the networking environment. As a result, unless your adapter card is an oddball or is very old, chances are good that Windows NT Server will locate it, correctly identify it, and load the proper drivers automatically.

That's the good news. The bad news is that, unlike the dynamic and participatory PnP environment, the Windows NT Server autodetection process is essentially passive and static. Although Windows NT Server can locate an adapter and will usually identify it correctly, it has no way of querying the adapter as to its actual settings. Neither does the adapter have any mechanism by which it can notify Windows NT Server or the computer BIOS that its settings are not the default settings. The result is that Windows NT Server autodetection fails for any adapter that is configured to other than its default settings.

NOTE Windows NT Server usually identifies installed adapters correctly. However, autodetection may fail in one common situation. If the installed adapter has both a native mode and an emulation mode, Windows NT may install drivers for the wrong mode, or may inform you that it has no driver available for the adapter. For example, many clone Ethernet adapters emulate the Novell NE2000 adapter. Although you may want to use the clone adapter in emulation mode, Windows NT Server may during installation detect the actual underlying adapter and configure itself on that basis. If this occurs, simply delete the adapter and re-install it manually as the emulated adapter.

If Windows NT Server apparently identifies your adapter correctly, but you can't get the adapter to talk to the network, the most likely cause is that the adapter is currently configured for an IRQ or Base Address other than the default. You can correct this problem either by reconfiguring the values used by Windows NT Server to correspond with the actual settings of the adapter, or by reconfiguring the adapter to correspond with the values expected by Windows NT Server.

TIP Don't paint yourself into a corner. Most modern network adapters are configured for IRQ, Base Address, and so forth under software control rather than by setting physical jumpers. Each adapter has its own dedicated utility program for determining the current settings and changing them. Unfortunately, many of these utility programs are DOS-based and won't run under Windows NT, even in a DOS box. This makes it impossible to reconfigure the adapter settings, or even to figure out how the adapter is currently set.

Before you go any further, either verify that the adapter utility runs properly under Windows NT server, or make a DOS-bootable floppy diskette and copy the adapter utility. Keep this floppy diskette handy. Ideally, tape it to the side of the server. When you need to make a change to the adapter configuration, down the server, boot the floppy diskette, make the changes, save them to the adapter's nonvolatile RAM, and reboot the server into Windows NT Server with the changed settings in effect.

To add and configure a network adapter, display the Adapters page of the Network property sheet. Installed adapters, if any, are shown in the Network Adapters pane. Further information about the highlighted adapter is displayed in the Item Notes pane. Select Add to display the Select Network Adapter dialog shown in Figure 3-9.

NOTE When Windows NT Server 4.0 shipped in July 1996, there was little choice but to use the adapter drivers bundled with the operating system. The adapter card manufacturers hadn't gotten around to writing drivers for Windows NT 4.0. Fortunately, drivers for numerous adapters cards were included, and they were of high quality.

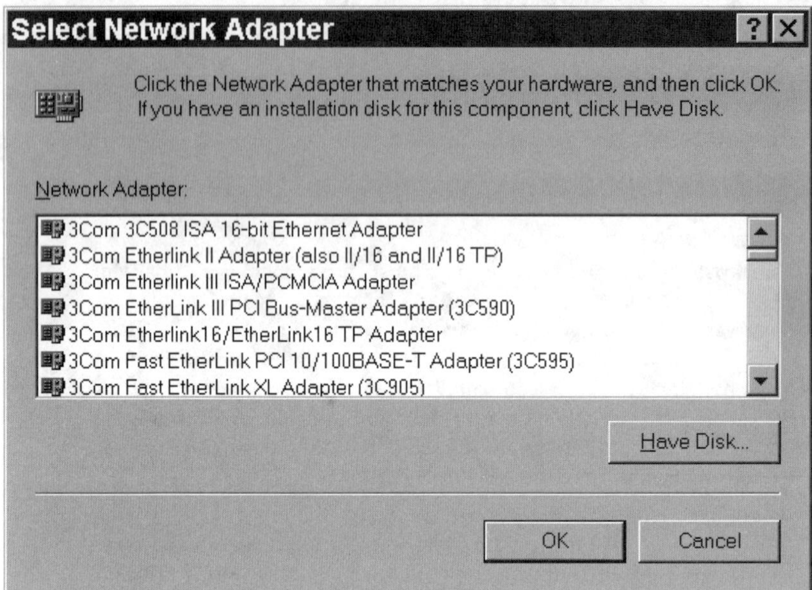

Figure 3-9. The Select Network Adapter dialog allows you to select the adapter to be installed

---

NOTE In the intervening months this situation has started to change. Most name brand adapters now ship with Windows NT Server 4.0 drivers included, and many vendors who do not bundle such drivers do make them available for download from their bulletin boards and web sites. Also, Microsoft frequently posts updated drivers for currently supported adapters and drivers for new adapters on their web site. You can install these updated and new drivers using the Have Disk option shown in Figure 3-9.

When you are installing a new adapter, the best way to proceed is as follows:

1. Check the adapter card manufacturer's web site for the latest released version of a production driver. Make sure you don't unintentionally get a beta or unsupported version of the driver. These are commonly posted, but should never be installed on a production server. If you find a release version driver with a relatively recent file date, chances are that this will be the best driver to use.

2. If you don't find a suitable driver on the manufacturer's web site, or if the driver appears to be an old version, check the Microsoft web site at *http://www.microsoft.com* for the latest version of the Microsoft driver for your adapter. Microsoft drivers are nearly always stable and fast, although they may not implement some special features supported by the manufacturer-provided driver, in particular, manageability functions.

3. If neither the manufacturer nor Microsoft has an updated driver available for your adapter, use the driver for your adapter that is bundled with Windows NT Server 4.0. It may not be the latest and greatest, but it will allow you to use your adapter, and it will be stable.

4. If your adapter is not listed in the Select Network Adapter pick list, you may still be able to use it if the adapter can emulate one of the adapters for which a driver is provided. Configure the adapter to emulate another adapter and install the driver for the adapter being emulated.

5. If none of these solutions is workable, chances are you need a new adapter. Bite the bullet and buy one.

Highlight the adapter to be installed and click OK to display the <adapter name> Adapter Card Setup dialog. In the example, I am installing a 3Com 3C509 Ethernet adapter. Windows NT Server presents the default values of 0x300 for the I/O Port Address and 10 for the Interrupt Number. As it happens, these values correspond to the actual card settings. Windows NT Server also presents the default value of 10 Base T for the Transceiver Type. Because my network uses 10Base2 Coax, I had to use the drop-down list to change the default value to Thin Net (BNC/COAX).

Click OK to continue installing the adapter. The exact sequence of steps depends on the particular adapter being installed and the type of server into which it is being installed. In this example, an ISA adapter is being installed in a server that has both a PCI bus and an ISA bus. Windows NT Server detects this situation, and prompts for more information. Depending on your server and the adapter you are installing, you may see similar dialogs, or you may not. You may also see one or more messages from Windows NT Server informing you that the configuration you are attempting to install appears to be incorrect.

After you have provided all of the information that Windows NT Server requires to install the adapter, it displays the Windows NT Setup dialog to prompt you for the location of the distribution files, defaulting to the location from which Windows NT Server was initially installed. Accept this default, or enter a new location where the distribution files can be found. Click Continue to begin copying files. Windows NT Server displays a status bar as the files are copied, and then returns you to the Network property sheet, with the new adapter now visible.

Click Close. Windows NT Server configures, stores, and reviews the bindings. If you have the TCP/IP protocol installed, the Microsoft TCP/IP Properties property sheet is invoked to allow configuring TCP/IP properties for the new adapter. Do so, if necessary, and click OK to complete the procedure.

Windows NT Server displays the Network Settings Change dialog to inform you that you must restart the server. As usual, click Yes to restart the server immediately and bring the changes you have made into effect, or click No to defer the changes until the next routine server restart. After the server restarts, the new adapter will be available for use.

NOTE You can remove or reconfigure an installed adapter by highlighting the adapter name in the Adapters page of the Network property sheet and clicking Remove or Properties.

Configuring Network Bindings

Microsoft uses the term *bindings* to refer to the logical connections between services, protocols, and adapters that are necessary for those elements to interact. For example, if you install both an NE2000 Ethernet card and the NWLink protocol in your server, these two elements must be joined by a binding before the NE2000 card can be used to communication IPX/SPX packets. Windows NT Server automatically configures appropriate bindings each time a network adapter, protocol, or service is installed or modified.

With respect to binding network adapters and protocols, Windows NT Server is similar to NetWare. Windows NT Server goes a step further, by also binding services to protocols and adapters, as well as binding services to other services. Most network administrators will not need to modify the bindings created by Windows NT Server.

You can view the bindings in effect for your server by displaying the Bindings page of the Network property sheet. The Show Bindings for drop-down list box allows you to determine how the bindings are shown. You may choose to display bindings for all services, all protocols, or all adapters. The bindings are displayed in the form of a hierarchical list such as that used by Windows NT Explorer. You can use the "+" icon at the far left to expand a particular branch of the display by a single level. You can also highlight a list element and then use the "+" key or the "–" key to fully expand or collapse that branch.

You may disable an active binding by highlighting it and clicking Disable. Similarly, you may enable an inactive binding by highlighting it and clicking Enable. You may also use Move Up and Move Down to rearrange the order of the bindings.

In this chapter:
- *Understanding Windows NT Partitioning and Filesystems*
- *Using Disk Administrator*
- *Working with Windows NT Server Disk Sets*

4

Managing Disk Storage with Windows NT

A few years ago, disk drives cost $10 per megabyte, a big drive held 250 MB, and a server with 1 GB of disk space was considered large. In 1997, disk drives cost closer to 10 cents per megabyte, a big drive holds 25 GB, and servers with 100 GB of disk space are common in the glass house, and not unusual even in branch offices. Although the scale has changed by two orders of magnitude, as have the prices, one thing remains true. The primary purpose of a LAN operating system is to share disk space among its users. Certainly, being able to share printers and to give workstations shared access to the Internet, fax servers, and other communications services is a major benefit, but sharing disk is the *sine qua non* of any network operating system.

Windows NT Server 4.0 provides all of the tools you need to install and maintain disk storage on your server. It supports a broad variety of disk types, disk models, and disk controllers—everything from obsolescent technologies like Enhanced Small Device Interface (ESDI) to the latest high-performance SCSI disk subsystems. Unlike NetWare 3.1x, which uses individual loadable .DSK disk drivers and character-based setup and maintenance programs, Windows NT Server provides a comprehensive, GUI-based utility called Disk Administrator that puts all the necessary disk management tools in one place. Like NetWare, Windows NT Server offers software-based RAID 1 mirroring and duplexing. Unlike NetWare 3.1x, Windows NT Server 4.0 offers native software-based RAID 0 striping for increased disk performance, and built-in RAID 5.

Windows NT Server uses many of the same terms related to disk storage that you are already familiar with. However, some of the terms used by Windows NT Server are unique. Throughout this chapter, I use the following terms:

Disk

A physical hard disk drive.

Partition

A logical division of a disk drive. Each disk has one to four partitions. Each partition may contain part of a *volume*, an entire volume, or several volumes. Volumes are described below.

Filesystem

A logical structure used to organize data on the partition. Each volume uses exactly one filesystem to store and organize its data. Windows NT Server uses the FAT filesystem and the NTFS filesystem.

Volume

A data storage unit visible to users of Windows NT Server. A volume is usually assigned a drive letter, e.g., *F:*, but may also be accessed by UNC share name, e.g., *servername**sharename*. A volume may occupy all or part of a partition, and may span partitions and disks. In addition to "ordinary" volumes located within partitions on a disk, each of the following items is also visible to and accessed by users as a volume.

Volume set

If you require a single volume that is larger than the largest available disk, you can create a volume set that spans multiple disks. The resulting volume set is visible to users as a single volume.

Mirror set

To increase data safety, Windows NT Server allows you to create a mirror set, which synchronizes the contents of one physical disk with that of another. If either disk fails, the data stored on the failed disk is retrievable from the mirrored copy on the other disk. Windows NT supports this function using either one host adapter to control both disks (referred to as "mirroring" by NetWare), or a separate host adapter for each disk in the mirror set (referred to as "duplexing" by NetWare). The mirroring function is provided by Windows NT Server itself, and is not dependent on special hardware. This function corresponds to RAID Level 1. The mirror set is visible to users as a single volume. Windows NT can boot from a mirror set.

Stripe set

Windows NT Server also provides software support for RAID 0, which it refers to as a stripe set. Stripe sets comprise two or more physical disk drives, and increase disk subsystem performance by writing alternate data blocks to alternate drives. Failure of one drive in the stripe set renders the data contained on the other drives unusable. The stripe set is visible to users as a single volume. Windows NT cannot boot from a stripe set.

Stripe Set with Parity

A stripe set with parity corresponds to RAID Level 5. At least three physical disk drives are combined into an array. Data and parity information is distributed across all of the drives that are members of the stripe set with parity. A stripe set with parity combines most of the increased data safety provided by a mirror set with most of the increased performance provided by a stripe set. The stripe set with parity is visible to users as a single volume. Windows NT cannot boot from a stripe set with parity.

Understanding Windows NT Partitioning and Filesystems

A new disk drive must first be prepared before it can be used by Windows NT Server to store data. The process of preparing a bare hard disk drive to store data requires three steps:

Low-Level Formatting

Also called *physical formatting*, records the tracks and sectors that will be used to store data. Low-level formatting occurs at the hardware level, and is independent of the way the disk will be divided and of the operating system that will use it.

Partitioning

Divides the physical disk drive into one or more logical sections, each of which can be formatted to store data in the form used by a particular operating system. For example, one physical hard drive may be partitioned into two segments, one to be used by DOS and the other by Windows NT Server.

Logical Formatting

Also called *high-level formatting*, creates the logical disk structure within a partition needed by a particular operating system to store its data. For example, the DOS partition mentioned above would be formatted for the FAT filesystem, and the Windows NT Server partition would be formatted logically to use the NTFS filesystem.

The following sections examine each of these steps in turn.

Choosing IDE Versus SCSI Disk Drives

In case you have somehow missed the obligatory discussion of IDE versus SCSI that seems to occur in every book and article about LAN disk storage, let me restate some of the issues briefly.

IDE in its current incarnations of Enhanced IDE (Western Digital) and Fast ATA (Seagate) is the fastest, most cost-effective storage technology for standalone PCs, usually beating SCSI on performance and always beating SCSI on price for individual workstations. The EIDE and Fast ATA specifications are almost identical functionally, and have overcome two of the drawbacks of older original IDE specifications relative to SCSI, namely, data transfer rate and maximum drive size. The newest and best SCSI drives are still larger and faster than the latest IDE drives, but for workstation purposes the differences are largely immaterial.

Where IDE still falls down relative to SCSI is in the number of devices that can be attached to the bus, and in the inefficiency with which it deals with multiple queued disk requests. IDE limits attached devices to four per channel, which is often inadequate for a server. More important, IDE services disk requests serially in the order that they are received. SCSI uses the concepts of command queuing, parallel execution, and elevator seeking to optimize disk access. Command queuing allows SCSI to deal with pending disk requests in the order that is most efficient, rather than on a simple first-in-first-out basis. Parallel execution allows SCSI to work simultaneously on multiple disk requests rather than serially on one request at a time. Elevator seeking allows SCSI to make the most of head movements—the slowest part of disk functioning—by retrieving one block of data "on its way past" to retrieving another block that is located farther away from the present position of the head.

In practical terms, almost any production server should ideally use fast-wide SCSI disk drives for its main disk storage. However, there's nothing wrong with using IDE drives on a small server, e.g., one that serves a branch office with only a few users. Although it's obviously impossible to set hard and fast rules, a server with 5 or 10 users running typical office applications can usually use IDE disk drives with no noticeable performance hit. If you have to build a small server within a tight budget, you are often better off using IDE disks and spending the difference that SCSI would have cost on more memory. A small server running IDE disks and 64 MB or 96 MB of system memory will often outperform a similarly priced server using SCSI disks, and only 24 MB or 32 MB of system memory.

NOTE For more detailed information about low-level filesystem structures, see the Microsoft Windows NT Server 4.0 Resource Kit and the Microsoft Windows NT Workstation 4.0 Resource Kit. The Workstation Resource Kit contains information about the fundamentals of Windows NT that applies to both the Server and Workstation versions of the software. The Server Resource Kit is really a supplement to the Workstation Resource Kit, and covers the extended features specific to Windows NT Server 4.0.

For more details about the low-level internals of the Windows NT 4.0 filesystem, see *Windows NT File System Internals*, by Rajeev Nagar, O'Reilly & Associates, Inc., 1997.

Low-Level Formatting

Conceptually, you can think of a new hard drive as a blank canvas. As the drive comes from the factory, it contains no information, but only an empty surface that, if prepared properly, can be used to store information. Low-level formatting that new hard drive lays down the tracks and sectors that will subsequently be used to store information. A typical low-level formatting program also performs an exhaustive surface test to locate flaws on the disk surface, and to mark these flawed areas as unusable by the system.

The low-level formatting program determines the number of tracks to be written to the disk, the size of each sector, and the number of sectors to be written to each track. The maximum number of tracks that can be written to the drive is determined by the hardware positioning mechanism used by the drive. Depending on the drive itself and the host adapter, sector size may be fixed or selectable. Almost all disk drives you are likely to encounter use a fixed sector size of 512 bytes. Again, depending on the disk drive and host adapter, the number of sectors per track may be the same for all tracks, or it may vary by track, with the longer tracks closer to the edge of the disk having more sectors per track and the shorter tracks closer to the center of the disk having fewer.

The low-level formatting program may choose these parameters based upon information provided by the firmware of the drive itself, or from information that you provide when you run the low-level formatting program. Using the parameters provided by the disk firmware or by the administrator, the low-level formatting program lays down the number of tracks specified, creates the number of sectors designated for each track, and writes error correction data and sector identification data to each sector it creates.

As a final step, the low-level formatting program performs a detailed surface test to verify that the information it has written is readable. If it determines that a sector cannot be read reliably, it "spares out" that sector, replacing it with an unused sector from a predetermined pool of spare ones.

NOTE This low-level format sparing process is conceptually similar to the NetWare Hot Fix function, but is static rather than dynamic. NetWare Hot Fix allows you to preallocate a portion of the disk as a Hot Fix area. A bad sector that develops during routine NetWare server operations can then be dynamically swapped for a good sector from the Hot Fix area, without impacting server operation.

Windows NT Server performs similar sector sparing repair operations automatically on NTFS formatted volumes, and does so without intervention by the administrator. If more bad sectors develop on a NetWare volume than the preallocated Hot Fix area has room to accommodate, the only permanent solution is to back up that volume, low-level format it, and restore the data. NTFS, on the other hand, does not require that you specify a size for the Hot Fix area; it simply spares sectors as needed.

Fortunately, the high reliability of modern disk drives has made development of bad sectors after the initial low-level format much less of a problem than was formerly the case. However, because a spared sector is logically assigned to a cluster, but physically located elsewhere on the drive, a cluster that contains a spared sector requires additional head movement to read or write, making both read and write operations to such clusters less efficient. Therefore, as good general practice, always choose the most rigorous surface test available when low-level formatting a disk that is to be used for Windows NT Server.

Low-level formatting considerations for SCSI drives

Always do a low-level format on a SCSI drive when you install it. If the drive is new, this process is required before you can store information on the drive. However, even if the drive has already been low-level formatted on another host adapter, you should repeat the low-level formatting process if you change to a different host adapter, even one of the same make and model. This is necessary because sector translation schemes and other low-level parameters can differ between the two host adapters, even if they are identical.

If you want to boot an Intel-based server from a SCSI drive, you must enable the SCSI host adapter BIOS and ensure that the CMOS settings for the server have no entries for SCSI disks.

Low-level formatting considerations for IDE drives

Integrated Drive Electronics (IDE) hard disk drives have some peculiarities all their own when it comes to low-level formatting. To understand why, it is useful to examine briefly the progress in head positioning methods used by disk drives.

Early PC disk drives used a stepper motor actuator similar to that used by floppy disk drives. The low-level format laid down tracks in a predetermined position. When the drive needed to read a track, the stepper motor moved the heads to where that track was "supposed" to be. Temperature changes caused read errors simply because the disk platters expanded and contracted, moving the tracks from where the stepper motor thought they should be. Stepper motor drives required a low-level format every six months or so to account for wear in the stepper motor mechanism and other components. Stepper motor drives can be identified immediately by their head geometry. If an old drive has an even number of heads, it's a stepper motor drive. For example, the classic Seagate ST-251 40 MB drive used 6 heads, 820 cylinders, and 17 sectors per track.

The next step up in actuator mechanisms was the voice coil. Voice coil drives were much more reliable than stepper motor drives, because they automatically accounted for environmental and physical changes to the drive and head mechanism. They did so by dedicating one surface to servo data. When a voice coil drive needed to read data, it first located the proper track by reading the information on the servo surface. Because all heads are physically aligned in a cylinder, correctly aligning the head for the servo surface automatically ensured that the heads for the data surfaces were also aligned properly. Voice coil drives could also be identified immediately by their drive geometry. They had an odd number of heads, because one was always used as a servo head. For example, the classic Seagate ST-4096 80 MB drive used 9 heads, 1023 cylinders, and 17 sectors per track.

As manufacturers strove to increase the capacity of disk drives and simultaneously reduce their size, the "wasted" servo surface became more and more irksome. When Compaq and Western Digital were designing the original IDE interface disk drives, they came up with the idea of combining the efficient utilization of surface provided by stepper motor drives with the precise head positioning benefits of voice coil drives. They did this by eliminating the dedicated servo surface used by earlier voice coil drives, and substituting embedded servo information. Embedded servo information means that the data needed to position the heads to a specific track is written to that track along with user data, rather than written to a dedicated servo disk surface.

Using embedded servo information allowed the disk surface to be used more efficiently, but it also meant that you could not low-level format an IDE disk using a generic low-level formatting program, because that generic program would be unable to write the necessary embedded servo information. IDE drives come from the factory with the low-level formatting already in place.

With some early IDE drives, running a generic low-level formatting program actually rendered the drive permanently unusable. Other IDE drives intercepted the low-level formatting calls, and instead of doing an actual low-level format, it simply wrote all zeroes to the disk surface. Still other IDE drives could actually be low-level formatted by using special software provided by the drive manufacturer, and specific to the model of drive being formatted. Modern IDE drives, and all Enhanced IDE (EIDE) drives, make provision at least for pseudo low-level formatting, and often for true low-level formatting. Refer to your hardware documentation or the manufacturer web site for instructions about doing a low-level format on your IDE drive.

Partitioning

The next step required to prepare a drive for use is called *partitioning*. Partitioning logically divides a drive into one or more segments, each of which can be logically formatted to store data in the format, or *filesystem*, used by a particular operating system.

The *Master Boot Record* on each physical disk drive contains a section called the *Partition Table*. The Partition Table tells the computer and the operating system how the hard disk is logically divided and how to access the information stored on that hard disk. Each physical disk drive must have at least one partition, and may have as many as four. For example, you might partition the main boot drive on your Windows NT Server computer to contain a small boot partition formatted for the DOS FAT filesystem, and a large partition formatted for the NTFS filesystem used by Windows NT Server.

There are two types of partitions. A *primary partition* is one from which the computer may be booted. Each primary partition is logically formatted as a single entity for a particular operating system and is assigned a single drive letter. A primary partition may occupy all or part of a physical hard drive, and a single hard drive may contain from zero to four primary partitions.

The second type of partition is called an *extended partition*. An extended partition is essentially a logical or virtual physical disk drive, which may itself be subdivided into multiple logical drives. A disk drive need not contain an extended partition. If it does, it may contain exactly one extended partition. The computer cannot be initialized from an extended partition, although the operating system files may be loaded from a volume located on an extended partition.

Extended partitions are neither formatted nor assigned drive letters. Instead, an extended partition is further divided, or subpartitioned, into logical drives, each of which may be logically formatted and assigned its own drive letter. Each of these logical drives may be treated as an independent entity. You might, for example, create an extended partition, subdivide it into two logical drives, and then format one of these drives for FAT and the other for NTFS.

The concept of extended partitions was originally devised to get around the limit of four partitions per physical hard disk drive, which limited that disk drive to being logically divided into four volumes. Although this may not seem like much of a limit, some operating systems place a small upper limit on the size of volumes, which meant that much of the disk space on a large disk drive would otherwise have been wasted. An extended partition entry in the partition table section of the master boot record resembles the entry for a primary partition. It differs from the entry for a primary partition by specifying only the starting point and size of the extended partition rather than including operating system and drive assignment information.

If the physical disk drive contains more than one primary partition, you may format each primary partition for a different operating system. If you do this, the formatting program uses the same values for sectors per track, tracks per cylinder, and sector size for all of the primary partitions located on the same physical drive. However, each logical partition may use a different value for sectors per cluster.

On a disk drive that contains multiple primary partitions, you can mark one of these primary partitions as active, which causes the computer to boot to the operating system contained within that partition. Using multiple primary partitions allows you to install and boot multiple operating systems that use different filesystems, e.g., Windows NT Server and UNIX, to the same physical hard drive. In order to allow the system to start, at least one partition must be marked active. Windows NT Server refers to such a partition as a *system partition*. A system partition contains the hardware-specific operating system bootstrap files needed to initialize the computer and begin the boot process. The system partition must be located on a primary partition. The concept of the system partition used by Windows NT Server corresponds to the concept of an active partition as used by MS-DOS and other operating systems.

A disk may also contain a *boot partition*, which may be located on either a primary partition or a logical volume within an extended partition. The boot partition contains the remainder of the operating system files needed to load and run the operating system. The system partition and the boot partition may be (and often are) the same, or they may be located in different partitions, including those located on separate physical disk drives.

NOTE For a typical Windows NT Server computer using a single hard disk, Microsoft recommends that you create a 10 MB DOS-formatted system partition, a 300 MB DOS-formatted boot partition, and allocate the remainder of the disk drive as an NTFS-formatted partition. They recommend this to make it easier to recover from a hard disk crash. Numerous low-level data recovery tools like the Norton Utilities are available for DOS-formatted volumes. Few such tools are available for NTFS-formatted volumes, and those that are have limited power when compared with their DOS siblings.

When you create primary and extended partitions on a physical disk drive, you are creating logical sections, each of which may be formatted for use by a particular type of filesystem. The first partition on a physical disk drive, whether that partition is a primary or extended partition, always begins at cylinder 0, head 0, sector 1. (For some reason lost in the depths of computing antiquity, tracks, cylinders, and heads are numbered starting at zero, whereas sector numbering begins with one. Go figure.) Cylinder 0 is always located on the outside edge of the platter, with higher numbered cylinders toward the center of the platter. Partition boundaries always correspond with cylinder boundaries, so the smallest partition you create comprises all of the tracks on one cylinder. The largest partition you can create is limited only by the size of the physical disk drive.

After Windows NT Server is installed and running on your server, you can use the Disk Administrator program to create new partitions and to manage existing ones. If you are installing Windows NT Server on a new computer, you may find either that the disk drive is empty and contains no partitions or that all of the disk space has been allocated to a partition containing another operating system. In either case, you need to create at least one partition to install Windows NT Server.

If the disk is empty, you can simply boot Windows NT Server from the included boot floppies and use Windows NT Setup to create one or more partitions for Windows NT Server. If the disk drive is partially or fully occupied by another operating system, chances are that you want to remove those partitions before installing Windows NT Server. Again, you can do this using Windows NT Setup to remove the unnecessary partitions, create new partitions as needed for Windows NT Server, and proceed with the installation.

For example, the computer that I'm using to write this chapter came with a 3 GB IDE hard drive. The drive was partitioned into a 2 GB volume with Windows 95 installed and a 1 GB unused area, apparently because the VFAT filesystem used by Windows 95 limits a volume to a maximum of 2 GB, and the technician who built the system didn't consider it worthwhile to create an extended partition to use the remaining disk space. I simply booted Windows NT Server from the floppy boot set and ran Windows NT Setup. I used Setup to delete the existing partition and create a single 3 GB NTFS partition for Windows NT Server.

Creating the first partition on a physical hard disk drive, whether it is a primary partition or an extended partition, creates the Master Boot Record (MBR) for that physical drive and then writes the MBR to the first physical sector on the disk drive. Subsequent changes to the partitioning of that drive, whether they are made by Windows NT Server or another operating system, update that single MBR.

To summarize:

- To be accessible to the operating system, each physical disk drive must contain at least one and at most four partitions. These partitions may be primary or extended partitions.
- A physical disk drive may contain from zero to four primary partitions, each of which is formatted as a single unit and assigned its own drive letter. Each primary partition is formatted for a single type of filesystem. Different primary partitions on the same physical disk drive may be formatted for different operating systems. A primary partition can be any combination of (a) a system partition, which is used to start the operating system, (b) a boot partition, which contains operating system files, or (c) a general-purpose partition, used to store user files.
- A physical disk drive may contain zero or one extended partitions. If the drive contains an extended partition, it may contain at most three primary partitions. An extended partition may be divided into one or more logical volumes, each of which may be formatted to contain a single type of filesystem. Different logical volumes within an extended partition can contain different filesystems.
- The system partition, also called the active partition, is a primary partition that contains the hardware-specific files needed to initialize the system and begin the boot process. Exactly one active partition must be present on the computer for it to boot.
- The boot partition contains the remaining files needed to run the operating system. The boot partition may be located on a primary partition, or on a logical volume within an extended partition. The boot partition may be (and often is) the same as the system partition.

Logical Formatting

Once you have low-level formatted the drive to create the basic logical disk structure at the hardware level and then partitioned the disk to create the logical volume structure, the next step is to format each volume with the operating system–specific high-level formatting program. This logical format writes information to disk that is needed by the filesystem, including:

- A partition boot sector for the filesystem that occupies that partition. Don't confuse the partition boot sector with the Master Boot Record. Information contained in the MBR applies to the entire physical disk drive, whereas information contained in the partition boot sector applies only to the partition to which it is written.
- The System ID Byte, which identifies the filesystem used to format the partition, and the type of partition. This byte can assume the following hexadecimal values:
    - 0x01 identifies a 12-bit FAT partition or logical drive.
    - 0x04 identifies a 16-bit FAT partition or logical drive.
    - 0x05 identifies an extended partition.
    - 0x06 identifies a BIGDOS partition or logical drive.
    - 0x07 identifies an NTFS partition or logical drive.
- Bad sector mapping information.
- Various information specific to the filesystem, including disk-free and disk-used data and the location of files and folders within the partition.

If Windows NT Server is already installed and running on the server, you can use Disk Administrator to create new partitions and format them for either the FAT or NTFS filesystem. If you are installing Windows NT Server on a new drive, you can use Windows NT Setup to create and format a primary partition for Windows NT Server. You may also use the DOS *FDISK.EXE* utility to create partitions and the DOS *FORMAT.EXE* utility to format them for the FAT filesystem, although doing so limits you to using hard drives that do not exceed 1,024 cylinders and partitions that do not exceed 2 GB.

Understanding Windows NT Server Filesystems

Windows NT Server 4.0 provides full support for two filesystems: The FAT (File Allocation Table) filesystem is the same as that used by MS-DOS and by Windows 95. The NTFS (New Technology File System) filesystem is the primary filesystem developed by Microsoft for Windows NT.

Windows NT Server also provides limited support for the HPFS (High Performance File System) filesystem originally developed by IBM for OS/2. Earlier versions of Windows NT provided full read-write support for HPFS formatted partitions. Windows NT 4.0 can read HPFS-formatted partitions, but cannot write to them. This limited support is intended to allow administrators to read the information stored on existing disk drives during the course of migrating to Windows NT 4.0.

The FAT filesystem

A primary partition (or a logical drive) that is formatted for the FAT filesystem can be accessed by the computer when it is running Windows NT, Windows 95, MS-DOS or OS/2. The FAT filesystem supported by Windows NT Server is essentially identical to the VFAT filesystem used by Windows 95. The FAT filesystem supports both the DOS 8.3 file naming convention, for compatibility with MS-DOS and OS/2, and the long file and folder names used by Windows 95 and Windows NT.

The FAT filesystem is an uncomplicated one, originally developed to support small hard drives and simple directory structures. The FAT filesystem stores data in clusters, which comprise one or more sectors. The number of sectors per cluster is fixed for any particular FAT volume, and depends on the total size of that volume. This is so because the size of the FAT is limited to a predetermined number of table entries. MS-DOS originally used a 12-bit FAT, which limited the number of entries in the FAT (and, so, the number of clusters that could be addressed) to 4,096. Later versions of MS-DOS up to and including Windows 95 used a 16-bit FAT, allowing up to 2^{16}, or 65,536 entries in the FAT. If each cluster contains only a single 512 byte sector, limiting the number of clusters to 65,536 allows a maximum volume size of (65,536 clusters x 512 bytes/cluster), or 32 MB. Table 4-1 shows the relation of volume size to cluster size using the FAT filesystem.

Table 4-1. The Relationship of FAT Partition Size to Cluster Size

Partition Size	Sectors / Cluster	Cluster Size
0 MB–32 MB	1	512 bytes
33 MB–64 MB	2	1 KB
65 MB–128 MB	4	2 KB
129 MB–255 MB	8	4 KB
256 MB–511 MB	16	8 KB
512 MB–1,023 MB	32	16 KB
1,024 MB–2,047 MB	64	32 KB
2,048 MB–4,095 MB	128	64 KB

With the FAT filesystem, a cluster is the smallest unit of disk space that can be allocated to a file, and only one file may be assigned to any particular cluster. As a consequence, any file, no matter how small, occupies at least one cluster. When a file exceeds the space available within the first cluster, a second cluster is allocated to that file. Space within the final cluster occupied by the file that is not needed to store file data cannot be used for any other purpose, and is referred to as slack space. On average, each file stored on a FAT filesystem wastes the equivalent of half a cluster's worth of disk space.

If a partition uses a small cluster size, or if most files are very large (and therefore fill multiple clusters completely), this wasted slack space is of little concern. However, if the FAT partition is large—and therefore has a large cluster size—or if many small files are being stored, the storage efficiency of the FAT filesystem decreases dramatically. In the worst case, a FAT partition that is 2 GB or larger, even a one-byte file occupies 64 KB of disk space. Large hard disks with many small files often have hundreds of megabytes of space devoted to cluster slack. This factor makes the FAT filesystem inappropriate for volumes larger than an arbitrary size of perhaps 511 MB.

The FAT filesystem uses the concepts of a root directory and a doubly linked list called the File Allocation Table to organize file storage. Each of the files and first-level directories contained within the root directory points to a FAT entry. This FAT entry contains the starting cluster number of the file or directory in question. If a file contains more than one cluster, each cluster points to the cluster number of the succeeding cluster. The final cluster points to a cluster that contains an 0xFFFF entry that indicates that the End of File (EOF) has been reached. FAT makes no attempt to optimize storage locations of files, and simply assigns the next available cluster to a file as it is written sequentially to the disk.

If the FAT is lost or corrupted, the files on a FAT filesystem volume can no longer be accessed. For this reason, the FAT filesystem maintains two identical copies of the FAT. If the primary FAT is corrupted, data from the secondary FAT is used to reconstruct it. Conversely, if the secondary FAT is damaged, it can be rebuilt by referring to the primary FAT.

The root directory contains an entry for each file and directory located at root level. The root directory must exist at a predefined location on the disk drive, and is limited to 512 entries. Subdirectories are really only ordinary files, but have a directory attribute bit set to indicate to the operating system that they contain a list of other directories and files. Subdirectories can grow to any size necessary. Directories contain one 32-byte entry for each file or subdirectory they contain. This entry contains the following information:

- File Name (8 bytes)
- File Extension (3 bytes)
- Date Created (2 bytes)
- Time Created (3 bytes)
- Date Last Modified (2 bytes)
- Time Last Modified (2 bytes)
- Date Last Accessed (2 bytes)
- Starting Cluster Number (2 bytes)
- File Size (4 bytes)
- Attributes (1 byte)

DOS applications running on a FAT filesystem store only a single date entry and a single time entry. These entries are set when the file is first created, and then modified when the file is again written to disk. This means that when a file is modified on a FAT filesystem by a DOS application, the original creation date and creation time data are lost. Also, DOS does not store or use the Date Last Accessed information. Windows NT Server stores and uses the extended date and time stamp information listed above, including the date and time last accessed, and the date and time created.

One byte, called the Attribute Byte, is used as a bit mask to store attribute information for the file or directory entry. Each bit within this byte is used as a flag to specify certain characteristics of the file. Two of the eight available bits are currently reserved and not used for any acknowledged purpose. The remaining six include:

Volume Label
: If set, this bit indicates that the file is a volume label for the disk volume upon which it resides. This bit is ordinarily under the control of the operating system, and is set when a volume is first formatted. It can be changed by the user, but only by using a sector editor or utility program. Do not confuse changing this bit with changing the volume label. This bit only indicates that the file contains the name of the volume. The actual volume name is contained within the file itself.

Directory
: If set, this bit indicates that the file is a directory, and contains a list of other files and directories.

Archive Needed
: If set, this bit indicates that the file has been created or modified since the last time a full backup was done. This flag is turned on any time a file is written to a volume formatted for the FAT filesystem.

Hidden
: If set, this bit indicates that the file or directory should not be displayed in a normal directory listing.

Read Only
: If set, this bit prevents a file from being deleted until the bit is toggled off.

System
: If set, this bit indicates that the file is an operating system file. This bit is nearly always set on in conjunction with the Hidden and Read Only bits.

The advent of long filenames and folder names with Windows NT 3.5 and Windows 95 presented a problem for the FAT filesystem. Older operating systems, like MS-DOS and OS/2, and older applications programs depended on the familiar DOS 8.3 naming convention. Supporting long names by simply allocating more space for file and directory names would render the resulting names unreadable and the volume inaccessible by these older operating systems and applications.

Microsoft used a clever workaround to allow long names while still maintaining backward compatibility for older operating systems and applications software that adhered to the older standard. Windows NT 4.0 and Windows 95 use the same method for creating long names, so a long file or folder name created with either can be accessed by the other. When a user creates a file or folder with a long name, the operating system first creates a standard 8.3 compliant name for that file or folder. This initial directory entry is readable by any software that understands the DOS 8.3 convention.

Windows NT then creates one or more additional supplemental file entries in the folder, whose sole purpose is to contain the remainder of the long name. Each of these entries contains 13 bytes of additional filename information, and Windows NT creates as many as are needed to contain the entire long name, up to the 255-character name limit. These additional characters are stored as Unicode, so each additional filename character requires two bytes of storage in the supplemental file. Windows NT toggles on the attribute bits for volume label, hidden, read only, and system to indicate that this is a supplemental file entry that contains long name data. Most MS-DOS and OS/2 applications do not display directory entries with this combination of attribute bits turned on, so these supplemental files are essentially ignored by most such applications. Note that the root directory of a drive has a limited capacity, and storing many long filenames (or a few very long filenames) will rapidly fill up the root directory.

TIP By default, Windows NT enables long name support for FAT volumes. You can disable support for long names on FAT volumes by making a manual change to the Registry to disable the 8.3 name creation process described above. Long name support is enabled or disabled globally for all FAT volumes on the server, and cannot be set per volume.

To disable long naming for FAT volumes, change the value entry NtfsDisable8dot3NameCreation in the subkey HKEY_LOCAL_MACHINE\System\CurrentControlSet\Control\Filesystem\ from a value of 0 to 1.

Doing so disables creation of 8.3 short filenames. Files and folders with long names created after this change will not be visible to MS-DOS and OS/2. Files and folders with long names that were created before the change are unaffected, and remain visible to MS-DOS and OS/2.

The NTFS filesystem

The NTFS filesystem is the native filesystem of Windows NT. Originally, NTFS stood for *New Technology File System*; now it stands for the Windows *NT File System*. Microsoft doesn't use the term *New Technology* much anymore. The NTFS filesystem combines fast performance and high reliability with efficient disk space utilization, and is optimized for large hard drives.

The NTFS filesystem stores extended attribute information about the characteristics of each file and folder on the volume, specifying ownership of the file or folder and controlling which users and groups are able to access it, and at what level. Unlike the FAT filesystem, which allows you to establish shares and control access only at the volume level, NTFS allows you to control access per user and per group down to the individual file level. These permissions control access both locally and across the network, and for both resources that are shared and those that are not.

The NTFS filesystem treats every object on the volume as a file. Every allocated sector on an NTFS volume belongs to one or another file, including the information that describes the filesystem itself. Everything contained within a file is an attribute. For example, the access control list for the file is a security attribute; the name of the file itself is a filename attribute; the user data contained within the file is a data attribute.

The NTFS filesystem uses the cluster as the fundamental unit of space allocation. The NTFS filesystem, like the FAT filesystem, by default determines the cluster size to be used according to the size of the volume being formatted. Table 4-2 lists the default cluster size used by NTFS when formatting volumes of different sizes. Unlike the FAT filesystem, which rigidly assigns a predetermined cluster size for any particular volume size, the NTFS filesystem allows the administrator to override the default cluster size and specify a different value for cluster size. You might, for example, increase storage efficiency on a large volume that is used to store many small files by setting the cluster size for that volume to a smaller value than the default. Conversely, on a smaller volume that is used to store a few large files, you might set the cluster size to a larger than default value.

TIP The **Tools ➤ Format** option of the Windows NT Disk Administrator GUI utility allows you to set the cluster size for a volume, but only to a maximum of 4 KB. You can use the command line utility *Format.com* to assign any cluster size to any volume, regardless of size.

WARNING The NTFS filesystem provides optional compression of volumes, folders, and files. NTFS compression can be used only on volumes whose cluster size is 4 KB or smaller.

Table 4-2. Default NTFS Cluster Sizes Depend on Partition Size

Partition Size	Sectors / Cluster	Cluster Size
< 512 MB	1	512 bytes
513 MB–1,024 MB	2	1 KB
1,025 MB–2,048 MB	4	2 KB
2,049 MB–4,096 MB	8	4 KB
4,097 MB–8,192 MB	16	8 KB
8,193 MB–16,384 MB	32	16 KB
16,385 MB–32,768 MB	64	32 KB
> 32 GB	128	64 KB

Formatting an NTFS volume first creates the Partition Boot Sector, which starts at sector 0, and may be as large as 16 sectors. The Partition Boot sector comprises, first, the BIOS Parameter Block, which describes how the volume is arranged and the structure of system files, and second, the bootstrap code that tells the computer how to boot the active operating system. In the case of Windows NT running on an Intel processor, the bootstrap code loads *ntldr* to initiate the boot process.

The NTFS format process next creates the Master File Table (MFT) and the various system files described in Table 4-3. These system files, referred to as *metadata files*, occupy the first 16 records of the MFT, and describe the filesystem structure. The metadata files are stored immediately following the MFT. The remainder of the volume is prepared to store operating system and user files.

Table 4-3. NTFS System (or Metadata) Files

System File	Filename	MFT Record	Purpose of File
Master File Table 1	*$Mft*	0	Lists contents of the NTFS volume.
Master File Table 2	*$MftMirr*	1	Mirrors first three records of $Mft to ensure that MFT will be accessible if a bad sector develops.
Log File	*$LogFile*	2	Logs transaction steps to ensure NTFS recoverability. Comparable conceptually to NetWare BACKOUT.TTS.
Volume	*$Volume*	3	Stores the name of the volume, the NTFS version number, and other volume characteristics.
Attribute Definition Table	*$AttrDef*	4	Lists attribute names, numbers, and descriptions.
Root Filename Index	*$.*	5	The root folder of the NTFS volume.
Cluster Bitmap	*$Bitmap*	6	Maps in-use clusters on the NTFS volume.
Partition Boot Sector	*$Boot*	7	Contains the bootstrap loader for the volume, if it is bootable.
Bad Cluster File	*$BadClus*	8	Location of all bad clusters on the volume.
Quota Table	*$Quota*	9	Currently unused. Intended to store user disk quotas for the volume, a function not supported by Windows NT 4.
Upcase Table	*$Upcase*	10	Maps lowercase characters to the corresponding Unicode uppercase characters.
		11–15	Reserved.

As I mentioned earlier, NTFS treats all objects on the NTFS volume as files. The characteristics of each file, including the actual data, are treated as attributes of that file. File attributes that are stored within the MFT record for that file are called *resident attributes*. Some file attributes, including the filename and the date/time stamps, are always resident attributes. File attributes that are too large to fit within the MFT record for the file are called *nonresident attributes*, and are assigned one or more clusters elsewhere on the volume. Table 4-4 lists the File Attribute types currently defined for the NTFS filesystem.

Table 4-4. NTFS File Attribute Types

Attribute Type	Contents
Standard Information	Time and date stamp and other basic information about the file.
Attribute List	Location of nonresident attribute records associated with this file.
Filename	The long filename, up to 255 Unicode characters, and the short, 8.3 filename.
Security Descriptor	Information about ownership and user and group access permissions for the file.
Data	The actual data contained in the file. NTFS permits a file to contain multiple data attributes, including one unnamed resident data attribute, and multiple named nonresident data attributes.
Index Root	Folder information.
Index Allocation	Folder information.
Volume Information	The name of the volume and the NTFS version used by the volume. This attribute is used only in the $Volume system file.
Bitmap	Maps records in use by the MFT or folder.
Extended Attribute Information	Used to support links to servers running OS/2. Not used by Windows NT.
Extended Attributes	Used to support links to servers running OS/2. Not used by Windows NT.

NOTE Like DOS, the NTFS filesystem is subject to *fragmentation*. Ideally, the clusters assigned to a file should be contiguous. Fragmentation occurs when some of the clusters belonging to a file are stored in noncontiguous areas of the disk. Fragmentation slows file access and causes the disk drive to work harder than it should. Although due to its superior architecture file fragmentation is not as big a problem with NTFS as it is with DOS, it's still worthwhile to do what you can to avoid or minimize it.

File defragmenting utilities for DOS are easy to find. Those for NTFS are less common. Two NTFS defragmenting utilities I have used and can recommend are the Speed Disk utility in Norton Utilities 2.0 for Windows NT from Symantec (*www.symantec.com*) and Diskeeper 2.0 from Executive Software (*www.execsoft.com*).

When they first use one of these NTFS defragmenting utilities, people who are used to DOS defragmenting utilities are invariably surprised. When you run a complete optimization with a DOS defragmenting utility, all of the files are defragmented and tightly packed at the front of the disk. When you do the same with an NTFS defragmenting utility, some files invariably remain fragmented, and the free space is scattered in chunks all over the disk. This isn't due to a defect in the NTFS defragmenting utilities. It occurs simply because these utilities cannot gain complete control over an NTFS drive as they can with DOS.

Choosing the Proper Filesystem

Choosing a filesystem for your server might seem like a no-brainer. After all, the FAT filesystem is a relic of MS-DOS, circa 1981. The FAT filesystem wasn't designed to handle large hard drives. It doesn't support the file and folder permissions you need to secure access to shared disk resources on your server, nor is it robust in terms of recoverability from disk errors. It uses an archaic and slow doubly-linked list to index disk contents, rather than the fast, efficient B-tree structure used by the NTFS filesystem. The FAT filesystem supports the Doublespace and Drivespace compression algorithms on systems running MS-DOS, but these compression algorithms cannot be used on a FAT volume if that volume is to be accessed by Windows NT.

You'd have to be nuts to use a FAT filesystem on any volume on your Windows NT Server, right? Well, not really. Although the NTFS filesystem is vastly superior overall to the FAT filesystem, for all its drawbacks the FAT filesystem does have a few advantages that are missing in the NTFS filesystem. The following sections examine some of the issues involved in choosing the best filesystem for the volumes on your Windows NT Server.

Access control and security

There's not much of a contest here. The FAT filesystem provides no access control or security at the local console. Anyone who can physically access the server can freely add, change, and delete files on a FAT volume. Things are only a bit better for FAT when looking at controlling access to shared disk resources across the network. You can create volume level shares on a FAT filesystem volume, and control access by user and by group. Access permissions are limited to the predefined levels, No Access, Read, Change, and Full Control. You cannot control access to individual files.

The NTFS filesystem, on the other hand, allows you to control access both at the local console and across the network. NTFS File Permissions and NTFS Folder Permissions, both covered fully in Chapter 6, *Controlling Access to Volumes, Folders, and Files*, allow you to specify which users and groups can access each shared folder and file, and at what level. You can assign a predetermined set of rights, e.g., Full Control or Add & Read, or you can use Special File Access and Special Directory Access permissions to create a custom set of permissions, e.g., granting a specific user or group all rights to a file except the Take Ownership right.

For these reasons, you will almost certainly want to use the NTFS filesystem for all of the general-purpose volumes on your server.

Performance and efficiency

Things get a little more complicated when you look at performance and efficiency differences between the NTFS filesystem and the FAT filesystem. In essence, the FAT filesystem is faster and uses disk space more efficiently on small volumes, especially those that contain few files, due to its lack of overhead and relatively small cluster size. Conversely, the NTFS filesystem is faster and uses disk space more efficiently on larger volumes, where overhead is less an issue and FAT cluster sizes begin to exceed those used by NTFS. There's no hard and fast break point, but, in general, consider using the FAT filesystem on volumes smaller than about 500 MB and the NTFS filesystem on those larger. This assumes, of course, that the security deficiencies of the FAT filesystem are not an overriding concern. Also, some applications insist (or strongly prefer) that you use one or the other filesystem. For example, SQL server likes to keep its log files on a FAT volume and its databases on an NTFS volume.

The FAT filesystem is simple, and introduces little overhead on small volumes. The NTFS filesystem, on the other hand, requires a certain amount disk space to store its system files and the log file regardless of the total size of the volume. On small volumes, overhead required by the NTFS filesystem can occupy several percent of the available disk space. The disk space overhead requirements of NTFS do not increase linearly with the size of the volume, however, and on large volumes NTFS overhead will be a small fraction of a percent of the available disk space.

Similarly, in terms of storage efficiency, although NTFS always allocates clusters more efficiently than FAT, this is a much less important issue for small volumes. For example, on a 100 MB volume, NTFS by default uses a cluster size of 512 bytes, whereas FAT uses 2 KB clusters. Because, on average, each file wastes half a cluster in slack space, the 100 MB NTFS volume loses 256 bytes per file to slack space, whereas the 100 MB FAT volume loses 1 KB per file to slack, a factor of 4.

On larger volumes, NTFS is much more efficient than FAT. For example, on my 3 GB system volume, NTFS uses 4 KB clusters, whereas FAT uses 64 KB clusters. The 3 GB NTFS volume loses an average of 2 KB per file to slack, whereas the 3 GB FAT volume loses 32 KB per file to slack. In other words, on this volume, FAT loses 16 times more disk space to slack than does NTFS.

In many environments, overall filesystem performance is a much more important concern than storage efficiency. Here, too, the story is mixed. On small volumes, the simplicity of FAT sometimes (but not always) results in better performance. FAT uses larger (and correspondingly fewer) clusters to store a given file. The smaller clusters used by NTFS, although they increase storage efficiency, can also result in increased fragmentation of files, and require an accordingly higher number of head positioning movements to retrieve those additional clusters. Also, the FAT folder is smaller and more quickly searchable than the NTFS folder.

On larger volumes, and on those that contain many files, the B-tree structure used by NTFS comes into its own. In essence, the lookup performance in a FAT directory is directly proportional to N/2, where N is the number of files. In an NTFS folder, lookup performance is proportional to Log N, again where N is the number of files.

Consider three directories in each filesystem, one that contains ten files, the second 100 files, and the third 1,000 files. With the FAT folder, the time required to do a lookup is linear in the proportions 5 to 50 to 500. It takes FAT ten times longer to do a lookup in a directory with ten times the number of files, and 100 times longer to do a lookup in the directory with 100 times the number of files.

It takes NTFS twice as long to do a lookup in the 100 file directory as it does in the 10 file directory, and three times as long to do a lookup in a 1,000 file directory as it does in the 10 file directory. That is, Log 10 = 1; Log 100 = 2; Log 1,000 = 3. In the smallest directory, FAT may do the lookup much faster than NTFS does. However, linear versus logarithmic means that as the number of files to be searched increases, NTFS rapidly overtakes FAT.

Another of the main reasons for the high performance of the NTFS filesystem is that it handles small files differently than it does large ones. All information about small files, including their data, is stored as resident attributes within the MFT. This means that only a single disk access is needed to locate the file itself and to retrieve its data.

Contrast this with the FAT filesystem, which requires a minimum of two disk accesses to retrieve even the smallest file; first a FAT lookup to determine the location of the cluster that contains the file data, and second, an access to actually read the data. If the file is located somewhere other than the root directory, additional disk accesses are needed to drill down through the directory structure. For example, to read the file *C:\Program Files\Microsoft Office\Office\Winword.exe* on a FAT volume requires the following steps:

- Read the root directory on *C:* to locate the *Program Files* directory.
- Read the first cluster of *Program Files* and search that directory to locate the *Microsoft Office* directory.
- Read the first cluster of *Microsoft Office* and search that directory to locate the *Office* directory.
- Read the first cluster of *Office* and search that directory to locate *Winword.exe.*

The B-tree structure used by NTFS avoids these additional disk reads, making it much more suitable for the deep directory structures common on file servers.

Using Disk Administrator

Disk Administrator is the primary Windows NT Server 4.0 GUI utility for disk administration. In general, Disk Administrator performs the same functions as the MS-DOS command-line utilities *FDISK* and *FORMAT*. In addition, Disk Administrator allows you to create and manage a variety of types of disk sets. Disk sets allow you to configure one or more physical volumes in various ways to enhance disk performance or data safety, and are fully described in the following sections.

Disk Administrator offers two views of the same data. The Disk Configuration view, as shown in Figure 4-1, is oriented toward the physical configuration of your disk drives, and allows you to map various logical configuration settings to the underlying physical disk drives that are available on the server. The Volumes view, as shown in Figure 4-2, focuses instead on the logical configuration of your disk storage subsystem and provides detailed characteristics of each volume created by Disk Administrator.

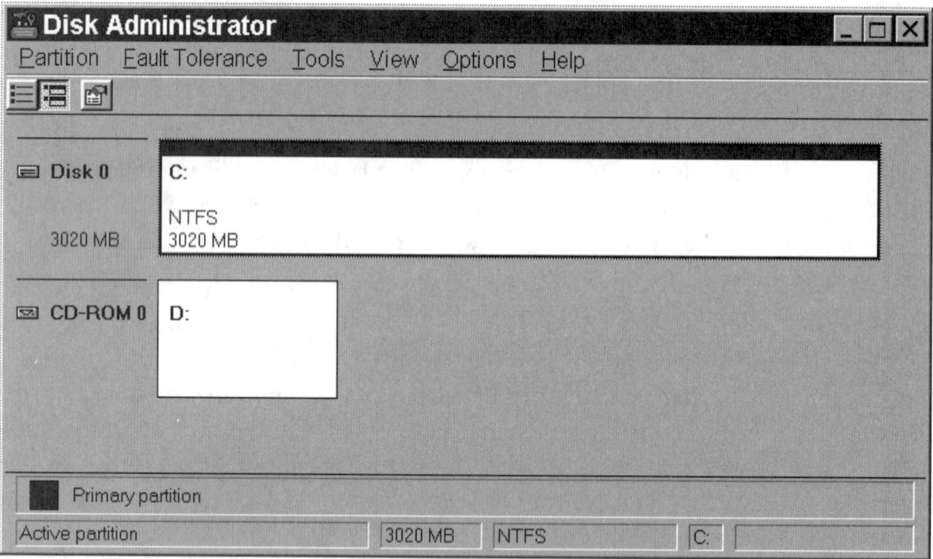

Figure 4-1. Disk Administrator is the primary Windows NT utility for managing disk storage; the Disk Configuration view displays information from a physical disk drive perspective

The designers of Disk Administrator consolidated a great many discrete functions into a single well-designed graphical utility. Because many of these functions are seldom used, and because the menu structure of Disk Administrator generally follows a first-to-last functional path, I have elected to cover the functions of Disk Administrator from a menu-based perspective. The following sections examine the functions provided within each main menu selection of Disk Administrator.

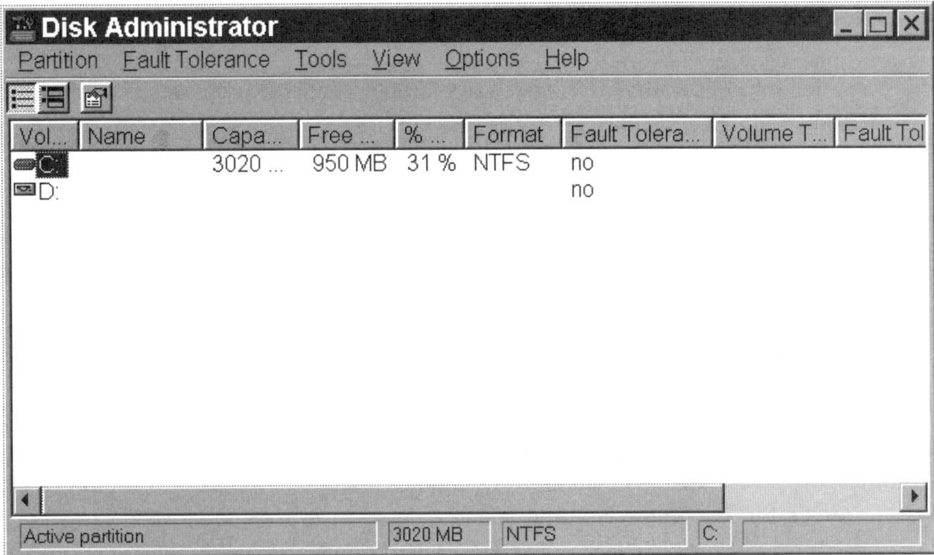

Figure 4-2. The Volumes view of Disk Administrator displays information from a logical disk configuration perspective

Using the Disk Administrator Partition Menu

The Disk Administrator Partition menu consolidates functions related to creating and deleting partitions, to creating and extending Volume Sets, to creating Stripe Sets, to selecting the partition to be booted, and to saving and restoring disk configuration information. The Partition menu includes the following options:

Create
: Invokes the Create Primary Partition dialog to create a new primary partition in an unallocated region on the selected disk, starting at the beginning of the an area of free space. This option is available only if the selected disk has both free space and no more than three existing partitions. You may assign all or part of the free space to the new primary partition. The primary partition will be assigned as a single volume and given a single drive letter.

Create Extended
: Invokes the Create Extended Partition dialog to create a new extended partition in an unallocated region on the selected disk, starting at the beginning of the area of free space. This option is available only if the selected disk has free space, and no more than three existing partitions, and no existing extended partition. You may assign all or part of the free space to the new extended partition. Once you have created the extended partition, you may use its space to create one or more logical drives, or you may assign part or all of the space to one or more volume sets or stripe sets.

Delete

Allows you to delete partitions, volumes, or logical drives. Windows NT displays a confirmation message before actually deleting the partition, volume, or logical drive. You cannot delete the partition that contains the Windows NT system files.

Create Volume Set

Invokes the Create Volume Set dialog. A volume set combines free space on one or more physical disks into a single logical partition. The purpose of a volume set is to create a single logical volume that is larger than the available space on any single physical disk. You may create a volume set using unallocated regions on from 1 to 32 disk drives. Once created, the volume set appears to Windows NT as a single volume. Data is written sequentially to the disks that comprise the volume set. That is, the space allocated to the volume set on one disk is completely filled before any data is written to an area on another disk that is allocated to that volume set. A volume set increases the maximum volume size available at the expense of risking your data. If one of the drives that contains a partition that belongs to a volume set fails, the data contained on other member partitions cannot be accessed.

Extend Volume Set

Invokes the Extend Volume Set dialog. Volume sets are dynamically extensible. That is, if your storage requirements grow beyond the size of a current volume set, you can increase the size of that volume set on-the-fly simply by adding another disk drive and allocating its space to the existing volume set. You needn't go through the process of backing up and restoring the existing data.

Create Stripe Set

Invokes the Create Stripe Set dialog. A stripe set combines free space on two or more physical disks into a single logical partition. The purpose of a stripe set is to increase disk subsystem performance by distributing reads and writes across multiple spindles. You may create a stripe set using unallocated regions on from 2 to 32 disk drives. What Microsoft calls a stripe set is actually RAID 0 implemented in software by the operating system.

Once created, the stripe set appears to Windows NT as a single volume. Data is written block-wise to the disks that comprise the stripe set. For example, if you write a file that contains four blocks to a stripe set that comprises three partitions on three physical drives, the first block may be written to the first drive, the second block to the second drive, the third block to the third drive, and fourth block to the first drive. Any file that contains more than one block is therefore stored on more than one physical drive. A stripe set increases read and write performance at the expense of risking your data. If one of the drives that contains a partition that belongs to a stripe set fails, the data contained on other member partitions cannot be accessed.

Mark Active

Marks that partition with an asterisk to indicate that this is the active partition, or the one from which the computer will boot, if a primary partition is selected on an Intel-based system.

Secure System Partition

Appears only on RISC-based systems. A check mark is displayed if the partition is secure. A secure partition can be accessed only by system administrators. If the partition is secure, clicking this option removes security for the partition. Changes to this option take effect only after the system is restarted.

Configuration

Displays the configuration menu, which you can use to search for a different configuration, and to save and restore configurations. Choose Save to write the currently defined disk configuration information to a floppy disk, including drive letter assignments, volume sets, stripe sets, stripe sets with parity, and mirror sets. Choose Restore to overwrite the current disk configuration information with that stored on a floppy disk created with the Save option. You can Search different installed versions of Windows NT and select a disk configuration from a list. Choosing another disk configuration overwrites the current disk configuration information, and discards any changes you have made during the current session.

Commit Changes Now

Changes that you make with Disk Administrator do not take effect immediately. You can choose this option while working with Disk Administrator to commit changes without exiting the program.

Exit

Quits Disk Administrator. If you have made configuration changes, Windows NT prompts you to save or discard the changes before the program terminates.

Using the Disk Administrator Fault Tolerance Menu

The Disk Administrator Fault Tolerance menu consolidates functions related to establishing and maintaining mirror sets and stripe sets with parity. A mirror set replicates the contents of one partition onto another partition on another physical disk drive, ensuring that, if one drive fails, its contents can be retrieved from the mirrored copy. A Windows NT mirror set corresponds to RAID 1 and to mirroring or duplexing in NetWare. A mirror set is the only disk set in Windows NT that the server can be booted from. A stripe set with parity distributes data blocks and parity blocks across several physical disk drives, and corresponds to RAID 5. NetWare offers no matching feature for stripe set with parity. The Fault Tolerance menu includes the following options:

Establish Mirror

Creates a redundant copy of one partition on another partition located on a different disk drive. The two disk drives may use the same host adapter (called "mirroring" by NetWare) or each may be connected to a different host adapter (called "duplexing" by NetWare). The two partitions are assigned the same volume label and drive letter. The purpose of a mirror set is to increase data safety by replicating each file to two physical disk drives. What Microsoft calls a Mirror Set is actually RAID 1 implemented in software by the operating system.

You may create a mirror set using unallocated regions on exactly two disk drives. Once created, the mirror set appears to Windows NT as a single volume. Data is written in parallel to the disks that comprise the mirror set, with any information written to one partition simultaneously written to the other member of the mirror set. If the disk drive containing one partition fails, all data is retrievable from the surviving partition.

Break Mirror

Breaks the selected mirror set into two individually addressable partitions, without deleting any information. You can use this option simply to break an existing mirror and use the resulting free space for other purposes. However, the most common use for this option is to recover from a disk failure in a mirror set. When one drive fails, you must first break the mirror set before undertaking repairs.

Create Stripe Set with Parity

Invokes the Create Stripe Set with Parity dialog. A stripe set with parity combines free space on three or more physical disks into a single logical partition. The purpose of a stripe set with parity is twofold. First, like an ordinary stripe set, the stripe set with parity increases disk subsystem performance by distributing reads and writes across multiple spindles. Second, the Stripe Set with parity increases data safety by storing parity information that allows the data contained on a failed drive to be reconstructed.

Once created, the stripe set with parity appears to Windows NT as a single volume. Data is written block-wise to the disks that comprise the stripe set with Parity, with parity blocks interleaved with the data on all disks. For example, if you write a file that contains four blocks to a stripe set with parity that comprises three partitions on three physical drives, the first data block may be written to the first drive, the second data block to the second drive, the third data block to the third drive, the fourth data block to the first drive, and the parity block for that file to the second drive. The data and parity blocks for any file therefore stored on at least two physical drives.

Any one disk drive in a stripe set with parity may fail without causing data loss. You may create a stripe set with parity using unallocated regions on from 3 to 32 disk drives, although using more than 5 or 6 disk drives is not a good idea. When one drive fails in a stripe set with parity, nearly all reads from or writes to that degraded set require a read from or a write to every drive that is a member of that set so that parity information can be used to reconstruct the data that was stored on the failed drive. If more than five or six disk drives are members of the stripe set with parity, the overall performance of the array can become so slow that it is effectively unusable. What Microsoft calls a stripe set with parity is actually RAID 5 implemented in software by the operating system.

Regenerate

To recover when a disk drive that is a member of a stripe set with parity fails, first replace the disk drive and recreate the partition used by the stripe set with parity. Then choose the Regenerate option, exit Disk Administrator, and restart the server. When the server restarts, it will reconstruct the data from the failed disk drive and write it to the replacement drive.

Although the regeneration process occurs in the background, it is very disk intensive because every data block and every parity block on all of the remaining good drives must be read so that the data to be written to the replacement drive can be reconstructed. While regeneration is occurring, the Disk Administrator status bar indicates that that stripe set is damaged. Once regeneration is complete, the Disk Administrator status bar again indicates that the stripe set with parity is healthy. Unless the stripe set with parity comprises few high-performance drives and is running on a very fast server, you will probably find that the stripe set with parity is effectively unable to service user requests during the regeneration process.

Using the Disk Administrator Tools Menu

The Disk Administrator Tools menu consolidates functions related to performing a logical format on a partition, to assigning a drive letter, and to viewing properties for a volume. The Tools menu includes the following options:

Format

After you have created a partition, you must first save the changes either by existing Disk Administrator or by committing the changes. Once you have done so, select the new partition and use the Format option to prepare it for use. You are first prompted to choose a filesystem, NTFS or DOS. After doing so, you may optionally enter a volume label to identify the volume.

If you are formatting a single partition as an ordinary volume, a partition that is assigned to a volume set, or one that is assigned to a stripe set, you may choose the Quick Format option. Using this option speeds up the formatting process considerably, because it skips checking for bad sectors during the format. The surface testing performed during a low-level format is ordinarily more intensive than that performed during the logical format, so it is normally safe to use Quick Format on a new drive, or one that has just been low-level formatted. Quick Format is not available for partitions that are members of a mirror set or a stripe set with parity.

If you are formatting the partition for the NTFS filesystem, you may click Enable Compression to cause Windows NT to store all data on this volume in compressed form.

Assign Drive Letter

MS-DOS and earlier versions of Windows automatically and dynamically assign drive letters to volumes. This means that if you add a new drive to a system, assigned drive letters for existing volumes can change. Windows NT allows you instead to assign a specific static drive letter to a volume, which can then be used to access that volume even if other drives are added to the system.

Select a volume and choose Assign Drive Letter. The Assign Drive Letter dialog appears. To assign a static drive letter, mark the Assign Drive Letter option button and select an available drive letter from the drop-down list, which presents only currently unassigned local drive letters in the range *C:* through *Z:*. On systems that have only an *A:* floppy drive installed, *B:* is also available to assign as a network drive letter. You may also mark the Do not assign a drive letter option button to create a volume with no drive letter assigned. Drive letter assignments take effect immediately.

Eject

Allows you to eject a CD-ROM disk from the drive. Choosing this option is functionally identical to choosing Eject from Windows NT Explorer or My Computer.

Properties

This option allows you to view and change properties for the selected volume. Choosing this option is functionally identical to choosing Properties from Windows NT Explorer or My Computer.

Using the Disk Administrator View Menu

The Disk Administrator View menu allows you to specify how Disk Administrator displays information about disks and volumes. Volume View, shown in Figure

4-2, displays detailed information about the characteristics of each volume. Disk Configuration View, as shown in Figure 4-1, focuses instead on the underlying disk drives. The View menu includes the following options:

Volumes
: Displays detailed logical information about each disk volume, including:

- *Volume.* The drive letter assigned to the volume.
- *Name.* The name of the volume.
- *Capacity.* The total space, used and free, on the volume.
- *Free Space.* The unused space on the volume.
- *% Free.* The percent of space unused on the volume.
- *Format.* The type of filesystem used by the volume. Valid filesystems include FAT, NTFS, HPFS, and CDFS (Compact Disc File System).
- *Fault Tolerant.* Yes, if this volume is a Mirror Set or a Stripe Set with Parity. No, if the volume is an ordinary volume, a Volume Set, or a part of a Stripe Set.
- *Volume Type.* Blank if this volume is an ordinary volume. Otherwise, indicates the type of disk set in use.
- *Fault Tolerance Overhead.* Disk space that would otherwise be available that was lost to creating a fault tolerant volume.
- *Status.* Ordinarily blank. Displays status of recoverable fault tolerant volumes when operating in degraded mode and during regeneration.

Disk Configuration
: Displays a bar for each physical disk drive available to Windows NT Server, including CD-ROM drives. Each bar is subdivided and labeled to show the logical volumes contained by each physical disk drive.

Refresh
: Rereads the current disk configuration information and updates the display.

Using the Disk Administrator Options Menu

The Disk Administrator Options menu allows you to specify which optional elements of the Disk Administrator program are displayed, and to set various options that determine how the display is configured. The Options menu includes the following options:

Toolbar
: If checked, displays the toolbar immediately beneath the main menu bar.

Status Bar
: If checked, displays the status bar at the bottom of the window. The status bar includes, from left to right, the type of partition, the amount of free disk space, the filesystem in use, the drive letter assigned to the volume, and the volume label.

Legend
: If checked, displays the legend at the bottom of the window, immediately above the status bar. The legend describes the colors and patterns used to describe each segment representing a logical volume.

Colors and Patterns
: Clicking this selection displays the Colors and Patterns dialog, which allows you to assign your choice of color and pattern to each type of disk entity displayed by Disk Administrator.

Disk Display
: Clicking this selection displays the Disk Display Options dialog, which allows you to choose equal length bars to represent each physical disk drive, regardless of its size, or bars which vary in length with the size of the physical disk drive they represent.

Region Display
: Clicking this selection displays the Region Display Options dialog, which allows you to choose—for all physical disk drives or for a specified disk drive—equal length bars to represent each logical disk region, regardless of its size, or bars that vary in length with the size of the logical disk region they represent. The final option is to allow Disk Administrator itself to decide how to size the disk region display, which is the default (and usually best) choice.

Customize Toolbar
: Clicking this selection displays the Customize Toolbar dialog, which allows you to add and remove icons to the toolbar. Icons are available for most of the menu functions in both views of Disk Administrator.

Working with Windows NT Server Disk Sets

If your server has more than one physical hard disk, Windows NT Server allows you to group these disk drives in different ways to accomplish various purposes, including enlarging the maximum volume size, increasing the disk subsystem performance, and improving data safety. Windows NT Server refers to these logical groupings of physical disk drives as disk sets. Windows NT Server supports four types of disk sets, called volume sets, stripe sets, mirror sets, and stripe sets with parity. Each of these disk set types is described in the following sections.

Volume Sets

A volume set allows a single logical volume to span partitions located on one or more physical disk drives. Using a volume set, you can combine free space on one or more disk drives to create a single logical volume. If you assign space from two or more disk drives, you can create a single logical volume that is larger than the largest physical disk drive in your server.

A volume set can span as many as 32 disk drives, and is dynamically extensible. That is, you can add more disk space to an existing volume set as needed without destroying the data already stored on the volume set. Data is written file-wise to a volume set sequentially. That is, files are written to the first partition in the volume set until that partition is full. Additional files are then written to the second partition in the volume set until it, too, is full, and so on. Windows NT Server cannot boot from a volume set.

There is really never a good reason to use a volume set. By its nature, a volume set does nothing to increase disk subsystem performance. Because losing one disk drive in a volume set causes all of the data stored on any partition assigned to that volume set to be lost, data stored on a volume set is actually more at risk than is data stored on a single partition that resides on a single physical disk drive. The likelihood that any one drive of the multiple drives assigned to a volume set will fail is correspondingly greater than the likelihood that a single drive will fail.

The only real purpose of a volume set is to create a single logical partition that is larger than the largest physical disk drive available. Using a stripe set with parity, described below, or a RAID 5 hardware solution is a much better way to create large logical volumes. Doing so not only provides a logical volume of whatever size is needed, but allows all of your data to be retrieved if a drive fails.

Creating a volume set

If you decide to ignore the very real drawbacks of volume sets and create one anyway, start Disk Administrator and proceed as follows:

1. From Disk Administrator Disk Configuration view, click the first area of free space to be assigned to the volume set to select it.
2. Hold down the `Ctrl` key, and click other areas of free space located on the same or other physical disk drives to add them to the space selected for the volume set.
3. After you have selected all areas of free space to be assigned to the volume set, click **Partition ➤ Create Volume Set**.
4. Disk Administrator displays the largest and smallest sizes available for the new volume set. Enter a size within this range and click OK. If you create a volume set that is smaller than the available space in the partitions you

selected in steps one and two, Windows NT Server creates the volume set using equal amounts of space from each free space area you selected.

5. To actually create the volume set, save the changes you have made either by exiting Disk Administrator or by clicking Commit Changes Now. Disk Administrator automatically restarts the server. After the server reboots, Disk Administrator automatically formats the disk segments newly assigned to the volume set without destroying data present on the first segment.

Extending a volume set

You can allocate additional disk space to an existing volume set without affecting the data stored on the existing volume set. To do so, take the following steps:

1. From Disk Administrator Disk Configuration view, click the existing volume set to select it.
2. Hold down the Ctrl key, and click other areas of free space that are to be added to the existing volume set.
3. After you have selected all areas of free space to be added, click **Partition ➤ Extend Volume Set**.
4. Disk Administrator displays the largest and smallest sizes available for the extended volume set. Enter a size within this range and click OK. Disk Administrator determines what portion of the available free space is needed to create a new volume set of the size that you specified, and assigns that space to the extended volume set.
5. Save the changes you have made either by exiting Disk Administrator or by clicking Commit Changes Now. Disk Administrator automatically restarts the server. After the server reboots, Disk Administrator automatically formats the disk segments newly assigned to the extended volume set without destroying data present on the first segment.

Deleting a volume set

You can delete a volume set, but only as a unit. Deleting a volume set deletes all data stored on that volume set and the partitions that comprise the volume set. To delete a volume set, take the following steps:

1. From Disk Administrator Disk Configuration view, click the existing volume set to select it.
2. Click **Partition ➤ Delete**.
3. Disk Administrator displays a warning message that all data will be lost. Click Yes to confirm deletion.
4. Save the changes you have made either by exiting Disk Administrator or by clicking Commit Changes Now. Disk Administrator deletes the volume set immediately.

Stripe Sets

Like a volume set, a stripe set allows a single logical volume to span partitions located on multiple physical disk drives. The purpose of a stripe set, however, is completely different. Reading data from and writing data to a stripe set is much faster than doing so to a single physical drive.

A stripe set can span from 2 to 32 disk drives, and is not dynamically extensible. That is, you cannot add more disk space to an existing stripe set without first destroying the data stored on the existing stripe set, and then recreating a new, larger stripe set. Data is written to a stripe set block-wise and in parallel. That is, a file to be written to a stripe set is broken into blocks, and different blocks belonging to a single file are written to different physical disk drives. The increased read and write performance of a stripe set is due solely to the fact that the work of reading or writing any particular file is distributed across several physical spindles and head mechanisms. Windows NT Server cannot boot from a stripe set.

There is almost never a good reason to use a stripe set. Although the stripe set provides greatly improved disk performance, similar (albeit usually somewhat smaller) performance benefits can be had using a stripe set with parity or RAID 5 hardware. Loss of one disk drive in a stripe set causes all of the data stored on any partition assigned to that stripe set to be lost, which puts any data stored on a stripe set in extreme peril. The more drives you assign to a stripe set, the more likely it is that at least one of those drives will fail in any given period, destroying the stripe set.

One situation in which using a stripe set may make sense is if you have an application, e.g., a database or imaging program, that creates large temporary scratch files. Because these files are transient, and losing them is therefore of no concern, storing them on a stripe set volume provides both efficient use of disk space and high performance without material risk.

Creating a stripe set

If you decide—despite the drawbacks listed above—to create a stripe set, start Disk Administrator and proceed as follows:

1. From Disk Administrator Disk Configuration view, click the first area of free space to be assigned to the stripe set to select it.
2. Hold down the `Ctrl` key, and click another area of free space located on a different physical disk drive to add it to the space selected for the stripe set. Repeat as necessary until you have assigned all desired areas to the stripe set.
3. After you select all areas of free space to be assigned to the stripe set, click **Partition ➤ Create Stripe Set**.

4. Disk Administrator displays the largest and smallest sizes available for the new stripe set. Enter a size within this range and click OK. Disk Administrator divides the total size of the stripe set you specify by the number of physical disk drives assigned to the stripe set, creating equal-sized unformatted partitions on each of the disk drives, and assigning a single drive letter to the stripe set.
5. To actually create the stripe set, save the changes you have made either by exiting Disk Administrator or by clicking Commit Changes Now.

Deleting a stripe set

You can delete a stripe set, but only as a unit. Deleting a stripe set deletes all data stored on that stripe set and the partitions that comprise the stripe set. To delete a stripe set, take the following steps:

1. From Disk Administrator Disk Configuration view, click the existing stripe set to select it.
2. Click **Partition ➤ Delete**.
3. Disk Administrator displays a warning message that all data will be lost. Click Yes to confirm deletion.
4. Save the changes you have made either by exiting Disk Administrator or by clicking Commit Changes Now. Disk Administrator deletes the stripe set immediately.

Mirror Sets

A mirror set replicates the contents of a partition located on one physical disk drive to an identical partition located on a second physical disk drive. A Windows NT Server mirror set corresponds to NetWare mirroring and duplexing. NetWare differentiates between mirroring, or replicating data to two disk drives controlled by the same host adapter, and duplexing, or replicating data to two disk drives, each of which is controlled by a different host adapter. Windows NT Server makes no such division. The disk drives that comprise a Windows NT Server mirror set can both use the same host adapter, or can each be controlled by a separate host adapter.

The primary purpose of a mirror set is to guard against data loss. If one of the physical disk drives assigned to the mirror set fails, the contents of that drive can be retrieved from the second physical disk drive in the mirror set. Another benefit of a mirror set is that, like a stripe set, reading data from a mirror set is much faster than reading it from a single physical drive. The increased read performance of a mirror set is due to the fact that the work of reading any particular file can be assigned to whichever physical drive happens to have its head mechanism closer to the file to be retrieved.

Because data must be written to both disk drives, a mirror set provides no increase in write performance relative to a single disk drive. In fact, write performance is usually somewhat poorer with the mirror set because the two writes must be synchronized and coherency must be maintained. Because most disks spend much more time reading than writing, the overall performance of a mirror set relative to a single disk drive is usually noticeably better.

A mirror set spans exactly two physical disk drives, and is not dynamically extensible. That is, you cannot add more disk space to an existing mirror set without first destroying the data stored on the existing mirror set, and then recreating a new, larger mirror set. Data is written to a mirror set just as it is written to a single physical disk drive. The only difference is that writes are replicated to both drives comprising the mirror set. Windows NT Server can boot from a mirror set. In fact, a mirror set is the only type of disk set from which Windows NT Server can be booted.

Using a mirror set make sense for most server environments. A mirror set provides two significant benefits. First, the extreme data redundancy—all data is duplicated—almost eliminates the risk of losing data because of disk failure. Second, a mirror set provides better disk performance than does a single disk drive, although the performance increase is smaller than that achieved with a stripe set.

Depending on your environment, using a mirror set can either be very expensive or dirt cheap. If your server has many large hard disk drives, purchasing a duplicate for each of them may be unfeasible, not only from the cost perspective, but from the aspect of finding enough free drive bays and power connectors. In this case, you should instead be considering using a stripe set with parity or, more likely, a hardware RAID solution. Conversely, if your server has only one (or a few) disk drives, purchasing a duplicate drive is relatively inexpensive, particularly considering the advantages that a mirror set provides for the money.

Microsoft recommends that a small server be configured with five disk drives. Two of these are configured as a mirror set, from which the server boots. The remaining three are configured as a stripe set with parity, described below, and are used to store user data. If you are building a small server, and five drives sounds like a lot to you, consider using only two drives configured as a mirror set to provide high data safety and reasonable high performance. With drives of 4 GB to 9 GB commonplace, and drives of 25 GB available, "small" becomes a relative term anyway.

NOTE A good big guy always beats a good little guy. Similarly, good hardware RAID always beats good software RAID. Although Microsoft has done an excellent job of incorporating high-performance, robust, and stable native software RAID support in the Windows NT Server operating system, even they admit that a hardware solution offers better performance.

If you want to mirror a server using SCSI disk drives, you will almost certainly find that your SCSI host adapter supports native hardware mirroring. If so, use it in preference to the software mirroring available with Windows NT Server. It will probably be faster, and will place no load on the server processor. Even if your existing SCSI host adapter does not offer hardware mirroring, it is probably worth the small additional cost to replace it with one that does.

If, instead, you are building a very small server that uses IDE disk drives, the software mirroring provided by Windows NT Server offers a very inexpensive way to improve disk performance and safety. For example, as this is written in early 1997, I find that I can implement mirroring on my main workstation (which runs Windows NT Server 4.0) for a total cost of about $300—the price of buying a second 3 GB EIDE disk drive.

Creating a mirror set

To create a mirror set, start Disk Administrator and proceed as follows:

1. From Disk Administrator Disk Configuration view, click the first partition to be assigned to the mirror set to select it.
2. Hold down the `Ctrl` key, and click an area of free space in a second partition of equal or greater size located on a different physical disk drive.
3. Click **Fault Tolerance ➤ Establish Mirror**. Disk Administrator creates a mirror partition the same size as the first partition in the free space on the second partition.
4. To actually create the mirror set, save the changes you have made either by exiting Disk Administrator or by clicking Commit Changes Now.

Breaking a mirror set

You can delete a mirror set, but doing so destroys the data in both mirrored partitions. Disk Administrator also allows you to remove the association between the mirrored partitions, which is referred to as breaking the mirror set. Breaking the mirror set does not destroy the data in either partition, but instead simply converts the mirror set into two independent partitions. After you have broken the mirror, you can manipulate each of the partitions as an individual unit.

The most common reason to break a mirror set is to recover from a failure of one of the disk drives that comprises the mirror set. To recover, you first break the mirror, then replace the failed drive, and finally reestablish the mirror set. You might also break a mirror set if you simply need to recover disk space used by the mirror set and assign it to a different use. To break a mirror set, take the following steps:

1. From Disk Administrator Disk Configuration view, click the existing mirror set to select it.
2. Click **Fault Tolerance ➤ Break Mirror**.
3. Disk Administrator displays a warning message. Click Yes to confirm that you want to break the mirror relationship and create two independent partitions.
4. Save the changes you have made either by exiting Disk Administrator or by clicking Commit Changes Now. Disk Administrator breaks the mirror set immediately.
5. Use Disk Administrator to reconfigure one or both of the formerly mirrored partitions.

Stripe Sets with Parity

A stripe set with parity distributes data blocks and parity blocks across three or more physical disk drives. A parity block for each stripe is calculated from the values of the data blocks within that stripe, and is then appended to that stripe. The corresponding parity blocks can be used to reconstruct the contents of data blocks lost due to failure of one of the physical disk drives which comprise the stripe set with parity. In industry-standard terms, a stripe set with parity is actually a RAID 5 array.

A stripe set with parity comprises from 3 to 32 partitions of similar size on different physical disk drives. Parity blocks and data blocks are distributed evenly across all of the partitions that comprise the stripe set with parity, but the net effect of using a stripe set with parity is that the equivalent of one partition is used to store parity information. For example, creating a stripe set with parity from three 1 GB partitions results in a single 2 GB logical volume being visible to the operating system, with the third 1 GB partition occupied by parity data. Creating a stripe set with parity from four 1 GB partitions results in a single 3 GB logical volume being visible to the operating system, again with the equivalent of one partition used to store parity information.

As with standard stripe sets, it's a good idea to restrict the number of physical drives assigned to a stripe set with parity, but for a different reason. When one drive fails in a stripe set with parity, no data is lost, but both read and write performance take a serious hit. This is because the system must recover the lost data by reading all data blocks that belong to that stripe and then using the data in the parity block to reconstruct the value of the missing data block. Thus, each logical read can require many separate physical reads combined with a calculation step. Writes to a degraded stripe set with parity similarly require many more disk operations. Increasing the width of the stripe by increasing the number of physical disk drives assigned to the stripe set with parity makes this problem worse. If you use a stripe set with parity, use no more than five or six physical disk drives in any one set.

The primary purpose of a stripe set with parity is to guard against data loss. If one of the physical disk drives assigned to the stripe set with parity fails, the data from that disk drive can be reconstructed as described above. Another benefit of a stripe set with parity is that, like a stripe set, reading data from a stripe set with parity is much faster than reading it from a single physical drive. The increased read performance of a stripe set with parity is due to the fact that the work of reading any particular file is distributed across several physical spindles and head mechanisms. Because the parity block need not be accessed (or calculated) under normal read conditions, a stripe set with parity typically offers read performance comparable to a stripe set of equivalent width.

The situation with write performance is not as happy. Because the parity block must be calculated and written for each write, a stripe set with parity write is noticeably slower than a stripe set write. Under some conditions, the stripe set with parity write is actually slower than a write to a single physical disk drive. However, the small percentage of writes relative to reads in a standard disk environment means that the overall disk performance of a stripe set with parity typically exceeds that of the single disk drive, and often approaches that of a stripe set.

A stripe set with parity spans at least 2, and as many as 32, physical disk drives, and is not dynamically extensible. That is, you cannot add more disk space to an existing stripe set with parity without first destroying the data stored on the existing stripe set with parity, and then recreating a new, larger stripe set with parity. Windows NT Server cannot boot from a stripe set with parity.

Using a stripe set with parity makes sense for many small servers. Relative to a single disk drive, it offers greatly increased data safety and a reasonable performance increase. Relative to a mirror set, it provides nearly as much data safety and equivalent performance while requiring fewer disk drives. If you do decide to use a stripe set with parity, your server will require at least four disk drives—three for the stripe set with parity and one to boot from.

Although you can use a stripe set with parity in a medium or large server environment, it makes little sense to do so. A hardware RAID 5 solution will provide better performance and maintainability while reducing the load on your system processor.

Creating a stripe set with parity

To create a stripe set with parity, start Disk Administrator and proceed as follows:

1. From Disk Administrator Disk Configuration view, click the area of free space on the first physical disk drive to be assigned to the stripe set with parity to select it.
2. Hold down the `Ctrl` key, and click at least two more areas of free space on two or more other physical disk drives to select them.
3. Once you have selected all of the areas of free space to be assigned to the stripe set with parity, click **Fault Tolerance ➤ Create Stripe Set with Parity**.
4. Disk Administrator displays the largest and smallest sizes available for the new stripe set with parity. Enter a size within this range and click OK. Disk Administrator divides the total size of the stripe set with parity you specify by the number of physical disk drives assigned to the stripe set with parity, creating equal-sized unformatted partitions on each of the disk drives, and assigning a single drive letter to the stripe set with parity. If you specify a value that cannot be divided evenly, Disk Administrator rounds to the nearest even value.
5. To actually create the stripe set with parity, save the changes you have made either by exiting Disk Administrator or by clicking Commit Changes Now.

Deleting a stripe set with parity

You can delete a stripe set with parity, but only as a unit. Deleting a stripe set with parity deletes all data stored on that stripe set with parity and on the partitions that comprise the stripe set with parity. To delete a stripe set with parity, take the following steps:

1. From Disk Administrator Disk Configuration view, click the stripe set with parity to select it.
2. Click **Partition ➤ Delete**.
3. Disk Administrator displays a warning message that all data will be lost. Click Yes to confirm deletion.
4. Save the changes you have made either by exiting Disk Administrator or by clicking Commit Changes Now. Disk Administrator deletes the stripe set with parity immediately.

Regenerating a stripe set with parity

Rebuilding a failed mirror set usually doesn't take long, typically several minutes. Essentially, all that must be done is to copy the contents of the original mirror partition to the partition on the newly installed disk drive, a process that doesn't require much in the way of system resources or time even for a very large drive.

Regenerating a failed stripe set with parity is another story entirely. Rather than simply copying data from one location to another, as is done when rebuilding a failed mirror set, all of the data from the failed drive must be reconstructed block by block and then written to the replacement drive. Although Windows NT Server allows you to regenerate the stripe set with parity in the background, for all intents and purposes this is seldom practical. Two bottlenecks intervene.

First, the process of regenerating the data is processor intensive. For stripes in which the failed drive contained the parity block, each data block in that stripe must be read, and then a new parity block must be calculated and written to the replacement drive. For stripes in which the failed drive contained a data block, all surviving data blocks and the surviving parity block must be read, and another calculation performed to derive the correct value for the missing data block, which must then be written to the replacement drive. These intense calculations put a noticeable load on the server processor. Second, regenerating the stripe set with parity is extremely disk intensive. Basically, during the regeneration process, all of the drives that are members of the stripe set with parity are continually reading and writing data. The combination of these factors means that doing a regeneration on a large stripe set with parity may take hours rather than minutes.

Let me first say that I have never had the misfortune of needing to regenerate a stripe set with parity on a production server. However, based on my experience with hardware RAID 5 under similar failure conditions, I can make the following observation with reasonable certainty. When you need to regenerate a degraded stripe set with parity, you will be faced with the proverbial rock and a hard place dilemma. You can wait for off-hours to do the regeneration, and in the interim allow users to continue to access the degraded stripe set with parity for normal operations, but, first, all redundancy is now gone, and second, the disk performance may be unacceptably slow. Or, you could attempt to get the server back up off its knees by regenerating while users continue to access the stripe set with parity. If you do this, you are almost guaranteed that disk performance will be inadequate. On balance, the best solution is usually to wait until after hours to do the regeneration, keeping your fingers crossed that another disk drive doesn't fail before you have the change to regenerate the array.

To regenerate a stripe set with parity, take the following steps:

1. From Disk Administrator Disk Configuration view, click the recoverable stripe set with parity to select it.
2. Hold down the `Ctrl` key, and click an area of free space at least as large.
3. Click **Fault Tolerance ➤ Regenerate**.
4. Exit Disk Administrator and reboot the server. When the server starts, it will begin recreating the data for the failed member of the stripe set with parity.
5. Monitor the Disk Administrator display. When the regeneration process is complete, the stripe set with parity will again appear as healthy.

5

In this chapter:
- *Understanding Windows NT Server Users and Groups*
- *Using User Manager for Domains*

Managing Users and Groups

The fundamental purpose of any network operating system (NOS) is to provide shared access to files, printers, and other resources assigned to the network. Just as important as the ability of the NOS to share these resources is its ability to control who may access them, and at what level. The ability of the NOS to control who may perform which administrative functions is another critical aspect of securing the network.

Both NetWare 3.12 and Windows NT Server use the concepts of user accounts and groups to identify network users and to assign privileges to them. Although there are many similarities between the concepts and methods used by both products to create and manage accounts and to assign privileges to them, there are also some key differences.

NetWare depends primarily on the character-mode program *SYSCON.EXE* to maintain users and groups, whereas Windows NT Server uses the Windows program User Manager for Domains. NetWare stores user and group information in the bindery, an object-oriented database that is local to each NetWare server. Windows NT Server stores user and group information in the Security Account Manager database, which is distributed across all domain controllers within the domain. With NetWare, all user and group management is by definition local to the server being managed, whereas with Windows NT Server, user and group management is done at the level of the entire network. With NetWare, therefore, you manage individual servers. With Windows NT Server, you instead manage the network as a whole.

NetWare 3.12 shows its age, both in the execution of its user and group management tools and the concepts upon which they are based. But with age comes maturity, and NetWare offers some capabilities that have not yet been incorporated in Windows NT Server, particularly those related to managing large corporate networks. For example, the NetWare accounting feature, which is used by many large companies to charge-back costs to users and departments based on actual usage of network services, has no equivalent in Windows NT Server.

In essence, then, relative to NetWare 3.12, Windows NT Server offers the advantages of providing more convenient user and group management tools, finer control, and a distributed management environment at the relatively small expense (for most administrators) of lacking a few capabilities that are sometimes used in large network environments. Let's take a look at how to manage users and groups with Windows NT Server.

Understanding Windows NT Server Users and Groups

As an experienced NetWare administrator, you are undoubtedly comfortable with the concepts of user accounts and groups. Windows NT Server uses these same general concepts, but with a couple of twists.

First, Windows NT Server differs from NetWare 3.1x in how privileges and levels of authority are assigned to individual user accounts and groups. NetWare uses the concepts of User Types and Security Equivalances to determine the level of authority enjoyed by a particular user account. For example, the Supervisor may assign a user account the User Type of *Workgroup Manager*. This automatically grants that account the level of authority that NetWare has predefined for that User Type, e.g., creating additional users and groups. To use Security Equivalences, you assign users and/or groups a Security Equivalence to an existing user with the desired level of authority. For example, on my NetWare 3.12 server, I have assigned my own account, *thompson*, security equivalence to the user *supervisor*, making the user account *thompson* a Supervisor Equivalent. Similarly, I have assigned the NetWare group *Administrators* as a security equivalent to user *supervisor*, with the result that any NetWare user account that is a member of the NetWare *Administrators* group is also a Supervisor Equivalent.

Windows NT Server does not use the concepts of User Types and Security Equivalances. Instead, you grant specific rights and permissions to either individual users or to groups. You may also assign a user account as a member of an existing group, whereby that user inherits the rights available to the group.

The second major difference between NetWare 3.1x and Windows NT Server results from the methods used by the two products to store user and group information. NetWare account information is stored in the bindery, an object-oriented database that resides locally on each NetWare server. Windows NT Server account information is stored in a distributed account database that is shared among all domain controllers within the domain. With NetWare, a user logs into a specific server to access the shared resources available on that server. To access resources on another server, the user must log into (or attach to) that server as well. With Windows NT Server, a user logs in to a domain, which automatically provides that user with access to the shared resources provided by all of the servers that are members of that domain.

The implications of this fact on managing users and groups on multiserver networks are profound. Consider two networks, one with four NetWare servers and the other with four Windows NT servers. To create a new user and grant that user access to all servers on the NetWare network, you must log in to each NetWare server in turn, create the user, and assign the appropriate rights for that user on that server. With Windows NT Server, you instead log in to the domain, create the user, and assign the appropriate rights and permissions. That user then has access to all of the resources for which he is authorized on any server that is a member of the domain. Similarly, if you need to change the rights and permissions assigned to a user on the NetWare network, you must do so on four separate servers. Doing the same on the Windows NT Server network requires only that you make a single change to the domain user record.

NOTE If you have a multiserver NetWare 3.1x network, one of the biggest advantages to installing even one server running Windows NT Server is that you can use it to centrally manage the user accounts on as many as eight NetWare 3.1x servers. This account management function is unidirectional. That is, changes made on the Windows NT Server computer are replicated to the managed NetWare servers; changes made locally to an individual NetWare server affect only that server, and are not communicated to the Windows NT Server computer. Implementing this feature requires the Directory Service Manager for NetWare component of the optional product Microsoft Services for NetWare, a $149 software package that is described fully in Chapter 20, *Managing Servers in a Mixed NetWare and Windows NT Server Environment.*

Windows NT Server uses the following terminology for managing users and groups:

Domain

A logical grouping of computers, including servers and workstations. A domain is to computers what a group is to users. Domains are commonly arranged either geographically or functionally. For example, a firm with offices in Chicago, Pittsburgh, and Winston-Salem might choose to establish a domain for each location. All servers and workstations physically located in the Chicago office would be assigned to the Chicago domain, and so forth. If the firm has, say, accounting, administration, and sales departments in each location, it might instead choose to create three domains named Accounting, Administration, and Sales. In this case, servers and workstations belonging to the accounting department, whatever their physical location, would be assigned to the Accounting domain.

Rights

Rights control who may perform specific actions. For example, members of the groups *Administrators* and *Server Operators* have the right to reset the clock/calendar on the server. Members of other groups do not have this right, and therefore cannot change the server time and date. Rights may be granted to both users and groups.

Permissions

Permissions control access to shared resources on the network. Granting a permission to a user for a specific resource allows that user to access the resource at the permitted level. For example, you might grant user *smith* the *read-only permission* to the shared folder *C:\WINNT*, allowing that user to read, but not change, the files contained in that folder. Permissions may be granted to both users and groups. Chapter 6, *Controlling Access to Volumes, Folders, and Files*, describes how to use permissions to control access to shared folders and files. Chapter 7, *Printing with Windows NT Server*, does the same for shared printers.

User

A user account contains all of the information needed for a particular user. The user account may be a Global Account, which is the type assigned to ordinary users in the domain, or it may be a Local Account, which is assigned to users from untrusted domains. The user account includes:

— *Identification Information*. The username and password needed to log on to the computer or domain. Although Windows NT Server does not allow a duplicate username, username is not the key field for this record. Windows NT Server assigns a unique Security Identification (SID) to each account when it is created. Deleting an account and then immediately creating a new account with the same name as the deleted account results in the new account having a different SID. All rights and other characteristics assigned to the original account are lost. The SID is manipulated internally by Windows NT Server, and cannot be modified by the administrator. Incidentally, the SID concept also applies to the server installation itself, and is the reason that you must reinstall Windows NT Server to convert a standalone server to a domain controller.

— *Group Information*. The groups to which this user belongs.

- *Rights and Permissions.* The rights and permissions assigned explicitly to this user, as opposed to the rights and permissions that the user inherits from group memberships.
- *Account Restrictions and Profile Information.* The location of profile information for this user, and the restrictions in effect for this user, e.g., account disabled, or logons limited to a particular time of day or to a particular workstation.

Group

Users may be assigned to one or more groups. Like a user account, a group may be granted rights and permissions. A user who belongs to a particular group is implicitly granted the rights and permissions that have been explicitly granted to that group.

Using groups properly allows you to manage user rights and permissions more efficiently. Instead of granting rights and permissions explicitly to each user, you create a group, grant the necessary rights and permissions to that group, and then assign multiple users to the group. When you need to change rights and permissions for several similar users who are all members of a particular group, you can modify them for the group rather than for each individual user.

You can grant specific rights and permissions to an individual user and thereby enhance that user's privileges beyond those enjoyed by the remaining members of the group. A user's effective rights and permissions are the cumulative total of the rights and permissions granted explicitly to the user and those inherited implicitly from all groups of which the user is a member.

Windows NT Server has two types of groups:

- *Global Groups.* A global group can contain only user accounts from the domain in which the group was created. A global group may be assigned rights and permissions in another domain if that domain trusts the domain to which the global group belongs. This allows users assigned to the global group to access resources on another domain without requiring that they have an account on that domain. A global group cannot contain other groups.
- *Local Groups.* A local group can contain both users and global groups. A local group can be assigned rights and permissions only in the domain in which it is created. Rights and permissions granted to a local group are inherited by all users and global groups that are members of the local group. You can assign global groups from several domains to a single local group, and then manage this local group as a single entity. This eases the burden of granting limited access to resources in your domain to users from outside your domain.

NOTE It's easy to confuse the purpose and function of local and global groups. Microsoft terminology seems just backwards, because local groups can contain users from any (global) domain, whereas global groups can contain only users from the local domain.

Everything becomes clear if you instead consider the local/global aspect from the standpoint of rights and permissions. Members of a global group can be assigned rights and permissions in both the local domain and in other trusted domains, whereas members of a local group can be assigned rights and permissions only in the local domain in which the local group was created.

Use global groups to manage rights and permissions for primary users—those from your local domain. Use local groups to grant limited rights and permissions to secondary users—those from remote untrusted domains.

Default Users

Windows NT Server creates two default user accounts when you install it. Windows NT Server refers to a default user as a *built-in account.* You can rename a built-in account, but you cannot delete it. Windows NT Server creates the following built-in users when you install it:

Administrator
: During installation, Windows NT Server creates the Administrator account automatically and prompts you for a password to be assigned to it. The Windows NT Administrator account corresponds directly to the NetWare 3.1x *supervisor* account. The Administrator account can be renamed, but it cannot be deleted. The Administrator account is automatically assigned to the Administrators local group, and to the Domain Admins and Domain Users global groups.

Guest
: The Guest account provides limited access to server resources, and is intended for infrequent, one-time, or casual users. The fact that the Guest account is created automatically and cannot be deleted disconcerts many system administrators new to Windows NT Server, who, when installing other network operating systems, would, for security reasons, delete the guest user account and similar accounts and groups as a matter of course. Fortunately, although it does not allow you to delete it, Windows NT Server installs the Guest user account securely by initially setting the account status to disabled and requiring that it be manually enabled before it has access to server resources. The Guest account is automatically assigned to the Domain Guests global group.

As a matter of good general practice, you should not use the Administrator account for routine operations. Instead, create a working account and assign it to the Administrators, Domain Admins, and Domain Users groups. Doing so creates an "Administrator Equivalent" account that has all of the rights and permissions possessed by the Administrator account itself.

Default Groups

Windows NT Server creates eleven default groups when you install it. Windows NT Server refers to a default group as a *system group*. You can modify the rights assigned to a system group, but you cannot rename or delete it. Windows NT Server creates the following standard system groups when you install it:

Account Operators
: Users assigned to this local group can create and manage user accounts and groups in the domain, but cannot grant rights to users. Account Operators can, however, assign users to groups created by an Administrator, whereby the users inherit the rights granted to those groups by the Administrator. The closest equivalent to the Windows NT Server Account Operator group is the NetWare user type *Workgroup Manager*. The Domain Admins global group is automatically assigned membership in the Account Operators group.

Administrators
: Like a NetWare 3.1x Supervisor Equivalent user, a user assigned to this local group has almost complete access to and control of the server. Users assigned to the Administrators group can access any file or directory on a FAT volume, but may be restricted by NTFS File Permissions or NTFS Directory Permissions from directly accessing resources on an NTFS volume. A member of this group who is prevented by NTFS permissions from accessing a disk resource can Take Ownership of the resource and thereby override NTFS restrictions. The Domain Admins global group and the Administrator user account are automatically assigned membership in the Administrators group.

Backup Operators
: Membership in this local group confers the rights needed to back up the server. These rights include logging on to the server locally, shutting down the server, and overriding NTFS File Permissions and NTFS Directory Permissions to the extent necessary to allow a user assigned to this group to back up files and directories to which that user account otherwise has no access. Membership in this group does not confer the right to view or change the files and directories for which access is granted, but merely to back them up. Note that users assigned to this group are not automatically given the right to restore the server. That right must be explicitly granted by an Administrator. No users or groups are automatically assigned membership in the Backup

Operators group, except that a user assigned to the local group Replicator is also assigned membership automatically in the Backup Operators group. There is no direct NetWare equivalent to the Backup Operators group. A NetWare user must be assigned Supervisor Equivalent status to be able to perform all of the functions of a Windows NT Server Backup Operator.

Domain Admins

Membership in this global group by default confers Administrator privileges. The user account Administrator is assigned membership in this group automatically, granting domain administration privileges to the local Administrator. The Domain Admins group is itself automatically assigned membership in the Administrators local group, which thereby grants any member of Domain Admins local administration privileges as well. You can remove the Domain Admins global group from the Administrators local group if you want to restrict the local authority of members of the Domain Admins group. Because NetWare does not support the domain concept, there is no NetWare User Type that is directly equivalent to Domain Admins. In a single server environment, the closest match is a Supervisor Equivalent user.

Domain Guests

Membership in this global group confers the limited rights associated with a guest account. By default, the user Guest is a member of the Domain Guests group, and the Domain Guests group is itself a member of the local Guests group. The built-in user account Guest is automatically assigned membership in the Domain Guests group.

Domain Users

Membership in this global group confers a standard set of rights adequate for "ordinary" users of the network. The Domain Guests group is itself a member of the local group Users. By default, all newly created users are assigned membership in this group. The built-in user Administrator is also automatically assigned membership in the Domain Users group.

Guests

Membership in this local group confers very limited privileges, and is intended for infrequent or one-time users. The global group Domain Guests is automatically assigned membership in the Guests group.

Print Operators

Membership in this local group confers the rights necessary to create and manage print shares in the domain, including logging on to the server locally and shutting down the system. There is no direct NetWare equivalent to the Print Operators group, although this group has powers similar to that of a NetWare user assigned as both a Print Queue Operator and a Print Server

Operator. No users or groups are automatically assigned membership in the Print Operators group.

Replicator

Membership in this local group confers the rights needed to support directory replication. No users or groups are automatically assigned membership in the Replicator group. Only those special users created when implementing directory replication services should be assigned membership in the Replicator group. No users or groups are automatically assigned membership in the Replicator group.

Server Operators

Membership in this local group confers a group of rights that are inferior only to those of Administrators. Members of the Server Operators group can both back up and restore files and directories, change the system time, force remote shutdown, log on locally to the server console, and shutdown the server. No users or groups are automatically assigned membership in the Server Operators group.

Users

Membership in this local group confers a standard set of rights adequate for "ordinary" users of the network. Local users (as opposed to global users) are assigned to this group. The group Domain Users is automatically assigned membership in the Users group.

NOTE One other system group, called *Power Users*, may or may not appear on your group list. If you install Windows NT Server 4.0 as a new installation, Power Users does not appear because it is no longer a standard system group. If instead you install Windows NT Server 4.0 as an upgrade installation on a server that had been running Windows NT Server 3.5x (or a beta version of Windows NT Server 4.0), this formerly standard system group will be imported, and will appear as a system group on your group list. The Power Users group corresponds closely in purpose to the User Account Manager user type in NetWare. Membership in the Power Users group extends the authority of a standard user account slightly, allowing it to create and manage other users. No users or groups are assigned automatically to the Power Users group.

Using User Manager for Domains

Windows NT Server stores user account and group information in an account database called the Security Account Manager database. In a domain environment, this database resides on the Primary Domain Controller and is replicated automatically to any Backup Domain Controllers that are members of the domain. If Windows NT Server is installed as a standalone server, the account database resides locally on that server, and is not distributed to other servers on the network.

Domain user accounts and groups are stored in the distributed account database on the Primary Domain Controller. These accounts give the user access throughout the domain to resources for which he or she has the necessary rights and permissions. Workstation user accounts and groups are stored in the local account database on the workstation in question, and control user access only on that particular workstation.

Windows NT Server provides one of two views of the same tool for managing users and groups, depending on the environment in which you run it. In a domain environment, the tool is called User Manager for Domains. In a standalone server environment, it is called simply User Manager. User Manager provides a subset of the tools provided with User Manager for Domains, and lacks only those tools used for managing domain-related items. Changes made with User Manager affect only the local account database on the computer running it. Changes made with User Manager for Domains affect the distributed account database on the Primary Domain Controller rather than just the local account database, and therefore impact the entire domain.

NOTE In this chapter, I assume that you will be working in a domain environment. Accordingly, I have used the User Manager for Domains version of the tool for screen displays. If, instead, you are using User Manager in a standalone server environment, the screens you see will be almost identical (lacking only the icons and menu options specific to managing domain-related items).

Use User Manager for Domains to create and maintain user accounts; to create and maintain groups; to set global account policies that affect all users in the domain; to assign explicit rights to users; to set Audit Policy for the domain; and to create and maintain trust relationships between domains.

Running User Manager for Domains

Windows NT Server automatically installs a copy of User Manager or User Manager for Domains as a Start Menu item when you install the operating system. To invoke User Manager for Domains, from the Start button, choose Programs, then Administrative Tools (Common), then User Manager (for Domains) to display the main window of User Manager for Domains. Individual user accounts are visible in the upper pane, and groups are shown in the lower pane. If more users or groups exist than can be displayed in the available space, User Manager for Domains provides a scroll bar to allow you to display the portion of the list that contains the item to be managed.

NOTE To use User Manager or User Manager for Domains to manage a computer or domain, respectively, your account must have administrator-level access for the computer or domain in question. You have the necessary level of access if your account is a member of the Administrators group, the Domain Admins group, or the Account Operator group for the computer or domain you want to manage.

You can also run User Manager for Domains from the Run dialog or a desktop shortcut, using command-line arguments to specify which domain or computer is to be managed. For example:

```
usrmgr TTGNET
```

This command invokes User Manager for Domains with the domain *TTGNET* active.

Use UNC syntax to specify the computer name, as follows:

```
usrmgr \\KERBY
```

This command invokes User Manager for Domains with the computer *KERBY* active.

NOTE You can manage the local Security Account Manager database only if the computer is a workstation or a standalone server. If you attempt to manage the local Security Account Manager database on a domain controller, you will instead be managing the Security Account Manager database for the entire domain.

This command-line method is useful primarily for creating desktop shortcuts that allow you to invoke User Manager for Domains for a particular domain or computer by simply clicking on a desktop icon. To create such a shortcut, right-click on an empty area of your desktop, select New and then Shortcut to invoke the Create Shortcut Wizard. Enter the program path, name, and command-line arguments when prompted, or Browse to select the file.

TIP If you browse for the file, don't forget to enter the command-line arguments manually to the executable filename filled in by the browsing procedure.

Adding and Managing Users

To begin adding new users or managing current users, log on to Windows NT Server with an account that has administrative privileges, and run User Manager for Domains. The application titlebar displays the name of the active domain or computer, which defaults to the current computer or domain. You can select a different domain or computer for which to modify the Security Account Manager database by choosing Select Domain from the User menu to display the Select Domain dialog. Enter the name of the domain or computer to be managed and click OK. If your connection to the remote domain or computer is via a dial-up or other low-speed link, you may optionally mark the Low Speed Connection check box.

Using the low speed connection option

Marking the Low Speed Connection check box (or choosing this option on the Options menu) modifies the functioning of User Manager for Domains in several respects, all of which are intended to make the application more responsive. These changes include:

- The user account list does not appear in the Username pane, and the Select Users option on the User menu is grayed out. You can use the New User option on the User menu to create a new user. You can also modify existing user accounts with the Copy, Delete, Rename, and Properties options. However, doing so requires that you know the exact username and enter it manually in the Manage User or Group Properties dialog.
- The group list does not appear in the Groups pane. You can modify existing local groups using the options on the User menu, or choose the New Local Group option to create a local group. Again, you must manually type the name of the local group to be managed into the Manage User or Group Properties dialog rather than picking it from a list.
- You cannot create or manage global groups.
- The options on the View menu are grayed out.

Windows NT Server never forces you to use the Low Speed Connection option, regardless of how slow your connection may be. Even when using a slow dial-up link, you can disable the Low Speed Connection option and use the full capabilities of User Manager for Domains. However, if the Security Account Manager database being managed via a slow link is very large, operations that normally require only seconds may instead take several minutes. You can toggle this option at any time. Doing so simply changes the options displayed by User Manager for Domains and controls the amount of data that will be exchanged between the application and the remote Security Account Manager database.

Creating new users and setting user properties

To add a user, choose the New User option from the User menu to display the New User dialog, as shown in Figure 5-1.

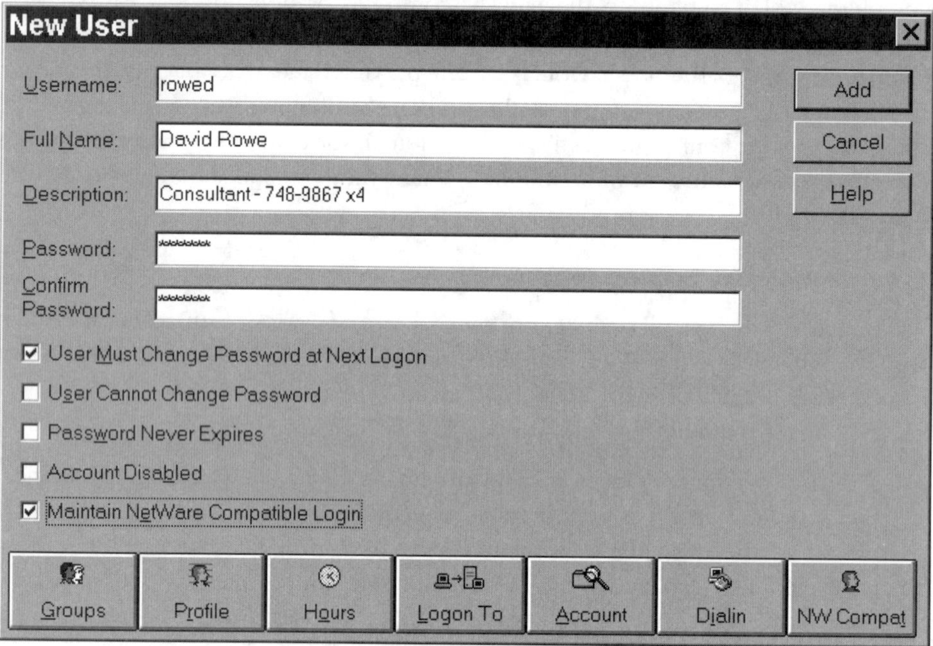

Figure 5-1. The New User dialog allows you to add a user and specify account rights and restrictions

---

NOTE Rather than recreating your entire user base in Windows NT Server, you may import existing user account information from your NetWare server by using the Directory Service Manager for NetWare, which is described in Chapter 20, *Managing Servers in a Mixed NetWare and Windows NT Server Environment,* or by using the Migration Tool for NetWare, which is described in Chapter 21, *Migrating to a Pure Windows NT Server Environment.*

Enter the account name for this user in the Username field. Although Windows NT Server automatically assigns an SID and uses it as the record key, you must still specify a unique value for Username. Many organizations standardize their user naming convention by creating eight-character usernames with the first six or seven characters of the last name followed by the first initial or first and middle initials. Using this scheme, or a similar one, makes it much easier to maintain user accounts, particularly in an internetworked heterogeneous environment.

TIP Windows NT Server allows account names as large as 20 characters using all but the few special symbols listed in the Help text for this function. However, it's a good idea to limit yourself to an eight-character name that uses only alphabetic and numeric characters. This ensures compatibility with other operating systems that have more limited user naming conventions.

Optionally, enter the user's complete name in the Full Name field. In particular, if your domain has many user accounts, decide ahead of time how you will enter this value, and then stay consistent. Windows NT Server allows you to display the user account list sorted either by Full Name or by Username. Entering some full names in the form "John Doe" and others as "Doe, John" makes it much harder to locate the proper account on server or domain with many accounts.

Next, enter and confirm the password you want to assign to the user. Windows NT Server displays asterisks as you type, and requires that you enter identical values in the two fields for the password to be accepted. Windows NT Server passwords may be as large as 14 characters, and are case sensitive. Depending on the settings in the Account Policy section, described later in this chapter, you may be permitted to leave the password fields blank, or you may be required to enter a password of at least the minimum length specified in Account Policy. For best security, enter a password of at least six (and preferably eight or more) characters, using a combination of letters and numbers.

TIP Now here's something you almost never see in print. An author recommending shorter passwords in preference to longer ones. If your network includes workstations that are providing peer-to-peer services, you may want to limit your passwords to eight characters. For example, a Windows 95 workstation that protects shared disk or printer resources with share level security (rather than user level security authenticated by a Windows NT Server or NetWare server) limits password length to eight characters. If your Windows NT Server user accounts have longer passwords, any user who attempts to log in to a Windows 95 shared resource will have to enter a password manually.

Next, mark the check boxes to specify how passwords will be controlled, as follows:

User Must Change Password at Next Logon
: Mark this check box to force a password change the first time the user logs on to the new account. Many administrators use blank passwords for new accounts to make it easier for the new user to get connected for the first time. Alternatively, some administrators set the password for the new account to the same value as the account name, or use a common word like "password" as the password. Obviously, any of these methods results in at least a short-term gap in security. If you use one of these methods, make sure that you set the account to force a password change the first time the new user logs on.

User Cannot Change Password
: Mark this check box to specify that only administrators can change passwords. Some companies that are very security conscious use this option to prevent users from choosing easily cracked passwords. However, a secure password policy also requires that passwords be changed frequently, so enabling this option will add significantly to your workload.

Password Never Expires
: If you have set a password aging value in Account Policy, marking this check box overrides the value set in Account Policy. Enabling this option violates a fundamental principle of password management, because a "permanent" password has a way of becoming known. Strangely, many administrators enforce frequent password changes on users, who have relatively limited privileges, but set the password status to permanent on their own accounts, which have high privileges. In the real world, what's sauce for the goose is almost never so for the gander.

Account Disabled
: Marking this check box makes the account temporarily unusable. You might do this, for example, if an employee is on vacation or a leave of absence. Simply clearing the box restores the account to its former status. Use this as an alternative to deleting the account, which would then have to be recreated when the employee returned to work.

Account Locked Out
: This check box is grayed out unless you have enabled Account Lockout in Account Policy. If Account Lockout is enabled, and a cracker attempts to break into a particular account, that account will be locked out in accordance with the parameters set for lockout. If Lockout Duration is set to "*Forever (until admin unlocks),*" an account once locked out remains so until the administrator manually reenables the account by clearing this check box.

Maintain NetWare Compatible Login

Mark this check box to active the NW Compat icon, described later in this section. This check box is present only if the optional File and Print Services for NetWare is installed.

Assigning group memberships. Next, specify the groups to which the new user will belong. To do so, click Groups to display the Group Memberships dialog, as shown in Figure 5-2. By default, new users are assigned membership in the global group Domain Users, which is displayed in the Member of pane. The available groups to which the user may be assigned membership are displayed in the Not member of pane. You can double-click a group name to move it from one pane to the other. Alternatively, you can select multiple groups using the standard Ctrl-click and Shift-click method and transfer them *en bloc* to the opposite pane using the Add or Remove button.

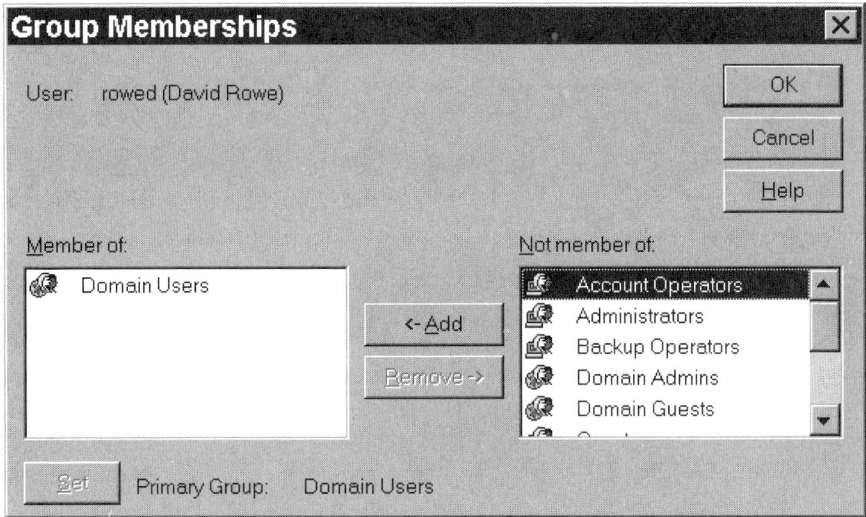

Figure 5-2. The Group Memberships dialog allows you to specify which groups the user is assigned to, and to set the primary group for the user

---

NOTE The Set Primary Group button allows you to specify a global group as the primary group for a user. This setting is meaningful only for users who are running Services for Macintosh or POSIX applications. You cannot remove a user from membership in its primary group. To change this setting, you must first assign the user to membership in at least one other global group, then Set Primary Group to one of these alternative global groups, and finally remove the user membership from the original primary group.

Setting profile and home directory locations. Next, specify home directory and profile information for the user. To do so, click Profile to display the User Environment Profile. You may optionally specify a user profile and logon script in the User Profiles section:

User Profile Path
: Enter the network path where the user profile will be located, using UNC syntax in the form *\\servername\profilepath\username*. To enforce a mandatory profile, open the Control Panel System applet, choose the User Profiles page, copy one of the existing profiles to the user profile path, and change *NTUser.dat* to have a *.MAN* extension.

Logon Script Name
: You may optionally assign a logon script to the user, which will run each time the user logs on. The script may be a batch file (*.CMD* or *.BAT*) or an executable (*.EXE*) file. Each time a user logs on, the authenticating server attempts to locate a logon script for that user in the logon script directory for that server. By default, logon scripts are located in the *\WINNT\system32\Repl\Import\Scripts* directory. Each user may be assigned his or her own unique logon script, or a single logon script may be shared by many users.

You may also optionally specify a home directory for the user, which may be assigned exclusively to that user or shared among many users. If assigned, the home directory becomes the default directory for all applications that do not themselves define a working directory. The home directory may be located on the user's local hard drive, or it may be a shared network directory. If the latter, the share must already exist, but Windows NT Server will normally create the home directory you specify on the fly. If you do not specify a home directory, Windows NT Server uses a default location, determined as follows: if you installed Windows NT Server 4.0 as a new installation, the default home directory is the root directory; if you installed Windows NT Server 4.0 as an upgrade, the default home directory is *\users\default*. You may specify the home directory using one of these options:

Local Path
: If the home directory is to be located on the local hard drive, enter the directory name here, for example, *c:\usr\rowed*.

Connect <drive-letter> To
: If, instead, the home directory is to be located on a shared network drive, use the scrolling pick list to select an available drive letter and then type a UNC location in the list box. If you are maintaining multiple user accounts simultaneously, rather than entering the user home directory, you can substitute the metatext value *%USERNAME%* as the final directory name in the path. Windows NT Server substitutes the actual username for each account.

If you have Microsoft Services for NetWare installed, you will see another home directory option named "N*etWare Home Directory Relative Path.*" To locate the user home directory on a NetWare volume, enter the path here, relative to root path of the server home directory, which by default is *\SYSVOL*.

Restricting logon hours

You may specify the days and times of day when this user is permitted to log on to the server. To do so, click the Hours icon to display the Logon Hours dialog. When you are maintaining existing users rather than adding a new user, you may also select multiple users and set Logon Hours for all of them simultaneously. The Logon Hours dialog changes slightly, presenting a scrolling list box showing the user account names. If you modify multiple users simultaneously who are currently set for different logon hours, User Manager for Domains presents a message box to inform you that the logon hours differ and will be reset before continuing.

By default, a newly created user is permitted to log on at all times. You can restrict specified days and times by clearing the boxes for those hours. To disable (or subsequently to enable) days and times, highlight the box or boxes in question and click Disallow or Allow, respectively. You can select all hours of a particular day by clicking that day's name in the left column. Similarly, you can select a specific hour for all days by clicking the gray box above the Sunday row.

The effect of restricting Logon Hours depends on two factors. First, the setting of the "Forcibly disconnect remote users from server when logon hours expire" check box in Account Policy determines the action that Windows NT Server will attempt to take when logon hours expire. If this check box is marked, Windows NT Server attempts to disconnect the user when logon hours expire. If this check box is cleared, Windows NT Server does not attempt to disconnect the user, but forbids that user from logging on again until a day or time when the user has access. The second factor is the operating system in use on the workstation. If the workstation is running Windows NT or Windows 95 and the Logon Hours expire, the user is first warned and then forcibly disconnected. If the workstation is running DOS or Windows 3.1x, the workstation is not disconnected when Logon Hours expire. Instead, it may continue to use all resources to which it is currently connected, but is prevented from accessing any new resources.

Limiting logon to specific workstations

You may restrict the user account to logging on from one or more specified workstations. To do so, click the Logon To icon to display the Logon Workstations dialog, shown in Figure 5-3. By default, the "User May Log On To All Workstations" option button is selected, allowing the user to log on from any workstation.

To restrict the user to specific workstations, mark the "User May Log On To These Workstations" option button and enter one or more workstations in the numbered boxes. Similarly, you may mark the "User May Log On To All NetWare Compatible Workstations" option button to allow the user to log on from any NetWare-compatible workstation. To restrict the user to specific NetWare-compatible workstations, mark the "User May Log On To These NetWare Compatible Workstations" option button and complete the Network Address field. The NetWare Compatible Workstations section of this dialog appears only if the optional File and Print Services for NetWare is installed.

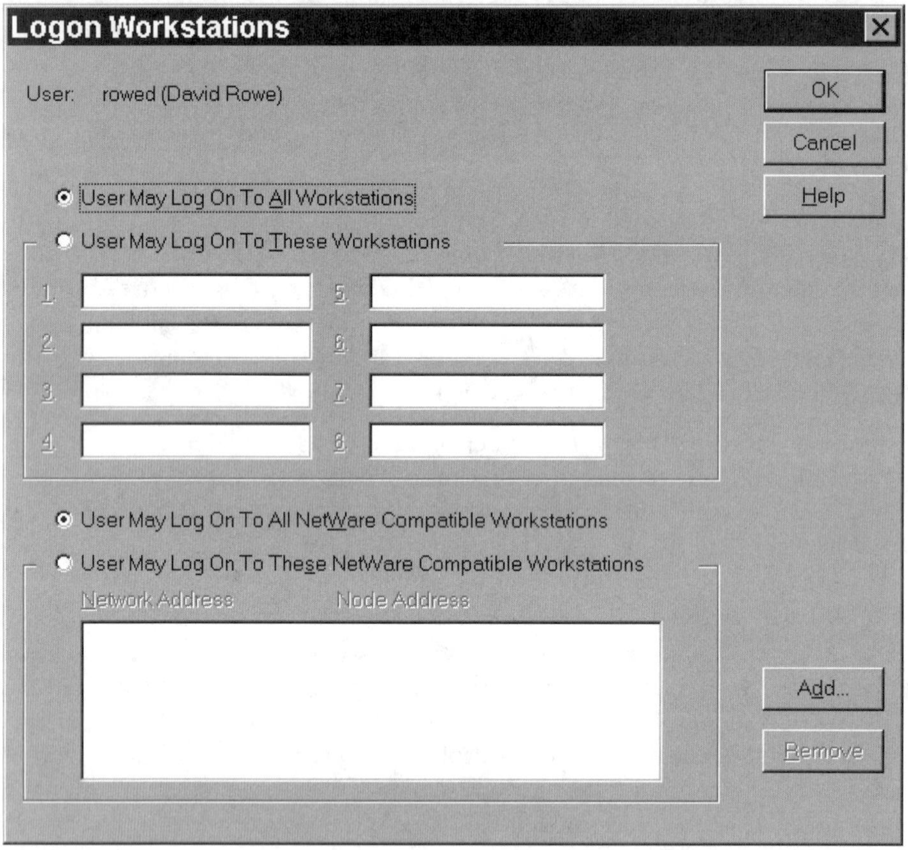

Figure 5-3. The Logon Workstations dialog allows you to control which workstations may be used by the user to log on to the network

Setting expiration and account type

You may specify the type of account to be created for the user and, optionally, a date upon which that account expires. To do so, click the Account icon to display the Account Information dialog. By default, Windows NT Server sets Account Expires to Never and the Account Type to Global Account.

You can specify an account expiration date by choosing the End of option button and using the scrolling list to specify a date. By default, Windows NT Server fills in a date 29 days in the future, allowing the user 30 days (counting the current day) of use. The account expires at the end of the day specified, unless Logon Hours restrictions further restrict the account. In this case, both the Account Expires date and the Logon Hours restriction determine in conjunction the last date and time that the user is permitted to log on. When the account expires, the user is permitted to remain logged on, but once disconnected is unable to reconnect. Setting an account expiration date is useful for setting up accounts for temporary employees that are valid only for the term of their employment, for setting up accounts for college students that expire at the end of the semester or term, and so on.

The account type may be set by selecting one of the option buttons, as follows:

Global Account
: This is the account type assigned to a normal user in that user's home domain. It allows the user to access local and global resource for which he or she is authorized. If your network includes multiple domains, each user should have only one global account in one of these domains. This allows the user to access resources in any domain for which he is authorized, while using only a single account name and password.

Local Account
: Create a local account in the current domain for a user whose main account is in a domain not trusted by the current domain, e.g., a non-trusted Windows NT Server domain or a LAN Manager domain. This allows the local account user to access resources in the current domain. A local account can access resources across the network, and can be assigned rights and permissions in the current domain, but cannot be used to log on interactively. A local account created in a trusted domain cannot be used in a trusting domain and does not appear in the user account list of the trusting domain.

Setting dialin permissions

If you want this user to be able to connect to the domain using Dial-Up Networking, click the Dialin icon to display the Dialin Information dialog. By default, Windows NT Server does not allow users to have dial-in access. Mark the "Grant dialin permission to user" check box to override this default and allow the user to use a Dial-Up Networking connection for network access.

In the Call Back section, mark one of the option buttons, as follows:

No Call Back
: This option is the default, and allows the caller to establish a network connection with the original telephone call. If the caller is using a Microsoft Dial-Up Networking client, the connection process can be fully automated to allow the caller to simply specify a phonebook entry and establish the connection without further input.

Set By Caller
: This option causes the Windows NT Server Remote Access Service (RAS) Server to prompt the caller for the telephone number at his or her location. Once this is provided by the caller, RAS Server drops the connection and places a call to the number provided by the caller. You can use this option to shift long-distance telephone charges from the caller to the RAS Server. Choosing this option also allows you to log the telephone numbers from which connections were initiated for security purposes.

Preset To
: This option is the most restrictive. When this option is active, the RAS Server receives the initial inbound call, identifies the caller, and then drops the connection. It then places a call to the preset number and establishes a network connection. This method is most suitable for DUN clients who are always at a known location, e.g., telecommuters, and for securing communications by limiting connections to predefined sites.

This dialog was added to Windows NT Server 4.0 as a convenience. With previous versions, the administrator was forced to set dial-in options in the Remote Access Admin application, making it necessary to use more than one program to set up new users. For more information about RAS, see Chapter 15, *Using Remote Access Service.*

The Add User Accounts Wizard

Windows NT Server 4.0 includes several Wizards of varying uselessness intended to automate the day-to-day procedures needed to manage and maintain a server. One of the more spectacularly useless of these is the Add User Accounts Wizard. In order to use it, you must already understand all of the issues involved in creating new user accounts, so it's no help in making things easier for a novice administrator. Conversely, using it to create a new user account requires more steps and takes longer than the method described in the preceding sections.

If for some reason you still want to give this Wizard a try, you can access it from the Start menu by choosing Programs, then Administrative Tools (Common), then Administrative Wizards to display the Administrative Wizards menu. Click Add

User Accounts and follow the steps presented by the Wizard to create a new user account.

Viewing and changing existing user accounts

To modify a single existing user account, highlight the Username in the Username pane of User Manager for Domains, and then choose Properties from the User menu to display the User Properties dialog. Alternatively, simply double-click the Username in the Username Pane to display this dialog. Make any changes needed, and click OK to save the changes, which take effect immediately.

NOTE The User Properties dialog is identical to that displayed when creating a new user account, except that the Username field cannot be modified in this dialog. To change the username for a user account, highlight the username in the Username pane of User Manager for Domains, and choose Rename from the User menu.

To modify multiple existing user accounts simultaneously, highlight the Usernames in the Username pane of User Manager for Domains, using the standard Shift-click and Ctrl-click conventions to select ranges of usernames. Choose Properties from the User menu to display the modified User Properties dialog, as shown in Figure 5-4.

Properties that are identical for all selected users are displayed as white check boxes, with or without a check mark. For example, the Accounts Disabled check box is cleared and has a white background, to indicate that none of the accounts for the selected users has been disabled. Similarly, the Maintain NetWare Compatible Login check box is marked and has a white background, which indicates that all three of these users maintain a NetWare login. Properties that have different values for different selected users are displayed as a marked check box with a gray background, as in the Passwords Never Expire check box.

Any changes you make within this dialog will be applied to all of the selected users simultaneously. If the current values for one or more of the selected users differ, User Manager for Domains will notify you of this fact and give you the opportunity to cancel the operation before it applies the new, uniform settings to the selected users.

Managing users from the command line

Although Windows NT is graphically oriented, it also provides various command-line utilities that can be used to accomplish many of the same tasks as their graphic counterparts. You can use the command *NET USER* to create, modify, and delete user accounts from the command line. When used without arguments,

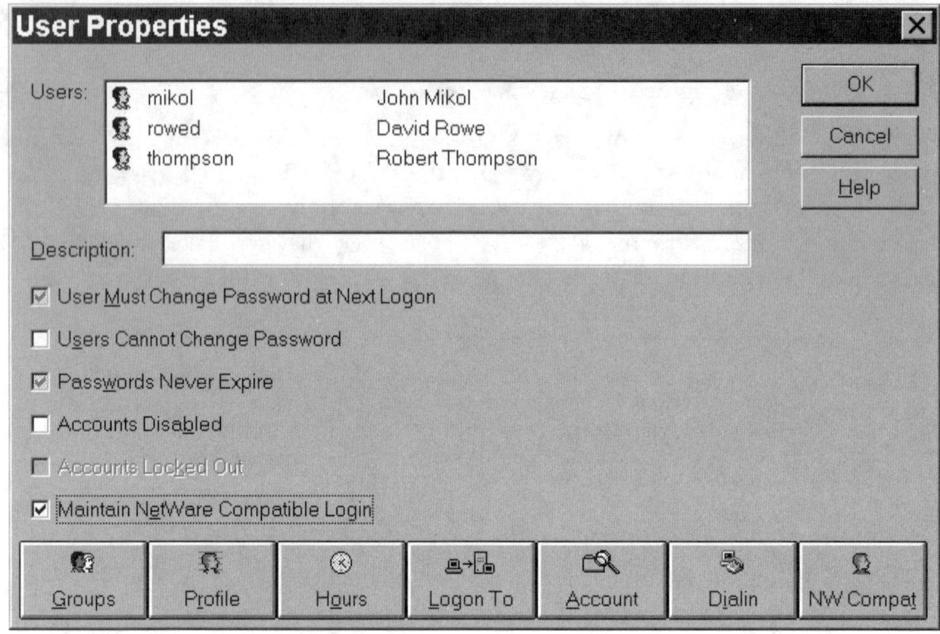

Figure 5-4. This modified version of the User Properties dialog allows you to modify settings for multiple existing user accounts simultaneously

NET USER simply returns a list of the users on the computer or domain. When used in the form *NET USER username*, it lists the account details for that user account.

The syntax of *NET USER* varies according to whether you want to add, modify, or delete a user, as follows respectively:

```
NET USER username {password | *} /ADD [options] [/DOMAIN]
NET USER [username [password | *][options]] [/DOMAIN]
NET USER username [/DELETE] [/DOMAIN]
```

Use the following command-line switches and arguments to modify the behavior of the *NET USER* command.

/ADD
: Add a user account to the user accounts database.

/DELETE
: Delete a user account from the user accounts database.

/DOMAIN
: This switch is useful only when you are using `NET USER` on a computer running Windows NT Workstation that is a member of a Windows NT Server domain. It causes `NET USER` to perform the specified operation on the PDC of the current

domain rather than on the user accounts database of the Windows NT Workstation computer. Using `NET USER` on a computer running Windows NT Server by default performs the operation on the PDC.

PASSWORD

Assign a password to, or change the existing password for, a user account. The password you specify must meet the minimum password length requirements in effect for the server or domain, and may be as long as 14 characters. You can also use an asterisk to specify that you should be prompted to type each password individually at the prompt.

USERNAME

The name of the user account, up to 20 characters, that is to be created, modified, deleted, or viewed.

Table 5-1 lists the options that you may specify when working with user accounts.

Table 5-1. Options for the NET USER Command

Option	Description
/active:{yes | no}	Activate or deactivate the account. Default is yes/active.
/comment:"text"	Enter a description of the account, enclosed in double quotes, using up to 48 characters.
/countrycode:nnn	Specify the language files to be used for help and error messages. Use zero for the default country code.
/expires:{date | never}	Specify a date when the account will expire, or that the account will never expire. Use the date form mm/dd/yy or dd/mm/yy, depending on the localization settings in effect.
/fullname:"name"	Enter the full name for the user, enclosed in double quotes.
/homedir:pathname	Specify the user home directory path, which must exist.
/passwordchg:{yes | no}	Specify whether the user can change his password. Default is yes.
/passwordreq:{yes | no}	Specify whether this account must have a password. Default is yes.
/profilepath[:path]	Specify a path for the user logon profile.
/scriptpath:pathname	Specify a path for the user logon script.

Table 5-1. Options for the NET USER Command (continued)

Option	Description
/times:{times | all}	Specify when this account is permitted to log on. Enter "all" if the user is always permitted to log on. Leave this value blank to prohibit the user from logging on at all. Enter value(s) for times as: day[-day][,day[-day]],time[-time][,time [-time]] where hours are specified in one-hour increments, using 12-hour (use a.m. or am and p.m. or pm) or 24-hour notation. Use full names, e.g., "Friday," or abbreviations, e.g., "Fri," for the day names. Use a comma to separate day and time entries. Use a semicolon to separate multiple day and time entries.
/usercomment:"text"	Specify a comment, enclosed in double quotes, for the account
/workstations:{computername[,...] | *}	List specific workstations, up to a maximum of eight, from which the user can log on to the network. If this value is blank, the user can log on from any workstation.

All of this begs the question, "Why would anyone in his right mind use that ugly old command-line utility when he could use the nice pretty graphic one?" Well, the graphic one is just perfect if all you want to do is add a user or two. It gets old pretty fast, however, when you need to do a bunch.

If you use User Manager for Domains, you have to create, modify, or delete each user individually. If instead you use `NET USER`, you can perform these operations *en masse* by creating a simple batch file, something like Example 5-1. The example creates several new users, deletes accounts for a couple of summer interns, and modifies the status of one intern account to inactive without deleting it.

Example 5-1. A Batch File that Uses NET USER to Modify the User Accounts Database

```
NET USER smithjp * /ADD /fullname:"John Smith" /times:all
NET USER joneslr * /ADD /fullname:"Linda Jones" /times:all
NET USER dennr * /ADD /fullname:"Robert Denn" /times:all
NET USER jenkinss * /ADD /fullname:"Sarah Jenkins" /times:all
NET USER intern1 /active:no
NET USER intern2 /DELETE
NET USER intern3 /DELETE
NET USER narevanl * /ADD /fullname:"Natalya Nareva" /times:all
```

If you need to create or modify only a few accounts, creating such a batch file is probably more trouble than it's worth. If you need to add hundreds of accounts, perhaps when creating a new domain, using a batch file can save you hours of pointing and clicking. Use Notepad or another ASCII editor to create the batch file. Create a template line for each type of action you want to take in the batch file, and use clipboard copy and paste to replicate it as many times as needed. By toggling your editor to overstrike mode, you can modify each line in a few seconds.*

NetWare administrators are lucky. Instead of using a batch file, they can import account information directly from a NetWare server using Migration Tool for NetWare or Directory Service Manager for NetWare. When you need to import user information from a UNIX host or another source, however, a batch file is often the only alternative to entering each user manually. If you can generate an ASCII file of users from the source machine or elsewhere, you can also use the mail merge function of your word processor to merge the user account information into the batch file automatically.

Adding and Managing Groups

To add new groups or manage current groups, log on to Windows NT Server with an account that has administrative privileges, and run User Manager for Domains. The standard Windows NT Server system groups are often adequate for small environments. In many small installations, ordinary users are assigned to the global group domain users. Network administrators and anyone else who requires a higher level of access are assigned to the group Administrators. If, instead, your firm is large enough to organize employees by department or work group, you can create new groups to correspond to each of these organizational structures.

For example, you might create new groups named Accounting, Administration, Manufacturing, Marketing, and Sales. You can then grant each of these groups the appropriate access level to various shared resources on the network, assigning each group full access to its own resources, and perhaps granting some groups limited access to the resources of one or more other groups. Assigning a user to the appropriate group automatically grants that user access to the shared network resources at the level specified for the group. Creating custom groups and assigning users to appropriate groups makes it easier to control access to shared network resources, because you need specify access levels only once for the entire group, rather than individually for each user.

Creating global groups

To create a new Global Group, from the User menu, select New Global Group to display the New Global Group dialog, as shown in Figure 5-5. Type a Group Name of up to 20 characters. You may use any character except those special

* For more on managing users and groups, see *Windows NT User Administration* by Ashley J. Meggitt and Timothy Ritchey, published by O'Reilly & Associates, Inc., October 1997.

symbol characters listed in the help file for this dialog. Optionally, type a Description for the new group. By default, the user who creates the group is assigned membership in that group. You can move users and groups back and forth between the Members pane and the Not Members pane by double-clicking the username or group name. Alternatively, you can use the standard Windows Shift-Click and Ctrl-Click conventions to select multiple users and groups simultaneously, and then move them between panes using the Add and Remove buttons. Once you have the Group Name, Description, and membership assignments the way you want them, click OK to create the group.

NOTE The New Global Group menu option is unavailable if you are using a Low Speed Connection, or if the computer you are administering is a Windows NT Server that is not configured as a Primary Domain Controller or a Backup Domain Controller.

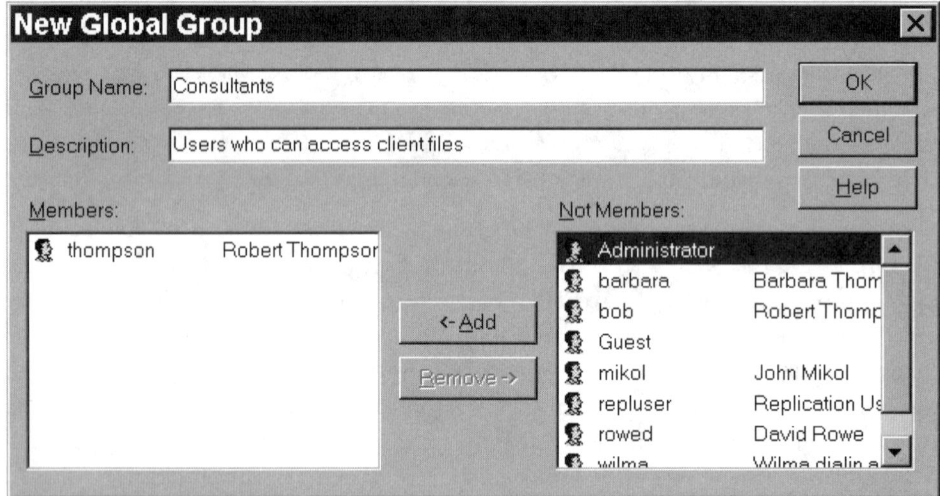

Figure 5-5. The New Global Group dialog allows you to name and describe the new group, and to assign members to it

Creating local groups

To create a new Local Group, from the User menu, select New Local Group Group to display the New Local Group dialog, as shown in Figure 5-6. Type a Group Name of up to 20 characters. You may use any character except those special symbol characters listed in the help file for this dialog. Optionally, type a Description for the new group. By default, no users or groups are assigned membership in the new local group.

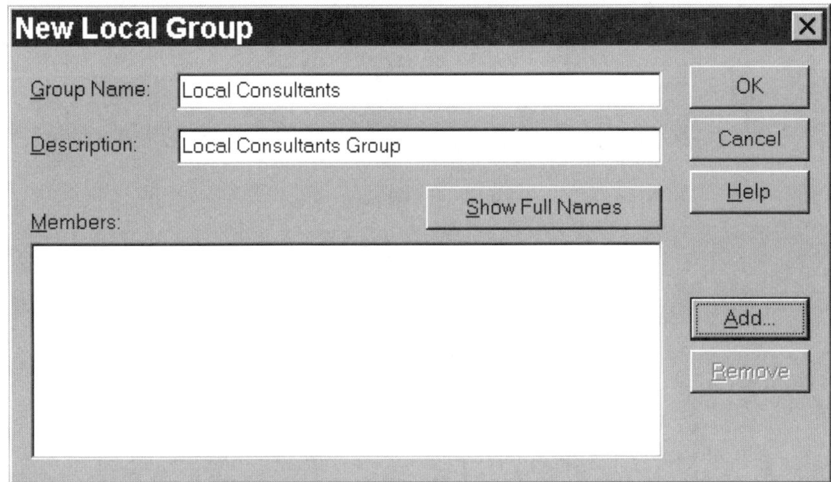

Figure 5-6. The New Local Group dialog allows you to name and describe the new group, and to assign members to it

Click Add to display the Add Users and Groups dialog, as shown in Figure 5-7. In the Names pane, double-click the names of a user or group to copy it to the Add Names pane. Alternatively, use the standard Windows Shift-Click and Ctrl-Click conventions to select multiple users and groups in the Names pane, and then click Add to copy them *en bloc* to the Add Names pane. Once you have all users and groups to be added displayed in the Add Names pane, click OK to return to the New Local Group dialog. User Manager for Domains assigns the users and groups you selected as members of the new local group. Use the Add and Remove buttons as needed until you have the Members pane correct. Press OK to create the new group.

Viewing and changing existing groups

To modify an existing local group or global group, highlight the group name in the User Manager for Domains group pane and then click Properties from the User menu. Alternatively, simply double-click the group name. In either case, User Manager for Domains displays the Local Group Properties dialog or the Global Group Properties dialog, as appropriate for the type of group you selected. These dialogs are identical to those shown above, except that the group name is displayed as an unchangeable label. You can select only one group to be modified at a time.

Unlike user account names, group names cannot be changed. If you find that you have assigned a group name that needs to be changed, the workaround is simply to copy the group to the new group name and then delete the original group. Be careful doing this unless you have just created the group and accidentally

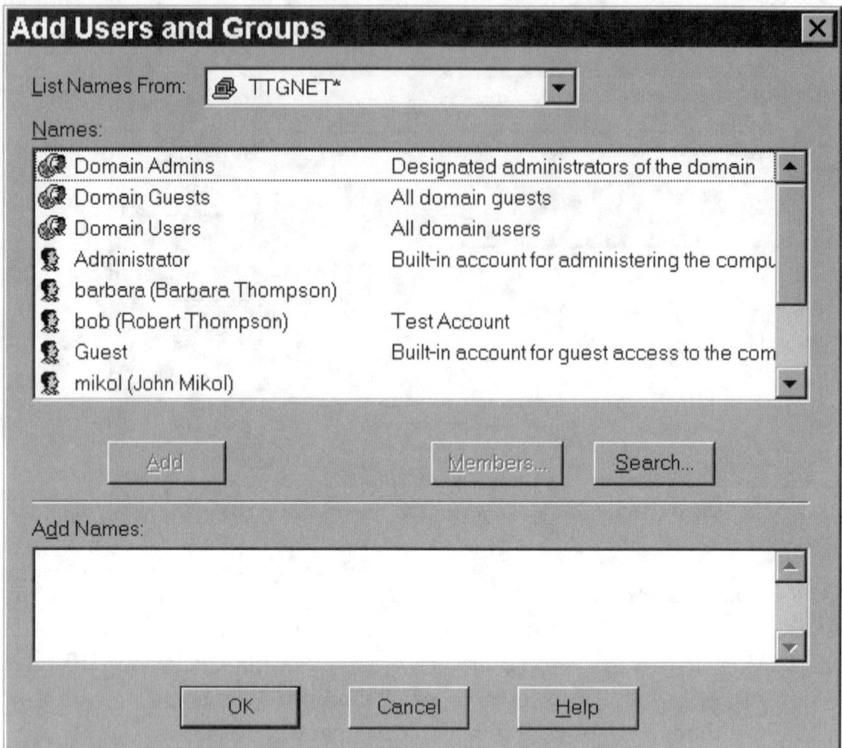

Figure 5-7. The Add Users and Groups dialog allows you to select users and groups to be added to the new local group

assigned a wrong name. Although the memberships and rights are copied to the new group, permissions remain with the old (and deleted) group name. Deleting an existing group can wreak havoc with you server, since users who depended on permissions inherited from that group may no longer be able to access network resources that they should be able to access.

The Group Management Wizard

Like the Add User Accounts Wizard, the Group Management Wizard, in theory at least, makes things easier for novice administrators and those who seldom perform administrative functions. Unlike the Add User Accounts Wizard, which is limited to creating new user accounts, the Group Management Wizard allows you both to create new groups and to modify existing ones. Like the Add User Accounts Wizard, the Group Management Wizard doesn't really make things much easier, and using it takes longer than just doing things the old-fashioned way.

If you want to see what you're missing by not using the Group Management Wizard, give it a try. From the Start menu, choose Programs, then Administrative Tools (Common), then Administrative Wizards to display the Administrative Wizards menu. Click Group Management and follow the steps presented by the Wizard to create a new group or to modify an existing one.

Managing groups from the command line

As with managing user accounts, Windows NT allows you to manage group accounts from the command line, using the *NET GROUP* command. You can use the command *NET GROUP* to create, modify the description of, or delete global groups, and to assign or remove user accounts from the group, all from the command line. When used without arguments, *NET GROUP* simply returns a list of the groups on the computer or domain. When used in the form *NET GROUP GROUPNAME*, it lists the user accounts that are members of that group.

The syntax of *NET GROUP* varies according to whether you want to add or delete a group, to modify the description of a group, or to add or delete users assigned to the group, as follows respectively:

```
NET GROUP groupname {/ADD [/COMMENT:"text"] | /DELETE} [/DOMAIN]
NET GROUP [groupname [/COMMENT:"text"]] [/DOMAIN]
NET GROUP groupname username [...] {/ADD | /DELETE} [/DOMAIN]
```

Use the following command-line switches and arguments to modify the behavior of the `NET GROUP` command:

/ADD
: Creates a new group, or add user account(s) to an existing group.

/COMMENT:"text"
: Adds or modifies a descriptive comment, enclosed in double quotes, for a new or existing group. The text may be as large as 48 characters.

/DELETE
: Deletes a group, or delete user account(s) from a group.

/DOMAIN
: This switch is useful only when you are using *NET GROUP* on a computer running Windows NT Workstation that is a member of a Windows NT Server domain. It causes *NET GROUP* to perform the specified operation on the PDC of the current domain rather than locally on the Windows NT Workstation computer. Using *NET GROUP* on a computer running Windows NT Server by default performs the operation on the PDC.

groupname

Specifies the name of the group to be added, modified, or deleted. If the groupname contains spaces, e.g., "Domain Admins," enclose it in double quotes to avoid an error message.

username

Specifies one or more user account names to be added to or removed from the group. If you specify multiple user account names on a single command line, separate them with spaces.

The ability to add and delete groups from the command line is all very well in theory, but in practice there is one real-world situation where the `NET GROUP` command is indispensable. Having used `NET USER` to create scores or hundreds of new users, you need a convenient way to assign each new user to the appropriate group(s). Example 5-2 expands the batch file shown in Example 5-1 to assign the newly created users to groups. The final two lines of this batch file now assign the user narevanl to the group MANAGERS and all of the new users to the group SALES.

Example 5-2. A Batch File that Uses NET USER to Modify the User Accounts Database

```
NET USER smithjp * /ADD /fullname:"John Smith" /times:all
NET USER joneslr * /ADD /fullname:"Linda Jones" /times:all
NET USER dennr * /ADD /fullname:"Robert Denn" /times:all
NET USER jenkinss * /ADD /fullname:"Sarah Jenkins" /times:all
NET USER intern1 /active:no
NET USER intern2 /DELETE
NET USER intern3 /DELETE
NET USER narevanl * /ADD /fullname:"Natalya Nareva" /times:all
NET GROUP MANAGERS narevanl /ADD
NET GROUP SALES smithjp joneslr dennr jenkinss narevanl /ADD
```

Setting Policies

User Manager for Domains allows you to set systemwide policies that affect account defaults, user rights, auditing, and trust relationships. These settings are made from the User Manager for Domains Policies menu, and each is described in one of the sections following.

Setting account policy

User Manager for Domains allows you to set global options for user accounts that control password policy and account lockout settings, functions performed in NetWare from the Supervisor Options menu of *SYSCON*. To modify Account Policy, from the Policies menu, click Account to display the Account Policy dialog, as shown in Figure 5-8.

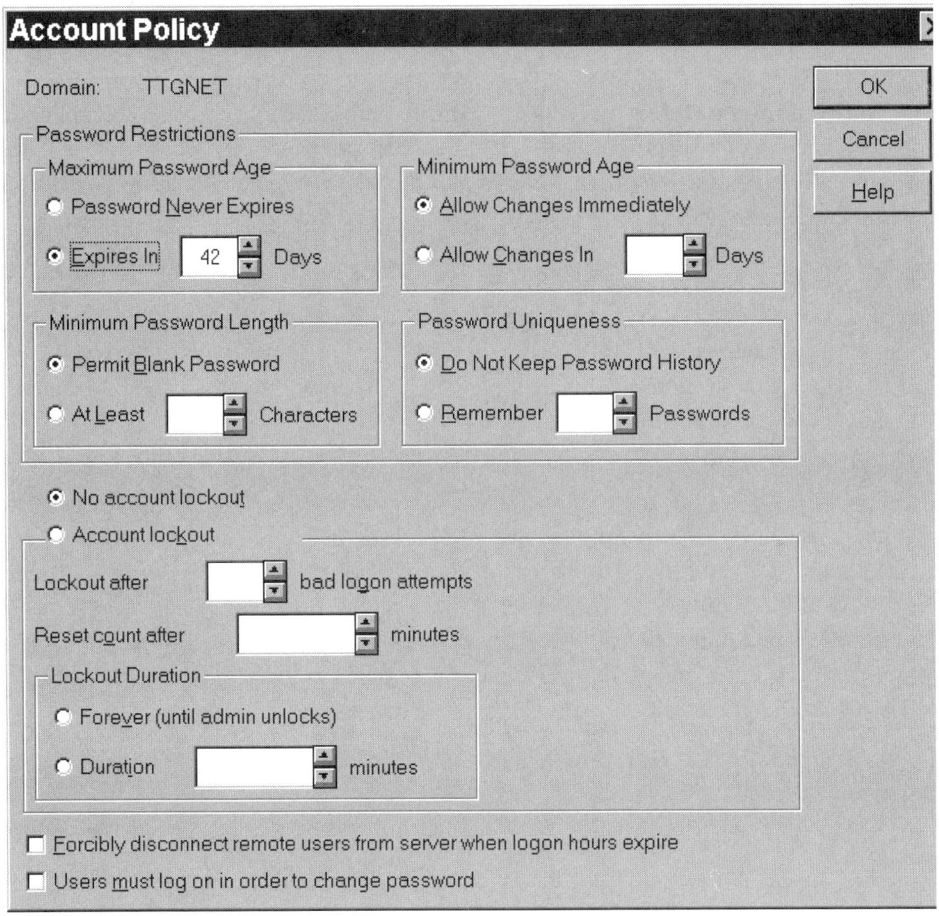

Figure 5-8. The Account Policy dialog allows you to control the expiration, length, and uniqueness of password, and to set parameters for account lockout

In contrast to the usual practices of Windows NT Server, where default values and settings tend to emphasize security at the expense of user convenience, the default Account Policy settings favor open access over securing the server. Account Policy options specify the parameters that will be used to create new user accounts, and have no effect on existing user accounts, except as noted. Nearly all administrators will want to change one or more of the default values in Account Policy to ensure that newly created accounts are more secure than they would be if the default values were used.

In the Maximum Password Age section, mark one of the option buttons, as follows:

Password Never Expires

Selecting this option allows a password to remain valid until the administrator either changes the password manually or clears the *Password Never Expires* check box for that account.

Expires in X Days

This option is enabled by default, with the value set to 42 days. You may set this value within a range of 1–999 days. If an account created with the Password Never Expires option is subsequently set to expire, the number of days until password expiration is determined from the day this option is set.

In the Maximum Password Age section, mark one of the option buttons, as follows:

Allow Changes Immediately

Selecting this option, which is enabled by default, allows users to change their passwords as often as they wish.

Allow Changes In X Days

Enabling this option requires users to wait X days between password changes, where X can range from 1–999 days. Use this option in conjunction with the Remember X Passwords option described below to enforce unique passwords. Setting this option to a reasonably high value prevents a user from circumventing the password history list by simply resetting his password repeatedly until his current (and desired) password ages out of the history list, and then resetting his original password as his new password.

In the Minimum Password Length section, mark one of the option buttons, as follows:

Permit Blank Password

This option is enabled by default, which allows user accounts with no password to exist. Some administrators enable this setting to make it easier for new users to get connected for the first time, although doing so obviously introduces at least a small potential security hole. If you choose to leave this option enabled, never clear the User Must Change Password at Next Logon check box in the User Properties dialog for newly created accounts. Otherwise, users will be able to continue using the account without assigning a password.

At Least X Characters

Choose this option to require a nonblank password. Use the arrow keys to set a value in the range of 1 to 14 characters. Microsoft sets the default value of this option, when selected, to six characters, apparently believing that this password size is a good compromise between security and user convenience. Many administrators are uncomfortable with so low a value, particularly since User Manager for Domains has no mechanism for verifying requested passwords against a dictionary, for generating a random list of secure passwords from which the user must choose, or otherwise ensuring that users do not choose passwords that are easily cracked. Neither does it make provision for requiring highly privileged accounts to use longer passwords than ordinary accounts are required to use. For these reasons, many administrators, particularly those for whom system security is a critical issue, set this value to between 10 and 14.

In the Password Uniqueness section, mark one of the option buttons, as follows:

Do Not Keep Password History
: This option, enabled by default, prevents Windows NT Server from keeping a list of the passwords used previously by each user account. Leaving this option enabled defeats the purpose of setting password lifetimes, because when a password expires, the user can simply change his or her password to a new password that is identical to the old one.

Remember X Passwords
: Setting this option causes Windows NT Server to maintain a password history list that contains X old passwords for each user account. When a user changes his password, either voluntarily or because his password expired, Windows NT Server compares the proposed new password against the history list for that user. If the password exists in the history list, Windows NT Server refuses to accept that password. The value of X may be set within the range 1 through 24. If you decide to enable this option, make sure also to set a reasonably high value for the *Allow Changes in X Days* option described above. If you do not do so, some users will simply reset their passwords repeatedly until the one they really want (the original one) has aged out of the password history list. The total number of days a user must wait before reusing a particular password is determined by the product of these two values. For example, if you have set these options to *Remember 10 Passwords* and *Allow Changes in 10 Days*, a user would have to wait for 100 days after a password expired before he or she would be able to again use it. In general, it is better to arrive at a particular value for this product by increasing the size of the history list rather than increasing the time required between changes. For example, if you want to require that at least 24 days pass before a particular password can be reused, keep 24 passwords in the history list and require only one day between changes, rather than the converse. This both maximizes the number of different passwords a given user will use, and offers the users maximum freedom to change their passwords as they want or need to.

Next, set values to determine if and when an account will be locked out. An account is locked out, or disabled, automatically by Windows NT Server when repeated unsuccessful attempts are made to log on to that account. Account

Lockout settings affect all accounts equally, except that the Administrator account can never be locked out. This makes the Administrator account a prime candidate for attempts by crackers to break into your system, because they know both the default account name and the fact that it is not subject to being locked out. For this reason, many administrators change the name of the Administrator account to something unlikely to be guessed by a cracker.

By default, Windows NT Server enables the *No account lockout* option button, disabling account lockout for that computer or domain. If you want to enable account lockout, as you almost certainly should, mark the *Account Lockout* option button and set the following parameters:

Lockout after X bad logon attempts

Specify the number of failed logon attempts, from 1 through 999, that can occur before Windows NT Server locks the account. Anyone can mistype a password once or twice. Three times begins to look like someone is attempting to crack the account. Although User Manager for Domains sets this value to 5 when account lockout is enabled, for most servers and domains, you should set this value instead to 3. If you require particularly long passwords, or if your users have particularly bad memories, you might want to set it to 5 or 6. If your network contains particularly sensitive information, or if you have been subject to cracker attacks, you might set it to 2 or even 1.

Note that only attempts at domain access via the network count against this number. Failed local attempts to access a workstation (or a server that is not configured as a domain controller) by entering a password at the Ctrl-Alt-Del logon screen or to bypass a password-protected screen saver do not count.

Reset count after X minutes

When account lockout is enabled, this value, by default 31 minutes, sets the period during which unsuccessful logon attempts continue to increment the counter described above. After the first unsuccessful logon attempt, this timer begins running. If another unsuccessful logon attempt occurs before this time period has expired, the counter for the number of bad logon attempts is incremented by one and the timer is reset. Bad logon attempts that occur within this time period are assumed to be made by a cracker. Bad logon attempts that occur separated by more than this value are assumed to be unintentional. This value can be set within the range of 1 through 99,999 minutes. Higher values secure your system better.

The two option buttons in the Lockout Duration section determine what action must be taken for an account to be reactivated once it is locked out.

Forever (until admin unlocks)

Choose this option if you want to require direct intervention by an administrator before an account can be unlocked. Once the account has been locked out, the administrator must clear the *Account Locked Out* check box on the User Properties dialog to reactivate the account manually.

Duration X minutes

This is the default option when account lockout is enabled. The value may be set within the range of 1 through 99,999 minutes, with 30 minutes the default. With this option in effect, once an account is locked out, a timer begins running. After this number of minutes, the account is unlocked automatically. During the period that this timer is winding down, the administrator may still clear the *Account Locked Out* check box on the User Properties dialog to reactivate the account manually.

Set the two final check boxes on the Account Policy dialog to specify how you want to handle users whose logon hours expire while they are connected and users whose passwords expire.

Forcibly disconnect remote users from server when logon hours expire

This check box determines what action Windows NT Server takes when a user with Logon Hours restrictions in effect reaches the limit of allowable hours. If the check box is unmarked, the default, Windows NT Server makes no attempt to disconnect the user, but does not allow him to log on again or to connect to additional server resources until the current system time and his Logon Hours settings allow him to do so. If this check box is marked, Windows NT Server attempts to actually disconnect the user from all servers within the domain, after warning him that it is about to do so. If that user is on a workstation running Windows NT Server or Windows NT Workstation, this option is enforced, and the user is actually disconnected. If instead he is running DOS or Windows 3.11 for Workgroups on his workstation, marking this check box has exactly the same effect as leaving it unmarked—the user may continue his session, but may not establish new connections.

Users must log on in order to change password

This check box determines whether a user can change an expired password himself, or if the administrator must do so. If the check box is unmarked, the default, a user whose password has expired may use the expired password to gain sufficient system access to reset the password himself. If this check box is marked, an expired password grants the user no access whatsoever, and the administrator must manually reset the password before that user account can access the system.

NOTE As an experienced NetWare administrator, you're probably wondering by now where to go to set accounting options and disk space quotas. The answer is, you can't. Windows NT Server makes no provision for charging out resources to users and groups. Nor does it allow you to set a limit on how much disk space can be used by a particular account. These two factors, probably more than any other, have given pause to administrators of large NetWare networks who are considering implementing Windows NT Server.

Granting user rights

NetWare uses the concept of User Types to control which actions can be performed by which users. NetWare defines various types of users, for example, Supervisor and Workgroup Manager, each of which has a predefined (and largely unchangeable) set of authorities. To down the server, for example, your account must be Supervisor or Supervisor Equivalent.

Windows NT Server instead uses the concept of User Rights to determine which user accounts can perform which actions. If for some reason, for example, you want an otherwise ordinary user account to be able to shut down the server, you can give it that power by granting that user account the User Right needed to perform that action. Granting User Rights allows you to control the power of particular user and group accounts much more finely than is possible in NetWare.

This flexibility is evidenced in many of the Windows NT Server standard system groups. For example, the fact that members of the Backup Operators group can back up data from anywhere on the server or domain, but cannot otherwise access the data, even to do a restore, is an artifact of the User Rights assigned to that group. You can modify the powers available to a user or group simply by granting additional User Rights or revoking existing ones. For example, you could enable members of the Backup Operators group to do both backups and restores simply by granting that group the additional User Right needed to do restores.

NOTE Don't confuse User Rights and Permissions. User Rights control who can perform which actions, e.g., resetting the clock/calendar on the server. Permissions instead control who can access which resources, e.g., shared volumes and printers.

Windows NT Server offers eleven Default User Rights, as follows:

Access this computer from network
A user or group assigned this right can connect to the computer from across the network, as opposed to being limited to logging in locally. When you grant this right in a domain environment (using User Manager for Domains), it applies to all domain controllers that are members of the same domain. When this right is applied to a computer running Windows NT Workstation, or to a computer running Windows NT Server that is not configured as a domain controller (using User Manager), it applies only to the specific computer being administered.

Add workstations to domain
Allows adding a computer to a domain, allowing that computer to recognize the user and global group accounts within that domain. Members of the Administrators and Account Operators groups are assigned this right automatically and irrevocably, and may grant this right to other users and groups.

Back up files and directories
This right overrides NTFS file permissions and NTFS directory permissions, allowing a user or group assigned this right to back up files and directories regardless of whether that user or group otherwise has access to those files and directories. This right explicitly grants only the ability to back up the files and directories. A user with this right cannot view or modify the files and directories unless other rights or permissions give him the ability to do so. When granted with User Manager for Domains, this right applies domainwide. When granted with User Manager, it applies only to the specific computer being administered. Note that this right gives the assigned user only the right to back up files and directories, and **not** the right to restore them (see "*Restore files and directories*" later in this section).

Change the system time
Allows the user to change the clock/calendar settings. When granted with User Manager for Domains, this right applies domainwide. When granted with User Manager, it applies only to the specific computer being administered.

Force shutdown from a remote system
This right is not yet implemented. When available, it will allow a dial-up or LAN-connected remote user to shutdown or restart the server. The lack of support for this feature is actually a downgrade from the prior version of Windows NT Server. The 3.51 Resource Kit included an unsupported utility that could be used to do a remote server shutdown. However, this utility had so many bugs and could cause so many serious problems when used that Microsoft recommended against using it. The 3.51 release mentioned that this

capability would be included in a future 3.51 service pack release or in Windows NT Server 4.0. So far, no joy.

Load and unload device drivers

A user or group granted this right can load and unload device drivers dynamically. When granted with User Manager for Domains, this right applies domainwide. When granted with User Manager, it applies only to the specific computer being administered.

Log on locally

This right allows the user to log on to the local console, as opposed to logging on over the network. When granted with User Manager for Domains, this right applies domainwide. When granted with User Manager, it applies only to the specific computer being administered.

Manage auditing and security log

This right gives a user the ability to manage auditing for files, folders and other objects, accessed from the Security page of the property sheet. When granted with User Manager for Domains, this right applies domainwide. When granted with User Manager, it applies only to the specific computer being administered.

The Manage auditing and security log right does not grant the user the ability to specify which security events are to be audited, as accessed from the Audit option on the Policy menu. That right is automatically granted to the Administrators group only, and cannot be assigned to any user that is not a member of the Administrators group.

Restore files and directories

A user or group granted this right can override NTFS file permissions and NTFS directory permissions, allowing that user or group to restore files and directories regardless of whether that user or group otherwise has access to those files and directories. This right explicitly grants only the ability to restore the files and directories. A user with this right cannot view or modify the files and directories unless other rights or permissions give him the ability to do so. When granted with User Manager for Domains, this right applies domainwide. When granted with User Manager, it applies only to the specific computer being administered. Note that this right gives the assigned user only the right to restore files and directories, and **not** the right to back them up (see "*Back up files and directories*" previously in this list).

Shut down the system

A user or group assigned this right may shut down the Windows NT Server. When granted with User Manager for Domains, this right applies domain-wide.

When granted with User Manager, it applies only to the specific computer being administered.

Take ownership of files or other objects

A user or group granted this right can take ownership of an object like a file or directory. Note that even a user who is a member of the Administrators group is limited in what he can do with objects owned by another user. However, a member of the Administrators group (or any other user assigned this right) can override in-place restrictions on the object by first taking ownership of the object and then manipulating it as the owner. When granted with User Manager for Domains, this right applies domainwide. When granted with User Manager, it applies only to the specific computer being administered.

NOTE The User Rights Policy dialog Grant To pane lists users and groups who have been granted the selected right. When viewing this list, or when granting additional users and groups a particular right, you may see a "group" named Everyone displayed as a selectable item. Unlike NetWare, which has an actual group named "Everyone," Windows NT Server uses the term *Everyone* simply to refer to all users who have a valid account on the server or domain. Everyone is not a real group at all in Windows NT Server, but is used instead simply as a collective noun.

In addition to the Default User Rights detailed above, Windows NT Server includes 16 Advanced User Rights. Advanced User Rights are useful primarily to those who are writing programs that will run under Windows NT. System Administrators will seldom have any need to modify them. The *Win32 Programmers' Reference* manual in the Win32 Software Development Kit (SDK) includes detailed information about Advanced User Rights, and may be ordered directly from Microsoft.

Act as part of the operating system

Allows a process to function in kernel mode rather than in user mode, gaining access to privileged functions of the microprocessor. Some subsystems are granted this right. No users or groups are granted this right by default, nor do they need it.

Bypass traverse checking

A user or group that is assigned this right can traverse a directory tree freely, even if he has no permissions in the portion of the tree being traversed. Note that this right confers only the "right of passage." Although a user assigned this right can freely enter and depart directories for which he has not been granted permissions, he cannot view or otherwise manipulate the contents of these restricted directories. By default, this right is assigned to everyone.

Create a page file

Allows the user to create a page file. This right is granted by default to the Administrators group.

Create a token object

Allows a user or a program to create access tokens. This right is restricted to the Local Access Authority. No users or groups are granted this right by default, nor do they need it.

Create permanent shared objects

Allows a user to create permanent shared system objects, e.g., *\Device*. No users or groups are granted this right by default, nor do they need it.

Debug programs

Allows users to debug various low-level system objects like threads. This right is granted by default to the Administrators group.

Generate security audits

Allows a user or program to create security audit log entries. No users or groups are granted this right by default.

Increase quotas

Allows a user to increase object quotas. This right is not currently implemented in Windows NT Server 4.0, although this right is granted by default to the Administrators group.

Increase scheduling priority

Allows a user to increase the priority assigned by the system to a process. This right is granted by default to the Administrators group.

Lock pages in memory

Allows a user to "set the sticky bit" on a page to prevent it from being swapped out from physical memory to disk-based virtual memory. No users or groups are granted this right by default.

Log on as a batch job

Allows a user to log on using a batch queue facility for deferred logons. No users or groups are granted this right by default.

Log on as a service

Allows a process to register with Windows NT Server as a service. By default, members of the Replicator group are granted this right.

Modify firmware environment values
: Allows a user to modify system environment variables (as opposed to the user's own environment variables, which may always be modified by the user). This right is granted by default to the Administrators group.

Profile single process
: Allows a user to use platform profiling capabilities on a process. This right is granted by default to the Administrators group.

Profile system performance
: Allows a user to use platform profiling capabilities on the system as a whole. This right is granted by default to the Administrators group.

Replace a process level token
: Allows a user to modify the Security Access Token for a process. This right should be limited to system processes. No users or groups are granted this right by default, nor do they need it.

To view and modify User Rights assignments, select User Rights from the User Manager for Domains Policies menu to display the User Rights Policy dialog. Use the Right drop-down list box to select a specific right to be granted or revoked. By default, only Basic User Rights are displayed in this list box. Mark the *Show Advanced User Rights* check box if you want to be able to select among all user rights.

When you select a right, the users and groups who have been granted that right appear in the Grant To pane. You can modify which users and groups are granted that right, as follows:

Revoke a User Right
: Revoke the selected right for a user or group by highlighting the user or group and clicking Remove and then clicking OK. That right will be unavailable to that user or group the next time it is invoked, although a right that is currently in use can remain in use. For example, if you revoke the *Back up files and directories* right, a user who is currently backing up the server will be able to complete that backup, but will not be permitted to start another.

Grant a User Right
: Grant a User Right to a new user or group by clicking Add to display the Add Users and Groups dialog. Select one or multiple users and groups in that dialog, and then click OK to return to the User Rights Policy dialog, with the selected users and groups copied to the Grant To pane. Click OK to grant those rights to the new users and groups. These new rights take effect immediately.

NOTE Strangely, although the User Rights Policy dialog makes it easy to determine which users and groups have been granted a particular right, the converse is not true. There is no convenient means to display all of the rights that have been granted to a specified user or group. The only way to determine this is to sequentially view each particular right to see if the user or group in question has been granted that right.

Setting audit policy

User Manager for Domains allows you to specify which of selected user activities will be tracked by auditing security events and writing the resulting transactions to the security log. To enable auditing, select Audit from the User Manager for Domains Policies menu to display the Audit Policy dialog, as shown in Figure 5-9.

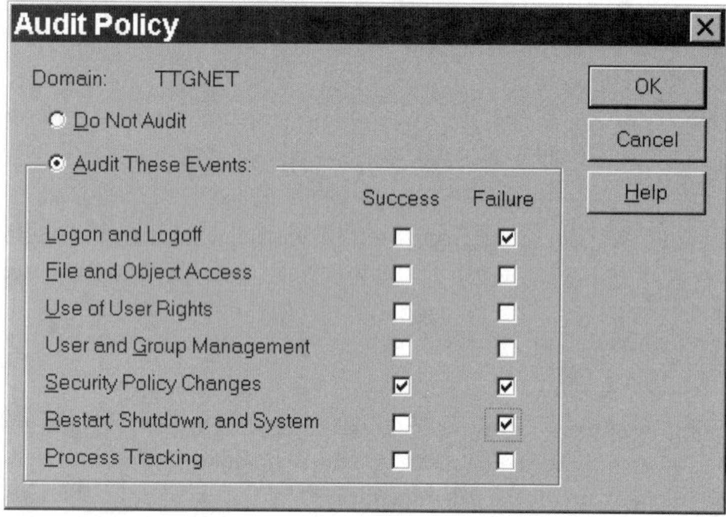

Figure 5-9. The Audit Policy dialog allows you to specify which, if any security events will be logged

In a domain environment, the settings you make to Audit Policy affects all domain controllers and other servers within the domain, because they share a common audit log. Audit Policy settings on a workstation or standalone server affect only the security log local to that computer.

By default, User Manager for Domains enables the Do Not Audit option button. To enable auditing of one or more types of security event, mark the Audit These Events option button, and then mark the event(s) you want to audit. The size of the audit log is limited, so think carefully before enabling auditing for any particular event. In particular, marking one or more of the check boxes in the Success column can result in rapid growth of the log file, since "Success" is the expected outcome of an event. Failures should be much less common, so it is usually safe to mark check boxes in this column for the security events that you want to log. In the example, the Audit Policy is set to record only failed attempts to log on or log off the server, and only failed attempts to down the server. Both columns are marked in the Security Policy Changes row to make sure that any attempts to change security policy are logged, whether or not they are successful.

You can view the security log (and alter its size) in Event Viewer. To use Event Viewer to view the security log, click the Start button, choose Programs, then Administrative Tools (Common), then Event Viewer. By default, Event Viewer displays the last type of log displayed, System, Security, or Application. If the System or Application log is active, click Log and then Security to display the Security Log. To modify the Event Log Settings, click Log and then Log Settings to display the Event Log Settings. Set the maximum size for the event log, and how overwriting will occur.

Setting trust relationships

Finally, User Manager for Domains also allows you to set up unidirectional and bi-directional trust relationships between Windows NT Server domains. Trust relationships allow user accounts in one domain (the *trusted domain*) to access resources in another domain (the *trusting domain*). Users and groups belonging to the trusted domain may hold user rights, permissions, and memberships in local groups in the trusting domain. You can set up trust relationships to allow users on a multidomain network to access resources from anywhere in the network structure by using a single logon account and password.

To add another domain as a trusted domain (one whose users and groups will be able to access resources on the domain being administered), click Add to display the Add Trusted Domain dialog. Enter the domain name and password and click OK. Windows NT Server first locates the domain controller for that domain, and then, if successful, inserts the new domain name in the Trusted Domains pane.

To add another domain as a trusting domain (one whose resources will be accessible by users and groups on the domain being administered), click Add to display the Add Trusting Domain dialog, as shown in Figure 5-10. Enter the domain name, enter and confirm the password, and click OK. Windows NT Server inserts the new domain name in the Trusting Domains pane, without first attempting to communicate with the domain controller for that domain.

Establishing a unidirectional trust relationship requires two steps, one in each domain. First, in the trusted domain, the administrator adds the other domain as a trusting domain. Second, in the trusting domain, the administrator adds the other

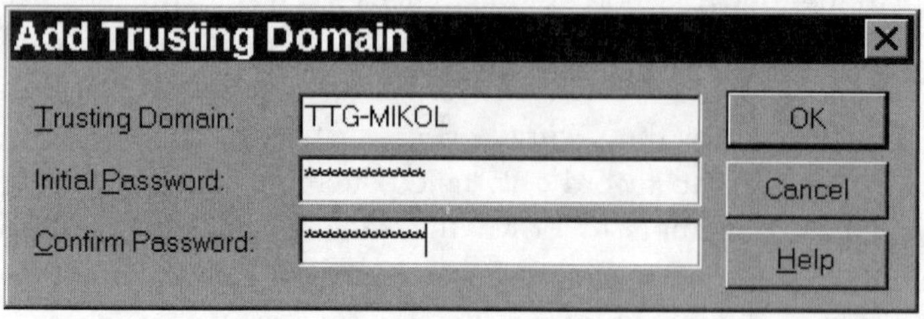

Figure 5-10. The Add Trusting Domain dialog allows you to add a domain that will be trusted by the domain being administered

domain as a trusted domain. Establishing a bidirectional trust relationship requires that each of these two steps be taken in each of the two domains for which the relationship is to be established.

In this chapter:
- *Understanding Shares*
- *NTFS Permissions*
- *Folder Replication*

6
Controlling Access to Volumes, Folders, and Files

One of the most important functions of any network operating system (NOS) is to provide clients with shared access to server disk resources—volumes, folders, and files. Just as important is the ability of the NOS to control access to these shared resources by allowing the administrator to specify who is permitted access, at what level, and when.

NOTE With the introduction of Windows 95, Microsoft began referring to directories as folders. They have continued this usage with Windows NT 4.0, but have not yet completed the transition. Some Windows NT Server program screens and help files continue to use the term *directory*. Throughout this chapter, we will use the newer (and preferred) term *folder* except when referring explicitly to a screen element that uses the older terminology.

Like NetWare, Windows NT Server provides a complete set of tools both to share disk resources and to control access to them. As is often the case, however, Windows NT Server does things just a bit differently.

Understanding Shares

With NetWare, simply mounting a volume makes that volume's resources available to any client authorized to access them. Windows NT Server requires the additional step of first creating a named *share*. No disk resource—volume, folder, or file—on the machine running Windows NT Server is accessible to network users until a share has been created for that resource and mapped to a *share name* browsable by network clients. Shares must be created at the console of the local machine upon which the share is defined. Even the administrator, who otherwise has full access to all network resources, cannot remotely access a local disk resource on the Windows NT Server unless a share exists for that resource.

Creating, Modifying, and Deleting Shares

To create, modify or delete a folder share, you must log on locally to the computer upon which the volume to be shared is physically installed. The account you use must be assigned to one or more of the groups, Administrators, Server Operators, or Power Users.

To create a new folder share, double-click My Computer to display a list of volumes and other resources available on the server. From the View menu, choose Details to display the detail view. You can also choose the rightmost icon on the toolbar to display the detail view. Double-click a volume to display a list of folders available on that volume. Icons associated with shared volumes and folders differ from those not shared. A hand holding the folder or volume icon indicates that the volume or folder has a share already in effect.

Right-click the folder you want to share to display the context-sensitive menu. Choose Sharing to display the Sharing page of the properties sheet for the selected folder, shown in Figure 6-1. In this example, we are establishing a share for the *Mercury* folder.

By default, the folder is marked as Not Shared. Mark the Shared As option button to establish the share. Windows NT fills in the folder name as the default Share Name. You may accept this name, or type a different name for the share. Whatever name appears in the Share Name box is the name by which network users will view and access the share. You may also enter a Comment to further describe the resource.

WARNING Some clients do not understand long file and folder names for network resources. Windows NT Server 4.0 automatically converts long filenames and long folder names to a form usable by DOS and Windows 3.x clients, which are limited to the original DOS 8.3 naming convention. Windows NT does not perform a similar conversion for share names, so exceeding the 8.3 convention in a share name may render that share inaccessible to some clients. Be careful how you name your shares.

By default, Windows NT sets the User Limit to Maximum Allowed. This means that the only limit to the number of users who may simultaneously access this shared resource is the number of users for which Windows NT is licensed. For performance reasons, you may want to limit the number of simultaneous users of

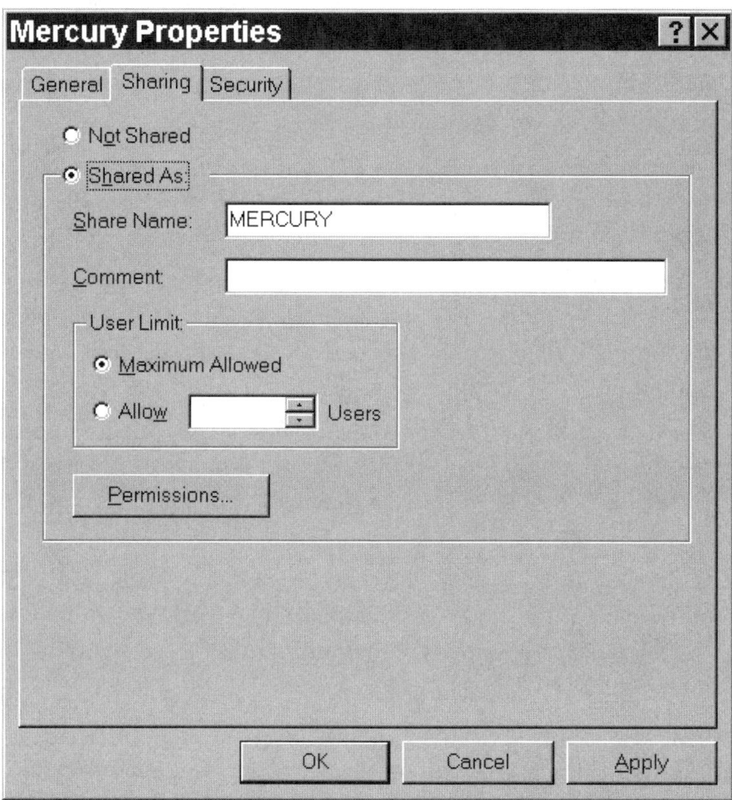

Figure 6-1. The <foldername> Property properties sheet allows you to specify share names, control how many users may access the share simultaneously, and to set permissions for the share

the share to something less than this figure. If so, use the up and down arrows to set Allow to the appropriate number of users. If you set a limit to the number of users allowed and that limit is reached, any additional users who attempt to access the share will be informed that the resource is temporarily unavailable.

Using Share Permissions

Share permissions specify which users and groups are allowed to access the shared disk resource, and at what level. Share permissions are a blunt instrument. If you use share permissions to give a user or group a particular level of access to a share, that user or group has that same level of access to the shared folder itself, to any subfolders within the shared folder, and to any files contained in that tree. NTFS directory access permissions and NTFS file access permissions are examined in the following sections. NTFS permissions function more like a scalpel, allowing you to specify very finely which users and groups have access to shared folders and files.

You can individually assign any one of the following four share permissions to any particular user or group defined for the share:

- *No Access* restricts all access to the share. A user or group assigned the No Access share permission cannot even view the share when browsing the network.
- *Read* allows a user or group to view a list of files within the folder, to change to a subfolder, to view the contents of files within the folder and its subfolders, and to execute program files. A user assigned the Read permission cannot create or write to a file or delete a file or subfolder.
- *Change* grants a user or group all of the rights of the Read permission. In addition, it allows the user to create new files and subfolders, to modify the contents of both existing files and those newly created, and to delete any file or subfolder.
- *Full Control* grants all of the rights of the Change permission. In addition, Full Control grants the user the right to add, modify, and delete NTFS permissions and to take NTFS ownership of resources within the share.

Remember that share permissions are the top level of access control in Windows NT Server. Restrictions you make with share permissions are absolute. Access rights you take away from a user or group by restricting share permissions cannot subsequently be returned by granting those rights using NTFS permissions. For example, if you create a new share and assign the group Everyone the Read permission for that share, that group can never have more than read-only permission to that share, although NTFS permissions can be used subsequently to further reduce the permissions available to the group Everyone.

WARNING NTFS permissions control access both by network users and by users who log on to the local server console. In contrast, share permissions control access only for those users who access the resource using the network. A locally logged on user can readily bypass share level permissions. The moral is that you should carefully control physical access to your server console.

By default, Windows NT Server assigns the Full Control permission to the group Everyone for a newly created share. This means that any user with a valid account on the server has the NetWare equivalent of Supervisor access to that share. Chances are you'll want to restrict access a bit more tightly on your new share, perhaps adding additional groups or individual users, each with a different level of share permissions. To do so, choose Permissions to display the Access Through Share Permissions dialog. By default, the group Everyone is assigned the Full Control permission to the new share.

To add permissions for selected users and groups, choose Add to display the Add Users and Groups dialog. Highlight a group name within the Names list box. You can use the standard Windows conventions to select multiple groups for which you want to assign the same share permissions. Pressing the Ctrl key while selecting a group name adds that group to those already selected. Pressing the Shift key while selecting a group name adds the range of groups between the group originally highlighted and the group upon which you Shift-click.

NOTE Choose Show Users to cause the Names list box to show individual users as well as groups. Highlight a group name and choose Members to display the individual users who are members of that group. Use either or both of these methods to set share permissions for individual users.

After you select the users and groups for which share permissions are to be added, choose Add to copy the selected users and groups to the Add Names list box. Use the Type of Access drop-down list to specify the access level to be granted to the selected users and groups. Choose OK to complete the procedure and return to the Access Through Share Permissions dialog. If you need to add other users and groups with different share permissions, repeat.

Use the Access Through Share Permissions dialog as needed to alter and maintain share permissions for the resource. You can alter the share permission assigned to a user or group by highlighting the user or group and choosing a different permission in the Type of Access drop-down list. You can also remove a user or group by highlighting it and choosing Remove. Once you have all of your users and groups assigned the appropriate permission level, choose OK to accept the changes and apply them to the share.

WARNING When you create a new share, always remember that Windows NT Server by default assigns full control to the group Everyone. Unless you really intend that any user with a valid account on the server should be able to do anything he wishes with this share, use either share permissions or NTFS permissions to further restrict access to the shared resource.

Aliasing Multiple Shares to a Single Resource

Windows NT Server allows you to assign multiple shares to a single resource. This allows different users and groups to use different names to access the same shared resource. For example, to allow users to access shared data files, you might establish a folder structure with a top-level folder named *sharedat*. You might create a sub-folder in the *sharedat* folder named *act* to contain the accounting department's shared data, another named *mkt* for the marketing folks, and so on.

To make things simple for the users, you might create the share *data*, map it to the *\sharedat\act* folder, assign the Accounting group Change permission, and assign everyone else the No Access permission. Similarly, you might map the *\sharedat\mkt* folder to the share *data*, giving the Marketing group Change permission and assigning everyone else the No Access permission.

Setting up this type of folder hierarchy has a couple of advantages. First, because all shared data resides within the *sharedat* folder tree, data backups are very straightforward. Second, a user in any department can access that department's shared data directory using the same share name. Regardless of what department you belong to, your shared data is always available in *data*. Having the same share name point to different physical folders also offers advantages in setting up shared applications programs across groups or departments, because the application always knows where its data is.

However, what happens if the marketing folks need access to the accounting department's data? You could modify the accounting share to give the marketing group access, but then the folks in marketing would have to deal with two shares with identical names, making errors much more likely to occur. This is where the ability of Windows NT Server to assign multiple share names to a single physical resource comes in handy.

Instead of changing the accounting share to give access to the Marketing group, you can create a new share mapped to the accounting data folder, and give only the Marketing group access to that share. You can use a distinctive share name to reduce confusion. For example, if the Marketing group requires only Read access to accounting data, create a share named *act_data* mapped to the *\sharedat\act* folder. Assign the Marketing Group the Read permission for the share, and assign everyone else the No Access permission. Users assigned to the Marketing group then have read-only access to the accounting data. They can't get mixed up about which data they're accessing. Their own shared data is still accessed using the *data* share name, while the accounting data is accessed using the share name *act_data*.

Creating an additional share for a resource is easy. To do this, in Windows NT Explorer, right-click the folder to be shared to display the context-sensitive menu. Choose Sharing to display the property sheet for the folder, and choose New Share to display the New Share dialog. Type a name for the new share in the Share Name box and, optionally, a description of the share in the Comment box. If you want to change the User Limit from the default Maximum Allowed to some smaller number, use the arrow keys to set the Allow box to the desired maximum number of concurrent users. Choose Permissions to display the Access Through Share Permissions dialog. Set permissions for users and groups as described in the preceding section. When you have finished assigning permissions, choose OK to return to the New Share dialog. If the new share is configured as you want, choose OK to establish the share.

TIP If you use the same share name to point to different folders or multiple share names to point to the same folder, it's a good idea to use the Comment field to more fully describe the share. Although users are limited in what is visible, it gets confusing for administrators, who can see everything.

Administrative Shares

In addition to shares that you create, Windows NT Server itself creates some shares automatically for administrative and management purposes. These shares, called *administrative shares*, are created when you install or reconfigure Windows NT Server. All servers include the following administrative shares:

- *ADMIN$* maps to the shared folder where Windows NT Server is installed. The Windows NT Server folder, by default *C:\Winnt*, is the only folder for which a share is automatically created during installation.
- *C$* maps to the root folder of drive *C:* on the server.

Most servers will also have some or all of the following administrative shares:

- *<drive_letter>$* maps to the root folder of each installed drive which has been assigned a drive letter. For example, if, in addition to drive *C:*, your server has drives *D:*, *E:*, and *F:* installed, these additional drives will be assigned the administrative shares *D$*, *E$*, and *F$*. The existence of a predefined root-level share for each drive allows an administrator to create additional share aliases for each of these resources from a remote workstation.
- *IPC$* refers to an Interprocess Communication resource. Windows NT Server allows a process or task to exchange data with another process or task using various IPC resources, including *mailslots*, *named pipes*, *queues*, *semaphores*,

shared memory, and *signals*. The IPC$ administrative share is most commonly used to support remote management and displaying shared resources on a computer.

- *NETLOGON* is used by Windows NT Server while processing domain logon requests. *NETLOGON* is the only administrative share that does not end in a dollar sign.
- *PRINT$* is used for remote printer administration.
- *REPL$* is created by Windows NT Server if you have configured the server as a replication export server.

WARNING Don't modify an administrative share unless you know exactly what you're doing and have a very good reason for doing it. Don't even think about deleting an administrative share.

TIP Administrative shares use the dollar sign as the final character of the share name, which renders the share invisible to browsing clients. Use the same technique with shares you create manually if you do not want the share to be visible to browsing computers. Anyone who knows the share name can still access the share, but only by explicitly typing the share name.

Viewing and Disconnecting Shares

Shared volumes and folders are flagged in the NT Explorer and My Computer displays using a special icon. Shared volumes are represented by a hand holding a drive icon, while unshared volumes are represented by the drive icon alone. Similarly, shared folders are represented by a hand holding a file folder. This makes it easy to determine whether or not the particular resource you are looking at is shared. However, there will be times when you need to view a consolidated list of all shares in effect on the server. To do this, from Control Panel, double-click Server to display Server status, as shown in Figure 6-2.

Choose Shares to display Shared Resources, as shown in Figure 6-3. The Sharename pane displays all shares, the number of concurrent users active for each, and the path to which each is mapped.

Highlight a Sharename. The Connected Users pane displays the names of all users of that share, how long each user has been connected in hh:mm format, and

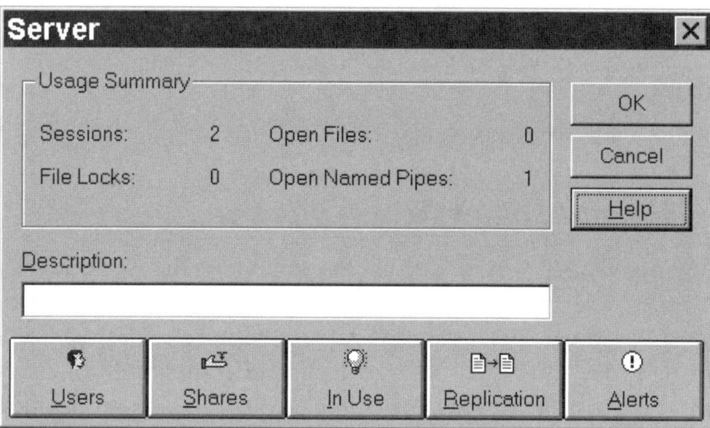

Figure 6-2. The Server status screen allows you to display and manage Users, Shares, and other aspects of server operation

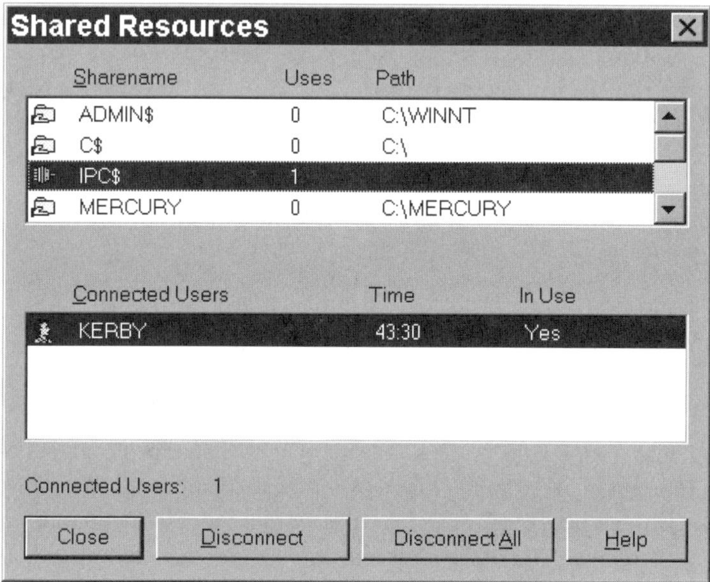

Figure 6-3. Shared Resources displays all shares in effect on the server, and allows you to disconnect all or selected users from the share

whether the share is currently in use. In the example shown, the server *Kerby* has been connected to the Interprocess Communication (*IPC$*) share for 43 hours and 30 minutes and is currently actively using the share. To disconnect one user from the share, highlight that user in the Connected Users list box and choose Disconnect. To disconnect all users from that share, choose Disconnect All.

WARNING Disconnecting a user may cause that user to lose unsaved data. Before disconnecting users from a share, notify them of the action you are about to take.

The Managing File and Folder Access Wizard

With the advent of Windows NT Server 4.0, Microsoft grafted the Windows 95 user interface onto Windows NT. Most aspects of the Windows 95 GUI have been ported to Windows NT Server, including Wizards. Because Wizards were designed primarily to help new or casual users to complete complicated or infrequently performed operations, it is curious that Microsoft chose to include Wizards in their server operating system. Presumably, most network administrators will opt for the finer control available when performing these operations manually rather than the simplicity offered by the Wizards.

Setting up shares is done infrequently enough that some administrators may find the Wizard helpful. A share created by the Managing File and Folder Access Wizard is no different from a share created manually. You can always go back and modify the share using the methods described in the preceding sections.

NOTE Microsoft can't decide what to call this Wizard. They refer to it sometimes as *Managing File and Folder Access* and at other times as *Managing Folder and File Access*. Here and elsewhere in Windows NT, as with the inconsistent use of *folder* and *directory*, Microsoft sometimes seems to be in accord with Emerson's remark that a foolish consistency is the hobgoblin of little minds.

To use the Managing File and Folder Access Wizard, choose **Start ➤ Programs ➤ Administrative Tools (Common) ➤ Administrative Wizards** to display the Administrative Wizards menu. Choose the Managing File and Folder Access menu option to display the opening screen of the Managing File and Folder Access Wizard. If the new share is to be on the local server, accept the default On my computer. If you want to create a share alias for an existing share on a remote system, choose On another computer.

If you are creating the new share on a remote computer, you have the opportunity to type a computer name or to browse the network to select the computer upon which the new share will be created. Once you have done this, Windows NT Server displays a list of volumes available on that computer. If instead you chose to create the share on the local server, Windows NT Server displays a list of local volumes upon which the share can be created.

Double-click the volume where the new share is to be created to display the folder tree of that volume. If you want to create the share for an existing folder, highlight that folder. If you want to create a new folder and share it, type the name of the new folder in the To create a new folder, type a new name box. If you are creating a new folder, Windows NT notifies you that the folder does not exist, and asks you to confirm its creation.

Windows NT displays the default permissions for the new share and gives you the opportunity to change them, as shown in Figure 6-4. By default, Windows NT gives the Full Control permission to members of the Administrators group and to System. The Creator/Owner is given the Special permission, and everyone else is given the Change permission. You may accept these default permissions by leaving the Keep the original permissions option button selected. To change the permissions, select the Change permissions option button and choose one of the option button selections within that pane. The Wizard limits your selections to only three choices:

Only I have access and full control
: Selecting this option gives the Full Control permission to the person who creates the share. It provides no access at all for any other user.

I have access and full control, everyone else can only read it
: Selecting this option gives the Full Control permission to the person who creates the share. All other users are assigned the Read permission.

Everyone has access and full control
: Selecting this option assigns the Full Control permission to any user with a valid account.

If you want to set permissions for the share other than those standard permissions offered by the Wizard, you must do this manually as described earlier in this chapter. If you find yourself in this situation, simply accept the default permissions for now. You can always change them later.

The Apply these permissions to all folders and files within this folder check box determines whether or not the permissions you are setting will affect existing folders and files within the newly shared folder. If you leave this box marked, permissions on existing folders and files will be changed to those you select in this screen. If you clear the check box, existing folders and files will keep the permissions already in effect for them.

The Wizard next prompts you to name the share. By default, Windows NT uses the folder name for the share name. You can override this choice simply by

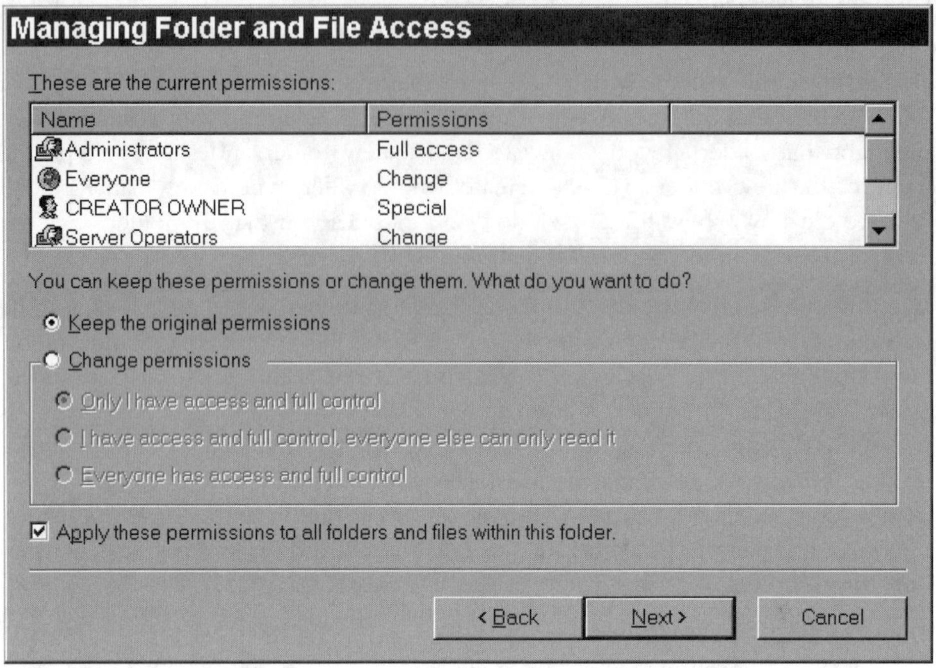

Figure 6-4. You may accept or change the default permissions for the new share

typing a different share name in the "*To rename this share, type a different name*" box. If you have clients running operating systems other than Windows 95 and Windows NT 4.0, remember to restrict the share name to the DOS 8.3 naming convention if you want this share to be accessible by these other clients. You may also optionally enter a comment to further describe the share in the Type a description for this share box.

You may also specify which network users are permitted to access this share. By default, the share is available only to Users of Microsoft Windows. If you have Services for Macintosh installed and enabled, you may mark the Macintosh users check box to grant access to these users. Similarly, if you have a NetWare gateway installed and enabled, marking the NetWare users check box grants access to these users. If either or both of these gateways are not installed and active, the respective check boxes are grayed out. When you have finished making selections, Windows NT presents a summary screen that displays the characteristics of your newly created share. Choose Finish to create the share. Windows NT notifies you that access was successfully set and asks if you want to set access for another folder or file.

NTFS Permissions

By now, you're probably wondering whether Windows NT Server provides anything like trustee rights and other access controls available with NetWare. The answer is yes, but not by using share permissions. Share permissions, again, are only the top level of access control in Windows NT Server, and are not really intended to offer fine control over the degree of access granted to individual accounts for specific resources. For that purpose, Windows NT Server allows you to set NTFS permissions at the file and directory level.

Prior to Version 4.0, Windows NT Server supported three filesystems. The DOS file system (File Access Table or FAT), offers little security, poor performance on all but the smallest servers, and a distinct lack of robustness. The High Performance File System (HPFS) originated on OS/2, and is a much better filesystem than DOS in all respects. The NT File System (NTFS) is the native filesystem for Windows NT Server, and is superior to HPFS in almost all respects. Volumes formatted as DOS or HFPS partitions can use only share permissions to control access to folders and files, effectively rendering these filesystems unusable for a production server.

With Windows NT Server 4.0, Microsoft eliminated all but read-only support for HPFS volumes, leaving only DOS and NTFS as filesystem choices for a new Windows NT Server. This is really no choice at all, because DOS is unsuitable as a server filesystem in every respect (unless, of course, you are using an application like SQL Server that really wants to store some or all of its files on a FAT volume). Fortunately, NTFS is fast, secure, and robust, making it effectively the only usable choice on Windows NT Server for all but specialized needs.

Like the DOS and NetWare filesystems, NTFS stores the name and size of each file and folder, as well as the date and time when the file was created or last modified. In addition, NTFS stores *extended attributes* for each file and folder. One of these extended attributes, called *permissions*, keeps track of which users and groups have access to the file or folder, and at what level. NTFS maintains two levels of permissions, as follows:

- *NTFS File Permissions* maintain information on a file-by-file basis concerning which users and groups are permitted to access that file, and at what level. For example, you might grant the system administrator and the Director of Accounting the Full Control permission for an accounting database file; members of the group Accounting, who need both to access and update that file, would have the Change permission assigned for that file; members of the group Purchasing, who need to look up information but not to change it, would have the Read permission assigned for that file.

- *NTFS Directory Permissions* maintain information about each directory (or folder) concerning which users and groups are permitted to access that directory, and at what level. For example, if your shared applications programs are stored in the *shareapp* directory, you might assign the system administrator the Full Control permission for that directory. Other members of the IS department might be assigned the Change permission for that directory, allowing them to update applications as needed. Everyone else might have the Read permission, allowing them to use the program but not to change or delete it.

By default, a user is granted the file and folder access permissions of the group to which that user is assigned. If, for example, you assign a new user to the group *sales*, that user automatically receives the access permissions in effect for that group. These implicit permissions are cumulative. That is, if a user is a member of more than one group, that user has all of the file and folder access permissions available to any of those groups.

Assigning permissions to groups, whenever possible, rather than to individual users, makes it easier to control access to files and folders. If you subsequently need to modify access permissions, it is much easier to make a single change to a group permission than to change each user's permissions individually.

NOTE Remember that NTFS permissions can only be used to further restrict the access level granted by the share permission in effect for a particular resource. Once share permissions have been used to revoke an access level, NTFS permissions can't be used to "add back" that level of access.

NTFS File Permissions

NTFS file permissions determine which users and groups can access a particular file, and at what level. NTFS file permissions for a particular file may be overridden by NTFS directory permissions set for the folder in which the file is contained. Microsoft defines standard permission sets which comprise various groupings of individual permissions. You can assign the following NTFS file permission sets to a file (individual permissions are shown in parentheses):

No Access (None)

Assigning the *No Access* permission set to a user or group restricts all access to that file, including the ability to view a directory listing of the file. Assigning *No Access* to an individual user restricts all access for that user, even if that user is a member of a group that would otherwise allow the user to access the file.

Read (RX)

Assigning the *Read (R)* permission set allows a user or group to view the filename within a directory listing and to read the file contents, but not to modify or delete it. Assigning *Read* permission implicitly assigns the *Execute (X)* individual permission as well, allowing the user to execute the file if it is a program. The Microsoft *Read* permission set corresponds to the Novell *Read* and *Filescan (RF)* trustee rights.

Change (RWXD)

Assigning the *Change* permission set grants the rights provided by the *Read* permission set, and adds the *Write (W)* and *Delete (D)* individual permissions. Users and groups assigned *Change* permission can modify and delete the file. The Microsoft *Change* permission set approximately corresponds to the Novell *Read, Filescan, Write, Create, and Erase (RFWCE)* trustee rights.

Full Control (All)

Assigning the *Full Control* permission set grants the rights provided by the *Change* permission set, and adds the rights to modify NTFS permissions for the file and to take ownership of it. The Microsoft *Full Control* permission set corresponds to the Novell *Supervisory (S)* trustee right.

Special Access

Special Access allows you to create a customized permission set for a file as an alternative to using one of the standard permission sets. You can specify any combination of individual permissions, including *Read (R), Write (W), Execute (X), Delete (D), Change Permissions (P),* and *Take Ownership (O).* You might, for example, have a shared database file that must be read and updated by a specified group. Although you could assign the *Change* permission set to that group, doing so would allow any member of that group to delete the file, either accidentally or intentionally. By assigning *Special Access* to that file, you can instead create a customized permission set that includes only the Read and Write individual permissions.

Modifying NTFS file permissions

To view and modify NTFS file permissions, use Windows NT Explorer and highlight the file or files for which NTFS file permissions are to be modified. Use the standard Windows conventions to highlight multiple files. Right-click the selected file or files to display the context-sensitive menu, and choose Properties to display the property sheet. On the Security page, choose Permissions to display the File Permissions dialog.

The individual users and groups for which NTFS file permissions already exist are shown in the Name list box, each with its corresponding permission set. To modify permissions for one of these users or groups, highlight the user or group and select a new permission set from the Type of Access drop-down list box. To remove permissions, highlight the user or group and choose Remove.

If you assigned one of the standard permission sets to the user or group being modified, choose OK to return to the property sheet, and then OK again to apply the new NTFS file permissions and to exit the property sheet. If instead you assigned the Special Access permission, the Special Access dialog shown in Figure 6-5 appears. In this example, Special Access permission is being used to create a custom permissions set that includes only the *Read (R), Write (W),* and *Execute (X)* individual permissions, revoking the *Delete (D)* individual permission previously assigned to the group Everyone. After you have marked the check boxes for the individual permissions you want to assign, choose OK to return to the File Permissions dialog, OK again to return to the property sheet, and OK one more time to assign the permissions and to exit the property sheet.

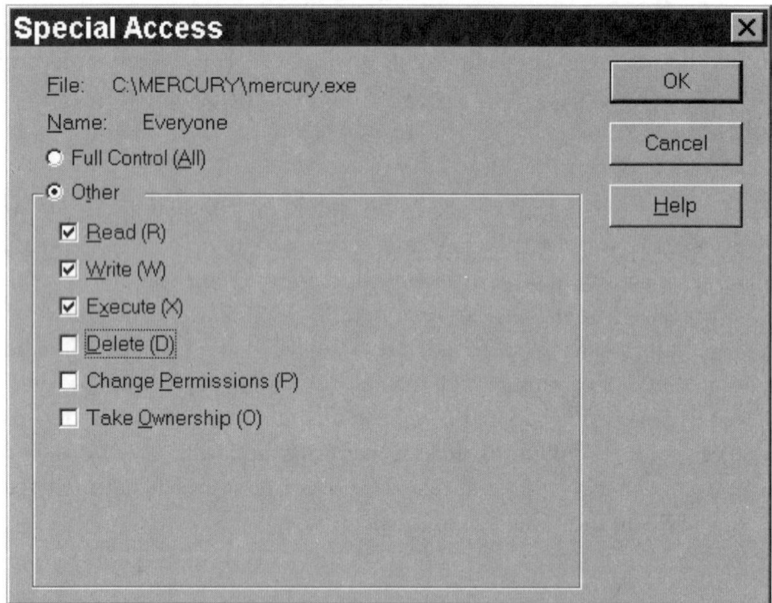

Figure 6-5. The Special Access dialog allows you to specify a custom set of NTFS permissions for the selected file

Adding NTFS file permissions

To add NTFS file permissions for new users and groups, take the steps described in the preceding section to display the File Permissions dialog. Choose Add to display the Add Users and Groups dialog, and use the List Names FROM dropdown list to select the domain or computer from which users or groups will be added. By default, only the available groups for the selected domain or computer are displayed in the Names list box. Choose Show Users if you want to display both users and groups in the Names list box. You can display the users for a particular group by highlighting that group and choosing Members. Double-click individual users or groups for which NTFS file permissions are to be added. As you select each user or group, it appears in the Add Names list box.

NOTE You can also use the standard Windows conventions to select multiple users or groups in the Names list box. When you have finished selecting multiple users and groups, choose Add to move your selections to the Add Names list box.

When you have selected all of the users and groups for which you want to set NTFS file permissions, use the Type of Access drop-down list to choose a permission set for the selected users and groups. Once you have done so, choose OK to return to the File Permissions dialog.

Windows NT Server allows you only to select among the four predefined permissions sets in this dialog. If you need to set Special Permissions for some or all of the selected users and groups, you must do so individually after the users and groups have been added. As a temporary measure, simply choose the closest standard permissions set here, and change permissions later as needed. After you have set Special Access permissions for any of the newly added users and groups, choose OK to return to the property sheet, and OK again to accept the changed permissions and exit the property sheet.

NTFS Directory Permissions

NTFS directory permissions determine the level of access granted to individual users and groups to a particular folder, the files within that folder, the subfolders of that folder, and the files within those subfolders. Setting NTFS directory permissions for a folder overrides the NTFS file permissions assigned to a file within that folder. As with NTFS file permissions, Microsoft defines standard permission sets which comprise various groupings of individual permissions.

You can assign the following NTFS directory permission sets to a folder (individual permissions that affect the folder itself are shown in the first set of parentheses; individual permissions that affect the files within the folder are shown in the second set of parentheses):

No Access (None) (None)

Assigning the *No Access* permissions set to a user or to a group restricts all access to the folder. Note that assigning *No Access* to an individual user restricts all access for that user, even if that user is a member of a group that would otherwise allow the user to access the folder.

List (RX) (Not Specified)

The *List* permissions set assigns the *Read* and *Execute* individual permissions at the folder level, and therefore allows a user or a group to view a listing of files and subfolders within the affected folder and also (via the *Execute* permission on the folder) allows users to make changes to subfolders within the folder. Because *List* does not define file access permissions for files contained within the folder and its subfolders, assigning *List* grants the user no access to those files. The Microsoft *List* permission therefore does not correspond directly to any specific Novell trustee right, but instead incorporates some, but not all, aspects of *Read (R), Filescan (F), Create (C),* and *Modify (M)* at the directory level.

Read (RX) (RX)

The *Read* permissions set incorporates the *List* permissions set at the directory level, and adds the *Read (R)* and *Execute (X)* individual permissions at the file level. The *Read* permissions set allows users to list the files within the folder and to read their contents, but not to create, modify or delete files. *Read* access also implies permission to execute a file if it is a program. The Microsoft *Read* permissions set corresponds to the Novell *Read* and *Filescan (RF)* trustee rights at the file level, and, with the differences noted above, to the *Read (R), Filescan (F),* and *Create (C)* trustee rights at the directory level.

Add (WX) (Not Specified)

The *Add* permissions set grants the *Write (W)* and *Execute (X)* individual permissions at the directory level, allowing a user or group so assigned to create both files *(W)* and subdirectories *(X)* within the directory. The Add permissions set by itself does not grant any other access to files or subdirectories, including those newly created. The Microsoft *Add* permissions set corresponds to the Novell *Create (C)* and *Write (W)* trustee rights at the directory level.

Add & Read (RWX) (RX)

The *Add & Read* permissions set combines the *Read* permissions set and the *Add* permissions set described in the two preceding items. Users and groups that are assigned this permissions set can create new files, change subdirectories, read files within the directories, and execute program files. The Microsoft *Add & Read* permissions set corresponds to the Novell *Read (R)* and *Filescan (F)* trustee rights at the file level, and to the Novell *Read (R), Filescan (F),* and *Create (C)* at the directory level.

Change (RWXD) (RWXD)

The *Change* permissions set grants all rights provided by the *Add & Read* permissions set, and adds the individual permissions to *Write (W)* and *Delete (D)* files, and to *Delete (D)* subdirectories. The Microsoft *Change* permissions set corresponds closely to the Novell *Read (R), Filescan (F), Write (W), Create (C), Erase (E),* and *Modify (M)* trustee rights at the file and directory level.

Full Control (All) (All)
The *Full Control* permissions set grants all rights provided by the *Change* permissions set, and adds the *Change Permissions (P)* individual permission and the *Take Ownership (O)* individual permission at both the file and directory level. The Microsoft *Full Control* permissions set corresponds to the Novell *Supervisory (S)* trustee right.

NTFS Directory Permissions are predefined groupings of individual permissions. For example, assigning the *Add & Read* permissions set to a folder simultaneously grants the *Read (R), Write (W),* and *Execute (X)* individual permissions at the directory level and the *Read (R)* and *Execute (X)* individual permissions at the file level. You can also use *Special Permissions* at the file or folder level to grant individual permissions in any combination to a folder, to the files contained within the folder, or both.

Special Directory Access
Choosing the *Special Directory Access* permissions set allows you to define a custom group of individual permissions at the directory level. You can assign any combination of *Read (R), Write (W), Execute (X), Delete (D), Change Permissions (P),* and *Take Ownership (O).* Permissions set here apply to the directory itself.

Special File Access
Choosing the *Special File Access* permissions set allows you to define a custom group of individual permissions at the file level. You can assign any combination of *Read (R), Write (W), Execute (X), Delete (D), Change Permissions (P),* and *Take Ownership (O).* Permissions set here apply to the files contained within the directory.

Modifying NTFS directory permissions

To view and modify NTFS directory permissions, use Windows NT Explorer to highlight the folder or folders for which NTFS directory permissions are to be modified. Use the standard Windows conventions to highlight multiple folders. Right-click to display the context-sensitive menu, and choose Properties to display the property sheet. On the Security Page, choose Permissions. If the directory has nonstandard (or no) permissions set, a warning appears. Choose Yes to confirm that you want to override the current permissions and set new permissions for the folder. The Directory Permissions dialog appears.

The individual users and groups for which NTFS directory permissions already exist are shown in the Name list box, each with its corresponding permissions set.

To modify permissions for one of these users or groups, highlight the user or group and select a new permission set from the Type of Access drop-down list box. To remove permissions, highlight the user or group and choose Remove.

To specify how the permissions you set will affect directories and files within the tree, mark or clear the *Replace Permissions on Subdirectories* check box and the *Replace Permissions on Existing Files* check box. These check boxes affect how the permissions flow through the tree as follows:

- If both check boxes are marked, the permissions you set affect the selected directory, its files, the subdirectories of the selected directory, and files contained within the subdirectories.
- If only the *Replace Permissions on Subdirectories* check box is marked, the permissions you set affect the selected directory and its subdirectories, but not the files contained within them.
- If only the *Replace Permissions on Existing Files* check box is marked, the permissions you set affect only the selected directory and the files contained within it, but not the subdirectories of that directory or the files contained within them.
- If both check boxes are cleared, the permissions you set affect only the subdirectory, but not files within it, the subdirectories of the selected directory, or files contained within the subdirectories.

If you assign one of the standard permission sets to the user or group being modified, choose OK to return to the property sheet, and OK again to apply the new NTFS directory permissions and to exit the property sheet. If instead you assign the Special Directory Access permission, the Special Directory Access dialog appears, which is analogous to the Special Access dialog (see Figure 6-5) described in the preceding section. After you have marked the check boxes for the individual permissions you want to assign, choose OK to return to the Directory Permissions dialog.

Note that if you assign a custom set of permissions that corresponds exactly to a standard set of permissions, Windows NT Server recognizes this fact, and simply uses and displays the standard set. If the Special Directory Access permissions you assign do not correspond to a standard permissions set, Windows NT displays the custom permissions set. Choose OK to return to the property sheet, and then OK again to assign the permissions and to exit the property sheet.

If instead you assign the Special File Access permission, the Special File Access dialog appears. You can use Special File Access permission to set individual permissions that will affect files within the directory. Mark the *Access Not Specified* option button to cause files not to inherit permissions from the directory. After you have marked the check boxes for the individual permissions you want to assign, choose OK to return to the Directory Permissions dialog, OK again to return to the property sheet, and OK for a third time to assign the permissions and to exit the property sheet.

Adding NTFS directory permissions

To add NTFS directory permissions for new users and groups, take the steps described in the preceding section to display the Directory Permissions dialog. Choose Add to display the Add Users and Groups dialog. Use the List Names From drop-down list to select the domain or computer from which users or groups will be added. By default, only the available groups for the selected domain or computer are displayed in the Names list box. Choose Show Users to display both users and groups in the Names list box. To display the users for a particular group, highlight that group and choose Members. Double-click individual users or groups for which NTFS directory permissions are to be added. As you select each user or group, it appears in the Add Names list box.

NOTE You can also use the standard Windows conventions to select multiple users or groups in the Names list box. When you have finished selecting multiple users and groups, choose Add to move your selections to the Add Names list box.

After you select all of the users and groups for which you want to set NTFS directory permissions, use the Type of Access drop-down list to choose a permission set for the selected users and groups. Once you have done so, choose OK to return to the Directory Permissions dialog.

Windows NT Server only allows you to select among the seven predefined permissions sets in this dialog. If you need to set Special Permissions for some or all of the selected users and groups, you must do this individually after the users and groups have been added. As a temporary measure, simply choose the most appropriate standard permissions set here, and change permissions later.

If necessary, set Special Access permissions for any of the newly added users and groups. After you have done this, choose OK to return to the property sheet and OK again to accept the changed permissions and exit the property sheet.

Folder Replication

Microsoft Windows NT Server offers a service called *Folder Replication*, for which NetWare 3.1x provides no equivalent capability. Folder Replication allows you to set up a process that automatically copies the contents of a specified folder to another computer or domain. Changes made to the files contained within the source folder, called the *export folder*, on the source computer, called the *export server*, are automatically synchronized on the destination computer, called the *import computer*, in the target *import folder*. The export folder and the import folder can be located on the same or different computers. If your Wide Area Network uses datacomm links fast enough to support the load, the two can be located in different cities, states, or even countries.

NOTE A computer running Windows NT Server can function as an export server, as an import computer, or as both simultaneously. A computer running Windows NT Workstation can function only as an import computer.

The Replication service does much more than simply copy files from the export folder to the import folder. Instead, it operates much like an ftp mirror program. Changed and newly created files and folders in the export folder are automatically copied to the import folder on the import computer. When files and folders are deleted from the export folder, they are also automatically deleted from the import folder. The contents of the import folder thus remain synchronized with those of the export folder.

The Replication service is a tool with many potential uses. Probably the most common of these is replicating a database between servers to spread the load and make backing up easier. Another common use is to replicate login scripts between domain controllers. This allows users to log on to the local server, which minimizes network traffic and distributes the burden of supporting logon and authentication between multiple servers. The replication service can be used any time you would like to have an automatically maintained copy of data reside on more than one server.

Setting Up a Replication User

The first step required to install and use the Replication service is to create a special *replication user* account, which must have the following characteristics:

Group Membership
: The replication user account must be assigned to the backup operators group. This ensures that the replication user will always have adequate permissions to access any file needed for replication.

Password Expiration
: The replication user account must be set to Password Never Expires.

Logon Hours
: The replication user account must not have any time-of-day or day-of-week access restrictions.

Account Name
: You may name this account anything you wish. However, the most likely name, *replicator*, is already in use as a group name, so you must choose something else. Most administrators choose something like *replicate* or *repluser* to make the purpose of the account clear from its name.

Creating a new user account and setting its properties are covered in Chapter 5, *Managing Users and Groups*.

Installing and Configuring the Directory Replicator Service

The next step required to install and use the Replication service is to install and configure the Directory Replicator service. To do this, from Control Panel, double-click the Services applet to display the Services dialog, as shown in Figure 6-6. In the example, the Directory Replicator service is highlighted. The Status is blank, which indicates that the service is not running. Startup is Manual, which means that the service must be started manually.

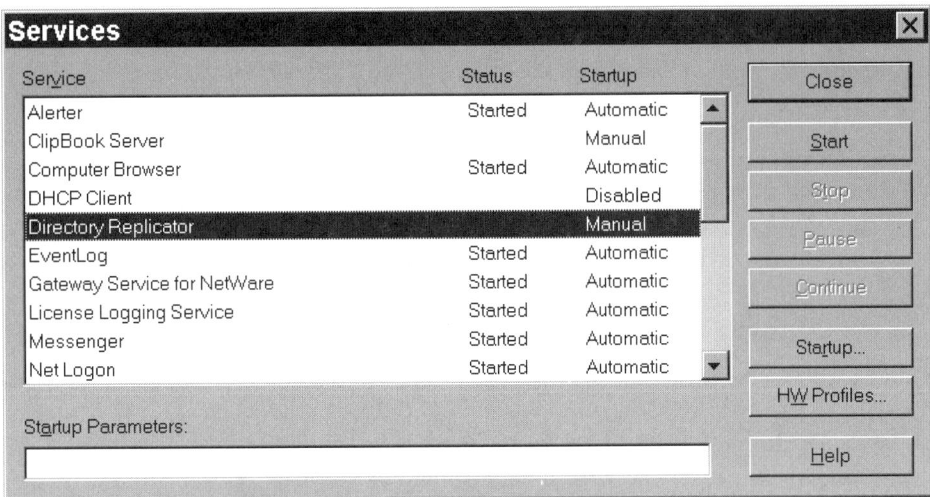

Figure 6-6. The Services dialog shows that the Directory Replicator service is not running and must be started manually

Highlight the Directory Replicator service and choose Startup to display the Service dialog. Under Startup Type, mark the Automatic option button if you want the Directory Replicator service to run automatically when you boot Windows NT

Server. Manual, the default setting, requires that you explicitly start the Directory Replicator service when you want replication to occur. Setting the Startup Type to Disabled prevents the service from running at all until you change the setting. Automatic is the best setting for most production environments.

Under Log On As, mark the This Account option button. Enter the account name, password and password confirmation fields for the replication user you created earlier. You may also use the ellipsis button next to the account name entry box to browse a list of available accounts. Verify that the information you entered is correct, and choose OK. Windows NT Server informs you that the account has been granted the Log On As A Service right and added to the Replicator group.

The Startup column reflects the choice you just entered for Startup Type. The Status column shows that the Directory Replicator service is not running. Start the Directory Replicator service manually by choosing Start. Windows NT Server displays a Service Control message to inform you that the service is being started. After a few moments, the Services dialog reappears, with the Status column set to Started, indicating that the Directory Replicator service is now running.

Configuring Replication

The next step is to configure the export server and the import computer. Remember that the Directory Replicator service must be running on both the export server and the import computer for replication to occur.

Configuring the export server requires that you provide two items:

- The From Path designates the source folder from which data will be exported. You can specify that only files in this folder be exported, or that the entire tree depending from the folder be exported. You can also specify that only particular subfolders be exported. If you have configured a subfolder to be exported, you can *lock* that folder temporarily or permanently to prevent its files from being exported. By default, Windows NT Server creates and configures the folder *C:\WINNT\System32\Repl\Export* as the export folder.
- The To List designates one or more import computers and/or domains to which data will be exported. Specifying a computer name causes data to be exported to that computer. If you specify a domain, all computers in that domain that are configured as import computers and have the Directory Replicator service running will receive the exported data. If you leave the To List blank, data is replicated to computers that are configured as import computers, have the Directory Replicator service running, and are members of the domain to which the export server belongs.

NOTE If you add a computer or domain name to the To List, Windows NT Server no longer exports data to the home domain automatically. To continue exporting data to the home domain, you must explicitly add the home domain to the To List.

Configuring the import computer is similar to configuring the export server, and also requires that you provide two items:

- The To Path designates the folder on the import computer to which imported data is written. Windows NT Server creates and configures the folder *C:\WINNT\System32\Repl\Import* by default as the import folder.
- The From List designates one or more export servers and/or domains from which data will be accepted. Specifying a computer name permits data to be imported from that computer. If you specify a domain, data will be accepted from any export server in that domain. If you leave the From List blank, data is accepted from any export server that is a member of the same domain as the import computer. As with exporting, a computer running Windows NT Server may be configured as an export server, as an import computer, or as both at the same time. To configure either an export server or an import computer, begin from Control Panel. Run the Server applet and choose Replication to display the Directory Replication dialog.

TIP Specifying domains rather than individual computers in either the To List or the From List may cause replication to work improperly or not at all if your servers are connected by a Wide Area Network. What's worse is that it may not be immediately apparent that replication is working improperly.

If this occurs, specify explicit computer names instead of domain names to solve the problem. The best rule of thumb is that if your export server and import computer are separated by a router, use explicit computer names rather than domain names in the To List and From List

Configuring an export server

To configure an export server, in the Directory Replication dialog, mark the Export Directories option button to activate this computer as an export server. Accept the default From Path or, optionally, enter an alternative folder from which data will be exported.

Leave the To List blank if you want to export only to one or more import computers that are members of the same domain as this export server. If you want to export only to specified import computers within the home domain, or to import computer(s) that are not members of the home domain, choose Add to display the Select Domain dialog. Domains found are displayed in the Select Domain pane. Double-click a domain name to display the individual computers that are members of that domain. Highlight a domain name or an individual computer and choose OK to add it to the To List and return to the Directory Replication dialog.

When you have configured the From Path and To List as needed, choose OK to close the Directory Replication dialog. Windows NT Server will now function as an export server.

Configuring an import computer

To configure an import computer, in the Directory Replication dialog, mark the Import Directories option button to activate this computer as an import computer. Accept the default To Path or, optionally, enter an alternative folder to which imported data will be written.

Leave the From List blank if you want this import computer to accept data automatically from any export server that is a member of the same domain. If you want to accept data only from specified export servers within the home domain, or from export server(s) that are not members of the home domain, choose Add to display the Select Domain dialog. Domains found are displayed in the Select Domain pane. Double-click a domain name to display the individual computers that are members of that domain. Highlight a domain name or an individual computer and choose OK to add it to the From List and return to the Directory Replication dialog.

When you have configured the To Path and From List as needed, choose OK to close the Directory Replication dialog. Windows NT Server will now function as an import computer.

7

Printing with Windows NT Server

In this chapter:

- *Windows NT Printing Overview*
- *Connecting Network Printers*
- *Managing Print Queues*
- *Managing Remote Printers*
- *Sharing Printing Resources with Other Operating Systems*

Sharing expensive printers has always been a primary *raison d'être* for local area networks. A decade or so ago, you might have been sharing a $3,500 Hewlett-Packard LaserJet that printed eight monochrome letter-size pages per minute (ppm) at 300 dots per inch (dpi) resolution. Today, you might be sharing a color laser printer or a 20 ppm monochrome laser printer that provides B-size output at 600 dpi, but that printer still costs $3,500. For most companies, financial realities dictate that the printers that most users really want on their desks must instead continue to be configured as shared resources. Although NetWare and Windows NT Server provide similar printing features, they address the task differently.

NetWare printing is queue based. With NetWare, a user print job is first delivered to a print queue, which is simply a special directory that temporarily stores the print data until it can be printed. Each print queue is managed by a print server. A print server may serve a single print queue, or it may serve multiple print queues located on one or more file servers. The print server periodically polls each print queue that it is responsible for managing (by default every 16 seconds) to determine if any print jobs are pending. If the print server finds a pending print job, and if the destination printer is available to print that job, the print server spools the job to the correct printer. Because a NetWare print queue simply stores pending documents passively where they await processing by the print server that manages that queue, it is referred to as using a "pull queue."

A NetWare print server may control one or several physical printers. These printers are of three types. First, a printer may be physically connected to a NetWare server running *PSERVER.NLM*, which allows the file server to function also as a print server. Second, a printer may be connected to a remote computer running *PSERVER.EXE*, which converts that computer to a dedicated print server. Finally, a printer may be connected to a remote computer running *RPRINTER.EXE*, which allows that workstation to function as a nondedicated print server. Many administrators have found that using *RPRINTER* to provide remote printing services is unworkable. They instead retire older 386 and 486 workstations to duty as *PSERVER.EXE* print servers.

Windows NT Server printing is printer based, and uses a push-based queue. Each print job is delivered to a queue that is associated with a particular physical printer (or printers). The queue itself then pushes the print jobs to the physical printer in sequence as it finishes each print job. Windows remote printing also takes a different approach. On a Windows SMB network, any client can designate a local printer as a shared network resource, thereby functioning as a print server. Windows never requires dedicated print servers, but instead allows SMB clients and servers to provide print server services as just another task. With Windows, sharing printers is as easy as sharing a disk volume.

Windows NT Printing Overview

Installing and sharing printers on a Windows NT network is straightforward. In fact, some administrators think that it is too easy. In a NetWare environment, setting up shared printers and controlling access to them is a matter for the administrator. In a Windows Networking environment, on the other hand, users can easily establish and control printer shares for their own locally attached printers by using the peer resource sharing functions built into all recent versions of Windows.

Novell NetWare 3.1x has always provided superior print sharing functionality and performance, allowing the administrator a great deal of flexibility in configuring shared printers and controlling access to them. As the new kid on the block, Windows NT Server had to go NetWare one better. It does so. Relative to NetWare, Windows NT Server provides the following capabilities that make printing easier and more flexible, both for administrators and users.

Browsing

With NetWare, only those printers explicitly configured by the administrator as shared are available to network users. Although printers connected to individual workstations can be made available to network users by running the DOS program *RPRINTER.EXE* on the workstation, this has never been an entirely satisfactory solution. Shared printers may be mapped to ports on a user-by-user basis via login scripts, or by using DOS commands at the prompt or in batch files. An unsophisticated user is limited to using those shared printers which have been predefined for him.

A client on a Windows NT Server network can instead simply browse the network for available Windows Network printers. Browsing for network printers may be done from Network Neighborhood and from the Add Printer Wizard. A user running either Windows NT or Windows 95 can dynamically select network printers from within the Print Setup dialog of an application program. A printer that is not browsable can be accessed directly by using its UNC name, in the form *\\KERBY\HP LaserJet 5P.*

Printing to other operating systems

In the absence of additional workstation client software or special gateway software installed on the server, NetWare clients are limited for all intents and purposes to printing to NetWare printers. Microsoft Networking clients, on the other hand, can browse to locate print servers running on other operating systems, including NetWare and UNIX, and print to the printers supported by those servers.

Remote Administration

Administering and controlling shared NetWare printer resources is a largely server-centric task. The Windows NT Server printing architecture allows the administrator to remotely administer print drivers, print servers, printers, and documents from any workstation connected to the network.

Centralized print driver support

With NetWare, print formatting is done at the workstation, before the print job is sent to the server. The appropriate print drivers must therefore be installed and maintained locally at each workstation. Windows NT Server can format print jobs at the server, allowing workstations to send unformatted data to the server for subsequent formatting and printing. Modern versions of Microsoft Windows, including Windows NT and Windows 95, support this server-based print processing, allowing print drivers to be installed and maintained only on the server.

NOTE Unlike NetWare, which can be configured to notify specific users when printing error conditions occur, Windows NT Server makes no such provision.

Microsoft uses somewhat different terminology than does Novell to refer to printing-related entities and services. In some cases, the same term is used to mean different things. In other cases, the same thing is referred to by different names.

Print Device

What Novell (and the rest of us) simply call a printer, Microsoft instead designates as a "print device." This term refers to the physical printer—the hardware that puts ink or toner on paper.

Printer

Microsoft uses the term *printer* to refer to the software interface that creates the logical connection between the operating system and the physical printer, or print device. A printer is a logical name that defines the port to which a print job is directed, how and when the print job will be spooled and printed, who may use the print device, and other aspects of controlling printing. One logical printer name may map to one or more physical print devices.

Printer Driver

A printer driver is a software interface that converts the text and graphics to be printed into the printer control language, e.g., PCL or Postscript, understood by the print device.

Queue

Microsoft refers to the list of documents awaiting printing as a queue. In NetWare, the print queue is a fundamental part of the printing architecture. NetWare users print documents to a queue. In Windows NT Server, the queue is simply the on-deck circle where documents are stored temporarily until a print device becomes available. Windows NT Server users print documents to a printer.

Spooler

In Windows NT Server, the spooler is simply a collection of Windows dynamic link libraries (DLLs) that together handle document printing. *Spooling* is the process of writing a document to disk as a *spool file* in preparation for printing.

Print Server

Microsoft refers to any computer, workstation, or server that receives and processes documents from clients as a print server. The NetWare environment allows print server functions to be provided either by loading *PSERVER.NLM* on the file server, or by creating a dedicated print server by running *PSERVER.EXE* on a PC. In the Windows Networking environment, any computer that is running Windows can be configured as a print server, and thereby share its local printer with network users.

Network Interface Print Device

Sometimes you need to place a shared printer at a location where, perhaps for space or security reasons, it is not convenient or desirable to install a PC to service it. Printers which connect directly to the network cabling system using a built-in or external network interface address this need, and are referred to by Microsoft as network interface print devices.

Connecting Network Printers

Windows NT Server allows you to configure two types of network printers, as follows:

Local Printer
: A printer that is defined, managed, and configured on the local Windows NT Server machine. A local printer may be (and often is) configured to send output to a print device that is physically connected to the Windows NT Server computer using a parallel or serial port, but it may instead be configured to send output to a print device that is logically connected via the network. For example, you might define a local printer for a remote network-connected HP JetDirect print device that communicates with the DLC protocol. In either case, the print server for the local printer is defined and managed locally.

Network Printer Server
: A printer that is connected to another machine, and for which all settings are managed by a print server that has been set up by an administrator of that other machine. A network printer server may be another computer running Windows NT, Windows 95, or Windows 3.11 for Workgroups. It may also be a remote print queue serviced by a NetWare server or a UNIX host.

Once configured, either type of network printer appears to clients as a shared resource on the server running Windows NT Server.

Installing a Local Printer

Windows NT Server makes it very easy to install and configure a local printer. Once installed, the printer can be made available as a shared resource to any or all network clients. To install a local printer on the server and share it, proceed as follows.

From My Computer, double-click Printers to display the Printers folder. If no printers have yet been installed on the server, the only item shown in this folder will be Add Printer. Double-click Add Printer to display the Add Printer Wizard, as shown in Figure 7-1. Because this printer will be connected directly to the server, accept the default selection of My Computer.

Next, specify the physical port to which the printer will be connected. You may, if necessary, add ports which do not appear in the Available ports pane by clicking Add Port. You may configure an existing port by selecting it and clicking Configure Port.

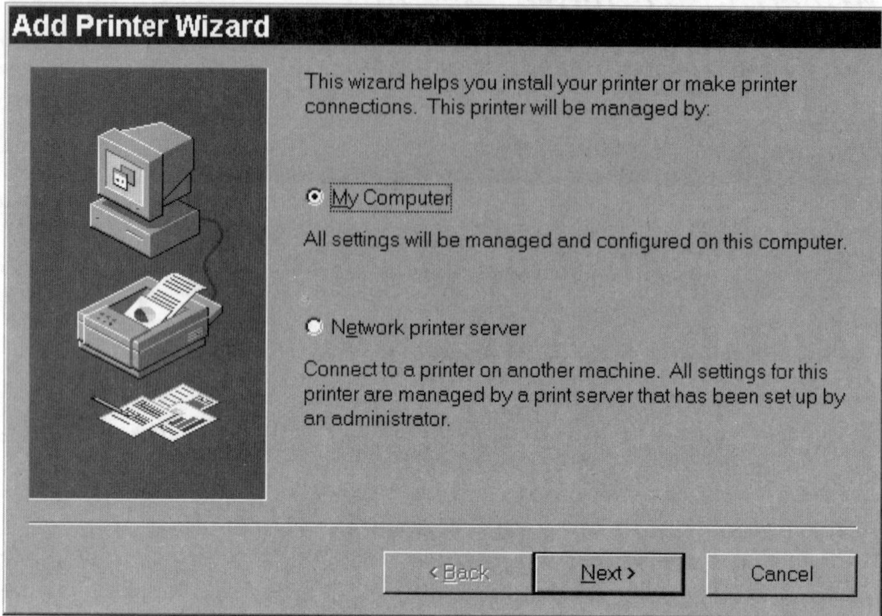

Figure 7-1. The Add Printer Wizard automates the process of installing shared network printers.

Parallel ports (LPTx:) can be configured only for Transmission Retry, which is set by default to 90 seconds. This value controls the duration for which the printer can remain nonresponsive before Windows NT Server notifies you. The default value is nearly always acceptable. Increase it only if you receive notifications that the printer is not responding when in fact it is simply busy processing data that has already been provided. This normally occurs only with parallel interface plotters.

Serial printers (COMx:) can be configured via drop-down lists for standard serial communications parameters, including Baud Rate, Data Bits, Parity, Stop Bits, and Flow Control. You can also use Advanced Settings to configure nonstandard values for COM1: through COM256: for Base I/O Port Address and Interrupt Request Line (IRQ). You don't normally need to alter these values unless you are connecting many serial devices to the server, perhaps using a smart multiport serial card.

NOTE The FIFO Enabled check box in Advanced Settings is marked by default if Windows NT Server detects a 16550 UART or other buffered serial port hardware. Windows NT Server grays out this box if it does not detect a buffered UART. If your serial ports use older 16450 UARTs, this check box should not be selectable. However, some serial ports, particularly those on smart multiport cards, may use 16450 UARTs with custom buffering hardware. These devices may report themselves to the system as 16550s. In general, if this check box is selectable, marking it is safe and will increase performance.

Finally, you may specify FILE: from the Available ports: pane as the destination for print jobs. Choosing this option causes formatted data to be "printed" to a specified disk file. This option is normally useful only in two situations. First, when debugging printing problems, it may be useful to capture an entire print job, including escape sequences and other printer control characters, to a disk file for review. Second, if you have an application that generates a log to a printer, but offers no option for capturing the log information to disk, you may redirect printer output to a disk file defined in Windows NT Server as a printer. If you set up a printer for this reason, make sure to define the printer manufacturer as "Generic" and the printer model as "Generic/Text Only" so that you can capture only ASCII text and not intermingle printer control characters.

Once you have selected and configured the port to be associated with the printer, the next step is to specify the make and model of the printer to be attached to that port. Windows NT Server ships with drivers for hundreds of printers. Highlighting the manufacturer name in the left pane displays a list of models made by that manufacturer in the right pane. Select the appropriate model and click Next to continue. Alternatively, if you have a new or updated driver on disk from Microsoft or from the printer manufacturer, click Have Disk and follow the prompts.

Next, enter a name for the printer. This is local Printer Name, by which the printer will be addressed and managed on the server to which it is attached. You will have the opportunity later to give the printer a share name, by which it will be accessed by users browsing the network.

Next, specify whether or not the printer will be available as a shared network resource, as shown in Figure 7-2. By default, Windows NT Server installs printers as Not shared, limiting them to use by the local machine. To share the printer with other network users, mark the Shared option button, and enter a value for Share Name. The share name (rather than the printer name) is what is seen by users who are browsing the network.

Using Printer Pools

Mark the Enable printer pooling check box if this printer will support two or more identical physical print devices as a printer pool. When this check box is marked, you can establish a printer pool simply by selecting two or more ports, each of which has a physical print device installed. Jobs subsequently directed to this printer are submitted in the form of a circular queue alternating among pool members. If the print device to which the job would normally have been submitted is busy with another job, the first job is simply routed to the next available printer in the pool.

There is no way to predict which print device within the pool will receive and print a particular document, although clients with the Windows Messenger Service installed are notified when their print job is completed and the physical port upon which it was printed. Unfortunately, Windows NT does not allow you to associate a discrete name for the physical printer with the port in a pooled environment. For most users, the port number alone will provide adequate identification only if the pooled printers are close together and each is labeled with its corresponding port number.

The installation procedure allows you to specify only a single printer model for the pool, with the assumption that all print devices within the pool are identical. It is sometimes possible to combine dissimilar but closely related printers within a single pool, if you are willing to accept the least common denominator limitations imposed by the less capable printers, and if the more recent printers offer a true and complete emulation of the earlier model. If, for example, you have an HP LaserJet III and a LaserJet IIID that you would like to assign as members of a single pool, you can do this at the expense of giving up the duplex printing capabilities of the IIID.

Printer pools are useful primarily in environments with extraordinarily heavy printing demands, and in which the pooled print devices can be located in close physical proximity. Otherwise, you run the risk of a user not knowing where to pick up his print job. In most office environments, you are better off simply defining each print device as a separate printer and siting the printers to provide easy access by the individual workgroups that each serves.

Windows NT Server provides special printing support to clients that are running Windows NT and Windows 95. When a Windows NT or Windows 95 client attaches to the printer server, the proper printer driver is automatically downloaded and installed on the client if this enhanced printing support is enabled. If you install an updated printer driver on the printer server, Windows NT clients automatically download and install the new driver, but Windows 95 clients must choose to manually update the driver. Earlier clients, including MS-DOS and

Windows 3.11 for Workgroups, can connect to a Windows NT printer server only by redirecting output to the UNC name of the resource, in this case *\\kerby\HPLJ-5*. Clients using these earlier operating systems must install the appropriate printer driver before connecting to the share.

This special support is enabled by default for clients running Windows NT 4.0 on the same type of processor used by the printer server, in this case an Intel processor. You can enable this support for Windows 95, for older versions of Windows NT, and for Windows NT 4.0 running on other types of processors by highlighting one or more selections in the lower pane before continuing. In this case, I've opted to install support for Windows 95.

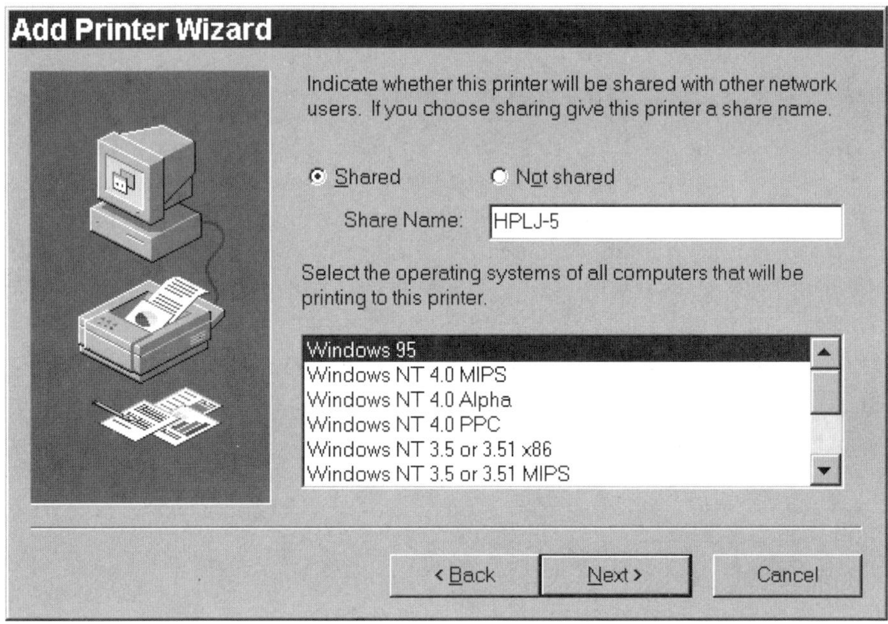

Figure 7-2. The Add Printer Wizard allows you to establish a share name to make the printer available to network users, and to install special printing support for recent versions of Windows

You are next prompted to decide whether or not to print a test page, with the default being Yes. The test page doesn't do much to test the extended capabilities of the printer, but it does at least allow you to verify that the printer is properly connected and that the server can print to it.

Windows NT Server next prompts you for the location of the distribution files needed to install the printer. By default, it suggests the drive and directory from which Windows NT Server was initially installed. If necessary, specify the correct location for the files, and click OK to continue. If the driver is already installed (for example, if you are installing a second identical printer on a different port)

Windows NT Server will offer you the choice of using the existing driver or overwriting it with a new driver.

If you selected enhanced printing support for one or more additional operating systems above, Windows NT Server next prompts you for the distribution files needed to install this support. Accept the default location, or enter a new location for these files. Installing enhanced support for Windows 95 requires distribution files located on the Windows 95 CD-ROM. Installing enhanced support for Windows NT 3.1 or Windows NT 3.5x requires the appropriate distribution CD-ROM for each version. The Windows NT distribution CD-ROM includes the support files needed for that version of Windows NT running on diverse platforms. After the files are copied, the new printer is installed, visible in the Printers folder and available for use by network clients.

Installing a Network Printer Server

You can also use the Add Printer Wizard to install a network printer server. A network printer server is a remote shared printing resource, i.e., one not physically connected to the server, but that is visible to the server in question. By installing this remote printing resource as a network printer server on the local server, clients of the local server can access this remote printing resource just as they would any other resource available on the local server.

For example, in this section, I establish a NetWare print queue running on the NetWare 3.12 server *theodore* as a shared resource on the Windows NT Server *kerby*. The fact that *kerby* is running the Gateway Service for NetWare allows it to see the NetWare print queue running on *theodore*, along with other shared NetWare resources. Once the network printer server has been installed and configured, the NetWare print queue is visible to local clients running Windows Networking as just another shared Microsoft Networking printer.

To install a network printer server, from My Computer, double-click Printers to display the Printers folder. If no printers have yet been installed on the server, the only item shown in this folder will be Add Printer. Double-click Add Printer to display the Add Printer Wizard. Because this printer will be a network printer server rather than a local printer, override the default selection of My Computer by marking the Network printer server option button.

The Connect to Printer dialog appears, as shown in Figure 7-3. In this case, I am running two networks, so entries appear for both NetWare or Compatible Network and Microsoft Windows Network. Double-clicking the entry for NetWare or Compatible Network displays the available servers. In this case, only one NetWare server, named *theodore*, is available. Double-clicking on *theodore* displays available shared printing resources. In this case, LASER_QUE is the only resource available.

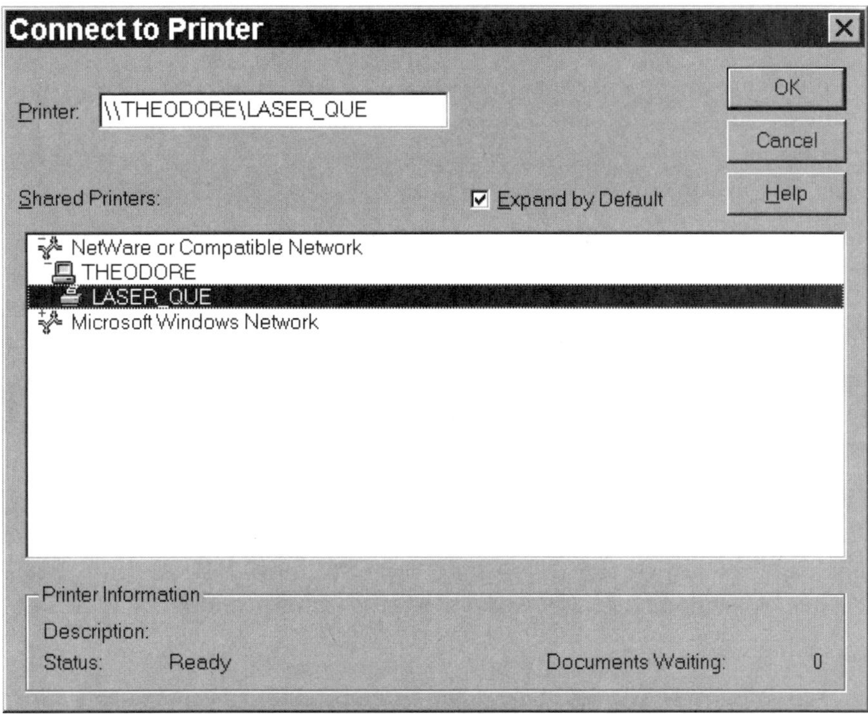

Figure 7-3. The Connect to Printer dialog allows you to browse for available shared network printing resources

The local machine does not have a printer driver installed that supports the remote print queue. Accordingly, Windows NT Server prompts to install an appropriate printer driver on the local server. As described in the preceding section, client machines running Windows 95 and Windows NT can install this printer driver automatically from the printer server running Windows NT. Clients running earlier versions of Windows must locally have an appropriate printer driver installed manually. Next, specify the manufacturer and model of the printer to be installed. In this case, the printer physically connected to the NetWare server is a Hewlett-Packard LaserJet III, so I install the driver for that printer.

After you install the appropriate printer driver, click OK to complete the installation. The Add Printer Wizard prompts you to specify whether or not to use the newly installed printer as the default printer for Windows programs. Specify Yes or No, and then click Next. A screen notifies you that the printer has been installed successfully. Click Finish to exit the Wizard.

Configuring Printer Properties

The next step is to configure the printer properties. Configuring the printer requires the Full Control access permission, which is given by default to members of the Administrators, Server Operators, and Print Operators groups. If you have upgraded from an earlier version of Windows NT Server, the Power Users group will also exist, and have the Full Control access permission by default.

Setting general properties

To configure the printer, highlight the printer name in the Printers folder, right, click to display the context-sensitive menu, and click Properties to display the General page of the <printername> Properties property sheet, as shown in Figure 7-4. You may enter a Comment and/or a Location to make it easier for users to determine where they can pick up their print jobs. You can use the drop-down list Driver to pick a different installed driver, or click New Driver to install an updated driver.

If you want to print a banner page to separate print jobs, click the Separator Page button to display the Separator Page dialog. You can enter the name of a .sep separator page, or browse for an existing page. Windows NT Server provides three default separator pages:

pcl.sep
: This separator page toggles the printer to PCL mode, for compatibility with Hewlett-Packard LaserJet printers running in PCL mode. It prints a banner page before each document.

pscript.sep
: This separator page toggles the printer to Postscript mode, but does not print a banner page.

sysprint.sep
: This separator page toggles the printer to Postscript mode, and prints a banner page before each document.

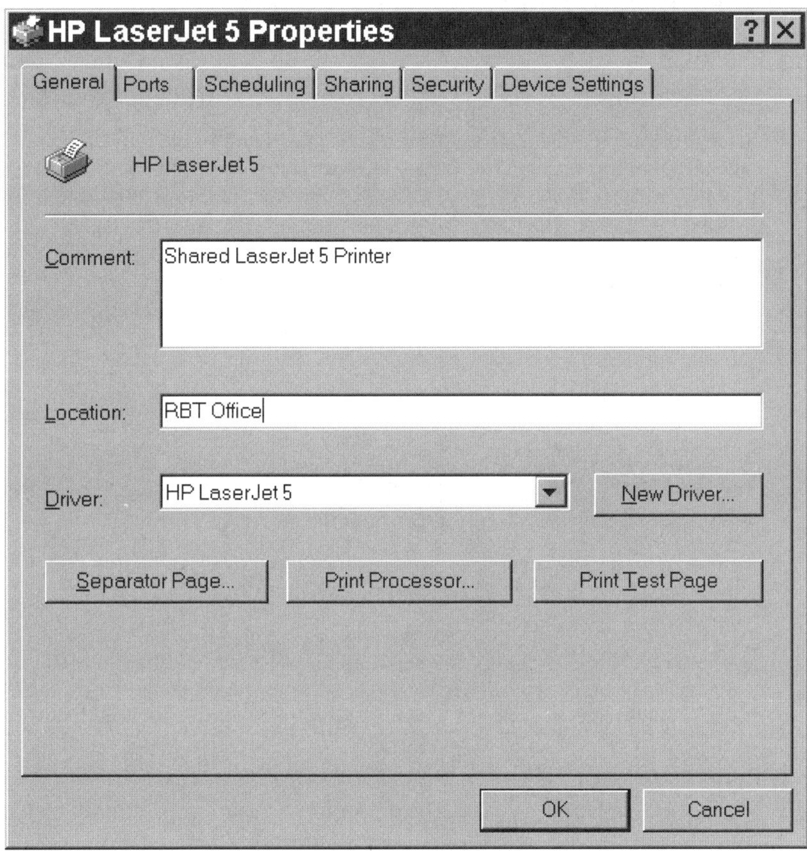

Figure 7-4. The General page of the <printername> Properties property sheet allows you to enter identifying information about the printer and to select driver options

You can also create a custom separator page using the commands listed in Table 7-1.

Table 7-1. Commands Available in Separator Page Files

Command	Description
\	The initial character of a separator page file is the single character to be used as the command delimiter, which must appear on the first line by itself. This table uses the backslash character as the command delimiter, but you can use another uncommon character at your option.
\B\M	Turn on block character printing using double-wide characters.
\B\S	Turn on block character printing using single-wide characters.
\D	Print the date the document was printed, using the format specified on the Date page of the Regional Settings applet in Control Panel.

Table 7-1. Commands Available in Separator Page Files (continued)

Command	Description
\E	Eject a page. Use this command at the beginning of the separator page file to force a form feed before printing the separator page, or at the end of the separator page file to force a form feed after completing the separator page. Depending on the characteristics of the individual printer, you may have to use zero, one, or two of these commands to print a separator page without printing wasted blank pages.
\Fpathname	Begin a new line and print the file specified by the fully qualified path name as unformatted raw text.
\Hxx	Send the hexadecimal control code, specified by xx, to your printer.
\I	Print the number of the document.
\Lxxxx...	Print the characters represented by xxxx... until another command delimiter is encountered or until the number of characters assigned as the width of the separator page is reached.
\N	Print the name of the user who submitted the document.
\n	Skip n lines, where n can range from 0 to 9.
\T	Print the time the document was printed, using the format specified on the Time page of the Regional Settings applet in Control Panel.
\U	Turn off block character printing.
\Wxx	Set the width in characters of the separator page to xx, where xx defaults to 80 and may be set within the range of 1 through 256. Received characters in a single line beyond the value assigned by \W are discarded.

You may click Print Processor to select a print processor other than the Windows print processor (*winprint.dll*) that is used by default. For example, if you install Services for Macintosh, the Macintosh print processor (*sfmpsprt.dll*) is available. If you install File and Print Services for NetWare, the NetWare print processor (*nwprint.dll*) is available.

The print processor works in conjunction with the printer driver to despool print jobs. The print processor formats the print job as needed, based on the data type of the print job, to allow the printer driver to print the job correctly. A given print processor may recognize several data types, or only one. For example, by default PCL printers use the EMF (enhanced metafile) data type, while Postscript printers use the RAW data type. A printer manufacturer may also provide a custom print processor to support its own printer drivers or to support custom data types different than those supported by the standard Windows print processor.

Setting ports properties

The Ports page, as shown in Figure 7-5, allows you to modify the port assignments that you made when you created the printer. You may add, delete, and configure ports; change the port to which the printer is assigned; and enable printer pooling. A printer can be assigned to only a single port if the Enable printer pooling check box is cleared. If it is marked, the printer may be assigned to any or all available ports. Assigning the printer to multiple ports establishes a printer pool.

Recent models of some laser printers are designed to communicate more detailed information to the printer server than just the traditional "paper out" and similar limited messages. For example, a print device with bidirectional support may notify the printer server that it is running low (but not out) in a particular paper bin or that the toner needs to be topped off. If your print device and printer driver both support bidirectional communications, mark the Enable bidirectional support check box to use these enhanced features. Note that bidirectional support is available only if the print device is physically attached to the server. Remote network printer servers do not support bidirectional communication even if both the print device and the printer driver support it.

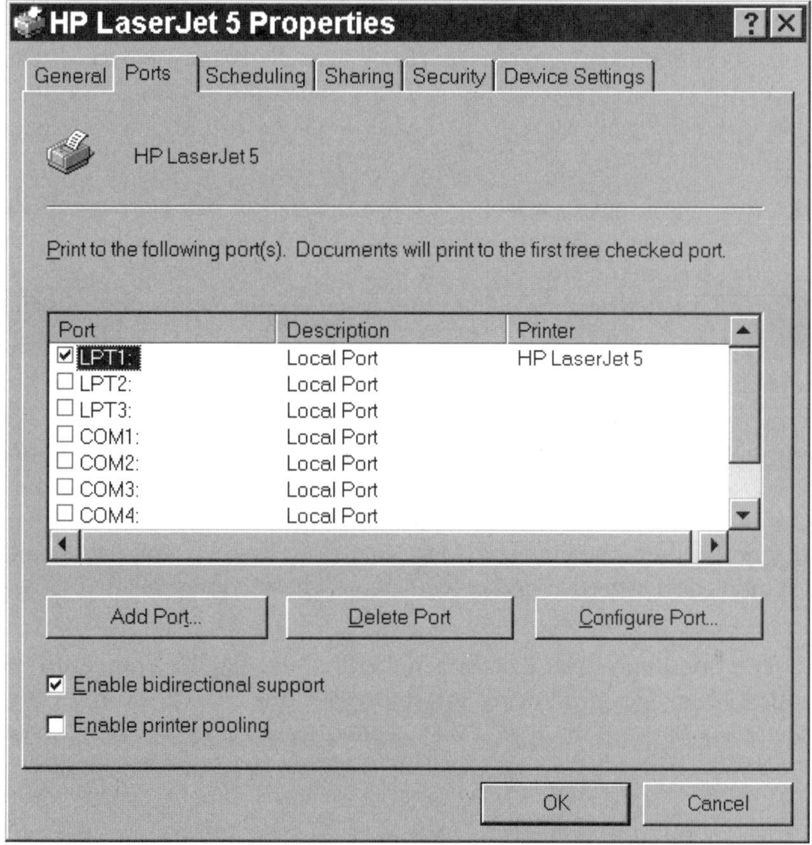

Figure 7-5. The Ports page of the <printername> Properties property sheet allows you to modify ports, enable bidirectional support and enable printer pooling

Setting scheduling properties

The Scheduling page, as shown in Figure 7-6, allows you to specify when the printer is available, to set priority, and to configure how the print spooling operates. The most common use for scheduling is to optimize use of existing printers by deferring lower priority print jobs to off-hours or times when the printer isn't busy printing higher priority jobs. You can do this by creating two printers for the same print device. Each printer may have different values for both the hours when it is available and the priority.

For example, I might create one printer named "LaserJet 5 – High Priority" and map it to the LaserJet 5 that is physically connected to LPT1. I assign this printer Always in the Available: section to ensure that jobs sent to it can be printed at any hour of the day or night. Values for Priority can range from 1 (lowest) to 99 (highest). Because I want this printer to have the quickest possible access to the physical print device, I assign it a priority of 99. This value guarantees that this printer has first claim on the print device unless it is currently printing another job.

I then create a second printer named "LaserJet 5 – Low Priority" and map it to the LaserJet 5 that is physically connected to LPT1. There are two ways to restrict this printer to using the print device only when it is not needed by a higher priority job.

First, I can set Available hours to a range of times outside normal working hours, e.g., from 7:00 p.m. through 6:00 a.m. If I do this, all print jobs sent to this printer during the working day are queued up, but actual printing begins only at the indicated start time. All queued documents are then printed sequentially in the order that they were sent to this printer.

Second, I can leave availability set to Always, but set the Priority on this printer to a value lower than the high priority printer assigned to the same port. Note that priority values are relative. If only two printers are assigned to the same print device, and the lower priority printer is assigned a priority value of 1, assigning the higher priority printer a value of 2 or 99 has exactly the same effect. When two or more printers are contending for the same print device, Windows grants access to that print device to the printer with the highest priority relative to the other claimants.

Specifying different priorities for the printers rather than limiting one printer to off hours offers the advantage of allowing lower priority print jobs to print at any time of day, as long as the print device isn't needed by a higher priority printer. The disadvantage to using this method is that once the lower priority printer is granted access to the print device, it may continue to use it until the print job is complete. If the low priority print job is a long one, a high priority print job may end up sitting in the queue while the lower priority job finishes printing. In an emergency, you can always abort the low priority job and allow the high priority printer to seize the print device.

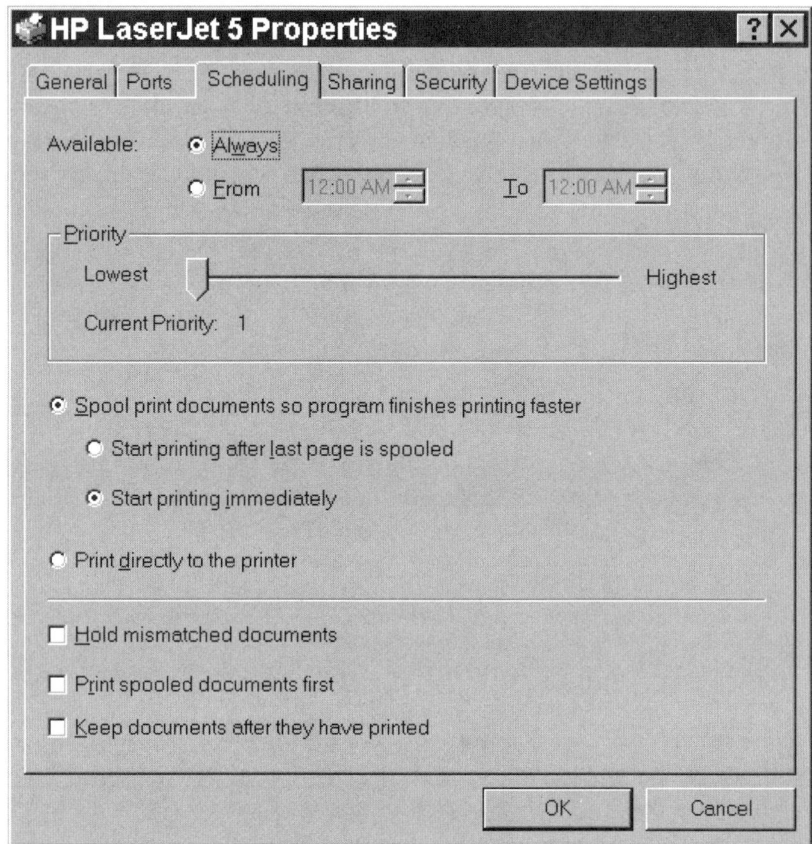

Figure 7-6. The Scheduling page of the <printername> Properties property sheet allows you to specify availability and priority values for the printer, as well as controlling various aspects of print spooling

The Scheduling page also allows you to control various aspects of print spooler functioning.

Spool print documents so program finishes printing faster

This option button causes Windows NT Server to spool print jobs to disk before delivering them to the printer. It is set by default, and is the alternative to printing directly to the printer. If you enable this option, you must select one of the options below:

— *Start printing after last page is spooled.* Choose this option if it is more important for you to keep the printer running constantly than it is to have user print jobs completed as fast as possible. When this option is enabled, a print job is not delivered to the printer until the complete job has first been spooled. This means that the print device never has to wait in the middle of a print job for an application to finish generating the print job.

— *Start printing immediately.* This is the default option. Choosing it allows user print jobs to complete as fast as possible, at the possible expense of causing the print device to pause during a print job while awaiting further data from the application that is generating the print job. With a page-printer print device such as a laser printer, the print job begins printing as soon as the first page is spooled to disk, rather than awaiting the complete print job being spooled before printing starts. With a character-oriented print device like a dot matrix printer, the print job begins printing as soon as the first character is written to the spooler.

Print directly to the printer

If you choose this option, print jobs are sent directly to the print device, without first being written to a spool file on the print server hard disk. Choosing this option can increase printing performance somewhat, at the expense of requiring significantly more server memory to accommodate pending print jobs.

You can also enable one or more of the following check boxes, all of which are disabled by default.

Hold mismatched documents.

If this check box is enabled and a print job arrives that requires a form that is not currently loaded, the spooler will hold that print job until the correct form is loaded. In the meantime, other print jobs that require the form currently loaded will be printed.

Print spooled documents first

Specifies how the actual printing order is determined based on when documents begin and finish spooling. If this box is enabled, print jobs are printed in the order that they finish spooling. If it is disabled, print jobs are printed in the order that they begin spooling. Enable this option in conjunction with the Start printing immediately option described above.

Keep documents after they have printed

If this option is enabled, print jobs are not deleted from the spooler as they are printed. This allows print jobs to be resubmitted from the print queue rather than from the original application that generated the print job. However, enabling this option requires that old print jobs be deleted manually to avoid consuming excessive disk space. This option is useful primarily as a "debug mode" when you are having problems with the printer.

Setting sharing properties

The Sharing page allows you to enable or disable sharing of this printer as a network resource. If you enable sharing, you can provide a share name by which the printer will be known to browsing clients. Windows NT and Windows 95 client computers can access a printer using either the printer name or the share name. Clients running other operating systems, like MS-DOS and Windows 3.11 for Workgroups, can connect only using the share name. If you have a mix of client types, be careful when you assign the share name. Older clients are restricted to using share names that comply with the MS-DOS 8.3 naming convention. Printers whose share names exceed this standard will be invisible to older clients. Unless you are absolutely certain that an older client will never need to access this printer, restrict yourself to using 8.3 share names.

NOTE If a client running a DOS application under Windows NT needs to print to a Windows NT printer server, it cannot use the printer mappings already established within Windows NT. Instead, that client must first invoke the NET USE command from within the DOS box to map a printer for that session. For example, the command `NET USE LPT1: \\KERBY\HPLJ-5` maps the local printer we created earlier to logical port LPT1: for the duration of the session.

You can also use the Sharing page to install printer drivers for other operating systems, as described earlier in this chapter in the section on installing the printer. Note that turning on sharing shares the printer for every protocol installed on the server. For example, if you have Services for Macintosh installed, the shared printer becomes available via AppleTalk.

Setting security properties

The Security page allows you to set permissions to control which users and groups can access the printer, and at what level. It also allows you to specify by user and by group which events, if any, trigger an entry to the audit log. Finally, as Administrator, you may also use the Security page to take ownership of a printer currently owned by another user.

Clicking Permissions displays the Printer Permissions dialog. By default, Windows NT Server assigns the Full Control access permission to the groups Administrators, Print Operators, and Server Operators. Everyone is given the Print access permission, allowing anyone with a valid account to print to this printer. The CREATOR OWNER of the printer has the Manage Documents access permission, allowing him limited rights to control the printer and the print queue.

If you are using only the standard Windows NT Server groups, these default permissions are probably just fine. If you have created custom groups, or if you need to control access to the printer more finely, use Add and Remove to specify which users and groups have access to the printer, and at what level.

Clicking Auditing displays the Printer Auditing dialog as shown in Figure 7-7. By default, printer auditing is disabled entirely. You can enable auditing of specified printing events for a particular user or group by using Add to add that user or group to the Name: pane and then marking one or more events. When a marked event occurs, an entry will be made to the audit log, and may be viewed using Event Viewer. Be careful about choosing who and what is to be audited, or your audit file may rapidly grow to an unmanageable size. In the example, I have chosen to enable auditing for all users, but only for the exceptional occurrence of a printing failure. In particular, be careful about enabling auditing for success of any event, which is, after all, the expected outcome.

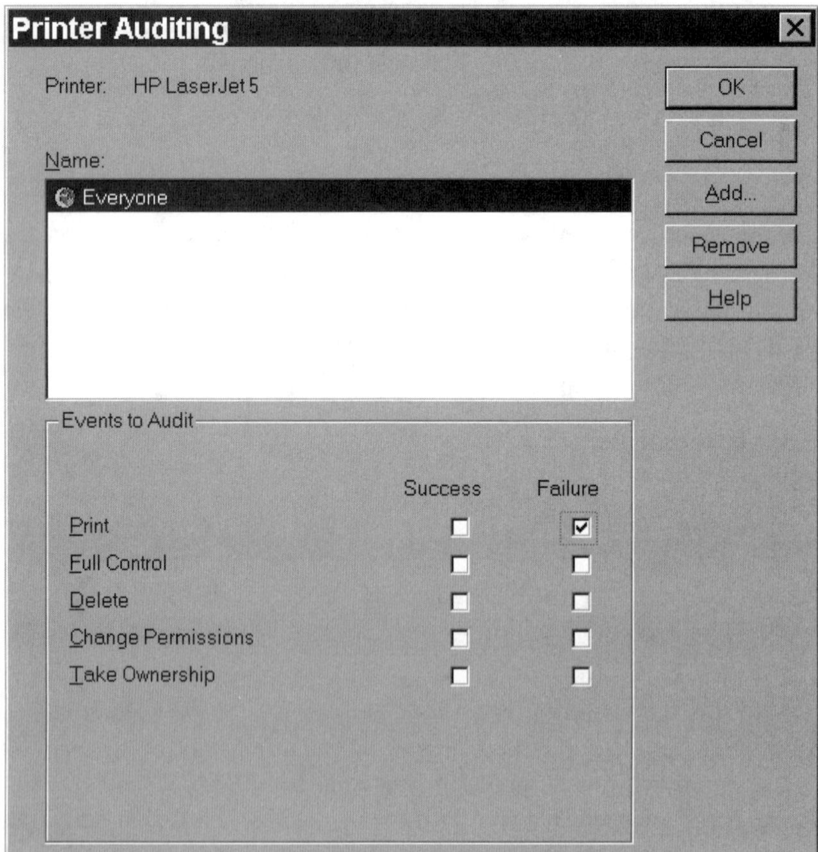

Figure 7-7. The Printer Auditing dialog allows you to specify, by user and group, which printing events will be recorded to the audit log

Clicking Ownership displays the Owner dialog. You can use this dialog to display the owner of the selected printer. As Administrator, you can also use this dialog if necessary to Take Ownership of a printer to override access controls which would otherwise prevent you from controlling the printer.

Setting device-specific properties

The Device Settings page, as shown in Figure 7-8 for a Hewlett-Packard LaserJet 5 printer, is specific to the individual print device installed. These settings characterize the properties of the physical printer, e.g., the amount of memory installed, the number and size of paper trays available, the number and type of font cartridges, etc. Note that, for any particular print device, the default values on this page are provided by the installed driver rather than by any interaction with the physical device itself. For example, for this printer, the driver assumes that the standard 2048 KB of memory is installed, but does not query the printer itself to determine its configuration.

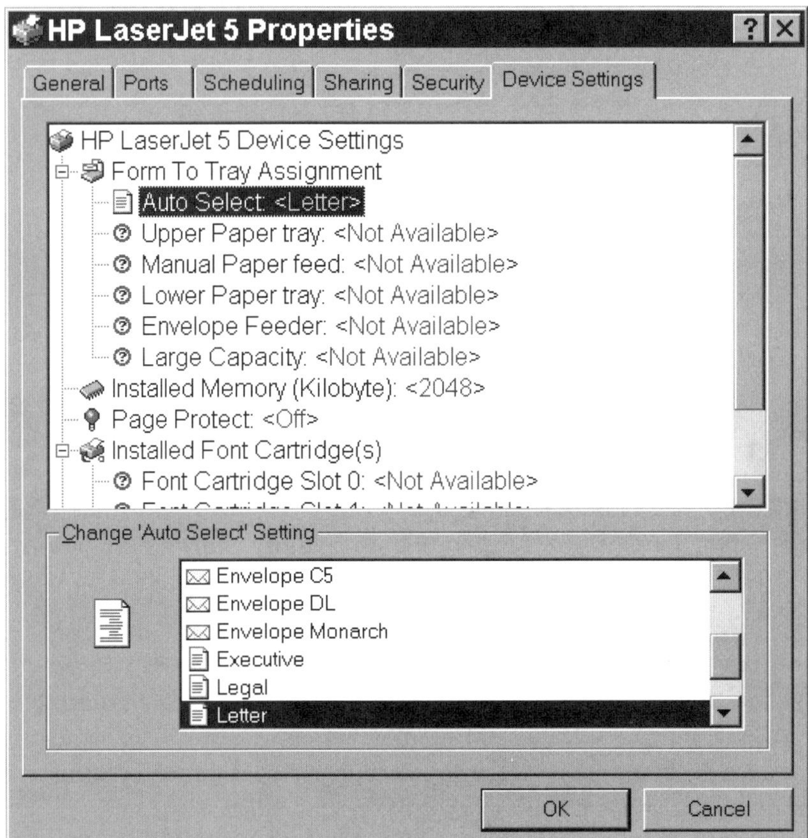

Figure 7-8. The Device Settings page of the <printername> Properties property sheet allows you to configure the physical properties of the print device

Configuring printer memory. Laser printers are the most common print devices used as network printers. Unlike dot matrix and ink jet printers, which print a single character at a time, laser printers are called page printers because they print an entire page as a single unit. This means that a laser printer must have at least enough memory to store all of the text, fonts, and graphics for the largest page that is to be printed.

In practice, a laser printer typically has more than this minimum amount of memory. A laser printer intended for use on a network usually has much more. For example, although Windows NT Server installed the LaserJet 5 with the default 2048 KB of memory, this particular printer actually has 8192 KB of memory installed. This additional memory can be used to buffer the remaining pages of the current print job, to buffer other pending print jobs, and sometimes to store downloaded soft fonts and standard forms on a semipermanent basis. Having adequate printer memory allows a network laser to perform much more efficiently. However, having that memory installed in the printer is not enough. Windows NT Server must know about the extra memory if it is to manage the printer effectively.

NOTE Nearly all laser printers allow you to determine the amount of memory and other options installed by simply printing a test page.

If the actual amount of memory installed in the printer is much more than the amount of memory that Windows NT Server thinks is present, Windows NT Server will act as though the printer is less capable than it actually is. For example, Windows NT Server might not download additional needed soft fonts to the printer because it believes that the printer has no room to store them. Instead, Windows NT Server will direct the printer to remove soft fonts that are not currently being used and to replace them with the soft fonts needed for the current job. It will then reload the original soft fonts when they are called for, removing other soft fonts that are temporarily unnecessary. This "churning" can reduce the efficiency of printing considerably.

Similarly, if the actual amount of memory installed in the printer is much less than the amount that Windows NT Server thinks is present, Windows NT Server will behave as though the printer had the additional memory. For example, it might attempt to download more soft fonts than the printer is capable of handling, causing the printer to dump some stored forms or to refuse temporarily to accept another print job so that it can make room for the additional fonts.

Using forms. Windows NT Server uses forms-based printing rather than tray-based printing. With forms-based printing, you define the type of form loaded in each paper tray. Users can then specify the type of form or forms to be used for their print jobs instead of specifying the particular tray.

For example, you might configure a printer to use letterhead form in the 100-page top tray, second sheet in the 250-page lower tray, inexpensive copy paper in the 2000-page bulk tray, and envelopes in the envelope feeder. A user who needs to print a draft job can then specify the "copy paper" form without knowing where that type of paper is physically located. Similarly, a user who needs to print a two-page business letter and envelope can specify a different form for each page of the document, automatically printing the first page on letterhead, the next on second sheet, and the final page on an envelope.

Each form definition includes the name of the form, its size, and the margins to be used when printing it. Windows NT Server installs default forms for your printer that correspond to various standard paper sizes and envelope types. You can also define custom forms that conform to the size and margin requirements of your letterhead and other forms particular to your business. Defining custom forms is described later in this chapter in the "Configuring Print Server Properties" section.

Using fonts. A font is a grouping of characters and symbols, called a character set, in various sizes and styles that all share the same type face. The type face is the overarching common factor that determines the font family. For example, Windows provides the *Times New Roman* serif face that corresponds closely with the standard copyrighted *Times Roman* face and the *Univers* face to correspond with the copyrighted Helvetica sans-serif face.

Within each face, a number of styles may be available. For example, any type face includes the Roman (or standard) style, the *italic* (or slanted) style, the **bold** style, and the ***bold italic*** style. Some type faces may include other styles, such as dark, extra bold, narrow, wide, and so on. For each face and style, characters are available in various sizes, which are measured in points, with a point being $1/72^{nd}$ of an inch. Discrete fonts are created in specific sizes, forcing you to choose one of the available sizes. For example, if a discrete font is available only in 6, 8, 10, 12, 14, and 18 point sizes and you really want to use 9 point, you're out of luck. You must pick either 8 or 10. Scaleable fonts, on the other hand, are created on the fly in any size specified. If you're using a scaleable font and what you need is a 13.5 point font, that's exactly what you can use.

Printer fonts are of two categories:

Raster fonts

These fonts, also called *bit-mapped fonts*, consist of a collection of individual bit maps, where each bit map corresponds to one particular character or symbol in one style, size, and orientation. Raster fonts are by their nature discrete fonts. They are, therefore, not scaleable, and cannot be rotated. This means, for example, that using a raster font to print a document in both portrait and landscape orientations requires two separate versions of the font.

Vector fonts

These fonts consist of a set of rules that can be used to draw any symbol included in the character set, in any size and in any supported style. For example, a Times-Roman vector font may include one rule that provides the information needed to create a capital A in the bold italic style. Using this rule, the processor can create a bold italic capital A in any size. Vector fonts often also include subsidiary rules, called hints, that are used to extend the basic rules to improve the rendering of very large or very small characters. Vector fonts are by their nature scaleable, and can be rotated to any angle. A single vector font can be used to print in both portrait and landscape orientations, and anything in between.

Windows print devices can use any of three types of fonts:

Device fonts

These fonts, also called hardware fonts, internal fonts, or printer fonts, are stored in the print device itself. They may be built into the printer ROM, or they may reside on plug-in font cartridges or cards. A particular printer may include both raster and vector device fonts. Device fonts have two advantages. First, because they are hardware-based, they are often faster and more efficient than alternative font types. Second, because they reside in ROM, they do not occupy printer RAM that might be used for other purposes.

Soft fonts

These fonts, also called downloadable fonts, are normally stored on the hard disk of the print server, although some high-end network printers include an internal hard drive devoted to storing soft fonts. Soft fonts can be installed from the Device Settings page of the printer property sheet. Soft fonts occupy printer memory that is often better used for other purposes. Most soft fonts are raster fonts, although some printers support the use of vector-based soft fonts designed for that particular printer.

In the past, soft fonts were a popular way to extend the capabilities of older generation printers that provided a very limited selection of device fonts. Nowadays, the advent of TrueType fonts and more capable printers has greatly reduced the need for soft fonts in most environments. Today, if used at all, soft fonts are usually limited to special purposes like generating IRS tax forms or printing specialized bar codes.

Screen fonts

These fonts are Windows NT fonts that can be used both to display characters on the screen and to print them on the print device. The advantage of using screen fonts is that, because the same font is used for both display and printing, what you see on your screen corresponds exactly with the printed output. This is particularly important if you are creating a newsletter, brochure, or similar item, where the unexpected line- and page-breaks that commonly occur with other types of fonts can wreck the entire layout. Screen fonts are available in raster, vector, and TrueType forms. Install screen fonts using the Fonts applet in Control Panel.

Setting document default properties

The preceding section discussed setting device-specific properties, those that correspond to the actual hardware of the print device. This section examines setting document defaults, those properties concerned with the document itself rather than with the hardware used to print it. For example, the location of a particular form is a device-specific property, while the form to be used to print a particular document is a property of that document. Device-specific properties, for example, may tell you that legal size paper is contained in the second tray; document properties specify that the document is to be printed on legal size paper.

Windows NT allows you to set document defaults for each printer. Like device-specific settings, document defaults are specific to a particular print device. These default values are used for all documents printed by that printer unless the properties of a specific document override those default values. Document properties associated with a particular document always override the default values set for the printer. A default property is used only if the document has no value set for that property.

To modify document defaults, highlight the printer name in the Printers folder, and choose Document Defaults from the File menu to display the Page Setup page of the <printername> Default Document Properties property sheet. Set the values for paper size, source, copy count, orientation, and duplexing to the most commonly used values for that printer. Use the Advanced page to set default values for printer specific document settings.

Configuring Print Server Properties

Server properties control the functioning of the local spooler and the available features of the print server to which the printer is connected. The server properties you set affect all printers supported by that server. You can use server properties to create custom forms that will be available to all printers, to modify port assignments, to specify location and error-logging for the spooler, and to set notification options.

To modify server properties, choose Server Properties from the File of the Printers folder. The Forms page of the Print Server Properties property sheet allows you to delete an existing form or to define a new form. To delete a form, simply highlight it in the Forms on <servername> pane and click Delete. To define a new form, first highlight an existing form and then mark the Create a New From check box. Enter a descriptive name for the new form in the Form Description for field. Specify the paper size and desired margins in the Measurement: section, and then click Save Form. The newly created form is immediately available to any of the printers supported by the print server.

The Ports page of the Print Server Properties property sheet allows you to add, delete, and configure ports. This page provides a subset of the control features available from the Ports page of the printer Property sheet, which was described in a preceding section. This page does not allow you to add printer devices to or remove them from a printer pool, nor does it allow you to change the physical port associated with a print device.

The Advanced page of the Print Server Properties property sheet allows you to specify the location of the spool folder, where spool files are written. It also allows you to specify the level of logging for the spooler and to determine whether or not Windows NT Server will notify you of errors and/or completion when remote documents are printed.

NOTE By default, Windows NT assigns the spool folder under the system root folder as *System32\spool\PRINTERS* and assigns the appropriate permissions to this folder. If you assign another folder located on an NTFS-formatted volume as the spool folder, make sure to assign the Change permission to anyone who needs to print using that server.

By default, all spooler events are logged to the system log, which can be viewed using Event Viewer. If you want to cut down on the number of entries made to the system log, clear the Log spooler information events check box, which causes routine spooler events to be written to the system log. Leaving the Log spooler warning events check box enabled causes nonroutine, potentially serious spooler events to be logged. Although you may clear this box, be aware that doing so eliminates the early warning that may allow you to prevent a failure of the print server. The Log spooler error events check box should never be cleared.

Managing Print Queues

With Windows NT Server, you manage both individual documents and the printer queue from the Printers folder.

To manage an individual document, double-click the printer name in the Printers folder to display the printer queue. Highlight the individual document to be managed, and use Document menu commands to control the document. When you are managing an individual document, you can:

- Pause printing the document
- Resume printing the document
- Restart printing the document from the beginning
- Cancel printing the document
- View and modify document Properties (Some of these document properties, e.g., the document priority, can be both viewed and modified; others, e.g., form name, orientation, and number of copies, can be viewed but not changed.)

To manage the printer itself, double-click the printer name in the Printers folder to display the printer queue. Use Printer menu commands to control the printer. When you are managing the printer queue you can:

- View a list of the documents queued up and awaiting printing
- Pause Printing all queued documents
- Resume Printing queued documents
- Purge Print Documents to cancel all print jobs on the printer

Managing Remote Printers

You can manage both local and remote printer servers for which you have the Full Control access permission from any workstation on the network that is running Windows NT 4.0 Server or Windows NT 4.0 Workstation. You can perform all of the same management functions on a remote printer server that you can on a local server, with one exception: to add, remove, or configure ports, you must be working on the local server. Clients running earlier versions of Windows NT can also manage remote printer servers, including those running

Windows NT 4.0, but are limited to viewing and controlling properties supported by the earlier version.

Any network client can check the status of a remote print server and manage any of his own documents that are queued on that server. A network client who has the Full Control access permission or the Manage Documents access permission for the remote print server can also manage documents owned by others. Managing the print queue on a remote print server requires the Full Control access permission for that server.

Sharing Printing Resources with Other Operating Systems

As this chapter illustrates, Windows NT Server provides extensive native printing support for Windows Networking clients. Windows NT Server also makes it easy for Windows Networking clients to use shared printing resources on other operating systems, and for clients on networks running other operating systems to use Windows NT Server shared printing resources. Your main interest in this area is likely to be sharing network printers between NetWare and Windows NT Server. However, it's so easy to provide printing interoperability between Windows NT Server and UNIX that you'll almost certainly want to do so if your network includes one or more UNIX hosts.

NetWare Printing Considerations

In an earlier section, I used a NetWare print queue as an example of how to set up a network printer server. Let's take a more detailed look at some of the options that allow NetWare clients to print to Windows NT Server printers and *vice versa.*

- The first key factor required to support bidirectional server-based printing interoperability between NetWare and Windows NT Server is that the two servers must share a common transport protocol. Given the dependence of NetWare on IPX/SPX transport, the easy answer is to install the NWLink IPX/SPX Compatible Transport on the server running Windows NT Server. This is not absolutely required. You can, for example, instead install dual protocol stacks and client software for both networks on all of the workstations, but it's much easier and cleaner to allow the servers to handle gateway duties.
- To allow Microsoft Networking clients to print to NetWare printers without first installing client software for NetWare on those clients, install the Microsoft Gateway Service for NetWare (GSNW) on the server running Windows NT Server. GSNW allows Microsoft Networking clients to access shared

NetWare resources as though they were shared resources available locally on the Windows NT Server. The remote printer server example earlier in the chapter used GSNW to allow a NetWare print queue to be installed as a printer on a print server running Windows NT Server. GSNW is bundled with Windows NT Server.

- To allow NetWare clients to print to Windows NT Server printers, install the File and Print Services for NetWare (FPNW) component of the optional package Microsoft Services for NetWare, described later in this book. Using this inexpensive optional software allows NetWare clients to see a Microsoft print server as a NetWare print queue, and to print transparently to it. It also allows NetWare clients to use shared Windows NT Server disk resources, and Windows Networking clients to access shared disk and printer resources on the NetWare server. Although the later items duplicate services provided by GSNW to some extent, FPNW provides much higher performance than GSNW. If you operate in a mixed Windows NT Server and NetWare environment, the smartest thing you'll ever do is spend $149 on Microsoft Services for NetWare.

TCP/IP and UNIX Printing Considerations

In shops that run both UNIX hosts and PC network operating systems like NetWare and Windows NT Server, there is often a great deal of printer envy on both sides of the aisle. The guys in engineering running UNIX workstations may have a $10,000 line printer and a $50,000 E-size plotter that the PC folks would love to get their hands on. Likewise, the PC folks may have a fast network laser, a thermal transfer color printer and a film output recorder that the UNIX guys would love to use. In the past, both groups often remained envious, because it was just too difficult and support-intensive to gateway printing services between the operating systems. Fortunately, Windows NT Server provides all the tools you need to bridge the gap without difficulty.

On the PC side, it requires only minimal effort to enable any network client that is capable of connecting to a server running Windows NT Server to print to network connected TCP/IP print devices and to printers physically connected to most UNIX boxes. TCP/IP printing support can be installed on a single server, which then gateways TCP/IP printing services.

Clients need not have special client software installed, and indeed do not need to be running TCP/IP transport. Clients can connect to the server running Windows NT Server using any supported transport protocol and client software, and submit documents to the print server. The print server submits the documents to the

TCP/IP print device. TCP/IP printers provided by the Windows NT Server machine appear to clients as would any other shared print resource.

The Windows NT Server machine providing these gateway services must have both the TCP/IP Protocol and the Microsoft TCP/IP Printing Service installed. To install either or both of these elements, double-click the Network applet in Control Panel. Install the TCP/IP Protocol from the Protocols page and the Microsoft TCP/IP Printing Service from the Services page. Installing and configuring protocols and services are fully described in Chapter 3.

From the opposite direction, to allow UNIX clients to print to Windows NT printers, you need only enable the TCP/IP Print Server component of the Microsoft TCP/IP Printing Service that is installed automatically with the service. In UNIX, a line printer daemon (*lpd*) runs as a process on the UNIX host, providing services similar to those provided by a NetWare print queue. In case you were wondering, a UNIX daemon is simply a background process that is not owned by any user. It is conceptually similar to an NLM in NetWare or to a system service in Windows NT Server. Daemons are used by UNIX to provide system services, including those required for printing. The UNIX line printer daemon is almost always named simply *lpd*. UNIX workstations that need to print to a UNIX *lpd* run a line printer remote (*lpr*) program to access the *lpd* running on the UNIX host. This *lpr* program is almost always called simply *lpr*.

The Microsoft TCP/IP Printing service provides both *lpd* and *lpr*. This offers a twofold benefit. First, Microsoft Networking clients that do not have an *lpr* client installed locally can print directly to a Windows NT Server print server, which then uses the *lpr* component of Microsoft TCP/IP Printing to communicate with the *lpd* running on the UNIX host. Second, the *lpd* component of the Microsoft TCP/IP Printing service appears to UNIX clients as just another *lpd*, allowing those clients to print directly to the Windows NT Server print server.

Installing an lpr printer

To install support to allow Microsoft Networking clients to print to UNIX printers from a print server running Windows NT Server, first make sure that you have installed the Microsoft TCP/IP Printing service mentioned above. Once you have done so, proceed as follows:

From the Printers folder, double-click the Add Printer icon to invoke the Add Printer Wizard. Accept the default My Computer option button to specify that the printer will be managed by Windows NT Server, and click Next to continue. In the second screen, click Add Port to display the Printer Ports dialog.

Highlight the entry for LPR Port and click New Port to display the Add LPR compatible printer dialog. If LPR Port does not appear as a choice, you have not installed the Microsoft TCP/IP Printing Service. Enter the name or the IP address in dotted decimal format of the UNIX print device which will provide lpd services. The UNIX print device may be a physical printer attached to the UNIX host, or it may be a direct-connect network printer, i.e., a printer that contains its own internal network interface card. If the latter, the direct connect printer interface must support *lpr/lpd*, and not all do.

Next, enter the name of the printer or print queue on the UNIX host to which print jobs are to be delivered. Click OK to install the LPR port and return to the Printer Ports dialog. Click Close to return to the Add Printer Wizard, which now displays the new port as available, in this case as *kiwi.ttgnet.com:lj*. Specify the manufacturer and model of the printer and provide a share name as described in the earlier section on adding printers. When you finish the Add Printer Wizard, the UNIX printer is browsable by Windows Networking clients, and may be printed to just as any other printer supported by the print server.

NOTE Microsoft provides a third component with the Microsoft TCP/IP Printing service. *LPQ.EXE* is a command-line only line printer query (*lpq*) utility. You can use it to check the queue status of a remote host running *lpd*. To do so, at the Windows NT command prompt, type:

```
LPQ -Sserver -Pprinter [-l]
```

where server is the name or IP address of the server providing *lpd* services, and printer is the name of the print queue on that server. The *-l* argument provides verbose output.

Enabling lpd on the print server

Configuring Windows NT Server to accept incoming TCP/IP print jobs from UNIX hosts or other systems running *lpr* is straightforward. The required *lpd* functionality is installed as the TCP/IP Print Server service when you install the TCP/IP Printing Service. To enable *lpr* clients to print to Windows NT printers, double-click the Services applet from Control Panel to display the Services dialog as shown in Figure 7-9.

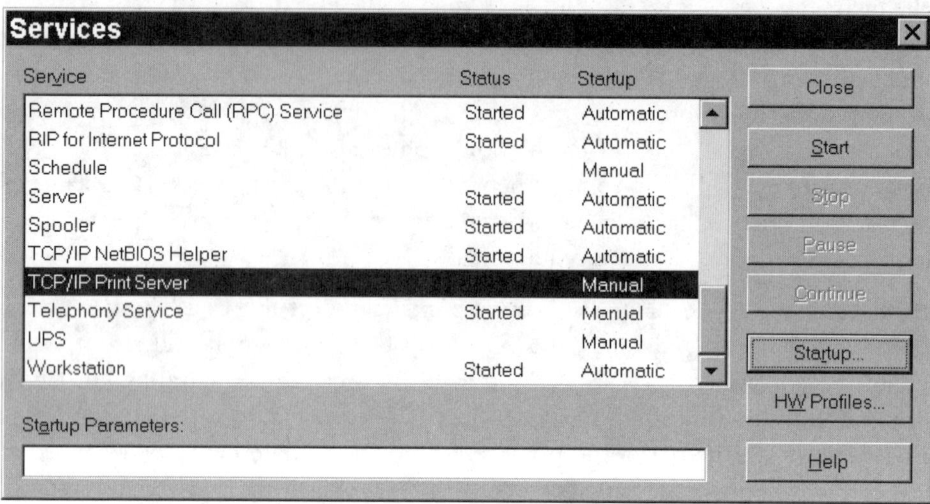

Figure 7-9. The TCP/IP Print Server service provides lpd services to remote lpr clients

By default, Microsoft leaves the TCP/IP Print Server service disabled by configuring it for manual startup. To start the service manually, highlight TCP/IP Print Server and click Start. If you want to start this service each time the server is booted, highlight TCP/IP Print Server and click Startup to display the Service dialog as shown in Figure 7-10. In the Startup Type section, choose the Automatic option button.

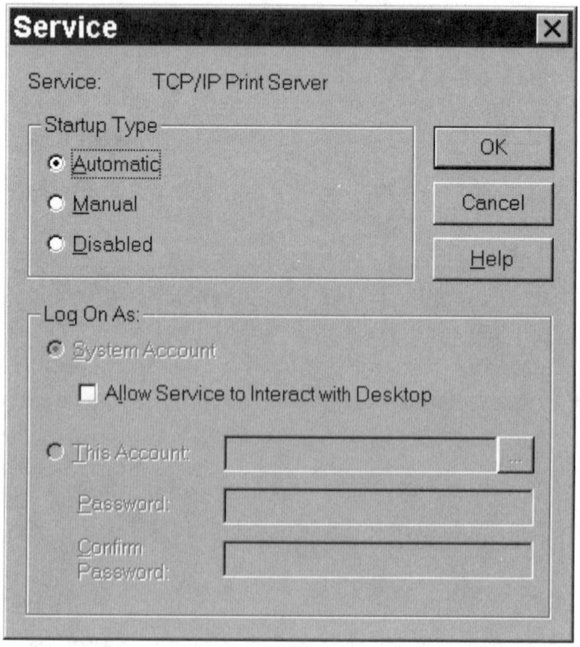

Figure 7-10. The Service dialog allows you to configure startup for the TCP/IP Print Server service

---

WARNING You cannot configure the TCP/IP Print Server service by individual printer. This service must log on using the built-in system account, and cannot be configured to use another account. The *lpd* service allows multiple printers to be addressed, and it directs print jobs to print devices using the printer name (as opposed to the share name for the printer). This means that, because the Spooler service also logs on as the system account, by default any *lpr* client can print to any printer visible to the server running the TCP/IP Print Server service. That is, any printer defined on that server as a Windows NT Printer, whether or not it is shared, can be printed to by any *lpr* client.

8

Backing Up Windows NT Server

In this chapter:
- *Choosing and Installing Backup Hardware*
- *Choosing Backup Software*
- *Developing and Implementing a Network Backup Plan*

Backing up is a lot like writing a check to pay for the fire insurance on your house. You'd just as soon not do it, but you do it anyway. The risk of not doing it is too horrible to contemplate. You write those checks and do those backups to protect yourself against something that may never happen. You willingly undergo frequent small pains to protect yourself against a catastrophic event like a house fire or a server crash. Just as you don't feel cheated if your house doesn't burn down, you shouldn't feel cheated if you never have to do a full restore.

Establishing and following a good backup policy serves four purposes:

- It guards against the wholesale loss of data that may occur when a hard drive fails. One of the most common reasons for small- and medium-size business failures is catastrophic data loss. A business that loses its customer lists and accounts receivable records and cannot reconstruct them isn't likely to stay in business for long.
- It allows you to keep a duplicate copy of your data stored off-site to protect against fires and other natural disasters. Even the best backup procedures won't protect you if all of your backup tapes go up in flames alongside your server.
- It provides a way to retrieve files that are accidentally (or maliciously) deleted. Users, and sometimes even administrators, may delete the wrong file or overwrite the new version with an old one. Having recent backups allows you to minimize the amount of work that must be redone. This is a particularly important issue with Windows NT Server, which, unlike NetWare, makes no provision for salvaging deleted files. With Windows NT Server running on NTFS partitions, once you delete a file, it's gone for good.

- It enables you to archive data for legal or tax reasons. Increasingly complex tax codes and the explosion of litigation often makes it essential to be able to reconstruct data from months or years past. Archiving a backup tape periodically allows you to do so.

Interestingly, many administrators of my acquaintance seem to be less concerned about backing up today than they were several years ago. Certainly, they still acknowledge verbally the importance of having good backups, but their actions speak louder than their words. Administrators who formerly did complete backups every night and a "snapshot" backup every day at lunch now make do with weekly complete backups and a daily partial backup. One administrator I know goes months between backups. The wonder is that he's still employed. There are some reasonable arguments for this growing laxity.

Hard drives are much more reliable nowadays, with some drives now listing a Mean Time Between Failures (MTBF) of 200,000 hours or more. Although that doesn't mean that your hard drive will really last 22 years, it's still an order-of-magnitude improvement in reliability over drives sold just a few years ago. The advent of RAID, and its increasingly common use in PC servers, means that even a catastrophic disk failure often causes no loss of data. Every month, it seems, larger hard drives are offered at lower prices. Server disk farms grow steadily larger, and the time available for backing them up shrinks. The storage capacity of mainstream tape drives hasn't been keeping up with the growth in hard disk capacity, making it more difficult to fit a complete backup in to the company schedule. All of these factors contribute to the increasing trend among administrators to depend more on the redundancy and reliability of their hardware and less on keeping a good set of backups.

This is a very short-sighted approach. Reliable disks with MTBFs of 20 years are great, but anyone who believes that a 200,000-hour MTBF means that his disk will last 20 years doesn't understand Poisson distributions. RAID is a wonderful technology, and you should have it on your server. RAID, however, protects only against disk crashes. It does nothing to secure your data against natural disasters, to help you retrieve an accidentally deleted file, or to archive data for historical purposes.

To protect your server against these things, you need good backups. There's no way around it. Any network that does not have a standardized backup procedure in place is an accident waiting to happen. Good backups don't just happen. You have to establish and follow a backup system that incorporates the proper hardware, the proper software, and the proper procedures. This chapter examines each of these three elements.

Choosing and Installing Backup Hardware

The first element needed to build a backup system for your network is suitable backup hardware. Traditionally, for most networks, this has meant some form of tape drive. Although alternatives to tape drives like recordable CD-ROM drives and magneto-optical drives are beginning to make some inroads, particularly for specialized needs, you will most likely find that one or another form of tape drive is most appropriate for your general backup needs.

If you're currently using a tape drive that was purchased more than a year or two ago, you might be surprised by what's out there now. In this section, I examine the particulars of tape drives based on three different technologies. One of them will almost certainly suit your requirements and your budget.

NOTE Tape drive manufacturers have fallen into the habit of exaggerating the capacities of their drives by a factor of two, by assuming that the data you are backing up can be compressed to one half its normal size, either by the backup software or by the drive hardware itself. This assumption may prove valid for an "average" volume with a normal mix of program, data, and compressed files. However, many volumes are far from normal in compressibility. A volume dedicated to images or other files that are stored in precompressed form may yield compression ratios of 1.1:1 or less, as may a volume that uses Windows NT Server's native compression feature. A volume that contains only spreadsheets, documents, and databases may compress by a factor of 3:1 or more. To avoid confusion, throughout this section, I use the native (or uncompressed) capacity when referring to the storage capacity of a tape drive.

Quarter Inch Cartridge (QIC) Tape Drives

Until recently, conventional wisdom held that QIC tape drives were suited only for backing up workstations. This was true for three reasons. First, QIC tape drives had native capacities ranging from about 100 MB to perhaps 1 GB, inadequate for all but the smallest servers. Second, QIC tape drives ran only on the floppy disk controller, limiting throughput to about 3 MB per minute, again inadequate for most servers. Third, unlike more expensive drives, QIC tape drives used a single head to both read and write data, requiring two separate passes for doing both a backup and a compare.

The advent of Travan technology and the availability of QIC tape drives that use ATAPI and SCSI interfaces has removed the first two of these objections. In particular, the latest Travan specification, called TR-4 or QIC-3095, allows native capacities of up to 4 GB per tape, which is competitive with the traditional helical scan drives described in the next section. Enhanced versions of Travan drives expected in 1997 will increase native storage capacity to 8 GB or more, making them suitable, at least in terms of storage capacity, for all but the largest servers. Several manufacturers are now shipping TR-4 drives that use SCSI interfaces, and at least one manufacturer (Seagate/Conner) is shipping a TR-4 drive that uses an ATAPI (IDE) interface. Either of these interfaces boosts QIC throughput by an order of magnitude, to something on the close order of 30 MB per minute native and 60 MB per minute compressed.

The upside to Travan drives is their low cost. The street price of Travan TR-4 tape drives as this is written is about $350, whereas a helical scan drive with comparable speed and capacity costs from $800 to $1,500. For very small servers configured with IDE disk drives rather than SCSI, the availability of ATAPI interface Travan TR-4 drives means that, for such servers, you can avoid introducing the added complexity and cost of SCSI just to support your tape drive. This increases the cost advantage of Travan further still.

Another, more subtle, cost issue is the matter of spare tape drives. No production server should depend on just one tape drive. If you have only one tape drive, Murphy's Law makes it likely that that tape drive will fail just when you most need it, usually when you're about to restore a tape to recreate a crashed disk drive. Having a spare tape drive installed and ready can make the difference between having your server back up and running quickly and having it down for an extended period.

One related and often overlooked factor in this equation is the issue of the compatibility of your tapes with multiple tape drives. Even if your tape drives are the same make and model, one tape drive may not read tapes written by the other. Helical scan tape drives are particularly subject to this problem, and, unlike that other helical scan device (the VCR), have no "tracking" knob to allow you to adjust for minor differences in head orientation between devices. Travan tape drives, as serpentine scan devices, are much less subject to such difficulties. A Travan tape written by any Travan tape drive should be readable on any other Travan tape drive of the same or higher level.

WARNING Although serpentine drives are normally less subject to interoperability problems between similar drives, this may turn out not to be the case with TR–4 drives. Several friends and I bought Seagate TapeStor 8000 IDE interface TR–4 drives in the spring of 1997. We gradually discovered that none of us were able to restore a tape made on another of these drives to our own drives.

When I contacted Seagate tape support about this problem, they responded that Seagate did not guarantee that tapes made on one Seagate TR–4 drive could be restored to a different Seagate TR–4 drive because of minor variations in head alignment between drives. This is surprising in light of the fact that TR–4 drives use preformatted tapes, which should minimize or eliminate alignment problems.

At this point, the issue is still up in the air. Clearly, it is unacceptable to depend on a tape drive whose tapes cannot be restored to a different drive. A drive can fail, or the server can be stolen or destroyed with the drive still in it. It would be nice to be able to restore surviving tapes on a different drive. On the other hand, our sample is small enough that the problems may be due to the individual drives themselves, or to the media we are using.

If you intend to depend on TR–4 drives to back up your server, it's worthwhile to verify that the tapes you write on your main drive can be read by your spare drive (and *vice versa*).

The downside to Travan drives is that you may end up spending enough extra on Travan tapes to offset the lower cost of the Travan drives themselves. While 8mm and DAT tapes can be purchased at street prices ranging from under $10 to perhaps $20, the street price of TR-4 tapes is closer to $40. If you use the common Grandfather-Father-Son tape rotation method that requires 21 tapes, you might spend more than $800 per set on Travan tapes. Using the same rotation method, DAT or 8mm tapes might cost from $150 to about $400.

The reason for this cost disparity in tapes is twofold. First, Travan is a patented proprietary technology, and Travan tapes are available only from the holders of those patents and their licensees. Second, and probably more important, is the fact that, unlike DDS and 8mm technology, QIC depends on the tape cartridge itself rather than the tape drive to maintain tape alignment. DDS and 8mm tape drives are expensive partially because they must be built to close tolerances to keep the tape aligned, but they can in turn use inexpensive tape cartridges with loose tolerances. On the other hand, QIC tape cartridges in general, and Travan cartridges in particular, must be built with extreme rigidity and fine tolerances to accommodate the lower tolerances of inexpensive QIC drives.

Give serious consideration to a Travan TR-4 drive if you can back up your server to a single tape, now and for the foreseeable future. If, instead, a complete backup will require multiple tapes, the additional cost of Travan tapes rapidly makes the use of Travan economically unattractive. The cost issue is really moot, however, because if the cost of Travan tapes is the deciding factor, you shouldn't be using Travan in the first place. You, instead, need to use a technology like 8mm or DLT that offers larger native capacity, faster throughput, and single pass backup/compare.

When Travan TR-4 drives began shipping in volume in late 1996, the drives shown in Table 8-1 were available.

Table 8-1. Travan TR-4 Tape Drives Shipping as of 9/97

Manufacturer	Model	Part Number	Interface	Street Price
Exabyte	Eagle TR-4I	604004-000	ATAPI/IDE	$350
IBM	TR-4	3502900	SCSI-2	$850
Seagate (Conner)	TapeStor 8000 (internal)	CTT-8000I	ATAPI/IDE	$350
Seagate (Conner)	TapeStor 8000 (internal)	CTT-8000S	SCSI/SCSI-2	$350
Seagate (Conner)	TapeStor 8000 (external)	CTT-8000E	SCSI/SCSI-2	$450

Since then, most of the major tape drive manufacturers have introduced Travan TR-4 drives, including Hewlett-Packard/Colorado and Wangtek. The only IDE interface TR-4 drives that I was able to locate were those made by Seagate and Exabyte/Eagle. The other manufacturers supply only SCSI versions. Interestingly, the price of TR-4 drives has remained relatively stable over the last several months. For the latest information about Travan TR-4 drives, check the manufacturers' web sites, five of which are shown here.

Name	URL
Colorado Memory Systems	*http://www.hp.com/cms/index.htm*
Core (Aiwa)	*http://www.aiwa.com/Qictape.htm*
IBM Storage Systems	*http://www.pc.ibm.com/options/#stor*
Exabyte	*http://www.exabyte.com/home/products.html*
Seagate/Conner	*http://www.conner.com/tape/prodmatrix.shtml*

Helical Scan Tape Drives

Helical scan tape drives are what immediately comes to mind when most people think about backing up a server, although perhaps not by that name. Chances are you're using one right now, in the form of 4mm DAT or 8mm, to back-up your NetWare server.

Serpentine scan tape drives (like QIC drives) record the first track from the beginning of the tape to the end of it, as shown in Figure 8-1. They then reverse and write the second track from the end of the tape to its beginning. This process continues until the backup is complete or the tape is full. Helical scan drives instead run the tape past a write head that rotates rapidly at an angle relative to the direction of the tape movement, as shown in Figure 8-2. If you could see them, the resulting tracks would appear as diagonal lines running from one edge of the tape to the other. In theory, a helical scan tape is filled by a single pass from the beginning of the tape to its end, and then rewound once. In practice, a full backup and compare operation with a helical scan tape drive may require as many as six passes, depending on the drive itself and your backup software. A serpentine scan tape, on the other hand, may make 60 or more passes through the drive before it is finally filled.

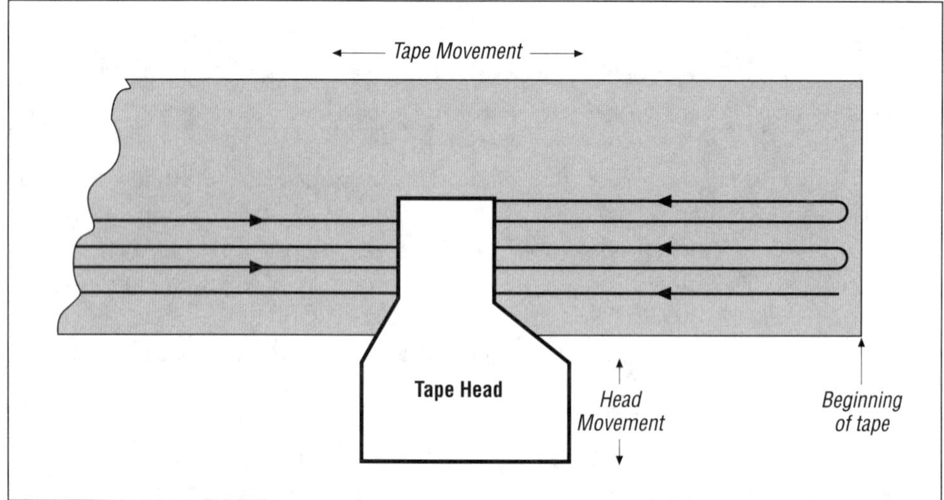

Figure 8-1. Serpentine recording uses relatively few tracks running the length of the tape

Helical scan tapes, like VCR tapes, do not need to be formatted before use. Serpentine tapes must be formatted before use, to lay down the tracks to which data will be written. Formatting a tape may take two hours or more, depending on your drive and the tape format. Tapes for most serpentine recording formats are available preformatted. It is well worth paying the extra charge, typically only a dollar or two, to save yourself the time and effort needed to format the tape. Some serpentine tape formats, e.g., TR-4, are available only in preformatted form.

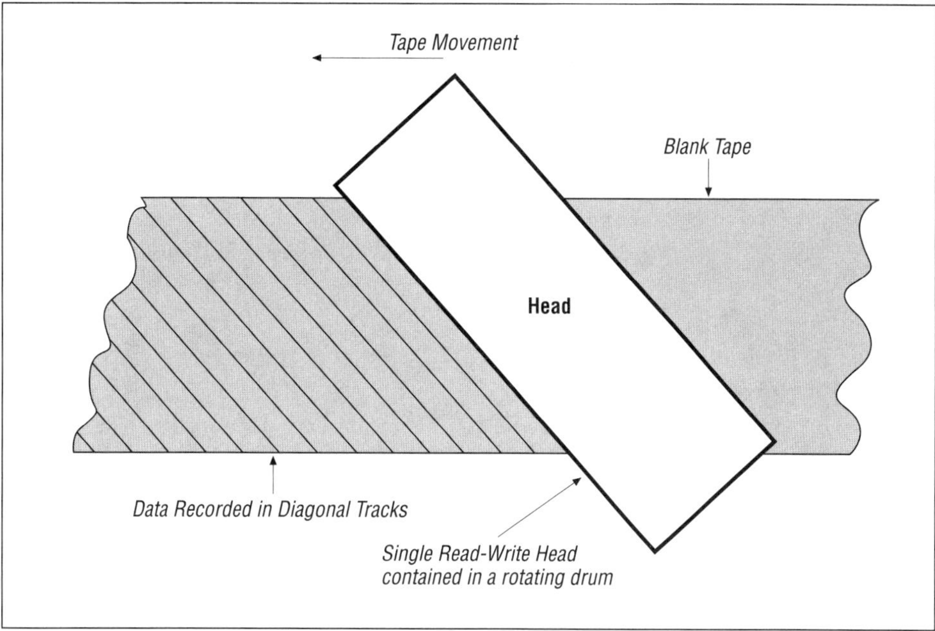

Figure 8-2. Helical scan recording uses many tracks running diagonally across the tape

---

TIP In particular if your tapes must be formatted before use, make sure to always have at least one blank, formatted tape on hand whenever you begin a backup. One of my friends ignored this advice recently, to his great regret. He'd been backing up one drive successfully to a single tape, but on this occasion, the software prompted for a second tape. He had a stack of blank but unformatted tapes available, but didn't want to wait the additional two hours that would be needed to format the tape before the backup continued.

Instead, he chose a tape from an existing backup set for another drive and overwrote it, intending to recreate that backup set soon thereafter. Of course, the backup set from which that tape had been removed was the only backup set for a drive that failed shortly thereafter, before he'd had a chance to back it up again. Locking the barn door after the horse had been stolen, he ran out and bought both a better tape drive and another disk drive to mirror the original drive. His data was still gone.

Helical scan drives have many advantages. They are a mature technology based on open standards. They are reasonably inexpensive, fast, reliable, and use inexpensive and readily available media. Until recently, helical scan drives were used almost universally for server backup. Today, these drives are increasingly under siege on the low end by Travan QIC drives and on the high end by Digital Linear Tape and other emerging technologies.

Helical scan tapes come in two broad varieties. Some drives use nominal 4mm tapes, actually measuring 3.81mm, that are based on media derived from that specified by the Digital Audio Tape (DAT) standard. Although more properly referred to as DDS drives, these 4mm drives are nearly always simply called DAT drives. Other tape drives use 8mm tapes derived from the Sony 8mm videotape standard. These drives are also commonly (and incorrectly) called DAT drives.

DDS tape drives

DDS tapes drives, more commonly called 4mm or DAT drives, are based on work done jointly by Sony and Hewlett-Packard to develop a data storage standard for drives and media based on the Sony DAT audio standard. DDS drives from participating manufacturers are certified by Hewlett-Packard to ensure compliance with the DDS formatting and data interchange standards. DDS tapes are similarly certified by Sony for compliance.

The original DDS specification, properly called simply DDS but often referred to as DDS-1, was adopted in 1989 and described a format that stored 1.3 GB on a 60 meter tape, with throughput of 183 KBps. The 1991 DDS-DC specification expanded capacity to 2 GB on a 90 meter tape, again at 183 KBps. The DDS-2 specification, released in 1993, increased the native storage capacity to 4 GB on a 120 meter MP+ tape, and also doubled the data transfer rate to 360 KBps. As this is being written in mid-1997, DDS-2 drives are the most capable DDS drives that are readily purchasable. The DDS-3 specification, developed in 1992 and adopted in late 1994, was originally intended to double capacity once again, to 8 GB native, but was subsequently extended to provide 12 GB native capacity on 125 meter MP++ media, with the data transfer rate again doubled to 720 KBps.

Although DDS-3 drives were originally to be available in late 1995 or very early 1996, and in fact Hewlett-Packard announced such a drive at that time, DDS-3 drives just began to ship in early 1997. Hewlett-Packard announced the availability of their C1537A DDS-3 tape drive in November, 1996. This drive had not appeared on the Hewlett-Packard web page by mid-December, and the vendors I contacted were unable to take firm orders or provide delivery dates. It appears, however, that the logjam is about to break, and DDS-3 drives should be available in quantity by the time you read this. The follow-on DDS-4 specification is scheduled for 1998, and will extend native capacity to 24 GB, using 180 meter tapes based on the so-called ME media. These drives will provide throughput of at least 1 MBps.

DDS tapes are inexpensive because the drives themselves take care of aligning the media, allowing the DDS tape cartridge to be relatively flimsy and to use low tolerances. Competing tape technologies instead depend on the tape cartridge to manage alignment, requiring that that cartridge be rigid, have very fine tolerances, and accordingly be expensive to manufacture. Name brand DDS-1 2 GB tapes are typically available at street prices under $10, with DDS-2 4 GB tapes running perhaps $15 each. DDS-3 12 GB tapes are available now from Hewlett-Packard at a list price of $26 each, although street prices are actually a bit higher.

You should replace DDS tapes fairly frequently. Most DDS tapes are rated for approximately 2,000 passes through the tape drive. Depending on the backup software you use and other factors, one backup operation may require six passes through the drive, so a tape cartridge should theoretically be discarded after 333 insertions. Because DDS tape cartridges are so inexpensive, many LAN administrators arbitrarily limit a tape to 100 insertions, and so, for example, erase and then discard a tape that has been used once a week after two years of use.

WARNING DDS tapes are manufactured to higher standards than are audio DAT tapes. You might be tempted to try to use an audio DAT tape in your DDS drive. Although an audio DAT tape will physically fit the DDS drive, it cannot be used reliably to store data. Most DDS drives will attempt to read an audio DAT tape, but will refuse to write to it. Some DDS drives will write to an audio DAT tape, apparently successfully. However, there is no guarantee that the stored data will subsequently be readable. DDS tapes intended for recording data are very inexpensive. Keep a good supply on hand.

The DDS drives themselves are considerably more expensive than the Travan QIC drives described in the preceding section, and less expensive than 8mm drives with similar capacity and performance. A name brand DDS-1 2 GB internal tape drive is typically street priced at $700, with similar DDS-2 4 GB drives costing perhaps $200 more. DDS-3 12 GB drives, when they finally become available, will likely fetch premium prices of $2,000 or more. DDS jukeboxes, also called autoloaders or tape libraries, are also available. These devices typically hold from six to eighteen DDS-2 tape cartridges, providing 24 GB to 72 GB of native storage. Their street prices range from about $2,500 to $7,000.

NOTE For the most up-to-date information about DDS, including technical papers, a list of certified drives, manufacturer contact information, and so forth, set your web browser to the Digital Data Storage Manufacturers' Group site at *http://dds-tape.com/*.

8mm tape drives

Exabyte pioneered the 8mm tape drive, basing it upon the Sony 8mm videotape standard. Although other manufacturers OEM Exabyte tape drive mechanisms and relabel the resulting drives with their own names, Exabyte remains the only mainstream 8mm tape drive manufacturer. Although many network administrators remain leery of this single-source aspect of 8mm drives, Exabyte has sold more than 1 million such drives.

Among network administrators of my acquaintance, the dialog between those in the Exabyte/8mm camp and those in the DDS camp has assumed almost the proportions of a religious debate. Both sides denigrate the reliability and performance of the hardware used by the opposing group. The reality is that both 8mm and DDS are good technologies. Because DDS reached at least a temporary plateau when DDS-2 drives first shipped, some DDS advocates have been forced to adopt 8mm for performance and capacity reasons. The imminent arrival of DDS-3 tape drives and autoloaders will doubtless reinvigorate this debate.

Exabyte manufactures a variety of 8mm tape drives and autoloaders, which differ widely in capacity, performance, features, and price (see Table 8-2). All Exabyte 8mm tape drives use the SCSI interface. At the lowend, the EXB-8700LT tape drive provides capacities and transfer rates comparable to Travan TR-4 drives, but at a street price nearly three times higher, or about $950. At the high end for individual tape drives, the Exabyte EXB-8900 Mammoth provides native tape capacities of 20 GB and throughput of 180 MB/min, allowing you to back up a 10 GB hard drive in one hour. At the very high end, the Exabyte EXB-480 Tape Library runs four Mammoth tape drives in tandem, providing 1.6 TB native capacities and throughput close to 1 GB per minute, allowing you to back up a 40+ GB disk farm in one hour.

Table 8-2. Representative Exabyte 8mm Tape Drives and Libraries as of 9/97

Model	Native/ Compressed Capacity (GB)	Native/ Compressed Transfer Rate (MB/min)	Number and Type of Drives	Tape(s)	Street Price
EXB-8700LT	5/10	30/60	-	1 x 112m	$950
EXB-8205XL	3.5/7	16/32	-	1 x 160m	$1,300
EXB-8700	7/14	30/60	-	1 x 160m	$1,200
EXB-8505XL	7/14	30/60	-	1 x 160m	$2,000
EXB-8900	20/40	180/360	-	1 x 170m	$4,300
EXB-10h Library	70/140	30/60	1 x EXB-8505XL	10 x 160m	$4,300
EXB-210 Library	200/400	180/360	1 x EXB-8900	10 x 170m	$8,500

Table 8-2. Representative Exabyte 8mm Tape Drives and Libraries as of 9/97 (continued)

Model	Native/ Compressed Capacity (GB)	Native/ Compressed Transfer Rate (MB/min)	Number and Type of Drives	Tape(s)	Street Price
EXB-220 Library	400/800	360/720	2 x EXB-8900	20 x 170m	> $18,000
EXB-440 Library	800/1,600	720/1,440	4 x EXB-8900	40 x 170m	> $30,000
EXB-480 Library	1,600/3,200	720/1,440	4 x EXB-8900	80 x 170m	> $50,000

Exabyte has had the 8mm market pretty much to itself since the mid-1980s. This is about to change. Sony recently announced a competing 8mm standard. The Sony SDX-300 tape drive uses the same Advanced Metal Evaporated (AME) media used by the Exabyte Mammoth drives to provide a 25 GB native capacity. The SDX-300c tape drive uses compression to achieve 50 GB per AME cartridge. These Sony drives are positioned to compete in both capacity and performance with the high-end Exabyte drives and the Quantum DLT drives. As of September, 1997, the Sony SDX-300 drives are shipping at a street price of around $4,500.

NOTE For up-to-date information about Exabyte 8mm tape drives and libraries, set your web browser to *http://www.exabyte.com/home/products.html*.

If you're interested in the Sony SDX-300 tape drives as an alternative to the Exabyte 8mm drives, set your web browser to *http://www.sel.sony.com/SEL*.

Digital Linear Tape Drives

Digital Linear Tape drives are the Rolls-Royce® of tape drives in terms of capacity, performance, reliability, and, unfortunately, price. Digital Linear Tape drives support native storage capacities as high as 35 GB per tape, offer sustained transfer rates of 5 MB/sec (10 MB/sec burst), have rated tape lives of 500,000 passes, and cost as much as a decent used car.

You don't buy a Digital Linear Tape drive just because you want to spend a lot of money, however. You buy one because it is the only realistic way to back up huge amounts of data in a short period of time. If, for example, you need to back up a 25 GB disk farm overnight, Digital Linear Tape provides both the tape capacity and the performance to get the job done within the allotted time.

NOTE Before you buy a Digital Linear Tape drive, make sure that the cost of the tapes needed to feed it won't be a stumbling block. Some administrators have been shocked to find that tapes run $100 apiece or so. Granted, most systems can be backed up to a single tape, but if your tape rotation plan requires many tapes or frequent archiving, you can easily find yourself spending much more on tapes than you did on the drive itself.

Digital Linear Tape technology was originally developed and implemented by Digital Equipment Corporation as a reliable high-capacity, high-performance backup solution for its large systems. Digital Linear Tape has since developed as an open standard, based on specifications from ANSI, ISO, ECMA, and other standards bodies. Digital Linear Tape drives are now available from DEC, Quantum, and others. For those who need truly gigantic backup capacities, Digital Linear Tape jukeboxes are available now that store 140 GB or more natively using seven or more Digital Linear Tape tapes (see Table 8-3).

Table 8-3. Representative Quantum DLT Tape Drives and Libraries as of 9/97

Model	Native/ Compressed Capacity (GB)	Native/ Compressed Transfer Rate (MB/min)	Street Price
DLT 2000xt	15/30	75/150	$2,600
DLT 4000	20/40	90/180	$3,000
DLT 7000	35/70	300/600	$8,500
DLT 2700xt	105/210	75/150	$6,500
DLT 4700	140/280	90/180	$9,500

Installing the Tape Drive

Once you have purchased an appropriate tape drive (better still, two of them) and physically installed it in the server, the next step is to install the necessary drivers to allow Windows NT Server to recognize the drive. To do so, run the Tape Devices applet in Control Panel.

If you have replaced an existing tape drive, the Devices Page displays the installed tape drive. Click the Drivers tab, highlight the driver for the installed tape drive, and click Remove. The driver remains loaded, so restart the server to remove it from memory before proceeding.

After the system restarts, again run the Tape Devices applet. Click Detect to cause Windows NT Server to scan for your newly installed tape drive. Windows NT

Server locates most tape drives successfully, including nearly all DDS drives, floppy interface QIC drives, IDE interface QIC drives, and SCSI minicartridge drives. If Windows NT Server locates your drive, it will prompt you for the location of the drivers for that tape device.

If Windows NT Server does not locate your tape drive, or if it incorrectly identifies your drive, click Add from the Drivers page to display the Install Driver dialog. In the Manufacturers pane, select either (Standard tape drives) to display a list of generic drivers, or a manufacturer name to display a list of tape devices made by that manufacturer. Highlight the specific device in the Tape Devices pane and click OK to install the driver. If you have a driver provided by the tape device manufacturer, or an updated driver from Microsoft, click Have Disk and follow the prompts to install the updated driver.

Restart Windows NT Server to load the driver for the newly installed tape drive. Run the Tape Devices applet again to verify that the driver loaded successfully and that your new tape drive is recognized by Windows NT Server. The new drive should be visible on the Devices page, with (Driver loaded) displayed immediately to the right of its name. Click Properties to display the <tape drive name> Properties property sheet. Verify that in the Device Status section, the message "The device is working properly" is displayed.

Choosing Backup Software

The second element needed to build a backup system for your network is suitable backup software. Most administrators choose one of three alternative solutions. First, you can use the limited version of Arcada Backup Exec that is bundled with Windows NT Server as Windows NT Backup. Second, you can use your existing NetWare backup software to back up the server running Windows NT Server. Third, you can purchase the Windows NT version of your NetWare backup product. Let's look at some of the advantages and drawbacks of each of these solutions.

Using Windows NT Backup

Using Windows NT Backup to back up your Windows NT Server has the following three advantages, one obvious and two more subtle:

Cost

Because Windows NT Backup is bundled with Windows NT Server, it costs you nothing beyond the price you pay for Windows NT Server itself, for the software at least. Although there are better places to economize than when purchasing backup software, third-party backup software is not inexpensive, and budget realities may dictate that you use what you have already paid for.

Compatibility

By definition, Windows NT Backup is fully compatible with Windows NT Server. A usable complete back up of your server requires that you do more than just copy the programs and data files to tape. You must also ensure that you have usable copies of the Registry, the Security Account Manager database, and other critical system files. Windows NT Backup is designed to back up these files. Using other backup software may result in a backup that is missing one or more critical files.

Exchange Server

Backing up a server that has files open at all times has always been a problem. This issue is particularly important if you are running one or more components of the Microsoft BackOffice suite. Some BackOffice programs, e.g., SQL Server, at least allow you to do a dump that can then be closed and backed up. Exchange Server, on the other hand, always has files open and makes no provision for doing a dump. Even if you shut down Exchange Server and then back up its files, you will find when you attempt to restore from that backup that Exchange Server will not load the restored files.

The only way to back up Exchange Server successfully is to use backup software specifically designed to work with it. A special version of Windows NT Backup is bundled with Exchange Server, and replaces the version of Windows NT Backup that comes with the operating system. Be careful when upgrading Windows NT Server. When doing so, more than one administrator has overwritten the Exchange-aware version of Windows NT Backup with an updated, but generic, version.

As a bundled version of the full-featured Arcada Backup Exec backup program, Windows NT Backup also has a few disadvantages.

Cost

Even though the Windows NT Backup software is free, you must provide a tape drive to use it with. Depending on the size of your server, this might be something as inexpensive as a $350 TR-4 Travan drive. More expensive tape drives are typically bundled with a more capable backup software package, rendering the question of using Windows NT Backup with them moot.

Automation

Windows NT Backup lacks the automation features that administrators have come to expect in a modern backup program. Although you can use the AT command and command-line arguments to automate Windows NT Backup to some extent, the minimal automation thus provided may be inadequate for your needs.

Compression

The most serious impediment to using Windows NT Backup in a production environment is that it does not support software compression. Assuming that your mix of programs and data would normally be compressed at 2:1, this has two implications, both bad. First, you are limited to only the actual native capacity of the tape drive. A data set that would fit comfortably on a single tape with compression may now instead require two tapes. Even worse for many administrators is that the doubled throughput provided by compression is lost. The backup that took one hour with compression may now take two hours.

It is likely that you will find that the limitations of Windows NT Backup make it unacceptable as your main backup software. However, you may find that Windows NT Backup is the best and most cost-effective solution for special purposes like backing up Exchange Server data. Many administrators use Windows NT Backup where it makes sense to do so, and depend on a full-feature third-party backup product for their main backup tasks.

For example, one administrator I know had tried for weeks to come up with a usable backup solution for Exchange Server 4.0, using his existing third-party backup software and jukebox. He purchased the Exchange Server agent for his third-party backup software, which in theory would allow him to do a complete backup of the Exchange Server database. When installing the agent, he learned that it supported Exchange Server 4.0 only through Service Pack 2. Since he was running Service Pack 3, he had to "downgrade" his installation by reinstalling Exchange Server, and then applying Service Packs 1 and 2. After several hours of effort, he was disgusted to find that the agent still didn't work properly.

On my recommendation, he went out and bought a $350 Seagate/Conner TapeStor 8000 Travan TR-4 tape drive with an IDE interface, and installed it in his $40,000 Compaq ProLiant server with the attached $60,000 jukebox. Kind of like replacing the hood ornament on your Mercedes-Benz with a rubber duck, but it works. Sometimes you can do with $350 worth of equipment what you can't do with $100,000 worth. He's now happily using his free Windows NT Backup and his inexpensive tape drive to back up his Exchange Server database at 2 GB/hour to $40 tapes.

Using Your NetWare Backup Software to Back Up Windows NT Server

Chances are that you are now using a major third-party backup software package like Cheyenne ARCserve, Arcada Backup Exec, or Legato NetWorker to back up your NetWare server. These products come in two varieties.

Server-based backup software
: These products run as a NetWare Loadable Module (NLM), and use a tape drive physically installed on the NetWare server. Most of these products come in two versions. The so-called single server version is capable of backing up only the volumes mounted on the server upon which it is installed. The more expensive version, typically called the "enterprise" version or something similar, makes provision for backing up volumes on remote servers and workstations to the same tape drive used to back up the main server.

  Because the NetWare server cannot directly "see" volumes on remote servers and workstations, server-based enterprise backup products instead depend upon agents. Agents are optional software modules that extend the base backup software running on the NetWare server to allow it to back up remote servers and workstations that are running other operating systems.

Workstation-based backup software
: These products run as DOS or Windows executables on a workstation equipped with a large tape drive. Again, these products are usually marketed in both basic and enterprise versions. The enterprise version allows you to use agents to back up volumes located on remote servers and workstations, whereas the basic requires that you use drive mappings to back up remote systems.

Using your existing server-based NetWare backup software to back up a remote Windows NT Server has some considerable advantages. First, of course, you've already paid for the software. It's already installed and running, and you know how to use it. Going this route allows you to avoid purchasing another expensive tape drive and the software to use with it. It also allows you to design a single backup operation that backs up all servers instead of having to do multiple backups on a server-by-server basis. Using properly designed agents allows you to back up not just the data, but also the critical system files (like the Registry and SAM database) from remote servers running Windows NT Server.

There are also some disadvantages to using your existing server NetWare backup software. First, you have no choice but to purchase a backup agent for Windows NT Server. These agents can be quite expensive, and in some cases, you may pay as much for the agent as you would for a standalone backup product to run on the other server. Agents also vary in features and quality. A poorly designed agent may only allow you to select specific volumes, rather than allowing you to specify individual directories and files.

Using existing workstation-based NetWare back up software to backup a remote Windows NT Server has many of the same advantages as using the server-based NetWare backup software. In addition to these advantages, you may not need to buy agent modules. You can instead map drives on your workstation to the volumes on the Windows NT Server, although using this method precludes backing up the Registry and SAM database. One administrator I know had a clever idea. He uses drive mappings to back up the data on his Windows NT Server machine to the expensive 8mm tape library that is connected to the workstation he uses to back up his NetWare server. He installed an inexpensive QIC-80 tape drive in his Windows NT Server computer, attaching it to the floppy disk controller. He uses the QIC-80 tape drive only to back up the Registry and other system files using Windows NT Backup.

For many administrators, a key disadvantage to using any of these NetWare backup methods to back up Windows NT Server is that the current tape drive may be nearing its capacity. If your current NetWare volumes can be backed up comfortably to a single tape, the last thing you want to do is add your Windows NT Server to the backup and find that you must now use multiple tapes. Another key issue is the time window available to do backups. If you're pushing it right now to do a complete backup during off hours, adding another server may make it impossible to do the complete backup in the time available. If you find yourself in this situation, consider establishing a separate backup procedure for your Windows NT Server rather than altering your existing backup procedures. It's better to have two separate backups using all complete backups than it is to have a single backup that requires you to use a mix of complete and partial backups.

Using the Windows NT Server Version of Your NetWare Backup Software

You will probably find that the third and final alternative, using the Windows NT Server version of your NetWare backup software, is the best solution. It is also likely to be the most expensive solution, since you must buy not only the backup software itself, but a capable tape drive to use it with.

Until recently, the crop of third-party backup packages for Windows NT Server was nothing to write home about. There weren't many available, and those that were tended to be less functional than their NetWare counterparts. Backup software developers wrote first for the gigantic NetWare market, and only later (if at all) for the tiny Windows NT Server market. The perceived momentum of Windows NT Server, the marketing clout of Microsoft, and the arrival of Windows NT Server v 4.0 changed all that. Today, new versions of backup software tend to be released first for Windows NT Server, and only later for NetWare.

Developing and Implementing a Network Backup Plan

The third and final element needed to build a backup system for your network is a suitable network backup plan. The best and most expensive tape drive and backup software is useless unless you develop and follow a plan to ensure that your data is backed up regularly and can be restored when necessary. Developing such a plan requires that you first understand the fundamentals of backup planning, and then that you apply them to the particulars of your environment.

Understanding Backup Types

In the early days of mainframe computers, backing up was conceptually simple. At some point every day, typically at 5:00 p.m. close-of-business, the glass house operators took the mainframe down and began copying the contents of the disk packs to large reel-to-reel tape drives. By the time the regular staff began arriving in the morning, the backup had been completed and the mainframe was again available for use. Every night, these backups copied the entire contents of the disk farm to tapes, which were then archived, typically in a fire-safe vault. The capacities of the tapes used often closely matched the capacities of the disks being backed up. With modifications to accommodate increased up-time requirements, this is essentially the same method used today to back up many mainframes.

Backing up a PC LAN today is a bit different. First, IS staff is often not available around the clock to perform the backup. Second, with LANs becoming increasingly critical to the core business of many companies, the LAN is often required to be up and available during times outside traditional business hours, reducing the time available for doing backups, called the backup window. Third, many PC LANs have immensely large disk subsystems, often 50 GB or more, that cannot be backed up to a single tape.

For many organizations, these factors in conjunction have ruled out the classic complete backup every night, both for PC LANs and sometimes for the heavy iron as well. As a result, methods were developed that combine less frequent complete backups, usually weekly, with daily (or more frequent) partial backups that copy only changed files. The first step to developing your backup plan is to decide which of these types of backup you will use.

File attributes and the archive bit

If you are fortunate enough to have both the backup hardware and the time necessary to use only complete backups, you don't much care about the status of any particular file. Whether a file was just created or modified today, or has been sitting unchanged on the disk since the server was first installed, it gets backed up every time.

If, instead, your circumstances require that you use some combination of complete and partial backups, the status of each individual file becomes critical. If the file was not created or modified since the last complete backup, you want to ignore it when doing partial backups. If the file has changed since the last full backup, it needs to be copied to the partial backup tape.

Deciding which files are candidates for copying during a partial backup has some subtle implications. Primitive partial backup methods depended upon the obvious indicator—the date and time stamp of a file—to decide whether that file should be backed up during a partial backup. This method is not completely reliable, because some operating systems allow an application to open a file, write to it, and close it without modifying the date and time stamp on that file. This is particularly common with *.ini* files and self-modifying executables. Some better method than simply examining the date and time stamp was clearly needed to determine whether a file should be backed up during a partial backup.

DOS, NetWare, and Windows NT Server all use the *archive bit* for this purpose. The archive bit is a single bit, stored with the directory listing for the file. When the file is created, or is subsequently written to, the operating system toggles this bit to on, or a value of one. When the file is backed up, the backup software can toggle the archive bit to off, or a value of zero. The backup software can therefore build a list of files that require backup simply by scanning the directory list to determine the status of the archive bit for each file.

In addition to the archive bit, the NTFS file system, like NetWare, stores extended file attributes. Although DOS stores only a single date and time stamp for each file, the extended attributes supported by NTFS include the date and time that a file was created, that it was last modified, and that it was last accessed. The last modified stamp can be used by the backup software to perform the daily copy backup described below. The last accessed stamp can be used to determine which files are so seldom used that they are candidates for migration to off-line storage.

Let's take a look at the five standard backup types recognized by Windows NT Server, and how these attributes are used by each of them.

Normal backup

What Microsoft calls a normal backup is called a "full backup" by most third-party backup software vendors. The Microsoft terminology is actually more accurate, since a so-called full backup doesn't necessarily back up every file on the volume.

Only the files that you have selected to be backed up are actually backed up during a normal or full backup. Depending on the directories and files you select, a normal backup might copy all files on multiple volumes, all files on a single volume, only the files in one directory, or even just one file.

Two factors characterize a normal backup. First, all selected files are copied to tape, regardless of how their archive bits happen to be set. Second, after completing the backup, the backup software turns off the archive bit on all files that were backed up.

If you use normal backups exclusively, doing either a full restore (if your disk crashed) or a partial restore (to retrieve an accidentally deleted file) is easy. You simply restore the appropriate files or volumes from the latest full backup tape or tapes. The only data you lose is from files that were created or modified since the backup was made. If the most recent full backup tape breaks or is otherwise unreadable, you can restore from the preceding day's set, losing only one day's work in the process.

In the best of all worlds, everyone would do only normal backups, and every normal backup would include all files on all volumes. The realities of limited tape capacities and short backup "windows" mean that many administrators must depend instead upon a combination of less frequent normal backups, typically weekly, and more frequent partial backups, typically daily.

Normal backups have two chief advantages over a scheme that depends on partial backups. First, because every backup tape includes every file on every volume, you always have multiple recent copies of every file available. If you use a normal/partial scheme and your last normal backup tape breaks when you are attempting to restore, you have to return to the normal backup tape made the week before, or worse, the month before. If you use all normal backups and a tape breaks, you use the tape from the previous day. Second, using all normal backups makes tape management much easier. Every tape includes every file.

One often overlooked advantage of using normal backups exclusively is that of increased coherency and currency. When you do a full restore from a normal backup, your disk is returned to its exact state at the time the normal backup was done. The only loss of data is from files that were created or modified recently, and the only deleted files that magically reappear are those that were deleted recently. On the other hand, if you use a combination of normal backups and partial backups, you may find files reappearing that were deleted a week ago (or a month ago).

If you find yourself constrained by either limited tape capacity or limited time for backups to using a mix of normal and partial backups, look into upgrading your back up hardware. Modern high-end tape drives allow you to store as much as

40GB on a single tape, and provide throughput approaching 4 GB per hour. It's an unusual server disk farm that can't be completely backed up overnight with such a tape drive. Even if your needs are more modest, it's worthwhile upgrading your backup hardware to match your hardware with your storage capacity and speed requirements. The advantages of using full normal backups exclusively are compelling.

If upgrading your backup hardware isn't a realistic alternative, spend some time thinking about the best way to implement a normal/partial backup scheme using the differential backup or incremental backup methods described in the following sections.

Differential backup

The differential backup is a partial backup. Differential backups copy a selected file to the backup media only if the archive bit for that file is turned on, indicating that it has changed since the last normal backup. A differential backup leaves the archive bits unchanged on the files it copies. Accordingly, any differential backup set contains all files that have changed since the last normal backup. A differential backup set run soon after a normal backup will contain relatively few files. One run soon before the next normal backup is due will contain many files, including those contained on all previous differential backup sets since the last normal backup. When you use a differential backup scheme, a complete backup set comprises only two tapes or tape sets: the tape that contains the last normal backup and the tape that contains the most recent differential backup.

Doing a full or partial restore from a differential backup set is nearly as straightforward as working with normal backup sets. You restore the appropriate files or volumes from the last normal backup set, followed by the files or volumes needed from the most recent differential backup set. The only data you lose is from files that were created or modified since the last differential backup was made. Again, if the most recent differential backup tape breaks, you can use the one from the preceding day and lose only one day's work.

Incremental backup

The incremental backup is another type of partial backup. Like differential backups, incremental backups copy a selected file to the backup media only if the archive bit for that file is turned on, indicating that it has changed since the last normal backup. Unlike the differential backup, however, the incremental backup clears the archive bits on the files it copies. An incremental backup set therefore contains only files that have changed since the last normal backup or the last incremental backup. If you run an incremental backup daily, files changed on Monday are on the Monday tape, files changed on Tuesday are on the

Tuesday tape, and so forth. When you use an incremental backup scheme, a complete backup set comprises the tape that contains the last normal backup and all of the tapes that contain every incremental backup done since the last normal backup.

Doing a full restore from an incremental backup set requires that you first restore the latest normal backup. You then restore every incremental backup tape, starting with the oldest incremental backup tape that was made after the normal backup you have just restored, and proceeding to the most recent incremental backup tape. Assume, for example, that you do a normal backup every Saturday and an incremental backup every weekday evening. If your hard drive fails on a Friday, to recreate it you first restore the normal backup tape from the preceding Saturday. You then restore the Monday incremental backup tape, followed by the Tuesday tape, the Wednesday tape, and (finally) the Thursday tape.

Doing a partial restore from an incremental backup set is even more problematic, because different files may reside on different tapes, depending on when the files were created or last modified. For example, if a user has accidentally deleted several files, you might take the scattergun approach and simply restore the user's home directory, first from the last normal backup tape and then sequentially from each intervening incremental backup tape. Doing so, however, may overwrite more recent versions of some files with older versions from last night's backup. To eliminate this problem, you must determine exactly which files need to be restored, and upon which tape the most recent version of each is located. Even if you keep backup logs with full detail, this is a time-consuming and error-prone process.

Another problem with incremental backups is that you lose the safety net of having multiple recent copies of your data stored on different tapes. If an incremental backup tape fails, all changed files written to that tape will be lost unless they were again changed and written to a later incremental backup tape. The affected files must be retrieved from the last normal backup tape, which may be several days out of date. In particular, those companies that do normal backups only once a month and depend on partial backups in the interim should avoid using incremental backups.

Copy backup

What Microsoft calls a copy backup is called a "full copy backup" by most third-party backup software vendors. A copy backup is identical to a normal backup with the exception of the final step. Whereas the normal backup finishes by turning off the archive bit on all files that have been backed up, the copy backup leaves the archive bits unchanged.

The copy backup is useful only in environments that use a combination of normal backups and incremental or differential partial backups. The copy backup allows you to make a duplicate "full" backup, e.g., for storage off-site, without altering the state of the hard drive you are backing up, which would destroy the integrity of the partial backup rotation.

Daily copy backup

The daily copy backup is a partial backup. It backs up only files created or modified on the day that the daily copy backup is run. The daily copy backup leaves the archive bit unchanged, and does not use the state of the archive bit to determine which files should be backed up. Assume, for example, that you have not backed up since the day before yesterday. Some of the files on your disk were created or changed yesterday and some today. If you run a daily copy backup today, it backs up only today's files, ignoring those changed yesterday, even though their archive bits are on, indicating that they need to be backed up.

NOTE It's easy for administrators to forget that they are not the only ones who can affect the archive bit. I once had a smart user who decided that, rather than depending solely on the network backup to protect his data, he would put his own backup method in place. He did so using the DOS *XCOPY* command to copy his data from his home directory on the network drive to his local hard drive. So that the batch file would run faster, he used the /a command-line argument, which copies only files that have changed and then clears the archive bit. He ran this batch file several times a day for a month or so, and was quite pleased with the results. Because files that had been deleted from the network drive would remain on his local drive, he periodically used *DELTREE* to delete everything from the local directory that contained his "backup" data and then refreshed it from the network copy.

Then one day he used *DELTREE* from higher in the directory structure than he intended, and wiped out his workstation hard drive. He used his local tape drive to restore from a month-old backup tape. Intending to refresh the data files on his local hard drive, he somehow managed to erase his batch file instead of his old data. When he recreated the batch file, he compounded his error by accidentally reversing the target and destination drives, causing the batch file to copy month-old files from his hard drive to the network drive instead of the converse. When we attempted to retrieve more recent versions of his files from tape, we of course found that his files never made it on to the differential backup tapes. We ended up having to restore them from the normal backup tape made the preceding weekend, losing nearly a week's worth of his work in the process. Some users are just too smart for their own good, or not.

Structuring Disk Organization to Optimize Data Storage and Backup

Different types of data require different types of backup. If your server is like most, you probably have a large amount of disk space occupied by files that are pretty much static. The Windows NT Server operating system itself and applications programs may easily occupy a gigabyte (or several gigabytes) of disk space. These files seldom need to be backed up. You might reasonably do a complete normal backup on these files when they are first installed, and then defer backing them up again until an application is updated or an operating system patch or new driver is installed.

Perhaps you have some large, infrequently updated files, e.g., a parts database or a corporate directory, that are stored in read-only form on the server for easy user reference. If these files are generated offline and never modified on the server, there is no need to back them up at all. You may also have a major database application that generates large temp files, which again require no backup at all.

On the other hand, there are files that need frequent backup. Your user directories are probably in a constant state of flux, with users creating and modifying word processing documents, spreadsheets, and mail files every minute of the day. Losing any of these files would be inconvenient at the least, and so you probably want to back them up at least once a day. You may also have one or more critical applications, like order entry and inventory databases, that support core business functions of your company. These you'd probably like to back up continuously.

Each of these types of files differs in how important it is to the company, how much time and effort would be needed to reconstruct it if you lost it, and how easy it is to back up. It makes sense to organize the volumes on your server so that different types of files can be stored on different volumes. For example, you might put the operating system and applications programs on the *C:* volume, frequently modified files like user home directories and active databases on the *D:* volume, and static files on the *E:* volume. Arranging your storage in this manner has two major advantages.

First, you can install underlying physical storage that is appropriate to the data type being stored. For example, you might set up a RAID 0 array (very fast, no redundancy) for the temporary files generated by your database application, RAID 3 (optimized for large records, with high redundancy) for your imaging application, RAID 5 (optimized for small records, with high redundancy) for your general user files, and RAID 1 (high read performance, with extreme redundancy) for your mission-critical database.

Second, segregating data on separate volumes according to how frequently it needs to be backed up makes it easy to make the most of your tape drive capacity and backup window. Say, for example, that your server contains 2 GB of system and application files, 4 GB of user data files, and another 4 GB of static reference databases, for a total of 10 GB. If you store all of these files on a single volume, you may well find that your tape drive cannot back up the entire volume to a single tape and that your overnight backup window isn't long enough to complete a normal backup. You find yourself doing a normal backup on Friday night and partial backups throughout the week.

If, on the other hand, you store each of these three types of data on its own volume, you can then back up the system and application files once in a while, the reference databases never, and the user files every night. Although you could use file and directory inclusions and exclusions to accomplish a substantially similar result, segregating data by volume provides a much cleaner and less error-prone solution. If you have only user data on a specific volume, you can simply do a normal backup each night for that volume. If you depend instead on file or directory exclusions, you may return in the morning to find (as I once did) that you forgot to exclude a huge database, and your backup software is waiting for the next tape.

For a single disk server, Microsoft suggests that you create a 10 MB FAT boot partition, a 300 MB FAT system partition, and devote the remaining space on the disk to an NTFS user partition. I suggest that you go further still, and segment your user storage area into separate volumes to which files will be assigned by type.

NOTE If you do arrange your volumes as suggested to optimize backup, make sure to do at least a differential backup frequently on the volume that contains the Registry and SAM database.

Choosing a Tape Rotation Method

A tape rotation method is a procedure that specifies when each particular tape will be used, and what will be backed up to it. For example, for a simple tape rotation scheme, you might label five tapes Monday through Friday and then do a complete normal backup to the corresponding tape each day. Some tape rotation methods are simple and use only a few tapes. Others are immensely complex and use many tapes. Choosing the tape rotation method that is most appropriate for your requirements is a critical step in developing and implementing a network backup plan.

To reduce matters to the absurd, you **could** back up to the same tape every day. Doing so would obviously expose you to several serious risks. First, you would have at most one backup copy of your data, and you would have no backup copies at all during the period that you were actually backing up to that single tape. Second, historical copies would be limited to a single day. If someone had accidentally deleted a crucial file two days ago and only noticed it today, you would have no way to retrieve the file, since the backup tape that contained it would already have been overwritten. Third, having only a single tape would require that you choose either to keep that copy off-site to guard against catastrophes or to keep the copy on-site so that it would be readily available when a restore was necessary. Fourth, if that single tape broke, your backup data would be lost. Fifth, this single tape would be used very heavily, making a breakage even more likely.

On the other extreme, one law firm for whom I did some consulting never re-uses a backup tape. Each evening, 365 days a year, they do a complete backup and compare of their "active" volumes to a new 8mm tape, which is then stored indefinitely in their vault. Inactive data is migrated to a "holding" volume, which is backed up to a WORM drive and then periodically archived to tape. They buy and use backup tapes by the case, but they regard the $10 daily cost of a new backup tape as a small expense relative to the benefit of being able exactly to reconstruct their data for any specified day.

NOTE Given the small cost of tapes relative to the value of the data they protect, and given the increasing importance of historical data in legal actions, it is perhaps surprising that more companies don't use the method described above. If you decide to archive tapes to preserve historical data, whether daily, monthly or quarterly, keep one potential pitfall in mind.

As anyone familiar with mainframe glass house environments is aware, the data recorded on magnetic tapes doesn't last forever. The magnetic flux that comprises the individual ones and zeroes of the data begins to weaken as soon as the tape is written. Over the course of several years, this weakening may render the tape unreadable. In general, the more densely that data is stored on a tape, the more subject that tape is to this problem.

Tapes need to be "refreshed" periodically to ensure that the data stored on them doesn't disappear entirely. Although data stored on tape should be readable for ten years or more (depending on the type of tape), many organizations that use tape archives do a refresh every three to five years. The only practical way to perform this refresh is to do a tape-to-tape copy. Doing so requires that you have two identical tape drives installed in the same machine, and that your backup software support a direct tape-to-tape copy.

Chances are, the best tape rotation method for your needs will fall somewhere between the extremes of always using the same tape and never reusing a tape. A good tape rotation method satisfies the following goals:

Availability
: When you need to do a restore, whether it be of a single file accidentally deleted or of an entire volume whose hard drive crashed, time is almost always of the essence. A proper tape rotation scheme will ensure that you always have the most recent copy of your backup data immediately available to restore.

Archiving
: Sometimes, the most recent version of your backup data isn't good enough. For example, perhaps a file was accidentally deleted or a database improperly modified some time ago, but only recently was this fact recognized. Your most recent backup may, for these reasons, be missing the file or may contain only the unusable version of the file. A proper tape rotation method will allow you to retrieve a version of that file from several days, weeks or months previous, before the file had been deleted or improperly modified. Tape sets created with the best and most powerful tape rotation methods allow you to select from multiple versions of the file, so that you can retrieve the most recent good version. A good tape rotation method also makes provision for periodically removing a tape from the rotation and archiving it for historical reasons.

Redundancy
: Tapes can break or be misplaced. Operators make mistakes and overwrite the wrong tape. A good tape rotation scheme recognizes these facts, and uses redundancy to make such problems less critical. One of the conundrums of developing a good tape rotation method is that you desperately want to have both of two conflicting benefits. You want the most recent version of your backup readily available when you need to do a restore. You also want the most recent version of your backup stored off-site to protect against a disaster.

Equalized Tape Wear
: Ideally, you would like each of the tapes in the rotation to be used as frequently as any other, equalizing the wear on the tape set. The simpler tape rotation methods usually fall down in this regard. For example, the popular Grandfather-Father-Son rotation, described below, requires writing to some tapes in the set once a week, to others once a month, and to still others only once a year. Although, for most users, equalizing tape wear is a less important consideration than the others described, doing so is desirable in that it minimizes the chance that a tape will break because it has been used too frequently.

A variety of standard tape rotation methods exist. Some are simple and use few tapes, at the expense of failing to meet completely one or more of the goals described above. Other tape rotation methods either meet or at least come close to meeting each goal, but at the expense of being difficult to manage and requiring many more tapes. Some of these methods use complete backups exclusively, whereas others use a combination of complete and partial backups. Some tape rotation methods can be modified to use either exclusive complete backups or a combination of complete and partial backups.

If you have a choice, pick a method that depends exclusively on complete backups. Use a tape rotation method that depends on partial backups only if you are forced to do so by limited tape drive capacity or a backup "window" that is too short to allow using all complete backups. When it comes time to restore, you will find that it makes your life much easier to have the entire data set in one place rather than distributed among two or more tapes.

Simple rotations

I spent some time one day in the communications room of the local Sheriff's department. I noticed that they recorded all incoming telephone calls on a large reel-to-reel tape recorder, with each phone line allocated a separate channel on the tape. On the wall was a large rack, which contained 30 tapes and one empty slot, with each tape numbered with a day of the month. The tape for that day was in the tape recorder and running. Each day, that day's tape was cycled back onto the rack and replaced with the following day's tape. That way, the Sheriff's department always had a record of all telephone calls they'd received during the preceding 31 days. Many network administrators use a similar simple rotation, although usually with fewer tapes. Let's take a look at some of these simple rotations.

Daily normal backup rotation. The simplest of rotations, assuming that you have both adequate tape drive capacity and a long enough backup window, is to do a complete normal backup each day. Most sites that use this method use ten tapes, labeled *Monday A* through *Friday A* and *Monday B* through *Friday B.* Using this method offers the considerable advantages of simple administration and extreme data redundancy. It's always obvious which tape you should be backing up to. If you start a restore and your most recent backup tape breaks, you simply use the next most recent tape. All tapes receive equal wear, and can be replaced periodically as a set. You can cycle each backup tape off-site as it is replaced by today's backup, leaving your most recent backup available on-site for easy restores, while having an off-site tape that is only one day old.

The sole disadvantage of this rotation is that you are limited to retrieving historical data from only two weeks prior, assuming that you use ten tapes. This problem is easily addressed. Simply add four quarterly tapes or twelve monthly tapes to the rotation, and do a duplicate backup to the appropriate archive tape at the end of each quarter or month.

Weekly normal backup with daily differential backup rotation. For small servers, this is probably the most commonly used rotation. In its simplest form, this rotation requires only three tapes, labeled *Weekly A*, *Weekly B*, and *Daily*. On the first and succeeding "odd" Fridays, you do a normal backup to the *Weekly A* tape. On the second and succeeding "even" Fridays, you do a normal backup to the *Weekly B* tape. Monday through Thursday, you do a differential backup to the *Daily* tape. This rotation has the advantages of being simple to administer and requiring very few tapes. It also has the following disadvantages:

- Historical data can be retrieved for a period of at most two weeks. If a user has accidentally deleted a file and does not realize it for a couple of weeks, that file may be gone forever. Similarly, the two-week horizon may cause problems if you find that your system has been infected by a virus. Ordinarily, you might retrieve older, known-good versions of files from backup. This rotation limits your ability to do this to a two-week period.
- If the *Daily* tape fails during a restore, you must return to the last normal backup weekly tape, which may cause you to lose as much as four days worth of data.
- Only a single current copy of the normal backup exists, so you must either keep it on-site for easy retrieval or off-site for safety.
- Tape wear is very uneven, since the *Daily* tape is used eight times more often than a weekly tape.

You can overcome some of these disadvantages simply by adding more tapes to the rotation and by making minor changes to the rotation itself. For example, to address the problem of off-site storage, you might add a couple of tapes to the rotation and use them to do a second complete normal backup each Friday, keeping one on-site and moving the other to safe off-site storage. Similarly, to address the broken *Daily* tape problem, you might add a second *Daily* tape and then alternate using the two *Daily* tapes. That way, if one *Daily* tape fails, you need return only to the previous day's backup rather than to the last normal backup. To address the historical data problem, you might add four quarterly tapes (or 12 monthly tapes), to each of which you would do a complete normal backup on the final day of the corresponding quarter (or month), and then store the tape.

Weekly normal backup with daily incremental backup rotation. This rotation requires six tapes, labeled *Weekly A*, *Weekly B*, *Monday*, *Tuesday*, *Wednesday*, and

Thursday. On the first and succeeding "odd" Fridays, you do a normal backup to the *Weekly A* tape. On the second and succeeding "even" Fridays, you do a normal backup to the *Weekly B* tape. Monday through Thursday, you do an incremental backup to the corresponding daily tape.

Although it is commonly used, and although it is superficially similar to the rotation described immediately above, using this rotation is in fact the worst possible choice, short of not backing up at all. Because it depends on incremental backups, each daily tape contains a different group of files. Doing a complete restore requires that you be able to restore the most recent normal backup tape and all subsequent daily tapes successfully. If any daily tape fails during the restore, you must either revert to the last normal backup, losing all subsequent changes to files, or else risk the incoherence in file versions that can be caused by restoring only some of the daily tapes.

I'm constantly amazed by the number of sites I find using this rotation. If you haven't started using this rotation, don't. If you're using it now, change to a rotation that will better secure your data.

The Grandfather-Father-Son rotation. The Grandfather-Father-Son (GFS) tape rotation method is probably more commonly used than any other. It's easy to manage, requires relatively few tapes, and is supported directly by every backup program on the market. A typical GFS rotation tape set requires 21 tapes, as follows:

- *Daily Tapes.* Label four tapes *Monday* through *Thursday.* Back up each day to the tape for the corresponding day, overwriting each tape once a week.
- *Weekly Tapes.* Label five tapes *Friday-1* through *Friday-5.* Back up each Friday to the corresponding weekly tape, using the *Friday-5* tape only in months that have five Fridays. Weekly tapes 1 through 4 are overwritten once a month, with *Friday-5* being overwritten less frequently.
- *Monthly Tapes.* Label twelve tapes *January* through *December.* Back up the first (or last) of each month to the corresponding monthly tape. Monthly tapes are overwritten only once a year.

The GFS rotation tape method meets most of the goals of an ideal tape rotation method. In terms of availability, you can always keep one or more recent tape sets on-site. In terms of archiving, it provides weekly granularity for the preceding month, and monthly granularity for the preceding year. In terms of redundancy, it provides numerous copies of both recent and older data. Older backup sets can easily be moved off-site. The only main drawback to using the GFS rotation is that tape wear is very uneven. Daily tapes are written once a week. Weekly tapes are written once a month (less frequently for the Friday-5 tape). Monthly tapes are written only once a year.

In a typical GFS rotation, the daily tapes are made using differential backup or incremental backup, and the weekly and monthly tapes are made using normal backup. If your tape drive capacity is large enough to do a complete backup on a single tape, and if your backup window is long enough to allow regular complete backups, you can just as easily use the GFS tape rotation method with complete backups exclusively.

The GFS tape rotation method can also easily be modified to suit your archiving requirements. Firms for which historical data is less critical might choose to create an archive tape only quarterly rather than monthly. Firms for which archived historical data is more important might instead choose to use a set of 52 weekly tapes, rotating them off-site and archiving them immediately as they are made.

The Tower of Hanoi rotation. The Tower of Hanoi tape rotation method is named after an ancient game that requires that rings of various sizes and colors be sequentially moved between a series of posts to finally arrive at an arrangement of specific rings in a specific order on specific posts. In the Tower of Hanoi tape rotation, individual tapes take the place of the rings, and backup sets take the place of the posts.

Using the Tower of Hanoi rotation requires that you periodically add new tapes to the set. New tapes are used more frequently than are older tapes, and each generation of older tape is used half as frequently as it was before the new tape was introduced to the set.

Like Tic-Tac-Toe, the Tower of Hanoi is "trivial" or "solved" in a mathematical sense. Attempting to manage it manually on a day-to-day basis is something else entirely. I know quite a few bright, well-organized people, but I've not met many administrators who could successfully manage a Tower of Hanoi rotation manually in the real world. If your backup software supports the Tower of Hanoi rotation directly, by all means use it. Tower of Hanoi does the best job of meeting all the goals of a good rotation method.

Off-Site Storage

Storing a recent full backup set off-site protects you against fire, other natural disasters, and theft. One administrator I know arrived at work one Monday morning to find that thieves had broken in and stolen his server. Apparently, the thieves planned to do regular backups, because they also made off with every one of his backup tapes. Fortunately, this administrator had just cycled a backup set off-site the preceding Friday. He was able to install a spare tape drive in a standby server, restore, and have his company back up and running late Monday afternoon.

If the off-site backup set had not been available, the company would have been unable to function properly for several weeks while data was being reentered from paper records. As it turned out, the administrator ended up getting a raise and a commendation for his foresight. Had he not had that off-site backup set, chances are that he would have been out of a job. In fact, everyone might have been unemployed, because the company itself would likely have folded. As things turned out, the theft resulted in only a minor inconvenience and the nagging worry that company data had been sold to competitors. It could have been much worse.

Although some companies depend on fire-safes and similar arrangements to protect backup tapes, nothing really replaces the security of having a complete set of data stored somewhere off premises. When deciding how to implement off-site storage, you must balance currency, accessibility, and convenience. Ideally, you'd like your off-site backup set to be absolutely current, to be readily accessible whenever you need it, and to require no extra work to maintain. Realities dictate, however, that you must balance these priorities.

NOTE If you decide to use a fire-safe to protect your backup tapes, make sure to get one rated for storing magnetic media. A typical fire-safe is designed to protect paper, and allows internal temperatures to reach levels that will destroy tapes. A fire-safe rated for tapes is much more expensive.

Because the off-site backup set is a last-ditch defense against data loss, many companies are willing to give up some currency in exchange for ease of administration. If this is your situation, you might, for example, cycle your next-most-recent normal backup set off-site as you complete the current normal backup set. Rather than modifying their normal backup rotation, some companies find it acceptable to run a special complete backup at the beginning of each month and store it off-site. It all depends on how much you are willing to risk losing.

Conversely, some companies regard having a current off-site backup as so important that they are willing to go to considerable pains to make it so. One company I know of maintains two complete backup workstations. The first is used to do the backups for the normal rotation. The second does a duplicate copy backup and compare each night. Upon arriving in the morning, the first duty of the administrator is to remove the off-site backup tape and deliver it to a business that provides tape depository services. He grabs his first cup of coffee on the way out the door.

Chances are that you won't need to go to these lengths with your off-site backup. Many administrators find that the best way to handle off-site storage is simply to take a recent backup set home with them periodically. Even during a widespread natural disaster, the chance of both the main backup set and the backup set stored at your home being destroyed is almost nil. If you do choose this method, make sure to get formal approval in writing before you take a backup set home. More than one system administrator has been shocked to find himself facing disciplinary action for removing company data from the premises.

Developing and Testing a Restore Plan Before It Is Needed

You back up so often and do a full restore so seldom that it's easy to lose track of the real purpose for doing the backups in the first place. Backups are simply a means to an end. What you really care about is being able to do a complete restore when necessary. No one tests a parachute by strapping it on and jumping out of a plane. If the parachute fails, you've discovered useful information, but it's far too late to do you any good. It's surprising how many otherwise competent network administrators use the equivalent of this "jump and hope for the best" method with their backups.

When a server goes down, it's usually a critical emergency both organizationally and from an economic point of view. People are unable to work, but are still collecting their salaries. Downtime may cost the company directly in lost sales and indirectly in degraded customer service. Even small organizations may count the cost of server downtime in thousands of dollars per hour. Larger companies may incur costs of tens of thousands or even hundreds of thousands of dollars per hour while the server is down. Even worse, your job is probably on the line, whether you know it or not.

For all of these reasons, it pays to have a well-conceived and well-tested restore plan in effect before events require that you put it into action. The problem is, although most administrators back up every day and may do partial restores of accidentally deleted files frequently, complete restores are few and far between. Other than a disk crash or a significant upgrade to the disk subsystem, few administrators have any reason routinely to do complete restores.

Having to do something you have little experience doing, and having to do it under the gun, is a recipe for disaster. More than one administrator of my acquaintance has found to his sorrow that his "last good backup" turned out to be unreadable or that the copy of the Registry on tape would not restore successfully. There's no good time to discover things like these, but finding them out in a practice run beats finding them out in a real emergency.

Although you may do a full compare on every backup you run, the only way to be absolutely sure that your backups will restore successfully is to do an actual restore. This presents an obvious problem for many administrators. Only a maniac would do a test restore that overwrites the working data on a production server, and yet you may not have another machine with enough disk space to accept a complete restore.

The best solution to this problem is to acquire such a machine, which can then also serve as a standby server if your main server fails. This spare machine needn't be equipped with all the bells and whistles of your main server, but it should have at least the same amount of RAM and disk space as the main server. Many administrators I know run $50,000 Hewlett-Packard NetServers or Compaq ProLiants as their main servers and use an $8,000 Gateway or Dell with 128 MB of RAM and several gigabytes of disk as a standby server.

The standby server may not have the ECC memory or the RAID array present in the production server, but it's capable of filling in for the main server on a temporary basis. If you do frequent test restores to this standby server, you also gain the advantage of having an in-place server that can be substituted quickly for a failed main server. Of course, the best solution is to duplicate your main server exactly, thereby avoiding problems like mismatched Registry configurations and so forth. If you have several identical production servers, buying an exact duplicate as a standby server is often a viable alternative. Otherwise, match the capabilities of the production server as best you can.

If you can't justify a standby server, but your main server has enough free disk space, another solution is to do a complete restore to the main server, but to a different volume or directory. Although many administrators routinely use this method to test backup integrity, it is inferior to the separate machine method, simply because you can't boot your restored data to test it, at least not without making significant changes to your main server.

If you have neither a spare server nor enough disk space on your main server to do a complete restore to an unused volume, the next best solution is to do a partial restore. If you find yourself forced to depend on this method, at least try to make the restore as realistic as possible. In particular, if your complete backup spans multiple tapes, make sure that the transition between tapes occurs successfully. Many administrators have found out the hard way that their first tape restores successfully but that the second stubbornly refuses to restore.

Creating and Maintaining a Formal Restore Emergency Kit

Being able to restore a failed server on demand is so important that it's well worth your time to create and maintain a formal restore emergency kit. When the alarm goes off in the fire station, you don't see the firefighters scrambling around trying to locate their hoses. Everything they need is already on the truck and ready to go. You should operate the same way. If the worst happens and you need to do a full restore, you don't want to spend time searching for the Windows NT Server CD or the current version of your backup software. You want everything in one place.

What you choose to include in your emergency kit will depend on your particular situation. If you have a standby server, the emergency kit can obviously be less extensive than if you must rebuild your production server from scratch. As a good starting point, consider including the following items:

Boot Disk and Diagnostics
: When faced with a dead server, your first task is usually to boot the server and run the hardware diagnostics. Make sure that the emergency kit contains everything you need to do so. You can't fix the server if you don't know what's broken.

Spare Hard Drive(s), Cables, and Host Adapter
: Most server hardware failures are disk related. Include one or more hard drives of the same type used in your server, along with spare cables and a host adapter. Make sure that the spare drive(s) are formatted and otherwise ready for use. Even if drive failures are covered by an on-site maintenance agreement, having a spare can mean the difference between having your server back up in an hour and waiting most of a day. It's also a good idea to include a spare network adapter card.

Spare Tape Drive
: If you use server-based backup, keep a spare tape drive in your emergency kit. If you back up your server from a workstation, the spare tape drive should be already installed in another workstation. Using workstation-based backup not only allows you to keep a spare tape drive online and ready. It also allows you to test periodically to ensure that each drive can read tapes made by the other.

Tools
: Make sure that your kit includes every tool necessary to open the server and replace components. Also make sure to have a copy of the key. Otherwise, you may find yourself using a can opener.

Windows NT Server CD
: I've seen more than one emergency kit that included everything except a copy of the network operating system. Store your distribution CD with the emergency kit, along with a copy of the emergency disk you created when you installed Windows NT Server. While you're at it, take five minutes to create a set of boot floppies from the CD. That's five minutes you won't have to spend when you're rebuilding your server under the gun.

Drivers, Updates, and Patches
: Include a copy of every single driver, update, service pack, and patch you've installed to your copy of Windows NT Server. Otherwise, you may find yourself desperately searching the Internet for a driver when you would otherwise already be doing the restore.

Backup Software
: You can't restore your data unless you have the software that you backed it up with. Keep a copy of the backup software distribution, along with any updates or patches, in your emergency kit.

TIP If you don't have a standby server, give serious consideration to building a spare system disk and storing it with your emergency kit. Having a prebuilt spare system disk can save you the two hours or so that it might take to install Windows NT Server and your backup software.

Having created a formal Restore Emergency Kit, many administrators consider the job to be done. They sit back and relax, figuring they've done a Good Thing. When it comes to an emergency kit, the job is never done. Every time you update drivers, add an application, or change server hardware, your emergency kit gets further out of date. When it finally comes time to do a full restore, you may find that the version 6.1 backup software that you carefully stored in the emergency kit won't restore your backup set that was made with version 7.0. Your production server is running Windows NT Server 4.0 with Service Pack 4 installed, but all you have in the kit is the original CD.

Although you might reasonably expect that restoring your current backup set will also restore the current configuration, there are times when you "can't get there from here." For instance, the current version of your backup software may be required to restore yesterday's tape, but it may run only if the current service pack is installed. Better safe than sorry. Make it a practice to update your emergency kit every time you touch your production server. Otherwise, you might just as well not create the emergency kit in the first place.

Also, consider who may need to use the emergency kit. If you are ill, at a conference, on vacation, or otherwise unavailable when it comes time to do a full restore, someone else will have to do the job. Make sure that your substitute knows where the kit is located and how to use it. It may seem silly to document procedures that you yourself are likely to be performing, but what's obvious to you may not be so obvious to your fill-in. Make sure that your substitute has everything needed for access, including keys to the server room and the administrator password. Otherwise, you're likely to find your well-earned vacation interrupted by a sudden trip home.

9

Working with the Windows NT Registry

In this chapter:

- *Registry Design Goals*
- *Understanding the Registry Structure*
- *How the Registry Supports Windows NT and Applications*
- *Editing the Windows NT Registry*
- *Securing and Auditing the Registry*
- *Working with Remote Registries*

Windows NT stores both hardware-specific and user-specific configuration information in a central hierarchical binary database called the Registry. The Windows NT Registry replaces the various ASCII text configuration files (including *autoexec.bat*, *config.sys*, *win.ini*, *system.ini*, and *protocol.ini*) used in LAN Manager and in earlier MS-DOS based Windows products like Windows 3.1 and Windows 3.11 for Workgroups.

The Windows NT Registry is in many respects comparable to the NetWare bindery, although the Registry contains a much broader scope of system and user information than the bindery. The Registry is just as critical to the correct functioning of Windows NT as is the bindery to NetWare. Like the bindery, the Registry is a "black box" to almost all users and to many administrators.

There is at least one major practical difference between the two. Almost no one modifies the NetWare bindery directly. You may run *bindfix.exe* periodically to clean up the bindery and make a backup copy of it. If the worst happens, you run *bindrest.exe* to restore the bindery from your backup copy. For almost all NetWare administrators, that's about the limit of their direct interaction with the bindery. The Windows NT Registry is much more accessible. As a Windows NT administrator, you will have the occasion to get your hands dirty by making direct modifications to the Registry. Sometimes, doing so is the easiest way to accomplish a particular task. Other times, it's the only way.

For many Windows NT administrators, including experienced ones, the Registry is both the least understood and the most intimidating aspect of Windows NT Server. It doesn't have to be. By making the effort to understand a few fundamentals about the structure and functioning of the Registry and the tools used to modify it, you can take control of your Windows NT Server at a level that many Windows NT system administrators will never reach.

Registry Design Goals

Microsoft learned their lesson with Windows 3.1x and LAN Manager. Both of these earlier products depended upon a variety of configuration files, most of which were stored as ASCII text, to record startup and configuration information. By the time Microsoft designed Windows NT, it had become abundantly clear that this multiplicity of text files made it difficult to manage a single server successfully and conveniently. Managing an environment with multiple servers, which was becoming much more common, was impossible under the constraints of *.INI* files.

The programmers and analysts who created Windows NT were many of the same people who had previously designed the Digital Equipment Corporation (DEC) VAX/VMS operating system, a serious minicomputer operating system. VAX/VMS itself uses methods that more resemble those used in Windows 3.1x than in Windows NT. No doubt the designers looked askance at the limitations of both the existing PC-based network operating systems and VAX/VMS, and were determined to do better with Windows NT. The bindery concept used by the then-current version of NetWare was certainly an improvement on *.INI* files, but the design team decided that they could do better. In particular, the bindery was designed to be a local resource, whereas Windows NT was to be designed from the ground up to function in a multiserver, heterogeneous environment.

The design team decided that the best way to accomplish the various design goals was to create a centralized hierarchical database in which all startup and configuration information would be stored. They named this centralized database the Registry. The primary design goals for this new Registry method of maintaining a database of configuration information, were as follows:

Centralized Configuration Data Repository

Windows 3.1x scatters files containing startup and configuration information all over your hard drive. The root directory of the boot volume contains the two startup files *AUTOEXEC.BAT* and *CONFIG.SYS*. The *\WINDOWS* directory contains various configuration files, including *WIN.INI*, *SYSTEM.INI*, *CONTROL.INI*, and *PROTOCOL.INI*. Application programs create their own *.INI* files, which may be stored in the application directory, the user data directory, the *\WINDOWS* directory, the *WINDOWS\SYSTEM* directory, or elsewhere. The most obvious primary design goal for the Registry was to gather all of this startup and configuration information in a central location, from which it could be administered. Another benefit of this centralized approach is that it makes possible distributing the database among multiple servers and administering the database remotely.

Enhanced Support for Multiple Users Sharing a Single Computer

Windows 3.1x makes very limited provisions for allowing more than one user to share a single computer. Only one *WIN.INI*, for example, can exist at any one time, forcing all users of the computer to use the settings contained in that one version of *WIN.INI*. A change made by any user affects all others. Because Windows NT was to be made available in both Server and Workstation versions, client-side issues like this were important design goals for the Registry. The registry allows each user to maintain a separate set of preferences for both operating system functions, such as desktop settings, and application functions, e.g., the most recently used list in Microsoft Word.

Multiple Level Storage Hierarchy

Windows 3.1x *.INI* files are flat. Although an *.INI* file can have more than one section, sections cannot be further subdivided into subsections. The increasing complexity of software and the design goal that the Registry contain comprehensive information about the system, its users, and the installed applications required that the Registry support nesting to allow this large amount of data to be stored and organized hierarchically.

Finer Granularity for Configuration Settings

One of the problems with *.INI* files is that they store information in large blocks, which can be protected only by using the gross access controls provided by DOS. For example, you might mark a particular *.INI* file as read-only, preventing accidental (or intentional) changes to that file. If you needed to allow a user to make a change to one aspect of system operation that was controlled by that *.INI* file, your only option was to remove the read-only attribute, allowing that user to change not only the desired aspect, but any aspect of system operation controlled by that *.INI* file. In addition, the control offered by this method was imperfect, since any reasonably knowledgeable user could simply remove the read-only attribute from a file he wanted to change.

The Registry was designed to allow each setting to be addressed individually, or as a defined group. For example, the Policy Editor allows you to view and modify Registry settings related to system policy, but not to access other Registry values. The Registry also controls access to each setting individually. It does so by using an Access Control List (ACL) to specify exactly which users and groups can access any particular Registry entry, and at what level. You might use this feature, for example, to grant general users read-only access to one particular Registry entry while allowing administrators full control of the same entry.

Extended Data Type Support

Windows 3.1x *.INI* files can store only ASCII text, and are limited to a maximum size of 64 KB. Both of these factors are a severe limitation for a modern network operating system. The design of the Registry specifies several supported data types, including binary. This allows almost any type of data to be stored in the Registry, including, for example, images. The only size limitations on Registry entries are the overall Registry Size Limit, discussed later in the chapter, and the fact that any one entry can have a maximum size of 1 MB.

NOTE Although Windows NT is strongly Registry-centric, it still supports *.INI* files, which is required to provide backward-compatibility with 16-bit Windows applications. This is necessary because access to the Registry is done using the Win32 API, which is not supported by 16-bit Windows.

Understanding the Registry Structure

The Registry database is organized using a hierarchical structure, similar to the inverted tree structure familiar to anyone who uses volumes, folders, subfolders, and files. In the Registry, the structure analogous to a volume is called a *subtree* or a *root key*. Each root key contains *keys*, which correspond conceptually to a top-level folder (one that is a child of the root folder). Keys may contain either *subkeys, value entries*, or both. Subkeys correspond to subfolders, and may themselves contain zero or more subkeys. The value entries contained within a key or subkey correspond to the files contained in a folder structure, and contain the actual data.

The final Registry organization entity is called a *hive*. A hive comprises a collection of keys, subkeys, and value entries that is rooted at the top of the Registry hierarchy. Each hive has two corresponding disk files, a main data file and a log file, that store the contents of the hive. It is easy to confuse hives and root keys. A hive maps to a physical disk file, and is therefore a "real" collection of data. A root key can instead be considered to be a logical view or filter of the underlying physical data contained within one or more hives. Some root keys, for example, HKEY_CURRENT_CONFIG, are not directly associated with any particular hive, but are instead simply pointers to the hive data mapped by another root key.

The Registry Hierarchy

The Windows NT Registry contains five subtrees, or root keys, as shown in Figure 9-1. Some of these subtrees contain hardware and software configuration information specific to the local computer. These computer-specific subtrees contain information about the hardware installed in that particular machine, the identity and location of software that is installed on the local hard drive, etc. Other subtrees contain information about the user currently logged on to Windows NT Server, and about other users who have accounts on that machine. These user-specific subtrees contain information about the personal settings of each user, e.g., drive and printer mappings. They also contain desktop settings, individual preferences for applications (for example, the most recently used file list), and other information particular to the individual user. Table 9-1 lists the root keys and the type of information stored in each.

Table 9-1. Windows NT Server Registry Subtrees

Root Key Name	Function
HKEY_CLASSES_ROOT	Stores the file associations that map a file extension to an application, e.g., *.doc* to Microsoft Word, allowing users to load the associated program by double-clicking on a file whose extension is associated with an application. Also contains the Object Linking and Embedding (OLE) associations contained in the Windows 3.x *REG.DAT* file. This key points to the subkey *\SOFTWARE\Classes* contained in the *HKEY_LOCAL_MACHINE* root key.
HKEY_CURRENT_USER	Stores user profile information for the user currently logged in to the system console, including user-level preferences for desktop settings, for system software and services, and for applications software. This key points to the corresponding key in *HKEY_USERS* for the current user.
HKEY_LOCAL_MACHINE	Stores machine-specific information about the local computer system, including: hardware configuration items like the installed processor and chipset, the bus architecture, the video chipset, and the disk I/O hardware; system software configuration information like loaded device drivers and installed services; security information; location and configuration of user applications.
HKEY_USERS	Stores all actively loaded user profiles, including the default profile and the profile of the currently logged in user in *HKEY_CURRENT_USER*. Users who connect to this server across the network do not have profiles stored in this root key. Their profiles are instead stored in the Registry of the local workstation they are using. Windows NT 4.0 implements significant changes in the way user profiles are used, making this root key useful primarily for backward compatibility with software that accesses it directly.
HKEY_CURRENT_CONFIG	This root key, new in Windows NT 4.0, is generated on the fly based on the hardware configuration specified by the current hardware profile. This key points to the subkey *\SYSTEM\CurrentControlSet\Hardware Profiles\Current* of the root name key *HKEY_LOCAL_MACHINE*.

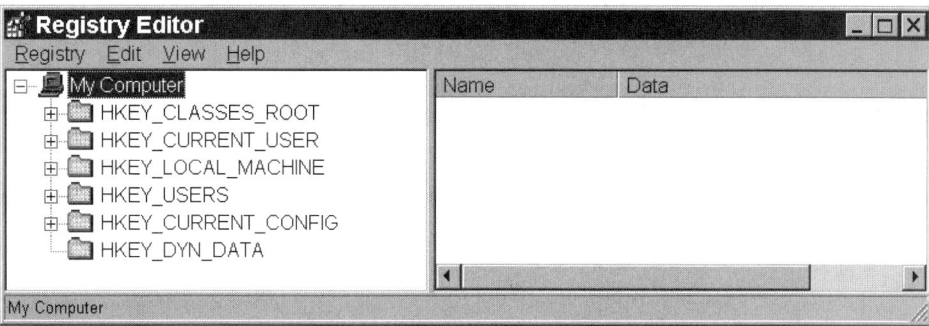

Figure 9-1. The Registry Editor displays the five root keys of the Windows NT Registry. HKEY_DYN_DATA is not a root key, as indicated by the absence of the plus sign to its left, but rather stores real-time dynamic data

Hives and Their Associated Disk Files

The Registry is divided into *hives*, apparently so called because someone at Microsoft decided that these structures resembled bee hives. A hive is rooted at the top of the Registry hierarchy, and contains keys, subkeys, and value entries.

Hive data is so important that Windows NT builds in fault tolerance to prevent a disk crash or sudden power failure from corrupting it. Each hive corresponds to two physical disk files. The primary file contains the master copy of the working data for that hive. The secondary file contains information necessary to recreate the primary file if it becomes corrupted.

By default, Windows NT stores both primary and secondary hive files in the *%SystemRoot%\system32\config* folder, where *%SystemRoot%* is a metavalue that maps to the drive and directory where Windows NT is installed. For example, on my computer, Windows NT 4.0 Server is installed in the *C:\WINNT* folder, so data for the hive HKEY_LOCAL_MACHINE\SOFTWARE can be found in the files *c:\WINNT\system32\config\software* and *c:\WINNT\system32\config\software.LOG*. You can store the hive files that contain user profile information in another location if you wish.

The two data files that correspond to each hive both use the hive name as the filename. The primary data file for each hive has no file extension. The secondary file for each hive has the extension *.log*, *.LOG*, or *.alt*. In Figure 9-2, the Windows NT Explorer displays the files associated with each of the hives.

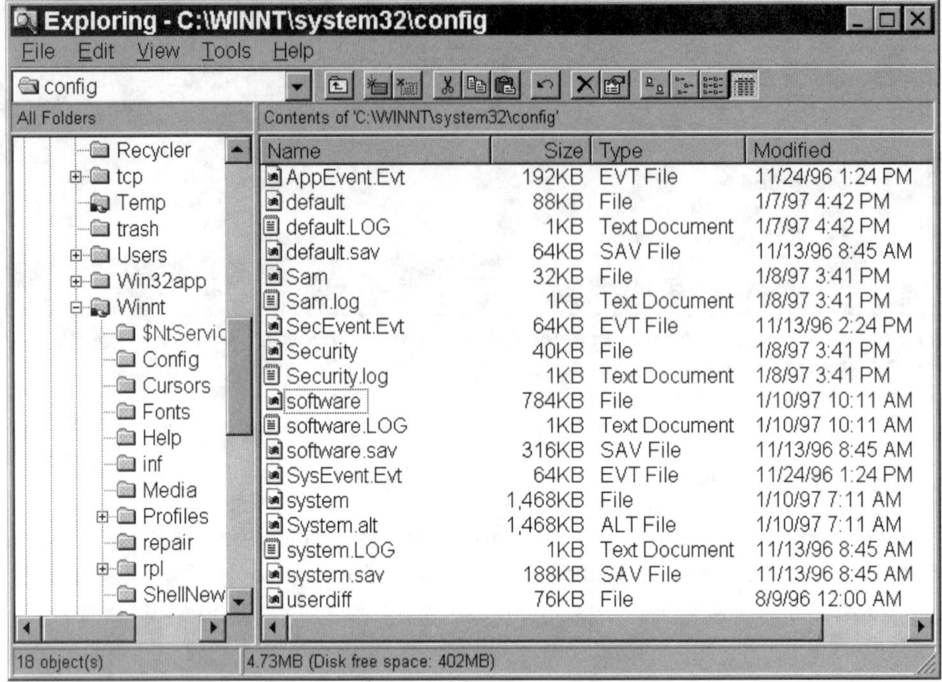

Figure 9-2. The Windows NT Explorer displays the files associated with the Registry hives

Windows NT Server has six standard hives. Table 9-2 lists the name of each hive, and the associated files that contain the data for each hive.

Table 9-2. Windows NT Server Registry Hives

Registry Hive	Associated Files
HKEY_LOCAL_MACHINE\SAM	*Sam* and *Sam.log*
HKEY_LOCAL_MACHINE\SECURITY	*Security* and *Security.log*
HKEY_LOCAL_MACHINE\SOFTWARE	*software* and *software.LOG*
HKEY_LOCAL_MACHINE\SYSTEM	*system* and *System.alt*
HKEY_CURRENT_USER	*User###* and *User###.log* *Admin###* and *Admin###.log*
HKEY_USERS\.DEFAULT	*default* and *default.LOG*

Hive fault tolerance

With one exception (the system hive described next), Windows NT uses these two files to provide fault tolerance for the hives. It does so by using the transaction processing concept of a two-phase commit. When a change is about to be written to a hive, Windows first copies the data to be changed to the log file, and verifies that the changed log file was written to disk successfully. It then places a flag in the primary hive file that indicates that it is being written to. The changes are then made to the primary hive file, the flag is removed, and the changed hive file is written to disk.

If a power failure or other system malfunction occurs during the write, it fails and the flagged hive file is left on disk. When the server is restarted, Windows NT sees the flag in that hive file, and recognizes that the hive needs to be rebuilt before proceeding. It uses the contents of the original primary hive file and the log file to reconstruct the primary hive file before continuing to boot.

NOTE The rebuild process can take several minutes, as I found out by experience while writing this chapter. I intentionally damaged a primary hive file and then rebooted the system. The system boot process appeared to proceed normally, but the logon prompt did not appear when expected. Instead, I spent several minutes staring at a blank green screen with only an hourglass displayed, listening to the disk churn away. After five minutes or so, the login prompt appeared and everything returned to normal.

Fault tolerance for the system hive operates a bit differently. Because the data contained in this hive is needed very early in the boot process, and is critical to the ability of the system to boot, the log file method is not used. Instead, Windows NT simply duplicates the contents of the primary system hive file to the *System.alt* secondary system hive file.

When a change is made to the primary system hive file, Windows NT inserts the "change in process" flag described previously before writing the changes to disk. Windows NT verifies that the changed primary system hive file has been written to disk successfully, and then removes the flag. After the primary system hive has been updated and unflagged successfully, the changed data is written to the *System.alt* secondary system hive file.

If the update to the primary system hive file fails for any reason, the next time Windows NT is started it notices that a flag is present on the primary system hive file and simply boots using the *.ALT* file, which is in an older but coherent state. It then copies the contents of the *.ALT* system hive file to the primary system hive file, restoring it to its former status. Changes made to the primary system hive file are lost and must be reentered. If instead it is the update to the secondary hive file that fails, the system simply restarts from the primary system hive file and copies the contents of it to the *.ALT* system hive file.

The last known good configuration

The subkey HKEY_LOCAL_MACHINE\SYSTEM contains critical startup information that Windows NT needs to boot successfully. This information is so important that Windows NT keeps at least three separate copies of it. The most recent version is contained in the subkey HKEY_LOCAL_MACHINE\SYSTEM\CurrentControlSet. Two older versions are also kept, initially in the subkey HKEY_LOCAL_MACHINE\SYSTEM\ControlSet001 and the subkey HKEY_LOCAL_MACHINE\SYSTEM\ControlSet002. As this information is updated, the control set numbers change. For example, on my workstation, Registry Editor displays the CurrentControlSet, ControlSet001, and ControlSet003.

When you change a value in the subkey HKEY_LOCAL_MACHINE\SYSTEM\CurrentControlSet, and restart the server, Windows NT writes the system configuration information as it existed before the change to one of the backup subkeys. If the change you make to the current control set causes the system to become unstable or unbootable, you can invoke the most recent of these backup copies by pressing the space bar when prompted during startup to use the last known good configuration.

NOTE Windows NT does not consider the boot process to have succeeded until a user has logged on to the console successfully. Once this occurs, Windows NT updates the last known good control set information.

Registry Keys and Value Entries

Conceptually, the structure of the Registry resembles the logical structure of a disk volume. Each of the root keys contains multiple *keys*, which are each containers for information. Each of these keys may contain *subkeys*, which correspond to subdirectories, and *value entries*, which correspond to files. Just as a subdirectory may contain only other subdirectories, only files, or both subdirectories and files, a key may contain subkeys, value entries, or both. Just as a file is the end point of the directory tree, a value entry terminates its own branch in the Registry structure.

A value entry comprises the following three parts, which are always displayed in the same order:

Name
: A (usually) descriptive name for the data contained within this entry, for example, *SecurityName*.

Data Type

A named standard definition of the type of data contained within the entry. For example, the data type named *REG_SZ* is used to store and represent human-readable data. Data types in the hexadecimal range from 00000000 through 7FFFFFFF are reserved for system use. Those in the range 80000000 through FFFFFFFF are reserved for applications. Table 9-3 lists the standard Registry data types currently defined and used by Windows NT 4.0 Server.

Value

The actual contents of the value entry, for example, *Basic Authentication*. The data contained here may be as large as 1 MB, depending on the data type specified for the entry.

The complete value entry is displayed by the 32-bit Registry Editor (*regedt32.exe*) in the form:

```
<Name> : <Data Type> : <Value>
```

Locating value entries within the registry

Right now, if someone asked me the filename of the program I'm running, I'd probably just say, *Winword.exe*. Of course, the real filename of that program, at least on my computer, is *C:\MSOffice\Winword\Winword.exe*. This is called the fully qualified pathname of that file. The reason that filenames must be unique within a given folder, but may be duplicated elsewhere in the folder structure, is that the actual name of the file includes not just the filename, but that file's location within the folder structure. Thus, two files with "identical" filenames in fact have very different names insofar as the operating system is concerned.

The Registry uses an analogous method to ensure unique naming. For example, the subkey:

```
HKEY_LOCAL_MACHINE\SOFTWARE\Microsoft\Internet Explorer\Security\Basic
```

contains the value entry:

```
SecurityName : REG_SZ : Basic Authentication
```

The actual or fully qualified name of that value entry is therefore:

```
HKEY_LOCAL_MACHINE\SOFTWARE\Microsoft\Internet Explorer
\Security\Basic\SecurityName
```

Just as many files with the same filename can exist in various folders on your hard drive, as many Registry value entries with the same name can also exist within different Registry keys. If you edit value entries manually, make sure that the value entry you are editing has not only the correct name, but is located in the correct key. This process is made even more confusing by the fact that, when examining keys, you are viewing a logical representation of the underlying phys-

ical data contained within a hive file. Changes you make to a value entry contained within one hive file will be reflected not only in the root key where the change is made, but within other root keys that also map to same value entry within the affected hive file.

Standard data types for value entries

The Registry defines the five standard data types, as shown in Table 9-3. In addition to these five standard data types, a sixth system-generated data type exists, named REG_FULL_RESOURCE_DESCRIPTOR. You cannot edit any value entry whose data type is REG_FULL_RESOURCE_DESCRIPTOR, or create a value entry with this data type.

Table 9-3. Windows NT Server Registry Data Types

Data Type	Purpose
REG_BINARY	Used to store binary data, including most hardware configuration information. You can display this data type as a hexadecimal value using Registry Editor, or in human-readable form using Windows Diagnostics.
REG_DWORD	Used to store data formatted as a double-word, or 4 bytes. Most parameters for device drivers and configuration settings for system services are stored in this format. You can use Registry Editor to display these values in binary, hex, or decimal form. For example: `InstallDate : REG_DWORD : 0x324dabe2`.
REG_EXPAND_SZ	Used to store expandable strings, or metatext, which are variables that are delimited with % signs, and are replaced with actual current values by a calling application. For example, on a typical server, the value *%SystemRoot%\Winhlp32.exe* might be replaced by the value *C:\WINNT\Winhelp32.exe*, where the actual Windows NT folder name replaces the metatext value.
REG_MULTI_SZ	Used to store lists or other entities that contain multiple values in human-readable form. List entries are separated by a NULL character, and the list is terminated by a double NULL character. `VideoBiosVersion : REG_MULTI_SZ : VGA/VBE BIOS, Version V2.1 Revision: 0.35 OS Version 1.00.06.CY1T.`
REG_SZ	Used to store string values representing human-readable text. `Title : REG_SZ : TCP/IP Protocol.`

Limiting Registry Size

The Registry stores so much information about so many aspects of the system running Windows NT Server that, left uncontrolled, it would simply continue to expand. Recognizing this problem, Microsoft gives you a mechanism to control this growth. The *Registry Size Limit* specifies the total amount of disk space allocated to Registry data.

In an environment where huge hard disks are available for pennies per megabyte, the reason for concern is not that the Registry might take a few more megabytes of disk space. Rather, the problem is that the Registry data is not only stored on the hard drive, but is loaded into the paged pool memory each time the server is booted. System memory is a much scarcer resource than disk space, and by limiting the size of the Registry on disk, you also limit the amount of paged pool memory devoted to storing Registry data.

Windows NT Server is hard-coded to limit Registry size to 25% of the size of the paged pool. That is, by default, no Registry key exists to specify the 25% limit. You should change the Registry Size Limit only on a Primary Domain Controller or on a Backup Domain Controller, and only if your network has so many user accounts that the default Registry size is inadequate to store the required information for all of them.

You can use either of two methods for setting a Registry Size Limit to a value other than the default. First, using the Registry Editor, you can modify the value entry for the Registry key:

```
HKEY_LOCAL_MACHINE\SYSTEM\CurrentControlSet\Control\RegistrySizeLimit
```

The value entry for RegistrySizeLimit must be specified as type REG_DWORD using a data length of 4 bytes, or it will have no effect. For example, to set RegistrySizeLimit to 20 MB, use the value 01400000, which will appear in the Registry Editor as 0x01400000 (20971520). If you have not previously modified the Registry Size Limit, you must create the key RegistrySizeLimit manually as described later in this chapter and then enter a value entry. If you have previously modified the Registry Size Limit, this key will already exist. You can then simply modify the value entry for that key.

The second (and recommended) method is to change the value for RegistrySizeLimit from the Performance page of the System Properties property sheet. You can view this property sheet either by right-clicking My Computer on the desktop and then choosing Properties or by double-clicking the System applet from Control Panel. In the Virtual Memory section of the Performance page, click Change to display the Virtual Memory dialog, as shown in Figure 9-3. Enter a decimal value for Maximum Registry Size (MB) and click OK to return to the System Properties property sheet. Click OK again to record the change and close the property sheet. Windows NT Server will prompt you to restart the server so that the change can take effect. After you have done so, if you use Registry Editor to examine the Registry, you will find that the RegistrySizeLimit key has been added and the value entry for it has been set to the value you entered for Maximum Registry Size (MB) above.

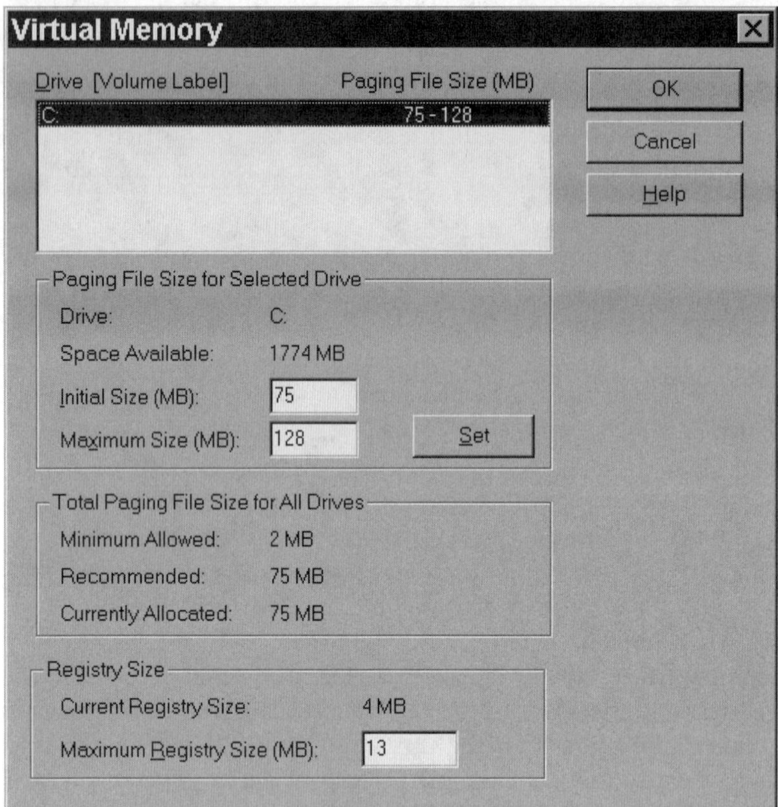

Figure 9-3. The Virtual Memory dialog allows you to specify a value entry for the RegistrySizeLimit key

Note that this value serves only to limit the maximum size to which the Registry can grow. Increasing this value does not preallocate the amount of disk space specified. A higher value simply allows the Registry to grow to that size if it needs to. Similarly, increasing this value does not guarantee that the required disk space will be available when needed.

How the Registry Supports Windows NT and Applications

The Windows NT operating system can both read data from the Registry and write data to the Registry, as can any application program. Changes made to the Registry may occur automatically, i.e., under control of the operating system or an applications program, or they can be a result of modifications made manually by the administrator or another user. The following interactions occur between the Registry and programs during routine system operations:

Registry Writes During Setup

Both the Windows NT setup program and setup programs for hardware and application software add or modify Registry information. A setup program almost always creates one or more new keys and/or subkeys and adds value entries for them. The setup program may also modify one or more value entries for an existing key or keys. For example, when I installed Microsoft Outlook, the setup program created a new key named HKEY_LOCAL_MACHINE\SOFTWARE\Microsoft\Office\8.0, which itself contains scores of new subkeys and value entries.

Registry Writes at Boot

Each time Windows NT starts, the *Hardware Recognizer* detects installed hardware and writes this current hardware configuration information into the Registry to ensure that Windows NT really has the hardware resources that it thinks it has. For Windows NT running on an Intel processor, these recognizer functions are performed by the utility program *NTDECTECT.COM* and by the Windows NT kernel program *NTOSKRNL.EXE*. Windows NT running on a RISC processor uses information provided by the firmware for the same purpose.

The Windows NT Kernel writes various information about itself to the Registry, e.g., build number and service packs installed, at boot time. As device drivers are loaded, they also report configuration information that is written to the Registry to describe the system resources that they consume, e.g., IRQ and base memory address. Similarly, various system services report status and other information as they are initialized, which may also be written to the Registry.

Registry Reads at Boot

In addition to writing to the Registry during boot, the Windows NT Server kernel also reads various information from the Registry. In particular, the kernel needs to know which device drivers should be loaded, in what order they should be loaded, and how they should be configured. As system services are initialized, they look to the Registry to determine how they should be configured initially.

Administrative Interaction with the Registry

Nearly any change that you make to the system configuration causes changed values to be written to the Registry. As an administrator, you can use any of the several tools provided by Windows NT to view the Registry and make changes to it. Some of these tools, e.g., Windows Diagnostics, allow you only to view a defined set of Registry parameters, but they display this information in an easily readable format. Other tools, such as Control Panel applets and the Policy Editor, allow you both to view and to change particular predefined subsets of Registry data indirectly. Other tools, like the various Registry Editors, allow you to view the entire Registry and make direct changes to it.

User Interaction with the Registry

User preferences and other user-specific information is written to the Registry of the local machine upon which the user is working. For example, settings for the current user for Microsoft Word are written to the key HKEY_CURRENT_USER\Software\Microsoft\Word\7.0\Data as a *REG_BINARY* value entry. To avoid uncontrolled growth of the server Registry, for users who log in across the network rather than logging in to the local console, this type of information is written to the Registry of the local workstation rather than to the Registry on the server.

Editing the Windows NT Registry

Windows NT provides numerous tools that allow you to modify the contents of the Registry. These tools vary in their power, in their ease of use, and in the scope of the information that can be displayed and altered. They also vary in how much inadvertent damage to the Registry can occur if you use them carelessly.

Using the Least Dangerous Tool for the Job

A typical Windows NT Registry is modified continuously. Some of these modifications are made casually, or implicitly. Other modifications are done on purpose, or explicitly, with the intention of modifying the behavior of the Registry. As common an occurrence as a local user opening and then saving a document results in implicit changes written to the Registry. The user has no intention of modifying the Registry by his actions, but the system itself makes changes to the Registry to keep current on the status of that user. Explicit changes are usually made by an administrator who is intentionally modifying the configuration of the system.

Explicit changes can be made using any of several tools provided by Windows NT Server. Some of these tools, like the Registry Editors described in the sections immediately following this one, are general-purpose ones that allow you to view and directly modify any aspect of the Registry. With this flexibility and power comes danger. Because these tools give you complete control over the Registry, you can easily make unintentional changes to the Registry that impair or even destroy the integrity of your Registry.

With this danger in mind, Microsoft created a variety of special-purpose tools. Some of these tools, like Windows NT Diagnostics, allow you to display (but not change) a broad variety of system information based on information retrieved from the Registry. Other tools, e.g., User Manager for Domains and the Control Panel applets, allow you to display and change information about a particular narrowly defined system function. Because these tools use standard Windows GUI conventions for editing, changing Registry values with them is much less error prone than doing so via direct Registry editing.

As a general precept, avoid editing the Registry directly unless doing so is absolutely necessary. Use the least powerful tool that will do the job. If you need to change network settings, do so from the Network applet in Control Panel rather than by using a Registry Editor. If you need to change RAS configuration settings, use Remote Access Admin. If you need to add or modify a user account, use User Manager for Domains. Using these special tools is not only safer but it's usually easier and much faster than to edit the Registry directly. Remember that, even as an experienced Windows NT administrator, each time you edit the Registry directly, you risk damaging the ability of your server to boot and run.

All of this said, there are times that you have no alternative to editing the Registry directly. Not all Registry keys and value entries are accessible using the special-purpose tools. The following sections cover the general-purpose Registry Editors and how to use them.

The Registry Editors

Microsoft actually supplies three versions of the Registry Editor, two of which are installed by Windows NT Setup. The two versions installed depends upon the configuration of your system, as follows:

- *regedt32.exe*. This is the 32-bit Registry Editor, and is the default Windows NT registry editing tool. Windows NT Setup always installs this program in the *%SystemRoot%\system32* folder. For example, on my server, this program is stored as *C:\WINNT\system32\regedt32.exe*.
- *REGEDT16.EXE*. If Windows NT Setup detects that you are installing Windows NT 4.0 in a directory where Windows 3.x is currently installed, or that you are upgrading an earlier version of Windows NT that had been installed over top of a Windows 3.x installation, Setup installs the 16-bit Registry Editor *REGEDT16.EXE* to the *%SystemRoot%* folder as the second registry editor.
- *Regedit.exe*. If you are making a new installation of Windows NT 4.0, or if you are upgrading an earlier version of Windows NT that had been installed to a clean hard drive, Setup installs the 32-bit Windows 95 Registry Editor *Regedit.exe* to the *%SystemRoot%* folder. For example, on my server, this program is installed as *C:\WINNT\Regedit.exe*.

The 32-bit registry editor—regedt32

The Windows NT Setup program always installs the 32-bit Registry Editor, which is named *regedt32.exe.* Regedt32 uses a tiled display reminiscent of the original Windows Program Manager. Each root key is displayed in a separate Window. Regedt32, shown in Figure 9-4, is the most powerful of the three Registry editing programs. Regedt32 offers more menu choices than the alternative Registry editor programs, and many of the menu choices have more options. The main drawback to using Regedt32 is that it allows you to work with only one root key at a time. If, for example, you are trying to locate a key with a particular name, but do not know within which root key it is contained, you must perform separate searches in each of the root keys.

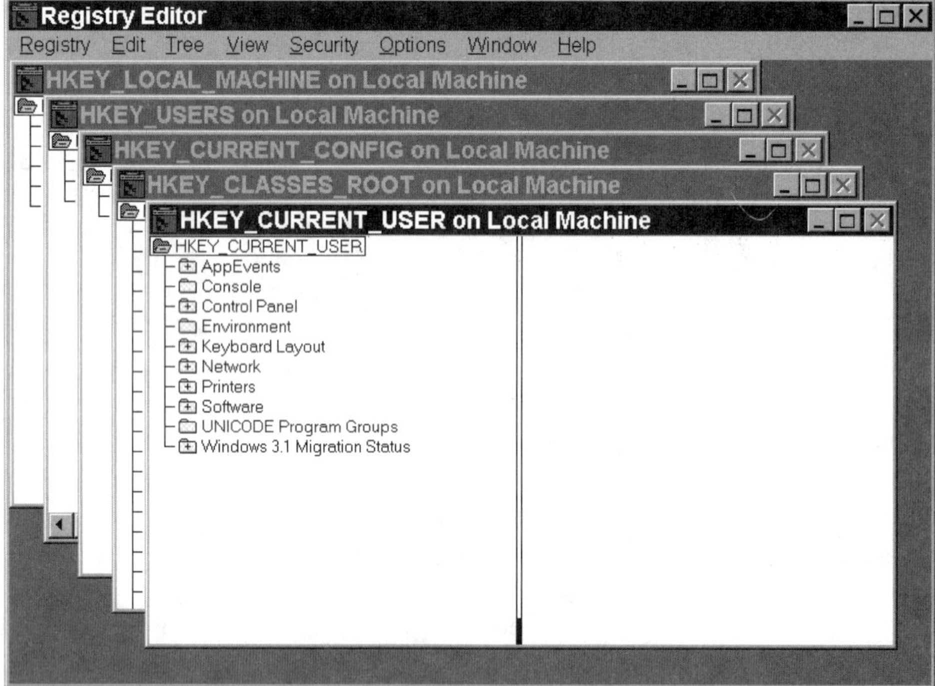

Figure 9-4. The 32-bit Registry Editor displays each root key in a separate window

The Windows 95 interface registry editor—regedit

Unless you install Windows NT Server on a system that previously had Windows 3.x installed, the Windows NT Setup program installs the Windows 95 Registry Editor *Regedit.exe* as the second Registry Editor. Regedit uses a hierarchical display reminiscent of the Windows 95/Windows NT Explorer. All root keys are displayed in a tree format. The root of the tree is the computer system upon which the Registry being edited is running. Regedit is less powerful than

Regedt32, but many people find it easier to use. Regedit offers fewer menu choices than Regedt32, and the menu choices have fewer options.

Relative to Regedt32, Regedit has two advantages:

Full Support for the Windows 95 Interface
: Unlike Regedt32, which uses the old-style Windows 3.x Program Manager interface to display each root key in a separate window, Regedit displays all keys in a single Explorer-like Window. Regedit displays context-sensitive menus when you right-click an item. These context-sensitive menus make it easy to modify the contents of a key, to search for values, and to perform other common editing functions. The Copy Key Name function is particularly useful when you need to prune and graft keys within the Registry because it allows you to copy the contents of a key to the clipboard and then paste it elsewhere. Regedt32, on the other hand, forces you to create keys manually.

Enhanced Searching Capabilities
: Regedt32 offers very limited searching capabilities. You can search only for a key, and only within a single root key per search. You may specify that the search be case sensitive and that only whole words be matched. Conversely, the Windows 95 Registry Editor allows you to perform a single search that crosses all root keys. You may search for any combination of keys, values, and data. You may specify an exact string match, but not that the search be case sensitive.

Relative to Regedt32, Regedit has two drawbacks:

Limited Support of Registry Data Types
: Regedit directly supports only the *REG_BINARY*, *REG_DWORD*, and *REG_SZ* data types. Data stored in *REG_EXPAND_SZ* and *REG_MULTI_SZ* is displayed in hexadecimal format, and can be edited only with the hex editor.

- *Lack of Security Support*. The interface of the Windows 95 Registry Editor was designed, obviously, with Windows 95 in mind. Because Windows 95 makes no provision for securing its Registry, this editor does not allow you to view or modify Windows NT Registry Security settings.

The 16-bit registration editor—REGEDT16

If you upgrade a system running Windows 3.x to Windows NT 4.0, or if you upgrade an earlier version of Windows NT that had been installed initially on a system running Windows 3.x, the Windows NT Setup program installs the 16-bit Registration Info Editor *REGEDT16.EXE* as the secondary Registry Editor. REGEDT16, shown in Figure 9-5, is a very limited tool. It allows you to edit the values originally contained in the Windows 3.x *REG.DAT* file, which maps the file associations and OLE data that correspond to those stored in the HKEY_CLASSES_

ROOT subtree in the Windows NT Registry. Figure 9-6 illustrates the type of edit that you can perform with the Registration Info Editor.

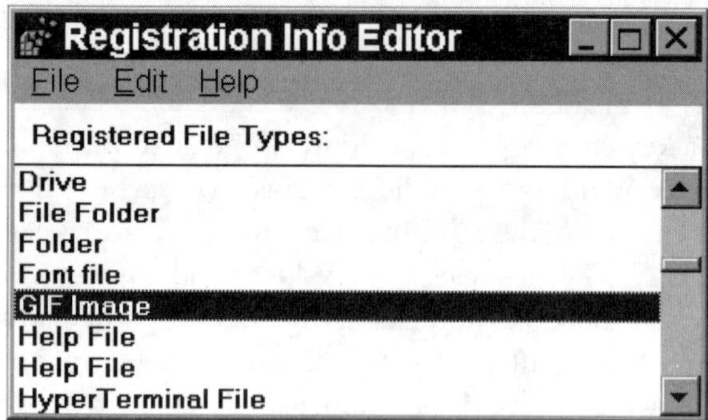

Figure 9-5. The 16-bit Registration Info Editor is intended for those upgrading to Windows NT from Windows 3.x

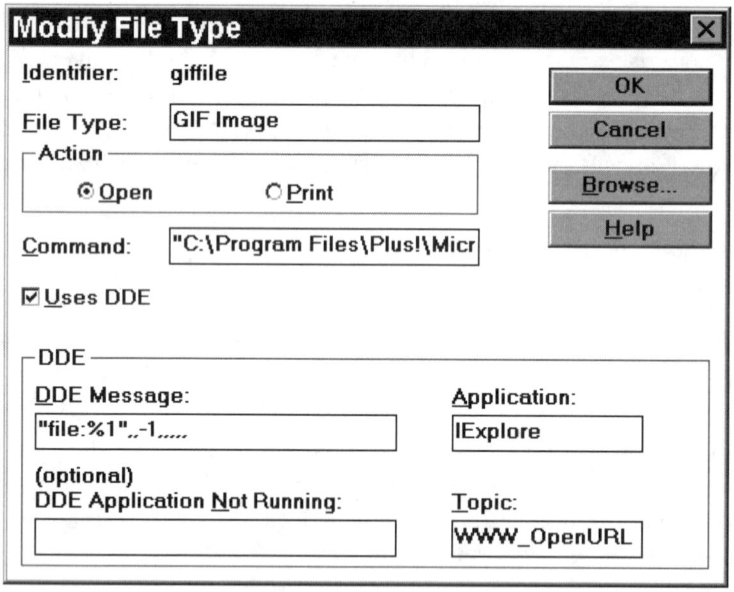

Figure 9-6. Using the Registration Info Editor to modify a file association

---

NOTE You will probably find, as I have, that you do most of your actual Registry editing with the 32-bit Registry Editor (*regedt32.exe*) because it is more powerful and flexible than Regedit. In fact, in any one session, I often use both tools. I use *Regedit.exe* for its superior search capabilities when I am trying to locate a particular key, and perhaps to copy that key. I use *regedt32.exe* to do the actual editing.

Backing Up the Registry

The Registry is designed to be fault-tolerant during routine system operations. When you take it upon yourself to edit the Registry manually, however, you're on dangerous ground. Changes you make for one purpose may have wholly unexpected results elsewhere. If you're very unlucky, you may unintentionally render the server unbootable. It only makes sense, therefore, to make a backup copy of the Registry before you start performing surgery.

The main reason that Microsoft recommends creating a 10 MB DOS-formatted boot partition and a 300 MB DOS-formatted system partition is to allow you easy access to these partitions if your server crashes. If your boot and system files reside on an NTFS-formatted partition and you crash your server by editing the Registry injudiciously, you may find that you have no alternative but to reinstall Windows NT from scratch. If instead the boot and system files are stored on a DOS-formatted partition, you can boot the crashed server from a DOS floppy, restore from the backup copy of the Registry, and restart the server in Windows NT. You can use any of the following methods to make a backup copy of the Registry.

Backing up with regedit.exe

You can use the Windows 95 Registry Editor to export a copy in ASCII text form of either the entire contents of the Registry or a selected branch. To do so, run *Regedit.exe*. Highlight the My Computer item at the top of the tree if you want to export the entire Registry, or highlight a branch if you want to export only the contents of that branch. From the Registry menu, choose Export Registry File to display the Export Registry File dialog.

Use the Save in pane to specify a folder where the backup copy is to be stored. Enter a File name for the backup copy, perhaps using today's date to ensure a unique name if you perform this procedure regularly. If you want to export a copy of the entire Registry, make sure that the Export range is set to All, which it will be by default if you selected My Computer before choosing the Export Registry File option. If you highlighted a branch before choosing the Export Registry File option, the Export range will be set to Selected branch and the name of the branch you highlighted will be filled in for you.

WARNING By default, *regedit.exe* sets the Save as type to Registration Files, and saves your backup copy with a *.REG* extension, resulting in a potentially hazardous situation. You might reasonably think that, when viewing files with Windows NT Explorer, double-clicking a file with a *.REG* extension would simply load the Registry Editor and allow you to view the contents of the backup file.

In fact, double-clicking a *.REG* file merges the contents of that file into the active Registry, something you probably didn't want to do. This action occurs immediately and without any warning message of what is about to occur.

You can avoid this potentially disastrous action by making sure that your backup Registry files do not have a *.REG* extension. To do so, either specify the Save as type as All (*.*) and assign your own extension to the backup file or rename the *.REG* file with a different extension immediately after you save it.

You can restore the Registry from a backup copy by simply reversing this process. To do so, start *regedit.exe* and choose Import Registry File from the Registry menu. Use the Import Registry dialog to specify the location of the backup Registry files. Highlight the file to be restored and click Open. The contents of the highlighted file are immediately merged into the active Registry.

Backing up with regedt32.exe

You can also use the 32-bit Registry Editor to save a copy of an individual root key or subkey in binary format. To do so, run *regedt32.exe*. Choose the appropriate root key Window, and highlight the key to be saved. From the Registry menu, choose Save Key to display the Save Key dialog. Use Save in to choose a location to store the backup copy and enter a name for that copy in the File name text box. Finally, click Save to write the copy to disk.

To restore a saved key, choose Restore from the Registry menu. Navigate to the location where backup copies of the keys are stored, highlight the desired filename, and click Open to restore the data. Windows NT displays a warning that Registry Editor is about to restore a key on top of the currently selected key, and will delete all existing subkeys and value entries when it does so. Click Yes to confirm the overwrite, or No to abort the restore.

Backing up with rdisk.exe

You can use the program *rdisk.exe*, which is located in the *%SystemRoot%\system32* folder, to create an emergency repair disk that contains your Registry information. By default, running rdisk does not back up the entire Registry, but saves only a subset of the Registry database. The purpose of *rdisk* is to provide a last-resort way of making a crashed server bootable, but not necessarily to restore the server to its former configuration. You can, however, cause *rdisk* to back up the entire Registry database by invoking it with the `/s` command-line switch.

Backing up with Regback.exe

Among the many programs included on the CD bundled with the Windows NT 4.0 Server Resource Kit is a group of utilities intended to make Registry management easier. Among these is *regback.exe*. *regback* is a command-line batch mode tool that allows you to make a snapshot of the entire Registry while the server is running and the hive files are open. The account you use when running *regback* must have the Backup files and directories User Right. You can start *regback* as *regback /?* to display the help screen. You may also start the program as *regback | more* to allow you to page through the available command-line arguments.

By default, *regback* backs up all Registry hive files in the *%SystemRoot%\system32\config* folder. You can use the following syntax to automatically back up all hives to the specified destination:

```
regback <destination>
```

For example, running *regback c:\archive* backs up all hives to the *c:\archive* `folder`. *regback* displays a warning if errors occur, or if one or more hives cannot be backed up automatically.

Editing Existing Keys and Value Entries

To edit a Registry key or value entry, first locate the key. I usually use the Windows 95 Registry Editor for this purpose. Once you have found the key you want to edit, run the 32-bit Registry Editor to do the actual editing. To do so, proceed as follows:

1. From the Start button, choose Run to display the Run dialog. Type the fully qualified pathname for *regedt32.exe*, in my case *C:\WINNT\system32\regedt32.exe*, in the Open text box. Alternatively, use Browse to locate the program. If you have run *regedt32* recently, you may also highlight the program name in the drop-down Open list. Once the program name is entered in Open, click OK to run the Registry Editor.
2. Click the window that contains the appropriate root key to highlight it, and then maximize that window for easier editing.

3. Expand the branch that contains the key to be edited. You can do this in any of the following ways:

   — Click the plus-sign that appears on the folder icon immediately to the left of the key name to expand that key. Similarly, click on the minus-sign to collapse the tree.

   — Highlight the key name and, from the Tree menu, choose Expand One Level, Expand Branch, Expand All, or Collapse Branch to modify the way the tree is displayed.

   — Highlight the key name and press Enter.

   — Double-click the key name.

4. Continue expanding branches until you have located the key to be edited. Once you have located the value entry to be edited, click to highlight it.

   In this example, I make a relatively innocuous change to the Registry, involving the settings for *regedt32.exe* itself. Currently, the program is set to delete without confirmation. This example changes that setting to require confirmation before deletion. The value entry for this setting is named ConfirmOnDelete and is located in HKEY_CURRENT_USER\Software\Microsoft\RegEdt32\Settings. Figure 9-7 shows the end result of drilling down through the Registry tree until the value entry is located.

5. Double-click the highlighted value entry to invoke the editor. *regedt32.exe* includes separate editors for binary values, string values, *DWORD* values, and Multi String values. In this case, the data type is *REG_SZ*, so the String Editor is automatically invoked.

6. Enter the new value and click OK to save it. In this case, I'm changing the value 0, which tells the Registry Editor not to confirm on delete, to 1, which tells it to prompt me before allowing deletions. The change is immediately reflected in the value entry displayed by the Registry Editor. Exit the Registry Editor to save the changes.

NOTE Many applications and services refer to the Registry to determine their settings, but do so only when they are first started. This means that you must usually exit the application and then load it again (or stop and restart the service) before changes to the Registry take effect. In this case, for example, even though ConfirmOnDelete shows a value of 1 or "true" in the Registry Editor display, I was able to create a new key and then delete it without having to confirm the deletion. A quick look at the Options menu verifies that Confirm on Delete remains unchecked.

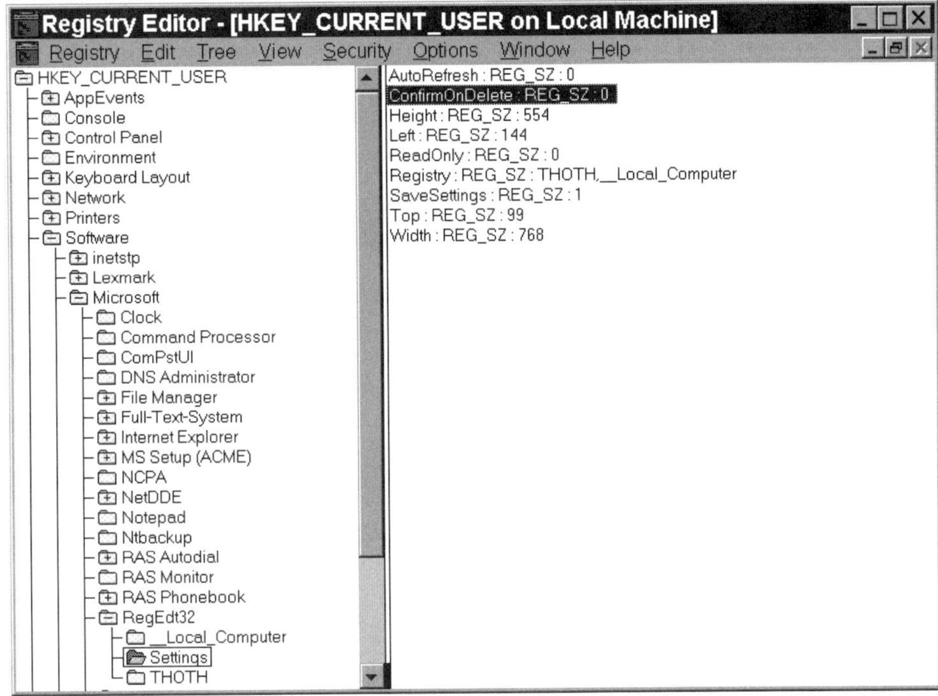

Figure 9-7. The Registry Editor displays the value entry to be modified

Creating Keys and Value Entries

Most administrators don't have occasion to create Registry entries manually very often. If you need to do so, it will probably be to fix an operating system bug or a problem with a driver. In cases like these, the vendor usually supplies detailed step-by-step instructions for making the change, that can be downloaded from its web page. Still, when you need to do this, you badly need to do it, so let's take a look at the process. In this example, I'll create a new key and enter a value to control the Registry size limit. As mentioned earlier in this chapter, the necessary value entry is located in the subkey HKEY_LOCAL_MACHINE\SYSTEM\CurrentControlSet\Control, and is named RegistrySizeLimit. To create this new value entry, proceed as follows:

1. Run *regedt32.exe*, and drill down to make HKEY_LOCAL_MACHINE\SYSTEM\CurrentControlSet\Control the current key.
2. From the Edit menu, click Add Value to display the Add Value dialog. Enter the name for the value entry, in this case RegistrySizeLimit, in the Value Name field. Data Type defaults to *REG_SZ*, but in this case needs to be changed to *REG_DWORD*. Use the drop-down list to specify the correct data type.

3. Verify that the Value Name and Data Type are correct, and then click OK to display the editor for the data type you specified. Because I specified data type *REG_DWORD*, the *DWORD* Editor is displayed. Enter a value in the Data field, making sure to use the radix indicated by the option button. In this case, I want to set the RegistrySizeLimit to 20 MB, which in hexadecimal notation is 1400000. You do not need to enter the "0x" portion of the string, which the display uses to indicate that the value is in hexadecimal. Click OK to save the new value entry, and verify that it is displayed correctly. Exit the Registry Editor.

NOTE You can also use the procedure described above to create a new key. To do so, simply choose Add Key from the Edit menu rather than choosing Add Value.

Securing and Auditing the Registry

You can use *regedt32.exe* to specify which users and groups can access which portions of the Registry, and at what level. For example, you might grant members of the groups Administrators and Domain Admins Full Control access to the entire registry, while restricting members of the group Users to Read access to all but specified portions. Other users may be assigned only certain higher-level permissions to specified portions of the Registry. You can also use *regedt32.exe* to determine, on a per-user and per-group basis, which Registry events are to be audited.

Assigning Registry Permissions

Regedt32.exe allows you to specify user and group access rights down to the individual key level. Access to individual value entries cannot be controlled, other than by controlling access to the key in which they are contained. In general, the default Registry permissions for an account correspond as you might expect to the general level of Windows NT permissions for the group to which that account is assigned. For example, an account assigned to the Domain Admins group will have default Registry permissions that grant it a high level of access, whereas an account assigned to Domain Users will have a corresponding lesser ability to make changes to the Registry. To set permissions that override these default permissions, proceed as follows:

1. In regedt32, highlight the key for which you want to set permissions. From the Security menu, choose Permissions to display the Registry Key Permissions dialog. In this example, I have chosen to modify permissions for the

entire root key HKEY_LOCAL_MACHINE. I could have modified those for only a subkey by highlighting that subkey before choosing Permissions.

2. The Registry Key Permissions dialog displays the name of the currently active key and its owner. Mark the Replace Permissions on Existing Subkeys check box if you want the changes you are about to make applied to the subkeys of the key being modified. Leave this check box blank if you want the changes to apply only to the active key.
3. The Name pane displays the users and groups who currently have access to the active key, and the level of that access. To modify the access level for an existing user or group, highlight that user or group. Click Add to add users and groups to the Name pane. Click Remove to delete an existing user or group.

NOTE You must choose the user or group to be modified individually. That is, the multiple-selection conventions of Windows do not operate within this dialog.

---

4. With the user or group to be modified highlighted in the Name pane, use the Type of Access drop-down list to specify an access level for that user. You may choose Read to grant read-only access, Full Control to grant complete access, or Special Access to grant customized access permissions. In this example, I am adding my own account, and granting Special Access. Choosing Special Access displays the Special Access dialog shown in Figure 9-8. You can use this dialog to grant customized access permissions to a user or group. These individual permissions are described in Table 9-4.
5. After you finish assigning permissions, click OK to accept the changes. These changes take effect the next time the Registry is accessed by the changed user or group.

Setting Registry Auditing

regedt32.exe allows you to specify, on a per-user or per-group basis, which Registry events will generate an entry in the audit log. As usual, you should be cautious about which events you choose to audit, and for which users. Otherwise, the size of your audit log can rapidly spiral out of control. To set auditing, proceed as follows:

1. In *regedt32*, highlight the key for which you want to set auditing. From the Security menu, choose Auditing to display the Registry Key Auditing dialog. In this example, I have chosen to set auditing for the root key HKEY_LOCAL_

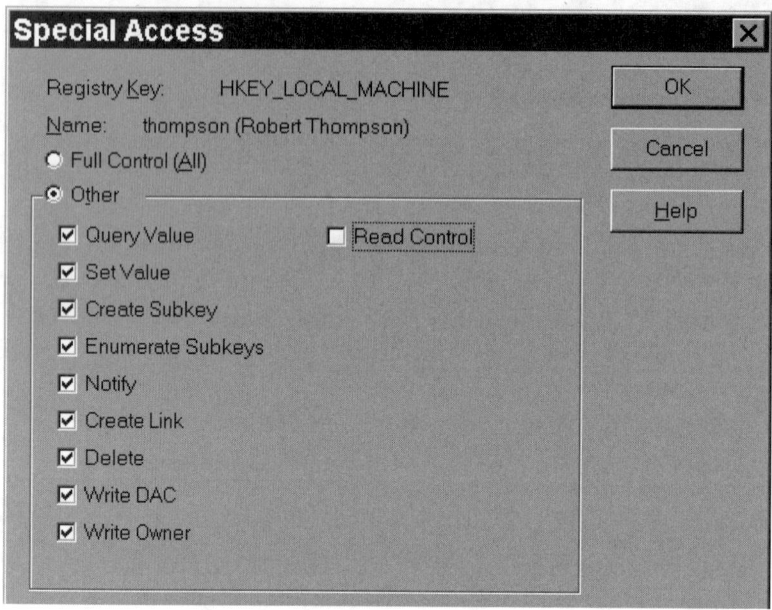

Figure 9-8. The Special Access dialog allows you to customize individual access permissions

Table 9-4. Custom Registry Access Permissions

Access Permission	Description
Query Value	Read a value entry from a Registry key.
Set Value	Modify a value entry within a Registry key.
Create Subkey	Create a new subkey within the Registry key.
Enumerate Subkeys	Identify subkeys within the Registry key.
Notify	Audit notification events from the Registry key.
Create Link	Create a symbolic link in the Registry key.
Delete	Delete the key, its subkeys, or value entries contained within the selected key or its subkeys.
Write DAC	Write a discretionary Access Control List to the selected key.
Write Owner	Take ownership of the selected key.
Read Control	Access the security information for the selected key.

MACHINE. I could have set auditing for only a subkey by highlighting that subkey before choosing Auditing.

2. The Registry Key Auditing dialog displays the name of the currently active key. Mark the Audit Permission on Existing Subkeys check box if you want the changes you are about to make applied to the subkeys of the key being modified. Leave this check box blank if you want the changes you make to apply only to the active key. By default, no Registry events are audited for

any user or group. Use Add to insert the users and groups for which auditing is to be set to the Name pane. You can also highlight an existing user or group and click Remove to eliminate auditing for that user or group.

3. When the Name pane displays the users and groups for which you want to set auditing, highlight one of these users or groups. As with setting permissions, you can work on only one user or group at a time. Mark one or more of the check boxes in the Events to Audit section. The example causes an audit entry to be generated when any audit event fails for any user in the HKEY_LOCAL_MACHINE root key or, because the Audit Permission on Existing Subkeys check box is marked, if such a failure occurs in any of its subkeys.
4. Click OK to save the changes you have made. If you marked the Audit Permission on Existing Subkeys check box, Windows NT displays a confirmation dialog to make sure that you really want to generate a log entry for any audit event within the subtree. The changes you have made take effect the next time the Registry is accessed by the changed user or group.

Working with Remote Registries

One of the nice things about the Registry is that it was designed to be a distributed database, accessible from any computer connected to the network. This means that you can work with the Registry on a given computer at the level granted by your account on that computer or in the domain of which that computer is a member. You can do so either from the console or from another workstation on the network. You may choose to use remote Registry editing for several reasons:

- The server whose Registry you want to edit may be locked away in a closet, making it more convenient to do the edits from your workstation than on the server console.
- The server may be located across town or across the country.
- You may need to edit the Registry on a user workstation running Windows NT Workstation. Even if that user has adequate permissions to edit his local Registry, you may prefer to do the job yourself instead of allowing the user to do it.
- The computer whose Registry requires editing may be running, but difficult to access. For example, a user may have set the background and foreground colors to blue on blue.

Although you can administer a remote Windows NT Registry from a workstation running Windows 95, or *vice versa*, instructions for doing so are beyond the scope of this book. Remote Registry editing between two computers that are running either Windows NT 4.0 Server or Windows NT 4.0 Workstation in any combination is very straightforward. To do so, proceed as follows:

1. Run *regedt32.exe* on the workstation to be used to edit the remote Registry. In this example, a computer named *kerby*, running Windows NT 4.0 Server, is running Regedt32 and will be used to edit the Registry on the remote server *thoth*, which is also running Windows NT 4.0 Server.
2. From the Registry menu, choose Select Computer to display the Select Computer dialog. Highlight the computer whose Registry is to be edited and click OK.
3. The Registry Editor window now displays two additional root keys, HKEY_LOCAL_MACHINE on *thoth*, and HKEY_USERS on *thoth*, as shown in Figure 9-9. It displays only these two root keys because the other root keys are either generated dynamically or are derived from the contents of these two main root keys.
4. Modify either of these two root keys as needed, using the same procedures you would use to edit the contents of a local key. Save the changes you have made and exit.

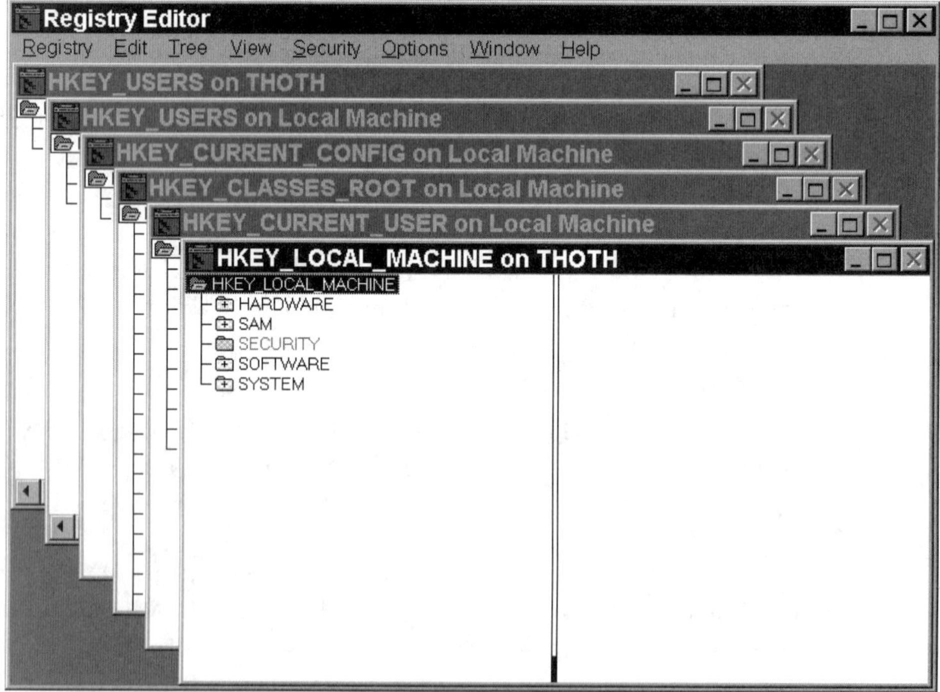

Figure 9-9. The main Registry Editor window displays two additional root name keys from the Registry on the remote server

In this chapter:
- *Monitoring Server Performance*
- *Optimizing Server Performance*
- *Monitoring Server Events*
- *Monitoring the Network*

10

Monitoring and Optimizing Server Performance

Many NetWare administrators take a minimalist approach to performance monitoring and optimization issues. They might reboot the server once a week or once a month to reclaim leaked memory. As new users are added to the server or additional NLMs are loaded, they might add a few megabytes of RAM. When performance eventually becomes unacceptable, they might upgrade to a faster processor, replace the disk drives with larger, faster ones, or simply replace the server.

This casual approach to performance considerations works pretty well with NetWare 3.1x, for several reasons:

- NetWare 3.1x doesn't make many demands on the hardware. Because it's written largely in assembler, it's small, fast, and performs well even when it's not fully optimized. Thousands of production NetWare 3.1x servers are still running on 486 and even 386 processors.
- NetWare 3.1x does a pretty good job of self-tuning. It makes the most of whatever resources you give it to work with. In most server environments, self-tuning does about 95% to 99% of the possible optimization. Any manual tweaks you make are simply to wring out that last percent or two.
- NetWare 3.1x functions in a relatively uncomplicated environment. A typical NetWare 3.1x server provides file and print services to local clients running IPX/SPX transport. NetWare generally doesn't have to deal with internetworks, support multiple transport protocols, function as an application server, and so on. The core file and print services provided by NetWare 3.12 have

been tweaked over the years by Novell, and require little user intervention to perform well.

- NetWare 3.1x is inherently a single-server environment. Although you may have many NetWare servers in your network, each is self-contained. Because the bindery database is local to each server, monitoring and tuning issues related to the interaction between servers do not arise.
- Finally, for many NetWare administrators, depending on self-tuning is Hobson's choice. NetWare 3.1x doesn't provide many performance monitoring and tuning tools, and those it does provide are not particularly easy to use.

The good news about Windows NT Server is that you can take pretty much the same approach without giving much up. Install Windows NT Server on a server that has a fast processor (or multiple processors), plenty of RAM, and fast disk drives. You'll find that, like NetWare 3.1x, Windows NT Server does a pretty good job all by itself of making the best use of the resources that you have provided. As demand on the server relative to the available resources increases, Windows NT Server continues to make rational resource allocation decisions.

As the server reaches the point of overload, it continues to juggle resources and demands gracefully. Performance gradually degrades, but nothing breaks. While writing this book, I built a test-bed server on an old Gateway 486/66 system with only 40 MB of RAM. As I started each chapter, I loaded the additional services that were the subject of that chapter. Eventually, this tired old server was running more processes than anyone could reasonably expect a production server to support. In addition to being a backup domain controller and running three transport protocols and the standard system services, this server was running the DHCP Server, the WINS Server, the DNS Server, a couple of Backup Exec services, and so on—a total of 28 services.

At some point, I consciously decided to see if I could break the server. I continued adding services—the IIS Web Server, an Exchange Server beta, an SNTP time server, and so forth—until I had a total of 50 services running on this server. Server performance—nothing to write home about initially—continued to degrade, but nothing failed. Response times became painfully slow, swapping became nearly continuous, but the server continued to function and to service user requests. Attempting anything even remotely similar on a NetWare 3.12 server would almost certainly have resulted in an abend and a server crash.

Various Windows NT services include their own tools, each focused on that particular service. For example, the DNS Manager application displays statistics related to performance of the DNS Server. In addition to these specialized tools,

Windows NT Server provides three primary general-purpose tools for monitoring and optimizing the operating parameters of your server. These tools include:

Performance Monitor
: This powerful tool, which originated in Microsoft System Management Server (SMS) 1.0, allows you to monitor the performance of virtually every aspect of your server and network. It provides real-time monitoring of the operating characteristics of the server, e.g., memory, disk, and processor utilization. You can display the data graphically, set traps to generate alerts based on threshold values, and log the data to a disk file for later review.

Event Viewer
: This tool allows you to view the System, Security, and Application log files maintained by Windows NT Server. These log files contain system-generated messages that report on system events of varying severity and importance, from simple Information messages to Warning messages that indicate potential developing problems to Error messages that indicate actual failures. Event Viewer also allows you to view system security events, those indicating success and failure of events that you have specified should be audited.

Network Monitor
: This tool provides many of the same functions of a network analyzer like Network General Sniffer®. It is a trimmed down version of the full-blown Network Monitor application bundled with Microsoft Systems Management Server. Its primary limitation *vis-à-vis* the full product is that it allows you to capture and examine only packets that are sent from or sent to the server upon which it is running. Even with this limitation, it is a very powerful tool for optimizing the network functions of your server.

In addition to these major tools, Windows NT Server includes *Task Manager* as a quick and dirty adjunct to the Performance Monitor. You can use Task Manager to get a snapshot of applications and services currently running on the server, along with the memory and CPU resource that each is consuming. Task Manager also provides a quick and easy way to locate and kill a process that is running out of control.

Monitoring Server Performance

Even though you can abuse Windows NT Server without breaking it, and even though it does a pretty good job on its own of managing its resources, it still pays to keep an eye on what's going on. By doing so, you can recognize developing problems early, while there's still time to fix them before they become critical.

You can also keep track of the bottlenecks that limit the performance of your server. Granted, when you locate and fix a bottleneck, another immediately crops up, but that's just the nature of any complex system. If, for example, your server is memory-bound and you add memory, you're then likely to find that disk I/O—or perhaps processor speed or network I/O—is now the limiting factor. You can never eliminate bottlenecks entirely, but Windows NT Server provides the tools you need to isolate them and make rational decisions about where to focus your efforts.

The primary Windows NT Server tool for general-purpose performance monitoring is named, reasonably enough, Performance Monitor, and is shown in Figure 10-1. Performance Monitor allows you to monitor the performance of virtually every aspect of your server. It provides real-time monitoring of the operating characteristics of the server, like memory, disk, and processor utilization. Performance Monitor can display performance data graphically, set traps to generate alerts based on threshold values, and log the data to a disk file for later review.

Like most Windows NT Server utilities, Performance Monitor is not limited to displaying data for the computer it is running on. You can use Performance Monitor to view data for other computers in the domain that are running Windows NT Server. You can also use Performance Monitor to view data for clients running Windows NT Workstation 4.0. Best of all, you can use Performance Monitor to view performance data for two or more computers simultaneously, which can be a very useful tool for balancing the load in a multiserver network. The ability to run Performance Monitor remotely also means that you can use it on a management workstation to monitor a server and thereby minimize performance degradation on the server caused by the Performance Monitor itself.

To start Performance Monitor, select **Start ➤ Programs ➤ Administrative Tools (Common) ➤ Performance Monitor**. The main Performance Monitor screen appears, as shown in Figure 10-1. By default, however, the screen is empty because you have not yet told Performance Monitor exactly what you want to monitor.

Understanding Objects, Counters, and Instances

Performance Monitor tracks the behavior of various system objects. Windows NT Server defines an *object* as a standardized entity that identifies a system resource. These resources may be physical or logical. For example, *Memory*, *Processor*, and *PhysicalDisk* are physical Windows NT objects, because they represent physical network resources. *Process*, *Thread*, and *LogicalDisk* are examples of logical objects, because they represent logical server resources or activities.

Performance Monitor associates one or more counters with each object. A *counter* is simply a way of characterizing the performance or behavior of one or more

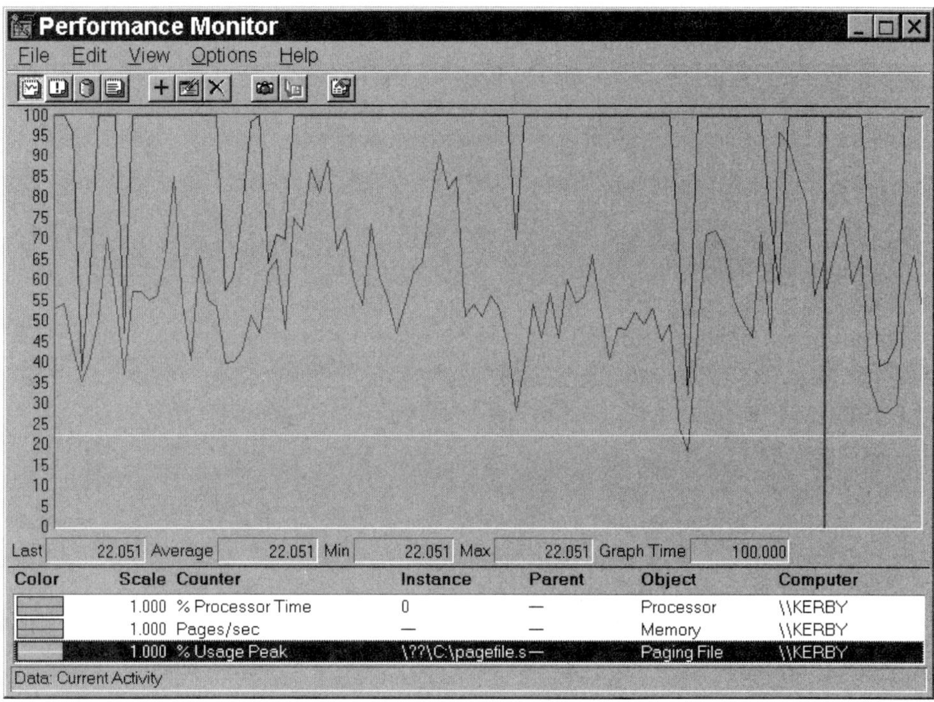

Figure 10-1. Performance Monitor uses Chart view to display counters for several critical system parameters (This is not a happy server. Processor utilization is spiking to 95%, and page faults are off the chart.)

aspects of an object. For example, the Processor object has several counters associated with it, including one named *% Processor Time.* This counter quantifies what fraction of the processor's available time is being spent performing actual work for user and system processes versus that being spent executing the idle process. Other counters associated with the Processor object measure other aspects of Processor operation.

Some counters are simple. They measure only one tightly defined aspect of an object. Other counters are complex. They measure a combination of several characteristics of the object and present the result as a single value. Still other counters are composite. They measure a combination of object characteristics that may also be viewed individually by examining the individual counters that make up the composite.

A counter is one of three types:

Instantaneous Counters

Display the most recent measurement as a snapshot value. For example, the Available Bytes counter of the Memory object displays the available virtual memory as of the moment the sample was taken.

Averaging Counters
: Display a value over a certain period of time, and can be identified by their names, which always contain *%* or */sec*. An Averaging Counter displays the results of the last two samples.

Difference Counters
: Measure the delta of a value by subtracting the most recent sample from the preceding one. If the difference is positive, it is displayed; if negative, zero is displayed. None of the counters that is currently supplied with the basic counter set in Performance Monitor is a Difference Counter, but this type of counter may be supplied with third-party applications and services.

The counters that are supplied with Windows NT Server are referred to as the *basic counter set*. Installing some applications, services, or hardware may also install counters, called *extensible counters*, that are specific to that item. These new counters may be installed in a new object or in an existing object. In some cases, the new counters are installed automatically with the new item. In others, the counters are supplied, but must be installed manually by following the instructions supplied with the item.

NOTE Some objects and their associated counters are found on any system running Windows NT Server. Others, for example the WINS Server object, exist only if the server in question is running a particular Windows NT service or application.

Performance Monitor provides a defined set of counters for each object. Some of these counters (and, indeed, some of the objects themselves) are primarily of academic interest. Either they measure values that are of little concern to most system administrators, or there's not much you can do with the information they provide anyway. Other counters, however, present information that is both critical to efficient server functioning and under the control of the system administrator.

Which counters are significant to you depends to a large extent on the way you are using your server. For example, on a server that is used primarily to provide file and print sharing services, counters that measure disk performance and network I/O performance are critical, and those that measure memory and processor somewhat less so. On a machine that is used primarily as an application server, counters that measure processor and memory are usually the most important, and those that measure disk and network I/O somewhat less so. Some counters, however, are important on nearly any server. Table 10-1 lists some of these important objects and counters, and details the significance of each.

Table 10-1. Important Performance Monitor Objects and Counters

Object	Counter	Description
Processor	% Processor Time	Measures how busy the processor is. This value is the percentage of time that a processor is executing a user or system process thread versus the time spent executing the Idle thread in the Idle process. This counter may occasionally spike to 100% on even lightly loaded servers. More important is its average value. If the average value exceeds 90% or so, consider replacing the processor with a faster model or adding another processor. On multiprocessor machines, each processor may have an instance of this counter. Note that some screen savers are notorious CPU hogs. In particular, the 3D OpenGL screen savers can consume 90% or more of the processor. If you must use a screen saver on your server, choose the Blank Screen option, which has nearly no impact on CPU utilization.
	Interrupts/sec	Measures how many hardware interrupts per second are occurring. A hardware device generates a hardware interrupt when it requires attention from the processor. When it receives an interrupt, the processor suspends normal thread execution and processes the interrupt. Some interrupt activity is always present, even on an idle server, for handling system events like clock interrupts. My server, for example, runs at about 100 interrupts/sec when completely idle. This value should be relatively stable on a production server. Major increases in this counter that occur without a corresponding increase in server load may be due to a hardware problem, e.g., a failing network interface card spewing interrupts. Always view this counter when you load a new device driver. Poorly written device drivers can cause huge increases in interrupt activity.
Memory	Available Bytes	Measures the amount of available virtual memory on the Zeroed, Free, and Standby lists, as an instantaneous snapshot value. Zeroed and Free memory is available for use immediately; Standby memory is that removed from a process working set.

Table 10-1. Important Performance Monitor Objects and Counters (continued)

Object	Counter	Description
	Page Faults/sec	A Page Fault occurs when a process attempts to access a virtual memory page that is not available in its working set in RAM. *Hard page faults* must be retrieved from disk, which greatly slows performance. Soft page faults are those that can be retrieved from the standby list, and therefore do not require disk I/O. If this value is high (or increasing), it is a sign that you need to add physical RAM to your server.
	Page Reads/sec	Measures how frequently the system needs to read pages from disk because of page faults, and therefore how badly page faulting is impacting performance. More than one page can be read in a single operation. This counter measures how often reads occur rather than how many total pages are read. This is the most important counter to monitor if you are concerned about page faulting affecting system performance.
Paging File	% Usage	The percentage of the space allocated to the page file that is actually in use. In rough terms, you can multiply this percentage by the size of the page file to determine how much more physical memory would be required in the server to minimize paging.
	% Usage Peak	The highest percentage usage of the page file. If this value frequently exceeds 90%, allocate more space to the page file. A 100% usage peak indicates that the server has, at least momentarily, run out of both physical and virtual memory.
Physical Disk	% Disk Time	The percentage of elapsed time that a disk drive is actually occupied in reading data from and writing data to disk. A value greater than about 67% indicates that the disk in question is a bottleneck.
	Avg. Disk Queue Length	The average number of read requests and write requests queued for the disk in question. A sustained average higher than two indicates that the disk is being over-utilized.
Network Interface	Bytes Total/sec	The rate that bytes, including data and framing characters, are sent and received on the network interface.
	Packets Outbound Errors	The number of outbound packets that could not be sent because of errors.
	Packets Received Errors	The number of inbound packets that had to be discarded because they contained errors that prevented them from being delivered to the proper destination protocol stack.

Performance Monitor allows you to monitor multiple *instances* of some objects and counters. For example, if your server has quad processors, you can monitor one instance of the Processor object for each physical processor. Similarly, if your server has multiple disk drives, you can monitor the counters for each individual PhysicalDisk object that corresponds with a disk drive. In fact, you can monitor multiple instances of a single object, although there is no point to doing so, because each instance simply replicates the other instances.

Configuring and Using Performance Monitor

Performance Monitor offers four views, as follows:

Chart
: The default view, Chart view, provides a near real-time display of system performance characteristics that you have specified. You may save your custom-defined charts as *.PMC* files and subsequently retrieve them for reuse.

Alert
: Allows you to set threshold values, or traps, for the minimum or maximum acceptable value for selected counters. When a counter exceeds (or falls below) the level you have defined, an alert is generated and logged to the alert file. You may also specify that other actions are to take place when an alert occurs. For example, you may specify that a particular program be run each time a specific alert is triggered, or that a notification message be sent to a specified computer. You may save custom-defined alerts as *.PMA* files and subsequently retrieve them for reuse.

Log
: Allows you to log the values of selected counters and subsequently to examine these logs. Logging is a very useful tool for determining trends over an extended period. It allows you to uncover potential performance problems that would not be immediately evident when using the shorter-term views provided by Chart view and Alert view. Custom-defined logs can be saved as *.PML* files, and reused later.

Report
: This view is similar in purpose to Chart view, but presents the captured data in textual form rather than graphically. Custom-defined reports can be saved as *.PMR* files, and reused later

NOTE You can save the current view at any time from the File menu. Choose *Save X Settings* (where X is Chart, Alert, Log, or Report) to save to the current settings file. Choose *Save X Settings As* to save the settings for the current view to another file you specify. You may also save the settings for all four views simultaneously by choosing Save Workspace.

Using Chart view

When you first start Performance Monitor, you are in Chart view. The display is blank because you have not yet specified any objects or counters to be monitored. This section examines the steps needed to configure Chart view to display the counters you select. To add a counter to Chart view, proceed as follows:

1. From the Edit menu, choose Add to Chart to display the Add to Chart dialog, as shown in Figure 10-2.

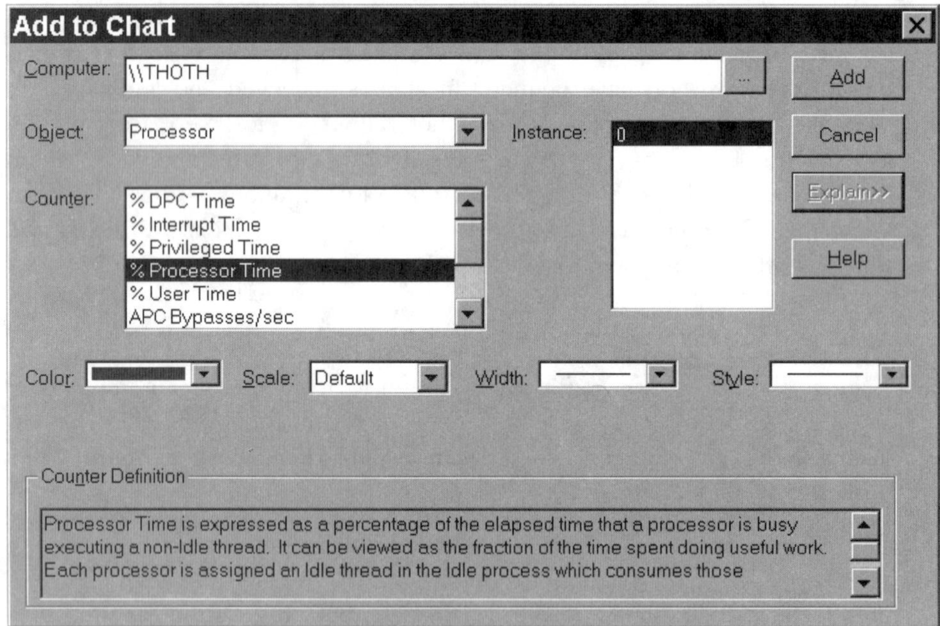

Figure 10-2. The Add to Chart dialog allows you to add one or more counters to be monitored

2. The Computer field defaults initially to the computer upon which Performance Monitor is running, and later to the machine for which a counter was last added. Accept this value, type a new computer name, or use the button to the right of the field to browse a list of available computers. One very nice

thing about Performance Monitor is that it allows you to display counters from multiple servers on a single Chart view.

3. Select an Object from the drop-down pick list. If multiple instances exist for the selected object, highlight one of these instances in the Instance pick list. Available counters for the selected object are shown in the Counter scrolling pick list. Highlight a counter to select it. Click Explain to display a pane that briefly describes the purpose of the highlighted counter.

4. Use the Color, Width, and Style drop-down pick lists to specify the line color and line type assigned to the selected counter, or accept the default values. These selections are useful primarily when you are monitoring counters for more than one server on a single chart.

TIP Assign a different Style to each server, and use the same color for the same counters. For example, I might assign a solid line to the server *kerby*, and a dashed line to the server *thoth*. I might then assign blue to the *% Processor Time* counter on both systems. When I view the chart, the color makes it immediately obvious which counter I am looking at, and the line style does the same for the server. Alternatively, some people find it more intuitive to assign color by server and line style by counter.

---

5. Use the Scale drop-down pick list to choose a decimal scaling value for the counter, or accept the default. The default value for scale varies according to the counter selected, and is appropriate for that counter under most circumstances. For example, *% Processor Time* uses a default scale of 1.000. Because the chart display ranges from 0 through 100, a scale of 1.000 means that 0% processor utilization appears at the bottom of the display, or 0, and 100% processor utilization at the top, or 100. Conversely, the Interrupts/sec counter may have an idle value of 100. Using a scale of 1.000 would place this idle value at the top of the chart, making it impossible to differentiate between no load and a heavy load. Accordingly, Performance Monitor assigns a default scale of 0.0100000 to this counter, meaning that a current value of 100 interrupts/sec is displayed on the chart as 1.0.

6. When you have completed your selections, click Add to add the counter to the Chart view. You may then repeat the process to add additional counters. When you have finished adding counters, click Done to return to Chart view. Figure 10-3 shows Chart view displaying the *% Processor Time* and *Pages/sec* counters for the servers *thoth* and *kerby*. For the purpose of illustration, just before capturing this screen shot, I started a file search on each server to locate all files that contained the text *the*, thereby ensuring high processor utilization and heavy page faulting.

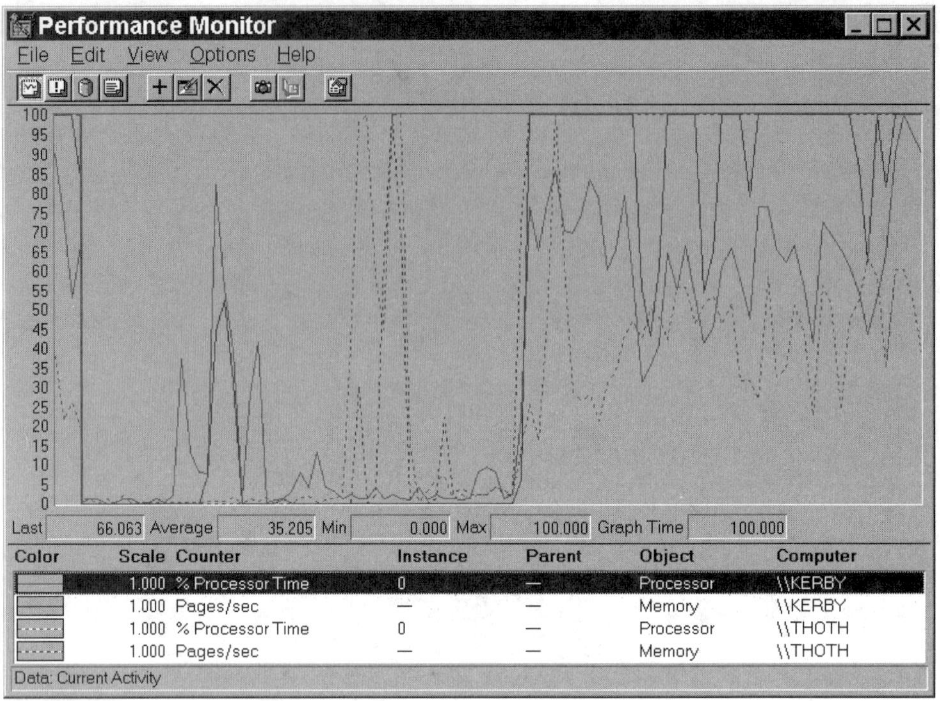

Figure 10-3. Chart view shows the % Processor Time and Pages/sec counters for the servers kerby (solid line) and thoth (dashed line)

The main pane of the Chart view displays updated values for each counter you have activated, condensing a lot of information into a small space. At times, you may want to view more detailed information for a particular counter. The bottom of the Chart view display contains a pane that lists each of the counters you have activated. It displays the icon associated with the counter (color and line type), the scale being used, the name of the counter, the instance (if applicable), the parent, the object of which the counter is a member, and the computer upon which the counter is being sampled.

To view detailed information about a particular counter, highlight that counter name in the lower pane. The last, average, minimum, and maximum values for that counter are displayed in the panes immediately beneath the main pane.

For example, in Figure 10-3, *% Processor Time* for *kerby* has varied over the course of sampling between 0% and 100%. The last sample was 66.063%, and the average over the graph time was 35.205%. For this counter, it is the average value that is important, and it shows that *kerby* is very lightly loaded. For other counters, the minimum or maximum value may be more important. For example, the % Usage Peak counter for the Paging File object should never approach 100%.

If it reaches 100%, that means that the system is running out of virtual memory, and that the size of the swap file needs to be increased.

NOTE Use the Options menu to set preferences for each view. For example, in Chart view, choose **Options ➤ Chart** to display the Chart Options dialog. You can choose among the available options to specify which screen elements are displayed, whether data is displayed as a graph (line chart) or a histogram (bar chart), whether the display is automatically refreshed and, if so, how often, and so on. The other views allow you to set preferences in similar fashion.

Using alert view

Alert view allows you to set threshold levels for selected counters. When the threshold value is reached, an alert is generated. To display the Alert view, choose **View ➤ Alert**, or press `Ctrl-A`.

Note that the counters you select in Alert view are completely independent of those you selected in Chart view. Chart view is intended for interactive monitoring of server performance, whereas Alert view is intended for setting traps to notify you of serious server events. Accordingly, you will often use a different group of counters for these two views.

The process of adding counters to Alert view is quite similar to that used to add counters in Chart view, so this section focuses on the differences. To add a counter to Alert view, select **Edit ➤ Add to Alert** to display the Add to Alert dialog box. Completing this dialog is very similar to completing the Add to Chart dialog described in the preceding section, but with the following differences:

Alert If pane
: This pane allows you to specify the threshold that triggers the alert. Select the Over option button for counters that are critical when they exceed the threshold value. For example, I have specified that an alert will occur if the *% Usage Peak* counter for the *Paging File* object goes over 95%. Select the Under option button for counters that are critical when they drop below the threshold value, e.g., the *Available Bytes* counter of the *Memory* object.

Run Program on Alert pane
: Allows you to specify a program to be run when an alert occurs. Select the First Time option button if you want the program to be run only for the first occurrence of the alert. Select the Every Time option button if you want the program to run for each occurrence of the alert. Enter the full name of the program to be run, including drive and path, in the text box.

TIP

Bizarrely, Windows NT Server offers no convenient mechanism for notifying an administrator of significant system events via email or pager. You can cause an alert notification message to be sent to a particular machine name, or to an account name for someone who is currently logged in, but not to an email address or to a pager.

One administrator I know (well, it's me) uses a particularly rococo workaround for this problem. I created a boilerplate text file in SMTP message format to correspond with each alert event. Each of these text files has a corresponding batch file that copies it to the *\mercury\smtpque* directory on my NetWare server. I configure each Alert to Run Program on Alert with the name of the appropriate batch file specified. When that alert occurs, the batch file runs, and copies the text file to the *Mercury* SMTP queue. *Mercury* handles it just as it would any other inbound message, and the message shows up at whatever workstation I happen to be logged into.

I also created two batch files named *in.bat* and *out.bat*, that copy one of two sets of text files to the directory where the alert batch files look. The "in" set of text files direct the mail message to my local mail account. The "out" set of text files direct the message to my pager. When I arrive at my desk, I run *in.bat*. When I leave, I run *out.bat*. Quite a lot of work to accomplish something the operating system should have done for me, but there it is.

To configure preferences for Alert view, select **Options ➤ Alert** from the main menu to display the Alert Options dialog. You can set the following options:

Switch to Alert View

This check box, if enabled, causes Performance Monitor to switch to Alert view when an alert occurs. This option is of limited practical utility, because if Performance Monitor is not running, it has no effect. If Performance Monitor is running minimized, the view changes, but the application does not maximize or otherwise notify you that an alert has occurred.

Log Event in Application Log

This check box, if enabled, causes an entry to be written to the application log when an alert event occurs. You can subsequently use Event Viewer to view this entry.

Send network message

This check box, if enabled, generates a network message when an alert event occurs. This message contains the names of the originating machine, the destination net name, the name of the counter, the threshold value specified for it, and the actual value reached.

Enter the account name or the machine name to be notified in the Net Name field, without using the double backslash. If you enter a machine name, the message is directed to that machine, regardless of who happens to be using it. If you enter an account name, the message is directed to the system where that account is logged in.

In order for network message notification to work, the messaging service must be running on the destination computer, and the net name must be registered. You can start the messaging service from a command prompt by typing *net start messenger*, or from the Control Panel Services applet. You can determine which net names have been registered by typing *net name* at the command prompt. The computer registers its own name when it boots, and the user account name is registered when that user logs in. You can add a name to a running machine by typing *net name <insert new name here> /add.*

Update Time pane

Choose the Periodic Update option button and enter an interval if you want Alert view to update automatically. Choose the Manual Update option button if you want Alert view to be updated only when you select **Options ➤ Update Now**.

Using log view

Log view allows you to log the values for selected objects to a disk file. This view is useful primarily for watching long-term trends on your server. To display the Log view, choose **View ➤ Log**, or press `Ctrl-L`. Note that Log view allows you to select only objects (rather than individual counters), and is completely independent of Chart view and Alert view.

The process of adding objects to Log view is a bit different from the process of adding counters to Chart view or to Alert view. To add an object to Log view, select **Edit ➤ Add** to Log to display the Add To Log dialog box.

In the Computer field, accept the default computer name, type a new name, or click the icon immediately to the right of the field to browse for a computer. The default computer name initially is the computer upon which Performance Monitor is running. After you have added an object, the default becomes the name of the last computer for which you added an object. After selecting the computer, highlight an object in the Objects scrolling pick list and click Add. You can add as many objects as you wish, from as many computers as you wish.

To begin using logging, switch to Log view and then select **Options ➤ Log** to display the Log Options dialog. Specify a location and name for the log file to create and save the log file. In the Update Time pane, mark the Periodic Update option button and enter an interval if you want logging to occur automatically. Otherwise, mark the Manual Update option button and select **Options ➤ Update Now** when you want to record information to the log.

Click Start Log to begin logging information to disk. Log view displays the log file name and the log interval, and displays and updates the file size and the status. Performance Monitor continues to collect data until you click Stop Log in the Log Options dialog. You may also select **Options ➤ Bookmark** to insert a text comment into the log file. This can be useful as a placeholder to indicate when you have made a change to the system so that you can subsequently analyze the log to determine the effects of that change. Performance Monitor automatically inserts a time- and date-stamped bookmark each time you start or stop logging.

WARNING Logging many objects, logging many machines, or using a short update interval both causes the log file to grow rapidly and may place a significant burden on the server. To minimize this impact, log only those objects needed to serve your purpose, and use the longest update interval feasible.

Unlike Chart view and Alert view, the data from Log view doesn't appear in the Performance Monitor window. To view logged data, first stop the logging process to close the log file. You cannot view data from an open log file. Once you have closed the log file, from Log view select **Options ➤ Data From** to display the Data From dialog.

Select the Log File option button, and type the full name of the log file, including drive and path. Alternatively, click the icon immediately to the right of the text box to display the Open Input Log File dialog and browse for the log file you want to use. After you select the appropriate log file, click OK to open it.

The next step is to specify which portion of the log file to view. By default, the entire log file is selected. To narrow this range, from Log view, select **Edit ➤ Time Window** to display the Input Log File Timeframe dialog. The bar in the top pane represents a time line for logged events, with the light gray vertical separators indicating bookmarks that delimit logging sessions.

In the Bookmarks pane, highlight the bookmark that indicates the beginning of the range you want to display, and then click Set As Start. Highlight the bookmark that indicates the end of the range you want to display, and then click Set As Stop. The time line bar in the top pane highlights the range you have selected in blue, with the starting date and time displayed above the bar, and the ending date and time displayed below it. Click OK to display the logged data.

Using Report view

Report view provides a text-based alternative to the graphics-based Chart view. Instead of displaying a real-time line chart or bar chart of counters, Report view displays the same data in tabular form. To display Report view, choose **View ➤ Report**, or press `Ctrl-R`. Like Chart view and Alert view, Report view allows you to select individual counters, rather than just objects. Report view is completely independent of Chart view, Alert view, and Log view.

The process of adding counters to Report view is similar to the process of adding counters to Chart view or to Alert view. To add a counter to Report view, select **Edit ➤ Add** to Report to display the Add To Report dialog box, as shown in Figure 10-4.

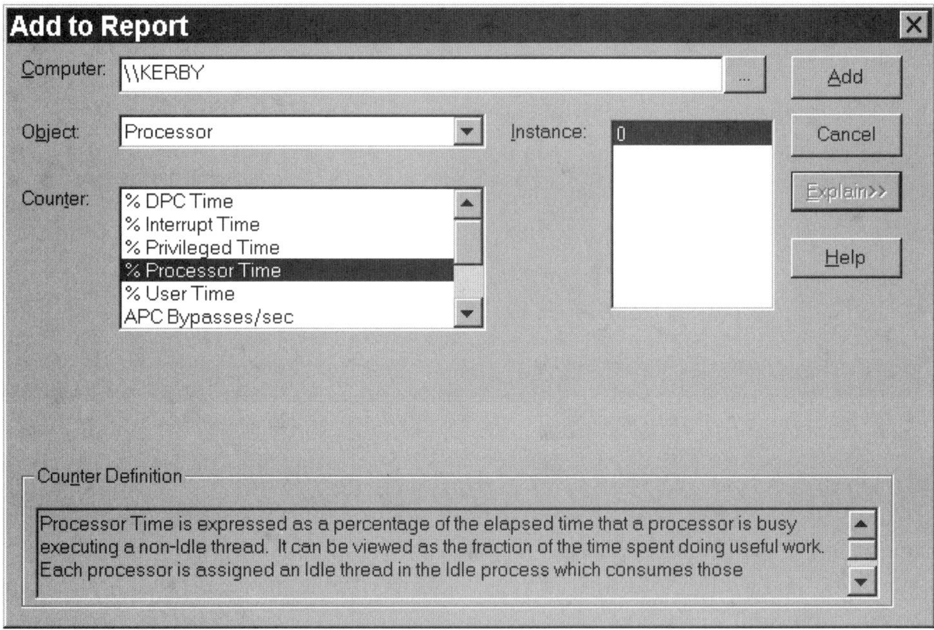

Figure 10-4. The Add to Report dialog box allows you to add counters for Report view

In the Computer field, accept the default computer name, type a new name, or click the icon immediately to the right of the field to browse for a computer. The default computer name initially is the computer upon which Performance Monitor is running. After you have added a counter, the default becomes the name of the last computer for which you added a counter.

After selecting the computer, highlight an object in the Objects scrolling pick list. A list of available counters for that object appears in the Counter pick list. Click Explain to display an information pane at the bottom of the dialog that describes each counter as is highlighted. Click Add to add the highlighted counter to Report view. You can add as many counters as you wish, from as many computers as you wish. When you have finished adding counters, click Done to return to Report view. Figure 10-5 shows an example of a completed Report view.

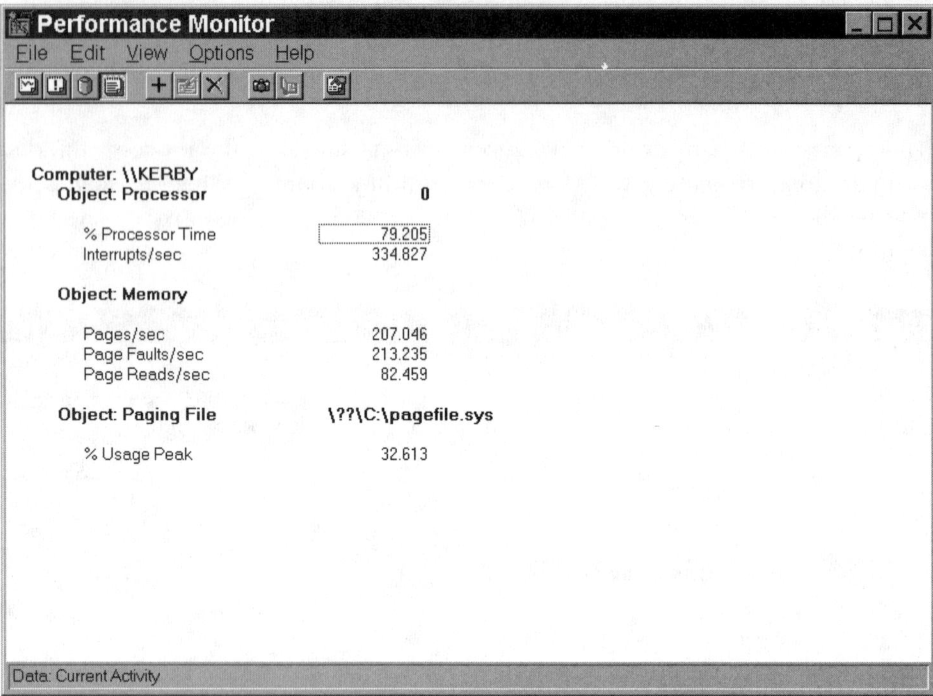

Figure 10-5. The Report view displays the selected counters, which are updated in real time

Optimizing Server Performance

After reading the preceding section, you might reasonably wonder exactly how to go about using the information you discover with Performance Monitor to improve the performance of your server. Which objects and counters should you look at, and how can you tell if one is too high or too low? Well, as usual, the frustrating answer is, "it depends."

The primary purpose of Performance Monitor is to uncover bottlenecks in your server environment. A bottleneck is simply a single choke point that by itself restricts the performance potential of your server. For example, if your processor utilization routinely borders on 100%, it doesn't matter that the server has the fastest disk drives available and plenty of memory. Your server can't go any faster because the processor is already pedaling as fast as it can.

If you eliminate a bottleneck, the overall performance of the server takes a substantial quantum jump. If you replace that processor with a faster one—or add another processor—the other system components will no longer be held back by the slow processor, and can achieve the higher performance that was always their potential.

When you locate a bottleneck, you might therefore expect that the next step is always to eliminate it. Not true. The next step is to determine what is causing it to be a bottleneck. Simply throwing hardware at a problem isn't always the best or most cost-effective solution.

For example, while writing this chapter, I noticed that my processor utilization was typically ranging from the mid-80s to the high 90s. Now, this is a small server on a small network, and it seemed that a 133 MHz Pentium and 64 MB of RAM ought to be enough to handle things. But, in thinking about it, I realized that I had more services and applications loaded on this box than any real production server would be expected to handle, so perhaps I really was processor bound. I might easily have decided that the quick fix was to replace my 133 MHz Pentium with a faster Pentium or a Pentium Pro, or to add a second processor.

As it turns out, that wouldn't have done anything to solve the problem. The real problem was that an RPC bug was causing the processor to sit there looping on a zombie process, eating CPU ticks in the process. I went to the Microsoft web site and found that they had posted a fix for that exact problem earlier that same day—talk about a timely solution. When I applied the hot fix, processor utilization dropped into the 2% to 5% range immediately and stayed there. If I had simply upgraded the processor, my server would have been looping much faster, but it would still have been sitting at 97% processor utilization.

The point is this. When you find a bottleneck, try to figure out what is causing it before you try to fix it. Otherwise, you'll spend a lot of time and money fixing things that aren't really broken.

Optimizing Memory Performance

Inadequate RAM is by far the most common reason for server performance problems, with Windows NT Server or any other network operating system. Windows NT Server 4.0 requires 16 MB of RAM. It says so right on the box. In fact, of course, 16 MB is a ridiculously low amount for a serious server. Although Windows NT Server will *load* in 16 MB, it won't actually do much afterwards.

Consider 24 MB—or, better, 32 MB—as a bare-bones minimum on a small production file and print server. If you are using the server as an application server, consider 64 MB to be the starting point, and install 128 MB or more if you possibly can. If your server RAM doesn't meet these realistic minimums, don't bother wasting your time using Performance Monitor to locate bottlenecks. It's pretty obvious where the bottleneck is. Add more RAM.

When you install Windows NT Server, a page file is created. The page file is an area of your hard disk that the system treats as virtual memory. When the physical memory (RAM) is inadequate to meet the demands of all of the processes running on the server, memory pages are swapped to and from the page file. The page file operates at hard disk speeds (~10 ms read times) rather than at memory speed (~100 ns read times). This disparity of 100,000 times means that every time the page file is used, the server takes a performance hit. In essence, virtual memory is nice to have as an emergency fallback, but you want to use it as little as possible.

If you think your server is equipped with a reasonable amount of memory, but you are still having performance problems that may be memory related, chances are that the problem is due to overuse of the page file. Check the following items to decide whether paging is slowing down your server:

- Examine the Pages/sec counter in the Memory object (subsequently referred to in the form **Memory ➤ Pages/sec**). If this value has a sustained average of 10 or more, your server may not have enough physical RAM. If this value reaches an average of 20, server performance will be significantly degraded because of the continuous swapping that is occurring. Before you decide to add RAM, check **Memory ➤ Available Bytes**. If this value is not shrinking when the Pages/sec counter is growing, the problem may not actually be a shortage of physical RAM. You may have an application that is doing a great deal of random disk I/O. For an example of this type of behavior, watch these counters while using **Start ➤ Find** to locate all files on your drive that contain the string "the." If you find that the problem is not due to excessive random I/O, the only solution is to increase the amount of physical RAM in your server.
- Examine **Memory ➤ Available Bytes**, which displays the amount of free physical memory. A consistent value below 4 MB indicates that substantial paging activity is occurring. Add RAM.
- Examine Memory ➤ **Committed Bytes**, which displays the amount of virtual memory that has been committed, as opposed to simply reserved. If this counter is greater than the amount of physical memory in the server, then the amount of physical memory may be inadequate to meet the demands of all processes that are currently active. Before you conclude that this is true, examine **Memory ➤ Pages/sec** and **Memory ➤ Page Faults/sec**. If the former is greater than 10 or so, and the latter is greater than **Memory ➤ Cache Faults/sec**, excessive paging is occurring.

  As **Memory ➤ Committed Bytes** nears the value for **Memory ➤ Commit Limit**, and the page file is at or near its allowable maximum size, your server is headed for serious memory problems. The Commit Limit counter specifies how much virtual memory can be committed without increasing the size of the page file. If both are maxed out, you're about to run out of both physical and virtual memory. This situation usually arises because a poorly written application is leaking memory. To determine the process that is causing the problem, use **Process ➤ Page File Bytes** or **Process ➤ Working Set** to examine each process that is a likely candidate. You can also use the Process Monitor utility, *PMON.EXE*, included on the Resource Kit CD.

- Examine your page file. If its current size is larger than its initial size (ordinarily the amount of installed RAM plus 12 MB), this means that Windows NT Server has found it necessary to expand the page file size during operations. This reduces server performance because it introduces page file fragmentation, which slows paging performance even more.

  The best solution to this problem is to never allow it to occur in the first place. Specify a very large page file when you install Windows NT Server—at least twice the size of the amount of physical RAM installed, and preferably three times the size. The initial page file is created in a single contiguous block of disk space, which avoids the fragmentation issue. If you're trying to fix this problem after the fact, the solution is a bit more involved, because disk defragmenting utilities currently available for Windows NT won't touch the page file.

  To fix the problem, first create a new, temporary page file of the appropriate size on another volume. Then, reduce the size of the current page file to zero and reboot the server, causing it to use the new page file. Delete the old page file, and then run a defragmenting utility on the original volume. Most defragmenters for Windows NT defragment only, however, and do not relocate files to eliminate gaps, and the whole point is to create a new page file that is contiguous. Accordingly, you may find yourself needing to do a full backup, format, and restore to fix the problem. It's much easier to do things right in the first place.

If your testing indicates that the server is memory-bound, there are a few things that you can do. First, you can relocate memory-hungry applications to another, more lightly loader server. Second, if the application in question can be run after hours, you can use the scheduler service and the *AT* command to do so. Realistically, however, the usual answer is simply to add memory to the server.

To determine how much memory to add, examine the **Paging File ➤ % Usage Peak** counter, and multiply that number by the size of the paging file. If you have more than one paging file, do so for each paging file and total the results. If, for example, your server has a single 100 MB paging file, and the % Usage Peak counter indicates that at most 30% of the paging file was in use, multiply 30% (0.3) times 100 MB to arrive at a total of 30 MB. That means that if your system had had 30 MB more physical RAM, minimal paging would have occurred. Round up to the next increment, and add 32 MB of RAM.

WARNING If you add memory to your server, you may also need to upgrade the secondary processor cache. Otherwise, you may find that the resulting reduced cache hit rates turn your memory-bound server into a processor-bound server. Some caching methods link required cache size relatively loosely to the main memory size, whereas others tie the required cache size closely to the main memory size. I recall one old Everex server that gave you no option. You had to upgrade cache when you added RAM, or the thing just didn't work.

If your server has a utility that allows you to monitor cache hit rate, use it. A value under 90% means that you probably need a larger cache, or one of a more efficient type. A value of 95% or more means that your cache is performing effectively, and that adding cache will yield only rapidly diminishing returns.

Optimizing Processor Performance

Processor utilization is unlikely to be a bottleneck on a file and print server. Even a relatively slow processor—like the 486/66 on my test bed server—can serve a reasonably large number of clients if all it has to do is share files and printers. On an application server, however, the story is different. Because an application server is actually executing programs on behalf of clients, it needs all the processor (and memory) you can give it. If your server is primarily providing file and print services and is running a fast Pentium or better, it's probably a waste of time to look at processor performance. If it's also providing application server functions, however, check the following items:

- Examine the **Processor ➤ % Processor Time** counter. If this value has a sustained average of 90% or more, your server may need a faster processor (or more processors), or it may not. You may have a poorly written client application or a system service that is consuming excessive processor ticks.

  To find out if this is the case, examine the **Process ➤ % Processor Time** counter for each instance of all likely processes, or use the *PMON.EXE* utility provided with the Resource Kit to view this data. Another quick way to get an idea of processor utilization is to use the Task Manager. To do so, press Ctrl-Alt-Del to bring up the Windows NT Security dialog, click Task Manager, and then the Processes tab. The resulting display shows each active process, the amount of memory it is using, its current CPU utilization, and the total CPU time it has consumed. You can sort on any of these values by clicking the column header.

  On a normal server, the System Idle Process will be at or near the top of the list in CPU utilization. If you find another process that is either consuming a large percentage of the CPU or has a high value for CPU Time, that process is a candidate for the culprit. You may find that you have a rogue process that is apparently running normally, but is consuming nearly all of the CPU. You may also find that you have a zombie process—one that you quit but it failed to go away.

For example, while writing this chapter, I exited Word one evening and went to bed. When I started work the following morning, I noticed that the system seemed to be responding very slowly. I used Task Manager to examine the running processes. I found that Word was still active, although the Applications tab showed it as "Not Responding." It was, however, taking 99% of the processor. Granted, Word is not the most usual application to be running on a server, but the concept remains the same. Any application or service may have a bug that causes the process to run out of control and consume processor resources.

- Examine the **Processor ➤ Interrupts/sec** counter to determine whether excessive processor utilization is due to a hardware device generating excessive hardware interrupts. On a normal server, this counter may have a value of 100 at idle, and perhaps 200 to 300 under load. If this value has a sustained average of 500 or more, you may have a hardware device—typically a network interface card or a disk host adapter—that is spewing spurious interrupts. If this value exceeds 1,000, you almost certainly have a hardware problem. To verify this, examine the **System ➤ System Calls/sec** counter, which measures the frequency of calls to Windows NT system service routines. If the Interrupts/sec counter value greatly exceeds the System Calls/sec counter, a malfunctioning hardware device is almost a certainty.

If your testing indicates that the server is processor-bound, there are several possible solutions:

- Relocate processor-hungry applications to another, more lightly loader server, or, if the application can be run after hours, use the scheduler service and the *AT* command to run it. If the application was written in-house, rewrite it to be more efficient in processor utilization.
- Use Task Manager to alter the priority of applications and services, or you can start them with a command-line switch to set their priority. By default, most applications and services run at Normal priority. You can right-click an image name in Task Manager and set the priority to Low, Normal, High, or Realtime. Whatever you do, don't run a processor-bound application at Realtime priority. You'll never get your server back.
- Upgrade the I/O controller drivers, or replace the controllers with better models. In particular, inexpensive or older SCSI host adapters and network inter-

face cards often place a large load on the processor. Early 100 Mbps network adapters were notorious for generating excessive processor loads. I recall seeing one model that, on its own and at idle, consumed more than 50% of a Pentium processor.

- Upgrade to a faster processor, or add additional processors. In a resource sharing environment, e.g., a file server, a faster processor will often provide more benefit than an additional processor. In a client/server environment that uses multiple threading, e.g., Microsoft BackOffice, multiple, slower processors will usually outperform a single faster processor.

Optimizing Disk Performance

Disk performance is critical to any server, both directly and indirectly. In a direct sense, high disk performance provides better response to users and applications by delivering data faster. Program load times are shorter, database files are searched faster, and so forth. In an indirect sense, high disk performance benefits paging file operations, and so benefits the overall performance level of any server that uses paging—which is to say, nearly any server.

If you think your server is disk bound, the first thing to do is check memory, as described in the preceding section. Disk bottlenecks are usually due to memory bottlenecks, and until you eliminate the memory bottleneck, it's almost impossible to resolve disk performance problems.

NOTE At this point in every Windows NT book I've seen, the author feels obligated to warn the reader that, to run Performance Monitor disk analyses, he must first load special drivers, and that these drivers shouldn't be left loaded because they adversely impact disk performance. Wrong.

Well, the part about the special drivers is right. You need to run *diskperf-y* from a command prompt and then restart the server before you can monitor Disk object counters. The part about them adversely impacting disk performance is a holdover from olden times, however. On a slow 486 server, these drivers cost you a performance hit in the 0.25% to 0.50% range. On anything faster, the theoretical performance hit is lost in the noise.

If you've eliminated memory bottlenecks on your server, it's worthwhile checking for disk bottlenecks, whether your server is primarily providing file and print services or is an application server. Check the following items:

- Examine the **Physical Disk ➤ % Disk Time** counter. This counter indicates the percentage of elapsed time that a disk drive is busy reading and writing. If this value has a sustained average of 70% or more, that physical disk is a bottleneck.

- Examine the **Physical Disk ➤ Current Disk Queue Length** counter. This instantaneous counter indicates the number of disk requests outstanding when the sample was taken. If this counter has a sustained value of two or more, that physical disk is a bottleneck.

If your testing indicates that the server is disk-bound, there are several possible solutions:

- Use the most efficient bus type available on your server for the host adapter. If you have ISA and EISA slots, put the host adapter in an EISA slot. If you have EISA and PCI slots, use a PCI host adapter. If you have ISA and VLB slots, use a VLB slot for the host adapter (but you really need a better server).
- Install a better host adapter. Inexpensive host adapters are often slow and inefficient, and place a significant burden on the processor. Better (and more expensive) host adapters transfer data faster, with less overhead, and do not load the processor. As a rule of thumb, if the SCSI host adapter you are using sells for less than $300, it may be causing a bottleneck.
- Move to a better drive technology. If you're using EIDE now, move to some form of SCSI. If you're running an older, slower, narrower type of SCSI, move to the latest, greatest, fastest, widest, highest numbered SCSI. When you choose drives, give greater weight to the seek time than to the transfer rate. Fast seeking, particularly on a server, is much more important than data transfer rate.
- Install more RAM in the server. Even if you are not memory-bound, Windows NT will devote additional RAM primarily to caching, improving the performance of the disk subsystem.
- Use RAID, as described in Chapter 4, *Managing Disk Storage with Windows NT*. RAID 0 striping and RAID 1 mirroring/duplexing can greatly improve disk subsystem performance by distributing activity among multiple spindles. RAID 5 striping with parity can achieve similar improvements at low cost, while protecting your data against drive failures.
- If your server has multiple disk drives, consider what data is stored on each. In my consulting practice, I often find a server that has multiple disk drives, but with 90% or more of the activity being serviced by only one of the drives. Distribute data across the drives to take advantage of having multiple spindles.
- Make sure that your disk drives do not become too full. Consider two disk drives whose specifications are identical except that one is 2 GB and the other 4 GB. If you store 1.9 GB of data on each drive, the larger drive will outperform the smaller drive every time, and by a significant margin. If both

drives have a 9 ms average seek time, the smaller drive will in fact require nearly 9 ms for the average seek because its heads may have to move anywhere on the disk surface. The larger drive, however, seeks much faster, because the drive heads spend all of their time on the half of the drive than contains data, giving the 4 GB drive an effective seek time of about 4.5 ms. Note that severe fragmentation can reduce the advantage of the larger drive.

- Use the NTFS filesystem on any but the smallest of disk drives. If you use the FAT filesystem on any drive larger than about 500 MB, performance suffers relative to NTFS.

Optimizing Network Performance

Here's a topic that's difficult to cover in any reasonable amount of space. Even scratching the surface would require an entire book, and treating this subject in depth would require a complete library. Still, there are some items that have a major effect on the efficiency of the network and that are easily checked. For more detailed information, see the Windows NT Server 4.0 Resource Kit.

Server optimization level

Windows NT Server has four preconfigured *server optimization levels*. These levels determine how various server resources (e.g., file cache) are allocated within the Server service, and what priority is assigned to various processes. Choosing the appropriate level for your server, depending on its usage pattern, is a very important factor in ensuring responsiveness.

To configure server optimization level, right-click the Network Neighborhood icon to display the Network dialog. Click the Services tab to display the Network Services page, and highlight the Server service. Click Properties to display the Server dialog. Choose one of the following option buttons:

Minimize Memory Used
: Choose this option button for a small server that supports 10 or fewer clients.

Balance
: Choose this option button for a general-purpose server in a medium environment—64 or fewer clients.

Maximize Throughput for File Sharing
: Choose this option button for a server on a large network that is providing primarily file and print sharing services. Setting this option enables LargeSystemCache in the Registry, giving file cache access priority over user application access to memory.

Maximize Throughput for Network Applications

Choose this option button for a server on a large network that is configured as an application server. Setting this option disables LargeSystemCache in the Registry, giving user application access priority over file cache access to memory.

Note that this setting benefits an application server only if it is running client/server applications that do not do their own caching. If you are running client/server applications, like Microsoft BackOffice, that do their own caching, choosing the *Balance* server optimization level will yield better overall network performance.

After you have set the appropriate server optimization level, close the Network dialog and restart the server so that the change will take effect. Examine the **Server ➤ Pool Nonpaged Failures**, the **Server ➤ Pool Paged Failures**, and the **Server ➤ Work Item Shortages** counters. If these counters are increasing, or if **Server ➤ Context Blocks Queued/sec** has a value greater than 20, the Server service is incapable of keeping up with I/O requests from clients. If the proper server optimization level is in effect, this may be caused by the server being overloaded due to inadequate processor, memory, or disk resources.

Workstation service (redirector object)

When users or applications access a redirected drive, the request is processed by the appropriate redirector. For example, the Windows NT Server Workstation service processes Windows Networking redirection requests, and the Gateway Service for NetWare processes NetWare redirection requests. The redirector forwards the request to the appropriate transport protocol, e.g., TCP/IP or NWLink, which places it on the network for transmission to the appropriate server. In general, the performance of the redirectors is strongly dependent upon the performance of the server. However, there are some issues specific to the redirectors to be considered.

- Examine the **Redirector ➤ Current Commands** counter. This counter indicates the numbers of redirection requests that are currently queued and awaiting service. If this value consistently exceeds the number of network interface cards installed in the server, a serious bottleneck exists.
- Examine the **Redirector ➤ Network Errors/sec** counter. Any nonzero value for this counter indicates that serious network communications problems exist. When a network error occurs, SMB requests are timing out, which requires the redirector to drop the connection, reconnect, and attempt to recover.

If you run multiple redirectors on the server, one of the most important things you can do to improve performance is select the proper provider order. When a network call occurs, Windows NT Server routes the call to the first provider listed, and awaits a response from this provider. If that provider responds that it is unable to service the call, Windows NT attempts the next provider, and so forth. For example, if *NetWare or Compatible Network* is the first Network Provider listed, and *Microsoft Windows Network* is the second, all network calls are routed to the *NetWare or Compatible Network* Network Provider before being routed to the *Microsoft Windows Network* Network Provider. If most network calls in fact need to be serviced by the *Microsoft Windows Network* Network Provider, using this Network Provider order slows performance needlessly by introducing an extra step for most network calls.

Because Windows NT Server uses providers in the order specified, and because the order that it selects itself may not be the most appropriate for your environment, you should examine provider order and configure it manually to match your environment. To do so, right-click the Network Neighborhood icon on the desktop, and select Properties to display the Network dialog. Click the Services tab to display the Services page, and then click Network Access Order to display the Network Access Order dialog. Expand the tree as necessary, highlight a service provider, and use Move Up and Move Down to rearrange the order in which providers are accessed.

Transport protocols

Transport protocols move data between stations on the network. Windows NT Server includes three major transport protocols—NBF (NetBEUI frame), TCP/IP, and NWLink. It also includes two minor transport protocols—DLC and AppleTalk. When Windows NT Server is operating in a NetWare environment, there are almost always at least two major transport protocols in use—TCP/IP and NWLink—and often all three are being used. If you have two or more transport protocols installed on your server, a potential bottleneck exists.

Network bindings describe the connection relationships between transport protocols, network interface cards, and system services. For example, if a network interface card is to be used to communicate IP packets and IPX packets, both the TCP/IP protocol and the NWLink protocol must be bound to that network interface card. Similarly, if the DHCP Server service is to communicate with TCP/IP on a particular network interface card, that service must be bound to the protocol and the card.

The first rule to follow to eliminate unnecessary transport protocol overhead is to bind only the transport protocols that are needed. For example, if you have a dial-up adapter that will be used only to provide a TCP/IP connection to a remote office, make sure that you don't have NWLink or NetBEUI bound to that adapter.

The second rule to follow is to arrange the order of the bindings to suit your own environment. When a connection to a shared resource is requested, the redirector simultaneously submits the request to all of the installed transport protocols. When it receives a response, it does not act upon it immediately, but instead waits until all higher priority transport protocols return a response. The location of a particular transport protocol on the bindings list determines its priority. Placing the transport protocol that will be used by most stations first on the bindings list decreases the average connection time.

To remove unneeded bindings, or to alter the order of necessary bindings, right-click the Network Neighborhood icon on the desktop, and select Properties to display the Network dialog. Click the Bindings tab to display the Bindings page. Use the Show Bindings for drop-down list to specify how you want the bindings displayed, and then expand the display as necessary to show the individual bindings you are interested in. Use Enable and Disable to set the correct bindings as active, and then use Move Up and Move Down to rearrange the access order.

Network Interface Card

The Network Interface Card (NIC) itself is a bottleneck on many servers. To determine if this is the case on your server, first calculate the throughput that your media access method provides. If you are running 10 Mbps Ethernet, for example, your total theoretical throughput is (10,000,000 bits/second) / 8 bits/byte, or 1.25 million bytes per second. Network overhead, collisions, and so forth, realistically limit actual Ethernet throughput to perhaps 80% or less of nominal—something less than 1 Mbps. Similarly, 16 Mbps Token Ring provides theoretical throughput of 2 million bytes per second, with actual throughput approaching that figure.

Next, examine the **Server ➤ Bytes Total/sec** counter. This counter measures the actual number of bytes per second that are sent by and received by the NIC. If this counter has a sustained value at or near the actual throughput of your NIC, then the NIC is a bottleneck. If the server itself is capable of substantially higher throughput (as is any modern server), this potential is wasted because the NIC is unable to transfer data any faster than it is already doing.

There are several possible solutions to this problem, but all of them require substantial changes to the network. You might segment the network into subnetworks; replace the existing media access method with a faster one (like 100BaseT, 100VG-AnyLAN, or FDDI); install a high-speed backbone to link servers; or install switching.

Monitoring Server Events

The second major monitoring tool provided with Windows NT Server is called *Event Viewer.* In Windows NT Server, an *event* is any anomalous occurrence that requires users to be notified. An event may indicate a serious problem, e.g., a failing hard drive that requires immediate attention. An event may also be simply informational, e.g., a notification that a program has initialized successfully. Windows NT Server automatically begins logging events each time it is started. Event records are written to an event log, which can then be viewed with Event Viewer.

Windows NT Server actually maintains three separate event logs, as follows:

Application Log
: This log maintains events related to applications. It is enabled automatically, and may be viewed by users and administrators. Which events are logged is determined by the programmer who wrote the application in question.

Security Log
: This log, disabled by default, maintains events related to system security, such as logins and logouts, changes to the filesystem, and so forth. Security logging is normally disabled because using it can adversely effect server performance. To use security logging, an administrator must first enable it by setting audit policy in User Manager for Domains. This log can be viewed only by user accounts that are assigned to the Administrators group. Which events are logged is determined by the administrator.

System Log
: This log maintains events related to hardware and low-level software components. It is enabled automatically, and may be viewed by ordinary users and by administrators. Which events are logged is hard coded into Windows NT Server.

The most serious events, e.g., a disk failure, are both recorded to the appropriate event log and cause a warning message to be displayed on the console. Less serious events—those that do not require immediate intervention by the administrator to prevent the server from failing or to return it to operation—are instead simply written to the event log. Inexperienced Windows NT Server administrators are often shocked when they first examine the event log to find the number (and seriousness) of events that had escaped their notice.

Events recorded to the event log are of five types, as follows:

Error
: This event type is flagged with a red stop sign icon, and indicates that a serious problem exists and should receive attention as soon as possible.

Events of this nature are those that can seriously impact operation of the server in whole or in part. For example, if a service fails to start when you boot the server, an Error event will be recorded to the event log.

Warning

This event type is flagged with a yellow bang icon, and indicates that a problem has occurred that is not adequately severe to be considered an error, but that nonetheless should be examined. If ignored, the types of problems reported as warnings may or may not develop into errors.

For example, a Warning event may inform you that you are running low on disk space. If you do nothing to resolve the problem, the next event may be an Error event informing you that you are now out of disk space. Conversely, you may receive a Warning event to inform you that a backup tape had a bad block. Although this may indicate a developing problem with the tape drive or the tape, chances are that you can safely ignore this warning for the time being, and simply keep an eye on the tape drive and the tape.

Information

This event type is flagged with a blue international information "i" icon, and indicates that a significant event has occurred, but completed normally with the expected results. For example, when the primary domain controller and backup domain controller synchronize successfully, an Information event record is written to the system log.

Success Audit

This event type is flagged with a gold key icon, and indicates that an audited security event was completed successfully. For example, if logons are being audited, a user successfully logging on generates a Success Audit event. This event type occurs only in the security log.

Failure Audit

This event type is flagged with a gray lock icon, and indicates that an audited security event was attempted unsuccessfully. For example, if a user attempts to log on using an incorrect password, a Failure Audit event would be written to the security log. This event type occurs only in the security log.

Viewing Events with Event Viewer

To start Event Viewer, select **Start ➤ Programs ➤ Administrative Tools (Common) ➤ Event Viewer**. The main Event Viewer screen appears, as shown in Figure 10-6, with the last log used displayed. If you want to use a different log, choose the log you want to view from the Log menu by clicking System, Security, or Application.

Each line of the Event Viewer display represents one event record. Reading from left to right, the icon specifies the event type, immediately followed by the local

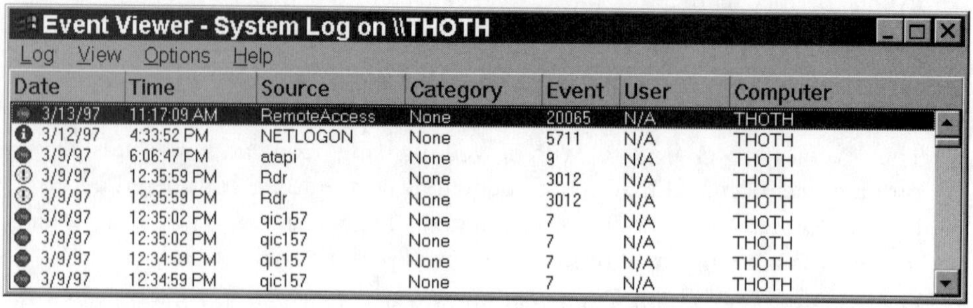

Event Viewer - System Log on \\THOTH

Log View Options Help

Date	Time	Source	Category	Event	User	Computer
3/13/97	11:17:09 AM	RemoteAccess	None	20065	N/A	THOTH
3/12/97	4:33:52 PM	NETLOGON	None	5711	N/A	THOTH
3/9/97	6:06:47 PM	atapi	None	9	N/A	THOTH
3/9/97	12:35:59 PM	Rdr	None	3012	N/A	THOTH
3/9/97	12:35:59 PM	Rdr	None	3012	N/A	THOTH
3/9/97	12:35:02 PM	qic157	None	7	N/A	THOTH
3/9/97	12:35:02 PM	qic157	None	7	N/A	THOTH
3/9/97	12:34:59 PM	qic157	None	7	N/A	THOTH
3/9/97	12:34:59 PM	qic157	None	7	N/A	THOTH

Figure 10-6. Event Viewer displays a system log showing Error, Warning, and Information events

date and time that the event occurred. The *Source* of the event is the name of the application software or system component that generated the event. For example, the first event shown was generated by the Remote Access service application, and the last event shown was generated by the qic157 tape driver. The *Category* field is used primarily in the security log, and provides a classification (originating with the event source) of the event. The *Event* field (actually the *Event ID*) is a number that identifies the particular event type. For example, the Event ID for the first event is 20065, which describes the event as `Internal Error: Disconnect operation on COM1 completed with an error`. In other words, the modem dropped carrier. The *User* field contains, if applicable, the account name of the client who generated the event The *Computer* field contains the name of the computer upon which the event occurred.

You can display the detailed record for an event by double-clicking it to display the Event Detail dialog, as shown in Figure 10-7. In addition to the information provided in summary view, the detailed record displays (sometimes) more helpful information in the Description pane. The Data pane, if it appears, contains a hexadecimal dump of data provided by the source of the event. This data is useless to most of us, but may provide a support technician with a lead to resolving the problem.

Viewing Events on a Remote Server

When you start Event Viewer, by default it displays the log files for the server upon which it is running. You can, however, use Event Viewer to view the event logs on a remote server. To do so, from the Log menu, choose Select Computer to display the Select Computer dialog. This menu option is available only if you are logged on as an administrator.

Initially, the Computer field is blank, and the Select Computer pane displays "working" as Event Viewer scans the network for other servers. Type the name of the server whose event log you want to view in the Computer field, or choose a server from the list presented in the Select Computer pane and click OK.

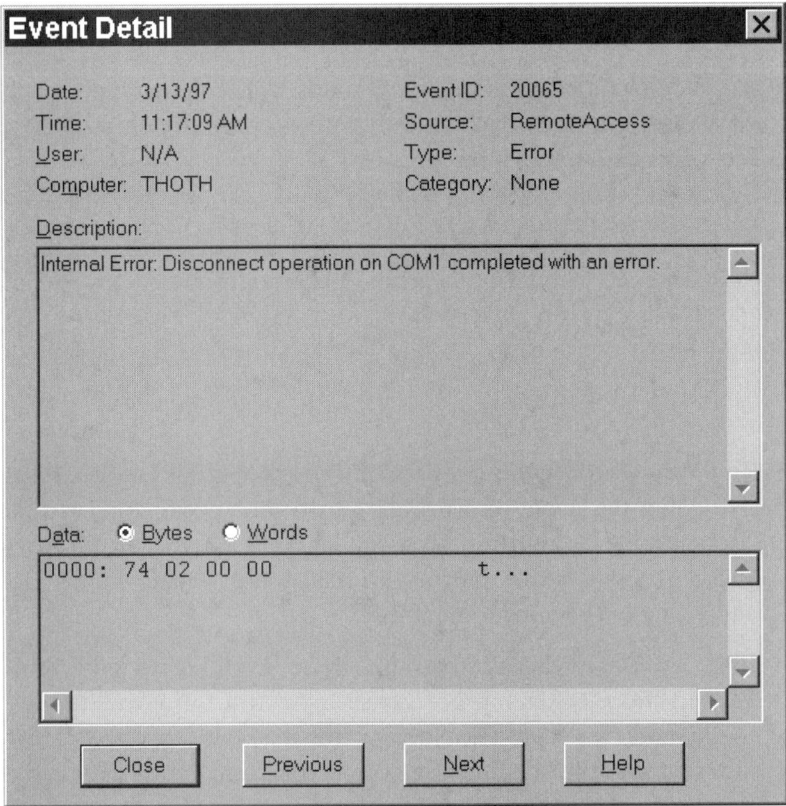

Figure 10-7. The Event Detail record provides additional information about the selected event

---

NOTE As far as I can determine, the Low Speed Connection check box does nothing. In other Windows NT Server applications, this option allows you to increase responsiveness over a slow connection at the expense of having fewer menu options available or being able to view less detailed data. In Event Viewer, however, no changes are apparent regardless of the state of this check box.

I first tested it by marking the check box and then connecting to my server *kerby*, which is on an Ethernet with the local server *thoth*. Thinking that perhaps Windows NT Server was smart enough to realize that I was lying to it, I then went to the trouble of establishing a dial-up connection between these two servers. No difference was evident. All menu options remained enabled, the same data was displayed, and the application seemed as responsive on the dial-up connection as it had on the local Ethernet.

Choosing Which Events to Display

Finding the one event—or a related group of events—that interests you in an event log with hundreds or thousands of entries sounds like a daunting prospect. Fortunately, Event Viewer provides two tools that allow you to display only a subset of the events contained in the event log.

Filtering events

The first of these tools is the event filter. To enable filtering, from the View menu, select Filter Events to display the Filter dialog, as shown in Figure 10-8. By default, the filter is set to perform no filtering at all. All events are displayed, regardless of date, type, or source. To display only a subset of events, enter values in the various sections of the Filter dialog.

The View From and View Through panes allow you to exclude all events except those that occurred within the range of dates and times you specify. This can be useful for analysis of problems after the fact—for example, if you return from vacation and someone tells you that the server was doing strange things last Tuesday around lunchtime but seemed to right itself.

In the Types pane, mark the check boxes for those event types you want displayed and clear the check boxes for those event types you want to filter out. You might use this feature when troubleshooting, for example, to display only Warning events—those that may have a bearing on the problem you're attempting to resolve.

You can use the Source and Category drop-down pick lists to limit display to only those events that originate from a particular source or category. Similarly, you can enter a value for the User, Computer, or Event ID fields to limit display to only those events that meet the criterion you enter.

Note that all of these filters are additive. That is, for example, if you enter values in the View From and View Through panes and then in the Types pane, mark only the Error check box, then the only events that will be displayed are Error events that occurred within the date range you specified.

Once you have created the filter you need, click OK to place it into effect. It remains in effect until you cancel it by selecting All Events from the View menu, or by clicking Clear in the Filter dialog to reinstate the default filter (which is no filter at all).

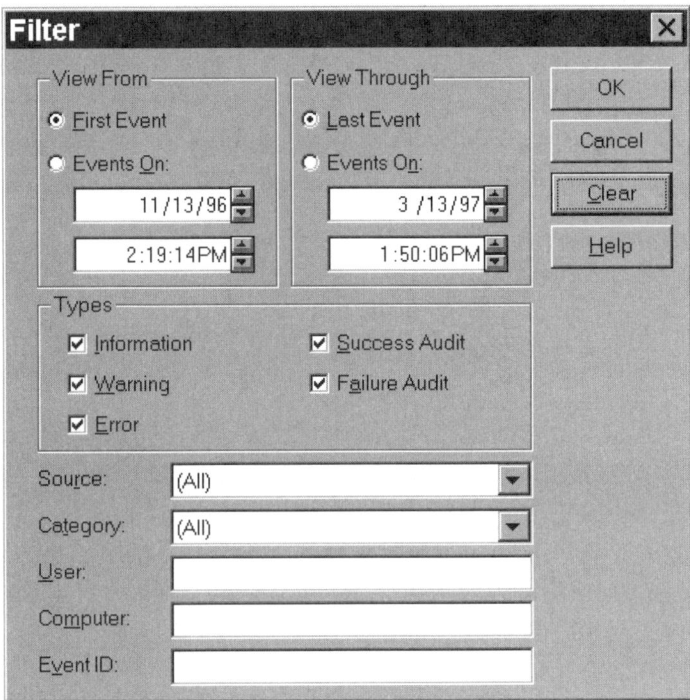

Figure 10-8. The Filter dialog allows you to choose which events will be displayed in Event Viewer

---

TIP Some administrators, particularly those of very busy servers, find it useful to leave filtering in effect at all times. You probably aren't too concerned with Information events or Success Audit events, so why have them cluttering up your Event Viewer display? In the Types pane, mark only the check boxes for Warning, Error, and Failure Audit to cut your event log down to size. One administrator I know filters everything but Error events, but then he also drives without a spare tire.

No matter what filter you put into effect, the less important events are still there if you need to look at them for some reason. They simply remain hidden during routine operations of Event Viewer.

Finding events

The second of these Event Viewer tools is the find function, which works in much the same way as does filtering. However, instead of causing the main Event Viewer window to display only a subset of events, the find function uses the criteria you specify to locate and sequentially display events. Invoke the find function by clicking Find from the View menu to display the Find dialog. Enter the search parameters as described in the preceding section, and click Find Next to display the first record that meets all of the criteria you specified. You can mark the Up or Down option button to specify the direction that the search will take from the current record. Unlike filtering, once it terminates, the find function has no effect on the main Event Viewer display.

Changing Log File Settings

Because events are generated frequently on a production server, simply continuing to log all events to a log file would eventually result in the log file filling the available disk space. To prevent this, Event Viewer places a maximum size limitation on each log file. Because the log files cannot grow without limit, some method must be used to specify what will occur when a log file reaches its maximum allowed size. You can modify these settings from the Log menu by clicking Log Settings to display the Event Log Settings dialog.

To modify the settings, first use the Change Settings for drop-down pick list to specify which log file—System, Application, or Security—you want to modify. Next, use the arrow keys to modify the Maximum Log Size field to the desired value. By default, it is set to 512 KB for each of the event logs, and may be increased or decreased in 64 KB increments. Finally, select one of the option buttons in the Event Log Wrapping pane to specify what action will be taken when the log file reaches its maximum allowable size.

NOTE If you select the Do Not Overwrite Events (Clear Log Manually) option button, you **must** clear the log manually from the Log menu by clicking Clear All Events. If you fail to do so, and the log file reaches its maximum allowable size, new events are simply not logged, and are lost.

Monitoring the Network

When you install Windows NT Server 4,0, you may optionally install a limited version of the Network Monitor application that is bundled with Microsoft Systems Management Server. Network Monitor, as shown in Figure 10-9, is a protocol analyzer and packet grabber that performs network analysis functions similar to those performed by such commercial products as Network General Sniffer®. Unlike many third-party protocol analyzers, Network Monitor uses what you have. It does not require a special NIC or promiscuous mode drivers to function.

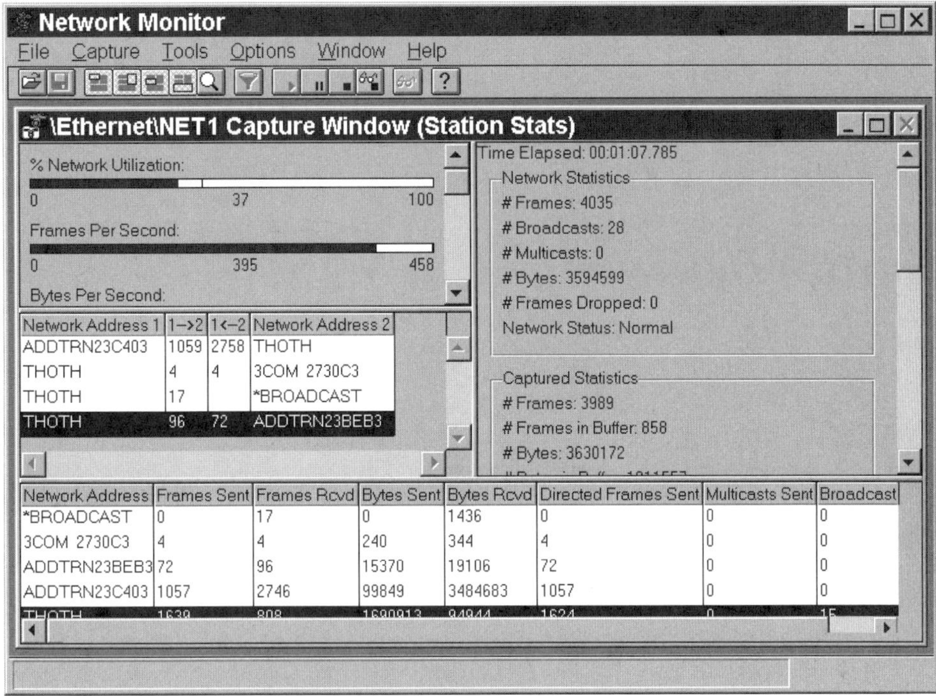

Figure 10-9. Network Monitor allows you to monitor server and network performance at the frame and packet level

Relative to the full version bundled with SMS, the limited version of Network Monitor that comes with Windows NT Server is primarily constrained by the fact that it can analyze traffic only on the server upon which it is installed. This makes the limited version useless for networkwide troubleshooting, but it remains very useful as a tool to analyze the performance of a particular server.

Using Network Monitor—and in particular interpreting the data that it collects—is well beyond the scope of this chapter. For further information about installing and using Network Monitor, refer to the Resource Kit.

11

In this chapter:

- *Understanding Networking Models*
- *The Internet Protocol Suite*
- *Understanding IP Addresses*

Understanding TCP/IP

The Internet arrived in the mass consciousness not long ago with all of the subtlety of a lightning strike. Just a couple of years ago, most people had never heard of the Internet, and even computer trade publications seldom mentioned it. Nowadays, you can't pick up the morning paper without seeing a feature article on the Internet or watch the evening news without hearing the anchor stumble over the network's web address. In a world where Tommy probably has his pinball machine connected to the Internet by now, chances are that you have at least some experience in working with TCP/IP and the Internet.

If you're a NetWare 3.1x administrator, though, your experience is probably limited to accessing the Internet as an ordinary user—using your web browser to read Novell technical bulletins or using your ftp client to download file updates and patches. Novell is a latecomer to the Internet, although they're making up ground fast with NetWare 4.11 and IntranetWare. NetWare 3.1x, conversely, provides very limited support for the TCP/IP protocol suite that forms the foundation both of the Internet and, increasingly, of corporate internetworks. Windows NT Server, on the other hand, was designed from the ground up to use TCP/IP.

This chapter examines the fundamentals of TCP/IP, and serves as a lead-in to the chapters that follow, which are devoted to the core TCP/IP services supported by Windows NT Server. If you're not completely clear about the differences between IP and IPX, or if you think a default gateway is an unmodified computer from South Dakota, you need to read this chapter. Much of what is discussed in the chapters following this one assumes that you have this basic understanding of the TCP/IP protocol suite. On the other hand, if at parties you often find yourself off in the corner with the other techies discussing the relative merits of RIP and OSPF, or if you lull yourself to sleep at night by calculating subnet masks in your head, you can probably safely skip ahead to the following chapter on Microsoft DHCP. If you don't know what DHCP is, you'd better read this chapter twice.

Understanding Networking Models

Networking is a complex subject. Attempting to understand it as a unified whole is nearly impossible. Breaking it down into related components allows you to understand each component individually. Once you understand each component in isolation, you can examine the interrelationship of these component parts and thereby gain a complete understanding of the whole. The mechanism used to break down the large topic of networking into smaller component parts is called a *networking model.*

NOTE It is important to understand that a networking model provides only a theoretical "big picture" framework for understanding the underlying network. At each level of the model, *protocols* are developed to specify in minute detail how each task will be accomplished. Actual products, called *implementations*, are then designed around these protocols.

For example, the Hewlett-Packard 10BaseT Ethernet card in my server is an *implementation* of the detailed IEEE 802.3 10BaseT *protocol,* which is itself generally described at Layers 1 and 2 of the OSI Reference *model* described in the following section.

TCP/IP networking was originally designed around a four-layer network model called the *DARPA model.* The DARPA model is also referred to as the *DoD model,* the *Department of Defense model,* the *Internet model,* or the *TCP/IP model.* The ISO, an international standards body, subsequently developed and promulgated a more detailed, seven-layer alternative model known as the *Open Systems Interconnect Reference model,* or, more commonly, the *OSI Reference model.* Figure 11-1 compares the DARPA Model and the OSI Reference Model.

The TCP/IP protocols originally described by the DARPA Model have become the most commonly used group of protocols worldwide, forming the foundation of both the Internet and of most corporate internetworks. However, the older DARPA Model itself has largely fallen into disuse, and the OSI Reference Model is used by nearly everyone to describe the TCP/IP protocol suite.

Conversely, although almost no one uses the OSI protocol suite originally described by the OSI Reference Model, almost everyone uses that model. As a result, we find a situation where the older protocols have become the standard, but are described by the newer model. Accordingly, I have stayed with common usage in using the OSI Reference Model as a theoretical framework to describe

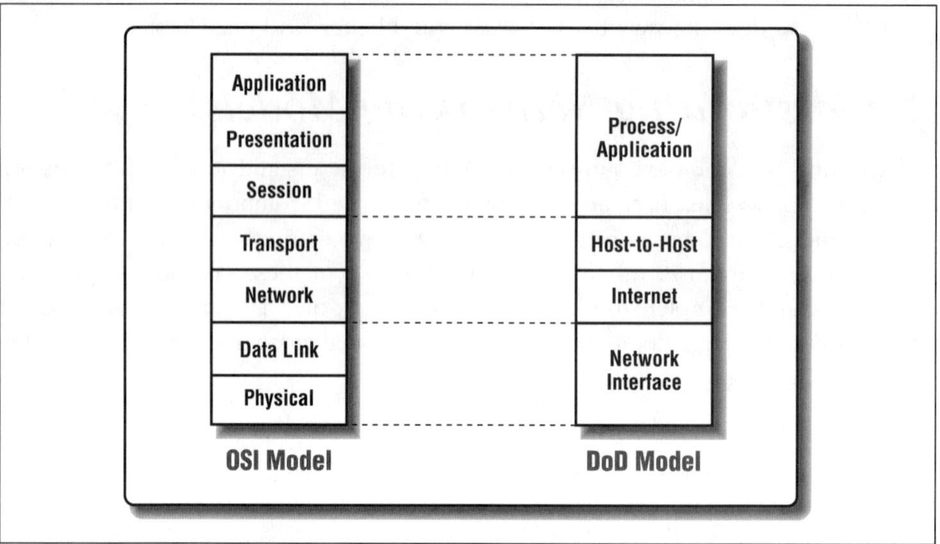

Figure 11-1. The DARPA Model and the OSI Reference Model are both used to describe TCP/IP networking

the TCP/IP protocol suite. The OSI Reference Model includes the following seven layers:

Physical Layer
: Describes the physical and electrical characteristics of the hardware used to connect to the network. The type of cable, the physical connectors used to terminate that cable, the voltages used for signaling, and so forth, are all defined at the Physical Layer. The OSI Physical Layer corresponds to the lower half of the DARPA *Network Interface Layer*, which is also called the *Local Network Layer*, or the *Network Access Layer*.

  Physical Layer protocols define how data will be placed on and retrieved from the network, which is called the *Media Access Method*. For example, IEEE 802.3 Ethernet and IEEE 802.5 Token Ring are defined at the Physical Layer. Data at the Physical Layer exist only as a series of electrical voltages, and have not yet been organized into frames, packets, or messages. In addition to network interface cards, *repeaters* function at the Physical Layer.

Data Link Layer
: Is responsible delivering error-free data on the local network. The Data Link Layer corresponds to the upper half of the DARPA *Network Interface Layer*. The Data Link Layer is conventionally divided into two sublayers, called the *Media Access Control (MAC) sublayer* and the *Logical Link Control (LLC) sublayer*. As the lower half of the Data Link Layer, the MAC sublayer provides the interface between the network hardware described by the Physical Layer

and the Data Link Layer. At the upper half of the Data Link Layer, the LLC sublayer defines the relationship between MAC sublayer devices and the logical drivers in the remainder of the Data Link Layer.

Data Link Layer protocols define how data will be organized, or *framed.* Data Link Layer *frames* organize the raw bit stream received from the Physical Layer into groupings of defined size and structure, which depend on the Media Access Method in use. For example, an Ethernet frame is typically 1,514 bytes, whereas a Token Ring frame is usually 4,202 bytes. In addition to organizing the data contained in the raw bit stream, header information is appended to each frame. The *frame header* includes administrative information like the size of the data block within the frame and the higher layer protocols for which the frame is intended. It also contains address information, e.g., the hardware (MAC) address of the source device and the hardware address of the destination device. Finally, the frame header contains checksum information that is used to ensure that the received frame was not corrupted during transmission. *Bridges* function at the Data Link Layer.

Network Layer

Is responsible for the timely delivery of data that it routes between networks. The Network Layer corresponds to the DARPA *Internet Layer.* The TCP/IP *Internet Protocol* (*IP*) and the Novell *Internet Packet Exchange* (*IPX*) protocol are examples of Network Layer protocols.

The Network Layer organizes data that it receives from higher layers into *packets.* In addition to the raw data, a packet incorporates a *packet header* that includes *network addresses,* also called *software addresses,* for the source and destination devices. Unlike the hardware addresses used in Data Link Layer frames, which limit delivery to destinations located on the same physical network, the network addresses used in Network Layer packets allow packets to be routed between networks. *Routers* function at the Network Layer.

Transport Layer

Is responsible for the reliable delivery of Network Layer packets. The Transport Layer builds and tears down connections, sequences packets, delivers and receives acknowledgments, and controls the flow of data. The Transport Layer corresponds to the DARPA *Host-to-Host Layer.* The TCP/IP *Transmission Control Protocol* (*TCP*) and *User Datagram Protocol* (*UDP*) are Transport Layer protocols, as is the Novell *Sequenced Packet Exchange* (*SPX*) protocol.

Session Layer

Is responsible for establishing and maintaining communications between applications for the duration of a session. Session Layer services include things like login authentication and error condition notifications. The Session Layer corresponds to the lower third of the DARPA *Process/Application Layer.*

Presentation Layer
: Is responsible for formatting, translating, and representing data, including functions like compressing and expanding data, encrypting and decrypting data, and translating between differing data formats. The Presentation Layer corresponds to the middle third of the DARPA *Process/Application Layer*.

Application Layer
: Is responsible for controlling the interface between network services and the applications being run by users. The Application Layer corresponds to the upper third of the DARPA *Process/Application Layer*.

Interlayer Communications

Each layer consumes services provided by the immediately adjoining lower layer, and, in turn, provides services to the layer above it. For example, the Data Link Layer is provided data in a raw bit stream from the Physical Layer immediately beneath it, formats that data into frames, and then provides it to the Network Layer immediately above it. Consider, for example, a source device and destination device connected to a local Ethernet LAN. The process of communicating data proceeds in the following fashion.

On the source device, data is first organized and formatted at the higher layers, and is then passed to the Transport Layer. At the Transport Layer, the data is organized into a TCP datagram. The Transport Layer passes the TCP datagram to the Network Layer, which adds network address header information and forms an IP packet. The Network Layer then passes the IP packet to the Data Link layer, which adds hardware address information to the IP packet and forms an Ethernet frame. The Data Link Layer then passes the Ethernet frame to the Physical Layer, which translates the Ethernet frame into a series of voltages that it places on the Ethernet cable.

At the destination device, the Ethernet card, functioning at the Physical Layer, retrieves the bit stream that had been placed on the wire by the Ethernet card on the source device. The Physical Layer passes this bit stream to the Data Link Layer, which uses it to reconstruct the original Ethernet frame. If the hardware address contained in that Ethernet frame is other than the address of the local Ethernet card, the frame is discarded. If the hardware address is that of the local Ethernet card, the Data Link Layer passes the Ethernet frame to the Network Layer. The Network Layer strips the frame header from the Ethernet frame, and extracts the IP packet that was encapsulated within that frame. The Network Layer then passes the IP packet up to the Transport Layer, which strips off the packet header, leaving only the TCP datagram that had been encapsulated within the IP packet. The Transport Layer then passes the TCP datagram up to the higher Layers for which it was intended.

In a functional sense, as shown by the dark lines in Figure 11-2, data originating at any layer is first passed down through the remaining layers on the source device, with header information being added at each layer, until it eventually reaches the Physical Layer and is placed on the wire. At the destination device, the process is reversed. The destination retrieves the data at the Physical Layer, and then passes it back up through the layers, stripping out header information at each layer, until it finally reaches the layer on the destination device that corresponds to the originating layer on the source device.

In a logical sense, as shown by the dotted lines in Figure 11-2, from the point of view of the communicating devices, the communication appears to be occurring directly between the layers in question. For example, when the source device forms a TCP datagram, it believes that it is transmitting that datagram directly to the Transport Layer of the destination device. All of the "plumbing" needed to actually effect the transfer—and supplied by the lower layers—is transparent to the upper layers.

The Internet Protocol Suite

The foundation of the Internet—and of most corporate internetworks—is the Internet Protocol Suite. Nearly everyone simply calls it TCP/IP, after two of its core protocols, *Transmission Control Protocol* (TCP) and *Internet Protocol* (IP). The protocols defined within TCP/IP are used to move information across the internet network. For this reason, TCP/IP is referred to as a "transport protocol" in casual conversation, although it incorporates protocols that function at all levels of the OSI Reference Model.

TCP/IP is only one of the transport protocols supported by Windows NT Server. The *NWLink IPX/SPX compatible transport* protocol provides native support in environments that include NetWare servers. The *NetBEUI* protocol is available for environments that include legacy Microsoft peer networking clients. TCP/IP can and does serve as the sole transport protocol in many Windows NT networks. It also coexists well with NWLink in networks that include NetWare servers.

This section examines the sources for the formal definition of the TCP/IP protocol, several of the major individual protocols that together comprise the suite, and how these protocols relate to the OSI Reference Model.

The Internet Activities Board (IAB)

It's easy to think of the Internet as being complete chaos. It sometimes appears that no one is in charge of anything, and that everyone can simply do as he pleases. In one sense, that's true, of course, as anyone whose mailbox has been

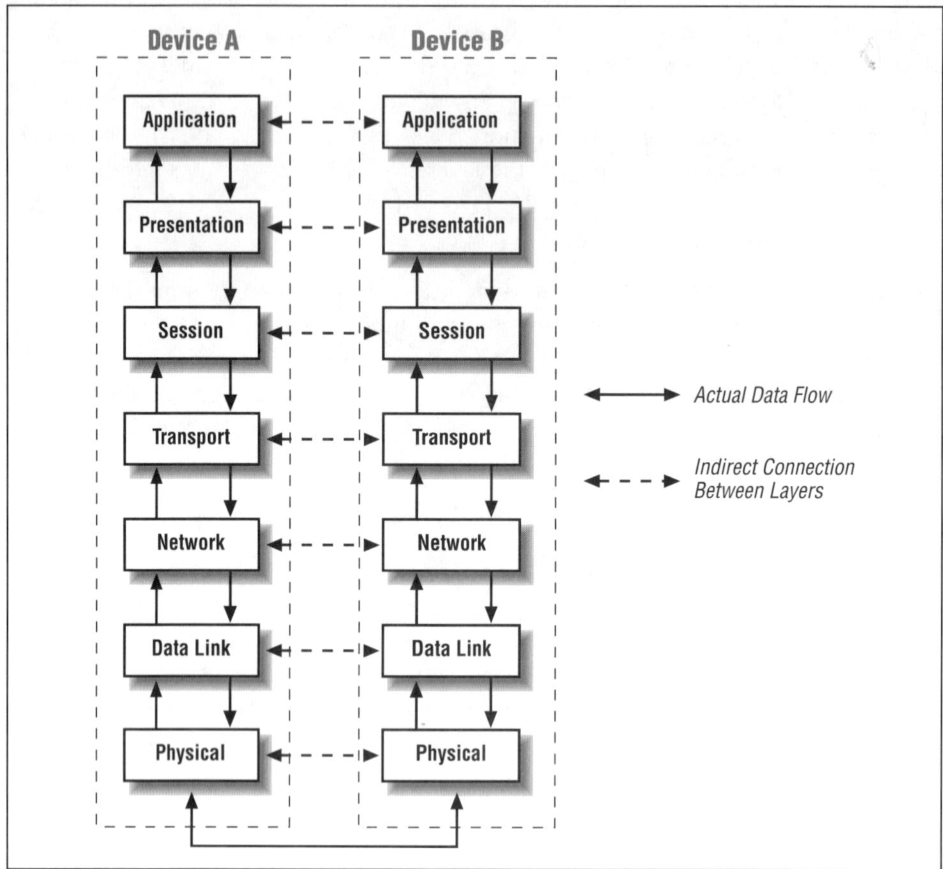

Figure 11-2. Interlayer communications occur sequentially in a physical sense, but directly between the layers in a logical sense

flooded with junk mail can attest. But in another, fundamental, sense, that's completely wrong. There aren't many restrictions on what you can do on the Internet, but there are a lot of restrictions that control how you do it.

Computers and networks are very literal things. You can let your imagination reign when you compose an email message or create a web page, but the fundamental low-level protocols that allow you to send that message or view that web page are defined in great detail. When it comes to the protocols used to move data through the network, if you don't play by the rules, you simply can't communicate. Obviously, someone or some group has to be responsible for defining and maintaining the rules that everyone plays by. For TCP/IP and the Internet, this group is called the *Internet Activities Board*, or *IAB*.

The IAB sponsors two key committees, called the *Internet Research Task Force* (*IRTF*) and the *Internet Engineering Task Force* (*IETF*). The IRTF is responsible for evaluating new technologies and their potential application to the Internet. The IETF develops new specifications and maintains existing specifications for the individual components of the TCP/IP suite.

When a new standard or a change to an existing standard is proposed, it is issued by the IETF as a *Request for Comment* (*RFC*). An RFC is a detailed technical document that concerns itself with a single, tightly focused issue. When a new RFC is issued, it is assigned a number in strictly sequential order, which serves to identify that RFC throughout its life. There are currently about 2,000 RFCs, many of which have been made obsolete by later documents with different numbers.

When an RFC is issued, there is period specified for open debate, during which anyone is free to respond to the RFC by suggesting additions or changes, or simply by criticizing what has been proposed. In response to the comments received, the RFC is modified and is then again distributed for comment. This process continues iteratively until a consensus is reached, at which point the RFC is adopted as a formal standard and promulgated. Although the time allocated for comments has by then passed, the final document is still called an RFC and is still identified by the number initially assigned to it.

NOTE You can retrieve any RFC by pointing your web browser to *www.internic.net.* RFCs are extremely technical (and often lengthy) documents that have little direct pertinence to the day-to-day concerns of most network administrators. If you never read an RFC, chances are your life will not be noticeably poorer for it. The important thing to understand is that the IETF defines TCP/IP using the RFC mechanism. If you really need to know more, you now know where to find it.

Major Components of the TCP/IP Suite

The entire TCP/IP suite includes scores of protocols, some of which are so esoteric or so limited in application that you are unlikely to ever hear of them, let alone use them. Without pretending to be exhaustive, this section examines some of the more important protocols that make up the TCP/IP suite. TCP/IP defines protocols that operate at all seven layers of the OSI Reference Model.

Although TCP/IP defines numerous protocols at the lower levels (Physical and Data Link Layers), these protocols are extremely technical, and of only academic interest—if that—to most network administrators. The protocols at the middle level (Network and Transport Layers) and upper level (Session, Presentation, and Application Layers) are more important to understand.

Some TCP/IP protocols straddle two or more OSI levels. For example, although the *Address Resolution Protocol* (*ARP*) and the *Reverse Address Resolution Protocol* (*RARP*) are assigned to the Network Layer of the OSI Reference Model, they in fact operate in the upper half of the Data Link Layer as well. Understanding exactly where a particular protocol fits in the model is not as important as understanding how it relates to other protocols within the suite. With that in mind, the following sections describe some of the more important components of TCP/IP.

Internet Protocol (IP)

The *Internet Protocol* (*IP*) operates at the OSI Network Layer. IP is a connectionless, unreliable protocol that offers best-effort delivery of routed datagrams. *Connectionless* means that no physical or logical connection exists between the source and destination hosts. *Unreliable* is not used in the everyday sense, but simply means that IP makes no provision for the source host to be notified of the success or failure of packet delivery to the destination host. The source host simply appends the network address of the destination host to the IP packet header and places the packet on the network. What happens after that is the responsibility of the network itself and the other protocols that make up the TCP/IP suite.

IP processing of outbound data begins when IP receives a segment of data, called a *message* or a *datagram*, from the Transport Layer above it. IP first determines the size of the message. Although IP is capable of handling data in blocks as large as 64 KB, it operates more efficiently with smaller block sizes, typically 1,460 bytes. If the message is too large, IP first *fragments* it into smaller chunks. It encapsulates each message (or message fragment) into a *packet*, which is the term used to refer to an organized assemblage of data at the Network Layer. A packet includes the data itself, the network (IP) addresses of the source and destination hosts, a checksum, and other administrative data. Once the packet is assembled, IP passes it to the Data Link Layer below it.

Departing for a moment from the discussion of IP and the Network Layer, the Data Link Layer encapsulates the packet into a *frame*, which is the term used for an organized assemblage of data at the Data Link Layer. The frame includes the data itself (the IP packet), hardware (MAC) addresses for the source and destination hosts, and other administrative information. Frames are specific to the media access method in use, e.g., Ethernet or Token Ring. Once the frame is assembled, the Data Link Layer delivers it to the Physical Layer, where it is placed on the network cable as a bit stream.

For inbound data, the process is exactly reversed. The Physical Layer retrieves the bit stream from the network cable, and passes it to the Data Link Layer as a frame. The Data Link Layer strips the frame header and extracts the encapsulated packet, which it then delivers to the Network Layer. IP, running at the Network Layer, then strips the IP header from the packet and extracts the message, which it then delivers to the Transport Layer.

Internet Control Message Protocol (ICMP)

The *Internet Control Message Protocol* (*ICMP*) operates at the Network Layer. ICMP is used to support the control messages exchanged between IP hosts to communicate error conditions and "out of band" administrative data. For example, if a router finds that one of its interfaces is no longer functioning, it communicates that fact to other routers on the network via ICMP messages. The most familiar use of ICMP is the *ping* utility used to verify that connectivity exists between two IP hosts.

Address Resolution Protocol (ARP)

The *Address Resolution Protocol* (*ARP*) operates at the Network Layer and the upper half of the Data Link Layer. ARP is used to resolve an unknown hardware (MAC) address from a known IP address. An IP host can use ARP to discover and map IP addresses to MAC addresses on the local network.

For example, the IP address for the default gateway is known to any IP host, but the MAC address that corresponds to that IP address must be discovered using ARP. To do so, the IP host sends an ARP message to the known IP address, requesting the host that owns that IP address to return its MAC address. As each IP host discovers address information via ARP messages, it stores these mappings to a local table. The mappings expire frequently to allow for physical changes to the network that involve a change to the MAC address of one or more of the hosts on the network.

Reverse Address Resolution Protocol (RARP)

The *Reverse Address Resolution Protocol* (*RARP*) operates, like ARP, at the Network Layer and the upper half of the Data Link Layer. As you might expect, it has exactly the opposite function of ARP. RARP resolves an unknown IP address from a known MAC address. RARP is largely obsolescent, although it remains a defined component of the TCP/IP suite, and some devices continue to use it. RARP has been largely superseded, first by the more recent BootP protocol, and subsequently by the even more recent DHCP protocol. The main disadvantage of RARP is that it resolves only the IP address of a host, requiring that you use other methods to determine other key TCP/IP configuration information like the subnet mask and the default gateway.

Transmission Control Protocol (TCP)

The *Transmission Control Protocol* (*TCP*) is one of the two key Transport Layer protocols. TCP is a connection-oriented, reliable protocol. *Connection-oriented* means that a logical connection (or session) exists between the source and destination hosts that are using TCP to communicate. *Reliable* is again not used in the everyday sense, but simply means that, during a TCP session, the destination host acknowledges each packet it receives, allowing the source host to know that the complete message has been received successfully.

The flip side to reliability is that the additional overhead required for reliable packet delivery makes TCP slower than the alternative. TCP is therefore used at the Transport Layer to support upper layer services, e.g., SMTP, FTP, Telnet, and HTTP, that require a reliable, streaming, connection-oriented transport and are willing to forego getting the highest available level of throughput in exchange for increased safety.

User Datagram Protocol (UDP)

The *User Datagram Protocol* (*UDP*) is the second major Transport Layer protocol. UDP is a connectionless, unreliable protocol. UDP is used instead of TCP to support those upper layer services that require the highest possible throughput and those that do not require reliability. UDP gains its higher performance relative to TCP by foregoing all of the overhead incurred by TCP to provide reliability. UDP simply places packets on the interface as quickly as possible, and doesn't worry about whether they arrive successfully at the destination. UDP is used mostly by upper layer services that exchange short, local messages, and by those that do not require the Transport Layer reliability provided by TCP because they provide their own built-in reliability. BootP, DHCP, and WINS are examples of upper layer services that use UDP transport.

NOTE The preceding sections describe some of the most important middle layer protocols. The following sections introduce some of the more important upper layer protocols supported by Windows NT Server. Entire books could be (and have been) written about these protocols. For more detailed information about the protocols that make up the TCP/IP suite, see *TCP/IP Network Administration 2nd ed.*, by Craig Hunt (to be published by O'Reilly & Associates, November, 1997).

File Transfer Protocol (FTP)

FTP is an upper layer client/server protocol that is used to do batch mode transfers of text and binary files between computer systems. FTP uses TCP at the

Transport Layer to ensure reliable file transfers. An FTP server can be configured to require a valid account name and password to log on, or it can allow anyone to log on anonymously—the familiar *anonymous FTP*.

Windows NT Server bundles a capable FTP server with the Internet Information Server module. It also bundles the rather Spartan character-mode FTP client, *\%SystemRoot\system32\ftp.exe*, which most people regard as being useful only for emergencies. Much better graphic mode FTP clients, e.g., WS_FTP and CuteFTP, are available for little or no cost from any shareware archive. For that matter, your web browser makes a pretty decent FTP client.

Trivial File Transfer Protocol (TFTP)

Like FTP, the *Trivial File Transfer Protocol* (*TFTP*) is another upper layer client/server protocol that is used to transfer data in batch mode. Although the names of the two protocols are similar, their purposes are quite different.

A host does not have to log in to a TFPT server before it transfers files. Because of this lack of login authentication, the types of files that TFTP is permitted to access and to transfer are quite limited. Only files whose permissions make them accessible to any user can be transferred with TFTP. Also, TFTP makes no provision for returning a list of directory names and filenames, so the TFTP client must specify the exact filename and location before initiating the transfer.

From the preceding description, it might seem that TFTP is a pretty worthless protocol, particularly on a server that also has an FTP server installed. TFTP doesn't do much, and it provides no security. However, the fact that it allows files to be retrieved without the client first logging in is the key. This single fact makes TFTP perfectly suited for its intended primary purpose, which is to "jump start" other hosts. For example, many routers have just enough intelligence in their bootstrap programs to establish a connection to a designated TFTP server and download their boot images from that server.

Because TFTP is designed to transfer small files to locally connected clients, it uses UDP at the Transport Layer rather than TCP. Although Windows NT Server does not include a TFTP server, numerous commercial, shareware, and public domain TFTP servers are available, as an Altavista search for "NT and TFTP" will quickly illustrate.

Hypertext Transfer Protocol (HTTP)

The *Hypertext Transfer Protocol* (*HTTP*) is an upper layer client/server protocol that, in conjunction with *Hypertext Markup Language* (*HTML*), forms the foundation of the World Wide Web. Windows NT Server bundles a full-featured HTTP server with the Internet Information Server module. It also bundles the top-notch HTTP client (or web browser) Internet Explorer.

Simple Mail Transfer Protocol (SMTP)

The *Simple Mail Transfer Protocol* (*SMTP*) is an upper layer client/server protocol that, in conjunction with *Post Office Protocol V3* (*POP3*), currently provides the foundation for Internet mail services. SMTP uses a store-and-forward, message switching model to deliver the mail. SMTP uses TCP at the Transport Layer to increase the likelihood that the message will eventually reach its destination. SMTP does not, however, guarantee successful delivery of any particular mail message.

An outbound mail message is transferred as a single entity from the originating SMTP host to the destination SMTP host, usually via intermediate SMTP hosts. The message is delivered to each successive SMTP host, where it is stored until it can be forwarded to the next SMTP host, and eventually reach its destination. At the destination, SMTP moves the message to the individual storage location, or mailbox, of the designated recipient. The recipient uses a POP3 mail client—or a mail client based on the more recent *Internet Mail Access Protocol V4* (*IMAP-4*)—to retrieve the message.

Microsoft does not currently bundle an SMTP server (or a POP3 server) with Windows NT. However, the Windows NT Server Resource Kit CD includes fully functional SMTP and POP3 servers that are suitable for those who need to provide simple Internet mail services. For those with more demanding mail environments, the optional Microsoft Exchange Server, includes full-blown SMTP and POP3 servers. Numerous commercial, shareware, and public domain alternatives are also available to provide these functions.

Microsoft provides numerous SMTP/POP3 clients, including the Exchange client, the standalone Microsoft Internet Mail package, and the mail module within Internet Explorer. Some of these clients are free for the download and others are included with optional packages like Exchange Server. In addition, nearly every third-party mail package available supports SMTP and POP3.

Telnet

Telnet is an upper layer terminal emulation protocol that is used to establish a terminal session across a TCP/IP link. Telnet uses TCP at the Transport Layer.

Most Telnet applications emulate a Digital Equipment Corporation (DEC) VT10x or VT20x terminal, although more advanced implementations may provide numerous terminal emulations, including Wyse and IBM 3270. Telnet is useful primarily for performing tasks like casual access to UNIX hosts and making programming changes to routers and similar devices.

Windows NT Server includes a serviceable if rather Spartan Telnet client, *\%SystemRoot\system32\telnet.exe*, which is all many administrators will need. Much better Telnet clients, e.g., QVTnet, are available for little or no cost from any shareware archive.

Simple Network Management Protocol (SNMP)

Simple Network Management Protocol (*SNMP*) is an upper layer protocol designed to support remote management of network components like servers, workstations, hubs, and routers. SNMP uses an agent/manager model that is analogous to the client/server model used by many other upper layer protocols.

SNMP agents are installed on devices that are to be remotely monitored and managed. SNMP agents are available for nearly any network component. The agent collects and stores protocol statistics, performance data, and other information about the device that it is running on. *SNMP proxy agents* run on a manageable (or smart) device, but are used to collect information about another, unmanageable (or dumb) device. For example, a proxy agent running on a router could be used to monitor traffic on a cable segment. Agents store their data in a local database called a *Management Information Base* (*MIB*).

An *SNMP manager* runs on a central management workstation. The manager can be used both to query individual agents about their status and to send commands to those agents to control the functioning of the device upon which the agent is running. In addition to their passive role of responding to queries and commands, some agents allow the manager to set traps. A *trap* is simply a threshold level or tripwire for a particular value that is being monitored by the agent. For example, you might set a trap on an agent running on a bridge to notify you if too many runt frames were occurring. When the value set for the trap is reached, the agent notifies the manager directly rather than waiting until the next time it is polled.

Domain Name Service (DNS)

The *Domain Name Service* (*DNS*) is an upper layer protocol that resolves unknown IP addresses from known host names. For example, when you point your web browser to *www.oreilly.com*, it uses DNS to determine the actual IP address of that host, which is needed to establish the session.

Microsoft Windows NT Server includes a full-featured DNS server, which is integrated with the DHCP server and the WINS server that also come with the operating system. DNS is covered in Chapter 14, *Using Domain Name Service*.

Dynamic Host Configuration Protocol (DHCP)

The *Dynamic Host Configuration Protocol* (*DHCP*) is an upper layer protocol that allows you to manage IP addresses and other TCP/IP configuration information from a central server, instead of maintaining this information at the individual client workstations.

Microsoft Windows NT Server includes a full-featured DHCP server, which is integrated with the DNS server and the WINS server that are also supplied with the operating system. DHCP is covered in Chapter 12, *Using Dynamic Host Configuration Protocol.*

Windows Internet Name Service (WINS)

The *Windows Internet Name Service* (*WINS*) is a semiproprietary Microsoft protocol used in the NetBIOS over TCP/IP (NetBT) environment. WINS is an enhanced implementation, or superset, of the formal Internet standards that pertain to NetBT, and is interoperable with other standards-based implementations of these RFCs. WINS servers dynamically register NetBIOS computer names and their associated IP addresses. WINS clients can query a WINS server to resolve an unknown IP address from a known NetBIOS computer name.

Microsoft Windows NT Server includes a full-featured WINS server, which is integrated with the DNS server and the DHCP server that are also supplied with the operating system. WINS is covered in Chapter 14, *Using Domain Name Service.*

Understanding IP Addresses

An *IP address*, also called an *Internet Address*, is used to identify each host on a network running TCP/IP transport. The IP address assigned to each device on the network must be unique within that network.

An IP address is a 32-bit number, which is conventionally divided into four bytes and expressed in *dotted decimal* format. A dotted decimal IP address comprises four values separated by periods, e.g., *192.168.169.0.* Because each value represents a byte, each can range from 0 through 255. The lowest possible IP address is therefore *0.0.0.0,* and the highest possible IP address is *255.255.255.255.*

The Internet Network Information Center (InterNIC)

The fact that IP addresses must be unique within a given network immediately raises an important issue. If your TCP/IP network is *private* (that is, not connected to the Internet), then you can assign any IP addresses you want to use. It's up to you to keep them straight and to avoid assigning duplicate addresses. If, on the other hand, your network will be connected to the public Internet, the IP address assignment issue becomes more complicated. You can't simply pick a set of addresses at random, because someone else may already be using them. Some central authority is needed to allocate and track IP addresses to ensure that no duplication occurs.

That central authority is called the *Internet Network Information Center*, or simply *InterNIC*. In addition to assigning IP addresses, InterNIC provides other important centralized Internet functions, including handling domain name registrations and other database services. InterNIC operations were formerly subsidized by the National Science Foundation, but that subsidy has been withdrawn, and InterNIC is now self-funding.

You can access InterNIC by setting your web browser to *http://www.internic.net*.

Network Address Classes

IP addresses are divided into two sections, which may vary in length, but which together must total 32 bits, as follows:

- The first, or leftmost, section of the IP address, called the *network number*, identifies the *network* to which the IP address is assigned. A network is a local group of interconnected machines that uses a *router* to connect to the outside world. The presence of the router delimits the boundary of the local network. All hosts on the local side of the router are members of the local network. All hosts on the remote side of the router are members of other networks. In fact, the router that connects a local network to the Internet is often called a *boundary router*.
- The second section, comprising the remainder of the IP address, is called the *host number*, and identifies a specific *host* on the network.

NOTE Don't confuse the term *host* when used in the Internet sense with its usage in conventional computing, where it typically means a large central computer. In the Internet sense, the term *host* is used to mean any device that must be assigned a unique address and be individually accessible. You may also hear a host referred to as a node. An old PC can be an Internet host, as can an individual router port, or even a communications link between two networks. In order to be accessible on a TCP/IP network, a device must be assigned a unique IP address. Any device that has an IP address is called a host.

InterNIC segments network addresses into five classes, each assigned an alphabetic label, A through E. The final two classes are not commonly used, and can safely be ignored. Class D is reserved for multicast use, and Class E is experimental. Classes A, B, and C, however, are in common use on the Internet. The difference between Classes A, B, and C is in how many of the four available bytes that comprise the IP address are assigned to the network address portion, and how many remain for use as the host address.

- *Class A network addresses* use only the first byte for the network address, leaving three bytes available for the host address. Class A network addresses are used only by huge organizations. A total of only 126 Class A network addresses are available. There are about 16,000,000 host addresses for each Class A network address.
- *Class B network addresses* use the first two bytes for the network address, leaving two bytes available for the host address. Class B network addresses are typically assigned to very large companies and Internet Service Providers. There are about 65,000 Class B network addresses available, and each Class B network address may contain about 65,000 hosts.
- *Class C network addresses* use the first three bytes for the Network Address, leaving only one byte available for the host address. Class C network addresses are typically assigned to small companies. Medium-size companies are often assigned a contiguous block of several Class C network addresses. There are about 16,000,000 Class C network addresses available, and each Class C network address may contain 254 hosts.

NOTE You can tell to which network class an IP address belongs simply by examining the most significant, or leftmost, three bits of the most significant, or leftmost, byte. In other words, the first number of an IP address determines the address class to which it belongs.

Reading from left to right, the 8 bits of a byte are assigned values of 128, 64, 32, 16, 8, 4, 2, and 1. The first byte of a Class A network address must begin with the bit pattern *0xx*, where x represents either a zero or a one. Because the leftmost bit must be zero in a Class A network address, the highest possible value for the first byte of a Class A address is 127. Because neither all zeroes nor all ones can be used as an address, the values for a Class A network address can range from 1 through 126, inclusive. Therefore, any IP address within the range *1.0.0.0* through *126.0.0.0,* inclusive, must be a Class A network address.

Similarly, the most significant 3 bits of a Class B network address must have the pattern *10x*. Because the leftmost (or 128-bit) bit must be one, the lowest possible value for the first byte of a Class B network address is 128. Similarly, because the second bit (or 64-bit) must be zero, the highest possible value for the first byte of a Class B network address is 191. Therefore, any IP address within the range of *128.1.0.0* through *191.254.0.0,* inclusive, must be a Class B network address.

The most significant 3 bits of a Class C network address must have the pattern *110*. Because the first two bits (the 128-bit and the 64-bit) must be one, the lowest possible value for the first byte of a Class C network address is 192. Because the third bit (or 32-bit) must be zero, the first byte of the Class C network address can be no higher than 223. Therefore, any IP address within the range of *192.0.1.0* through *223.255.254.0,* inclusive, must be a Class C network address.

The following sections examine each of these network address classes in more detail.

Class A network addresses

Because Class A network addresses use only the first byte of the IP address as the network address portion, very few Class A network addresses are available. You might expect that a one byte value would allow as many as 256 Class A network addresses, but because of the way that the address space is calculated, this figure is further reduced to only (2^7 - 2) or 126 addresses. The remaining values within the first byte are reserved for Class B and Class C network addresses, as described in the following sections.

NOTE Because a valid address at whatever level can never comprise all binary zeroes or all binary ones, you will see values in the form (2^x - 2) throughout these sections. The -2 portion reflects the fact that neither all zeroes nor all ones is a valid address.

Because only one byte is used for the network address portion of a Class A network address, three bytes (or 24 bits) remain for use as the host address portion (see Figure 11-3). This means that a Class A network can support as many as (2^{24}-2) or 16,777,214 hosts. Class A network addresses are obviously intended for huge networks. Nearly all of the active Class A addresses were originally assigned in the very early days of the Internet.

Today, only the national government of a major country or a huge multinational corporation could even hope to be assigned a Class A network address. As a matter of fact, in a public-spirited effort to help reduce address space problems, some of the organizations that originally held Class A network addresses have returned them to InterNIC for recycling, and now instead use multiple Class B network addresses.

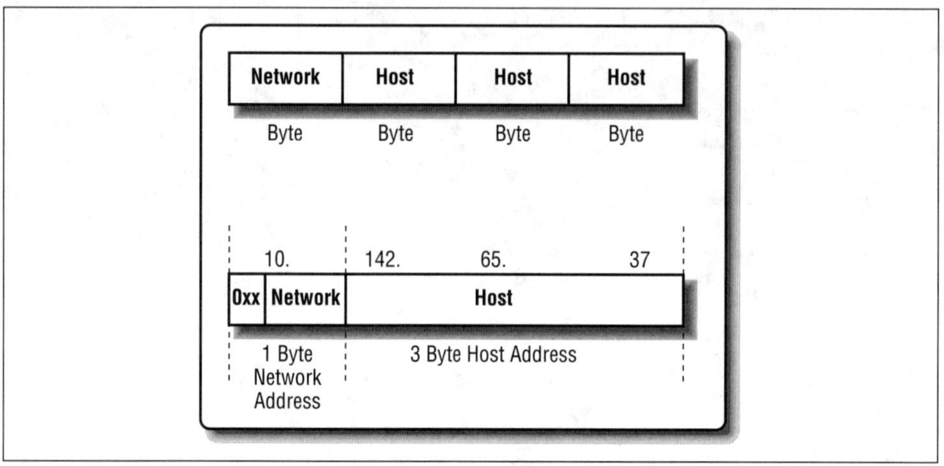

Figure 11-3. An Internet Class A network address uses one byte, leaving three bytes available for the host address

Class B network addresses

Class B network addresses use the first two bytes of the IP address as the network address portion and the remaining two bytes for the host address portion (see Figure 11-4). As a result, there are (2^{16}-2) or 65,534 Class B network addresses available, each of which provides 65,534 host addresses. Class B network addresses were originally intended for medium-size companies, but nowadays, for all practical purposes, InterNIC assigns Class B network addresses only to large companies (e.g., Microsoft and Novell) and to large Internet Service Providers. Organizations that in the past would have qualified easily for a Class A network address are now being asked to make do with multiple contiguous Class B network addresses.

Class C network addresses

Class C network addresses use the first three bytes of the IP address as the network address portion and the remaining one byte for the host address portion (see Figure 11-5). As a result, there are (2^{24}–2) or 16,777,214 Class C network addresses available, each of which provides (2^{8}–2) or 254 host addresses. Class C network addresses were originally intended for small companies. Organizations that in the past would have qualified for a Class B network address are now

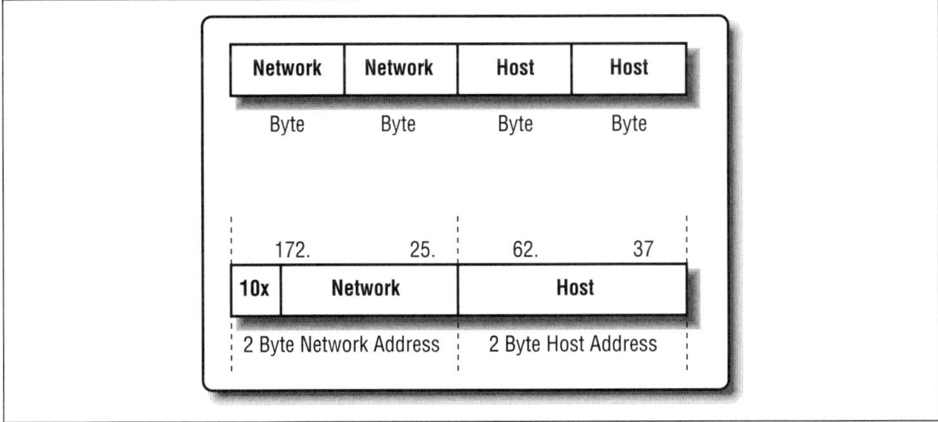

Figure 11-4. An Internet Class B network address uses two bytes, leaving two bytes available for the host address

being asked to make do with multiple contiguous Class C network addresses in lieu of a single Class B network address.

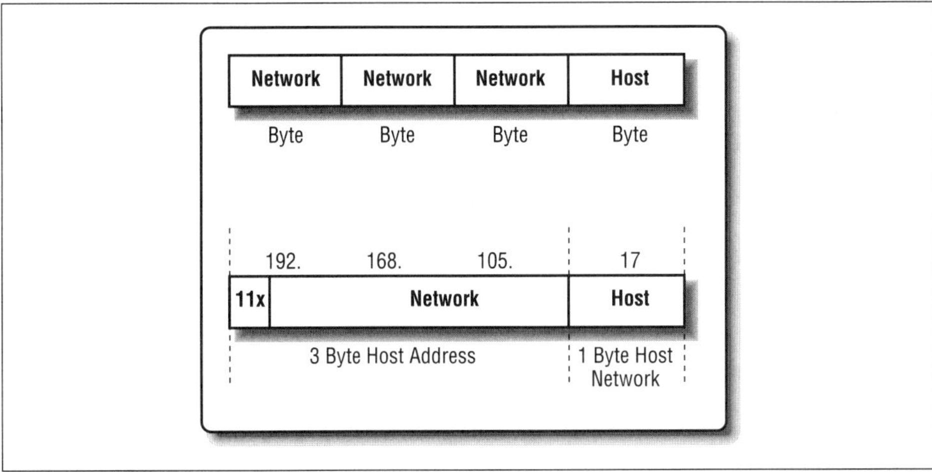

Figure 11-5. An Internet Class C network address uses three bytes, leaving only one byte available for the host address

---

NOTE Although you are unlikely to encounter either of them, two other address classes exist. Class D addresses are reserved for multicast use. Their initial bytes are in the 224 through 239 range, inclusive. Class E addresses are experimental, and range from 240 through 255.

Managing IP Addresses

The block of IP addresses that you receive, either directly from InterNIC or from your Internet Service Provider (ISP), specifies only the network address. It's up to you to assign individual IP addresses from this range to specific hosts on your network, and to otherwise manage the IP address space assigned to you.

In the following sections, I use a fairly typical situation to describe IP address management. These sections assume that a small business has applied for and been granted a Class C network address by InterNIC. This business has a home office, which is connected to the Internet, and two remote offices. All three locations are to be connected by a small private internetwork.

Assigning IP addresses to hosts

Neither InterNIC nor your ISP cares which of your hosts are assigned which IP addresses, as long as you use the network address they assigned to you. Assume that you have been assigned the Class C network address 192.168.169.0. This gives you a block of 256 IP addresses to work with, ranging from 192.168.169.0 through 192.168.169.255.

NOTE As it happens, 192.168.169.0 is one of the network addresses reserved by InterNIC for private networks. As such, no network using this address can ever be connected to the public Internet. RFC1597 lists the other network addresses reserved for private networks.

Because all hosts must be assigned a nonzero host number—that is, no host address may comprise all binary zeroes—the lowest address you can actually assign to a host is 192.168.169.1. Similarly, because the host address 255 (all binary ones) is reserved for broadcasts, the highest address you can actually assign to a host is 192.168.169.254. You, therefore, have only 254 usable IP addresses, rather than the nominal 256. You can assign these IP addresses to particular hosts in one of two ways, described in the following sections.

Assigning static IP addresses. A *static IP address* is one that is manually assigned to a particular host on a permanent—or at least a semipermanent—basis. A static IP address is so called because it does not change routinely.

How you assign a static IP address to a particular host depends on that host. With some operating systems, e.g., MS-DOS and NetWare 3.1x, the IP address may be defined in an ASCII configuration file. Many network hardware components, e.g., routers, are programmed via a terminal session, with the static IP address and other information you provide during this session stored in nonvolatile RAM. You set the IP address for some other network hardware using DIP switches. Computers running Windows NT and Windows 95 are set from the Network applet in Control Panel, and so on.

Using static IP addresses can be a viable solution on a small network, particularly if it doesn't need to accommodate roving users. If your network comprises one or two servers and a dozen or two workstations, all located at a single site, using static IP addresses may be workable. The larger the network grows, and the more frequently it is added to and changed, the less satisfactory static addressing becomes.

This is so because any address change made to key network components requires you to visit each workstation and make the appropriate changes to it manually. For example, all of your workstations may point to a primary Domain Name Server (DNS) located locally and a secondary DNS located at your ISP. If your ISP installs a new DNS with a different IP address, you must visit each workstation on your network individually and change the IP address for the secondary DNS. If you don't know what a DNS is, don't worry. DNS is covered in great detail in Chapter 14, *Using Domain Name Service*. The point is that address changes for key network components, although they may occur relatively infrequently, do occur, and each such change requires a lot of manual effort to accommodate it.

NOTE One of the most important drawbacks of using static IP addressing is that it may effectively lock you into your current ISP. If your network uses a network address assigned by your current ISP, changing ISPs requires that you give up that network address. For the new ISP, you use either a network address assigned by that ISP or one assigned to you directly by InterNIC. In either case, you must reconfigure every host on your network to use the new addresses. This fact argues strongly against not only using static addressing, but against using a network address assigned by an ISP.

Unfortunately, using a network address assigned directly by InterNIC is becoming increasingly difficult, and is likely to become more so. First, many ISPs will no longer allow you to use your own network address; second, InterNIC is likely in the near future to begin charging thousands of dollars per year for directly assigned network addresses; third, and most important, upstream service providers may arbitrarily—and with no notice—decide to stop routing your traffic if you use a directly assigned network address. If using a directly assigned network address becomes impracticable for whatever reason, the best plan is to keep your options open by avoiding the use of static IP address assignments.

If your network is very small, you could probably live with these problems. Granted, visiting 10 or 25 workstations is a royal pain, but you can probably drop everything and get the job done in a couple of hours, or perhaps a day at most. If your network is large, however, the problem becomes correspondingly larger. If you have dozens of servers and hundreds (or thousands) of workstations located at several sites, a simple change may require that several skilled staff members spend days or weeks making that change. Bad as this is, it's the least of the problem. Even worse is the fact that until a workstation is updated, it loses TCP/IP connectivity. Waiting an hour or two to get your Internet access back is one thing; waiting a week or two is quite another. Clearly, some better method is needed for managing IP addresses, particularly in larger networks.

Assigning IP addresses dynamically. The answer to this problem is called dynamic IP addressing. A *dynamic IP address* is one that is automatically assigned to a host on a temporary basis. A host that uses dynamic IP address assignment may have one IP address today and a different one tomorrow or next week.

With dynamic IP addressing, a fixed pool of IP addresses is established on a central server. These addresses are then assigned to hosts by the central server as needed. A host does not own the IP address assigned to it. It merely borrows, or *leases*, the IP address for a particular period of time. When the host is finished using the IP address, or when the lease period expires, ownership of the IP address is returned to the central host for eventual reassignment.

NOTE Dynamic IP addressing is managed in the Windows NT environment by the *Microsoft Dynamic Host Configuration Protocol* server, or *DHCP* server. DHCP is covered fully in Chapter 12, *Using Dynamic Host Configuration Protocol.*

Using dynamic IP addressing doesn't completely eliminate the need to use static IP addresses. At a minimum, for example, the server providing DHCP services must itself be assigned a static IP address. In most networks, there are several other hosts that should also be assigned static IP addresses. For example, you almost certainly will want to assign static IP addresses to your routers, file servers, application servers, print servers, and other shared devices that are accessed by ordinary network clients. You should also assign static IP addresses to devices, like web servers, that are accessed by outside users via the public Internet. In other words, you want these shared devices to be easy to find, and the way to make it so is to assign them static IP addresses.

Using DHCP to provide dynamic IP addressing solves nearly all of the problems caused by static IP addressing in one swell foop. Making major changes to your TCP/IP network, called *recasting* or *renumbering*, requires only two steps. First, you assign new static IP addresses to those few devices that are using them. Next, you alter the range of addresses assigned to the IP address pool on the DHCP server. Completing the entire process may take only a few minutes or a few hours, rather than the days or weeks that might be needed to renumber a network that used static IP addressing.

Using subnets

Only a couple of years ago, getting a Class C or even a Class B network address was pretty straightforward. If your company was "larger than small"—say Fortune 5,000 or better—you could spend a few hours completing the template needed to request a Class B network address and expect that InterNIC would grant your Class B network address in a few days.

The fact that most of the more than 64,000 host addresses provided by a Class B network address would be wasted by most holders of a Class B network address was of no concern to anyone. After all, there were more than 64,000 Class B network addresses available, and no great likelihood that that many organizations would want one. Why try to conserve something that appeared to be an unlimited resource?

Similarly, if you were a small company with three sites, you could apply for three Class C network addresses and expect InterNIC to grant them almost without question. The fact that you might have, say, only 14 hosts at each of these sites meant that you wasted 240 addresses of the 254 available in each Class C network address. No one cared. There were more than 16 million Class C network addresses available, and it seemed that there was no possibility that they would run out.

Nowadays, things have changed. The dramatic growth of the Internet and the perceived shortage of Internet address space that resulted from this explosive growth have caused InterNIC to clamp down on new requests for network addresses. A company that formerly would have been routinely granted a Class B network address is now assigned multiple Class C network addresses instead. The small company with multiple sites is now granted a single Class C network address and told to make do with it.

Even ISPs have become very conservative about how many addresses they will assign. Today, you have to spend an inordinate amount of time to justify each and every network address you request, and even then you probably won't get as many as you ask for. One alternative is to lie, and I know a few people who have done so and gotten away with it. As far as I know, there's still no law against it. If you have three sites with 15 computers each, you might slip while filling out the form and accidentally say that you have three sites, each with 150 computers. That ought to guarantee you three Class C network addresses without much problem. So, what should you do if you're too honest to lie and, based on the honest information you provide, InterNIC or your ISP won't give you a network address for each of your sites?

Say, for example, that you have three sites. The home office has a server or two, 15 or 20 workstations, and a router. Each of the two branch offices has a server, several workstations, and a router. What you would like to do is create three separate networks and then join them into a private internetwork. You might, for example, have an Internet connection at the home office, and want to link the home office to two branch offices across town using ISDN connections. That way, all three locations can communicate with each other, and all three can access the Internet without your having to install and pay for three separate Internet connections.

You wanted a Class C network address for each of the sites, but InterNIC or your ISP refused to assign you more than one Class C network address. How should you proceed? Again, I'll use the private Class C network address 192.168.169.0 for the example.

At first glance, the solution might seem obvious. Why not simply divide up the available IP addresses between the sites? You might assign the IP address range 192.168.169.1 through 192.168.169.154 to the home office, the range 192.168.169.155 through 192.168.169.204 to the first branch office, and the range 192.168.169.205 through 192.168.169.254 to the second branch office. This would give the home office 154 IP addresses to work with, and each of the branch offices would have 50. Problem solved, right?

Well, not really. There's a major fly in the ointment here. To understand the problem, you must first understand a little bit about how data is transferred between networks.

Consider what occurs when a host elsewhere on the Internet needs to send a packet to a host on your network. The remote host recognizes that the destination host is not on its own network, and therefore sends the packet to its own default gateway (or router) for onward forwarding to the destination. The remote router checks its own routing table to determine whether it has a direct route to the destination network. If it does, it forwards the packet directly to the destination network. If it does not, it forwards the packet to an intermediate router that is "nearer" to the destination network, as determined from its routing table.

Eventually, the packet arrives at a router on a network that is a direct neighbor of your own network. This router receives the packet and prepares to forward it to your network. This is where the problem arises. The remote router doesn't forward the packet directly to the IP address of the destination host on your network; it forwards the packet to the border router that serves the network of which the destination host is a member. The way that it identifies that border router is by its network address. However, we have three separate networks (remember that a router delimits a network) with three separate routers, but only one network address among them.

Which of your routers should the router on the neighboring network deliver the packet to? The home office router? The router in the first branch office? The router in the second branch office? All of the above? None of the above? How can it even tell the difference, since all three of your routers have the same network address? It can't. The real answer is none of the above, since TCP/IP networks in general, and the Internet in particular, simply don't work this way. Each network (and each border router) must have a unique network address.

After reading this, it may seem to you that, by granting you only one network address, InterNIC is telling you that you can have a network at only one of your three sites. This isn't really the case, however. You can have your three networks, but you'll need to take that one network address and somehow turn it into at least three unique network addresses. The way that you do so is called *subnetting*.

Remember that InterNIC (or your ISP) assigned only the first three bytes of your Class C network address. Although many people think that a network address must occupy some whole number of bytes, it is really simply a bit mask of arbitrary length. As it happens, nothing limits a network address to ending on a byte boundary. As you will recall, that final byte of your Class C network address is yours to do with as you please.

One of the things you can do with it is split it up. Rather than using all 8 bits for the host address, you can use some smaller number of bits for the host address and then append the remaining bits to the existing 3 byte network address. For example, rather than using a 3-byte (24-bit) network address with a 1-byte (8-bit) host address, you might assign the most significant 3 of "your" bits to the network address (thereby creating a 27-bit network address) and retain only the least significant 5 bits for the host address. By doing so, you've magically subdivided (or *subnetted*) your single network address into multiple network addresses, at the expense of having fewer bits available for the host address portion.

The number of bits you reserve for the host address versus the number of bits you allocate to expanding the network address determines how many additional network addresses, called *subnets*, are available, and how many hosts each subnet can contain. Table 11-1 lists the possible ways to subnet a Class C network address.

Table 11-1. Available Subnets for a Class C Network Address

Host Address Bits	Subnet Address Bits	Subnet Mask	Number of Subnets	Hosts per Subnet	Total Hosts per Network
7	1	128	0	126	0
6	2	192	2	62	124
5	3	224	6	30	180
4	4	240	14	14	196
3	5	248	30	6	180
2	6	252	62	2	124
1	7	254	126	0	0

Note first the first and last rows of the table. Recall that neither a network address nor a host address can comprise all binary zeroes or all binary ones. Allocating only one bit to either purpose by definition forces it to assume one or the other of the forbidden values, so assigning either 1 bit or 7 bits to the subnet address is not possible.

The second row of the table uses 2 bits for the subnet address. These two bits can assume the values 00, 01, 10, or 11. The first and last of these values are forbidden by convention, leaving the two values 01 and 10 available for subnet addresses. The six remaining bits are assigned to the host address, allowing 2^6 (or 64) possible values for host address. Again, a host address of all binary zeroes or all binary ones is forbidden, leaving (64 – 2) or 62 possible host addresses. Assigning 2 bits to the subnet address therefore yields two subnets, each of which may contain as many as 62 hosts. The final column simply multiplies the number of subnet addresses available by the number of hosts per subnet. In this case, using subnetting has given us two network addresses at the expense of allowing only 124 host addresses on the network rather than the 254 host addresses that we started with.

The remaining rows of the table show the effect of increasing the number of bits assigned to the subnet address. As you increase the number of bits assigned to the subnet address, the number of available subnets increases, but each can contain many fewer hosts. In practical terms, most Class C network addresses that are subnetted use either 2, 3, or 4 bits for the subnet address. Assigning 5 bits to the subnet address yields 30 subnets, each with only 6 host addresses, a configuration that is not often useful. Assigning 6 bits to the subnet mask yields 62 subnets, but each can contain only two host addresses, presumably a router and one computer.

Subnetting a Class C network address is often a useful workaround in small environments, but there is no guarantee that it can solve the problem of an inadequate number of network addresses. The hard and fast relationship between the number of subnet addresses and the number of host addresses per subnet can prove an insuperable obstacle. For example, if you need more than two network addresses, you have no alternative but to assign 3 or more bits to the subnet address. This in turn limits the maximum number of host addresses to at most 30 per subnet. If at least one of your sites requires more than 30 host addresses, then subnetting won't solve your problem. You have no alternative but to apply to InterNIC or your ISP for one or more additional Class C network addresses.

Although this section focuses on subnetting a Class C network address, subnetting is also a useful tool for Class A and Class B network addresses. In fact, it's more a way of life on larger networks. Class A and Class B network addresses assign three full bytes and two full bytes, respectively, to the host address, leaving much more room to operate.

Class A networks are almost always subnetted at the byte level (using the entire second octet) to provide 254 subnets, each of which is the equivalent of a Class B network. Class B networks are often subnetted at the byte level (using the entire third octet) to provide 254 subnets, each of which is equivalent to a Class C network. Class B networks are also often subnetted at the bit level, using only a portion of the third octet. This yields fewer subnets, but allows each to contain more host addresses.

Understanding subnet masks

The *subnet mask*, also called the *netmask*, is the decimal value of those bits that you allocated to the subnet address. For example, if you used a 3-bit subnet address to divide your network into six subnets, each with 30 host addresses, then you add the values of the three most significant bits to determine the subnet mask. In this case, those values are 128, 64, and 32, which total 224. Similarly, if you used a 4-bit subnet mask to divide your network into 14 subnets, each with 14 host addresses, then you add the values of the four most significant bits—128, 64, 32, and 16—to arrive at a subnet mask of 240. Figure 11-6 shows a network subnetted with 3-bit and 4-bit subnet masks.

Class A, Class B, and Class C network addresses have default subnet masks, which in each case assumes that the network address is not subnetted. The default subnet mask for a Class A network address is 255.0.0.0; for a Class B, 255.255.0.0; and for a Class C, 255.255.255.0. If you used a 3-bit subnet address to divide your Class C network address, you would use a subnet mask of 255.255.255.224, with the value for the final octet calculated as described in the preceding paragraph.

The subnet mask is a key piece of TCP/IP configuration information. To understand why, remember two items. First, a router delimits a network (or a subnetwork). Second, when a host needs to send a packet to another host, it first

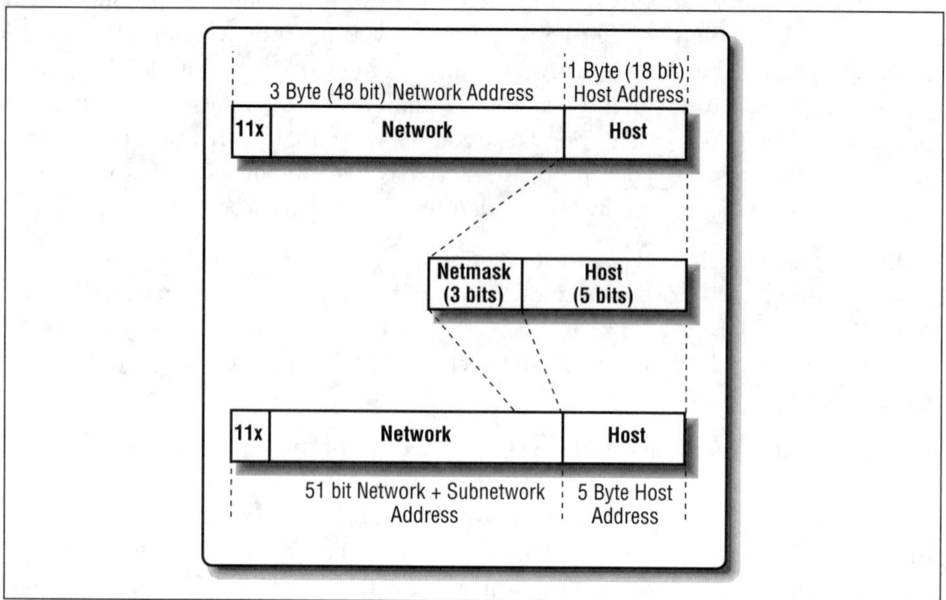

Figure 11-6. The subnet mask specifies the configuration of the subnet

decides whether the destination host is on its own network. If it is, the source host sends the packet directly to the destination host. If the destination host is on a different network, the source host sends the packet to a router for delivery to the remote network. The source host decides if the destination host is on its own network by comparing its own network address with the network address of the destination host. If they are the same, the source host assumes that the destination host is on its own network and sends the packet directly.

This works fine as long as the network has not been subnetted. On an unsubnetted Class C network, for example, if the first three octets of the destination address match those of the source address, the source host can be certain that it can communicate directly with the destination host. The situation is a bit more complicated if subnetting is being used.

Consider the following three arbitrarily chosen IP addresses: 192.168.169.100, 192.168.169.161, and 192.168.169.188. The first octet tells us that these host addresses are members of a Class C network. That the first three octets are identical tells us they are members of the *same* Class C network. If 161 needs to send a packet to each of the other two hosts, and the network is not subnetted, there's no problem. By definition, all three host addresses are members of the same network, and 161 can send a packet directly to either of the other host addresses.

Consider what happens, however, if this Class C network is subnetted with a 3-bit subnet address. Unless you have a black belt in IP subnetting, looking at dotted decimal IP addresses doesn't tell you much. If you convert the final octet to binary, things become a lot clearer:

Decimal	Binary
100	01100100
161	10100001
188	10111100

Looking at the first three bits—those that comprise the subnet address—quickly tells you that the host address 100 is a member of subnet 011, whereas host addresses 161 and 188 are members of the subnet 101. Because host 161 has a subnet mask of 224 decimal (or 11100000 binary), it knows that the most significant three bits of the final octet are actually part of the network address rather than the host address.

When host 161 needs to send a packet to host 188, it first examines the network address of the destination host—192.168.169—and finds that the destination host is a member of the same network. So far, so good. Because it has a nonzero subnet mask, host 161 realizes that it is a member of a subnet. Host 161 then applies the subnet mask to determine how many bits of the final octet should be considered as a part of the network address instead of the host address. Because its subnet mask is 224, it realizes that the most significant three bits of the final octet are actually a part of the network address, and compares those three bits of its own address with the corresponding three bits of the destination address. It determines that both addresses have a subnet address of 101, and that they are therefore both members of the same subnet. Host 161 can send the packet directly to host 188.

Conversely, when host 161 needs to send a packet to host 100, it first examines the network address of the destination host—192.168.169—and finds that the destination host is a member of the same network. Again, so far, so good. Host 161 then examines the extended portion of the network address, and finds that host 100 is a member of a different subnet—011 to be exact. Host 161 realizes that it cannot send the packet directly to host 100, and instead must deliver it to a router for subsequent forwarding to the proper subnet.

NOTE If, for example, you were using a 4-bit subnet mask instead of a 3-bit subnet mask, each of the example host addresses—100, 161, and 188—would be members of a different subnet—0110, 1010, and 1011, respectively.

The default gateway

The *default gateway*, also called the *default router*, is the final key piece of IP configuration information. Every IP host must have a default gateway defined if it is to communicate outside its own subnet.

If your network uses static IP address assignment, the IP address of the default gateway is one of the items that you must specify when you are configuring a host. If your network uses DHCP for dynamic IP address assignment, the IP address of the default gateway is specified during configuration of the DHCP server, which then provides the IP address of the appropriate default gateway to each client it serves.

As I mentioned in the preceding section, any IP host can communicate directly with another IP host that is on the same network (or subnetwork). If, however, the destination IP address is on a different network or subnetwork, the source IP host has no means to deliver the data directly. Instead, the source host sends the packet destined for a foreign network to the IP address of a local router, called the default gateway.

When the default gateway router receives the packet, it must determine what action to take. The router examines the packet's destination network address and compares it with the entries in its own routing table. If it finds the destination network address, the router forwards the packet, using the interface specified in the routing table. For example, the router may determine that one packet should be routed to an Ethernet interface that connects to a router located on the next floor; another packet may be routed to the T1 interface that connects that router to the Internet; still another packet may be routed to a dial-up interface that connects that router to another router at a branch office.

Routing table entries are of three types:

Static
: A static routing table entry, usually called simply a *static route*, is created manually by the network administrator. Static routes can be used as the only type of routes in a simple network, and are also used in more complex networks to ensure that a default route exists.

Protocol
: A protocol routing table entry, usually called simply a *dynamic route*, is one that is created automatically by the interaction of the various routers on the network. Dynamic routes are updated whenever external conditions change. For example, if a T1 interface connected to a router fails, that router will inform other routers on the network that the route represented by that interface is no

longer available. Dynamic routes are constantly updated to account for changing environments.

Connected
: A connected routing entry is created automatically for each installed interface on a router.

Classless Interdomain Routing (CIDR)

The traditional IP address assignment method that InterNIC uses—granting addresses in Class A, B, or C blocks—introduces two serious problems. Neither of these problems was apparent in the early days of the Internet, but both have become increasingly critical as the Internet continues to expand dramatically.

Granularity
: The smallest block of addresses that can be assigned to a network is a Class C network address—256 IP addresses. Most Class C networks use only a small number of the assigned addresses. The perceived shortage of IP address space makes it desirable to minimize this wastage. In particular, the Class B network addresses commonly assigned to ISPs were often utilized very inefficiently, with customers being granted large blocks of addresses, many of which remained forever unused.

Routing Table Growth
: Under the current system, Class C network addresses are assigned on a first-come, first-served basis, which means that there is no correlation between network address and physical location. As a result, a very high percentage of Class C network addresses end up as individual routing table entries, which must be proliferated to all of the core routers on the Internet backbone. To reduce the load on the backbone routers, it would be very desirable to aggregate as many smaller address blocks as possible into single larger address blocks, which require only one routing table entry.

The solution to both of these problems is called *Classless Interdomain Routing* (*CIDR*), described in RFC1518 and RFC1519. CIDR defines IP addressing schema and address aggregation methods designed to minimize the size of the top-level Internet routing tables. At the same time, CIDR reduces the granularity in IP address assignments. With CIDR, IP addresses can be assigned in blocks that correspond with any power of two. For example, the small company that previously would have been granted a Class C network address (with 256 IP addresses) can now instead be granted 16, 32, 64, or 128 IP addresses.

NOTE CIDR uses a different syntax to refer to IP address blocks. It specifies the number of bits allocated to the network address. For example, a traditional Class C network address assigns three bytes, or 24 bits to the network address. With CIDR, the equivalent block of addresses is designated /24. Similarly, a 2-byte Class B network address is identified as a /16. CIDR, however, is not limited to byte boundaries. An ISP using CIDR can assign you a block of IP addresses that closely corresponds to the number you actually need. For example, the ISP might assign you a /26 block, which comprises 64 IP addresses, or a /23 block, which comprises 512 addresses.

The best way to understand CIDR is to think of it as "supersubnetting" or better still as "supernetting/subnetting." In a traditional routed IP network, the subnet mask is a property of the individual host and the subnet to which it is assigned. The upstream network is not aware of the subnetting details, or even that subnetting is being used. With CIDR, the subnet mask becomes an integral part of the routing tables themselves, and of the protocols being used.

Traditionally, an IP route pointed to an IP address, which was broken down (according to its network address class) into network address bits and host address bits. With CIDR, a route instead comprises both an IP address and a subnet mask. This allows networks to be divided into subnets, as before, but it also allows networks to be combined into supernets, as long as they share a common network prefix.

Although CIDR is becoming increasingly common, two barriers have prevented its universal adoption.

- Using CIDR requires that the routers at both the ISP and the customer site be upgraded to support CIDR-aware protocols, namely, *Routing Information Protocol V2* (*RIP-2*), *Open Shortest Path First V2* (*OSPF v2*), and *Border Gateway Protocol V4* (*BGP-4*). ISPs have been quick to convert, mainly because it is in their own interest to do so. Their customers, however, have been much slower about taking the CIDR plunge. Although the necessary router software upgrades are usually inexpensive or free, the process of upgrading can be time consuming and disruptive. Also, many customers' perception is that upgrading to CIDR doesn't really buy them much. In fact, if anything, it takes them in a direction that they don't want to go.
- Using CIDR requires that the customer renumber his entire IP network. This process is time consuming, error prone, disruptive, and expensive—particularly for networks that use static IP address assignment. It also, by definition, requires you to give up the IP addresses that you obtained directly from InterNIC and instead use IP addresses that you "borrow" from the ISP.

All of this will change nearly overnight, probably before you read this book. As this is written, there is no charge for a network address block. Sometime in 1997, this free ride is likely to end. Free network addresses will go the way of free domain names. One proposal is to charge a $2,500 annual fee to anyone who registers one or more network address blocks, with additional charges fixed on a declining scale based on the number of addresses registered.

It will no longer be economically feasible to register small numbers of C blocks directly. All but the very largest providers will find that it makes economic sense to get their IP address blocks from their own providers rather than registering them directly. Ultimately, only a handful of very large providers will register network addresses directly. Everyone else will get their network addresses from their upstream providers. This is the entire point, of course. When network addresses are being managed by only a few providers, the problem of IP address fragmentation and huge routing tables goes away.

In the short term, this change is likely to have two negative effects. The price of Internet access may increase, because someone has to pay for those IP address blocks, directly or indirectly. Also, many small ISPs are likely to fail, or to be absorbed by larger providers. Paying for IP addresses will be a significant burden for small operators, who are unable to distribute the relatively large fixed costs over a large number of address blocks.

In the long term, however, the widespread adoption of CIDR will have a positive effect. Prices for Internet access may eventually stabilize at a lower level, and CIDR will be at least in part responsible. Today, a core router for the Internet backbone might cost $100,000 or more, simply because you need one hell of a router to handle 30 MB routing tables with an acceptable level of performance. CIDR will eventually have the same kind of impact on the size of routing tables that PKZip has on the size of a text file—routing tables will shrink to a tiny fraction of their current size. All of a sudden, you'll be able to use a $10,000 router to accomplish the same job that used to require a $100,000 router.

12

Using Dynamic Host Configuration Protocol

In this chapter:
- *Why DHCP Is Needed*
- *How DHCP Works*
- *Planning for DHCP*
- *Installing the DHCP server Service*
- *Managing DHCP with DHCP Manager*
- *DHCP Relay Agent*
- *Maintaining and Troubleshooting DHCP server*

The Microsoft Dynamic Host Configuration Protocol (DHCP) server is a Windows NT Service that automatically assigns IP addresses to clients running DHCP client software. By using DHCP, you can centralize the management of IP addresses, netmasks, and other IP configuration information, greatly reducing the amount of administration needed to maintain a network running TCP/IP transport.

A DHCP client does not have a permanently assigned, "hard-coded" IP address. Instead, at boot time, the DHCP client requests an IP address from the DHCP server. The DHCP server has a pool of IP addresses that are available for assignment. When a DHCP client requests an IP address, the DHCP server assigns, or *leases*, an available IP address from that pool to the client. The assigned IP address is then owned by that client for a specified period, called the *lease duration*.

When the lease expires, that IP address is returned to the pool and becomes available for reassignment to another client. When a client reboots, it checks to see if its lease is still valid. If so, it continues using the same IP address. If not, it requests a new IP address from the DHCP server. Servers and other computers that should always have the same IP address may be assigned a permanent IP address using a DHCP *permanent lease*.

Many people believe that DHCP is a proprietary Microsoft protocol. It is not, although Microsoft was instrumental in having DHCP adopted as a formal Internet standard. The Internet community has long recognized that a dynamic means of assigning IP addresses to clients was needed, both to reduce the administrative load of manually managing IP addresses and related information like subnet masks and default routers, and to increase the efficiency with which the limited IP address space is allocated.

DHCP extends an earlier protocol called BOOTP, which provided similar, although more limited, functionality. DHCP added several new configuration options and the ability to allocate reusable network addresses automatically. DHCP and BOOTP clients are largely interoperable, and some network components still depend on BOOTP. BOOTP and DHCP are defined in the following Internet Requests for Comment (RFCs), which you may retrieve with your ftp client at *ds.internic.net/rfc* or with your web browser at *www.internic.net/ds/dspg2intdoc.html:*

RFC951 Bootstrap Protocol
: This RFC, dated 9/1/85, originally defined the BOOTP protocol, and was subsequently updated by RFC1532, RFC1395, and RFC1497.

RFC1533 DHCP Options and BOOTP Vendor Extensions.
: This RFC, dated 10/8/93, makes obsolete RFC1497, and specifies the current set of valid DHCP options, which are tagged data items stored in the options field of a DHCP message.

RFC1534 Interoperation Between DHCP and BOOTP.
: This RFC, also dated 10/8/93, defines the interactions between DHCP and BOOTP network clients.

RFC1541 Dynamic Host Configuration Protocol
: This RFC, dated 10/27/93, makes obsolete RFC1531, and defines the current implementation of DHCP.

RFC 1542 Clarifications and Extensions for the Bootstrap Protocol
: This RFC, also dated 10/27/93, makes obsolete RFC1532, and defines the functioning of relay agents, a matter of particular concern to those who are running DHCP on a routed network.

DHCP uses a clientserver architecture. DHCP servers are available for many operating systems, including UNIX, Novell NetWare 4.1x, and, of course, Windows NT Server. Similarly, DHCP clients are available for nearly any client operating system. A workstation running any standards-compliant DHCP client software can communicate with, and be serviced by, any standards-compliant DHCP server. The Microsoft DHCP implementations for both client and server comply fully with the relevant RFC standards.

Microsoft has taken things a step further by integrating DHCP functions on both the client and the server with Microsoft Domain Name Service (DNS) and Microsoft Windows Internet Naming Service (WINS) functions. The one downside is that, in order to get the maximum benefits from this tight integration, you must run Microsoft operating systems on all of your servers and clients. Given the realities of today's environment, that's not much of a hardship for many administrators. NetWare servers, Macintosh clients, and other non-Microsoft DHCP devices on your network can still participate, although with a somewhat reduced level of integration.

Why DHCP Is Needed

DHCP has become a practical necessity for large IP networks for two reasons. First, each host in a TCP/IP network must have a unique IP address. This simple fact has caused a tremendous amount of annoyance and extra work for network administrators, and has resulted in more than a few crashed networks. In the early days of TCP/IP networking, there was no automated alternative; you had to assign an IP address manually to each host. Even today, many networks continue to use manual assignment and tracking of IP addresses.

Assigning IP addresses manually is practical only for small networks. As the size and complexity of the network increases, using manual IP address assignment becomes increasingly unworkable. Each time a workstation, server, network printer, router, or other host is added or relocated, someone must determine a valid IP address, ensure that that IP address is not already in use by another host, record the assignment of that address, and then finally configure the host manually for that IP address. This process requires expert staff time and is always prone to error. Accidentally duplicating an IP address will at best cause a communication failure on both affected hosts. At worst—if the duplicated IP address belongs to a server, router, or other critical network component—the duplicate IP address may cause the entire network to crash. Microsoft TCP always checks to see if its address is a duplicate by issuing an ARP before using the address.

The second motivation for using DHCP is that the perceived shortage of IP network addresses has made it necessary to use IP host addresses more efficiently. Only a few years ago, getting a Class C network address (256 IP addresses) was a matter of simply asking InterNIC to assign one to you. Requests for as many as 16 contiguous C blocks were routinely honored by InterNIC without much formality. If you said you needed it, they gave it to you. Even getting a Class B network address (256 C blocks, or 65,536 IP addresses) required minimal paperwork and justification.

Nowadays, it's a struggle to get InterNIC to assign even a single Class C network address. Getting multiple C blocks assigned requires spending hours or days completing detailed justifications, network plans, and so forth. Getting a B block assigned is almost impossible unless you are applying on behalf of a Fortune 500 corporation, and even then it's not a foregone conclusion.

The large granularity of network addresses—a C block is the smallest unit that can be assigned—means that many IP addresses are wasted. Consider a small branch office with a router, a server and seven workstations. If that branch office is assigned a Class C network address, only 9 of the available 256 IP addresses are in use. The remaining IP addresses cannot be used except at that branch office, and so are wasted. In the past, this didn't much matter, because network addresses were free and were easily available from a seemingly inexhaustible supply. Some large companies with many small remote sites wasted 90% or more of the many IP addresses assigned to them.

Network addresses are assigned by InterNIC on a first-come, first-served basis, which means that there is absolutely no correlation between network address and geographic location. For example, InterNIC assigned my company (located in Winston-Salem, NC) the Class C network address 204.238.30.0. The network address immediately preceding mine, 204.238.29.0, is assigned to Warner Brothers Imaging Technologies in Sherman Oaks, CA. The network address immediately following mine, 204.238.31.0, is assigned to the Bead Gallery in Juneau, AK.

A side effect of this policy has been the explosive growth of routing tables. Each individually assigned network address requires a routing table entry in every router on the backbone. A contiguous block of, say, 16 Class C network addresses assigned to the same network requires only a single routing table entry. Those same 16 C blocks, if assigned individually to different companies (and different networks), require 16 individual routing table entries. As of early 1997, the routing tables on the Internet backbone have grown to more than 30 MB.

Understanding InterNIC-Assigned IP Addresses Versus ISP-Assigned IP Addresses

InterNIC strongly encourages you to use IP addresses assigned to you by your Internet Service Provider (ISP) rather than applying directly to InterNIC for your own block of addresses. They do so both to avoid wastage of IP addresses and to slow the growth of routing tables.

However, there is a downside to using addresses provided by your ISP, and you won't hear either InterNIC or your ISP talking much about it. Addresses provided by your ISP belong to the ISP rather than to you. This means they aren't portable. If you decide to change ISPs, you have no option but to recast your IP address assignments networkwide to use the addresses provided by your new ISP. In effect, using addresses provided by an ISP locks you into that ISP.

At first, InterNIC simply recommended that you use ISP-provided IP addresses, but that didn't accomplish much. Most administrators were concerned about address portability, and so simply continued to apply to InterNIC when they needed additional network address blocks. Seeing this, and still determined to slow the growth of routing tables, InterNIC next began warning applicants for network address blocks that there was no guarantee that individually assigned blocks would be routable in the future.

Apparently, this hasn't worked either, because InterNIC now proposes to charge for directly assigned IP addresses. Under this proposal, any organization to which InterNIC directly assigns a network address must pay a $1,000 annual fee, with additional charges assessed based on the number of IP addresses assigned. If this proposal is implemented, you will see the wholesale abandonment of Class C network addresses. Almost everyone will use network addresses provided by his ISP.

So, what relationship exists between the source of your IP addresses and using DHCP? Simply this: implementing DHCP on your current network will allow you to recast your IP addressing much more easily when (not if) you find yourself switching to addresses provided by your ISP. If you are using DHCP when the time to recast arrives, you will need to change only the DHCP server configuration and the few static addresses assigned to servers and routers, including the DHCP server. If you are not running DHCP, you will need to change the IP configurations individually for each machine on your network.

Understanding IP Address Translation

When you're designing (or redesigning) your IP network configuration, consider also the related issue of network address translation. InterNIC reserves the Class A network address 10.0.0.0 for private networks. This means that anyone can use this network address for an internal IP network, but that network can never be connected directly to the Internet. The huge address space provided by a private Class A network address gives you great flexibility in configuring your internet IP network. This wouldn't be a very good tradeoff, however, if it prevented your users from accessing the Internet and prevented outside Internet users from accessing your public servers. Fortunately, there are a couple of ways around this problem.

Network address translators

A network address translator (NAT) may be software running on your border router (the one that connects your network to your ISP), or it may be a separate box. On the public (or Internet) side, the NAT uses the network address assigned to you by your ISP, typically one or more Class C network addresses. On the private (or internal) side, the NAT uses the Class A private network address. The NAT can map public Internet addresses to private internal addresses either statically or dynamically.

Static address mapping allows you to make privately addressed resources, e.g., a web server or a mail server, available to outside Internet users. For example, you might assign your public web server an internal address of 10.0.1.1. Then, if your ISP has assigned, for example, the Class C network address 204.179.186.0 to the public side of your NAT, you might establish a static mapping of the public Internet address 204.179.186.128 to the private internal address 10.0.1.1. Users on your internal IP network can then access the web server by pointing their browsers to 10.0.1.1. Outside Internet users can access the same web server at 204.179.186.128.

Dynamic address mapping allows your internal users to share the limited number of public Internet IP addresses. For example, if an internal user with the private IP address 10.0.1.200 wants to access the Microsoft web site, he must be assigned a public Internet address so that the Microsoft web server has a valid address to which it can send the requested pages. To meet this requirement, the NAT temporarily maps the private 10.0.1.200 address to a public address, say, 204.179.186.54. For the duration of his session, that user is visible to the public Internet as address 204.179.186.54.

If you have a public C block (with 256 addresses) and only a few dozen—or a few hundred—internal users, it might seem that contention for public addresses would be a relatively minor concern. After all, chances are that only a small percentage of these users would be accessing public Internet hosts at any one time. In fact, contention for the limited number of public addresses is a more important issue than it might at first seem. Here's why. When the user mentioned above hits the Microsoft homepage, there might be 28 images on that page. As the web page loads, a separate HTTP session is initiated to download each of the images. The NAT treats each of these sessions as an individual entity, and maps a separate public IP address for each. On this basis, two or three users doing heavy web access could easily occupy all of the available public IP addresses.

The solution to this problem is called *overloading*, which is not supported by all NATs. A NAT that does not support overloading has no alternative but to assign a new public IP address as each session is established. A NAT that does support overloading instead reuses the same IP address, but assigns a different TCP port number to each session. The NAT then redirects inbound packets to the appropriate private IP address based on the TCP port number associated with the individual packet.

If you decide that a NAT is appropriate for your environment, you must also consider some Domain Name Service (DNS) issues. DNS is covered fully in Chapter 14, *Using Domain Name Service*, but for now, be aware that:

- You must maintain two separate sets of DNS servers, one internal and one external.
- The internal DNS servers must act as root name servers for the private network.
- The internal DNS servers must be authoritative for your domain. If they are not, communications between your internal and external DNS server can corrupt the cache of both.

Proxy servers

The second way to do IP address translation is to use a proxy server. At its simplest level, a proxy server is simply an agent that isolates one end of a connection from the other. For example, if you Telnet from your workstation to a UNIX host, and then run Telnet on that UNIX host to connect to another host, the UNIX host is functioning as a proxy server.

Whereas a NAT does pure address translation, ignoring the contents of the packets it processes, a proxy server is a protocol-specific gateway. That is, a proxy server is limited to handling the protocols for which it was designed. If, for example, you install a proxy server that supports HTTP and FTP (a common combination) but not Gopher, your internal users will not be able to access Gopher servers located on the public Internet. A proxy server establishes a "stateful" connection between itself and the internal client for the duration of a session. The connection to the public Internet may be stateless, as for example, when you use a proxy server to access an external web server.

Although proxy servers are popular in a corporate world increasingly concerned about Internet security, using one has two significant drawbacks relative to using a NAT. First, when you install a proxy server, any host you want to be accessible to the public Internet must be located outside your private network, sited between the proxy server and your ISP. Although some might look upon this "firewall" feature as an advantage, all it really does is limit your flexibility. You can easily accomplish exactly the same thing with a NAT simply by not mapping a static address for the host you want to be inaccessible to the public Internet. The second drawback of a proxy server is cost. A NAT is typically available as a low-cost or no-cost software option for your border router. A proxy server may be a standalone box or it may be software running on one of your servers. In either case, the proxy server is typically relatively expensive even in its base configuration.

How DHCP Works

Now that we know why using DHCP is desirable, if not essential, let's take a look at how it actually works. When you install the Microsoft DHCP server, a DHCP server database is created. This database contains two types of information. First, it contains static configuration data supplied by the administrator using DHCP Manager. These static data include the range of IP addresses available to the DHCP server for assignment to DHCP clients, and various DHCP options set by the administrator. The DHCP server database also maintains dynamic configuration data that is modified continuously by the interactions between the DHCP server and its clients, e.g., those IP addresses that are currently in use and to which clients they are assigned.

NOTE Although this chapter focuses on the Microsoft DHCP implementations for both server and client, the Microsoft DHCP server also supports third-party DHCP clients, and third-party DHCP servers also support Microsoft DHCP clients. Basic DHCP functionality is provided by any combination of DHCP server and client. The availability of extended DHCP functions is determined by which DHCP options are supported by both the DHCP server and the DHCP client being used.

Windows NT, Windows 95, and LAN Manager 2.2c provide native Microsoft DHCP support. To use Microsoft DHCP on Windows 3.11 for Workgroups clients, install the 32-bit TCP/IP VxD from the file *TCPIP32B.EXE*, which is available free from Microsoft. To use Microsoft DHCP on MS-DOS clients, install the Microsoft Network Client v 3.0 with the real-mode TCP/IP driver.

When a DHCP client boots, the DHCP server supplies it with the IP configuration information needed by that client to participate in the TCP/IP network. This configuration information includes:

IP Address
: Each client network adapter that is bound to the TCP/IP protocol requires a unique IP address. The DHCP server supplies this IP address from its available pool. If a client has more than one network adapter bound to TCP/IP, the DHCP server supplies one IP address for each such adapter.

Subnet Mask
: If IP packets are to be routed correctly to their destinations, the client must know to which subnet it is assigned, which is determined by the subnet mask. The DHCP server assigns a subnet mask to the client based on which subnet (or logical network) that client is a member of.

Default Gateway
: Local IP packets—those whose destination IP address is on the same subnet as is the source IP address—are delivered directly. Packets destined for a remote network must be delivered to a local router that connects the local network to remote networks. This router is called the default gateway.

Other IP Configuration Parameters
: Other optional IP configuration data, e.g., domain name, may be assigned to DHCP clients. If such parameters have been assigned by the administrator, the DHCP server also delivers them to the DHCP client at boot time.

The TCP/IP configuration parameters that are eventually assigned to the DHCP client are negotiated by messages exchanged between the DHCP server and the DHCP client in the following sequence:

1. When the DHCP client boots, it broadcasts a *Dhcpdiscover packet* to the DHCP servers to request TCP/IP configuration information. Because the client does not yet have an IP address assigned, the source address for the Dhcpdiscover packet is set to 0.0.0.0. If the DHCP client receives no response to the first Dhcpdiscover packet, it again broadcasts a Dhcpdiscover packet. The DHCP client repeats this process four times, at intervals of approximately 2, 4, 8, and 16 seconds. If the DHCP client receives no response to any of these broadcasts, it waits 5 minutes and begins the process again. In Windows 95, the DHCP client displays a message box to inform you that no DHCP server was found, and asks if you want to see DHCP error messages in future. If you elect to suppress such messages, that choice is permanent, which makes troubleshooting more difficult later on.

2. When a DHCP server receives a Dhcpdiscover packet, it returns a *Dhcpoffer packet* that contains an IP address chosen by the DHCP server from the available IP addresses assigned to its pool, or a reserved lease. The Dhcpoffer packet also normally includes other TCP/IP configuration parameters, e.g., subnet mask and default gateway. More than one DHCP server may respond to the Dhcpdiscover packet. If so, each DHCP server returns a Dhcpoffer packet, and the DHCP client responds to the first Dhcpoffer packet it receives, whether the responding DHCP server is located on the client subnet or another subnet.

3. The DHCP client responds to the Dhcpoffer packet by sending a *Dhcprequest packet.* This packet contains the IP address offered by the DHCP server, and notifies the DHCP server that the client wants to use the IP configuration information provided in the Dhcpoffer packet. If the DHCP client determines that one or more of the TCP/IP parameters provided by the Dhcpoffer packet is invalid, the DHCP client instead returns a *Dhcpdecline packet* to notify the DHCP server of the problem.

4. When the DHCP server receives a Dhcprequest packet, it returns a *Dhcpack packet* to acknowledge the request and to notify the responding DHCP client that the negotiated TCP/IP parameters are reserved for that client. When the client receives the Dhcpack packet, it begins participating in the TCP/IP network using the agreed-upon TCP/IP configuration. If the IP address initially proposed is now in use by another client or has otherwise become invalid, the DHCP server instead returns a *Dhcpnack packet* to notify the client of that fact. When a client receives a Dhcpnack packet, it restarts the DHCP negotiation process by broadcasting a Dhcpdiscover packet. Microsoft TCP clients must also ARP to make sure the address is unique.

A DHCP client that has no further need to participate on the TCP/IP network can also issue a *Dhcprelease packet* to notify the DHCP server of that fact. When the DHCP server receives a Dhcprelease packet from a client, it cancels the lease on the IP address allocated to that client. This can be forced by using *ipconfig* or *winipcfg*.

NOTE When a DHCP client has been configured to use a static IP address, or when the client is rebooted after already having been assigned an IP address by the DHCP server, the DHCP client issues a Dhcprequest packet instead of a Dhcpdiscover packet. The Dhcprequest packet includes the IP address formerly assigned to that client, and notifies the DHCP server that the client would like, if possible, to be assigned the same IP address that it had been using.

The DHCP server honors this request—unless the IP address in question has already been assigned to a different client in the interim—by returning a Dhcpack packet. If the requested IP address is not available, the DHCP server instead returns a Dhcpnack packet to inform the client that it must restart the DHCP negotiation by broadcasting a Dhcpdiscover packet.

Understanding DHCP Scopes

A DHCP *scope* is a collection of IP configuration information that defines the IP parameters that will be used by all DHCP clients on a particular subnet. Each subnet may have exactly one DHCP scope, which comprises a single contiguous range of IP addresses. Each DHCP scope is defined by the administrator using the DHCP Manager application. A DHCP scope defines the following information:

Name
: Identifies the subnet served by this DHCP scope. May be as large as 128 characters, and may use any combination of letters, numbers, and hyphens.

Comment
: Further describes the DHCP scope, if necessary.

IP Address Inclusion Range
: Defines the contiguous range of IP addresses assigned to the IP address pool by specifying the beginning and ending IP addresses in that range. These are the IP addresses available to the DHCP server for assignment to DHCP clients.

IP Address Exclusion Range
: Specifies one or more IP addresses (or contiguous groups of IP addresses) within the IP Address Inclusion Range that are not available to the DHCP server for assignment to DHCP clients. Excluding IP addresses allows you to reserve a range of IP addresses that can be manually assigned to DHCP servers, routers, and other devices that require a static IP address.

Subnet Mask
: Defines the subnet mask that identifies the logical network to which the IP address belongs.

Lease Duration
: Defines the period for which the DHCP server "lends" or *leases* the IP address to a DHCP client. The lease duration may be unlimited, or may be specified in days, hours, and minutes.

In addition to the DHCP scope characteristics described above, you can use DHCP Manager to modify the following optional DHCP scope items:

Deactivate
: Immediately releases the reserved IP address when a computer is physically removed from the network, and returns that IP address to the pool available for reassignment. This option is particularly useful if you have notebook users who frequently connect to and then disconnect from your TCP/IP network. It is moot if your network comprises only hard-wired desktop systems.

Renewal
: Determines the renewal period for leased IP addresses. By default, the renewal process occurs when half of the lease duration has expired.

Reserve
: Allows you to reserve one or more IP addresses and assign them to devices like DHCP servers and routers that require a static IP address. You needn't use this option. You can simply exclude an IP address range and assign IP addresses from that range to servers and routers as needed. However, using this option maps the assignments of static IP addresses to devices, and allows you to view those assignments in DHCP Manager.

NOTE With the release of Windows NT Server 4.0 Service Pack 2 (SP2), Microsoft added support for a new DHCP feature called *superscopes*. By using superscopes, you can:

- Support DHCP clients in a multinetted environment, i.e., a local network that comprises multiple subnets (or logical networks) on a single physical network. Prior to SP2, Windows NT Server 4.0 did not allow addresses from multiple scopes to be assigned to a single physical network, and the only workaround was to install a separate network adapter to support each IP subnet. The DHCP server supplied with SP2 allows you to create multiple scopes and then group them together into a superscope.
- Support DHCP clients on a remote multinetted network via a bootp relay agent.

Understanding DHCP Options

In addition to the standard DHCP scope configuration parameters described in the preceding section, you can use DHCP Manager to configure the DHCP options defined by RFC1533 and RFC1541. DHCP options are used to configure advanced TCP/IP settings like WINS and DNS integration.

You can specify DHCP options individually for each DHCP scope, or globally for all DHCP scopes. DHCP option values defined globally are used for all DHCP scopes except under the following circumstances. First, if a global DHCP option is also defined for an individual DHCP scope, the value set for the individual DHCP scope overrides the global setting, and is used for that DHCP scope. Second, DHCP options set for an individual DHCP client override both global and scope DHCP option settings, and are used for that DHCP client.

The Microsoft DHCP server can control most of the DHCP options defined by RFC1533 and RFC1541. Microsoft DHCP clients, however, understand only a subset of these DHCP options. Setting values for DHCP options that are not so marked affects only third-party DHCP clients that understand the DHCP option in question.

NOTE At this point in a DHCP chapter in most books, you'd find a 5 page table listing the 60 or so individual DHCP options supported by Microsoft DHCP. Because most DHCP administrators will never need to set most of these options, it seems a waste of space to reproduce such a table here.

You can find a detailed list of DHCP options on pages 408 through 413 of the Networking Guide supplied with the Windows NT Server 4.0 Resource Kit. If you don't have the Resource Kit, you can retrieve the same information directly from InterNIC at *http://www.internic.net/rfc/rfc1533.txt* and *http://www.internic.net/rfc/rfc1541.txt* using your web browser.

A Microsoft DHCP packet can contain up to 312 bytes of DHCP option data, which is more than sufficient for most DHCP configurations. However, this 312-byte limit is fixed. Some third-party DHCP servers and clients allow you to use *option overlays*, which store additional DHCP option data in unused space in the DHCP packet. Neither the Microsoft DHCP server nor Microsoft DHCP clients support the use of option overlays. If you attempt to specify a complex DHCP option configuration—one that requires more than 312 bytes of storage—option data beyond the 312-byte limit is truncated and ignored.

Understanding DHCP Databases

The Windows NT Server 4.0 DHCP server service uses the same database engine as Microsoft Exchange Server 4. Installing DHCP server automatically creates the following database files in *%SystemRoot%\system32\Dhcp:*

dhcp.mdb
: The main DHCP server database file.

Dhcp.tmp
: The swap file used when indexing the main DHCP database file. According to Microsoft, this file may remain as an orphan after a crash. However, I found that this file existed in the DHCP directory on a server that had had DHCP server freshly installed, and had not crashed.

j50.chk
: A checkpoint file, used to maintain and verify database coherency.

j50.log
: Contains a log of DHCP transactions. May be used after a DHCP server crash to roll back the DHCP database to a coherent state.

j50?????.log
: Another file whose contents are used to recover the DHCP database after a crash. On my server, the actual name of this file is *j50000A2.log*.

res?.log
: I have no idea what this file is for, and was unable to find any information about it anywhere. If you know, please let me know.

The DHCP database is modified dynamically. Each time a DHCP client boots and is assigned TCP/IP configuration parameters by the DHCP server, these changes are recorded to the DHCP database. Similarly, as DHCP client leases expire, these changes are also recorded.

WARNING The DHCP database remains open at all times while the DHCP server is operating. Do not attempt to delete or modify any of these database files.

Because the DHCP database files are always open, it is impossible to back them up using traditional means. To ensure that critical DHCP data is not lost, Windows NT Server automatically backs up the DHCP database to the *%SystemRoot%\system32\Dhcp\backup* folder. Once written, these files are then closed, and so can be backed up normally.

NOTE By default, Windows NT Server backs up the DHCP database every 60 minutes, which is usually more than sufficient protection. However, if your network is very large (or very small), you may want to change the default backup frequency. You can do so by modifying the Registry value entry *BackupInterval* in *HKLM\SYSTEM\CurrentControlSet\Services\DHCPServer\Parameters*.

The default value for *BackupInterval* is 0x3C (or 60 minutes). If you have many DHCP clients, particularly ones that connect to and disconnect from the network frequently, setting the *BackupInterval* to a smaller value—perhaps 0x14, or 20 minutes—makes sense. Similarly, if your DHCP environment is small and relatively static, setting *BackupInterval* to a larger value—perhaps 0xF0, or 240 minutes—risks little (but also gains little).

If your primary backup program can be run from a batch file, you can use it to backup the main DHCP database. To do so, create a batch file that shuts down the DHCP server (closing the database), runs the backup program, and then restarts the DHCP server. Controlling the DHCP server from the command line is described at the end of the following section on installing DHCP server.

Planning for DHCP

Installing the Microsoft DHCP server is so easy that some administrators install it without much thought, and paint themselves into a corner by doing so. In a typical network, the DHCP server places such small demands on server resources that you can easily forget that DHCP is even there. That's a mistake. Once it is installed, the DHCP server becomes a mission-critical component of your network. If the main DHCP server fails and you do not have a standby DHCP server available, all of your workstations lose TCP/IP connectivity at the end of their lease, or when they reboot.

The size and complexity of your network largely determine how much DHCP planning you need to do. You might be able to plan DHCP for a small network in a few minutes on the back of an envelope. Planning DHCP for a large, complex internetwork may require much more effort. Before you install DHCP, spend some time thinking about how you want DHCP to work for you and how you will cope with a failure.

Planning DHCP for a simple network—one in which all devices are connected to a single logical segment—is pretty straightforward. A simple network may use repeaters to extend the reach of its physical segment; it may also use bridges to connect multiple physical segments into a single logical segment; it does not, however, use routers to link multiple logical networks (or subnets) into a single network—with one exception—a simple network may include a border router that is used to link that network to the public Internet. Take the following steps to plan and implement DHCP:

1. Determine which hosts on the network require static IP addresses and which can use dynamically assigned IP addresses. For those that require static addresses—typically DHCP servers, WINS servers, DNS servers, web servers, and the border router—record the IP addresses in use.
2. You may use a single DHCP server to support all of the clients on a simple network if you are willing to forego DHCP server redundancy. If you decide that you must have redundancy, as you probably should, determine how to implement it. If you have a second server on the network that can run the Microsoft DHCP server, you will always have at least the first of the following options, and perhaps the second as well.

   — Configure the second server as a standby DHCP server, which will be used only if the primary DHCP server fails. You can use the Windows NT Replicator service to store a nearly real-time copy of the DHCP database on the second server.

   — The Microsoft DHCP server cannot use shared scopes. That is, IP addresses assigned to the address pool on one DHCP server cannot also be assigned to a second DHCP server. However, if you have enough IP addresses available, you can configure both servers to be available simultaneously. During routine network operation, DHCP clients might receive their addresses from either server, depending on which responded first. If one of the DHCP servers fails, the other would remain available to support clients.

     For example, if you are using an Internet Class C address block, and you have fewer than 100 devices that will use dynamic address assignment, you might assign the IP host addresses in the range 1 through 99 to the first DHCP server and the host addresses in the range 100 through 199 to the second DHCP server. Devices that require static IP addresses would be assigned host numbers in the range 200 through 254, which would be excluded on both DHCP servers. Although running two DHCP servers is fine in theory, some administrators have found that attempting to do so causes problems. Instead, they simply keep a good backup of their DHCP database, and are prepared to restore it to another server if necessary.

   If you have only one server running Windows NT Server on the network, you can also use a third-party DHCP server, e.g., one running on a UNIX host, to provide redundancy. You can implement this sort of redundancy using either method described above—as a standby DHCP server or using independent DHCP scopes.

3. Install the Microsoft DHCP server and create a scope, excluding the IP addresses used by devices that are assigned static IP addresses. Use DHCP Manager, if necessary, to define DHCP options for the scope. Start the scope before rebooting the clients.
4. Enable the DHCP client software on each of the clients you want to use dynamic addressing. Reboot the client and verify that it has been assigned a TCP/IP configuration by the DHCP server and is functioning correctly. For Windows 95 clients, for example, use *Winipcfg.exe* for this task.

Planning DHCP for an internetwork is considerably more involved than doing so for a simple network. If you will be implementing DHCP on an internetwork, see the Windows NT Server Resource Kit for more information and planning aids.

Installing the DHCP Server Service

To install the DHCP server service, take the following steps:

1. Right-click the Network Neighborhood icon on your desktop, and then click Properties to display the Network property sheet. Click the Services tab to display the Network Services page, as shown in Figure 12-1.
2. Click Add to display the Select Network Service dialog. Windows NT builds a list of available network services, and displays them in the Network Service pane.
3. Highlight Microsoft DHCP server and click OK. Windows NT displays the Windows NT Setup dialog to prompt you for the location of the distribution files. Accept the default location, or specify a new location, and then click Continue. Windows NT copies the distribution files and then displays an informational message.

NOTE Any server running the Microsoft DHCP server service must itself be assigned a static IP address. That is, a DHCP server cannot obtain its own IP address from another DHCP server.

---

4. Click OK to close the informational message box and return to the Network property sheet, which now shows Microsoft DHCP server as an installed service. Click Close to complete the installation. If this server was configured previously to obtain its IP address from a DHCP server, the TCP/IP property sheet will be displayed, allowing you to enter a static IP address for the new DHCP server. Windows NT Server configures, stores and reviews the bindings, and then displays the Network Settings Change dialog. Click Yes to

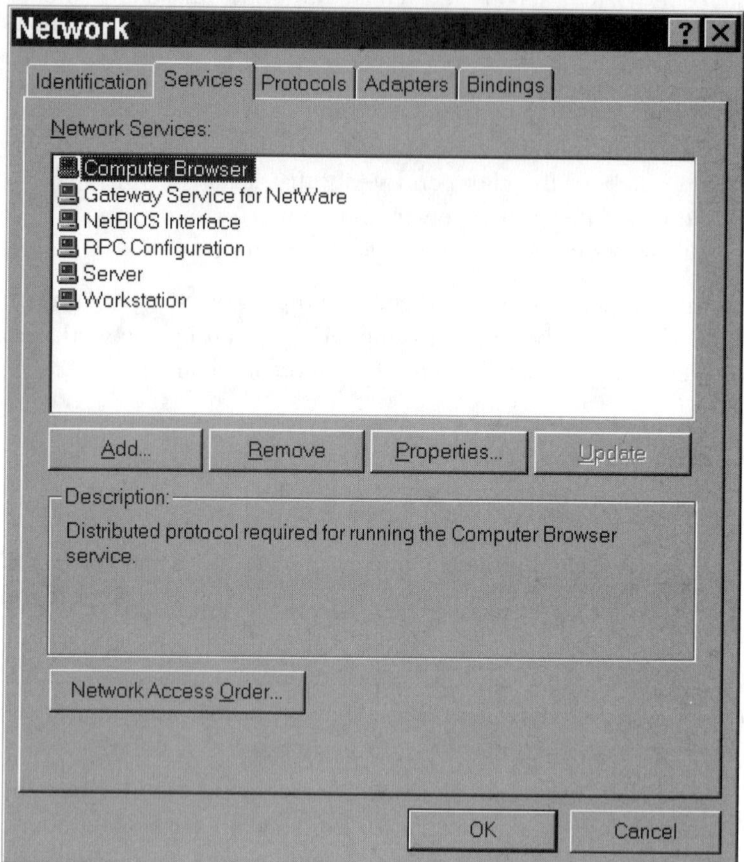

Figure 12-1. The Network Services page allows you to install a new service

restart the server immediately, or click No to wait until the next routine server restart to make the DHCP server service available.

NOTE Windows NT Server configures the DHCP server service by default to start automatically each time the server is booted. You can use the Services applet in Control Panel to modify the startup settings for the DHCP server service, or to start, stop, pause, or continue the DHCP server service.

You can also control the DHCP server service from the command prompt, using the commands *net start dhcpserver*, *net stop dhcpserver*, *net pause dhcpserver*, and *net continue dhcpserver*. These commands are useful primarily for creating batch files to backup your server, including the DHCP server database, during off hours. You can stop the DHCP server service, run the backup, and then restart the DHCP server service, all from within a batch file.

For more extensive command-line control, use the *dhcpcmd* utility included in the Windows NT Server Resource Kit. This program allows you to perform numerous tasks related to managing your DHCP server, including: adding additional IP address ranges to an existing scope; adding a reserved IP to an existing scope; listing IP lease information in detailed form, optionally including hardware information; displaying DHCP server statistics; and displaying and setting DHCP server parameters.

Managing DHCP with DHCP Manager

After you have installed the DHCP server service, you use DHCP Manager to configure and manage it. Before the DHCP server can support clients, you must complete the initial configuration steps described in the following section. After you have configured the DHCP server, you can use DHCP Manager to reconfigure the DHCP server as necessary, and routinely to view the status of the DHCP server and DHCP clients.

Defining a DHCP Scope

After you have installed the DHCP server and restarted the server, the next step is to define a DHCP scope. The DHCP scope determines the range of IP addresses that will be available for assignment to DHCP clients, and specifies other IP configuration information. To define a DHCP scope, proceed as follows:

1. From the Start button, choose **Programs ➤ Administrative Tools (Common) ➤ DHCP Manager** to start DHCP Manager.
2. In the DHCP servers pane, highlight the DHCP server for which you want to create a DHCP scope. From the Scope menu, select Create to display the **Create Scope ➤ [machine-name]** dialog, as shown in Figure 12-2.
3. Define first the range of IP addresses that will be allocated to the IP Address Pool. These are the IP addresses that the DHCP server service has available for assignment to DHCP clients. Enter values for the Start Address and End Address to define this range. The example uses IP addresses from my company's Internet Class C address 204.238.30.0. I have subnetted this Class C address using a 3-bit subnet mask into 6 subnets, each with 30 host addresses. I have assigned the entire range available in the fifth subnet to the DHCP server.

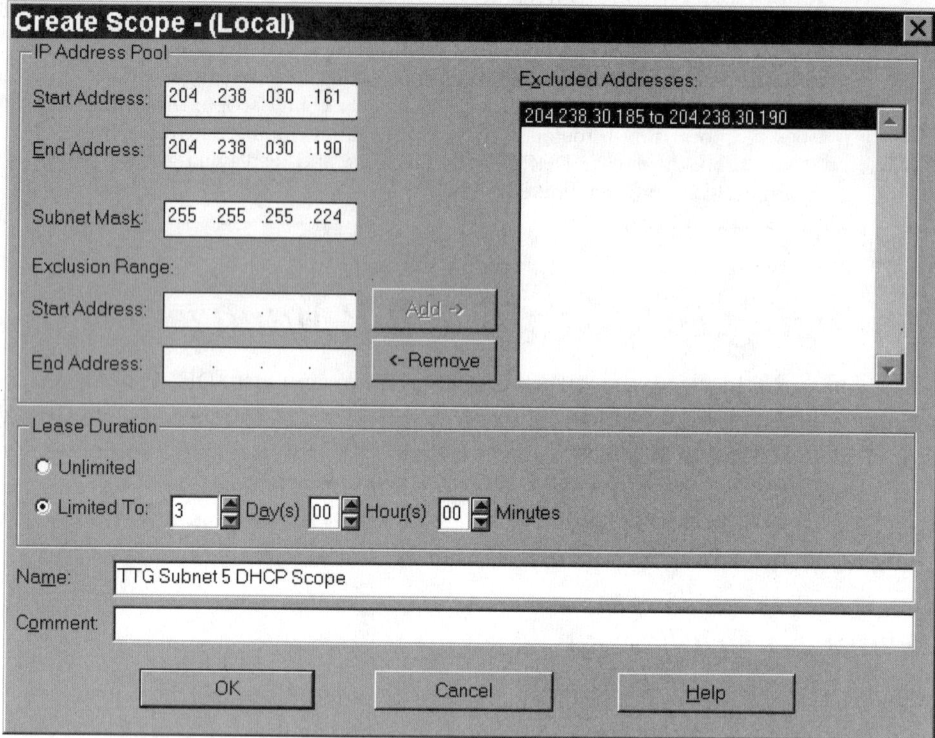

Figure 12-2. The Create Scope–<machine-name> dialog allows you to define the properties of the DHCP scope, including the range of addresses included in and excluded from the scope, the subnet mask, and the lease duration

---

WARNING Do not include the first and last host addresses in the range when defining the DHCP scope. For example, to use the entire Class C network address 204.179.186 for the DHCP scope, assign the range 204.179.186.1 through 204.179.186.254 to the scope. Do not use 204.179.186.0 through 204.179.186.255. You don't want DHCP to assign the host address 0 to any device. You really don't want DHCP to assign the host address 255 (broadcast) to a device.

---

4. Enter a valid value for Subnet Mask. The value you enter here must correspond to the range of addresses you entered in the step immediately preceding. For example, I entered the value 255.255.255.224 here because it corresponds to the 3-bit subnet mask in use. If, instead, I had assigned the entire unsubnetted Internet Class C address 204.238.30.0 to the DHCP server, I would have specified a subnet mask of 255.255.255.0.

5. Define the range of addresses that will be excluded from the IP address pool. Excluded IP addresses are not available to the DHCP server service for assignment to clients. You assign addresses from the excluded range to hosts that must have a static IP address, e.g., the DHCP server itself. Under Exclusion Range, enter values for Start Address and End Address and then click Add to define an excluded range of IP addresses and display it in the Excluded Addresses pane.

   You may repeat the process to exclude additional ranges, if necessary. You may also exclude a single IP address by entering its value in the Start Address field, leaving the End Address field blank, and clicking Add. Ordinarily, the only reason to use more than one exclusion range is to accommodate existing hosts that require static IP addresses, and whose current addresses you do not wish to change. In the example, I reserve the IP addresses in the range 204.238.30.185 through 204.238.30.190, inclusive.

TIP Define the DHCP scope to include the entire subnet, and then use exclusions to reduce the size of the available pool. For example, if you want to assign only 10 pooled addresses from the Class C network address 204.179.186, do not specify 204.179.186.1 through 204.179.186.10 as the DHCP scope. Instead, specify 204.179.186.1 through 204.179.186.254 as the DHCP scope, and then exclude 204.179.186.11 through 204.179.186.254.

Either method of restricting the number of addresses assigned to the pool works, at least until you need more pooled addresses. If you defined a small DHCP scope, you must remove the existing scope and create a new one, not something to be undertaken lightly on a production server. If you instead used exclusions to limit the number of pooled addresses, you can simply reduce the size of the excluded range in the existing DHCP scope, which automatically increases the number of available pooled addresses on the fly.

When working with C-block size network addresses, the common convention is to assign the host address 200 to the router for that subnet. Most administrators define the DHCP scope to include the entire C-block, and then exclude host addresses 200 through 254, reserving that range for routers, servers, RAS adapters, and other devices that require static addresses.

---

6. The next step is to specify the period for which IP addresses will be leased. By default, Windows NT Server uses a value of three days, which is appropriate for most environments. If you have relatively few hosts competing for relatively many available IP addresses, you may wish to set a higher value. If IP addresses are in shorter supply relative to the number of hosts contending for them, or if you have many notebook users plugging into and unplugging from your network frequently, you may wish to set a shorter lease duration.

7. Enter a Name, and optionally a Comment, to identify the DHCP scope. Click OK to create the new scope. DHCP Manager displays a message to inform you that the new scope has been created but has not yet been activated. Click Yes to activate the new scope.

Defining a DHCP Superscope

To define a DHCP superscope, take the following steps:

8. Use DHCP Manager to create two or more DHCP scopes, as described in the preceding section.
9. Set global or scope properties for each scope individually, and then activate the scope.
10. After you have created, configured, and activated each of the individual scopes that are to be grouped into a superscope, select the DHCP server in the left pane.
11. Select the Scope menu, and then select Superscopes to display the Superscopes dialog.
12. Click Create Superscope to display the Create Superscope dialog, type a name for the superscope in the Superscope Name field, and then click OK to return to the Superscopes dialog, where you will find the name of your new superscope selected and displayed in the Superscope Name drop-down list.
13. Use the Add and Remove buttons to move scopes from the Available Scopes pane to the Child Sub-Scopes pane. Move scopes to the Child Sub-Scopes pane in the reverse order that you want them to be used. That is, scopes are added sequentially, with each newly added scope appearing at the top of the Child Sub-Scopes pane. Scopes are used in the order that they appear, from first at the top to last at the bottom. When all of the scopes that you want to combine into the superscope appear in the Child Sub-Scopes pane in the proper order, click OK to create the superscope and return to the main DHCP Manager window.

WARNING If the superscope is on a local multinet—one not connected via a DHCP relay agent—and if the Registry value entry *IgnoreBroadcast-Flag* is set true, then each logical subnet must be directly accessible to the DHCP server. In other words, a local route must exist for each subnet. If all of the logical subnets are connected to a single physical network adapter, you can meet this requirement by assigning multiple IP addresses to that single adapter.

Setting DHCP Options

Before the DHCP server can support clients properly, you must first set various DHCP options. You can do so by choosing one of the following options from the DHCP options menu of DHCP Manager.

Scope
: Displays the DHCP Options: Scope dialog, which allows you to define the DHCP options to be used for the currently selected DHCP scope.

Global
: Displays the DHCP Options: Global dialog, which allows you to define the DHCP options to be used for all DHCP scopes on the selected DHCP server.

Defaults
: Displays the DHCP options: Default Values dialog, which allows you to define the standard DHCP options to be set whenever a new DHCP scope is defined, and to add, edit, or delete custom DHCP option types.

Which DHCP options need to be set depends upon your own environment. At a minimum, you should configure the following DHCP options:

Option 003
: *Router.* Defines the default gateway to be used by DHCP clients.

Option 006
: *DNS servers.* Defines IP addresses for one or more Domain Name Service (DNS) servers to be used by the DHCP clients.

Option 015
: *Domain Name.* Defines the Internet domain name to which DHCP clients belonging to this scope are assigned.

If you are running Windows Internet Naming Service (WINS) servers, you should also define the following two DHCP options, which are further explained in *Chapter 13, Using Windows Internet Naming Service:*

Option 044
: *WINS/NBNS Servers.* Defines IP addresses for one or more WINS/NBNS (NetBIOS Name Servers) servers to be used by DHCP clients.

Option 046
: *WINS/NBT Node Type.* Defines the NetBIOS over TCP/IP node type, as defined in RFC1001 and RFC1002, where type 01 equals b-node, type 02 equals p-node, type 04 equals m-node, and type 08 equals h-node. On multi-homed servers (those with more than one adapter), one node type is assigned to the computer and used by all adapters.

To set the DHCP options required for minimum TCP/IP connectivity, proceed as follows:

1. From DHCP Manager, click DHCP Options, then Scope to display the DHCP Options: Scope dialog.
2. In the Unused Options pane, highlight *003 Router* and then click Add to move it to the Active Options pane.
3. Highlight the Active Option to be modified, in this case *003 Router*, and click Value. The dialog box alters, as shown in Figure 12-3, to display a pane listing currently assigned values for the selected DHCP option.

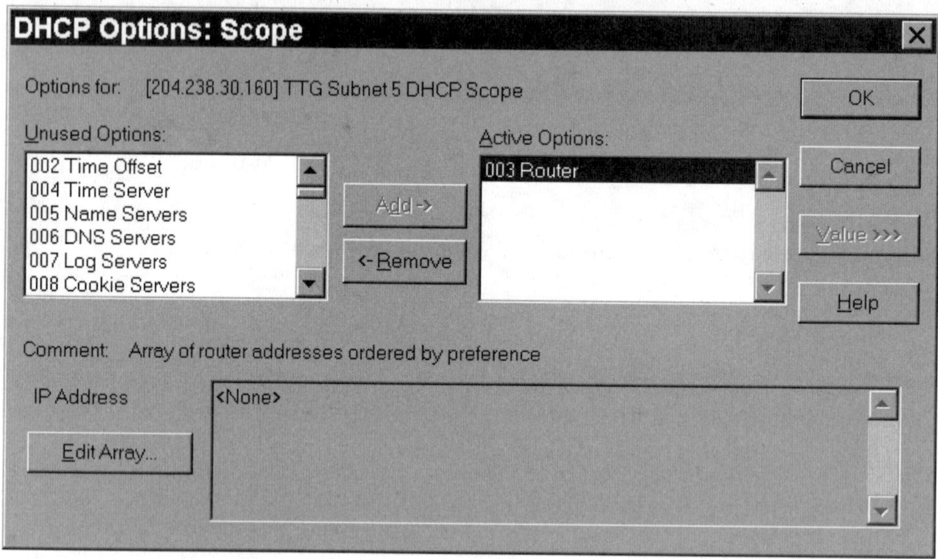

Figure 12-3. The DHCP Options: Scope dialog displays assigned values for the selected DHCP option

4. Click Edit Array to display the IP Address Array Editor. Enter the IP address for your router (default gateway) in the New IP Address field, and click Add to insert it into the IP Addresses pane. If you do not know the IP address of the router, type its fully qualified Internet name (e.g., *kiwi.ttgnet.com*) in the Server Name field and click Resolve. Windows NT resolves the IP address for the host, and inserts it into the New IP Address field. You don't need the domain name. If it is NT, WINS will find it; however, if your DNS is UNIX, that has to be configured and working right on the host machine for this to work.

   You may repeat this procedure to enter IP address values for additional routers. However, only the first value listed will be used (as the default gateway) unless the server listed as the default gateway fails or is otherwise unavailable. If this occurs, the second address listed will be used as the default gateway, and so on. Use the Up and Down arrows to rearrange IP addresses so that the host you want to use as your default gateway is shown first. Click OK to save your changes and return to the DHCP Options: Scope dialog. The Active Options pane now displays 003 Router with the IP address you assigned showing in the lower pane.

5. In the Unused Options pane, highlight *006 DNS servers* and then click Add to move it to the Active Options pane. Repeat step four to add IP address values for both your Primary and Secondary DNS servers. Again, use the Up and Down arrows to ensure that your Primary DNS server is listed first.
6. In the Unused Options pane, highlight *015 Domain Name* and then click Add to move it to the Active Options pane. The modified DHCP Options: Scope dialog box is displayed. Enter the Internet Domain Name, e.g., *ttgnet.com*, in the String field. Do not enter the Windows NT Domain name here.
7. Click OK to save your changes and return to the main DHCP Manager screen. The DHCP options you have set and the values assigned for them are displayed in the Option Configuration pane. Verify that you have set all necessary DHCP options to the correct value, and then exit DHCP Manager. The changes you have made to the DHCP configuration take effect immediately. Any DHCP client that now boots will use the currently defined options. Any DHCP client that is already connected to the network will not use the modified DHCP options until the next time that client is booted and needs to renew its lease.

NOTE The DHCP configuration illustrated in this section prepares the DHCP server to support basic TCP/IP connectivity. If your network includes WINS servers, you must also set DHCP Option *044 WINS/NBNS Servers* and DHCP Option *046 WINS/NBT Node Type*. These options are set using a procedure similar to that described above for the required DHCP options.

Adding Client Reservations

You can use DHCP Manager to configure static TCP/IP configuration information for a specific client, which is called making a *client reservation*. To add a client reservation, take the following steps:

1. Click Add Reservations from the Scope menu to display the Add Reserved Clients dialog.
2. Enter the IP address to be reserved for that client in the IP Address field. In the example, the IP address 204.238.30.164 is being reserved.

3. Enter the MAC address of the network adapter in the Unique Identifier field. The MAC address is the hardware address of the network adapter. In the example, the client has an Ethernet network adapter whose MAC address is 00-40-33-23-C0-53.
4. Enter the Internet name of the machine (not including the Internet domain name) in the Client Name field. In the example, the full Internet name of the computer is *sherlock.ttgnet.com*, so I have specified the client name as *SHERLOCK*. The Client Name field is really only a convenience for the administrator. It provides a more meaningful description of the client when viewing the display of active leases. Because the client doesn't register its name with the server, the server cannot provide this information. If the Client Name field is not completed, all you will see in the display of active leases is the IP address and the reservation in use.
5. You may optionally enter a value in the Client Comment field that further describes the client.
6. When you have completed the required fields, click Add to create an entry in the DHCP database for this client reservation and return to the main DHCP Manager screen. Exit DHCP Manager. The changes you have made to the DHCP configuration take effect immediately. Any DHCP client that now boots will use the currently defined options. Any DHCP client that is already connected to the network will not use the modified DHCP options until the next time that client is booted.

Viewing, Modifying, and Deleting Active Leases

You can use DHCP Manager to view or delete active leases for ordinary DHCP clients and to view, modify, or delete active leases for Reserved DHCP clients. The options you have available depend on the type of DHCP client that is selected.

Viewing and deleting active leases for ordinary DHCP clients

To work with an ordinary DHCP client—one that is assigned its TCP/IP configuration information dynamically by the DHCP server—take the following steps:

1. Click Active Leases from the Scope menu to display the Active Leases–<Scope Name> dialog, as shown in Figure 12-4. You may choose the way in which clients are sorted by marking either the Sort leases by IP address option button or the Sort leases by Name option button. Reserved DHCP clients are indicated by the word Reservation appearing next to the IP address and client name. All other clients shown are ordinary DHCP clients. In this example, only one DHCP client is visible because I have configured only that one client on my test network to use DHCP.

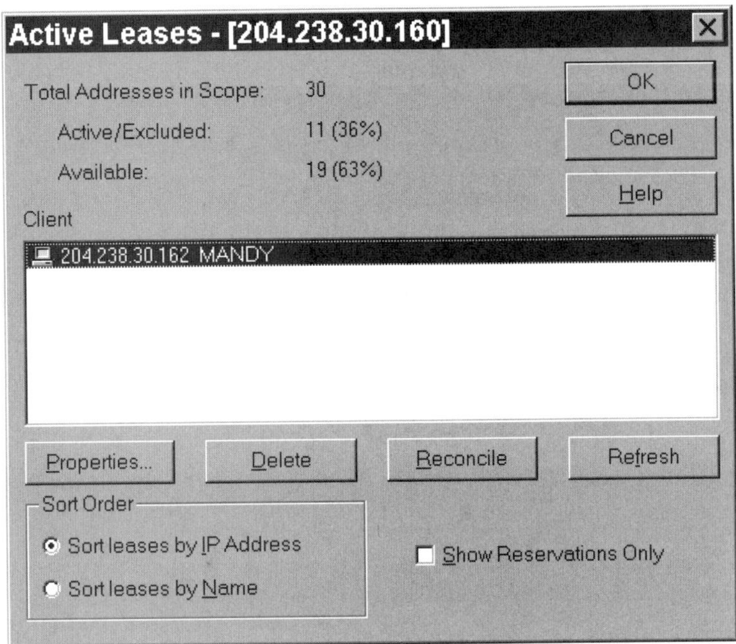

Figure 12-4. The Active Leases–<Scope Name> dialog allows you to view, modify, and delete active leases

2. Highlight the client that you would like to view or delete, and take one of the following actions:

   — To view the status of the selected DHCP client, click Properties to display the Client Properties property sheet for that DHCP client. The property sheet displays the IP address currently assigned to the selected DHCP client, the MAC address, the client name, and any comments entered for that client. It also displays the date and time when the currently active lease will expire. If you want to enter a reservation for a client, this is a good place to cut the MAC address from and then paste it.

     All of these properties except IP address are grayed out, indicating that they cannot be modified. Although it appears that the IP address field is active and may be changed, attempting to do so simply causes the machine to beep at you.

   — Or, to delete a DHCP client, highlight that client and click Delete.

3. Click OK to save the changes you have made and return to the main DHCP Manager screen. Exit DHCP Manager. The changes you have made to the DHCP configuration take effect immediately. Any DHCP client that now boots will use the currently defined options. Any DHCP client that is already connected to the network will not use the modified DHCP options until the

next time that client is booted. The client can also force a renewal/release by running *Winipcfg.exe*.

Viewing, modifying, and deleting active leases for reserved DHCP clients

To work with an reserved DHCP client—one for which you have created a manual reservation—take the following steps:

1. Click Active Leases from the Scope menu to display the Active Leases–<Scope Name> dialog. You may specify client sort order as described in the previous section. You may also mark the Show Reservations Only check box if you want to display only DHCP clients for which you have created a client reservation manually. For this example, I reconfigured *MANDY* as a reserved DHCP client.
2. If you want to delete the reserved client, simply highlight its name and click Delete. If instead you want to view properties for the reserved client or to modify it, highlight it and click Properties to display the Client Properties property sheet, as shown in Figure 12-5.

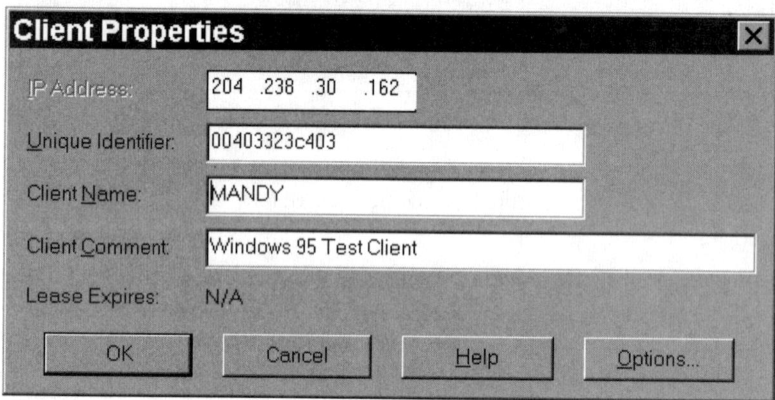

Figure 12-5. The Client Properties property sheet allows you to view, modify, and delete active leases for a reserved DHCP client

3. Modify the values for Unique Identifier, Client Name, and Client Comment as necessary. The value for Unique Identifier must correspond to the actual MAC address of the network adapter installed in that client. The value for Client Name is informational only; changing it has no effect on the actual computer name of that client. Similarly, the value for Client Comment is free text.

NOTE You cannot directly modify the IP address for a reserved client. Instead, you must first delete that client and then add a new reservation with the new IP address by clicking Add Reservations from the Scope menu.

---

4. The Options button appears on the Client Properties property sheet only for reserved clients. To modify DHCP options for the selected reserved client, click Options to display the DHCP options: Reservation dialog. Set DHCP options for this client as described in the preceding section on setting DHCP options. Note that the settings you make here apply only to this client. When you have finished setting DHCP options for this client, click OK to return to the Client Properties property sheet.
5. When you have finished making changes, click OK to save your changes and return to the Active Leases–<Scope Name> dialog. Click OK again to save your changes and return to the main DHCP Manager screen. Exit DHCP Manager. The changes you have made to the DHCP configuration take effect immediately. Any DHCP client that now boots will use the currently defined options. Any DHCP client that is already connected to the network will not use the modified DHCP options until the next time that client is booted and needs to renew its lease. Creating a reservation also allows BootP clients to get an address.

Reconciling leases

Information about active DHCP leases is stored in both the DHCP database and the Registry of the machine running the DHCP server service. For a variety of reasons, it is possible that the information stored in these two locations will become unsynchronized. The Registry may show one or more IP addresses as leased, or in use, whereas the DHCP database shows that these same addresses are available for assignment.

If this occurs, you can use the following procedure to run a consistency check between the two databases. Running this procedure lists inconsistent IP address assignments, and reconciles the actual state of the DHCP environment—as reflected in the DHCP database—with the incorrect information maintained by the Registry. To reconcile leases, take the following steps:

1. Select Active Leases from the Scope menu to display the Active Leases–<Scope Name> dialog.
2. Click Reconcile. If the databases are consistent, DHCP Manager displays a message informing you of that fact. If reconcile finds inconsistencies, it lists the inconsistent addresses.

Run this reconciliation procedure any time the server crashes. You should also run it each time you restore the DHCP databases from backup. Reconcile is nondestructive. You may run it any time to ensure that the DHCP database and the Registry are in sync. Microsoft recommends doing so routinely. Some administrators do so for the warm, fuzzy feeling, but if you have several scopes, reconciling frequently is time consuming and provides little benefit.

NOTE Reconcile operates on individual scopes. If your DHCP server supports multiple scopes, you must run reconcile individually for each scope.

DHCP Relay Agent

If you plan to use DHCP in a routed network, you may have a problem. Some routers forward DHCP message packets properly, whereas others simply discard them. Routers that handle DHCP message packets properly are called RFC1542-compliant. Many routers, particularly those that are intended primarily as IPX routers and route IP only as an adjunct, are not RFC1542-compliant.

If you find yourself with noncompliant routers and still must use DHCP across an IP internetwork, you have three choices. You can install a DHCP server on each IP subnet; you can replace or upgrade your routers to make them RFC1542-compliant; or you can use the DHCP relay agent. For detailed information on this subject, see the Windows NT Server Resource Kit.

Maintaining and Troubleshooting DHCP Server

Once it has been installed and configured correctly, the DHCP server requires little routine maintenance and is unlikely to have many problems. However, Murphy's Law still applies, so let's look at some of the problems that can occur with DHCP server and how to go about resolving them. One of the following problems will likely be your first sign that all is not right with the DHCP server:

- One or more clients receives the warning message "The DHCP client could not renew the IP address lease." Or, a user will find that he can't access the web or that a program won't function. Note that if the user once turns off the DHCP error notification, he will never be notified again of what's causing the problem.
- When you attempt to use DHCP Manager, you receive a warning message.
- When you attempt to start the DHCP server service or the DHCP client service, you receive a warning message that the service cannot start.

If either of the first two problems occurs, first verify that the DHCP server service is started. You can do so by running the Services applet from Control Panel. The Status column should report "Started" for both the DHCP client service and the Microsoft DHCP server service. If either or both of these services is not running, first attempt to start the service by highlighting its name and clicking Start. If the service starts successfully, verify that the problems you were experiencing have been resolved.

TIP Don't forget to use Event Viewer to check the log for error messages. Although these error messages are sometimes cryptic and of little use—my favorite being "The service did not start because the service could not start"—they sometimes provide enough information to at least get you started in the right place. To run Event Viewer, from the Start Button, choose **Programs ➤ Administrative Tools (Common) ➤ Event Viewer**. Make sure that you are viewing the correct log file. DHCP error messages are logged to the System log.

If the third problem occurs, or if you are unable to start the service using the procedure described immediately above, more drastic measures are called for. First, notify everyone that the server is going to be shut down. If your communications problems are severe, or if some of your clients are not running Windows NT or *Winpopup.exe*, you may have to do this using some other method than a broadcast to clients. Power down the server and allow it to remain down for at least a minute.

Once your drives have all spun down, turn the power back on, and watch the console for warning messages as the server restarts. Most of the time, you will find that the service has started normally. If not, take a club to it. Get to a command prompt, type *net start dhcpserver*, and then press Enter. The service should start normally. If it doesn't—and I've never had a server that recalcitrant—the next step is to restore the DHCP database from backup.

TIP Windows NT includes several command-line utilities that are helpful in diagnosing TCP/IP problems. Although many administrators seldom use them—and some don't even know that they're there—these utilities can provide essential information. Familiarize yourself with at least the following utilities:

Ipconfig. Displays the current Windows NT IP configuration.

Netstat. Displays protocol statistics and current TCP/IP connections.

Ping. Allows you to verify that at least minimum TCP/IP connectivity exists between two hosts.

Tracert. Displays the path, including intermediate hops, that connects two hosts, allowing you to determine at what point TCP/IP connectivity is being lost.

Restoring the DHCP Database

If the procedures described in the preceding section fail, or if they apparently succeed but the problems persist, the only alternative is to restore the DHCP database from a known-good copy. To restore the DHCP database, take the following steps:

1. If the DHCP server service is running, stop it. Use the Services applet from Control Panel or the command *net stop dhcpserver* to do so.
2. For safety's sake, copy all of the files located in the folder *%SystemRoot%\system32\Dhcp* and its subfolders to another location.
3. In the folder *%SystemRoot%\system32\Dhcp*, delete the files *Dhcp.tmp, j50.chk, j50.log*, and *j50?????.log*.
4. Restore a good backup copy of *dhcp.mdb* to *%SystemRoot%\system32\Dhcp* and restart the DHCP server service.

Rebuilding the DHCP Database on Another Server

If your DHCP problems arise as a result of hardware problems on the machine running the DHCP server service, you may have no alternative but to rebuild the DHCP database on another server. To rebuild the DHCP database, take the following steps:

1. If it is at all possible, attempt to retrieve a copy of the DHCP database from the failed server by stopping the DHCP server service and making a copy of the database as described above. Otherwise, you must use your most recent good backup of the DHCP database.
2. If it is not already running Windows NT Server 4.0, install the operating system on the new server.

WARNING The DHCP database must reside in the same location on the new server as it did on the old. That is, if the DHCP database was stored in *C:\WINNT\system32\Dhcp* on the original server, it must also reside in the *C:\WINNT\system32\Dhcp* on the replacement server. If Windows NT Server is installed in a different folder on an existing replacement server, you must reinstall Windows NT Server to the original *%SystemRoot%* before proceeding.

---

3. Verify that the DHCP server service is stopped on the replacement server.
4. Use the Registry Editor to restore the DHCP Registry Keys from backup copies made from the original server.

5. Restore the DHCP database files to the DHCP data directory on the replacement server and restart the server.

You can also use this procedure if you simply want to remove the DHCP server from one server and relocate it to another. If you do so, you will find that DHCP Manager still shows the original scope because Registry entries remain on the original server. Run reconcile, as described earlier in this chapter, to remove DHCP lease information from the Registry of the original server.

13

Using Windows Internet Naming Service

In this chapter:
- *Why WINS Is Needed*
- *How WINS Works*
- *Installing the WINS Server Service*
- *Managing WINS with WINS Manager*
- *Maintaining and Troubleshooting WINS*

The Microsoft Windows Internet Naming Service (WINS) server is a Windows NT Service that allows client computers to locate NetBIOS resources in routed TCP/IP networks. By using WINS, you can establish a centralized dynamic database that maps NetBIOS resource names to IP addresses. WINS overcomes the administrative burdens and functional limitations associated with using other methods NetBIOS name resolution like static *LMHOSTS* files and IP broadcasts. WINS is to NetBIOS and Microsoft Networking what the Domain Name Service (DNS) is to TCP/IP and the Internet.

Historically, Microsoft Networking meant small, peer networks running NetBIOS. The NetBIOS environment was really designed with small networks in mind. It was never intended to function in a large-scale network environment, let alone in a TCP/IP internetworking environment. Microsoft, however, with its roots in small networks, was committed to supporting NetBIOS. When Microsoft decided to extend their mandate from peer networks to encompass the enterprise, they had little choice but to find a way to incorporate the NetBIOS user base into their enterprise schema. Their solution to this problem is the Windows Internet Naming Service.

As is the case with DHCP, many people incorrectly believe that WINS is a purely proprietary Microsoft protocol, although this time they have somewhat more justification. WINS is in fact a proprietary Microsoft implementation of the following generic NetBIOS-over-TCP/IP Internet standards:

- *RFC1001. "Protocol Standard for a NetBIOS Service on a TCP/UDP Transport: Concepts and Methods."* This RFC, dated 3/1/87, provides an overview of NetBIOS over TCP/IP protocols, focusing on underlying concepts rather than on implementation details.

- *RFC 1002. "Protocol Standard for a NetBIOS Service on a TCP/UDP Transport: Detailed Specifications."* This RFC, also dated 3/1/87, defines the detailed implementation issues for NetBIOS over TCP/IP, including packet definitions, protocols, and so forth.

As you might guess simply by looking at their dates, neither of these RFCs explicitly mentions either Windows or WINS. Because WINS deals with NetBIOS names, which are for all practical terms limited to Microsoft networking, WINS has a much stronger Microsoft cachet than does DHCP. WINS implementations are, however, not limited to running on Windows NT Server. For example, SAMBA running on UNIX provides WINS server functionality, and can support Microsoft WINS clients. For all intents and purposes, if someone tells you he is running WINS, it's almost a certainty that he's doing so on Windows NT Server.

Like DHCP, WINS uses a client/server architecture. The WINS server is bundled with Windows NT Server. WINS clients are bundled with or available for various Microsoft client operating systems, including MS-DOS, Windows 3.1x, Windows 95, and Windows NT. Microsoft WINS is tightly integrated on both the client side and the server side with Microsoft Dynamic Host Configuration Protocol (DHCP) functions and with Microsoft Domain Name Service (DNS) functions. As was noted in the previous chapter, in order to get the maximum benefits from this integration, you must run Microsoft operating systems on all of your servers and clients. NetWare and Macintosh clients and other non-WINS compliant devices on your network can still participate in WINS, although at a reduced level of integration.

NOTE Microsoft wants very much for people to think of Windows NT Server as an enterprise-level operating system. Accordingly, much of the technical documentation for products like DHCP, WINS, and DNS focuses on implementing these products in very large-scale environments.

Issues like planning for WINS network traffic and distributing the load across WINS servers located in different time zones are important if you have dozens of sites, hundreds of servers, and thousands of clients. My network isn't on this scale, and yours probably isn't either. If it is, refer to the relevant planning sections in the Windows NT Server 4.0 Resource Kit. Otherwise, you can safely disregard these issues. This chapter focuses on the environments typical to small and medium-size businesses.

Why WINS Is Needed

People prefer to use names to identify items; computers are more comfortable using numbers to accomplish the same task. If you want to access the O'Reilly & Associates web site, you'd probably prefer to do so using its URL—*www.oreilly.com*. Your computer, on the other hand, needs the numeric IP address—204.148.40.9—that corresponds to this URL.

Each workstation, server, and other host on a Microsoft network running TCP/IP can be uniquely identified by at least two names and two addresses, as follows:

- *Computer Name*. The Windows computer name, as displayed in the Identification page of the Network property sheet. The computer name must be unique within the Windows NT domain. For example, my test server has the Windows name *kerby*, and is a member of the Windows domain *ttgnet*. Its full computer name, therefore, is *\\ttgnet\kerby*. The computer name is assigned by the system administrator.
- *DNS Host Name*. The Internet name of the computer, as displayed in the Microsoft TCP/IP Properties dialog for the TCP/IP Protocol in the Network property sheet. The DNS host name must be unique within the Internet domain. For example, the fully qualified domain name (FDQN) *kerby.ttgnet.com* refers to a host named *kerby* in the Internet domain *ttgnet.com*. Other hosts named *kerby* may exist elsewhere on the Internet, but only one host named *kerby* may exist within the *ttgnet.com* Internet domain. The DNS host name is assigned by the system administrator.
- *Hardware Address*. The MAC address of the network adapter installed in the device, as displayed in the Network–Transports page of Windows NT Diagnostics. For example, the hardware address of *kerby* is 00-40-33-23-BE-B3, which is the hard-coded "serial number" assigned to my Ethernet card by its manufacturer. Although a few network adapters allow an administrator to alter the hardware address, most do not.
- *IP Address*. The Internet address assigned to the host. For example, the IP address of *kerby.ttgnet.com* is 204.238.30.161. The IP address for a particular host may be assigned manually by the administrator, or it may be assigned automatically by DHCP.

NOTE Although nothing requires that the NetBIOS computer name and the DNS host name be identical for a particular machine, most administrators choose to use the same name for both purposes. Doing otherwise is a leading cause of insanity among network administrators.

Some means is needed to translate back and forth between people-friendly names and the corresponding computer-friendly addresses. This process is called *resolution*. Resolving an unknown address from a known name is called *address resolution*. Resolving an unknown name from a known address is called *name resolution*. The following sections examine name space issues and the alternative methods available for name resolution on a Microsoft network.

Understanding Name Spaces

Conceptually, at least the following two methods can be used to organize naming for computer systems within a network:

- *Flat name space*. Uses a simple one-part name to identify each host. Using a flat name space, each host name must be unique within the network. For example, once the name *kerby* has been assigned to a host, no other host on that network can subsequently be assigned the name *kerby*.
- *Hierarchical name space*. Subdivides the network into multiple named parts, typically referred to as *domains*. Each host name must be unique within any particular domain, but may be duplicated in other domains on the same network. For example, a host named *kerby.ttgnet.com* and another host named *kerby.oreilly.com* may exist within the same network—in this case, the Internet.

Originally, both NetBIOS and TCP/IP used a flat name space. This was a workable solution in the early days of networking, when few networks existed and those that did were seldom interconnected. In today's environment, however, using a flat name space is inadequate, for the following reasons:

- *Limited name availability*. A good computer name is short, easily remembered, and meaningful. For example, *kerby* is a pretty good computer name, whereas *a304js#9eqt$p16* is not. Obviously, there are a relatively small number of such short, desirable names. In a flat name space, all the "good" computer names would be taken quickly, and you would find yourself assigning essentially random names to your hosts. Imagine, for example, that only one host named *www* was allowed on the Internet, and it was already in use. What would you name your web server?
- *Centralized administration requirements*. In a flat name space, you have no way of knowing which names have already been used by other administrators. To ensure unique names, a centralized naming authority would be needed. When you needed a name for a new host, you would have to apply to this central authority, which would assign you a name. You probably wouldn't get the name you wanted, and you'd have to wait to get it. Neither of these limitations is acceptable in today's fast-moving network environment.

> My editor tells me that, when he was with DEC, their whole engineering net had a flat name space. Once consequence was that it took about six weeks to apply for and get a name for a new machine. As terminals began to be replaced by workstations, the flood of name requests brought the whole system to its knees.

Clearly, something better than a flat name space is needed. That something is a hierarchical name space, structured as an inverted tree. Just as an inverted tree directory structure allows you to have duplicate filenames in different directories, an inverted tree naming structure allows you to have duplicate computer names in different domains.

Using a hierarchical name space also minimizes or eliminates the need for a central administrative authority. In a hierarchical name space, administration devolves to the local level. If, for example, you're the administrator responsible for the domain *ttgnet.com*, you can name your hosts anything you'd like. Duplicate names are not a problem, because it's easy for you to keep track of which names you've already assigned within your domain.

A central naming authority may still be needed, depending on the name space in question. For example, Internet names are centralized at the first and second levels. You cannot, for example, just decide on your own that your Internet domain will be *widget.com* or *gadget.org*. Internet names at the first level, e.g., *.com* and *.org*, and at the second level, e.g., *widget* and *gadget*, are administered by InterNIC. Once InterNIC has assigned you a second-level domain name like *widget.com*, you are free to assign your own host names within that domain. InterNIC takes care of guaranteeing uniqueness at levels one and two; it's up to you at the third and lower levels.

The degree to which a central naming authority is necessary is determined by the extent to which the networks in question are interconnected. In the case of the Internet, such an authority is absolutely required simply because—by definition—all hosts and networks on the Internet are connected to all other hosts and networks.

On the other hand, any large-scale interconnection of networks running Microsoft Networking is by nature private. You can name your Windows NT domain anything you please. In fact, given the Windows NT installation default, it's a safe bet that a significant number of Windows NT domains are named simply "DOMAIN." This doesn't cause any problems because, although many of these identically named networks are internetworked with TCP/IP, they do not communicate across the internetwork using Microsoft protocols.

Both TCP/IP and NetBIOS originally used flat name spaces. Both, however, can now use a hierarchical name space. The TCP/IP hierarchical name space is administered by the Domain Name System (DNS). NetBIOS hierarchical names are administered by NetBIOS Scopes, which are similar conceptually to the DHCP scopes described in the preceding chapter. You must use the hierarchical name space for any TCP/IP network that connects to the Internet. NetBIOS under Windows NT uses a flat name space.

Resolving NetBIOS Computer Names Under Windows NT

Windows NT provides the following methods of resolving computer names to IP addresses:

IP Broadcast

In the absence of any of the other methods described below, a client can resolve a NetBIOS computer name into an IP address by using IP broadcasts. To do so, the client broadcasts IP packets that contain a message that says something like, "Is there a computer on this network whose NetBIOS name is such-and-such? If so, please send me your IP address." If a host hears its own NetBIOS name in such a broadcast, it returns its IP address to the source IP address of the broadcast packet.

Static Mapping Files.

These files maintain a static database that maps computer names to their corresponding IP addresses. The file *Hosts* maps DNS names to IP addresses. The file *Lmhosts* maps NetBIOS computer names to IP addresses. Static mapping files may be installed locally (on the workstation) or centrally (on a server).

Windows NT Server installs the file *c:\WINNT\system32\drivers\etc\Lmhosts.sam* as an example *Lmhosts* file and the file *c:\WINNT\system32\drivers\etc\Hosts.sam* as an example *Hosts* file. Both of these example files are liberally commented to describe their structure and function.

NetBIOS Name Server (NBNS)

An NBNS uses a client/server architecture to maintain a centralized, dynamic database that maps NetBIOS computer names to IP addresses. Clients that need to resolve an IP address for a known NetBIOS computer name query the NBNS, which resolves the IP address and returns it to the client. RFC1001 and RFC1002 define a generic NBNS. The Windows NT WINS server is a standards-compliant superset of that generic NBNS.

Domain Name Service (DNS) Server

A DNS server uses a hierarchical client/server architecture to maintain a distributed, dynamic database that maps Internet host names to IP addresses. A DNS client (called a resolver) queries the DNS server to resolve an unknown IP address from a known Internet host name. If the DNS server can resolve the query locally, it does so and returns the IP address to the client. If the local DNS server cannot resolve the query using its local database, it queries other DNS servers to complete the resolution.

Which method or methods is best for you depends on your own environment. For any network, using IP broadcasts is the choice of last resort. First, IP broadcasts generate a large amount of network traffic. Second, IP broadcasts work only within a subnet. That is, they don't cross routers.

You may not need WINS at all. Static mapping files are often a workable choice for small networks, particular those that comprise only a single subnet and are not subject to having computers added and removed frequently. Although using local static mapping files is an administrative nightmare, using global static mapping files stored centrally on a server may be the best way to go on a small, simple network.

For most networks, the two dynamic name resolution methods, WINS and DNS, are the best choices. The Microsoft implementations of WINS and DNS are designed to work together, and to interoperate with the Microsoft DHCP server. DHCP is covered in the chapter immediately preceding this one; DNS is covered in the chapter immediately following this one.

How WINS Works

NetBIOS over TCP/IP (NetBT) is the session-level network service used to provide NetBIOS naming support in the Windows NT environment, both via broadcast name resolution and via WINS. The two sides of the naming coin are called *name registration* and *name resolution*. Name registration is the process by which each computer is allocated a unique computer name. A computer normally registers its name when it boots. Name resolution is the process described above, by which the unknown numeric address is determined from the known computer name. The following sections examine, first, the various NetBT modes used during the naming process, and then the actual processes of name resolution and name registration.

Understanding NetBT Modes

NetBT defines several modes by which NetBIOS computer resources are identified. These modes differ in terms of which resources they use to resolve addresses, and in which order. They include:

- *b-node*. Stands for broadcast-node and depends entirely on IP broadcasts to resolve names. For example, in a b-node environment, if a computer named *kerby* wants to communicate with a computer named *thoth*, *kerby* broadcasts a message to the entire subnetwork that asks *thoth* to respond with its IP address. *kerby* waits a specified time for a response, and, if it receives no response, rebroadcasts the request.

b-node has two significant drawbacks. First, in all but the smallest network, the amount of IP traffic it generates loads the network unnecessarily. Second, as noted earlier, most routers discard these broadcast messages rather than forwarding them, which limits b-node to use on a single subnet.

- *p-node*. Stands for point-to-point-node. Uses point-to-point communication with a name server to resolve names. p-node attempts to resolve both of the problems listed for b-node. In a p-node environment, computers neither originate IP broadcasts nor reply to them. At boot time, each computer registers itself with the NBNS. Using p-node, if *kerby* wants to communicate with *thoth*, *kerby* directly queries the NBNS, which returns the IP address for *thoth*. *kerby* then communicates directly with *thoth*, without using IP broadcasts.

  p-node solves both of the problems of b-node. Bandwidth is used more efficiently because p-node does not use IP broadcasts. Name resolution can occur across a routed internetwork because the queries are directed to name servers with defined IP addresses. p-node introduces a couple of problems of its own, however. First, all clients must know the address of the NBNS. This requirement is typically accommodated by setting options 44 and 46 on the DHCP server. The second problem is more serious. p-node introduces a single point of failure. If the designated NBNS fails, all clients that depend on it are unable to communicate until the problem is resolved.

- *m-node*. Stands for mixed-node. First uses b-node to resolve the name via IP broadcast. If this fails, then uses p-node to resolve the address from the name server. m-node was created as an attempt to solve the problems associated with b-node and p-node by essentially combining these two earlier methods.

  In an m-node environment, a client first uses b-node for name registration and name resolution by IP broadcast. If this fails, presumably because the name to be resolved is on the far side of a router, the client then uses p-node to attempt to use an NBNS for registration and resolution. In theory, m-node offers a couple of advantages. First, because m-node defaults to using IP broadcasts, nodes on the local subnet can be resolved even if an NBNS is unavailable. Second, by using its fallback to p-node, m-node allows names to be resolved across routers. Balanced against these advantages is the continued dependence of m-node on IP broadcasts.

- *h-node*. Stands for hybrid-node. First uses p-node to attempt to resolve the address using the name server. If the name server is unavailable, or if the name in question is not registered in that name server's database, then uses b-node to attempt to resolve the name using IP broadcasts.

Reading through the description of m-node, it might seem that the designers of m-node got things exactly backwards. After all, p-node is both more efficient than b-node and works across routers. Wouldn't it be better to try the more efficient p-node first and then use b-node only as a fallback if there is no NBNS available? Well, yes it would, and that's exactly what h-node does.

h-node goes further, however. Rather than simply reversing the order in which b-node and p-node are used, h-node makes intelligent choices based on the existing environment. If p-node fails because the NBNS is down, h-node periodically repolls the NBNS. If the NBNS returns to service, h-node reverts to using p-node. Also, when h-node is operating in b-node and is unable to resolve an address, it will attempt to use the static mapping file *Lmhosts* to resolve the name.

Windows NT supports all of these modes. Which of them NetBT uses by default depends on the configuration of both the server and the clients. If the WINS server is installed on the server, WINS-enabled clients use h-node and non-WINS clients use b-node. If no WINS server or other NBNS is available on the network, all clients use b-node by default, unless an *Lmhosts* static mapping file exists. If the local *Lmhosts* static mapping file exists, the client first uses b-node IP broadcasts to resolve the name, and then, if necessary, the client attempts to resolve the name using the *Lmhosts* static mapping file. This method, called *modified b-node*, allows name resolution across routers in a b-node environment, and is the default method used by Windows 3.11 for Workgroups clients.

WARNING During the transition to using WINS, you may find yourself thinking that it would be useful to run a hybrid environment, with some hosts using b-node and others using p-node. Although doing this can solve some migration problems, such an environment threatens the stability of your network. The danger is this: your p-node hosts ignore IP broadcasts, whereas your b-node hosts use only IP broadcasts. This leaves open the possibility that a b-node host and a p-node host may have identical NetBIOS names, with results that are unpredictable to say the least.

A better solution is to use WINS proxy agents during the transition. A WINS proxy agent is a WINS-enabled computer that uses an NBNS to provide name resolution as a surrogate to one or more non-WINS clients. A non-WINS client uses b-node IP broadcasts as usual to resolve names. When a WINS proxy agent hears an IP broadcasts for a computer that is not on the local subnet (or that is running p-node), it intercepts the broadcast, queries the NBNS server on behalf of the non-WINS client, and returns the response to the non-WINS client. This solution is much cleaner—and much safer—than depending on a hybrid b-node/p-node environment.

WINS Versus IP Broadcast in Mixed Environments

If all of this discussion of NetBT modes and IP broadcasts makes you think that manually managing NetBIOS naming in a complex network is almost impossible, you're right. WINS is Microsoft's solution to the problems of administering NetBIOS naming on a complex network. WINS uses a distributed dynamic database to map NetBIOS computer names to IP addresses. Machines register themselves with the WINS server when they boot. The WINS server records the NetBIOS name and IP address of each WINS client. Subsequently, WINS clients use p-node to query the WINS server, which looks up the NetBIOS name provided, resolves the corresponding IP address, and returns this information to the requesting client.

By itself, WINS really does little that you can't accomplish using other methods. WINS simply makes the entire NetBIOS naming process automatic and transparent to both users and administrators. WINS is dynamic in the sense that, rather than depending on static mapping data entered by an administrator, it uses the information provided automatically by the WINS clients to update and maintain its database. WINS is also dynamic in the sense that it interoperates with the Microsoft DHCP Server and the Microsoft DNS Server.

This means, for example, that if a roving user plugs his notebook computer into the network and boots it, several things happen. First, the notebook client is assigned an IP address by the DHCP server; next the notebook client registers its own NetBIOS computer name and the IP address provided by the DHCP server with the WINS server; if the Microsoft DNS Server is available, the client also registers its DNS name and IP address with the DNS server.

WINS also makes life much easier in a routed network. Because WINS uses p-node, queries to the WINS server are directed to the explicit IP address of that WINS server, allowing it to be either local (on the local subnet) or remote (on the other side of a router). On a Windows NT network running WINS, users can browse network resources whether they are local or remote. If the Windows NT network is not running WINS, local users cannot by default browse remote resources.

NOTE The above statement is not strictly true. You can enable browsing for remote resources on a non-WINS network, but doing so takes a little bit of work. First, at least one machine on each side of the router must be running Windows NT—in either the Server or Workstation flavor—to act as a master browsers for the local subnet. Second, you must manually configure an *Lmhosts* file on each of these Windows NT machines with an entry for the Windows NT domain controller on the other side of the router. All things considered, it's easier just to run WINS.

In a WINS environment that includes some clients that use WINS (h-node) and others that depend on IP broadcasts (b-node), differences exist in how clients resolve, register, release, and renew names. The following sections examine these differences.

WINS versus IP broadcast for name resolution

Name resolution is the process by which a client computer submits the NetBIOS name for another host with which it wishes to communicate and in turn receives the IP address of that destination host. The name resolution process differs between WINS-enabled clients operating in a WINS environment and non-WINS clients only in that the WINS-enabled clients first attempt a WINS lookup. If that lookup fails, the subsequent process is identical for either type of client.

A WINS-enabled client attempts to resolve a name in the following sequence:

1. If the WINS client cannot resolve the name from its local cache, it first uses h-node to send a *name query request* directly to the IP address of its designated WINS server. The name query request UDP packet includes the NetBIOS name of the computer to be resolved. The WINS server resolves the IP address that corresponds to the NetBIOS name and returns the IP address to the WINS client. The WINS client then uses that IP address to establish a session directly with the target computer.

NOTE In response to a name query request, the WINS server examines its database and then returns the IP address that maps to the NetBIOS computer name provided by the WINS client. The WINS server does not do any checking or verification. That is, simply because the WINS server returns an IP address does not guarantee that the computer associated with that IP address is not turned off or otherwise inaccessible.

---

2. If the WINS query fails, and the WINS client is configured as h-node, it then sends a b-node IP broadcast packet containing a name query request. If the target computer is on the same subnet, it returns its IP address to the querying computer and a direct session is established.

3. If the IP broadcast name query request fails to return an IP address, the WINS client next examines its local *Lmhosts* file and, if the local *Lmhosts* contains an `#INCLUDE` statement pointing to a remote *Lmhosts* file on a server, examines the remote *Lmhosts* file as well.

NOTE Any Microsoft Networking client can be configured to use WINS in at least one way, and possibly two ways, depending on the network configuration.

1. On any network, you can configure a Microsoft Networking client to use WINS by explicitly setting the IP configuration for that client individually to point to the IP addresses for a Primary WINS server and a Secondary WINS server. Clients so configured use h-node automatically. This method requires manual configuration of each client.

2. On a network that includes a DHCP server, you can set DHCP Option 044 (WINS/NBNS Servers) and DHCP Option 046 (WINS/NBT Node Type) to configure WINS automatically on all Microsoft clients. Enter the IP addresses for one or more WINS servers for DHCP Option 044. Set DHCP Option 046 to any of three values: 02 (p-node); 04 (m-node); or 08 (h-node).

A client that is not WINS-enabled attempts to resolve a name in the following sequence:

1. The non-WINS client sends a b-node IP broadcast name query request packet. If the target computer is on the same subnet, it returns its IP address to the querying computer and a direct session is established.
2. If the IP broadcast name query request fails to return an IP address, the non-WINS client next examines its local *Lmhosts* file and, if the local *Lmhosts* contains an #INCLUDE statement pointing to a remote *Lmhosts* file on a server, examines the remote *Lmhosts* file as well.

WINS versus IP broadcast for name registration

Name registration is the process by which a computer reserves a NetBIOS name for itself that is unique within the network. The name registration process differs significantly between WINS-enabled clients operating in a WINS environment and non-WINS clients.

A WINS-enabled client operating on a network that includes a WINS server registers its NetBIOS computer name using the following procedure:

1. The WINS client sends a *name registration request* packet directly to the IP address of its associated WINS server. This packet includes the NetBIOS name by which the client wishes to be known.
2. When it receives the name registration request packet, the WINS server examines its database. If the requested name does not already exist in the database, the WINS server creates a database entry for that name that includes the

NetBIOS computer name, the associated IP address, and a unique incremental version number for the transaction. It then sends a *positive name registration response* packet to the client that generated the name registration request to notify that client that its desired NetBIOS name has been registered successfully.

3. If the requested NetBIOS computer name is already registered in the database to a different IP address, the WINS server attempts to resolve the conflict. To do so, it first challenges the current entry to determine if the host will actually respond. If the currently registered host does respond, the WINS server sends a *negative name registration response* packet to the host that submitted the name registration request packet to inform it that the NetBIOS name it wants to use is already in use by another host. This is invisible to the client. The only indication that something is wrong is that you can't connect to the network.

A non-WINS client, or a WINS client operating on a network that has no WINS server accessible, registers its NetBIOS computer name using the following procedure:

1. The client sends a *name registration request* packet via IP broadcast to the entire local network. This packet includes the NetBIOS computer name by which the client wants to be known, and the IP address of that client. If no challenge is received to this name registration request packet, the client assumes that the NetBIOS computer name is available, and begins using it.
2. If another client on the local network has already claimed that NetBIOS computer name, that client sends a *negative name registration response* packet to the host that is trying to register the duplicate name.

Once a client has successfully claimed a NetBIOS computer name via IP broadcast, it has two responsibilities. First, when it receives a name query packet via IP broadcast that is directed to its own NetBIOS computer name, it must respond to that broadcast by directing a *positive name query response* packet to the IP address of the host that generated the name query. This positive name query response includes the responding host's IP address, which allows a direct session to be established between the querying and responding hosts. Second, the client must defend its turf against any other client on the local subnet that attempts to register the NetBIOS computer name that it is already using. To do so, it generates a negative name registration response packet whenever it receives an IP broadcast name registration request that contains its own NetBIOS computer name.

WINS versus IP broadcast for name release

Name release is the process by which a computer discontinues using a NetBIOS name and makes that name available for use by other clients. The name release process differs significantly between WINS-enabled clients operating in a WINS environment and non-WINS clients.

A WINS-enabled client operating on a network that includes a WINS server releases its NetBIOS computer name for reassignment to another client. The WINS server takes several actions, some of which occur in any event, and others of which occur only if another client requests the released name, as follows:

- When a WINS client is shut down normally, it informs the WINS server that it will no longer be participating on the network. The WINS server marks the database entry for that client as *released* but takes no further immediate action.
- If the original WINS client subsequently reconnects to the network while the status of the database entry remains as released, the WINS server issues no challenge, but instead simply honors the client's request for its original NetBIOS computer name and updates the WINS database to reflect the fact that the client is now connected.
- If the original WINS client does not reconnect to the network, and so the released entry remains unused for a certain period (specified in WINS Manager), WINS marks the entry *extinct*. It then assigns a new incremental version number and broadcasts this changed information to the other WINS servers with which it is partnered on the network.
- If, while the database entry is marked released, a different client (one with an IP address different from that of the original client) requests the released name, the WINS server immediately grants the request. It need not issue a challenge because the released status of the database entry indicates that the original client has relinquished its claim on the name. This situation commonly occurs when you are upgrading computers or when a roving user first disconnects a portable computer from the network and then reconnects using a different IP address assigned by DHCP. This one is all a matter of timing. If the WINS timeout is longer than the DHCP timeout, you get a new IP address. Otherwise, the address remains the same.
- If the original WINS client was not shut down properly, e.g., the power failed or someone simply powered down the computer, the WINS server is not aware that the client is no longer participating on the network, and accordingly leaves its associated database entry marked as active. When that WINS client or another client subsequently attempts to register the NetBIOS computer name, the WINS server believes that the name is already in use, and

accordingly issues a challenge to the registered owner of the name. Because that computer is no longer active, the challenge fails and the WINS server is free to reassign that name to the requesting client.

A non-WINS client, or a WINS client operating on a network that has no WINS server accessible, releases its NetBIOS computer name as follows:

- If the non-WINS client is shut down normally, it sends an IP broadcast message to release the name reservation. Other computers on the network that have cached this name and its associated IP address clear the entry from their cache. Because the original client is no longer defending its name by issuing negative name registration response packets in response to name registration request packets, any other client on the local network can register the name successfully.
- If the non-WINS client is shut down improperly, it has no opportunity to broadcast a name release packet, and so it continues to appear to the other hosts on the local subnet as an active computer. This situation is resolved in one of two ways. First, because the client is no longer able to generate positive name query response packets in response to name query packets, the other computers on the network will eventually become aware that the client is no longer active on the network. Second, if another client subsequently attempts to register the same name and is not challenged by the original client with a negative name registration response packet, the other computers on the local network recognize immediately that the original client is no longer active. In either event, the other computers on the local network clear the registration information for that client from their caches.

WINS name renewal

Name renewal is the process by which WINS-enabled client computers periodically renew their name registrations with the WINS server. Non-WINS clients have no analogous function.

When a WINS client initially registers its name with the WINS server, the WINS server returns a message to that client, informing it when it will need to renew the registration. By default, the WINS server renewal period is set to four days. If you frequently add and remove computers from your network, you may wish to set the renewal period shorter than four days because when a computer is removed from the network, the computer name remains on browse lists for the remaining duration of the renewal period, and can drive other users crazy. You may also configure an entry as *static*, which means that it is permanent and never need be renewed.

Understanding WINS Databases

WINS uses the same database engine as Microsoft Exchange Server 4 and the Microsoft DHCP Server. The WINS database is modified dynamically. Each time a WINS client registers with the WINS server, releases its name, or renews its name, these changes are recorded in the WINS database.

The WINS database can grow to whatever size is necessary to store the registration data for the WINS clients it supports. The size of the WINS database varies according to the number of clients registered, but not necessarily in direct proportion. Because the WINS database stores both current and historical configuration information, it gradually grows over time. A newly installed WINS database occupies about 2 MB.

Installing WINS automatically creates the following database files in *%SystemRoot%\system32\wins*:

wins.mdb
: The main WINS database file. This file contains two tables. One table maps IP address to Owner ID, and the other table maps Owner ID to IP address.

winstmp.mdb
: The swap file used when indexing the main WINS database file. According to Microsoft, this file may remain as an orphan after a crash. However, I found that this file existed in the WINS directory on a server that had had WINS freshly installed, and had not crashed.

j50.chk
: A checkpoint file, used to maintain and verify database coherency.

j50.log
: Contains a log of WINS transactions. May be used after a WINS crash to roll back the WINS database to a coherent state.

j50?????.log
: According to Microsoft, another file whose contents are used to recover the WINS database after a crash. On my server, this file did not exist when WINS was initially installed, and was not created when I intentionally crashed WINS.

res?.log
: I have no idea what this file is for, and was unable to find any information about it anywhere. If you know, please let me know.

WARNING The WINS database remains open at all times while WINS is operating. Do not attempt to delete or modify any of these database files.

WINS interval timers

WINS defines four timers, which are used to determine how and when automatic changes are made to the WINS database. These timers are described in more detail in the section on configuring WINS, but for now, consider them as follows:

Renewal Interval
: Specifies how frequently, in hours, minutes, and seconds, a WINS client must reregister its name with the WINS server.

Extinction Interval
: Specifies, in hours, minutes, and seconds, the minimum duration between the time that a WINS client releases its name and the time that that name will be marked extinct in the WINS database.

Extinction Timeout
: Specifies, in hours, minutes, and seconds, the minimum duration between the time that an entry is marked extinct and the time that that name will be deleted from the WINS database by scavenging.

Verify Interval
: Specifies, in hours, minutes, and seconds, how often the WINS server must revalidate active names that originated on a remote WINS server and were replicated to the local WINS server.

Scavenging the WINS database

If left to itself, the WINS database would simply continue to grow, with released entries, expired entries, and orphan entries continuing to occupy space. WINS uses a process called *scavenging* to clean-up the database by removing these obsolete entries. WINS automatically scavenges the database periodically. How frequently it does so is determined by the relationship between the Renewal Interval and the Extinction Interval, which are defined when WINS is configured. You may also scavenge manually at any time by selecting the Initiate Scavenging option from the Mappings menu of WINS Manager. Windows recovers space in the WINS database using a process called *compaction*, which reclaims empty but allocated space within the database. Compaction occurs automatically under Windows NT Server 4.0 during idle time after database updates.

Scavenging updates the database in various ways, depending on the current status of each original entry and the status of the timers, as follows:

Owned Name Entries.

These are database records that originated on the local WINS server (the one that is being scavenged). Scavenging affects these entries as follows:

- If a name is Active, but the Renewal Interval has not expired, that database entry is left unchanged.
- If a name is Active, and the Renewal Interval has expired, that name is marked Released.
- If a name is Released, but the Extinction Interval has not expired, that database entry is left unchanged.
- If a name is Released, and the Extinction Interval has expired, that database entry is marked Extinct.
- If a name is Extinct, but the Extinction Timeout has not expired, that database entry is left unchanged.
- If a name is Extinct, and the Extinction Timeout has expired, that database entry is deleted.

Replica Name Entries.

These are database records that originated on a remote WINS server and were replicated to the WINS server being scavenged. Scavenging affects these entries as follows:

- If a name is Active, but the Verify Interval has not expired, that database entry is left unchanged.
- If a name is Active, and the Verify Interval has expired, that database entry is revalidated.
- If a name is Extinct or Deleted, whether or not the Extinction Interval has expired, that name is deleted.

Backing up the WINS database

Because the WINS database files are always open, it is impossible to back them up using traditional means. Windows NT Server can be configured to back up the WINS database periodically without manual intervention. However, unlike the DHCP databases (which are backed up automatically to a predetermined folder by installation default), you must take explicit action to cause this periodic backup to occur. You do so simply by using the WINS Manager once to do a manual WINS backup to a WINS backup folder that you specify. Backing up the WINS data on a typical server takes only a few seconds. Once you have specified a back up folder in WINS Manager, the system automatically backs up the WINS data every three hours by default.

If your primary back up program can be run from a batch file, you can use it to back-up the main WINS database. To do so, create a batch file that shuts down the WINS server (closing the database), runs the backup program, and then restarts the WINS server. Controlling the WINS server from the command line is described at the end of the following section on installing the WINS server. Even more simply, just backup the back-up data files created by WINS Manager.

Installing the WINS Server Service

Install the WINS service from the Network Services page of the Network property sheet (**Control Panel ➤ Network ➤ Services** tab). Select Add to display the Select Network Service dialog (see Figure 13-1), where you can highlight Windows Internet Name Service for installation.

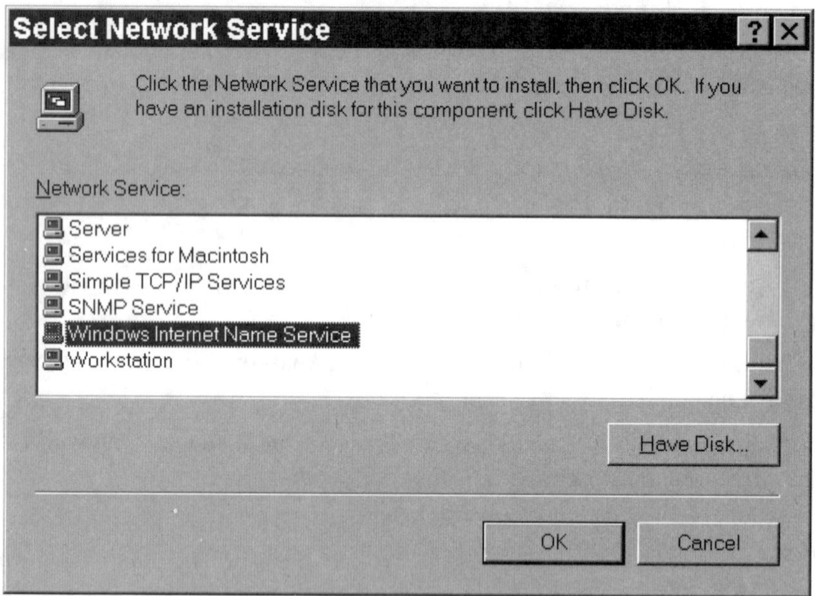

Figure 13-1. The Select Network Service dialog displays a list of services available to be installed

Windows NT displays the Windows NT Setup dialog to prompt for the location of the distribution files; accept the default or specify a new location as appropriate. Windows NT copies the distribution files and returns to the Network property sheet, which now shows WINS as an installed service. When you close the installation dialog, Windows NT configures, stores, and reviews the bindings, and then asks if you want to restart your computer to activate the WINS settings.

NOTE Windows NT Server configures the WINS server service by default to start automatically each time the server is booted. You can use the Services applet in Control Panel to modify the startup settings for the WINS server service, or to start, stop, pause, or continue the WINS server service.

You can also control the WINS server service from the command prompt, using the commands *net start wins*, *net stop wins*, *net pause wins*, and *net continue wins*. These commands are useful primarily for creating batch files to back up your server, including the WINS server database, during off hours. You can stop the WINS service, run the backup, and then restart the WINS service, all from within a batch file.

The Windows NT Server Resource Kit includes several enhanced tools for managing WINS, including the *WINSCL.EXE* command-line administrative tool; the *WINSDMP.EXE* command-line dump utility that exports the WINS database to a *.csv* text file; and the *WINSCHK.EXE* command-line tool that allows you to verify WINS database coherency and to monitor replication activity. If you plan to use WINS, the resource kit is a worthwhile purchase, if only for the bundled utilities.

Managing WINS with WINS Manager

Installing WINS adds the WINS Manager application to the Administrative Tools (Common) program group. You can use WINS Manager to configure and control all aspects of WINS server operation. At this point, the WINS server is installed and the WINS database has been created, but the WINS server has not yet been configured. The following sections describe how to use WINS Manager to configure and manage the WINS server.

The WINS servers pane displays a list of known WINS servers. By default, WINS Manager displays WINS servers using their IP addresses. You can use the Address Display pane in Options–Preferences to cause WINS servers to be displayed by name only, by IP address only, or by both name and IP address. WINS Manager can manage multiple WINS servers, but only one at a time. Select the WINS server to be managed or viewed by double-clicking the address or name of that server in the WINS servers pane. Note that single-clicking the server highlights it, but does not actually select it.

The Statistics pane displays a summary of the most important statistics related to the functioning of the selected WINS server. You can clear the statistics for the selected WINS server by selecting Clear Statistics from the View menu. You can update the statistics for the selected WINS server by selecting Refresh Statistics from the View menu, or by double-clicking the server address or name in the WINS servers pane

The topmost block displays the time the WINS server was started, when the database was initialized, and when the statistics were last cleared. The Last Replication Times section lists the last time replication occurred automatically (Periodic); by a manual replication initiated by the administrator (Admin Trigger); or by Net Update. Total Queries Received and Total Releases are the heart of the Statistics pane. On a normally functioning WINS server, the values for each of these for Total and Successful should continue to increment as clients connect to and disconnect from the network routinely. The values for Failed should remain very low. An occasional failure is not cause for alarm.

For more detailed information about the selected WINS server, choose Detailed Information from the Server menu to display the Detailed Information message box. This lists the name and IP address of the WINS server; the transport protocol it is using; how long it has been connected; the last time its address changed; the last time scavenging occurred; the number of unique registrations, conflicts, and renewals; and the number of group registrations, conflicts, and renewals.

NOTE The WINS Server Statistics pane displays statistics for only one WINS server at a time. You can also use the Performance Monitor application to display statistics for all WINS servers at the same time.

Configuring the WINS Server

To configure the WINS server, take the following steps:

1. From the WINS Manager Server menu, choose Configuration to display the WINS Server Configuration–(Local) dialog box. Click Advanced to display the extended dialog, as shown in Figure 13-2.
2. In the WINS Server Configuration pane, accept the default values, or set new values for the following WINS timers. The default values are suitable for nearly any WINS environment. None of the WINS administrators I know use anything other than the defaults for these timers.
   — *Renewal Interval.* Specifies how frequently, in hours, minutes, and seconds, a WINS client must reregister its name with the WINS server. This counter defaults to a value of 144 hours, or 6 days. WINS clients by default renew their names every two days. Setting this value high reduces

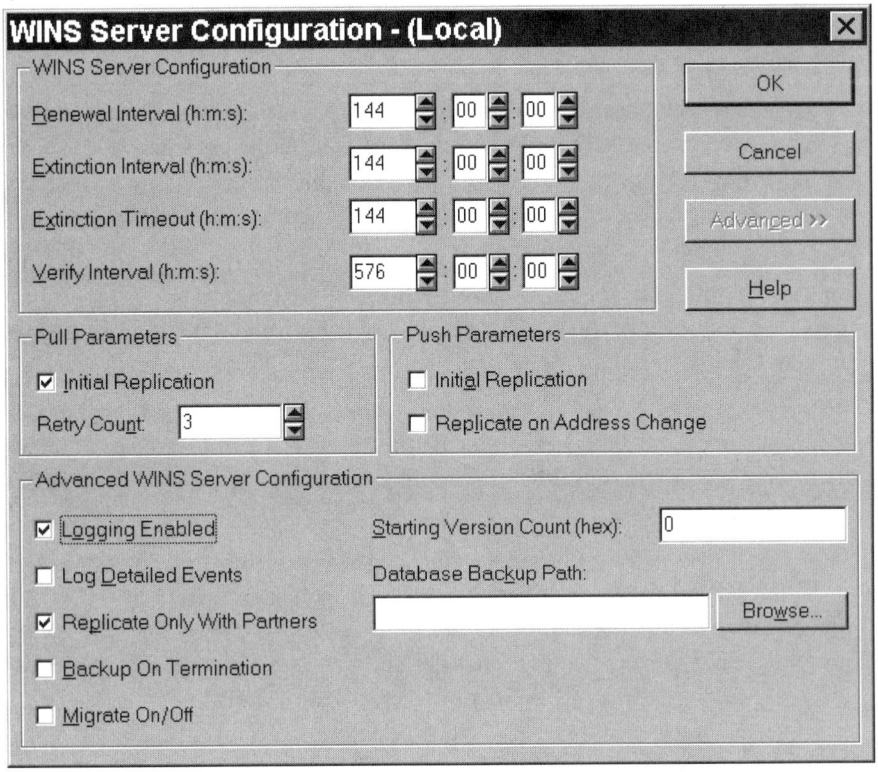

Figure 13-2. The WINS Server Configuration dialog, showing advanced configuration options

network bandwidth demands. Doing so has few drawbacks, particularly if most or all of your clients are desktop systems. If you have many roving users, you can set this value lower to cause the WINS database to be updated more frequently. If possible, leave this value set to at least the default interval to allow for long weekends.

— *Extinction Interval.* Specifies, in hours, minutes, and seconds, the minimum duration between the time that a WINS client releases its name and the time that that name will be marked extinct in the WINS database. The default value for this counter depends on the renewal interval and on the maximum replication interval between WINS partners. Six days is both the maximum allowable value and the default value if you run a single WINS server.

— *Extinction Timeout.* Specifies, in hours, minutes, and seconds, the minimum duration between the time that an entry is marked extinct and the time that that name will be deleted from the WINS database by scavenging. The default value for this counter depends on the renewal interval and on the maximum replication interval between WINS partners.

The default value for a single WINS server is 144 hours, or 6 days. The maximum allowable value is 9,999 hours, 59 minutes, and 59 seconds.

— *Verify Interval*. Specifies, in hours, minutes, and seconds, how often the WINS server must revalidate active names that originated on a remote WINS server and were replicated to the local WINS server. The default value for this counter depends on the extinction interval, but if installation defaults are used, this value is set to 576 hours, or 24 days, which is also the maximum allowable value.

3. If you plan to run multiple WINS servers that will be configured as replication partners, set values in the Pull Parameters and Push Parameters panes, as follows:

   — *Pull Parameters–Initial Replication*. Marking this check box, which is enabled by default, causes the local WINS server to pull replicas from its partners whenever the WINS server is started or replication parameters are changed.

   — *Pull Parameters–Retry Count*. Specifies how many times this WINS server will immediately retry pull replication if it is unable to connect to a pull partner on its first attempt. The duration between retries is determined by the value for Replication Interval specified in the **Options ➤ Preferences** dialog described later in this section. If replication fails after the specified number of retries, WINS resets this counter, waits approximately three times the Replication Interval, and the again begins attempting to replicate.

   — *Push Parameters–Initial Replication*. Marking this check box, which is cleared by default, causes the local WINS server to inform its pull partners when the local WINS server is started.

   — *Push Parameters–Replicate on Address Change*. Marking this check box, which is cleared by default, causes the local WINS server to inform its pull partners that the local WINS database has changed whenever an address mapping changes.

4. In the Advanced WINS Server Configuration pane, set the following parameters:

   — *Logging Enabled*. Marking this check box, which is enabled by default, causes WINS to log changes to the WINS database.

   — *Log Detailed Events*. Marking this check box, which is cleared by default, causes WINS to generate detailed logging. Enabling this function causes very rapid growth of the log file, and can adversely impact WINS server performance. Use it only when troubleshooting WINS problems.

— *Replicate Only With Partners.* Marking this check box, which is cleared by default, causes the local WINS server to inform its pull partners when the local WINS server is started.

— *Backup On Termination.* Marking this check box, which is enabled by default, allows the local WINS server to replicate only with other WINS servers that have been configured as partners. If this check box is cleared, the administrator can initiate a replication manually with any other WINS server.

— *Migrate On/Off.* The setting of this check box, which is cleared by default, determines how WINS resolves the collision when a new name entry received from a replication partner is identical to a name assigned a static mapping in the local WINS database. Enabling this check box allows the static database record to be dynamically updated. Leave this check box cleared unless you are updating to Windows NT Server from another operating system.

— *Starting Version Count (hex).* Leave the value in this field alone, unless you experience corruption of your WINS database. If this occurs, specify a value here that is higher than the highest version number counter for this WINS server database on any replication partner. WINS itself will verify that the value you select is high enough, and will correct the value you supplied to a higher number if necessary. This field may be set to a value as high as $2^{31}-1$.

— *Database Backup Path.* If you want WINS to back up its database automatically, specify a value for this field. If you do not specify a value here, you can still back up the WINS database, but you must do so manually using the Mappings–Backup Database option, and specifying the destination folder each time. If you specify a folder in this field, WINS Manager will also automatically use that folder as the restore source when you restore the database.

Configuring WINS Server Replication Partners

If your network is very small, you might not need to run WINS at all. If your network serves only one small or medium-size workgroup, you might decide to run only one WINS server. If your network serves a medium to large company at a single location, running multiple WINS servers offers redundancy if one of them fails. On very large, enterprise-level, multisite networks, running multiple WINS servers is almost mandatory, both for redundancy and for load sharing.

If you plan to run multiple WINS servers, you need to consider *replication* issues. Replication is the process by which a WINS server automatically distributes its database to other WINS servers running on the network. These other WINS servers are referred to as *replication partners*. A *pull partner* is a WINS server that initiates replication by asking other WINS servers to send their data to it. A *push partner* is a WINS server that initiates replication by sending its data to other WINS servers. In most WINS environments, all of the WINS servers should be configured to be both push and pull partners with the other WINS servers on the network.

Configuring replication is pretty straightforward. In this section, we start with two newly installed WINS servers. One of them is running on the Windows NT Server primary domain controller *thoth.ttgnet.com*, whose IP address is 204.238.30.165. The second is running on the Windows NT Server backup domain controller *kerby.ttgnet.com*, whose IP address is 204.238.30.161. The initial display in WINS Manager shows only the local WINS server. In this case, it happens to be *kerby*, which I just finished installing.

To configure replication partners, from the WINS Manager Server menu, choose Add WINS server to display the Add WINS server dialog. Enter the computer name or the IP address of the remote WINS server and click OK to return to the WINS Manager main screen. In the WINS servers pane of WINS Manager, double-click the IP address of the remote WINS server (in this case, 204.238.30.165) to select it. Note that single-clicking the WINS server highlights it, but does not select it. After you select the WINS server, choose Replication Partners from the WINS Manager Server menu to display the Replication Partners—(204.238.30.165) dialog, as shown in Figure 13-3.

WARNING This process is confusing, at least to me. Inevitably, it seems, I end up trying to configure a WINS server as its own replication partner. Fortunately, WINS Manager recognizes the absurdity of this situation, displays a warning message, and refuses to proceed until you select an appropriate partner. If this happens to you when you are trying to configure two WINS servers as replication partners, just select the other WINS server. If you are configuring three or more WINS servers as replication partners, you simply have to pay close attention to what you are doing.

In the WINS server pane of the Replication Partners dialog, highlight the IP address of the local WINS server—in this case, 204.238.30.161. In the Replication Options pane, mark the Push Partner check box to select the server as a push partner. A check mark appears in the Push column of the WINS server pane next to the IP address of the local WINS serverWINS server. Mark the Pull Partner check box to select the server as a pull partner. A check mark appears in the Pull column of the WINS server pane next to the IP address of the local WINS server.

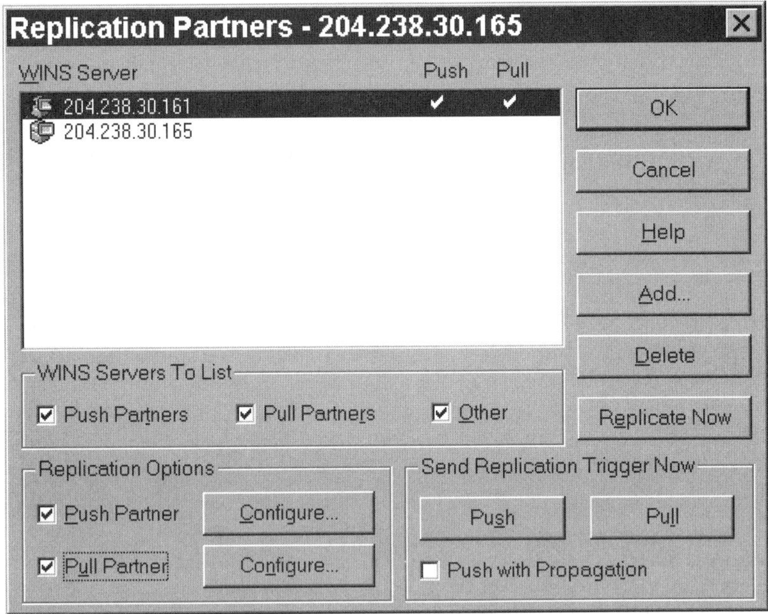

Figure 13-3. The Replication Partner dialog allows you to configure replication partner relationships and to specify how and when replication occurs

This indicates that the selected WINS server (204.238.30.165) is now configured as both push and pull partners with 204.238.30.161 (see Figure 13-4).

NOTE If you need to modify the list of available WINS servers, click Add to display the Add WINS server dialog or click Delete to remove the selected WINS server from the list of replication partners. The Replicate Now button forces an immediate WINS database replication between the replication partners you have already configured.

After you have added all of your WINS servers and established the replication relationships, next configure the partnership properties for each WINS server. In Replication Options, click Configure to display the Push Partner Properties dialog. Enter a value in the Update Count field. This value determines how many changes must be made to local database records before WINS will push an update to the pull partners of this server. You may also click Set Default Value to revert to the default update count specified in the **Options ➤ Preferences** dialog, described later in this section. Setting a low value for this field causes replication updates to occur more frequently, which keeps the databases on the replication partners more closely synchronized at the expense of increasing bandwidth consumption.

Next, click Configure to display the Pull Partner Properties dialog. Enter a value in the Start Time field to specify when replication should begin. Set the Replication Interval field to specify how often you want pull replication to be initiated. By default, Replication Interval is set to 30 minutes, which is appropriate for most WINS environments. You may also choose Set Default Values to revert to the default values specified in the **Options ➤ Preferences** dialog, described later in this section.

NOTE If you return to the WINS Manager main screen, and then double-click the local WINS server (204.238.30.161) to select it, and then display the Replication Partners—(204.238.30.161) dialog for that WINS server, you will see that the local WINS server is now also configured as a Push and Pull partner with the remote WINS server (204.238.30.165), as shown in Figure 13-4.

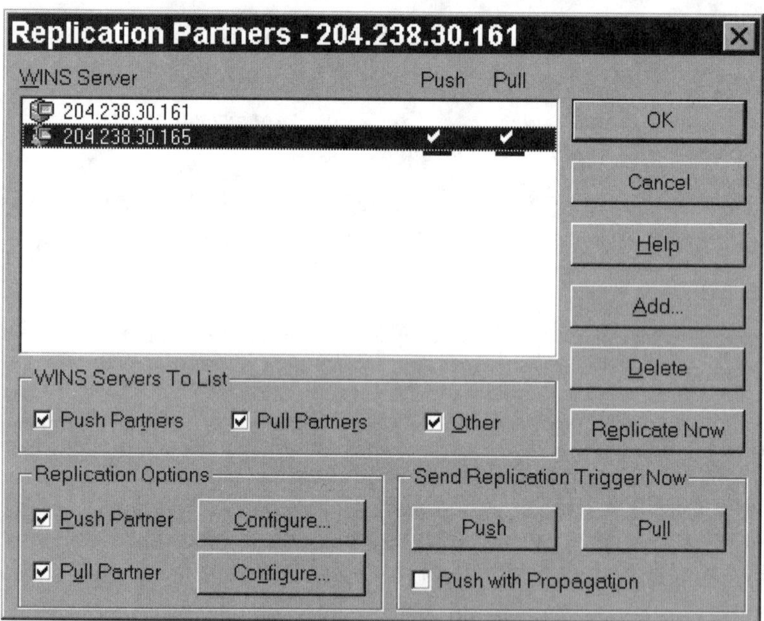

Figure 13-4. The Replication Partners–(204.238.30.161) dialog shows the other side of the coin—that 165 is both a push and pull replication partner of 161

Setting WINS Server Preferences

Choose the Preferences option from the Options menu of WINS Manager to display the Preferences dialog. Click Partners to display the extended version of the Preferences dialog, as shown in Figure 13-5. This dialog allows you to set various parameters that specify how WINS Manager itself functions.

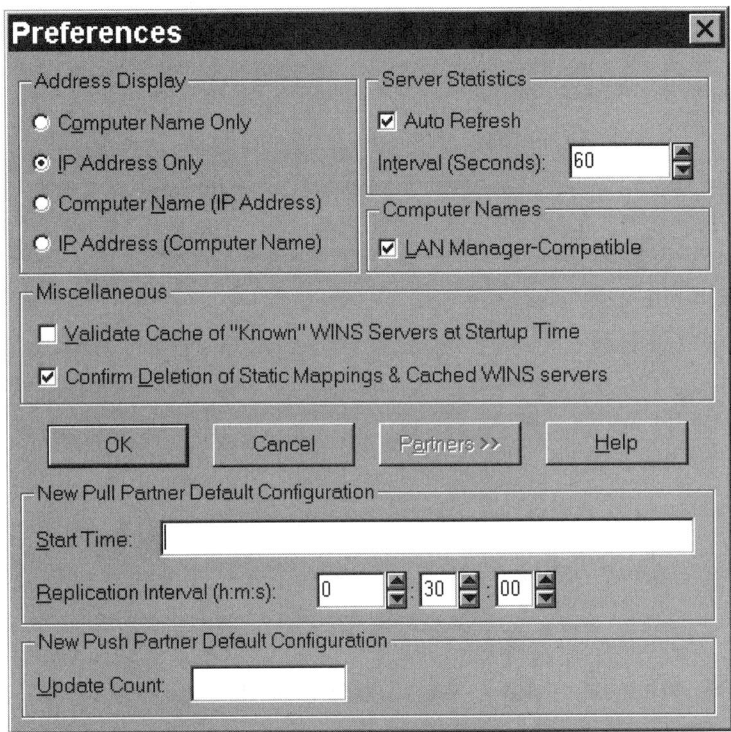

Figure 13-5. The Preferences dialog allows you to configure WINS Manager to function using your preferences

You may set the following preferences:

Address Display pane
: Choose one of the option buttons to specify how you want address information to be displayed throughout WINS Manager. The options are pretty much self-explanatory. You can choose to display only the computer name, only its IP address, or either one followed by the other in parentheses.

Server Statistics pane
: If you want the server statistics to be updated automatically in the Statistics pane of WINS Manager, mark the Auto Refresh check box and specify how frequently you want updates to occur by entering a value for Interval (Seconds). If you clear the Auto Refresh check box, the display will be updated only when you click **View ➤ Refresh Statistics** or press F5.

Computer Names pane

Standard NetBIOS computer names can be up to 16 bytes long. Microsoft, originally with LAN Manager and subsequently with all of their networking products, elected to limit NetBIOS computer names to 15 bytes and to use the remaining byte as a special hexadecimal flag character to indicate the type of host or service represented by the name, as follows:

— `00`: A standard NetBIOS computer name, or Workstation Service Name.

— `03`: Used by the Messenger Service. Registered with the WINS server as the messenger service on the WINS client, and is appended to the computer name and the name of the current user.

— `06`: Owned by the RAS Server service.

— `1B`: Indicates that the name so flagged is owned by the master browser. Identifies the Primary Domain Controller to allow clients and other browsers to contact the domain master browser.

— `1F`: Owned by the NetDDE service.

— `20`: Server service name used for resource shares.

— `21`: Owned by a RAS client.

— `BE`: Owned by the Network Monitor Agent.

— `BF`: Owned by the Network Monitor utility.

The LAN Manager-Compatible check box is marked by default. Because Windows NT Server also uses LAN Manager naming conventions, you should leave this check box marked unless your network accepts NetBIOS names from non-Microsoft sources. The most common reason for clearing this check box is if you are running IBM/Lotus Notes, which uses the standard, 16-byte NetBIOS naming convention.

- *Miscellaneous pane.* The options displayed in this pane allow you to determine how WINS handles validation of other WINS servers at startup, and how it handles deletions of static mappings and cached data.

  — *Validate Cache of "Known" WINS Servers at Startup Time.* Mark this check box, which is disabled by default, if you want the WINS server to query the list of WINS servers for available servers each time it is started.

  — *Confirm Deletion of Static Mappings & Cached WINS Servers.* Mark this check box, which is enabled by default, if you want to see a warning message each time a static mapping or a cached WINS server is deleted.

- *New Pull Partner Default Configuration pane.* Specifies the default values that will be used for Start Time and Replication Interval when you create a new pull partner. Also, clicking Set Default Values in the Pull Partner Properties dialog causes the current values for the selected partner to revert to this default.

- *New Push Partner Default Configuration pane.* Specifies the default value for Update Count that will be used when you create a new push partner. Also, clicking Set Default Value in the Push Partner Properties dialog causes the current value for the selected partner to revert to this default.

Managing the WINS Database

There is little need for an administrator to make routine changes to the WINS database in most WINS environments. WINS clients interact automatically with WINS servers, and the replication partners exchange information among themselves without manual intervention. Sometimes, however, the WINS administrator will find it necessary to view the WINS database or to make manual changes to it. In particular, if you have b-node clients operating on your network, you will need to create static mappings for them. The following sections describe how to view and modify the WINS database.

Viewing the WINS database

To view the WINS database, from WINS Manager, choose Show Database from the Mappings menu to display the Show Database–<WINS Server ID> dialog, as shown in Figure 13-6. Note that the title bar displays the location of the database you are working with. In this case, it happens to be the WINS database on the local server.

The upper half of the screen displays information and options that allow you to control which data will be displayed, and how it will be displayed, as follows:

Display Options–Owner section
: Choose the Show All Mappings option button to display every mapping in the selected WINS database, regardless of which WINS server owns it. Choose the Show Only Mappings from Selected Owner option button and then select one of the WINS servers in the Select Owner pane to display only mappings owned by the selected WINS server. The Highest ID column in the Sort Owner pane shows the highest WINS version number of records owned by the associated WINS server in the database of its replication partners.

Display Options–Sort Order
: Choose one of the option buttons in this section to specify how the list of mappings will be displayed. The first three choices are self-explanatory. The last two require some explanation:

  — *Sort by Version ID.* Choosing this option button causes the list of mappings to be sorted by WINS version ID number, which is ordinarily a pretty useless sort order. However, if a WINS server fails or the database is corrupted, you need to take remedial action, as described in the troubleshooting section that follows. One of the things that you need to do to reconstruct a WINS server database is determine the highest WINS version ID number that was in use on the problem server. This option button allows you to do so.

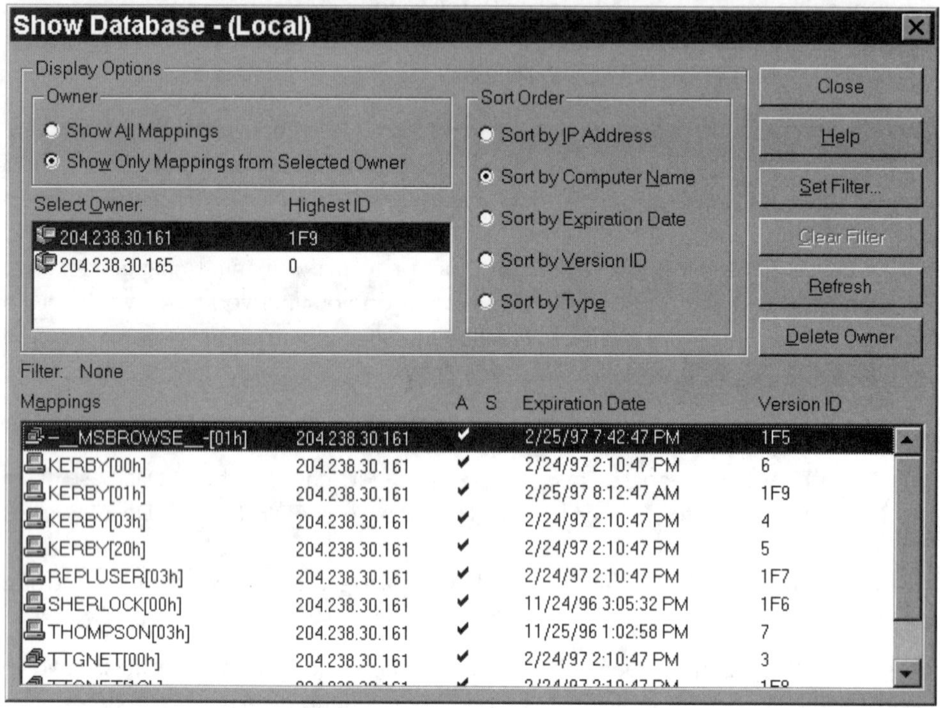

Figure 13-6. The Show Database–<WINS Server ID> dialog allows you to display mapping records from the selected WINS database

— *Sort by Type*. Choosing this option button causes the list of mappings to be sorted by type. In addition to an ordinary computer name used by a regular WINS client (called a *Unique* name), WINS recognizes four special types of NetBIOS computer names, called *Group*, *Domain Name*, *Internet Group*, and *Multihomed*. These special names are described in the following section on using static mappings.

You can also use the following buttons to specify which mappings will be displayed, and how:

Set Filter

Use this button to create a filter that limits the range of IP addresses or computer names displayed in the Mappings list. When you click Set Filter, the Set Filter dialog is displayed. You can filter by computer name by entering part or all of a name in the Computer Name field, using an asterisk as a final wildcard character. You can filter by address by entering part or all of an IP address in the IP address field, using one or more asterisks as wildcards. Mappings are displayed only if they match the filter in effect. For example, if you enter a filter of 204.238.30.*, mappings with any address that begins with 204.238.30 will be displayed, whereas all others will be suppressed.

If a filter is currently in effect, the name or address of that filter is displayed immediately above the Mappings pane, and the Clear Filter button is activated. Click Clear Filter to remove the filter and display all mappings.

Refresh
Click this button to query the WINS database and display an updated list of mappings.

Delete Owner
Use this button to remove the mappings for one or more WINS servers from the Mappings list. To do so, highlight a WINS server in the Select Owner pane and then click Delete Owner. Mappings for the selected WINS server are removed from the Mappings list. Note that on larger networks, it can take literally hours to delete a record.

The lower half of the screen displays the Mappings list, each line of which corresponds to a single database record. Note that a single entity has multiple database entries, one for each of its functions. The first column displays three elements:

- An icon that indicates the mapping type. In this example, the icon associated with the first and last entries resembles several computers, indicating that this entry is of the Group, Domain Name, Internet Group, or Multihomed type. The icon associated with the other entries is a single computer, indicating that these entries are of type Unique. Double-clicking an individual entry displays the View Mapping dialog. This dialog shows the Name of the mapping; the Mapping Type, e.g., Unique, Group, etc.; and the IP address. You can modify the IP address to specify a new static mapping address for that entry.
- The NetBIOS computer name that is mapped.
- The hexadecimal flag byte, described earlier in this chapter. Recall that Microsoft NetBIOS names use only the first 15 of the 16 available characters, and reserve the final character as a flag byte to indicate type.

The remaining columns provide additional information for each mapping, including the IP address; a check mark to indicate that the mapping is A or active; a check mark to indicate that the mapping is S or static; the expiration date of the record; and the WINS version ID number for the mapping.

Using static mappings

Ideally, you'd prefer that every host on your network be WINS-aware and use h-node name resolution. In the real world, this usually turns out not to be the case. Chances are you'll have at least one device on your network that is limited to using b-node for name resolution. In the normal course of things, this might cause problems, because b-node devices are unaware of h-node devices, and *vice versa.* WINS, however, makes provision for accommodating b-node devices in an h-node environment. The method it uses to do so is called *static mapping.*

Static mapping allows you manually to create WINS database entries that associate a specific NetBIOS computer name and IP address with a b-node device. To create a static mapping entry, proceed as follows:

1. From WINS Manager, choose Static Mappings from the Mappings menu to display the Static Mappings–<WINS Server ID> dialog. By default, this dialog displays all active static mappings. You can use the Set Filter button and Clear Filter button as described in the preceding section to display a subset of the static mappings in the database, filtered by computer name or IP address.

NOTE Changes you make to the WINS database using the Static Mappings dialog occur in real time. That is, if you mistakenly add an entry, you must delete it manually. Similarly, if you delete an entry accidentally, the only way to recover it is to recreate the entry.

---

2. Click Add Mappings to display the Add Static Mappings dialog. Enter the Name of the host and its IP address in the appropriate fields. Specify the type of host by choosing one of the Type option buttons, as follows:

   — *Unique.* An "ordinary" client, i.e., that the host name and IP address have a one-to-one mapping.

   — *Group.* Defines the host as a member of a normal group, or one in which individual IP addresses are not stored for each member.

   — *Domain Name.* Defines this host as a member of a Domain Name group. See WINS help or the Resource Kit for more details.

   — *Internet Group.* Defines this host as a member of a user-defined group that associates multiple IP addresses with multiple computer names in a many-to-many mapping. See WINS help or the Resource Kit for more details.

— *Multihomed.* A multihomed host has more than one IP address associated with a single unique computer name. Choosing this option button invokes another dialog that allows you to enter additional IP addresses for this entry, to a maximum of 25. See WINS help or the Resource Kit for more details.

3. When you have finished entering information for a static mapping entry, click Close to save that entry and return to the Static Mappings–<*WINS Server ID*> dialog. If you need to create more static mapping entries, instead click Add, which saves the current entry and then displays an empty Add Static Mappings dialog.

You can view and modify existing static mapping entries either by double-clicking the entry or by highlighting the entry and then clicking Edit Mapping to invoke the Edit Static Mapping dialog described above. Similarly, you can delete a static mapping entry by highlighting it and clicking Delete Mapping.

NOTE If you need to create static mapping entries for many hosts—perhaps when you are first installing your WINS server—there is an alternative to entering them individually as described above. Create and save a file in *Lmhosts* format that contains a name and IP address for each host for which you need to create a static mapping entry. Then in the Static Mappings–<*WINS Server ID*> dialog, click Import Mappings and specify the location of the file you just created in the Select Static Mappings File dialog that appears. WINS Manager creates a static mapping entry for each of the records in the file.

Backing up and restoring the WINS database

WINS can back up its databases automatically, although by default it does not do so. To cause WINS to do periodic automatic backups, from the WINS Manager Server menu, choose Configuration, click Advanced, and then Browse to display the Select Backup Directory dialog. Select a folder and then click OK to insert that folder name into the Database Backup Path field. The folder you specify must be located on a local disk drive; WINS will not back up to a network drive.

The Database Backup Path is used as the destination for automatic backups. It is also used as the default source location when you choose Restore Local Database from the Mappings menu. Finally, it is used as the default destination when you initiate a manual backup by choosing Backup Database from the Mappings menu. When you restore or perform a manual backup, WINS Manager gives you the opportunity to specify a different path before proceeding.

Maintaining and Troubleshooting WINS

Once it has been installed and configured correctly, WINS requires little routine maintenance, and is likely to have few problems. When problems do occur, they are usually minor and affect only one or a few clients. The following list describes four of the most common minor problems that might occur with WINS and how to go about resolving them:

Clients receive "network path not found" messages
: This problem may occur in environments with a mix of h-node and b-node hosts, and in those with multiple WINS servers configured as replication partners. If this problem occurs, the first step is to look up the name in question in the WINS database. If the name does not exist, check to see if the destination host uses b-node. If so, you must enter a static mapping for the b-node host in the WINS database. If an entry for the destination host does exist in the local WINS database, but that host is connected to a subnet served by a different WINS server, then the most likely cause is that that host's IP address is no longer the same as the value stored in the local WINS database. To resolve the problem, perform a push replication from the remote WINS server to the local WINS server to replicate the changed information to your local database.

WINS returns "duplicate name" messages
: This problem also occurs in environments with multiple WINS servers configured as replication partners. It occurs when a static mapping record exists for a particular name in the local database, and a remote database attempts to replicate that same name to the local database. To resolve the problem, first examine the local WINS database to determine if a static mapping record exists for that name. If so, delete it.

WINS database backup fails
: If you receive an error message during backup of the WINS database, the most likely cause is that the backup folder you specified initially in WINS Manager is located on a network drive. WINS requires that its backup folder be located on a local drive. You will also receive a similar message if the drive containing the backup folder has inadequate space to complete the backup.

WINS replication fails
: If you receive an error message reporting a replication failure, by far the most likely cause is a simple configuration error. A WINS server can be configured as a push partner, as a pull partner, or as both push and pull. Normally, in an environment with multiple WINS servers configured as replication partners, each WINS server should be configured as both a push partner and a pull

partner with each other WINS server. If you receive an error message reporting a replication failure on a newly installed or recently reconfigured WINS server, verify that the partnership settings are configured correctly between the WINS servers. You can do so by using the Registry Editor to examine the values for the Registry subkeys *Pull* and *Push* in the key *HKLM_SYSTEM\CurrentControlSet\Services\Wins\Partners*.

If you haven't made any changes recently to your WINS servers, then an incorrect configuration is unlikely to be the cause of the replication problem. In this case, the most likely cause is a simple network communication problem. The two WINS servers obviously can't replicate if they can't talk to each other. Use the *ping* utility to verify that IP connectivity exists between the two servers.

NOTE Performing any of the problem resolution measures described in this section requires that you be logged on to the server with an account that is a member of the Administrators group.

The following two problems (or widespread client problems of the sort described earlier) indicate more severe problems with WINS:

- When you attempt to use WINS Manager to connect to a WINS server, you are unable to do so and receive a warning message.
- When you attempt to start the Windows Internet Name Service service or the WINS client service, you receive a warning message that the service cannot start.

If the first problem occurs, first use *ping* to verify that IP connectivity exists between the workstation you are using and the WINS server in question. If you can ping the server successfully, next verify that WINS is running on that server by running the Services applet from Control Panel. The Status column should report "Started" for both the Windows Internet Name Service service and the WINS client service. If either or both of these services is not running, first attempt to start the service by highlighting its name and clicking Start. If the service starts successfully, verify that the problems you were experiencing have been resolved.

TIP Don't forget to use Event Viewer to check the log for error messages. To run Event Viewer, from the Start button, choose **Programs ➤ Administrative Tools (Common) ➤ Event Viewer**.

If the second problem occurs, and you are unable to start the service using the procedure described earlier, the next step is to shut down the server. Before doing so, notify everyone that the server is about to be shut down. If you experiencing severe WINS problems, you may have to notify your users using some method other than a broadcast to clients. Once all clients have disconnected safely, shut down the server, turn the power off, and allow the server to remain down for at least a minute.

Once your drives have all spun down, turn the power back on, and watch the console for warning messages as the server restarts. Most of the time, you will find that WINS starts normally. If WINS still does not start, from the command prompt, type *net start wins*, and press Enter. WINS should start normally. If WINS still refuses to start, or if WINS appears to start properly but you still cannot access the WINS database with WINS Manager, there are two alternatives remaining. Before attempting either, back up your existing WINS database. Make sure that you are not backing up bad data over good, and that you have a copy of your last-known-good WINS database backup stored in a safe location before proceeding.

Restore the WINS database

The penultimate measure to correcting WINS problems is to revert to an earlier version of the WINS database. You can restore the WINS database using WINS Manager or by manually copying files.

— To restore using WINS Manager, select Restore Local Database option from the Mappings menu, enter the location of the backup WINS database files, and click OK to confirm.

— To restore manually, first stop any running WINS services as described earlier in this section. Next, delete all files in the *\%SystemRoot\system32\wins* folder, and copy a known-good earlier version of *wins.mdb* to this folder. Finally, restart WINS using the command-line procedure described earlier.

- *Reinstall WINS.* If you are running a small network with a simple WINS environment—one without replication partners, numerous static mappings, and so on—the quickest and easiest fix is sometimes simply to reinstall WINS. Even if your WINS environment is more complex, you may have no alternative to reinstalling WINS if you find that all of your existing WINS database copies are corrupt.

  To reinstall WINS, from Control Panel–Services, shut down any WINS services that are currently running. Next, from the Services page of the Network property sheet, highlight Windows Internet Name Service and click Remove, but don't restart the server just yet. First, delete the *\%SystemRoot\system32\wins* folder and all of its files and subfolders. Restart the server and install WINS as described earlier in this chapter. Restart the server once more. The WINS database will be rebuilt dynamically as the clients access it. In a small environment, removing and then reinstalling WINS may be quicker and less disruptive than attempting to fix the existing installation.

Rebuilding the WINS Database on Another Server

If your WINS problems arise as a result of hardware problems on the machine running the WINS server service, you may have no alternative but to rebuild the WINS database on another server. To rebuild the WINS database, take the following steps:

1. If it is at all possible, attempt to retrieve a copy of the WINS database from the failed server by stopping the WINS server service and making a copy of the database as described above. Otherwise, you must use your most recent good backup of the WINS database.
2. If it is not already running Windows NT Server 4.0, install the operating system on the new server.

WARNING The WINS database must reside in the same location on the new server as it did on the old. That is, if the WINS database was stored in *C:\WINNT\system32\wins* on the original server, it must also reside in the *C:\WINNT\system32\wins* on the replacement server. If Windows NT Server is installed in a different folder on an existing replacement server, you must reinstall Windows NT Server to the original *%SystemRoot%* before proceeding.

---

3. Verify that the WINS server service is stopped on the replacement server.
4. Use the Registry Editor to restore the WINS Registry Keys from backup copies made from the original server.
5. Restore the WINS database files to the WINS data directory on the replacement server and restart the server.

You can also use this procedure if you simply want to remove the WINS server from one server and relocate it to another.

14

Using Domain Name Service

In this chapter:
- *Why DNS Is Needed*
- *How DNS Works*
- *Installing the Microsoft DNS Server Service*
- *Managing the Microsoft DNS Server*

The Microsoft Domain Name Service (DNS) Server is a Windows NT Service that allows client computers to resolve an unknown IP address from a known Internet name. By using DNS, you can establish a centralized, dynamically updated database that maps Internet names to IP addresses. DNS overcomes the administrative burdens and functional limitations associated with using static HOSTS files. DNS is to TCP/IP and the Internet what the Windows Internet Name Service (WINS) is to NetBIOS and Microsoft Networking.

Microsoft is late to the party with a DNS server for Windows NT. Although they made a DNS server for Windows NT Server 3.51 available, it offered limited functionality and was not well integrated with the other TCP/IP services provided by Windows NT. Most administrators considered this early Microsoft effort to create a DNS server as an interesting oddity, but certainly not as a product that they would even consider using in a production environment. The DNS server included with Windows NT Server 4.0 is worth serious consideration. It corrects the problems and missing functionality of the 3.51 DNS server, and adds some bells and whistles all its own.

If you're now on the Internet or running a private TCP/IP network, chances are you're using UNIX to provide DNS services—probably one or more UNIX boxes at your site for primary DNS and another UNIX box at your ISP for secondary DNS. You might wonder why you should even bother looking at the Microsoft DNS Server. After all, if it's not broke, don't fix it, right?

Well, there are a couple of reasons why you might consider changing to the Microsoft DNS Server. First, it is fully compliant with Internet standards, and interoperates well with UNIX-based and other DNS servers, so using it doesn't paint you into any corners. Applications running on any platform can use the Microsoft DNS Server for name resolution. Second, it is integrated with Microsoft DHCP and

Microsoft WINS, which can make your life a lot easier. Finally, the Microsoft DNS Server includes the DNS Manager, a graphic application for managing DNS. If you've ever struggled with maintaining the configuration files used by most DNS servers, you will appreciate just how much easier and faster it is to use DNS Manager.

Like DHCP and WINS, DNS uses a client/server architecture. The DNS server is bundled with Windows NT Server. On the client side, DNS differs from DHCP and WINS in that the DNS client, also called a *resolver*, exists at the application level rather than at the operating system level. The DNS protocols are well defined, and any DNS client can use any DNS server for name resolution services.

Why DNS Is Needed

In the very early days of the Internet, no mechanism existed to resolve unknown IP addresses from a known host name. To connect to a remote host, you had to specify its IP address directly. If you didn't know the IP address, you couldn't connect to the host. This was bad enough when the Internet comprised only a handful of hosts located at a few universities and government sites. It rapidly become completely unworkable as additional hosts were connected to the Internet.

The next step was to allow the use of a host name as an alias for an IP address. For example, the host *thoth.ttgnet.com* corresponds (as of this writing) to the IP address 204.238.30.165. Although host names are convenient for people, who can remember names more easily than numbers, the Internet protocols must still use the underlying IP address to connect to a host. This made it necessary to have some mechanism to map host names to IP addresses.

Initially, that mechanism was a static *hosts* file, which contained a simple list of names and their associated IP addresses. Initially, this file was centrally administered on the Internet, and each site would periodically download the most recent copy. As the number of hosts connected to the Internet continued to grow, this solution became impracticable.

Although better than the alternative of using IP addresses directly, hosts files have some problems of their own. Because hosts files are static, each time a host name needs to be added, the change must be made manually to each hosts file. Because hosts files are often stored on the local hard disk of the client, making even a minor change requires an on-site visit to each client.

Another problem with hosts files is that they are inherently flat. In order to resolve a host name, your hosts file must contain an entry for that specific host name. For example, if your hosts file has entries for *thoth.ttgnet.com* and *kerby.ttgnet.com*, but not for *theodore.ttgnet.com*, then you will be unable to resolve *theodore.ttgnet.com*. A hierarchical arrangement would be preferable, because under such an arrangement, being able to resolve the IP address for, say, the parent *ttgnet.com* would also allow you to resolve the IP addresses for hosts that are children of *ttgnet.com*.

Yet another, more subtle, problem of hosts files is that using them loses one of the chief advantages of using host names rather than IP addresses. Because hosts files map host names to IP addresses statically, any change made to the IP address of a host causes the hosts file to point to an incorrect IP address. If instead we had a dynamic method of mapping host names to IP addresses, we could, for example, point our web browser to *www.oreilly.com*, and not really care what the underlying IP address was. If the system administrator at O'Reilly moved the web server to a computer with a different IP address, this change wouldn't affect our ability to resolve the correct address, since the resolution would be dynamic.

Using hosts files is a workable alternative if you need to map one (or a few) host names to IP addresses. It becomes increasingly unworkable as the number of host names to be mapped increases. In today's Internet environment, with literally millions of hosts connected, using hosts files for anything but very specialized purposes—like mapping a limited number of hosts as a fallback for times when the DNS server is down—is too absurd to even consider. Also, there are still major applications that require either standard local hosts files or proprietary hosts files located in the application directory.

Clearly, some better alternative means of resolving IP addresses from host names was needed. Three characteristics are desirable in such a system. First, it should be distributed, so that changes are proliferated automatically to all participating hosts. Second, it should be dynamic, so that received changes are incorporated into the local database automatically, instead of requiring manual intervention. Third, it should be based on a hierarchical naming method to minimize the size of the database by allowing child names to be resolved from known data concerning the parent. Such a system exists now, and is called the Domain Name Service, or DNS. DNS is fundamental to the functioning of the Internet and of corporate TCP/IP networks.

How DNS Works

DNS is based on an organized naming structure that uses *DNS domains*, which are usually called simply *domains*. Each domain may contain both hosts and other domains, which may also be referred to as *subdomains*. A domain normally contains one or more *DNS servers*. A DNS server maintains a dynamic database that maps host names to their corresponding IP addresses. DNS servers respond to client queries by returning the IP address that corresponds to the host name provided by the client, or by returning the host name that corresponds to the IP address provided by the client. If a DNS server does not have the necessary information stored in its local database, it can query other DNS servers to determine the correct answer. The following sections describe in more detail how DNS functions.

WARNING Do not confuse DNS domains (also called *Internet domains*) with Windows NT domains. The two are entirely unrelated, although to avoid confusion it is often a good idea to organize and name your Windows NT domain(s) to correspond with your DNS domain(s). For example, my company was assigned the DNS domain name *ttg-net.com.* I named my Windows NT domain *TTGNET.*

One exception to this is when you use a firewall to isolate your private network from the public Internet. In this case, it may make sense to use completely different names for your private, internal Windows NT domain and your public Internet domain. That way, it's always clear to users when they are working internally and when externally.

Understanding Domain Naming Conventions

The Internet domain name system comprises a distributed database of names. These names are arranged in a hierarchical structure, called the *domain name space*, that resembles an inverted tree. At the top of this pyramid is the *root* of the domain name system, which is actually named *null*, but is conventionally represented by a single dot. Figure 14-1 illustrates the hierarchical nature of the domain name space.

Root is at the zeroth level of the tree. Immediately beneath root are several first-level domains, called *top-level domains.* The top-level domains are organized into two separate hierarchies, called the *organizational hierarchy* and the *geographical Hierarchy.* Each is intended for a different purpose, and each is managed by a different organization, but both are branches of root.

The organizational hierarchy

The organizational hierarchy contains seven top-level domains. An organization is assigned to one of these top-level domains based on the type of activity it engages in, as follows:

com
: Used by commercial firms, e.g., *microsoft.com, ibm.com, oreilly.com.* The com top-level domain is also used as a catch-all for entities that do not fit any of

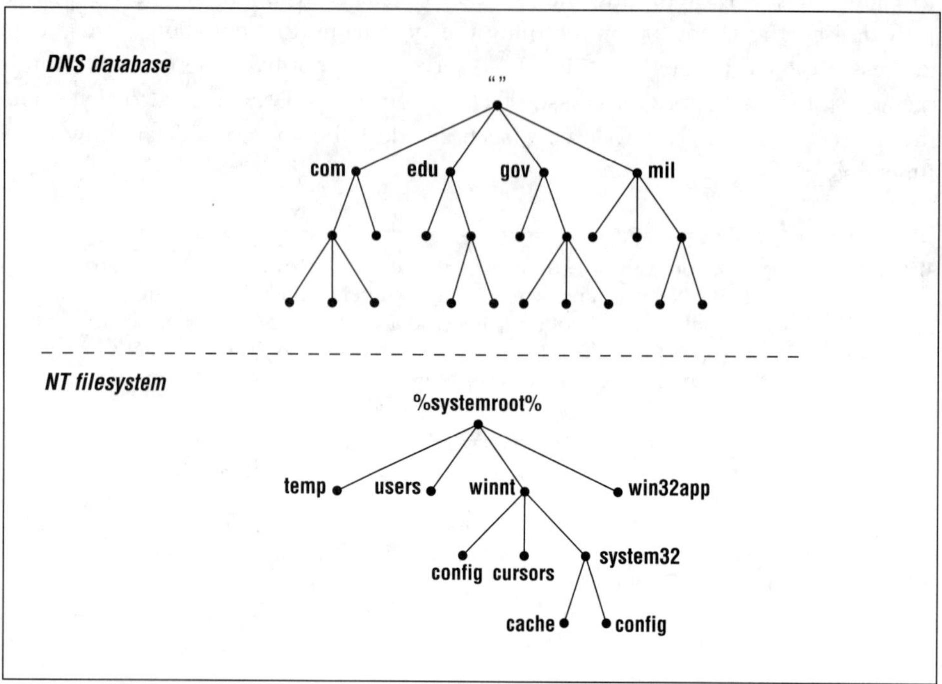

Figure 14-1. The Domain Name Space uses a hierarchical structure much like that used to organize folders and files on a disk drive

the other categories. Many individuals have registered domain names in the com name space.

edu

Used by four-year colleges and universities, e.g., *harvard.edu, princeton.edu, yale.edu.* Other educational institutions—K-12 public schools, private schools, community colleges, etc.—are assigned elsewhere in the domain name space.

gov

Used by United States federal government agencies, e.g., *epa.gov, fbi.gov, nasa.gov.* State and local government agencies are assigned elsewhere in the domain name space, as are foreign government agencies.

int

Used by international governmental or quasi-governmental organizations, e.g., *nato.int.*

mil

Used by United States military organizations for hosts that contain only nonclassified data, e.g., *army.mil.* The secure military communications network is completely separate from the Internet.

net

Used by companies and organizations that provide network infrastructure services, including Internet Service Providers (ISPs) and Network Service Providers (NSPs), e.g., *ibm.net, internic.net, mci.net.*

org

Used by nonprofit entities, including those engaged in advocacy, political parties, research groups, and public service organizations, e.g., *cato.org, redcross.org, libertarian.org.*

The geographical hierarchy

The geographical hierarchy is organized by political subdivision, and contains numerous top-level domains. Each country is assigned a top-level domain, designated using the ISO 3166 country code. For example, the United States is assigned the top-level domain *.us*; Australia, *.au*; and Canada, *.ca*. One departure from correct nomenclature is the top-level domain for Great Britain. For consistency, it should be *.gb*, but by long-standing convention, Great Britain uses the *.uk* top-level domain for United Kingdom.

At the second level and below, the method used to organize domain names in the geographical hierarchy is chosen by the national authority to which the top-level domain has been delegated. In some countries, smaller geographic or political subdivisions are used for domain naming at the lower levels. For example, in the United States, the *.us* domain is further subdivided into states, and then into cities.

Some countries graft the organizational hierarchy into the geographical hierarchy. For example, Australia assigns domain names to organizations beginning at the third level. The top level is *.au*; the second level is occupied by organizational hierarchy domains: *.com, .edu*, etc. For Australian domain names, this makes the second level effectively the top level. For example, the domain name assigned to IBM in Australia is *ibm.com.au*. Similarly, the University of Melbourne is assigned the domain name *unimelb.edu.au.*

Delegation

The *Internet Assigned Numbers Authority* (*IANA*) owns and manages the Internet domain name space. IANA, using a process called *delegation*, assigns responsibility for managing portions of that space to various organizations. For example, IANA delegated the *.com* and *.edu* top-level domains to InterNIC, allowing InterNIC to control who may register a domain name within those top-level domains, and how they may do so. Similarly, IANA assigns control of the top-level domains within the geographical hierarchy to authorities within the countries in question, and allows them to assume responsibility for managing their portions of the address space.

Each top-level domain can contain an unlimited number of *second-level domains*. A domain that is the child of a parent domain is called a *subdomain* of the parent domain. An entity that has been delegated authority for a particular address space may further delegate authority for subsets of that space (see Figure 14-2).

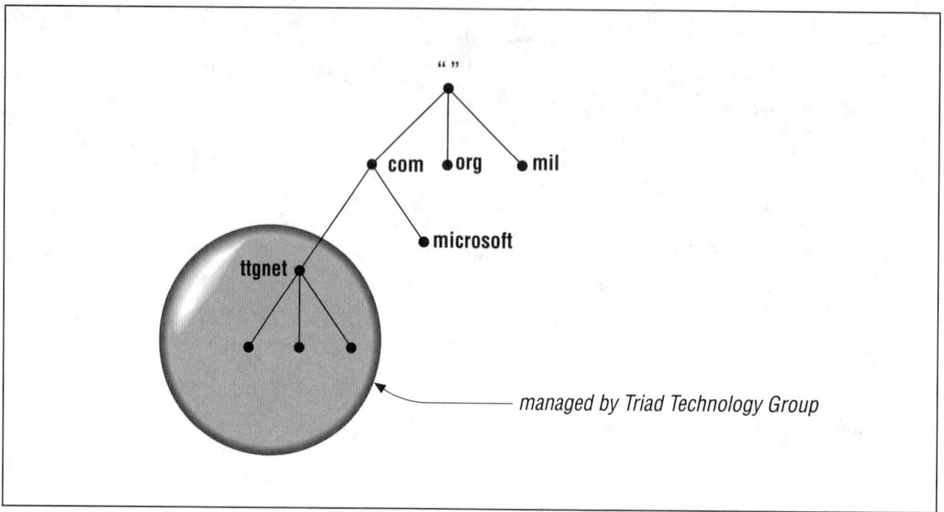

Figure 14-2. Delegation allows responsibility for managing subdomains to be distributed to the organization that uses the subdomain

For example, when I registered my company domain name (*ttgnet.com*) in the *.com* domain, InterNIC—which manages the *.com* top-level domain—delegated authority for the *ttgnet.com* subdomain to me. I may assign names to individual hosts within the *ttgnet.com* domain. I may also, if I wish, create subdomains and subsubdomains within the *ttgnet.com* domain. For example, if I had a main office in Winston-Salem, NC and a branch office in Rural Hall, NC, I might create the subdomains *ws.ttgnet.com* and *rh.ttgnet.com*. I might just as easily name these subdomains *main.ttgnet.com* and *branch.ttgnet.com*. How I name subdomains and hosts within my domain is completely up to me.

Zones versus domains

It is important to understand the distinction between DNS domains and DNS zones. A domain is a logical grouping that encompasses the domain itself, all subdomains of that domain, and all hosts within that domain and its subdomains. A *zone*, on the other hand, is an administrative grouping that may encompass parts of domains, entire domains, and groups of domains.

Registering a Domain

Any person or organization is permitted to register one or more domain names within the geographical hierarchy. A few types of organizations, e.g., K-12 schools and local governments, can register domain names **only** within the geographical hierarchy. The organizational hierarchy and the geographical hierarchy are not mutually exclusive. You can register one—or several—domain names within each hierarchy. For example, although IBM has registered the domain *ibm.com* in the organizational hierarchy, they could just as easily have instead registered the geographical hierarchy domain name *ibm.armonk.ny.us.*

The organizational hierarchy is where the action is. Most commercial firms—both inside and outside the United States—choose to register in the *.com* top-level domain. A major reason for this preference is that organizational hierarchy domain names tend to be short, sweet, and easy to remember, whereas geographical hierarchy names tend to be long, ugly, and easy to forget.

For example, in the organizational hierarchy, my company domain name is *ttg-net.com.* I wanted to register *ttg.com,* but that domain name was already in use when I registered my domain. Because my company happens to be located in Winston-Salem, NC, its geographical hierarchy domain name would be something like *ttg.winston-salem.nc.us,* a considerably less desirable domain name.

The matter of domain name length can be critical. Theoretically, the domain name system places few restrictions on the length or content of names. However, some software severely limits the number of characters that it will accept for a domain name. For example, one well-known (non-Microsoft) operating system accepts only 12 characters for the domain name, including periods.

For more information about registering a domain within the organizational hierarchy, set your web browser to *www.internic.net* and choose the link for Registration Services. For more information about registering a domain in the *.us* domain, set your web browser to the US Domain Registry at *www.isi.edu/in-notes/usdnr/.* For more information about registering a geographical hierarchy domain elsewhere, set your web browser to *rs.internic.net/help/other-reg.html.*

Rather than being a purely logical grouping, a zone has physical reality, as reflected in the existence of a *zone file,* which contains database records for only that zone. A DNS server may manage one or several zone files. Each zone is anchored at a domain node, which is referred to as the *root domain* of that zone. The zone may encompass the complete domain, or only a portion of it, as shown in Figure 14-3.

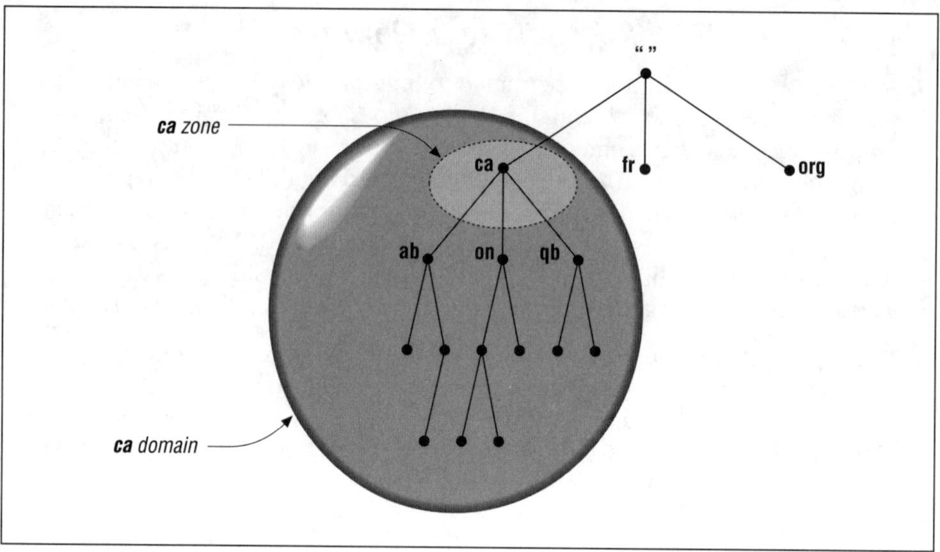

Figure 14-3. Zones versus domains

DNS Servers

The foundation of the domain name system is a network of *domain name service servers*, more simply called *DNS servers*. A DNS server stores information about the domain name space and about the zone of which it is a part. A DNS server may be assigned responsibility for one or more zones. Such a DNS server is referred to as being *authoritative* for that zone.

DNS servers get their information in one of two ways. First, all DNS servers receive and store information provided by other DNS servers. When configuring a DNS server, you provide information about other DNS servers within the same domain. Second, some DNS servers contain information that is entered manually by the administrator of the domain and zone. DNS servers are grouped by type, according to the source of their data, as follows:

Primary
: A primary DNS server contains information about the local zone entered manually by the domain or zone administrator. When you need to add hosts to a domain, or create a subdomain, you do so on the primary DNS server.

Secondary
: A secondary DNS server receives zone information from other DNS servers that are authoritative for the zone or zones in question. The process of replicating this data from one DNS server to a secondary DNS server is called a *zone transfer*, and amounts more or less to a simple file copy. The primary

purpose of a secondary DNS server is to provide redundancy for the primary DNS server.

Master
: The DNS server that provides zone information to a secondary DNS server is referred to as a master DNS server. If both DNS servers are located in the same zone, the master DNS server is simply another name for the primary DNS server for that zone. If the secondary DNS server is requesting information from a different zone, the master DNS server located in that zone may be a primary DNS server or a secondary DNS server for that zone.

Caching
: This is something of a misnomer, because all DNS servers cache information that they resolve while servicing client queries. However, a caching DNS server is one whose only job is to resolve client queries, cache the results, and then return them to the client who generated the query. In other words, a caching DNS server is not authoritative for any zone, and contains only data that it has discovered in the process of resolving queries.

Note that these designations are not absolute. You cannot refer to a particular DNS server as simply a primary or secondary DNS server without also considering the zone. For example, the primary DNS server for one zone may be the secondary DNS server for another zone, and vice versa.

There are several good reasons to have at least two DNS servers. First and foremost, InterNIC requires it. Before InterNIC will assign a domain name, they generally require that you designate both a primary and a secondary DNS server for that zone, and that both of these DNS servers be active and responding to queries. Another obvious reason is redundancy. If your primary DNS server fails, the secondary DNS server can continue to service client queries. If your network connects several sites, placing DNS servers at the remote sites minimizes traffic across the WAN link. Finally, if your organization is very large, using multiple DNS servers allows you to distribute the burden of responding to DNS queries across several servers.

The DNS Resolution Process

DNS resolution begins when a DNS client (or resolver) queries a DNS server. For example, if you are using Internet Explorer and want to browse the O'Reilly and Associates web site, you might enter the URL *www.oreilly.com*. The DNS resolver built into Internet Explorer sends the name *www.oreilly.com* to the designated primary DNS server, requesting that the DNS server return the associated IP address.

If the DNS server finds the IP address for *www.oreilly.com* in its cache, it immediately returns that address to the client that originated the query. If the information is not in the cache, the DNS server must use the services of other DNS servers to resolve it (see Figure 14-4).

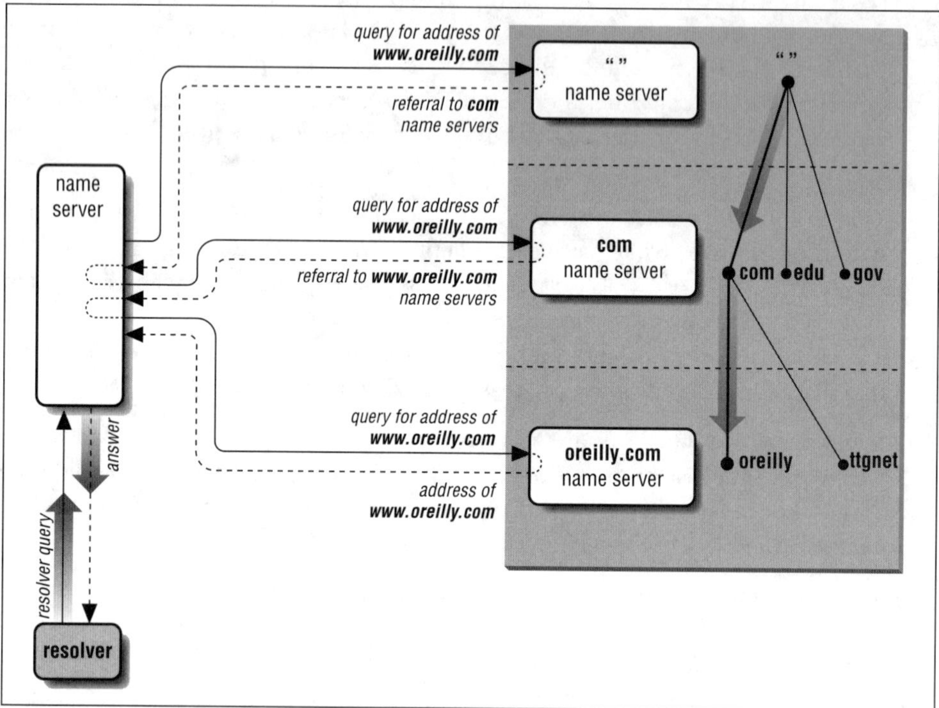

Figure 14-4. DNS uses an iterative process to resolve name queries

The local DNS server begins this process by querying the root DNS server to determine the IP address of the *.com* DNS server. Once the result is returned by the root DNS server, the local DNS server stores this information in its cache, and then queries the *.com* DNS server to determine the address of the DNS server that is authoritative for the *oreilly.com* domain. Once it obtains this information, the local DNS server again stores the newly obtained data in its cache and then queries the *oreilly.com* DNS server to determine the correct IP address for the host *www.oreilly.com*. Once it receives the response, the local DNS server stores the information in its cache and returns the result to the client that made the initial query.

NOTE Actually, the local name server will almost never need to resolve the addresses of the root DNS server and the top-level DNS servers. This information will almost always be retrievable from its cache. InterNIC periodically publishes an updated list of the root name servers.

Because the DNS server caches each newly discovered piece of information, if you or another client subsequently queries the DNS server to resolve *www.oreilly.com,* the DNS server can return the address directly from its cache, rather than repeating the resolution process. Similarly, because the address of the authoritative DNS server for *oreilly.com* is cached, a subsequent client query for the address of another host in the *oreilly.com* domain, e.g., *ftp.oreilly.com,* can be resolved by querying the *oreilly.com* DNS server directly, rather than by starting at the root name server. Finally, because the address for the *.com* DNS server is cached, the local DNS server can directly query the *.com* DNS server to resolve the address of another member of the *.com* domain, e.g., *microsoft.com.*

DNS query types

Until this point, I've simply said that a client queries a DNS server, without examining how this process occurs. A DNS client query can actually be any one of three types, as follows:

Recursive Query
: When a client makes a recursive name query, it requires the DNS server to respond in one of two ways: First, the DNS server, if it is able to resolve the query using its local data files, returns the IP address that maps to the host name provided by the client. Second, if the DNS server is unable to resolve the required IP address, it must return an error message to the DNS client, stating that the query is unresolvable. The DNS server is not permitted to refer the querying DNS client to another DNS server.

Iterative Query
: When a client makes an iterative name query, and the DNS server is able to resolve the query from its local database, it returns the IP address to the client. If the DNS server is unable to resolve the exact domain name or host name specified by the client, the DNS server returns the best information that it does have available. This information comprises a pointer to another DNS server that is authoritative for a domain higher in the name space. The DNS server returns the location of the authoritative DNS server that is "closest" to the query made by the client.

For example, if the client queried for the address of *www.oreilly.com*, and the DNS server did not have an address for that host in its cache, but did have the address of the authoritative DNS server for *oreilly.com* cached, the DNS server would return the latter to the client. The client can then query the *oreilly.com* DNS server to determine the IP address of *www.oreilly.com*. If the DNS server did not have the address of the *oreilly.com* DNS server cached, but did have the address of the *.com* DNS server, it would provide the latter information to the client. The client would then query the *.com* DNS server to determine the address of the *oreilly.com* DNS server and, having received that information, query the *oreilly.com* DNS server to determine the address of *www.oreilly.com*.

Inverse Query

When a client makes an inverse query, also called a reverse query, it provides an IP address and asks the DNS server to resolve the host name associated with that address. For example, the client might ask the DNS server to resolve the IP address 204.148.40.9. The DNS server resolves this IP address to the associated host name (*www.oreilly.com*) by using reverse lookup, which is described further in the following section on DNS databases.

Time to live

The fact that DNS servers cache information that they learn in the process of resolving queries brings up a possible problem. If address information is being cached by the DNS server, how can we ensure that the data does not become obsolete? The solution to this problem is contained in the data that is returned in response to the query.

When the local DNS server receives a response to its query, that response includes not only the address information it requested, but also a value for *Time to Live* (*TTL*). The TTL value specifies the period for which that data is valid. The local DNS server continues to cache that data only until the TTL period has expired, and then removes it from the cache. A subsequent query for that same information will then be resolved as described above, allowing the DNS server to periodically refresh its information.

The value for TTL is controlled by the administrator of the DNS server being queried. For example, if the *oreilly.com* administrator plans to make significant changes to her network in the near future—perhaps moving the web server to a computer with a different IP address—she might reduce the TTL value on his DNS server. Queries for the IP address of *www.oreilly.com* would be returned with the short TTL value, causing them to expire quickly on the remote DNS servers. Once the *oreilly.com* administrator had made the changes to his network, he might then TTL to a higher value, allowing remote DNS servers to cache the new address of the web server for a much longer period.

Like many things in life, choosing a value for TTL involves tradeoffs. Setting a short value ensures that the data cached on remote DNS servers is more likely to be accurate, but at the same time causes more queries to be generated and consumes additional bandwidth. Setting a long value on TTL minimizes the number of queries that are received and uses less bandwidth, but any change you make to your network will be proliferated throughout DNS much more slowly. The rule of thumb is simple. If your network is relatively stable, set a long TTL value. If you plan to make significant changes to the network—particularly to the addresses of hosts that are visible on the public Internet—revise your TTL value downward shortly before you make the change, and then back upward after the change has been implemented.

Forwarders, Slaves, and Firewalls

The increasing perception of the Internet as an insecure environment has led many corporations to install firewalls to isolate their private internal TCP/IP networks from the public Internet. At the same time, these firms need to provide Internet access to their employees and to allow users elsewhere on the Internet to access at least some parts of their corporate network.

For many firms, the solution to this conundrum is to divide their corporate network in two by installing a firewall. The bulk of the network is private, and is located "inside the firewall." Those hosts, e.g., web servers and mail servers, that need to be accessible to the public Internet are sited between the firewall and the ISP, or "outside the firewall." The divided nature of such a network brings up several DNS issues.

If a DNS server cannot resolve a client query by using its local database, its next step is to query other DNS servers. If the local DNS server in question is located inside the firewall, and if the name to be resolved is on the public Internet, the local DNS server may need to query a DNS server located outside the firewall. Chances are, however, that you don't want the DNS servers inside your firewall communicating freely with DNS servers on the public Internet.

The solution in this environment is to use two sets of DNS servers, as shown in Figure 14-5. The first, external, set of DNS servers, located outside the firewall, communicates normally with other DNS servers on the public Internet. The second, internal, set of DNS servers, located inside the firewall, provides all DNS name resolution services for any host sited behind the firewall. If the internal DNS server is unable to resolve the query from its own database, it passes the query to one of the external DNS servers, which resolves the query and returns the answer to the internal DNS server.

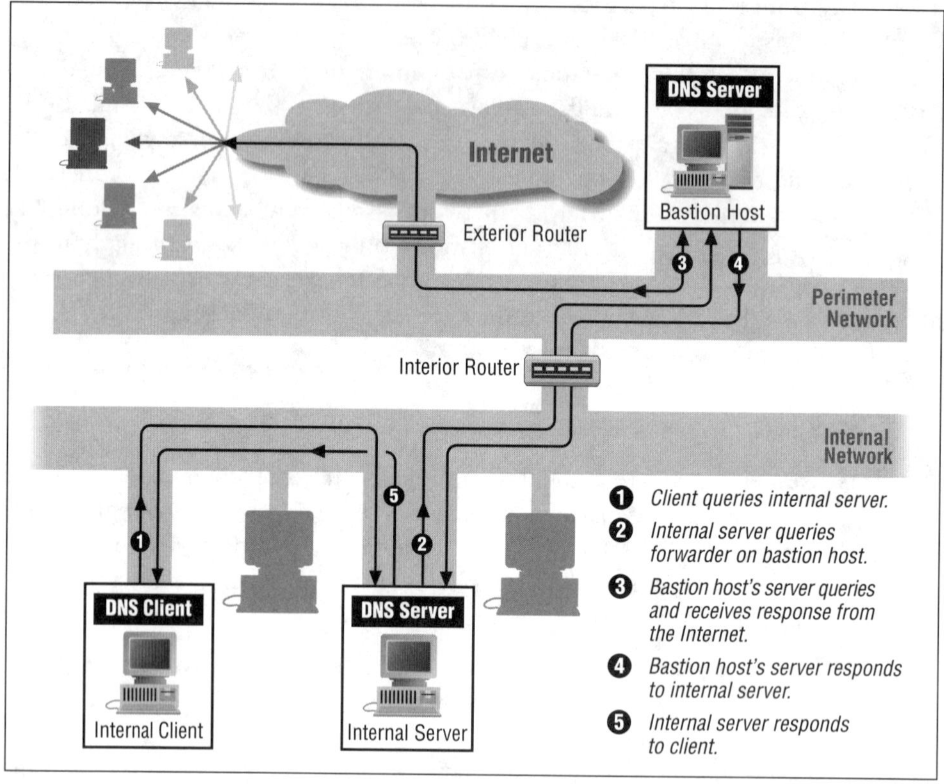

Figure 14-5. Forwarders and slaves allow DNS to function in a firewall environment

Using this method, an external DNS server is configured as a DNS *forwarder*. A forwarder interacts with other DNS servers on the public Internet just as you might expect. It contacts other DNS servers as necessary to resolve queries that it is unable to resolve from its own zone files, and it responds to queries that it receives from other DNS servers. It does not distribute information about the hosts inside its firewall to other hosts on the Internet.

An internal DNS server is configured as a DNS *slave*. Slave DNS servers provide all DNS name resolution services to hosts inside the firewall. If a slave DNS server is able to resolve a query from its local database, it returns the answer to the client that generated the query. Like any other DNS server, if a slave DNS server is unable to resolve the query locally, it queries another DNS server. What characterizes a slave DNS server is that it is limited in terms of which other DNS servers it is permitted to query.

A slave DNS server may query only its designated forwarders, the IP addresses of which are entered when the slave DNS server is configured. When the slave DNS server is unable to resolve a query locally, it passes the request to one of its designated forwarders. The forwarder then attempts to resolve the request, first using its own zone files, and then, if necessary, querying other DNS servers on the public Internet. If the forwarder resolves the query successfully, it returns the response to the slave DNS server, which in turn passes the response to the host that originated the query. If the slave DNS server is unable to resolve the query, either locally or by querying the forwarder, it returns a failure message to the host that initiated the query. The slave DNS server does not attempt to contact any other DNS server to resolve the query.

The Microsoft DNS Server

The Microsoft DNS Server bundled with Windows NT Server 4.0 complies with all relevant Internet standards, including RFC1033, RFC1034, RFC1035, RFC1101, RFC1123, RFC1183, and RFC1536. The Microsoft DNS Server is also fully compatible with and interoperable with the popular Berkeley Internet Name Domain (BIND) implementation of DNS.

NOTE Microsoft themselves state in published material that "The book *DNS and BIND*, published by O'Reilly and Associates, is a valuable resource. The Windows NT DNS essentially conforms to this book."

As a standards-compliant DNS server, the Microsoft DNS Server uses the same database files and resource records types used by other DNS servers. As usual, however, Microsoft has attempted to improve on the existing standard. With the Microsoft DNS Server, they have done so in two respects:

Improved Integration
: The Microsoft DNS Server is integrated with Microsoft WINS and with the Microsoft DHCP Server. Using all three of these services on the network allows clients that use NetBIOS computer names and are assigned a dynamic IP address by the DHCP server to participate fully in DNS.

Improved Management
: Traditional implementations of DNS are managed by creating and maintaining ASCII text configuration files. Microsoft DNS Server is maintained using the graphical DNS Manager application.

DNS resource records

DNS stores information about host names, IP addresses, and so on as *resource records*. Different types of resource records are stored in various files, which together comprise the DNS database. Table 14-1 describes the resource record types recognized by Microsoft DNS Server. The sections that follow describe the files that contain these resource records, and the purpose of each file.

Table 14-1. DNS Resource Record Types Supported by the Microsoft DNS Server

Type	Description
A	The *Address* (A) resource record maps a host name to an IP address. The inverse of the A resource record is the PTR resource record, which maps an IP address to a host name.
AAAA	The AAAA address record maps a host name to an IP v6 address.
AFSDB	The *Andrews File System Database* (AFSDB) resource record specifies the location of an AFC cell server or the authenticated name server for a DCE cell.
CNAME	The *Canonical Name* (CNAME) resource record is used to create an alias for a host name. For example, O'Reilly & Associates runs their web server on a machine whose actual name is *helio.oreilly.com*. By creating a CNAME record that maps the alias *www.oreilly.com* to the host *helio.oreilly.com*, the O'Reilly administrator can allow users to access the web server as *www.oreilly.com*. If the administrator moves the web server to a different host, he need only edit the CNAME record to point to the new host.
HINFO	The *Host Information* (HINFO) resource record specifies the type of hardware and the operating system used by a host, as defined in RFC1700.
ISDN	The *Integrated Services Digital Network* (ISDN) resource record is analogous to the A resource record, but instead of mapping a host name to an IP address, it maps a host name to an ISDN address. An ISDN address looks much like an ordinary telephone number, with a country code, an area code, an exchange prefix, and a number. An ISDN address may also include a subaddress, which is used to enable optional ISDN features. The ISDN resource record is used in conjunction with the RT resource record described below.
MB	The *Mailbox* (MB) resource record is experimental, and maps a specific DNS server to a specific mailbox. See RFC1035 for further details.
MG	The *Mail Group* (MG) resource record is also experimental, and specifies a mailbox that is a member of a mail group for a specified domain. See RFC1035 for further details.
MINFO	The *Mailbox Information* (MINFO) resource record is also experimental, and specifies a mailbox that manages a designated mail group or mailbox. See RFC1035 for further details.
MR	The *Mailbox Rename* (MR) resource record is also experimental, and specifies a mailbox name that is a proper rename of a designated mailbox. See RFC1035 for further details.

Table 14-1. DNS Resource Record Types Supported by the Microsoft DNS Server (continued)

Type	Description
MX	The *Mail Exchange* (MX) resource record maps a DNS domain name to a particular mail server, allowing that server to process inbound mail destined for that domain name. This processing may consist of delivering the mail message to the local mailbox of the addressee, passing it to a different MTA, delivering it via SMTP to the destination mail server or an intermediary mail server, or simply queuing it for a specified period. Say, for example, that you have registered the domain name *mycompany.com*, but have only a dial-up connection to the Internet via your ISP at *yourisp.net*. Ordinarily, to receive mail, you would have to use an email address that was something like *yourname@yourisp.net*. If your ISP creates an MX record for *mycompany.com*, then its mail server can process inbound email addressed to *<anyone>@mycompany.com*. In this case, the ISP mail server would simply queue any message traffic destined for *mycompany.com* for subsequent retrieval by dial-up users.
NS	The *Name Server* (NS) resource record identifies a DNS server for the domain in question. NS records exist for every DNS zone and for every reverse zone.
PTR	The *Pointer* (PTR) resource record maps an IP address to a host name in a reverse zone—those in the in-addr.arpa domain. The PTR resource record is the inverse of the A resource record described above, which maps a host name to an IP address.
RP	The *Responsible Person* (RP) resource record identifies a technical contact for a DNS domain, zone, or individual host. The RP resource record includes the email address of the designated person in DNS format. That is, a dot is used rather than a @ to separate the account name from the host, e.g., *postmaster.oreilly.com* is used rather than *postmaster@oreilly.com*. The RP resource record also includes a pointer to additional information about the person. There can be zero, one, or several RP resource records associated with any particular host, zone, or domain.
RT	The *Route Through* (RT) resource record designates an intermediate host to be used to route packets to the destination host. The RT resource record is analogous in purpose and usage to the MX resource record, but is used with the ISDN resource record and the X.25 resource record.
SOA	The *Start of Authority* (SOA) resource record is the initial record in the database file of each DNS server, and specifies the DNS server that is authoritative for that domain. DNS Manager creates the SOA record automatically each time you create a new zone.
TXT	The *Text* (TXT) resource record maps ordinary descriptive text to objects within the DNS database. For example, you might use a TXT resource record to identify the location of a host or to specify contact information.
WINS	The *Windows Internet Name Service* (WINS) resource record is generated automatically when a Microsoft DNS server is configured to enable WINS. The WINS resource record contains the IP address of the designated WINS server to be used for WINS resolution.
WINS_R	The *WINS Reverse Lookup* (WINS_R) resource record is created automatically when WINS reverse lookup is enabled on the Microsoft DNS Server. This record instructs the DNS server to use the *nbtstat* command to resolve a reverse lookup query.

Table 14-1. DNS Resource Record Types Supported by the Microsoft DNS Server (continued)

Type	Description
WKS	The *Well-known Service* (WKS) resource record identifies a combination of protocol and port number that maps to a standard service. This record can map any protocol listed in *\%SystemRoot%\system32\drivers\etc\Protocol* and any service listed in *\%SystemRoot%\system32\drivers\etc\Services*. For example, tcp port 110 maps to the pop3 service.
X.25	Like the ISDN resource record, the X.25 resource record is similar to an A resource record, but maps host names to the X.121 addresses used by the X.25 network. The X.25 resource record is used in conjunction with the RT resource record described above.

DNS database files

The Microsoft DNS Server stores DNS information as resource records in several files, including one or more *zone files*, the *cache file*, and the *reverse lookup file*. Together, these files comprise the DNS database. Each of these files is examined in the following sections.

Zone files. The *zone file* is the main database file for each DNS zone. It contains one or more resource records for each host that is a member of that zone. It may also include resource records that serve other purposes, e.g., MX resource records and CNAME resource records.

Creating a zone with DNS Manager automatically creates the associated zone file. Using DNS Manager, you then enter resource records for that newly created zone file. Alternatively, you may create a zone file (or edit an existing zone file) with any ASCII editor. Also, you may import an existing zone file from any RFC-compliant DNS server.

Zone files are named in the form *zonename.dns*, and are stored in the *\%System-Root%\system32\Dns* folder. Any primary or secondary DNS server must have at least one zone file, and may have several—one for each zone it serves. Example 14-1 shows the zone file for *ttgnet.com*.

Example 14-1. The zone file ttgnet.com.dns for ttgnet.com

```
;  Database file ttgnet.com.dns for ttgnet.com zone.
;       Zone version:  3
;
@                        INSOAkerby.ttgnet.com.thompson.ttgnet.com.(
                         3            ; serial number
                         3600         ; refresh
                         600          ; retry
                         86400        ; expire
                         3600       ) ; minimum TTL
;
;  Zone NS records
```

Example 14-1. The zone file ttgnet.com.dns for ttgnet.com (continued)

```
;
@                         INNSkerby
;
;  WINS lookup record
;
@                         0INWINS204.238.30.161
;
;  Zone records
;
bambamIN A 204.238.30.102
barneyIN A 204.238.30.98
bettyIN  A 204.238.30.100
dino IN  A 204.238.30.103
fred IN  A 204.238.30.97
gatewayINA204.238.30.189
gazooIN  A 204.238.30.104
humphreyINA204.238.30.167
kerbyIN  A 204.238.30.161
kiwi IN  A 204.238.30.188
mandyIN  A 204.238.30.162
notebookINA204.238.30.187
pebblesINA204.238.30.101
poo  IN  A 204.238.30.168
sth-gwIN A 204.238.30.125
theodoreINA204.238.30.163
thothIN  A 204.238.30.165
valentineINA204.238.30.166
wilmaIN  A 204.238.30.99
www  IN  CNAMEkerby
```

The zone file has the following components:

- The first section is a comment, identified by the use of semicolon to begin the lines. This section defines the zone filename, the zone that it identifies, and the zone version number.
- The first resource record, identified by an @ symbol in the left column, defines the Start of Authority (SOA) record for this zone. The @ symbol is shorthand for the origin, which comes from the boot file. For example, if the primary is *ttgnet.com*, the @ symbol represents *ttgnet.com*. The *IN* in the second column defines the record as being of the *INternet* class. Although other record classes exist, none are in common use. The SOA record includes the name of the DNS server, the responsible person, and various values that control zone transfers, which are described later in this chapter.
- The second resource record is a Name Server (NS) record that defines the DNS server for this zone. Because only one DNS server had been defined when this file was created, only one NS record appears. In a normal file, at least two NS records will exist, describing the primary and secondary DNS servers.

- The third resource record is a WINS record that defines the WINS server for this zone. Again, because only one WINS server had been defined when this file was created, only one WINS record appears. In a normal file, two or more WINS records will appear.
- The final section includes several Address (A) resource records, one for each host in the zone. The first column of each of these resource records specifies the host name, which does not include the DNS domain; the second column defines the record as a member of the INternet class; the third column defines the record as an address record; and the fourth column specifies the full IP address associated with the host name.

Cache files. The *cache file* contains NS resource records and A resource records that allow the Microsoft DNS Server to locate the Internet root name servers, which are used to resolves queries outside the local zone. Installing the Microsoft DNS Server automatically creates the file *\%SystemRoot%\system32\Dns\Cache.dns*, which contains the current mappings for the root name servers. Example 14-2 shows, in its entirety, the *Cache.dns* file that was created when I installed the Microsoft DNS Server.

Example 14-2. The Cache File Contains Mappings for the Internet Root DNS Servers

```
.    IN   NS   E.ROOT-SERVERS.NET.
E.ROOT-SERVERS.NET.INA192.203.230.10
.    IN   NS   I.ROOT-SERVERS.NET.
I.ROOT-SERVERS.NET.INA192.36.148.17
.    IN   NS   F.ROOT-SERVERS.NET.
F.ROOT-SERVERS.NET.INA192.5.5.241
.    IN   NS   G.ROOT-SERVERS.NET.
G.ROOT-SERVERS.NET.INA192.112.36.4
.    IN   NS   A.ROOT-SERVERS.NET.
A.ROOT-SERVERS.NET.INA198.41.0.4
.    IN   NS   H.ROOT-SERVERS.NET.
H.ROOT-SERVERS.NET.INA128.63.2.53
.    IN   NS   B.ROOT-SERVERS.NET.
B.ROOT-SERVERS.NET.INA128.9.0.107
.    IN   NS   C.ROOT-SERVERS.NET.
C.ROOT-SERVERS.NET.INA192.33.4.12
.    IN   NS   D.ROOT-SERVERS.NET.
D.ROOT-SERVERS.NET.INA128.8.10.90
```

The first line of the cache file is an NS resource record that identifies the name server for a domain. In this case, the domain is . (root), and the associated DNS server is *E.ROOT-SERVERS.NET*. The second line of the cache file is an A resource record that maps the name *E.ROOT-SERVERS.NET* to the IP address 192.203.230.10. The remaining lines of the cache file go on to map several more root name servers using similar resource record pairs.

Note that the *Cache.dns* file designates nine root name servers, which can be used interchangeably. All of the root name servers contain the same information, which is replicated between them continually. There are multiple root name servers for two reasons:

Redundancy
: The entire DNS resolution process is based on the fact that a root name server will be available any time one is needed. If only one root name server existed and it failed, the Internet would be out of business until the root name server was again available. Multiple, widely dispersed root name servers remove this single point of failure, and also guard against network communication failures that temporarily render one or another of the root name servers inaccessible.

Load sharing
: Because the root name servers are at the top of the DNS tree, they are accessed frequently by other, subordinate DNS servers. The rapid growth of the Internet has dramatically increased the burden on the root name servers, which now process thousands of queries per second. Recently, DNS resolution failures that occur because a root name server did not respond to a query have become much more common. The use of multiple root name servers allows the burden to be spread across many servers.

NOTE The names and addresses of the root name servers are changed more frequently than you might expect. InterNIC periodically posts an updated cache file with the current names and addresses of the root name servers. You can retrieve the current version at *ftp://rs.internic.net/named.cache.*

If your network uses a firewall to isolate it from the public Internet, or if you simply have a private TCP/IP network, you should replace *Cache.dns* with an identically named and structured file that contains your own, private "root" name servers.

Reverse lookup files. The *reverse lookup file* contains PTR resource records that map IP addresses to their corresponding host names. In a non-DNS environment, a host that needs to resolve an unknown host name from a known IP address uses RARP broadcasts to do so. If DNS is available, the host can instead use it to resolve the unknown host name. The most common application for such reverse lookups is a secure environment that restricts access to IP addresses on an approved list. Reverse lookups are also useful when troubleshooting a TCP/IP network.

Because there is no natural correlation between IP addresses and DNS domain names, some mechanism is needed to map IP addresses to host names. To address this lack, the *in-addr.arpa* domain was created to map IP addresses to host names. One problem arises in doing creating such a mapping file. Whereas the host names become more specific as you move from right to left, IP addresses become more specific as you move from left to right. To resolve this problem, the *in-addr.arpa* data structure reverses the order of the IP address to correspond with that of the host name. Example 14-3 shows the reverse lookup zone file for *ttgnet.com*.

Example 14-3. The reverse lookup zone file for ttgnet.com

```
;  Database file 30.238.204.in-addr.arpa.dns for 30.238.204.in-addr.arpa zone.
;      Zone version:  21
;
@    IN   SOA kerby.ttgnet.com.thompson.ttgnet.com.(
     2         ; serial number
     3600      ; refresh
     600       ; retry
     86400     ; expire
     3600      ) ; minimum TTL
;
;  Zone NS records
;
@    IN   NS  kerby.ttgnet.com.
;
;  Zone records
;
100  IN   PTR betty.ttgnet.com.
101  IN   PTR pebbles.ttgnet.com.
102  IN   PTR bambam.ttgnet.com.
103  IN   PTR dino.ttgnet.com.
104  IN   PTR gazoo.ttgnet.com.
125  IN   PTR sth-gw.ttgnet.com.
162  IN   PTR mandy.ttgnet.com.
163  IN   PTR theodore.ttgnet.com.
165  IN   PTR thoth.ttgnet.com.
166  IN   PTR valentine.ttgnet.com.
167  IN   PTR humphrey.ttgnet.com.
168  IN   PTR poo.ttgnet.com.
187  IN   PTR notebook.ttgnet.com.
188  IN   PTR kiwi.ttgnet.com.
189  IN   PTR gateway.ttgnet.com.
97   IN   PTR fred.ttgnet.com.
98   IN   PTR barney.ttgnet.com.
99   IN   PTR wilma.ttgnet.com.
```

The reverse lookup file has the following components:

- The first section is a comment, identified by the use of semicolon to begin the lines. This section defines the reverse lookup filename, the reverse lookup zone that it identifies, and the zone version number.
- The first and second resource records are the SOA and NS records described in the preceding section on zone files.
- The final section includes several Pointer (PTR) resource records, one for each host in the zone. The first column of each of these resource records identifies the host by specifying the final octet of its IP address. Note that only the final octet is used because this reverse lookup file applies to a Class C network address. If, instead, it applied to a Class B network address, this column would include the third and final octets, and so on. The second column defines the record as a member of the INternet class; the third column defines the record as an pointer record; and the fourth column specifies the fully qualified DNS name associated with the IP address.

Installing the Microsoft DNS Server Service

Install the Microsoft DNS Server service from the Network Services page of the Network property sheet (**Control Panel ➤ Network ➤ Services** tab). Select Add to display the Select Network Service dialog where you can highlight Microsoft DNS Server for installation.

Windows NT displays the Windows NT Setup dialog to prompt for the location of the distribution files; accept the default or specify a new location as appropriate. Windows NT copies the distribution files and returns to the Network property sheet, which now shows the Microsoft DNS Server as an installed service. When you close the installation dialog, Windows NT configures, stores, and reviews the bindings, and then asks if you want to restart your computer to activate the DNS settings.

NOTE Windows NT Server configures the DNS server service by default to start automatically each time the server is booted. You can use the Services applet in Control Panel to modify the startup settings for the DNS server service, or to start, stop, pause, or continue the DNS server service. You can also control the DNS server service from the command prompt, using the commands *net start dns*, *net stop dns*, *net pause dns*, and *net continue dns*.

Managing the Microsoft DNS Server

Installing DNS adds the DNS Manager application to the Administrative Tools (Common) program group. You can use DNS Manager to configure and control all aspects of DNS server operation. At this point, the DNS server is installed and the DNS database has been created, but the DNS server has not yet been configured. The following sections describe how to use DNS Manager to configure and manage the DNS server.

WARNING When you install the Microsoft DNS Server service, DNS Manager automatically adds the newly created server to the Server List. You can also use DNS Manager to manage other DNS servers—both those from Microsoft and those from third parties.

To add an existing DNS server to the Server List, highlight Server List and choose New Server from the DNS menu to display the Add DNS Server dialog. Enter the name or the IP address of the DNS server to be added, and click OK.

When you add a DNS server, DNS Manager automatically creates several files. These files include the *Cache.dns* file needed to locate the Internet root name servers, and the *0.in-addr.arpa*, *127.in-addr.arpa*, and *255.in-addr.arpa* files needed to prevent reverse lookup queries and broadcasts from reaching the root name servers.

Configuring the DNS Server with DNS Manager

After you have installed the Microsoft DNS Server, the next step is to configure it by creating zones, specifying the parameters that control DNS functioning, adding resources records, and so forth. The following sections provide an overview of these tasks. However, DNS is a very complex topic, and a full explanation of each variable and setting is well beyond the scope of this book. For a comprehensive explanation of DNS, see *DNS and BIND*, 2nd ed., by Paul Albitz and Cricket Lin (O'Reilly & Associates, 1997).

Creating a new zone

The first step required to configure the DNS server is to define one or more zones. Before creating a new zone, make sure that the TCP/IP configuration information is set correctly for the computer running Microsoft DNS Server. In particular, verify that IP address, Internet host name, and Internet Domain name are correct. These values are used when creating the new zone.

To create the new zone, start the Domain Name Service Manager (**Start button ➤ Programs ➤ Administrative Tools (Common) ➤ DNS Manager**). In the Server List pane, highlight the name of the DNS server to be configured. From the Server menu, choose DNS and then New Zone to create a new zone. DNS Manager displays the first screen of the Creating new zone for <DNS server name> Wizard.

By default, neither option button in the Zone Type pane is selected. Mark the Primary option button if this will be a primary DNS server, or the Secondary option button if it will be a secondary DNS server. In this case, the Microsoft DNS Server is being installed as the first DNS server, so no other zones exist. I, therefore, marked the Primary option button.

NOTE If you mark the Secondary option button, the Zone and Server fields activate, allowing you to enter values for these fields. You may also point to an existing zone to fill in the appropriate values for these fields automatically.

In the second screen of the Creating new zone for <DNS server name> Wizard, enter the zone name. This is the domain name, e.g., *ttgnet.com*, that is at the root of the DNS name space segment whose resource records will be managed in this zone. DNS Manager fills in the zone file name by appending *.dns* to the zone name you provide. In this case, the default zone file name is *ttgnet.com.dns.* Accept the suggested filename, or enter a different name for the zone file. When you click Next, DNS Manager informs you that all necessary information has been entered, and prompts you to continue. Click Finish to create the zone file. DNS Manager automatically creates the zone and the associated zone file.

WARNING You can create subdomains within a zone to further subdivide the name space managed by the DNS server. For example, I might choose to create subdomains for the Winston-Salem and Rural Hall sites by creating *ws.ttgnet.com* and *rh.ttgnet.com* within the *ttgnet.com* zone.

Use DNS Manager to create one or more subdomains within a zone. To do so, right-click on the zone name in the Server List pane, and select New Domain to display the New Domain dialog. Enter a name for the subdomain in the Domain Name field and click OK.

Creating a reverse lookup zone

The next step needed to configure the DNS server is to create a reverse lookup zone. To do so, follow the procedure described in the preceding section to create a new primary zone. When prompted for the Zone Name, enter the reverse lookup zone name in *in-addr.arpa* format. That is, reverse the network address portion of the IP address in dotted decimal format, and append the string *.in-addr.arpa.*

For example, the IP address of the new DNS server *kerby.ttgnet.com* is *204.238.30.161.* This is a Class C network address, which means that the first three octets comprise the network address. To name the reverse lookup zone, I therefore use the first three octets of the address *204.238.30* and reverse them to *30.238.204.* I then append the string *.in-addr.arpa* to arrive at the final reverse lookup zone name of *30.238.204.in-addr.arpa.* For a Class B network address, use only the first two octets, reversed. For a Class A network address, use only the first octet.

When you create a new primary zone, always create the reverse lookup zone immediately. If you do so, when you subsequently enter A resource records in the primary zone, DNS Manager automatically creates the associated PTR resource records in the reverse lookup zone. If you have not created the reverse lookup zone before entering A resource records, you must enter the reverse lookup PTR resource records manually.

Modifying zone properties

Once you have created the primary and reverse lookup zones, the next step is to set properties for the zone. To do so, right-click the zone name in the Server List pane and select Properties to display the Zone Properties–<zone name> property sheet, as shown in Figure 14-6.

The Zone Properties–<zone name> property sheet contains four tabs, as follows:

General

This page allows you to view and change the name of the zone file associated with the zone. You can also change the zone type from primary to secondary and *vice versa.* If you change a primary zone to a secondary zone, specify one or more IP Masters (primaries) for the secondary zone, and the order in which they should be used.

SOA Record

This page allows you to change the settings for the Start of Authority record, which designates the authoritative name server for the domain. You can change the primary name server DNS name and specify the responsible person (RP) mailbox DNS name. Note that the default RP value is the account that was used to install the DNS server.

A *zone transfer* is the process by which a primary DNS server distributes data to secondary DNS servers. In essence, it is a simple file copy from the

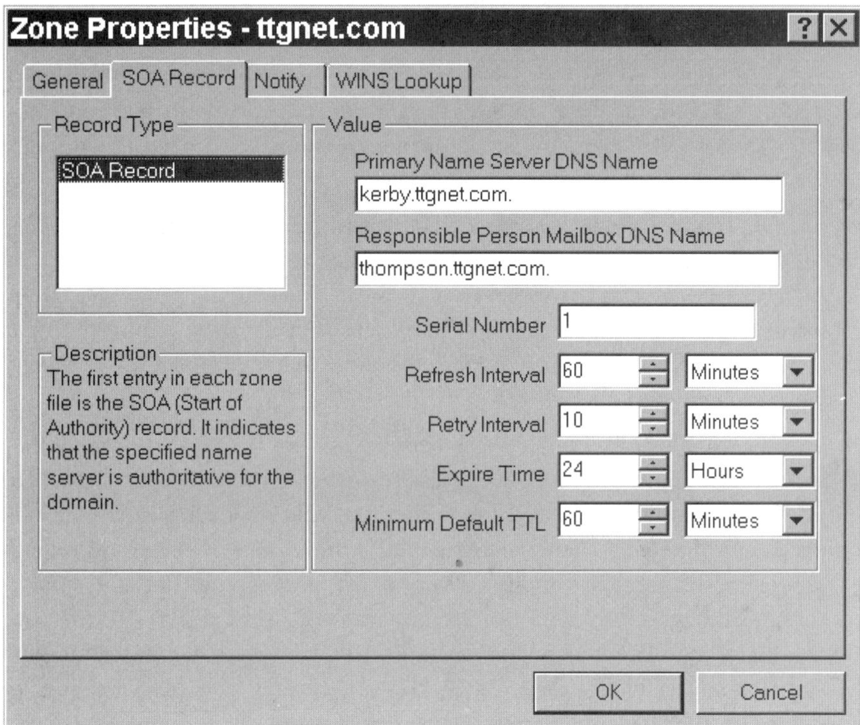

Figure 14-6. The Zone Properties—<zone name> property sheet allows you to configure the zone

primary to the secondary. Values set in the SOA record control the timing of zone transfers. You may set the following values:

Serial Number. This value is automatically incremented each time a change is made to DNS zone data, and determines when zone transfers are automatically initiated. A secondary DNS server stores the serial number associated with the zone data it last retrieved from a primary DNS. When a zone transfer is about to be initiated, the secondary DNS compares the serial number of its data with the current serial number on the primary DNS server. If the serial number on the primary DNS server is higher, the secondary DNS server knows that its data is out of date, and transfers the current data from the primary DNS server. You should not normally modify this value. However, you can increase it arbitrarily to force a refresh of the secondary DNS data.

Refresh Interval. This value, 60 minutes by default, tells the secondary DNS servers how frequently to check the primary DNS server for changes. Setting a low value here means that the secondary DNS servers are more likely to be current, but may also result in more frequent zone transfers and increased network traffic. If the data on your primary DNS server changes relatively infrequently, setting a low value here can ensure that new data is propagated quickly without greatly increasing the number of zone transfers.

Retry Interval. If the secondary DNS server is unable to contact the primary DNS server, this value, 10 minutes by default, specifies how long the secondary DNS server should wait before again trying to contact the primary DNS server.

Expire Time. This value, 24 hours by default, specifies how long a secondary DNS server will continue to respond to queries after it fails to contact its primary DNS server. The assumption is that the zone data on the secondary DNS server becomes more and more dated, and that after the expire time has passed, the secondary DNS server must assume that its data is now invalid and stop responding to queries.

Minimum Default TTL. When a DNS server resolves a query from another DNS server and returns the answer, it also includes a Time to Live (TTL) value, described earlier in this chapter. The TTL value specifies how long the recipient is permitted to cache the returned value. DNS Manager by default sets the TTL to 60 minutes, which is a very short time. If your network configuration is relatively stable, you can set this value to several days. If you are about to make significant changes to your network, e.g., moving your web server to a computer with a different IP address, several days before doing so, reset the TTL value to a small number to ensure that the changes you make are propagated in a timely manner. Note that you should not make the TTL lower than the Refresh Interval.

Notify

This page allows you to specify which secondary DNS servers will be notified when the database of the primary DNS server changes. Enter the IP addresses of the secondary DNS servers to be notified. You may also mark the Only Allow Access From Secondaries Included on Notify List check box to limit access to listed secondary DNS servers.

WINS Lookup

This page allows you to enable and configure WINS resolution. To enable WINS resolution, mark the Use WINS Resolution check box and enter the IP address of one or more WINS Servers. The Settings only affect local server check box determines what data is transferred during a zone transfer. Leave this box unmarked if you want to transfer WINS records during a zone transfer. Mark the box if you want to prevent WINS records from being transferred.

Creating and modifying new host DNS resource records

Compared with other DNS servers, the Microsoft DNS Server does a lot of the work for you. For example, DNS Manager automatically creates and maintains an

A resource record and a PTR resource record for any host that is running DHCP and/or WINS. Chances are, however, that at least some of your hosts are not WINS-enabled or DHCP-enabled, and for these hosts you must enter A resource records and PTR resource records manually.

To create a host resource record, right-click the zone name in the server list, and then select New Host to display the New Host dialog. When you enter the Host Name, specify only the actual host name—including the domain name portion causes an error message. Enter the IP address associated with the host. If you want to create a reverse lookup PTR resource record, mark the check box. When you have entered all of the information for the new host, click Add Host to generate the resource record(s) for that host and display an empty New Host dialog.

When you have finished adding new hosts, click Done. Highlight the zone name in the Server List pane to display the newly created A resource records in the Zone Info pane, or highlight the reverse lookup zone name to display the newly created PTR resource records. Click **View ➤ Refresh** to ensure that all records are displayed. You can modify the values for an existing host simply by double-clicking the host name in the Zone Info pane to display the Properties sheet for that host.

Creating and modifying nonhost DNS resource records

Although DNS Manager creates many of the required A and PTR host resource records for you, it's still up to you to create the supplementary resource records manually. To create a nonhost resource record, right-click the zone name in the server list, and then select New Record to display the New Resource Record dialog.

In the Record Type pane, use the scrolling pick list to select the type of resource record to be created. The fields in the Value pane change according to the record type you select. In the example, I am creating a CNAME resource record to create an alias for *kerby.ttgnet.com* named *www.ttgnet.com*. This will allow users to access my web server, which runs on *kerby*, by using the URL *www.ttgnet.com*. Note that this web server is part of a private intranet, and is located behind a firewall. In other words, you can't get to it, so don't even try.

15

Using Remote Access Service

In this chapter:
- *Introduction to the Microsoft Remote Access Service*
- *Installing and Configuring Remote Access Service*
- *Managing Remote Access Service*

This chapter describes how to install, manage, and use the Microsoft Remote Access Service (RAS). RAS duplicates (and extends) the remote node functionality provided by Novell NetWare Connect (NC). It supports as many as 256 dial-up clients (versus 128 for NC) and comes bundled with NT Server, whereas NC is an optional product, licensed per user at a cost of hundreds or thousands of dollars over the cost of NetWare itself.

The proliferation of notebook computers and the need for traveling salespeople and others to access the corporate network has made products like these increasingly popular. Not a few new installations of NT Server in NetWare shops have been made primarily or solely to provide these remote access functions.

Also, although RAS supports a reasonable number of remote users perfectly well running on the main NT Server, many administrators find that attempting to run the NC NLM on the main NetWare server is an imperfect solution. Accordingly, all but the smallest NC installations typically run on dedicated hardware, further increasing the cost of using NC for remote access versus using NT RAS. RAS also provides a usable alternative for linking remote branch offices, using PPTP and the Internet to provide an inexpensive and secure connection.

NOTE Terminology can get confusing. The Remote Access Service, or RAS, is actually a group of three related Windows NT services. A server running the Remote Access Service is called a Remote Access Service Server, or a RAS server. A RAS server answers incoming calls from remote clients, and provides them with network connections. A workstation running the client software needed to access a RAS server may be called either a RAS client or a Dial-Up Networking (DUN) client—both mean exactly the same thing. When Windows NT Server is used to place a call to another Windows NT server for the purpose of establishing a network connection, it is referred to as a DUN Client. Both RAS server (inbound) and DUN (outbound) connections depend on the underlying group of Windows NT Server services that comprise RAS.

A RAS server can also provide services to clients other than Microsoft RAS clients. For example, a UNIX client running PPP can access a RAS server. Conversely, a Microsoft RAS client can access a remote access networking server other than Microsoft RAS server, e.g., a Telebit NetBlazer terminal server.

Introduction to the Microsoft Remote Access Service

Windows NT Server RAS allows remote computer systems to connect to the Windows NT Server computer using Dial-Up Networking. Once a link has been established, the remote client has a direct network connection to the RAS server, and can access resources on the server and on the network to which the server is connected. This section introduces some fundamental remote access concepts and examines how RAS operates.

Remote Node Versus Remote Control

The term *remote access* is used by different people to mean different things. Remote access products fall into one or both of two categories, called *remote control* and *remote node*. The distinction between these two types of remote access is important, and is illustrated in Figure 15-1.

Remote control software

Products like Carbon Copy and pcAnywhere are called remote control applications. Remote control software comes in two parts. The host portion of the remote control software runs on the remote access server connected to the local area network. The client portion is installed on the notebook or other remote client. The client software passes keystrokes and mouse movements from the remote workstation to the host portion of the remote control software. The host portion in turn acts upon these keystrokes and passes screens back to the remote client.

Using remote control requires that each connected remote user have a corresponding local LAN-connected workstation. Depending on the remote control software you are using, this local computer may be a physical PC, or it may be a virtual PC created on the remote access server by the remote control host software. All processing occurs on the local computer, just as it would on any other local LAN workstation. The remote control software allows you to control this local workstation from your remote client system.

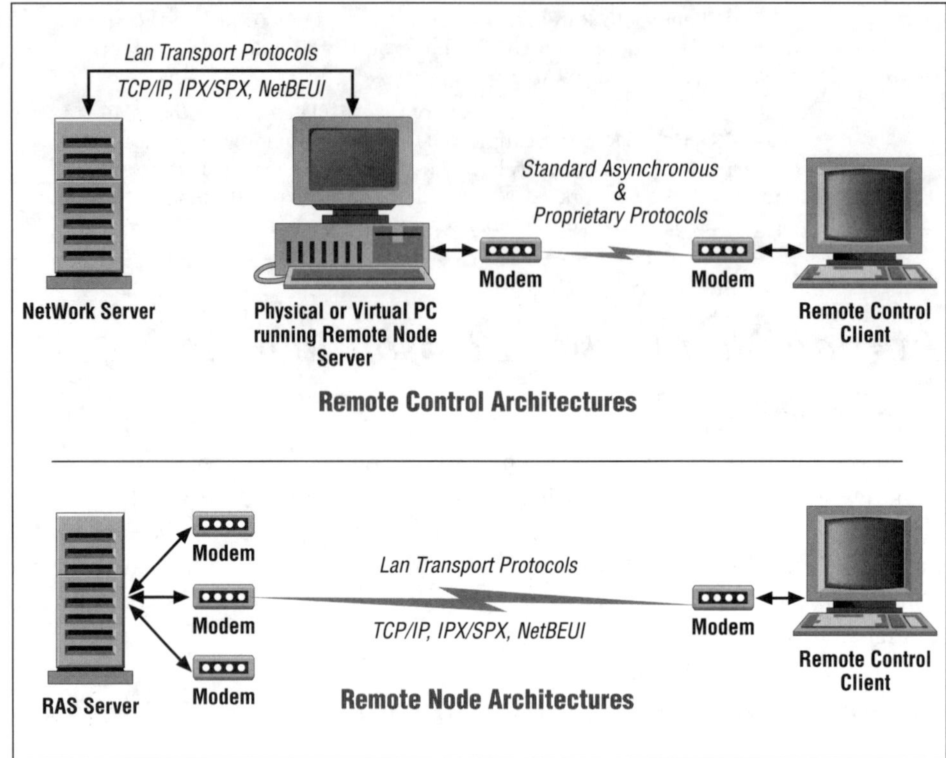

Figure 15-1. Remote access uses standard asynchronous protocols to link the remote client and the server, whereas remote node provides a full network link between remote client and server

When you connect to a remote LAN using a remote control product, the link itself uses only standard dial-up asynchronous protocols to establish and maintain the connection. Proprietary protocols allow the host and client portions of the remote control software to communicate and coordinate activities. Network transport protocols like TCP/IP, IPX/SPX, and NetBEUI are restricted to the LAN, and are not passed across the connection to the remote client. The remote client thus does not actually participate as a network workstation, but merely controls the functioning of the locally connected network workstation from a distance.

Remote node software

Products that provide this type of remote access use industry- and Internet-standard dial-up networking protocols like Point-to-Point Protocol (PPP) to communicate standard Transport Layer and Network Layer protocols like TCP/IP, IPX/SPX, and NetBEUI between the remote access server and the remote client, establishing a true network connection between them. Once connected with a remote node product, the remote workstation can participate as a full network client, just as though it were locally connected to the LAN.

The only real differences between the local node and the remote node workstations exists at the Physical Layer and the Data Link Layer. Where the local workstation may be using Ethernet on unshielded twisted pair cable to connect to the network, the remote workstation substitutes dial-up or ISDN link. At the Network Layer and above, the two workstations are fully equivalent, albeit with a considerable differential in the speed of the connection.

A remote node connection is superior to a remote control connection in nearly every respect. In particular, remote node offers advantages in two areas, scalability and maintainability.

In terms of scalability, consider first where the actual processing occurs under each of the two schemes. With remote control, processing occurs on the locally connected workstation, whereas the remote client functions essentially as a terminal, simply passing keystrokes in and receiving screens in return. The locally connected workstation may be a physical PC, or it may be a virtual PC created on the remote control host system. In either case, the burden of processing remains at the central location. To add remote ports, you must in the first case add more physical PCs to the network. In the second case, you must create additional virtual PCs on the remote access server, which may well require adding more processors or additional memory to the remote access server host. With the remote node solution, on the other hand, all processing occurs on the remote client, removing that burden from computers located at the central site.

Remote node applications like Windows NT Server RAS can easily support dozens or hundreds of remote access ports with minimal resources at the central site. Adding more ports to a remote node server is usually a simple matter of adding the physical ports, and perhaps adding a few megabytes of additional memory to the server. Adding more ports to a remote control server is much more expensive and complex. You must add physical PCs to the network, or add additional processors to the remote access server. You don't want to use inexpensive or cast-off PCs as the local PC either, because the local PC is doing the actual processing. You can use the latest, fastest Pentium notebook as your remote client, but if the local PC is old and slow, the performance experienced by the remote user will reflect that fact. For any but the smallest installations, remote control is often an order of magnitude or more expensive than a remote node solution.

In terms of maintainability, remote node wins hands down. If you visit a typical remote control central site, you see stacks of PCs dedicated to serving remote users. Each of these PCs must be purchased, installed, and maintained. Just managing the cabling necessary to connect all these dedicated PCs to the network is enough to give many administrators nightmares. On the other hand, if you visit a typical remote node central site, you see a single remote access server supporting the same (or a larger) number of clients.

Even this isn't the worst of it. One of the most common problems experienced with remote control applications is caused by conflicts in video settings (e.g., resolution and color depth) between the local dedicated PC and the remote client. For all practical purposes, you usually have little choice but to standardize on a least common denominator for these settings, usually plain vanilla 640X480 VGA in 16 colors. Otherwise, a remote client using an older, less capable notebook will be unable to access your remote access server. Remote clients with the latest, greatest notebooks that can run 1024X768 resolution in 64K colors then often find themselves running vanilla VGA full time, wasting much of the capability of their expensive computers. Remote control software vendors have taken steps to ameliorate some of these problems, but the reality is that maintaining a Remote Control server and its clients is still a labor-intensive process, with many opportunities for conflicts and errors.

Remote control software does have a single advantage over remote node software. If your application requires that a large amount of data be sent across the remote link, remote node software can become unusable. For example, if you load Microsoft Word from the server in a remote control environment, the local dedicated PC loads Word at LAN speed from the server, taking perhaps 15 seconds. If you try to do the same in a remote node environment, it may take an hour or more for the Word application to be transferred across the slow dial-up link from the server to the remote client.

The solution to this problem is usually easy. Simply install Word and your other applications on the hard drive of each remote client system. That way, huge program files and overlays are loaded from local disk and only data needs to be transferred across the slow dial-up link. This works well in most environments. One exception is when you need to access a server resident database application that is written using traditional methods which ship large amounts of data back and forth between the server and the client. A well-written client/server database application eliminates this problem, since the actual processing occurs on the server, and only queries and responses are passed between the server and the client. Note that you can't take the "well-written" part for granted. Many poorly written client/server database applications actually generate as much or more LAN traffic as do traditional database applications.

Remote Access Service Overview

A Windows NT Server Remote Access Service configuration includes the following elements:

Remote Access Service Server
: Remote Access Service is a group of Windows NT services. A server running these services is called a Remote Access Service Server, or RAS server.

Remote Access Service Protocols
: Two separate types of protocols are involved in Remote Access Service. LAN protocols are those used to provide the remote workstation with connectivity to the local area network. Windows NT Server RAS supports the NetBEUI, TCP/IP, and the NWLink IPX/SPX Compatible Transport LAN protocols. Remote Access protocols are used to establish and maintain the link between the remote workstation and the RAS server over which the LAN protocols are used to communicate data. Remote Access protocols supported by Windows NT Server RAS include the Point-to-Point Protocol (PPP), the Microsoft RAS Protocol, and the Point-to-Point Tunneling Protocol (PPTP).

Remote Access Service Connections
: Some means of connecting the remote client to the RAS server is needed for communications to occur. Windows NT Server RAS allows you to use standard telephone lines, ISDN lines, or an X.25 connection for this purpose.

Remote Access Service Clients
: In order to connect to the RAS server, the remote workstation must be running RAS client software. RAS client software is available, either bundled or as an option, for all modern Microsoft operating systems, including Windows NT Server, Windows NT Workstation, Windows 95, Windows for Workgroups, and MS-DOS. Once the client software is installed and configured and a RAS link is established, the client can access resources on the RAS server as though it was connected locally, using the standard means available to the operating system for accessing network resources. For example, a connected remote client running Windows 95 could use the Windows 95 Explorer to browse network resources. Non-Microsoft PPP clients, e.g., UNIX systems, can also connect to and use network resources using RAS (see Figure 15-2).

Remote Access Service server

A Remote Access Services Server, usually called simply a RAS server, is a computer running Windows NT Server with the Remote Access Service installed and running. The Remote Access Service is actually a group of three Windows NT Server services. The *Remote Access Server* service provides the core RAS services. The

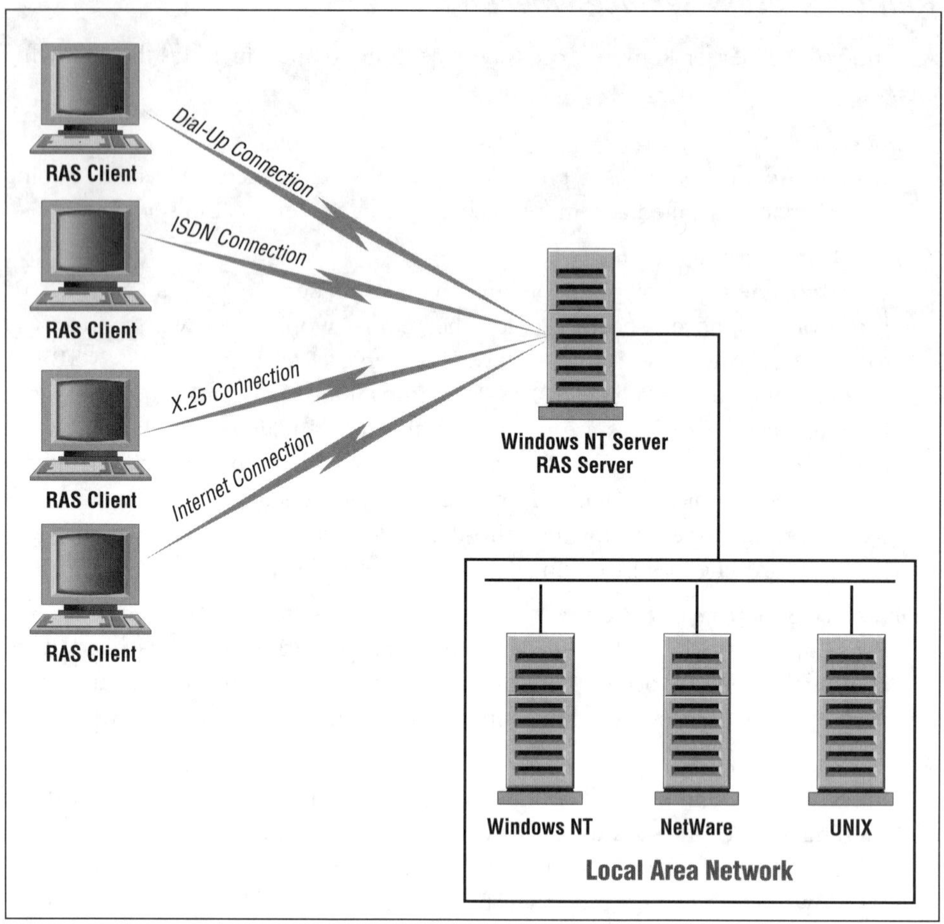

Figure 15-2. Windows NT Server RAS support client connections via standard dial-up lines, ISDN lines, the X.25 packet switching network, and the Internet, and allows those remote clients to access TCP/IP, IPX/SPX, and NetBEUI resources on the local network

Remote Access Connection Manager service and the *Remote Access Autodial Manager* service provide supplementary services that support the core RAS service.

Remote Access Service supports as many as 256 RAS ports, each of which allows an individual remote user or a remote network to connect to your RAS server. For a small RAS server, you may configure the two (or four, depending on your server hardware) internal serial ports as RAS ports. For a medium RAS server, you may install one or more multiport serial cards like those available from DigiBoard, Star Gate Technologies, and others to support RAS ports in groups of 8, 16, or more. Large RAS servers can be configured to use rack-mount modular modem pools like those available from U.S. Robotics, Cisco, and others.

Depending on the number of RAS ports to be installed and how much excess capacity exists on your main Windows NT Server machine, you may elect to run the RAS server on the main server, or you may dedicate a machine as a RAS server. RAS makes minimal demands on system resources. Most existing Windows NT Server machines can easily support one or two RAS ports using the internal "dumb" serial ports, particularly if they use the newer buffered 16550A UARTs rather than the older 16450 unbuffered UARTs. Similarly, using a "smart" multiport serial card with an on-board communications processor will almost certainly allow you to add 8, 16, or even 32 RAS ports to an existing server without adversely impacting its performance. If you need to configure a RAS server with more than 16 or 32 ports, install a separate machine running Windows NT Server to function as a dedicated RAS server.

You are given the opportunity to install and configure the Remote Access Service when you install Windows NT Server. If you elect not to do so, you may install RAS at a later time by invoking the Remote Access Setup routine, as described later in this chapter.

NOTE If the machine upon which you install Windows NT Server has no network adapter installed, the setup routine assumes that that computer will use RAS to connect to a remote network. Accordingly, it automatically invokes RAS Setup.

The *Remote Access Setup* program allows you to configure global options that affect the functioning of the RAS server as a whole. These global options include the LAN protocols available for dial-out, the LAN protocols available for dial-in, the encryption method to be used, and whether Multilink will be used for channel aggregation. These global settings affect all RAS ports. You may also configure each RAS port individually to specify whether that port will be available for dial-out only, dial-in only, or both dial-out and dial-in.

The *Remote Access Admin* program allows you to start, stop, pause, and continue the RAS server itself, to grant permissions to users, to monitor RAS and port statistics, and to view and disconnect current RAS users. You can also use the *Dial-Up Monitor* program to perform similar functions.

Remote Access Service protocols

Windows NT Server RAS uses two different types of protocols to establish and maintain connectivity between the RAS server and the RAS Client. LAN protocols like TCP/IP, IPX/SPX, and NetBEUI provide LAN connectivity between the server and the client. Remote Access Protocols like Point-to-Point Protocol (PPP), Point-to-Point Tunneling Protocol (PPTP), and Microsoft RAS Protocol control the communication of data across the wide area network (WAN) link. In essence, the

Remote Access Protocols provide the highway to link the RAS server and the RAS Client, and the LAN protocols manage the traffic (LAN packets) carried by that highway.

Remote Access Service LAN protocols. Windows NT Server RAS supports the same transport protocols as those available for local connections, namely, TCP/IP, NWLink IPX/SPX Compatible Transport, and NetBEUI. This range of protocol support means that you can provide RAS clients with access to nearly any resource connected to the local network, including UNIX hosts, the Internet, NetWare servers, and connected peer networks running Microsoft Networking.

When you install and configure RAS, all of the transport protocols in use on the local server are automatically enabled for both inbound and outbound RAS connections. RAS LAN protocol support is specified globally for all ports, so if you enable or disable a transport protocol, you do so for all ports. For each transport protocol that you enable, you specify whether remote clients using that protocol can access only the server upon which RAS is running or can access the entire network. You might, for example, allow remote clients using NWLink to access the entire network, while limiting remote clients using TCP/IP to accessing only the RAS server.

If you configure TCP/IP to allow access to the entire network, you must also specify how IP addresses will be assigned to remote clients running TCP/IP. If you configure NWLink to allow access to the entire network, you must also specify how IPX network numbers will be assigned to remote clients running NWLink. Remote clients running NetBEUI can be restricted to accessing only the RAS server or can be granted access to the entire network without additional configuration.

Using TCP/IP with RAS

The TCP/IP transport protocol is the foundation of the Internet, and is also the protocol chosen by most network administrators to support their wide area networks. Windows NT Server RAS provides complete support for remote clients running TCP/IP.

IP address assignment

Windows NT Server allows TCP/IP clients to themselves specify the IP address to be used, or to be assigned an IP address by the server. In the former case, you must configure the RAS server to allow the clients to request a specific IP address. From the client side, the IP address to be used is entered as a part of the phonebook entry for the RAS server, or is specified by the remote caller at the time the call is initiated. In the latter case, the RAS server can assign an IP address to the remote client in one of two ways.

First, you may allocate a pool of IP addresses for RAS clients. When a RAS client using TCP/IP establishes a connection to the RAS server, it is assigned an available IP address from the pool for the duration of the connection. When the call is terminated, the pooled address becomes available for reassignment to a subsequent caller. Second, you may configure RAS to use a DHCP server located on your network. In this case, the RAS server again automatically assigns each RAS client running TCP/IP an IP address when the connection is made, and then recycles the address when the connection terminates. The advantage to using DHCP is that you avoid fragmenting your available IP addresses by dedicating some of them to RAS clients. With DHCP, a RAS client is assigned an IP address as needed from the pool used by all TCP/IP clients on the network, local or remote.

DNS and WINS name resolution

Running TCP/IP requires that some means be made available to resolve host names to numeric IP addresses. Windows NT Server provides four methods for doing so: the Domain Name Service (DNS) Server; the Windows Internet Naming Service (WINS); the *hosts* and *lmhosts* files; and broadcast resolution. RAS clients running TCP/IP can use any or all of these means of name resolution.

NOTE By default, RAS clients are automatically assigned to the same DNS and WINS servers used by the RAS server itself. You can override this automatic assignment, if necessary, but only by editing the Registry. This is one of the very few operations in Windows NT Server networking that requires manual Registry editing.

Using NWLink with RAS

Using the NWLink IPX/SPX Compatible Transport protocol makes it easy for your RAS clients to access NetWare server resources on the LAN. So long as the remote client has a NetWare redirector installed, NWLink provides the transport necessary to allow it to communicate with NetWare servers. A RAS server configured to support NWLink can also provide the IPX network number, the IPX routing, and the Service Advertising Protocol (SAP) services needed by the RAS client to access Novell file and print services.

By default, the IPX network number needed by the client is provided by the RAS server, using any of the following methods:

Randomly Generated Network Numbers
: You can configure RAS to generate a random network number for each RAS NWLink client as that client connects to the RAS server. The RAS server generates a random network number, and then uses NetWare RIP (not to be

confused with Internet Routing Information Protocol) to ensure that that network number is not already in use on the network before assigning it to the RAS client.

Network Numbers Assigned from a Pool
: You can override automatic network number assignment and specify that RAS NWLink callers are to be assigned a network number from a predefined static pool of network numbers. Because each connected NWLink RAS client has a separate, manually assigned network number, this method gives you more control over network number assignment, making it easier to monitor and secure your network. If you choose this method, make sure that the network numbers you assign to the pool are not currently in use and are not otherwise subject to being assigned automatically by another server.

Single Network Number Used for All Clients
: You can also configure the RAS server to assign a single network number to all connected RAS NWLink clients. Doing so has the drawback that clients are no longer uniquely identified by network number, making monitoring and security of the network more difficult. However, many administrators find this minor loss acceptable, because using a single network number allows all RAS NWLink clients to share a single routing table entry and minimizes RIP broadcasts.

The last method of assigning network numbers is to allow the RAS NWLink client to request a specific network number. This method is seldom used because it introduces a security hole whereby a RAS NWLink client can request, intentionally or otherwise, the same IPX network number used by an earlier caller and thereby gain unauthorized access to the resources available to the earlier caller.

Using NetBEUI with RAS

Windows NT Server 4.0 RAS supports NetBEUI primarily for backwards compatibility with earlier versions of Microsoft operating systems. If all of your RAS clients are running up-to-date versions of Microsoft operating systems, i.e., Windows 95 or Windows NT 4.0, you have no need of NetBEUI support on your RAS server. On the other hand, if you have RAS clients running early versions of Windows NT, Windows 3.11 for Workgroups, or the MS-DOS RAS client, then you must install NetBEUI support to allow these clients to access your RAS server. Even if all of your RAS clients are running current versions of Windows, you must also install NetBEUI support if those clients need to access a locally attached peer network that supports only NetBEUI.

Remote Access Service remote access protocols

The second protocol component of Windows NT Server RAS is the Remote Access Protocol support that establishes and maintains the physical link between the RAS server and the RAS client. This physical link provides a "tunnel" through which the LAN protocols described in the preceding section route the actual data packets used to communicate data between the RAS client and the local network.

Windows NT Server 4.0 RAS supports four of these Remote Access Protocols: Point-to-Point Protocol (PPP); Serial Line Internet Protocol (SLIP); Microsoft RAS Protocol; and the NetBIOS Gateway. The Point-to-Point Tunneling Protocol is a special case. It can be considered both a Remote Access Protocol and a connection method, and is described in the following section. SLIP, the Microsoft RAS Protocol, and the NetBIOS Gateway are supported primarily for backwards compatibility with earlier standards.

- *SLIP* is an old and obsolescent UNIX protocol that has been largely superseded by PPP. Windows NT Server 4.0 RAS supports SLIP only for outbound calling, and only then to access UNIX hosts that do not offer PPP support. SLIP supports only the TCP/IP protocol.
- *Microsoft RAS Protocol* is a proprietary NetBIOS implementation used by previous versions of RAS, including those in Windows NT 3.1, LAN Manager, Windows 3.11 for Workgroups, and MS-DOS. A RAS client connecting to an older RAS server must use NetBEUI transport. The RAS server then provides gateway support to that client, allowing it to access resources on TCP/IP, IPX/SPX, or NetBEUI servers. Again, in the Windows NT 4.0 environment, this protocol is useful for placing outbound calls to RAS servers running older versions of RAS and for receiving inbound calls from older RAS clients.
- *NetBIOS Gateway* is the mechanism by which earlier versions of RAS provided RAS clients with connectivity to TCP/IP and IPX/SPX resources on the local network. The NetBIOS Gateway translates packets from the NetBEUI form used by the RAS connection to TCP/IP or IPX/SPX packets as needed to access resources on a LAN running multiple protocols. The NetBIOS Gateway is an imperfect solution at best, because it does not allow remote clients to run applications that require native TCP/IP or IPX/SPX support. Windows NT Server RAS defaults to using the NetBIOS Gateway for RAS clients running NetBEUI.

The Remote Access Protocol of choice is PPP. PPP is an Internet-standard group of protocols that function at the Physical, Data Link, Network, Transport, and Session Layers of the OSI Reference Model to provide numerous services, from framing at the lower layers to authentication at the higher layers. As an Internet standard, PPP is broadly supported throughout the industry. Running PPP on your

Windows NT RAS server allows interoperability between your server and remote access servers and clients from other manufacturers.

PPP also supports the use of multiple protocol stacks, allowing you to run any combination transport protocols, including TCP/IP, IPX/SPX, and NetBEUI, on your servers and clients. Applications written to the Windows Sockets API, the NetBIOS interface, or the IPX interface can communicate successfully using a PPP connection. A PPP connection is established and negotiated using the following steps:

1. The PPP client system initiates a call to the RAS server.
2. The RAS server answers the call and negotiates PPP framing rules with the caller. This step establishes a PPP connection between the two systems and allows subsequent frames to be communicated.
3. The RAS server negotiates with the client to determine the PPP authentication method to be used, i.e., PAP, MS-CHAP, or SPAP. The method ultimately selected depends on the capabilities of the client and upon the configurations of both the RAS client and the RAS server. If the client supports MS-CHAP encryption and the RAS server is configured to require it, all subsequent frames exchanged between the systems are encrypted.
4. After authentication is complete, the client requests that the server provide a TCP/IP, IPX/SPX, or NetBEUI connection. The server enables the requested protocol and configures itself to provide it (see Figure 15-3).

Remote Access Service connections

Windows NT Server 4.0 RAS allows you to support remote clients directly using standard telephone lines, ISDN lines, or the X.25 data network. You can also allow remote clients to access local network resources across the Internet.

Standard telephone lines. Doubtless, the most common means used to connect RAS clients to a RAS server is a standard telephone line and modem. This method is simple, relatively inexpensive, and provides adequate performance for most applications. Windows NT Server 4.0 supports hundreds of models of modem, including the latest V.34 modems that offer 33.6 Kbps throughput. Even if your modems are not on the Windows Hardware Compatibility List, chances are good that you will be able to use them without difficulty.

Windows NT Server successfully detects most modems automatically, making installation very straightforward. It also supports several rack-mount modem pool devices, including those from U.S. Robotics and others. Windows NT Server 4.0 RAS supports the enhanced features of modern modems, including error checking and data compression. The software compression used by Windows NT Server RAS is nearly always more efficient than modem hardware compression, because

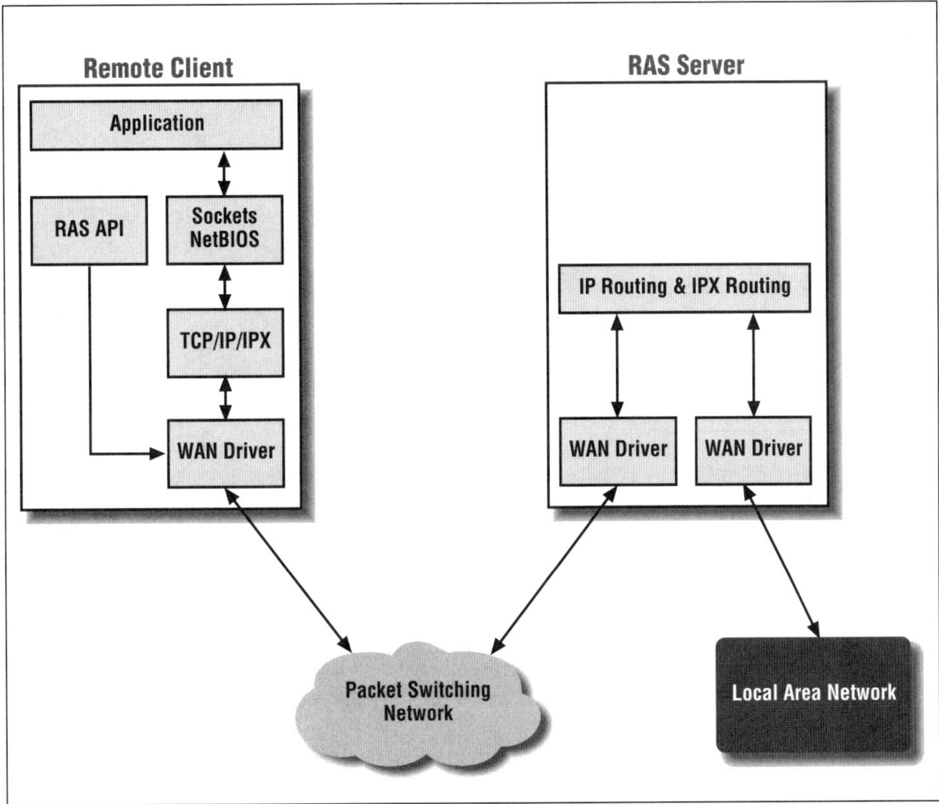

Figure 15-3. The Remote Access Service PPP Architecture links the remote client to the RAS server using WAN drivers, and routes IP and IPX packets internally to the locally connected LAN

the software compression algorithm can "see" more of the data simultaneously than can the modem compression algorithm.

WARNING If your modems use MNP5 rather than V.42bis for data compression, make sure to turn off hardware compression. Windows NT Server RAS applies an efficient software data compression scheme before sending data to the modem. Attempting to use MNP5 compression on already-compressed data can cause that data actually to increase in size, slowing throughput. V.42bis is smart enough to recognize data that has already been compressed, and does not attempt further compression.

ISDN. You can use Integrated Services Digital Network (ISDN) to provide end-to-end digital data communication between the RAS server and a fixed point, such as the home of a telecommuter. As ISDN lines become more ubiquitous, this may change. Some day, roving users may be able to use ISDN from their hotel rooms or while waiting for a plane, but right now those users are limited to standard dial-up connections.

Standard dial-up telephone lines provide nominal data rates as high as 33.6 Kbps, although realistically this speed is often limited by line conditions to something in the mid-20s or lower. ISDN uses one or two 64 Kbps B-channels to provide cumulative throughput as high as 128 Kbps, although the top speed is often limited to 115 Kbps because of limitations in PC serial ports. ISDN connections therefore run at approximately four times the speed of a dial-up connection.

When you use standard telephone lines to connect to a RAS server, you are reminded frequently by delays and slow response that the server is at the other end of a very long wire. If you look at the numbers alone, you might reasonably believe that an ISDN connection would provide noticeably better performance than a dial-up connection using standard phone lines, but that it would appear closer in "feel" to a dial-up connection than to a local LAN connection. Strangely, this is not the case. With ISDN, most users feel as though they are connected locally to the server. There are still response lags, certainly, but overall the ISDN connection performs much like the local LAN connection.

There are three drawbacks to ISDN relative to standard telephone lines:

Availability
: ISDN is not yet widely deployed, so you may not be able to get it even if you want it. Even if the telephone company central office that serves your location offers ISDN service, you may be located too far from the CO switch. ISDN is typically limited to 18,000 feet of copper between the switch and the user demarc.

Incompatibilities and lack of standardization
: Although using a standard phone line and modem is pretty much plug and play, using ISDN can be a hair-pulling experience. Just getting connected to someone at the phone company who knows anything at all about ISDN can be nearly impossible. Even using the same make and model of ISDN adapter on both ends of the connection is no guarantee of trouble-free connections. Attempting to use different equipment at each end is almost a guarantee that you will experience problems. Even once the ISDN line is installed, configured properly and working, your troubles are not necessarily over. One day you may find that your ISDN line has suddenly stopped working for no apparent reason. It can take days, or even weeks, to get such a problem resolved.

Cost

This may or may not be a major factor. Telephone companies are all over the map when it comes to charging for ISDN service. Some local phone companies provide flat rate (or unmetered) ISDN service at a reasonable monthly charge. Others may provide unmetered ISDN, but at a very high monthly rate. Others may charge a low monthly rate for ISDN, but insist on a per minute charge for all usage, typically a cent or two per minute per B channel. At first glance, this may not sound like much, but when you add up the number of minutes in a month and multiply by the per minute charge, you find that you can easily run up phone bills of several thousand dollars a month for each ISDN line under such a billing arrangement. Still other phone companies offer you the worst of both worlds by charging both a high monthly fee and per minute charges.

Don't let this turn you off to the idea of using ISDN. For most RAS servers, the advantages of using ISDN are worth the hassles involved in getting it installed and running. Various organizations are defining standards for ISDN that will eventually make using it as routine as using a voice telephone line. Phone companies are gradually getting their acts together, with the goal of providing the same level of support for ISDN lines as you have come to expect for voice lines. Likewise, equipment manufacturers are making strides toward ensuring that their equipment is interoperable with equipment from other manufacturers. The long-term outlook for ISDN is good, although it is likely that just as ISDN matures, other technologies like xDSL will overtake it in popularity.

X.25. X.25 is an obsolescent but universally available data communications service. Originally designed and implemented when the telephone network infrastructure was still largely analog, X.25 offers limited speed (up to 56 Kbps) and devotes a great deal of overhead toward ensuring reliable delivery of packets. X.25 provides connection-oriented, reliable packet switching services at the Network Layer, allowing it to be used for either static point-to-point connections via permanent virtual circuits or for switched connections via switched virtual circuits.

X.25 requires a Packet Assembler/Disassembler (PAD) on each end of the connection. At the originating end, the PAD converts a serial byte stream into packets and places them on the X.25 network. The destination PAD receives the packets and reconverts them to a serial byte stream. Many routers have, or can be, upgraded to provide PAD functionality.

X.25 is not the protocol of choice for most wide area networks. However, it remains an ITU (formerly CCITT) standard and is available worldwide. The low speed and relatively high cost of X.25 limit it to applications where it is the only game in town. In third-world countries X.25 is often the means available to connect a WAN. If your WAN is limited geographically to the United States and other developed countries, X.25 is usually not a cost-effective choice.

Windows NT Server RAS supports X.25 using PADs and X.25 smart cards. You can also use a modem to establish a link as needed to dial-up X.25 providers like SprintNet.

Point-to-Point Tunneling Protocol (PPTP). The Point-to-Point Tunneling Protocol (PPTP), jointly developed by Microsoft and U.S. Robotics, is a proposed Internet standard that supports the creation of secure virtual private networks using insecure public data networks like the Internet for transport. To all intents and purposes, PPTP allows you to incorporate the Internet as a part of your corporate Intranet, without sacrificing security. Many corporations that, because of security concerns, now use private leased data lines to link branch offices will find that PPTP offers the same or higher level of security while allowing them to use their current Internet connections to replace the leased lines.

PPTP uses the RSA Data Security, Inc. RC-4 encryption algorithm and the Data Encryption Standard (DES) to ensure that packets intercepted between the source and destination servers cannot be read by the eavesdropper. After PPTP is used to establish a secure virtual circuit between the two servers, that circuit can be used as a tunnel to carry packets from various transport protocols, including TCP/IP, IPX/SPX, and NetBEUI. The transport datagrams are envaginated within IP packets for transmission to the recipient, where they are processed and decrypted by PPTP and passed in unencrypted form to the standard protocol stack.

Using PPTP to its maximum advantage requires not just that the end points be running PPTP, but that the Internet Service Provider at each end and the intervening routers also be PPTP-aware. PPTP is currently implemented on Windows NT Server 4.0 and the U.S. Robotics Total Control Enterprise Hub. The latest release of the Cisco IOS operating system also provides PPTP support, and other big-name router vendors are coming on board quickly. It is likely that by 1998 the majority of the Internet will support PPTP, making it a viable secure transport protocol for general usage.

Multilink channel aggregation. Windows NT Server 4.0 provides a service called Multilink that allows you to combine multiple communications channels into a single virtual communications channel that provides higher throughput. For example, you might use Multilink to combine two 28.8 Kbps dial-up channels into a single 56 Kbps virtual channel.

Multilink allows you to combine dial-up connections, ISDN connections, or a combination of the two. Multilink gives you the flexibility to create a communications channel that is just fast enough for your needs. For example, you might want to provide a link between your home office and a branch office across town to be used to exchange email and do an occasional file transfer. In the past, if you found that a single V.34 28.8 Kbps link was not quite fast enough to serve your needs, your alternative was to install a dedicated leased line at a cost of perhaps several hundred dollars per month. Using Multilink, you can instead simply install another dial-up connection at each end and join the two to provide 56 Kbps throughput between the servers.

Remote Access Service clients

Windows NT Server 4.0 RAS supports Microsoft clients running Windows NT, Windows 95, Windows for Workgroups, LAN Manager, or MS-DOS. RAS also allows PPP clients, e.g., UNIX hosts, to establish a connection. The capabilities of each of these clients vary in terms of protocols and authentication methods supported, as follows:

Recent versions of Windows clients
: The RAS client software supplied with Windows NT 3.5x and higher and with Windows 95 supports all of the features of Windows NT Server 4.0 RAS. These clients connect to the RAS server using PPP, and can use any authentication method supported by NT Server 4.0 RAS. Because they connect using PPP, these clients can establish direct network connections using TCP/IP, IPX/SPX, or NetBEUI transport. Windows NT 4.0 clients support PPTP connection. PPTP support for the Windows 95 RAS client has been announced, and should be available by the time you read this.

Windows NT 3.1, Windows for Workgroups, LAN Manager, and MS-DOS clients
: These clients use the Microsoft RAS protocol to connect to a RAS server running any version of Microsoft RAS. Because this client does not use PPP, it can establish a direct network connection only using NetBEUI. These clients can use the RAS NetBIOS Gateway to access NetBIOS servers running TCP/IP and IPX/SPX applications, but they cannot use applications that require native client support for TCP/IP or IPX/SPX.

PPP clients
: Windows NT Server 4.0 RAS supports non-Microsoft PPP clients directly. RAS negotiates PPP authentication with such clients automatically, and does not require any special settings or configuration to do so. The PPP client can establish a direct network connection using any combination of TCP/IP, IPX/SPX, or NetBEUI transport protocols.

Remote Access Service as an Alternative to NetWare Connect

Novell NetWare Connect has probably been responsible for more copies of Windows NT Server being purchased than have all the efforts of Microsoft's Marketing Department. It's not that NetWare Connect isn't a good product. It is. It's simply that Microsoft bundles remote access as a standard part of its operating system, whereas Novell positions remote access as an expensive option to NetWare.

Consider the relative costs involved in creating a remote access solution with Windows NT Server versus doing the same with Novell NetWare Connect 2. Windows NT Server out of the box supports up to 256 remote clients. Novell NetWare Connect is licensed per user, with a 2-user version list priced at $395, an 8-user version at $1,495, and a 32-user version at $4,495. Matching the number of users supported natively by Windows NT Server with NetWare Connect carries a suggested retail price of $35,960.

NetWare Connect also tends to be more hardware intensive than Windows NT Server RAS. Small Windows NT Server RAS configurations, perhaps 2 to 16 ports, can often run on the main Windows NT Server machine without noticeably affecting performance. On the other hand, Novell, acknowledging that all but the smallest NetWare Connect installations should run on a dedicated server, bundles a NetWare runtime license with the 8-user and 32-user versions of NetWare Connect.

In larger configurations, the fact that NetWare Connect allows a maximum of 128 remote clients per server versus the 256 remote clients per server support by Windows NT Server RAS can become a major cost issue. Adding just one more client to NetWare Connect requires that you buy another server. Conversely, Windows NT Server RAS can easily be expanded incrementally on a single server. As the number of RAS ports grow, you can simply add more RAM and perhaps another processor now and then.

Although there is a great deal of overlap in functionality between Microsoft NT Server RAS and Novell NetWare Connect, there are also some differences. Novell NetWare Connect offers the following advantages:

Remote Control support

NetWare Connect supports both remote control and remote node applications. Microsoft Windows NT Server RAS provides only remote node functionality. As I mentioned earlier in this chapter, remote node is a more generally useful technology. However, there are times when remote control is just what you need to get the job done. For example, a corporate help desk might use remote control to "look over the shoulder" of a remote user while resolving a problem.

Asynchronous services for LAN users.
: Windows NT Server RAS is used primarily to provide network connections to remote dial-up users. NetWare Connect does this as well, but it also provides asynchronous connection services to the local users on the LAN. For example, the NetWare Asynchronous Services Interface (NASI) support included with NetWare Connect allows you to establish a central modem pool and allow any user on the LAN to access a pooled modem via the network. Windows NT Server RAS doesn't offer equivalent functionality, but this lack won't be noticed by most network administrators. The use of NASI and similar technologies to provide shared asynchronous services to network users is much less important now than it was only a couple of years ago due to the rapid proliferation of services on the Internet. Few users have any need to call bulletin boards and similar dial-up services nowadays.

Client support
: In addition to the DOS and Windows clients supported by Windows NT Server RAS, NetWare Connect offers full support for Macintosh clients. Windows NT Server RAS does support the Macintosh, but only as a generic PPP client. If you need to support remote Macintosh clients and require that the remote client software support full authentication and security features, NetWare Connect is the obvious choice.

Management
: NetWare Connect includes NetWare ConnectView 2, a Windows-based management application that offers considerably more power and sophistication than the equivalent Remote Access Admin application used to manage Windows NT Server RAS. The maturity of NetWare as a network operating system and of Novell as an NOS vendor is obvious when these two products are compared. Remote Access Admin offers a full assortment of the basic tools needed to manage RAS servers, but it goes no further. ConnectView 2, on the other hand, goes beyond the basics. For example, NetWare ConnectView 2 allows you to implement full cost accounting and auditing for the service, even to the extent of allowing differing costs to be assigned to different types of connections.

If what you need is a remote access server to provide network connections for dialin clients running MS-DOS and Windows, NetWare Connect 2 is overkill in terms of functionality, hardware requirements, and cost. Windows NT Server RAS will do the same job much more economically, and also provides PPTP, Multilink, and other server-to-server connection tools that NetWare Connect 2 does not provide. Using NetWare Connect 2 makes sense only if you require one or more of the capabilities unique to it and are willing to pay the price for them.

Installing and Configuring Remote Access Service

You are given an opportunity to install and configure the Remote Access Service when you install Windows NT Server. If you elect not to do so at install time, you may install RAS at any time thereafter by following the steps described later in this section. To install RAS separately, you must be logged on to the server as an administrator.

The only things needed to install RAS are one or more modems, ISDN terminal adapters, or X.25 PADs, an available serial port for each device, and the necessary connections to the telephone company or other service provider. Beyond these fundamental requirements, consider the following issues when deciding how to configure your RAS server:

Small RAS configurations

If you plan to install only one or two RAS ports, you can do so on your main Windows NT Server system using its standard serial ports and ordinary external modems. Almost any system running Windows NT Server has sufficient resources to support such a configuration without a noticeable impact on performance. Even if you don't plan to provide RAS services to general users, it's worthwhile to install this minimum RAS configuration if only to support remote server maintenance.

Medium RAS configurations

If your RAS configuration will be somewhat larger, say 8 to 16 ports, you can install one or more multiport serial cards in your main server. These cards have on-board processors that off-load much of the burden of handling communications I/O from the main server, allowing it to support many more RAS ports without degradation. In fact, a well-designed multiport serial card with an efficient driver can actually make fewer demands on server resources when running 16 clients simultaneously than those made by only 2 clients running on standard 16550 serial ports.

Large RAS configurations

Any RAS configuration with more than 16 ports (32 at the outside) should be run on a dedicated Windows NT Server system. With large configurations, attempting to use individual modems connected to multiport serial cards becomes increasingly difficult, if only from the standpoint of attempting to manage the rats' nest of cables required to connect all the individual components. For large configurations, investigate the rack-mount solutions available from U.S. Robotics and others.

NOTE Whether your RAS server has 1 port or 256 ports, make sure that every hardware component you install appears on the Windows NT Hardware Compatibility List (HCL). Although even Microsoft admits that you can successfully use modems that do not appear on the HCL, doing so almost ensures that you will have problems sooner or later. Don't even think about attempting to use a multiport serial card or rack-mount modem chassis that does not appear on the HCL. You'll waste a lot of time and money, and in the end it probably won't work well, if at all.

Installing Remote Access Service

Install the Remote Access Service from the Network Services page of the Network property sheet (**Control Panel ➤ Network ➤ Services** tab). Select Add to display the Select Network Service dialog where you can highlight Remote Access Service for installation.

Windows NT displays the Windows NT Setup dialog to prompt for the location of the distribution files; accept the default or specify a new location as appropriate. After Windows NT copies the distribution files, RAS Setup searches your hardware configuration to determine whether one or more RAS-capable devices (e.g., modems) are already installed. If RAS Setup routine locates one or more such devices, it proceeds directly to configuring those devices, which is described in the following section. If RAS Setup finds no RAS-capable devices, it displays a dialog that prompts you to install a RAS-capable device.

If you choose to install a modem, RAS Setup invokes the Install New Modem wizard. If you choose not to install a modem, RAS Setup terminates. Later you can install a modem and run RAS Setup to install it as a RAS-capable device.

If you mark the "Don't detect my modem; I will select it from a list" check box, or if Windows NT Server is unable to detect the installed modem, you will be given the opportunity to select the installed modem from a list of available modems for which Windows NT Server has drivers. If your modem is not on this list, but you have a Windows NT 4.0 driver provided by the modem manufacturer, you may install the new modem using the Have Disk option.

I have successfully installed many different modem makes and models using Windows NT Server autodetection, and have never seen it fail to detect the installed modem and configure it properly. However, I have also received many reports from those who were not so fortunate, so it seems likely that Windows NT automatic modem detection is an imperfect method at best. Be prepared to specify your modem manually.

Make sure that the modem to be configured is turned on. Also, make sure that no program is using the modem. In particular, non-TAPI compliant communications software monopolizes the modem, making it unavailable to other Windows programs, including the Install New Modem setup routine. Click Next to continue installing the modem. Windows NT Server scans all installed communications ports to detect a physically installed modem. When it locates an unknown modem attached to a communications port, it then queries the modem repeatedly, using the modem's response strings to isolate the make and model of the modem. If this process detects one or more modems, Windows NT Server displays the Install New Modem screen showing the type of modem detected on each active communications port.

Verify that the modem type displayed is correct. If it is not, click Change to display a list of available modem makes and models, and specify the correct modem manually. After you have done so, click Next to display the Location Information dialog.

Use the What country are you in now? drop-down list to select your country. Type your area or city code in the What area (or city) code are you in now? field. If your telephone system requires that you dial a special code for an outside line, enter it in the If you dial a number to access and outside line, what is it? field. Select the Tone dialing or Pulse dialing option button, as appropriate. Click Next. Windows NT Server installs your modem using the parameters you have provided, and displays a message to notify you that the modem has been set up successfully. Choose Finish to complete installing the new modem. Windows NT Server displays the Add RAS Device dialog with the newly installed modem selected.

At this point, the modem is available to Windows NT Server, but has not yet been configured as a RAS Device for use by the Remote Access Service. Use the RAS Capable Devices drop-down list to select a device to be installed as a RAS Device. Click OK to install this RAS-capable device as a RAS device and proceed to Remote Access Setup. You may also click Install Modem to install another modem or Install X25 PAD to install an X.25 Packet Assembler-Disassembler. X.25 is a slow, expensive data communication technology that is obsolescent in the United States, although its near-universal availability often makes it the only usable connection method elsewhere in the world, particularly in third-world countries.

Configuring Remote Access Service

After you have installed one or more RAS-capable devices as RAS devices, you must then configure each RAS device and port. Remote Access Setup allows you to specify the following items for each installed port:

- Whether that port will be used to dial out only, to receive calls only, or to do both. By default, Windows NT Server configures RAS ports to receive calls only.
- Which transport protocols are supported for inbound and outbound calls, and how they are to be configured. Windows NT Server supports NetBEUI, TCP/IP, and IPX in any combination for inbound and outbound calls.
- What authentication method, if any, will be required to establish a RAS connection.
- Whether Multilink will be enabled to allow channel aggregation.

To configure a RAS Device, display the Remote Access Setup dialog. If you are installing Remote Access Service, this is done automatically as a part of setup. You may also run Remote Access Setup any time you need to reconfigure RAS devices. To do so, display the Services page on the Network property sheet, highlight Remote Access Service, and click Properties.

If your server already has one or more modems installed as RAS Devices, examine the Remote Access Setup dialog Type column carefully. Windows NT Server 4.0 uses a new type of modem driver, which is displayed in this column as (unimodem). If a currently installed modem is instead shown as Modem (modem.inf), this indicates that it is using the old type of modem driver. Delete that device and reinstall it. Otherwise, RAS will not work properly. If you made changes to the standard *modem.inf* file for that modem to modify the behavior of that modem, save a copy of *modem.inf* before deleting it. Highlight the RAS Device to be configured and click Configure to display the Configure Port Usage dialog.

Windows NT Server assumes that a RAS port will be used to support callers dialing in to the RAS server, and therefore by default configures RAS Devices to Receive calls only. If this port will instead be used only to place outgoing calls, click the Dial out only option button. If the port will be used for both inbound and outbound calls, click the Dial out and Receive calls option button. When the port is configured properly, click OK to return to the Remote Access Setup dialog.

Click Network to display the Network Configuration dialog. The appearance of this dialog differs, depending on the settings you made for the port in the Configure Port Usage dialog, as follows:

- If you configure the port as Dial out only, Windows NT Server displays the Network Configuration dialog. This version of the dialog allows you only to specify which transport protocols will be available for outbound calls.
- If you configure the port as Dial out and Receive calls, Windows NT Server displays the Network Configuration dialog, as shown in Figure 15-4. This version of the dialog allows you to set options for both inbound and outbound calls.
- If you configure the port as Receive calls only, Windows NT Server displays the Network Configuration dialog similar to Figure 15-4, but with the check boxes for Dial out Protocols grayed out and inactive.

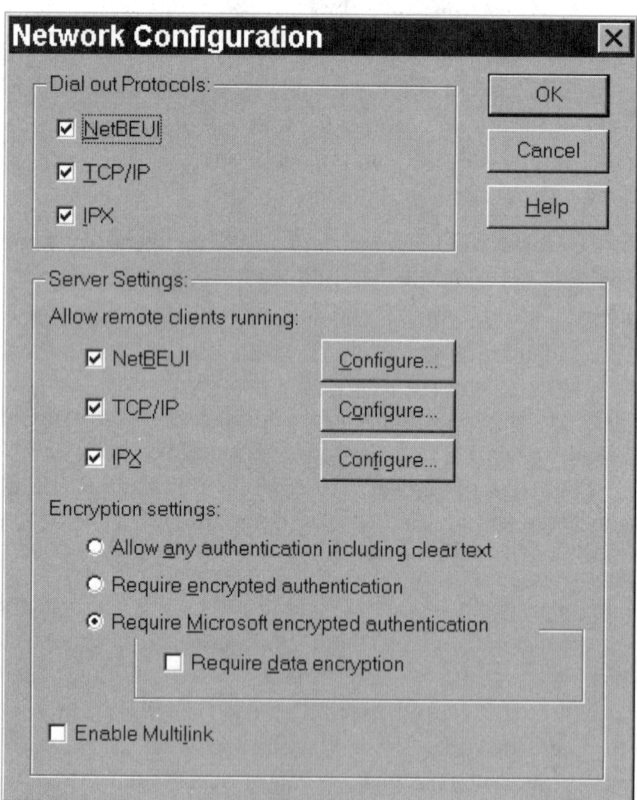

Figure 15-4. If the RAS Port is configured as Dial out and Receive calls, the Network Configuration dialog allows you to specify the transport protocols to be used for outbound calls and to specify and configure the protocols to be used for inbound calls; it also allows you to specify the encryption settings to be used and whether Multilink is to be enabled

If this port is configured either as Dial out only or as Dial out and Receive calls, mark the check boxes for the protocols you want to be available for outbound calls. By default, Windows NT Server enables all installed protocols for dial out. If a protocol is not installed, the check box for the protocol will be inactive (grayed out) and cannot be selected. If this port is configured either as Receive calls only or as Dial out and Receive calls, configure the Server Settings pane as follows:

- If you want the server to support dial-in clients using NetBEUI transport, mark the NetBEUI check box. Click Configure to display the RAS server NetBEUI Configuration dialog. By default, Windows NT Server selects the Entire network option button, which allows dial-in NetBEUI callers to access resources on the RAS server as well as resources on any other machine on the network. If you want to limit callers to accessing resources on the RAS server only, mark the This computer only option button. Click OK to return to the Network Configuration dialog
- If you want the server to support dial-in clients using TCP/IP transport, mark the TCP/IP check box. Click Configure to display the RAS server TCP/IP Configuration dialog, as shown in Figure 15-5. By default, Windows NT Server selects the Entire network option button, which allows dial-in TCP/IP callers to access resources on the RAS server as well as resources on any other machine on the network. If you want to limit callers to accessing resources on the RAS server only, mark the This computer only option button.

  Specify next how you want to assign IP addresses to dial-in TCP/IP clients. By default, Windows NT Server marks the "Use DHCP to assign remote TCP/IP client addresses" check box. If there is a DHCP server on your network, it is usually best to allow Windows NT Server to assign an IP address for each dial-in TCP/IP client.

  If there is no DHCP server on your network, or if you simply want to assign IP addresses to dial-in users from a predefined static pool of addresses, mark the Use static address pool option button. Enter the first IP address in this range into the Begin field, and the last IP address in the range into the End field. At least two IP addresses must be assigned, one for the dial-in client and another for the RAS server adapter. The address range you assign must be valid for the IP subnet to which the RAS server belongs.

  You may exclude one or more IP addresses within the assigned range by entering an address or range of addresses to be excluded in the From and To fields and then clicking Add to display them in the Excluded ranges list box. You may make an excluded address or range of addresses again available by entering it in the From and To fields and then clicking Remove.

  Mark the "Allow remote clients to request a predetermined IP address" check box if you want the dial-in TCP/IP caller to be able to request a specific IP address. If a remote client enters a specific IP address when initiating a dial-up networking session, the server grants that address if possible. Otherwise, the caller is assigned an IP address by the DHCP server or from the static address pool, according to how you have configured the item immediately preceding.

When you have finished configuring TCP/IP options, click OK to return to the Network Configuration dialog.

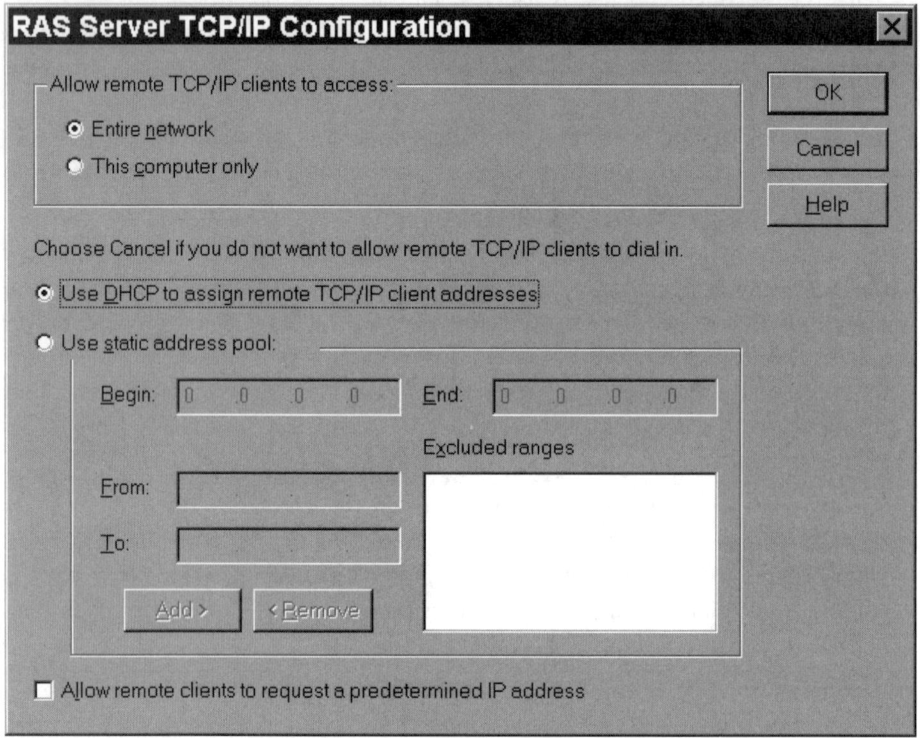

Figure 15-5. The RAS server TCP/IP Configuration dialog allows you to specify whether dial-in TCP/IP callers can access only the server or the entire network, and how IP addresses will be assigned to remote TCP/IP clients

- If you want the server to support dial-in clients using IPX transport, mark the IPX check box. Click Configure to display the RAS server IPX Configuration dialog, as shown in Figure 15-6. By default, Windows NT Server selects the Entire network option button, which allows dial-in IPX callers to access resources on the RAS server as well as resources on any other machine on the network. If you want to limit callers to accessing resources on the RAS server only, mark the This computer only option button.

Specify next how to allocate numbers to dial-in IPX clients. By default, Windows NT Server marks the Allocate network numbers automatically option button. This allows Windows NT Server to locate unused network numbers and assign them as needed to dial-in IPX clients. Mark the Allocate network numbers option button if you prefer to assign a range of network numbers to be used by dial-in IPX clients. Enter the first network number in the From field. Windows NT Server automatically determines the number of network numbers needed for the number of RAS ports defined and enters the last network number in the To field.

By default, Windows NT Server marks the Assign same network number to all IPX clients check box. This reduces network overhead by minimizing RIP broadcasts because a single routing table entry serves all active dial-in IPX clients. Clearing this check box causes each dial-in IPX client to be assigned its own network number. This makes each dial-in IPX client individually identifiable, but greatly increases network overhead because a discrete routing table entry must now exist for each active dial-in IPX client.

The Allow remote clients to request IPX node number check box is cleared by default, which requires dial-in IPX clients to use the IPX node number supplied by RAS. Marking this check box allows the remote client instead to request a specific IPX node number, which opens a security hole in RAS, because a dial-in IPX client can then spoof a previously connected dial-in IPX client by requesting the same node number as that client. This allows the spoofer to access the network resources available to the previously connected authorized IPX client. The only reason I know to enable this check box is if you happen to be using one of the very few applications that will only communicate with clients that use predefined node numbers.

When you have finish configuring IPX options, click OK to return to the Network Configuration dialog.

Select one of the three available encryption settings, as follows:

- *Allow any authentication including clear text* allows RAS to use any authentication type requested by the client, including Microsoft Challenge Handshake Authentication Protocol (MS-CHAP), Shiva Password Authentication Protocol (SPAP), and Password Authentication Protocol (PAP). Use this setting if one or more of your dial-in clients do not support enhanced authentication protocols. This setting offers the least restrictive and least secure means of authentication available for RAS.
- *Require encrypted authentication* allows a dial-in client to be authenticated using any means except PAP, which sends unencrypted passwords across the

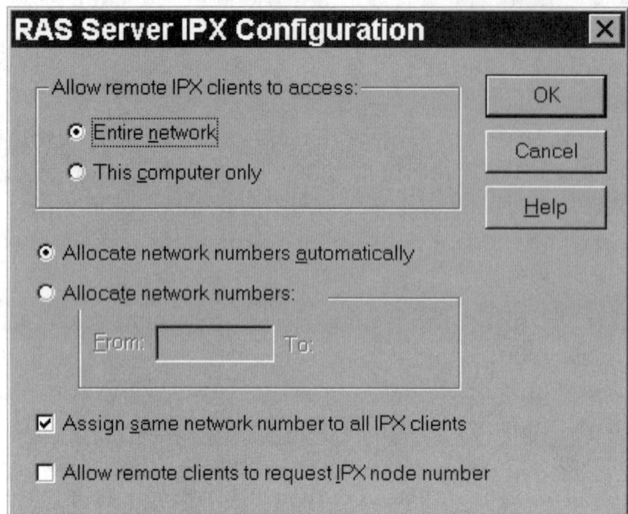

Figure 15-6. The RAS server IPX Configuration dialog allows you to specify whether dial-in IPX callers can access only the server or the entire network, and how network numbers will be assigned to remote IPX clients

connection. This setting offers a high degree of security, at the expense of not allowing clients that support only PAP from connecting to the RAS server.

- *Require Microsoft encrypted authentication* requires that a dial-up networking client use the MS-CHAP protocol for authentication. MS-CHAP establishes a dialog between the RAS server and the client making the connection to determine the most secure means of authentication and subsequent data communication supported by both the server and the client. MS-CHAP uses the RSA Data Security, Inc. RC-4 algorithm to ensure data security. This setting offers the highest level of security, at the expense of further restricting which clients are able to access the RAS server to those that support MS-CHAP authentication.

TIP If you choose Require Microsoft encrypted authentication, you should also mark the Require data encryption check box. Doing so causes all data communicated between the RAS server and the remote client to be encrypted with the RC4 algorithm, rather than just passwords being encrypted. This ensures that even if the data stream is intercepted, that data will remain unintelligible to the eavesdropper.

Mark the *Enable Multilink* check box if you want to enable Multilink functionality. Multilink allows you to combine two or more physical connections into a single logical connection to increase throughput. For example, you might combine two

ISDN connections, each of which provides 128 Kbps throughput, to yield a logical connection that provides 256 Kbps throughput. Multilink can be used to combine multiple ISDN connections, multiple dial-up connections, or a combination of the two.

To use Multilink, both ends of the connection must have Multilink enabled. Because Windows NT Workstation does not support Multilink, this essentially restricts the use of Multilink to joining two servers running Windows NT Server. Multilink is most useful as an alternative to high-speed leased data lines when you need to connect two Windows NT Server computers at remote locations, but find that a single ISDN connection does not offer sufficient throughput. The cost of two ISDN connections at each end may be significantly lower than the cost of the dedicated high-speed leased line that would otherwise be needed to link the two sites.

After you complete the Network Configuration dialog, click OK to return to the Remote Access Setup dialog. If you have additional RAS ports to be configured, you may do so by repeating the procedure just described if that port or ports will be configured differently. If additional ports are to be configured identically to that just completed, use the Clone button to replicate additional ports based on the settings you have just made.

After you have finished configuring ports and global RAS settings, click Continue. Windows NT Server installs RAS, configures the bindings, and finally displays a Setup Message to inform you that RAS has been installed successfully. Click OK to return to the Network property sheet. Click Close to complete the installation. Windows NT Server configures, stores, and reviews the bindings, and then displays the Network Settings Change dialog to inform you that you must restart the server for the changes to take effect. Click Yes to restart the server immediately, or click No to defer these changes taking effect until the next time the server is routinely restarted.

Managing Remote Access Service

After you have installed and configured RAS ports and restarted the server, RAS is immediately available for use. RAS requires little day-to-day routine management. When RAS is initially installed, and later only as needed, you should do the following:

Configure Remote Access Startup

Remote Access Setup by default configures RAS to start automatically each time the server is started. You may also reconfigure RAS to run only when you explicitly start the RAS service.

Authorize users for remote access

Users must be explicitly granted permission to use remote access. You can grant this permission on a user-by-user basis with either the User Manager for Domains application or the Remote Access Admin application.

You can also monitor Remote Access Server on a routine basis using the Remote Access Admin application described later in this section.

Configuring Remote Access Service Startup

Installing RAS actually installs three separate Windows NT Server services, including the *Remote Access Autodial Manager*, the *Remote Access Connection Manager*, and the *Remote Access Server*. When you restart your server after installing RAS, all three RAS services are started automatically. By default, both the Remote Access Autodial Manager service and the Remote Access Server service are configured to start automatically, and the Remote Access Connection Manager is configured for Manual Startup.

NOTE Although the Remote Access Connection Manager service is configured by default for Manual Startup, it starts each time the server is booted if either the Remote Access Server service or the Remote Access Autodial Manager is configured for Automatic Startup. This occurs because both the Remote Access Server service and the Remote Access Autodial Manager are dependent on the Remote Access Connection Manager, which must therefore be started before either the Remote Access Server service or the Remote Access Autodial service can be started.

To configure remote access startup parameters, From Control Panel, double-click the Services applet to display the Services dialog. Use the scrollbar to display the three remote access services.

Highlight the service to be configured, and click Startup to display the Service dialog. In this example, I am configuring the Remote Access Autodial Manager service. In the Startup Type pane, select one of the option buttons to specify how the service will be started. Choosing Automatic causes the service to start each time the server is booted. Choosing Manual causes the service to start only when you explicitly order it to do so by highlighting the Service name in the Services dialog and clicking Start. Choosing Disabled causes the service to be unavailable until its Startup Type is reset to either Automatic or Manual. Click OK to return to the Services dialog. Click Close to save the settings and exit the Services dialog.

NOTE A service configured for Manual Startup can also be started by another service that is dependent upon the Manual service. Setting Startup Type for a service to Disabled can cause other services to fail at startup, if they are dependent upon the Disabled service. If you plan to run the Remote Access Service in a production environment, it is best to leave startup parameters configured at default values.

WARNING Do not modify the values in the Log On As pane. These values are set correctly by Remote Access Setup. Changing them can cause RAS to fail or to behave unpredictably.

Setting Remote Access Service User Permissions

After you have installed and configured RAS, the next step is to specify which users will be permitted to use Remote Access. As a security measure, all users by default are denied permission to use Remote Access, including even Domain Admins. You can grant dial-in permission for users with the User Manager [for Domains] application or with the Remote Access Admin application.

To grant dial-in permission for users with the User Manager [for Domains] application, from the Start button, choose Programs, then Administrative Tools (Common), then User Manager [for Domains] to run the User Manager [for Domains] application. Double-click a Username to display the User properties dialog for that user, as shown in Figure 15-7.

Choose Dialin to display the Dialin Information dialog. Mark the Grant dialin permission to user check box. Call Back allows the RAS server to place an outbound telephone call to the remote client. You can use call back options both to enhance RAS security and to shift long-distance telephone charges from the remote client to the RAS server location. Mark one of the Call Back option buttons, as follows:

No Call Back
: Choosing this option disables call back and allows the remote caller to connect immediately with the RAS server to establish a network session. With No Call Back selected, only one telephone call is needed to establish a RAS session—that call originally placed by the remote client to the RAS server.

Set By Caller
: Choosing this option causes RAS to prompt the remote caller for the telephone number from which he is calling. Once the remote caller provides the telephone number, RAS drops the connection and immediately dials the telephone

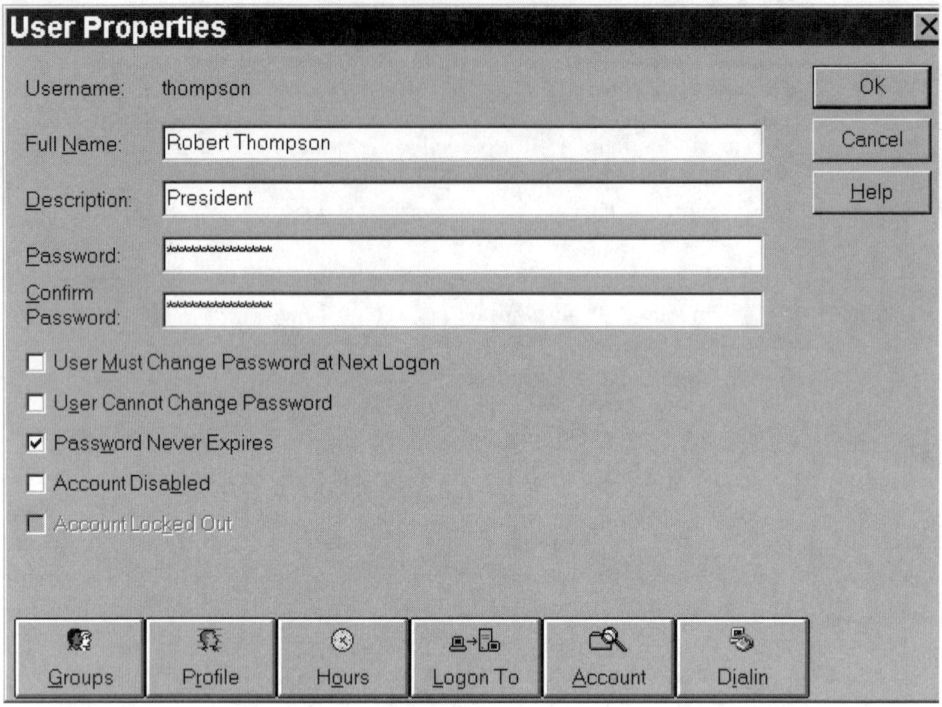

Figure 15-7. The User Properties property sheet allows you to set dial-in permissions and other account parameters for the selected user

number specified. Using this option enhances RAS security because RAS logs the telephone numbers it calls back. If a security breach is suspected, you can review this log later to determine the telephone number of the remote caller in question. This option is also ideal for roving users, e.g., traveling sales-people, because it allows long-distance telephone charges to accrue to the RAS telephone line rather than to the telephone line being used by the remote caller.

Preset To

Choosing this option causes RAS to drop the connection as soon as it establishes the identity of the remote caller. RAS then calls the predefined telephone number and establishes a network connection. This option is useful in two situations. First, it offers the highest security, since a RAS connection for a particular user can be made only to a specifically predefined telephone number. Second, because it does not require the remote caller to enter a call back telephone number, it combines security and simplicity for nontechnical users who will be using RAS to connect from only a single location, e.g., telecommuters working from home.

After you have configured the Dialin Information dialog, click OK to return to the User Properties property sheet. Click Close to return to the User Manager [for Domains] application. Close User Manager [for Domains]. Alternatively, you can grant dial-in permission for a user with the Remote Access Admin application. To do so, from the Start button, choose Programs, then Administrative Tools (Common), then Remote Access Admin to run the Remote Access Admin application, shown in Figure 15-8.

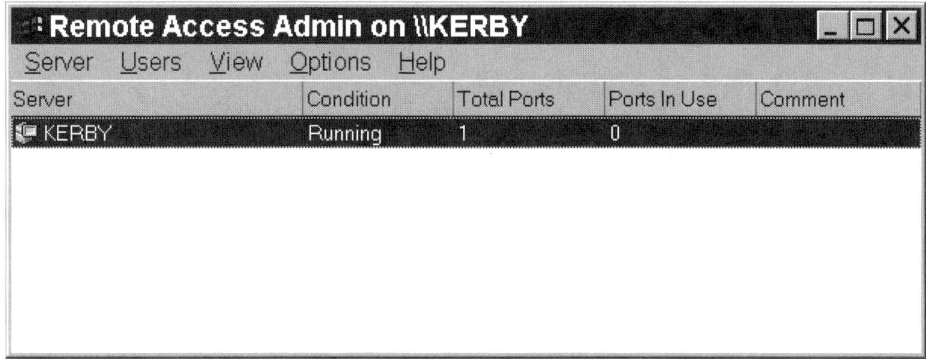

Figure 15-8. The Remote Access Admin application offers an alternative method for granting dial-in permission to selected users

From the Users menu, click Permissions to display the Remote Access Permissions dialog, as shown in Figure 15-9. In the example, the Remote Access Service is running on *kerby*, which is a Backup Domain Controller for the *TTGNET* domain. Because the user account information resides on the Primary Domain Controller *thoth*, Windows NT Server displays a Remote Access Admin message to inform you that the changes will be made to the master user account database on the Primary Domain Controller.

In the Remote Access Permissions dialog, highlight a user. Mark the *Grant* d*ialin permission to user* check box to allow that user to access the RAS server. Use Grant All or Revoke All to grant or revoke permissions simultaneously for all listed users to avoid having to do so for each user individually. Set Call Back for each user as described in the preceding section. When you have finished setting permissions, click OK to return to the Remote Access Admin application main screen. Close Remote Access Admin.

NOTE The Grant All and Revoke All global settings affect only the Grant dial-in permission to user check box. You must still set Call Back settings individually for each user if they are to be other than the default value of No Call Back.

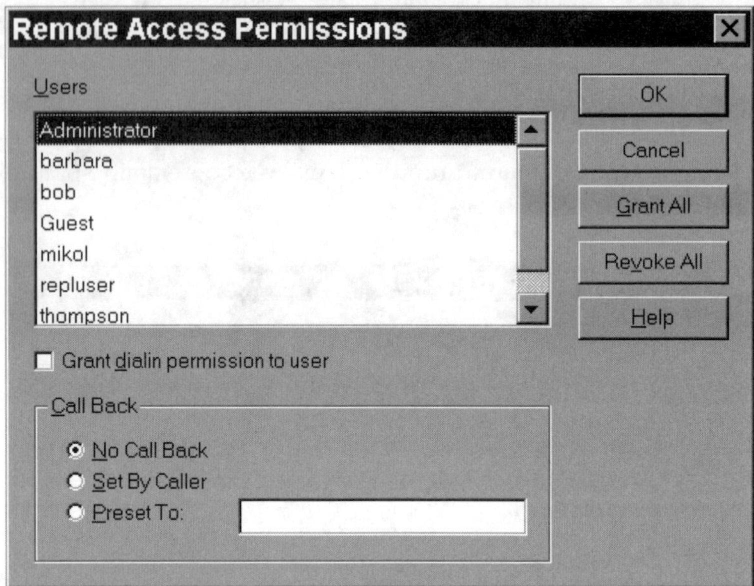

Figure 15-9. The Remote Access Permissions dialog allows you to grant and revoke dial-in permissions for a specified user or for all users in the account list

Managing the RAS server with Remote Access Admin

The Remote Access Admin application allows you to monitor and control your RAS server(s), both locally and across the network. If you run Remote Access Admin on a server that has RAS installed and running, Remote Access Admin displays the data for that server by default. If you run Remote Access Admin on a server that does not have RAS running, Remote Access Admin notifies you that RAS is not running on that server, and allows you to choose a different server or domain to administer.

You can use Remote Access Admin to:

- Monitor and control RAS ports
- Start, Stop, Pause, and Continue the Remote Access Service itself
- Select a Domain or Server to be managed
- Set User Permissions
- Display active users (those currently connected to the RAS server)

To run the Remote Access Admin application, from the Desktop, click the Start button, highlight Programs, then Administrative Tools (Common), then click Remote Access Admin. Windows NT Server displays the Remote Access Admin in <domain-name> main screen.

The Remote Access Admin main screen displays for each RAS server, the Server name, its condition (e.g., running, paused), the total number of RAS ports installed on that server, the number of ports currently in use by connected RAS clients, and any comment associated with the RAS server.

The choices available on the Remote Access Admin Server menu allow you to view and control Communication Ports; Start Remote Access Service; Stop Remote Access Service; Pause Remote Access Service; Continue Remote Access Service (if you have paused it); Select Domain or Server to be managed; or Exit. All of these choices are self-explanatory except perhaps the Communication Ports option.

To view and manage Communication Ports, from the Server menu, click Communication Ports to display the Communication Ports dialog. This dialog displays all active RAS ports for the selected RAS server. Installed but currently unused ports are not shown. For each active port, the dialog displays the Port name, the User currently connected to that port, and the date and time when the connection was established.

Viewing the status of a RAS port

To view the status of a particular RAS port, click the Port to be viewed to highlight it, and click Port Status to display the Port Status screen shown in Figure 15-10. View the statistics for the port you selected in the preceding step, or use the Port drop-down list to select a different RAS port. Click Help for a detailed explanation of each item, including the normal status of that item and possible explanations for abnormal values. Click Reset at any time to reset the counters for all values. Clicking Reset does not reset the port itself, but only zeroes out the accumulated values displayed for that port. When you are finished viewing statistics, click OK to return to the Communication Ports dialog.

Disconnecting a RAS user

To disconnect a user, highlight that port and click Disconnect User to display the Disconnect User dialog. Click OK if you simply want to disconnect the user at the moment. Mark the Revoke Remote Access Permissions check box before clicking OK if you want both to disconnect the user and at the same time revoke his RAS privileges.

Sending messages to connected RAS clients

To send a message to all connected RAS clients, click Send to All to display the Send Message dialog. If the message requires more than one line, remember to use Ctrl-Enter to start each new line. Pressing Enter by itself sends the message. This counterintuitive procedure will doubtless cause you to send many incomplete broadcast messages, as it has me and every other RAS administrator I know.

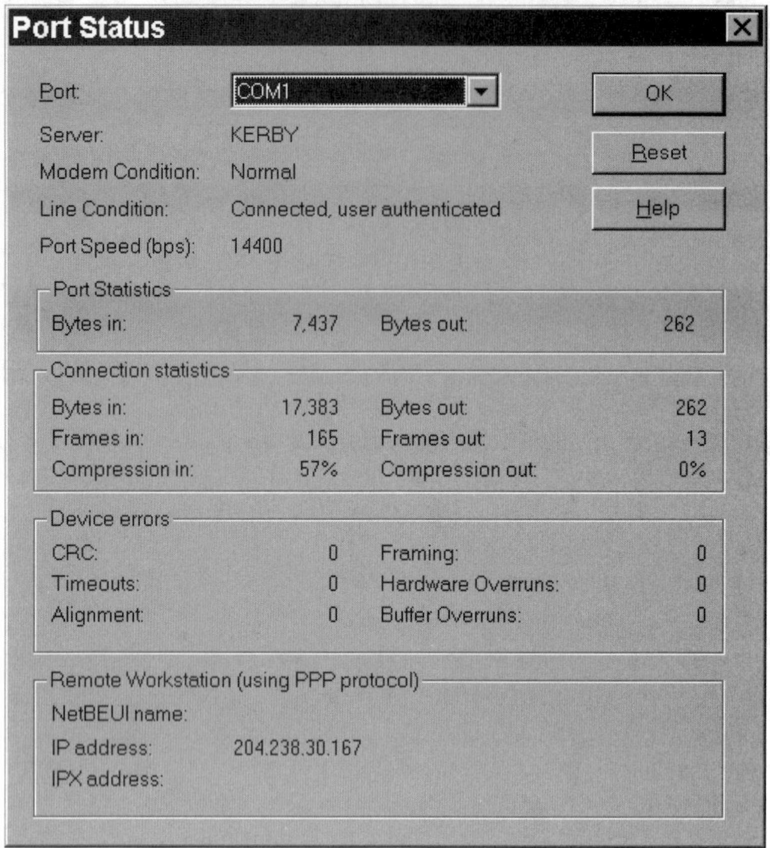

Figure 15-10. The Port Status dialog displays the characteristics of the connection on the selected port, statistics for the port and connection, any errors that have occurred, and the network protocols being used

If you need to send a message to one specific connected RAS client, highlight that port and click Send Message.

NOTE You can send messages to a RAS client only if that client is running the messenger service. If you attempt to send a message to client who is not running the messenger service or is otherwise incapable of receiving messages, Windows NT so notifies you.

Managing connected RAS users

The Remote Access Admin Users menu offers two choices. The first choice, Permissions, was covered earlier in the Setting Remote Access Service User Permissions section. The second choice, Active Users, allows you to display information about each connected RAS user, to disconnect users, and to broadcast messages to users.

To view and manage active Users, from the Users menu, click Active Users to display the Remote Access Users dialog. This dialog displays all active RAS Users, the RAS server to which they are connected, and the date and time that the session was established. The Disconnect User, Send Message, and Send To All functions work as described in the preceding section.

To view detailed information for a specific user, highlight that user and click User Account to display the User Account information screen shown in Figure 15-11.

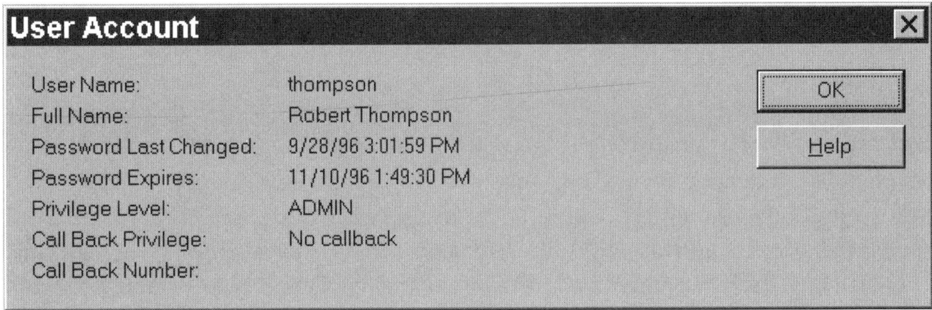

Figure 15-11. The User Account information screen displays the detailed account information for the selected RAS user

---

NOTE If you are connected to the RAS server being managed by a dial-up or other low-speed connection, choose Low Speed Connection from the Options menu. Doing so minimizes the amount of data that is transferred across the link in the interest of performance, at the expense of making some options unavailable.

Using the Dial-Up Networking Monitor

Windows NT Server provides a second tool for managing RAS, called the Dial-Up Networking Monitor. The Dial-Up Networking Monitor allows you to display statistics for RAS ports and manage users. Invoke the Dial-Up Networking monitor by double-clicking its icon in Control Panel. The Dial-Up Networking Monitor Status page displays, for the selected device, the condition, device and connection statistics, and errors. The Summary page displays a hierarchical tree of all connected networks and users. The Preferences page allows you to configure sound and video options for the Dial-Up Networking Monitor.

16

Microsoft Tools for NetWare Integration

In this chapter:

- *NWLink IPX/SPX Compatible Transport Protocol*
- *Gateway Service for NetWare*
- *Migration Tool for NetWare*
- *Microsoft Services for NetWare*
- *Coexistence, Migration, and Transition*

With Windows NT Server, Microsoft has created a world-class PC LAN operating system. The Microsoft marketing machine has positioned Windows NT Server well, and done everything possible to ensure that it gains market share rapidly at the expense of Novell NetWare. The Microsoft PR people have done yeoman duty to gain *mind share* for Windows NT Server. The systems designers and programmers have made sure that all the right pieces are in place to ensure that Windows NT Server does everything NetWare does, and does it at least as well.

All these things are necessary if Windows NT Server is to prevail in its struggle to become the dominant PC LAN operating system, but they are not in themselves sufficient. To succeed in the world of computing, it's not enough to have the best product. The history of computing is littered with great products that withered on the vine. You must also make your product easy to integrate into the existing scheme of things. People don't change their overall way of doing things to accommodate a new product, even if it's a great one.

From the beginning, Microsoft has been smart enough to realize that, if Windows NT was to make serious inroads in the corporate LAN environment, it had to play nice with NetWare. Vendors of other competing LAN operating systems—including Microsoft's earlier LAN Manager product—had tried to go head to head against NetWare without notable success.

Their common mistake was to expect LAN administrators to replace NetWare entirely with their product, or, what was almost as bad, to run their incompatible product side by side with NetWare. These products offered few or no tools for integration with and migration from NetWare; their client software could not access NetWare servers; NetWare client software could not access their servers; they were fundamentally incompatible even at the OSI Network and Transport layers. Potential customers stayed away in droves.

With Windows NT Server, Microsoft avoided all of these errors. They realized that, if Windows NT Server was to be regarded as an easy fit in existing networks, several things had to happen. First, if you don't use the same fundamental protocols as NetWare, interoperability is a nonstarter, so Windows NT had to support Novell's native IPX/SPX Network Layer and Transport Layer protocols. Second, at the Session Layer and above, Windows NT Server uses the Server Message Block (SMB) protocol, while NetWare uses the NetWare Core Protocol (NCP). Because these protocols are fundamentally incompatible, some means had to be found to gateway them bidirectionally. Third, no LAN administrator in his right mind wants to make wholesale changes to the client software installed on existing workstations, so some means had to be found to allow NetWare clients to access Windows NT servers transparently, and *vice versa.*

Microsoft also realized that making all of these things happen was up to them. With the overwhelmingly dominant network operating system in their corner, Novell had no incentive to make it easier for a competing product to get its foot in the door. Accordingly, Microsoft set out to build all of the bridges needed to allow Windows NT Server to fit smoothly into NetWare networks. If something could be done along the way to allow Windows NT Server to make up for some of the deficiencies of NetWare, so much the better. Here's what Microsoft came up with:

NWLink IPX/SPX Compatible Transport protocol
: NWLink is the Microsoft version of the Novell IPX/SPX protocol. NWLink is fully compatible and interoperable with Novell IPX/SPX on every level, and supports all of the frame types that are supported by Novell IPX/SPX. Installing NWLink on Windows NT Server allows NCP clients—those running only NetWare client software—to access shared resources and applications on the servers that are running Windows NT Server. NWLink can coexist with other transport protocols running at the same time on Windows NT Server, including TCP/IP and NetBEUI. Installing and configuring NWLink is covered in Chapter 3, *Configuring Windows NT Server Networking.*

Gateway Service for NetWare (GSNW)
: GSNW is a Windows NT Server service that allows a computer that is running Windows NT Server to act as a gateway to one or more NetWare servers. Before Version 4.0, GSNW supported NetWare 2.x and 3.x servers fully, and supported NetWare 4.x servers only if they were running in bindery emulation mode. In Version 4.0, GSNW also fully supports NetWare 4.x servers running NDS. Using GSNW allows SMB clients—those running only Microsoft Networking software—to access shared disk and printer resources on your NetWare servers. GSNW is covered in Chapter 18, *Using Gateway Service for NetWare.*

Migration Tool for NetWare (MTNW)

MTNW is a Windows NT Server application that can automatically port the contents of one or more NetWare servers to Windows NT Server. MTNW can transfer user and group accounts, volumes, directories, and files (including their security information), and login scripts. Running MTNW does not change the NetWare server in any way. You can use MTNW as a coexistence tool, e.g., simply to replicate the user and group account structure of a NetWare server to the Windows NT server that will run beside it indefinitely. You can also use MTNW as a one-time tool, to convert the contents of a NetWare server to the Windows NT server that will replace it. MTNW is covered in Chapter 21, *Migrating to a Pure Windows NT Server Environment.*

These three products are supplied standard with Windows NT Server. Microsoft also sells an optional $149 software product, called the *Microsoft Services for NetWare (MSNW)*, that includes the following NetWare integration utilities:

File and Print Services for NetWare (FPNW)

FPNW is a Windows NT Server service that allows a Windows NT server to emulate a NetWare 3.12 server. With FPNW running, workstations that have only NetWare client software installed can access shared Windows NT Server disk and printer resources transparently, as though those resources were located on an actual NetWare server. Chapter 19, *Using File and Print Services for NetWare,* is devoted to FPNW.

Directory Service Manager for NetWare (DSMN)

DSMN is a Windows NT Server service that allows you to manage bindery-based NetWare servers from within Windows NT Server. Rather than maintaining user and group accounts locally at each NetWare server, you can use DSMN to maintain this information centrally on Windows NT Server, and replicate it automatically to the managed NetWare servers as changes are made to the central database. DSMN is covered in detail in Chapter 20, *Managing Servers in a Mixed NetWare and Windows NT Server Environment.*

Given Microsoft's focus on coexisting with NetWare servers—and eventually replacing them—it may seem surprising that they didn't simply choose to bundle these two utilities as well. It's probably not a coincidence that Microsoft bundles every tool you need to do a one-step migration from NetWare to Windows NT Server, but makes you pay extra for a separate product if you want the two to coexist.

The following sections examine each of these five NetWare interoperability tools in a more detail, describing what each one does, and why you'd want to use it. I'll try not to sound like a Microsoft PR flack, but these really are excellent tools.

NWLink IPX/SPX Compatible Transport Protocol

If Windows NT Server is to be fully interoperable with NetWare, it needs to support compatible protocols at each layer of the OSI model. At the lower layers—Physical and Data Link—there isn't much of a problem. Everyone uses the same Ethernet or Token Ring cards connected to the same twisted pair or coax cabling.

At the middle layers—the Network and Transport layers—there was a problem. In NetWare, the middle layers are owned by IPX/SPX, while early Microsoft Networking products used NetBEUI transport for the same purposes. If they wanted to be compatible with NetWare, Microsoft had little choice but to create their own version of the Novell IPX/SPX protocol. They did, and in the process gained the world record for the longest protocol name—the NWLink IPX/SPX Compatible Transport protocol, which I'll just call NWLink from here on.

NWLink is completely compatible with Novell IPX/SPX, and interoperates flawlessly. NWLink supports all of the frame types that Novell IPX/SPX uses. Specifically, NWLink supports Ethernet 802.3 for compatibility with NetWare 3.11 and earlier networks; Ethernet 802.2 for compatibility with NetWare 3.12 and 4.x networks; the interim Ethernet SNAP (subnetwork access protocol); and Ethernet II for compatibility with heavy iron, UNIX, and the Internet. In a Token Ring environment, NWLink supports standard Token Ring framing and Token Ring SNAP.

NWLink also allows you to specify frame type autodetection, which generally works correctly. Autodetection may fail if your network runs multiple frame types or if you have multiple adapters installed in the server. To avoid such problems, I usually bypass autodetection and specify frame types explicitly.

Windows NT Server and NWLink also support the internal routing functions ("bridging" in former Novell-speak) that NetWare provides to allow a single server to connect multiple segments. If you enable RIP for NWLink, Windows NT Server can route IPX/SPX using the Novell RIP protocol (not to be confused with Internet RIP).

NWLink forms the foundation of Microsoft's NetWare integration strategy. All of the other products mentioned in this chapter—Gateway Service for NetWare, Migration Tool for NetWare, File and Print Services for NetWare, and Directory Service Manager for NetWare—require NWLink.

In fact, although Microsoft created NWLink primarily for NetWare compatibility, many Windows NT Server networks that are not connected to NetWare servers use NWLink as their primary (or only) transport protocol, particularly those networks that are not routed or connected to the Internet. In a simple local network, NWLink provides the performance of TCP/IP while avoiding its complexity. If yours is such a network, NWLink may be the only transport protocol required.

Gateway Service for NetWare

With NWLink taking care of compatibility at the middle OSI layers, the next step was to look at compatibility at the upper OSI layers—the Session Layer and above. At this level of the OSI model, NetWare uses the NetWare Core Protocol (NCP), and Windows NT Server uses the Server Message Block (SMB) protocol. If Microsoft (SMB) clients were able to access NetWare (NCP) resources, some means was necessary to translate SMB messages to and from NCP.

The Gateway Service for NetWare (GSNW) is a Windows NT Server service that allows a server running Windows NT Server to act as a gateway to one or more NetWare servers. It does so by translating SMB queries from Microsoft clients to NCP messages, and presenting them to the NetWare server. When the NetWare server responds, GSNW translates the NCP responses from the NetWare server to SMB messages and redirects these to the Microsoft client. GSNW is a unidirectional gateway in the sense that it performs these gateway services only for SMB clients communicating with NCP servers, and not the converse.

GSNW serves as a local NetWare redirector for the Windows NT server upon which it is installed, allowing that server to access shared disk and printer resources on NetWare servers connected to the network. GSNW also serves as a proxy redirector for Microsoft Networking clients connected to the server upon which it is running, allowing those clients to access shared NetWare resources while running only the Microsoft Networking client software.

Deploying GSNW provides the following benefits:

- Allows you to use whatever primary transport protocol you wish to connect clients and servers, without losing connectivity to NetWare resources. For example, you might choose TCP/IP as your strategic corporate protocol to support connection to intranets and the Internet, while maintaining the tactical advantages of continuing IPX/SPX connectivity with NetWare servers.
- Allows remote dial-up users, and those connected via a routed TCP/IP network, to access locally shared NetWare file and print resources. By using GSNW in conjunction with the Windows NT Remote Access Service (RAS), you can provide dial-up users that are running either Windows Networking software or NetWare client software with the same secure and reliable connection to shared NetWare resources.

- Allows you to stage network upgrades, by permitting older and newer technologies to coexist side by side until you have the time and resources available to complete the upgrade.

Against these advantages, you must weigh two serious disadvantages, each of which springs from the fact that GSNW services are supplied via a single, shared session with the NetWare server, as follows:

- GSNW provides much lower performance than a direct, native NetWare connection. Like any situation that introduces a gateway, protocol overhead is responsible for some of this lost performance. By far the larger problem, however, is that all GSNW clients are contending for the available throughput of a single NetWare session.
- GSNW security is pretty much an all-or-nothing proposition. Although each GSNW client is logged in to the Windows NT Server individually, access to shared NetWare resources is funneled through a single connection, which, obviously, may have only one set of rights assigned. This means that **any** GSNW client has **all** of the rights available to any other GSNW client. You can avoid this problem to some extent by defining more than one share for the same NetWare resource, and then assigning different Windows NT Server users and groups rights to those shares. However, you are limited to using share-level permissions—No Access, Read Only, Change, and Full Control—to effect these security differences, which is often insufficient granularity.

Installing, configuring, and using GSNW is relatively straightforward, and requires the following steps:

- Create the group NTGATEWAY on each of the NetWare servers that are accessible to Microsoft clients.
- Create a gateway account on each NetWare server, assign it to the NTGATEWAY group, and grant it the trustee rights and other permissions that you want available to users of the gateway.
- Install the Gateway Service for NetWare.
- For a NetWare 2.x server, a NetWare 3.x server, or a NetWare 4.x server running in bindery emulation mode, specify a Preferred Server. For a NetWare 4.x server running NDS, specify a Default Tree and Context.
- Enable the gateway and define shares to map NetWare disk volumes.
- Use the Add Printer Wizard to add a network print server, selecting a NetWare printer, and share this printer.

After you have performed these steps, Microsoft Networking (SMB) clients can access shared NetWare disk and printer resources just as though they were Windows NT Server shared resources.

NOTE The version of GSNW supplied with Windows NT Server 4.0 has been significantly upgraded from the version supplied with Windows NT Server 3.51. GSNW v3.51 provided access only to bindery-based NetWare services—those available on 2.x and 3.x NetWare servers, and on 4.x servers running bindery emulation. GSNW v4.0 also allows users to access NDS-based NetWare resources. GSNW v 4.0 users may navigate NDS trees, print from NDS, run 4.1 login scripts, and authenticate to NDS-based servers.

Migration Tool for NetWare

The Migration Tool for NetWare (MTNW) is a Windows NT Server application that serves two purposes. First, you may use it, as the name implies, as a migration tool to do a one-time transfer of the information on your NetWare servers to Windows NT Server, just before shutting down your NetWare servers forever. Second, you can use it on a continuing basis as an integration tool in an environment where NetWare and Windows NT Server will coexist indefinitely. Microsoft hopes that you will choose the first usage. Realistically, most of us will choose the second.

MTNW makes it easy to replicate user accounts, group accounts, volumes, directories, and files from one or more NetWare servers to Windows NT Server. If the target Windows NT server is running File and Print Services for NetWare, which is described in the following section, you can also migrate NetWare login scripts.

Microsoft Services for NetWare

Although the optional $149 product called Microsoft Services for NetWare is new as a product to Version 4.0, it simply incorporates enhanced versions of two NetWare integration utilities—File and Print Services for NetWare and Directory Service Manager for NetWare—that were formerly available as individual $99 products. Microsoft apparently figured that, if you needed either of them, you probably needed both. They're right.

Microsoft Services for NetWare is an important tool for anyone who administers a network that includes both Windows NT servers and NetWare servers. If you plan to have NetWare and Windows NT Server coexist—either during an extended transition or semipermanently—MSNW is essential. Even if you plan to do a complete transition to Windows NT Server over a weekend or holiday, having MSNW at hand will be a lifesaver if you find that getting all of your clients upgraded is going to take a bit longer than you planned.

File and Print Services for NetWare

Like GSNW, File and Print Services for NetWare (FPNW) addresses compatibility at the upper layers of the OSI model. The purpose of FPNW, however, is exactly the converse of GSNW. GSNW allows Microsoft (SMB) clients to access NetWare servers; FPNW allows NetWare (NCP) clients to access Windows NT servers.

Running the FPNW service on a Windows NT server allows it to emulate a NetWare 3.12 server. NetWare clients see the FPNW server as just another NetWare server, and can use the shared disk and printer resources on that FPNW server directly, without first installing Microsoft Networking client software. When you drop the first Windows NT server into your NetWare shop, FPNW addresses the urgent problem of allowing all those existing NetWare clients to have immediate access to the resources on the new Windows NT server.

GSNW is a gateway, or proxy redirector, which is subject to all of the security compromises and performance problems that it implies. FPNW is much more than a simple gateway. Installing FPNW essentially adds native direct support for NCP to Windows NT server. Unlike GSNW users, who must share the throughput available on a single session to the NetWare server. FPNW users each establish a separate session to the Windows NT server.

On the downside, this means that you must purchase a Windows NT Server client access license for each FPNW client who will access the FPNW server. On the upside, this also means that the security and performance problems that are inherent in a gateway are not an issue with FPNW. You use the same tools to control access to shared resources for FPNW clients that you do for ordinary Windows NT clients. The performance experienced by FPNW clients is essentially identical to that of ordinary SMB clients. In fact, NetWare clients usually find that an FPNW server appears to be at least as fast as a real NetWare 3.12 server.

Because it provides top-notch security and performance, FPNW is perfectly suitable as a permanent part of your network. If you install FPNW, you will never be forced to upgrade your existing NetWare clients.

NOTE The version of FPNW supplied with Windows NT Server 4.0 has been significantly upgraded from the version supplied with Windows NT Server 3.51, although it is still limited to bindery emulation mode clients. With v4.0, FPNW adds enhanced support for remote management. You can now use Windows NT Administration Tools for Windows 95 to administer FPNW, as well as the web administration tool for Windows NT Server. Microsoft also enhanced FPWN multiprocessor support, as well as overall performance. Finally, FPNW now uses the standard Windows 95/Windows NT 4.0 interface, rather than the Windows 3.x interface used by its predecessors.

Directory Service Manager for NetWare

One of the major hassles of administering a NetWare network with multiple bindery-based servers is that, if you want to make a change to a user account or group, that change must be entered individually for each server that it affects. If you have many NetWare servers, and in particular if those servers are widely scattered geographically, a simple user add can involve a lot of work, even when using the NetWare remote administration tools. If you have to make an actual on-site visit to each server to get the job done, adding one user can take all day. Don't laugh. I know of more than one NetWare administrator who, because of corporate security concerns, is forced to work only at local consoles. Microsoft's answer to this problem is called Directory Service Manager for NetWare (DSMN).

DSMN is a Windows NT Server service that allows you to grant bindery-based NetWare servers membership in the Windows NT Server domain, and subsequently to manage those servers using Windows NT Server tools. Once the NetWare servers are assigned to DSMN, you no longer use *SYSCON* and other NetWare utilities to maintain users and groups. Instead, you use User Manager for Domains to make all ongoing changes to the user account and group account structure of the managed NetWare servers. DSMN then propagates these changes back to the managed NetWare servers. All of this is done without requiring that any additional software be added to the NetWare servers or that any changes be made to them.

DSMN also includes user utilities with the same names as the NetWare user utilities they replace. From the users' point of view, they simply continue to use the same utilities to change their passwords. However, these homonymous DSMN utilities update the Windows NT Server account database, rather than updating the local NetWare bindery. These changes are subsequently automatically propagated to the member NetWare servers, keeping the user and group account information synchronized.

DSMN includes the following features and benefits:

Standard Interface
: DSMN allows you to use standard Windows point-and-click conventions to propagate user and group account information from NetWare 2.x/3.x servers—and from NetWare 4.x servers that are running bindery emulation mode—to the Windows NT account database.

Flexibility
: DSMN allows you to specify how passwords are set initially on propagated accounts, to specify which users and groups are to be propagated in each direction, to handle duplicate account names, etc.

Trial Propagation

DSMN allows you to do a trial run before you actually propagate account information, to ensure that the propagation will have the results you expect.

Database Safety

The all-important NetWare bindery is relatively unprotected on a standard NetWare server. Although you can use BINDFIX periodically to duplicate the contents of the bindery, and your backup software may store a good copy of the bindery, NetWare itself does little on a routine basis to protect the bindery. DSMN automatically backs up the user and group account information, and can replicate the account database to any computer on the network.

Easy Administration

Using DSMN allows you to maintain all account information centrally. You can use Windows NT Server remote administration tools on a client that runs Windows 95 or Windows NT Workstation to maintain your account database from anywhere on the network, including a dial-up RAS connection.

Single Network Logon

Using DSMN allows you to maintain only one user account entry for each network user. In addition to the obvious administrative advantages, this also benefits the users. Each user uses the same account name and password, whether he is logging on to a local NetWare server, a local Windows NT server, or a dial-up RAS server.

Authentication

Windows NT can authenticate users for applications running on Windows NT Server. This extends the advantages of a single network logon to include applications security.

Coexistence, Migration, and Transition

Microsoft differentiates between coexistence, which they define as maintaining both NetWare servers and Windows NT servers on your network on a continuing basis, and migration, which they define as a planned, orderly movement from NetWare to Windows NT Server that takes place in a relatively short period of time. In practice, the difference is usually one of intent, and can be hard to discriminate when looking at any particular network.

Few networks will include both NetWare 3.1x servers and Windows NT servers on a permanent basis. The NetWare servers will eventually be phased out, upgraded to Windows NT Server, or perhaps upgraded to NetWare 4.x. Conversely, few networks will be migrated from NetWare 3.1x to Windows NT Server overnight. There are just too many issues that need to be resolved to make this practical. In short, for most companies, the process that will occur is better thought of as a transition that will require a greater or lesser amount of time.

You can use the tools described in this chapter in various combinations either to ease the long-term coexistence of NetWare and Windows NT Server on your network, or to expedite the migration from NetWare to Windows NT Server. The following sections briefly describe the actions you need to take in either situation.

Coexistence

By far the most common situation is one in which NetWare and Windows NT Server must coexist on the network—sometimes for weeks or months, and sometimes indefinitely. In outline, take the following steps to allow NetWare and Windows NT to coexist peacefully on your network:

1. Build a new Windows NT server. Install the NWLink protocol to provide interoperability between NetWare and Windows NT Server at the network and transport layers.
2. Install the Gateway Service for NetWare to provide Windows NT Server with the local redirector needed to allow it to communicate with the NetWare server. If you have Microsoft Networking clients that need casual access to your NetWare server, enable and configure a gateway. If your Microsoft Networking clients will be using NetWare resources more heavily, install NetWare client software on each of them.
3. Install and configure File and Print Services for NetWare, to allow NetWare clients to access shared resources on the Windows NT server.
4. Install and configure Directory Service Manager for NetWare, to allow you to maintain user accounts and group accounts centrally by using User Manager for Domains. Add your NetWare server to your Windows NT Server domain.
5. Use Directory Service Manager for NetWare to replicate the existing NetWare user and group account structure on the new Windows NT Server. Verify that each account is NetWare-enabled, to ensure that it will be accessible using NetWare client software.
6. If necessary, use the Migration Tool for NetWare to replicate some or all of the directories and files on the NetWare server to the Windows NT server.

At this point, you have completed all the basic tasks needed to allow NetWare and Windows NT Server to coexist. NetWare clients can access shared disk and printer resources on both NetWare servers and Windows NT Server. Windows Networking clients can also access resources on either type of server. You have centralized user and group account management on Windows NT Server. The two operating systems will play well side by side until you finally get around to taking down your NetWare servers, if ever.

Migration and Transition

Broadly speaking, there are two possible types of transition from NetWare to Windows NT Server. A sudden transition, or a migration, is a clean break. It occurs all at once, typically over a weekend or a holiday. If this is the type of transition you plan, the following outlines the general steps you must take:

1. Build a new Windows NT server. Install the NWLink protocol to provide interoperability between NetWare and Windows NT Server at the network and transport layers.
2. Install the Gateway Service for NetWare to provide Windows NT Server with the local redirector needed to allow it to communicate with the NetWare server.
3. Use the Migration Tool for NetWare to replicate all of the users and groups and all of the directories and files that reside on the NetWare server to the Windows NT server. Verify that all information has been migrated correctly, and clean up any minor problems that occurred.
4. Shut down the NetWare server.

At this point, your new Windows NT server contains all of the user and group accounts and all of the directories and files that were on the NetWare server. However, you still have one big problem. None of your clients can access the new server. They have only NetWare client software installed, and all of them are pointing to a server that no longer exists.

There are two ways to eliminate this problem. The hard way is to visit each of your clients, install Microsoft Networking client software on it, and point it to the new server. The easy way is to install File and Print Services for NetWare on the new server, giving the FPNW server the same name as the old NetWare server.

In my experience, this kind of sudden transition from NetWare to Windows NT Server is a pretty rare event. Few companies are prepared to take such a large step. Even for those that are, other factors often militate against it. For example, you may be running an NLM-based database application that is not available as a Windows NT Server application. Or you may have your corporate mail system running reliably under NetWare and not want to change it. Usually, there's at least one thing running on NetWare that is impossible or inconvenient to move to Windows NT Server.

Even if you develop what you think are complete plans for an immediate migration and then attempt to implement it, what may occur is that one or another key element doesn't perform as expected. You might, for example, have verified that your key database program is available for Windows NT Server and that it loads and runs successfully. Only after you have migrated to Windows NT Server and begun running the database in a production environment do you find that the Windows NT version is not as well tuned as the NLM-based version you had running on NetWare, and provides inadequate real-world performance. The only solution may be to revert to the NetWare version.

Incidentally, don't get me wrong. Although NetWare NLM-based applications have a built-in advantage because they run in Ring 0—buying performance at the potential expense of safety—vendors are focusing much of their attention nowadays on their Windows NT Server versions. It's almost as likely that the Windows NT version will outperform the NLM version as is the converse. The point is that you don't really know what's going to happen until you actually do it.

The prudent course is to plan for coexistence even if your real intention is simply to migrate. Purchase and install FPNW and DSMN. If the best happens, and your migration proceeds without a hiccough, you haven't lost much—only the minimal cost of MSNW and the hour or so needed to install and configure them. If, on the other hand, unforeseen problems occur during or shortly after your migration, you have all the required pieces in place to fall back to a coexistence strategy.

In this chapter:
- *Using License Manager*
- *Using Network Client Administrator*
- *Building Universal Clients*

17
Building Clients for Mixed NetWare and Windows NT Server Environments

This chapter focuses on client-side issues. Now there's a scary thought. The last thing in the world you probably want to do is change the client software on your workstations. You may have dozens or hundreds of workstations, all configured to work with your NetWare servers, and all of which are working well. Obviously, you would prefer to avoid the cost, effort, and disruption involved in doing wholesale workstation upgrades. Well, the good news is that you can integrate Windows NT Server into your network without changing a thing on any of your client workstations. The Microsoft FPNW utility, described in Chapter 19, *Using File and Print Services for NetWare*, allows NetWare clients to access shared resources on Windows NT Server.

Even so, you need to be aware of the client-side issues that arise when you install Windows NT Server in a NetWare shop. Although what you have in place may be good enough. You may have sufficiently few workstations on your network that it makes sense to upgrade them *en masse* to take advantage of the benefits provided by modern workstation operating systems like Windows NT Workstation 4.0. Even if such a wholesale replacement is not in the cards, you probably add new workstations to your network periodically, and replace older ones. When you have to make a site visit anyway, it only makes sense to get the client side right while you're there.

Given the limited inroads that Windows 95 has made in corporate LANs, many of you have a client environment that comprises mostly Windows 3.11 for Workgroups running Novell ODI NIC drivers and the VLM requester. Some of you will be using mostly Windows 95 clients with the Client for NetWare Networks, or perhaps the Novell client for Windows 95. Others—an increasing number—will be using Windows NT Workstation 4.0 clients with the Client Service for NetWare, or perhaps the Novell client for Windows NT. Most of you probably have a mixed environment of Windows 3.11 for Workgroups, Windows 95, and Windows NT workstations running a mix of client software.

This chapter begins with an overview of License Manager, the Windows NT Server application used to maintain access licenses. It continues with a brief description of using Network Client Administrator to create network installation disks and installation disk sets. The final section describes how to build universal clients—those equally capable of accessing NetWare servers, Windows NT servers, UNIX hosts, and the Internet—on the three primary OS platforms—Windows 3.11 for Workgroups, Windows 95, and Windows NT Workstation 4.0.

Using License Manager

Tracking NetWare licenses is easy because you've licensed a certain number of concurrent users on each NetWare server. You don't need to worry about exceeding the license count because NetWare won't let you. If users are unable to log on because of insufficient licenses, you'll hear about it soon enough. Tracking Windows NT Server licenses can be a bit more difficult, both because of the distributed nature of a typical Windows NT Server network and because of the additional flexibility that Windows NT Server gives you in terms of how licenses are purchased and assigned.

Although it might be possible to track licenses manually on a small Windows NT Server network, doing so would be both time consuming and error prone. On large Windows NT Server networks, manual tracking would be next to impossible. Recognizing this problem, Microsoft includes the License Manager utility with Windows NT Server.

License Manager automatically tracks and manages license usage throughout your organization. Like user account data, this licensing data is stored on the PDC and replicated automatically to each BDC. You can use License Manager to view the status of per-server and per-seat licenses throughout the organization, to manage licensing by adding and removing licenses as needed, and to view license usage statistics for each user.

Viewing License Usage

To start License Manager, from the Start button, select **Programs ➤ Administrative Tools (Common) ➤ License Manager** to display the Purchase History page of License Manager, as shown in Figure 17-1. Purchase history displays a single line for each licensing transaction that has occurred, which includes the date of the transaction, the product that was licensed, the number of licenses added or removed, the person who modified the license count, and an optional comment. These transaction records cannot be deleted or edited. If you make a mistake when entering the licenses originally, you must first create a reversing entry, and then enter the proper number and type of licenses, yielding a total of three entries for that single transaction.

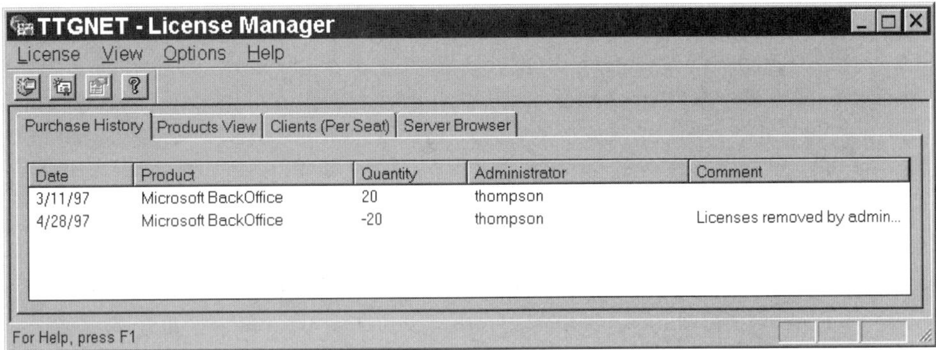

Figure 17-1. The License Manager Purchase History page lists the licenses you have added and removed

To view the license status by product, click the Products View tab to display the Products View page. License Manager displays a line for each licensed product, which includes the product name, the number of per-seat licenses purchased and in use, the number of per-server licenses purchased, and the maximum number used.

To view the license status by client, click the Clients (Per Seat) tab to display the Clients (Per Seat) page. License Manager displays a line for each client that is currently using one or more licensed products. This line includes columns listing the username, the number of valid licenses being used, the number of products being used without a license (if any), and a list of the products in use.

To specify the domain or server for which licenses are to be viewed, click the Server Browser tab to display the Server Browser page. After a brief pause during which it scans your network to discover the Windows NT servers present, License Manager displays a hierarchical tree that lists each domain present in your enterprise network and, for each domain, the servers that are members of that domain. Double-click a server name to display the products licensed per server for that server, and the license count for each.

Managing Licenses

Windows NT Server License Manager gives you a great deal of flexibility in managing the licenses you buy. You can, for example, remove unnecessary licenses from one server and add them to another server. The following sections describe using License Manager to change licensing modes, to add and remove per-server licenses, and to add and remove per-seat licenses.

Changing licensing mode

Microsoft allows you to make a one-time change from per-server licensing to per-seat licensing. To change the licensing mode, click the Server Browser tab to display the Server Browser page. Double-click a domain name to display a list of servers within that domain. Double-click a server name to display a list of products that are licensed per server on that server. Double-click a product name to display the Choosing Licensing Mode dialog.

In the Licensing Mode pane, mark the Per Seat option button, and then click OK. Windows NT Server displays a warning. If you are sure you want to convert your per-server licenses to per-seat licenses, click Yes to make the change. Otherwise, click No to abort the change and return to the Choose Licensing Mode dialog.

If you click Yes, License Manager displays the Per Seat Licensing dialog. Click Help to display the license agreement. If you agree to its terms, mark the I agree that check box and click OK to activate the per-seat licenses. Otherwise, click Cancel.

Adding per-server mode client licenses

To add client access licenses in per-server mode, take the steps described in the preceding section to select the appropriate server and product and to display the Choose Licensing Mode dialog. Click Add Licenses to display the New Client Access License dialog. Although it appears that the Product field drop-down list will allow you to select different products, only the product selected in the preceding step is available. Use the Quantity field spinner to select a number of licenses to be added. Enter a short description in the Comment field, if needed. Click OK to add the licenses. Read and accept the license agreement to place the new licenses into effect.

Removing per-server mode licenses

You can also use License Manager to remove per-server licenses. Why would you want to remove licenses? So that you can use them on a different server. Microsoft allows you to move licenses around freely. If, for example, you have a total of 100 per-server client licenses and two servers, and you want to assign 58 licenses to one of the servers and the other 42 licenses to the other server, simply add and remove licenses as needed to make the numbers come out right.

To remove client access licenses in per-server mode, take the steps described in the preceding section to select the appropriate server and product and to display the Choose Licensing Mode dialog. Click Remove Licenses to display the Select Certificate to Remove Licenses dialog. In the Serial Number column, highlight the certificate for which you want to remove licenses. Use the Number of Licenses to remove spinner to specify the number of licenses to be removed and click Remove to remove the licenses.

Adding and removing per-seat mode client licenses

When you add client licenses in per-seat mode, you are adding them to a pool of available licenses, and not for individual users or particular servers. These licenses are issued to users on a first-come, first-served basis, for each product they access. If more users access the product than you have licenses for, license violations will result. You are responsible for making sure that you have enough per-seat licenses to ensure that each user who accesses a product has a valid license for that product.

To add client access licenses in per-seat mode, from the License menu click New License to display the New Client Access License dialog. This is the same dialog used for adding per-server licenses, except this time the Product field drop-down list is active. Use it to select the product for which you are adding per-seat licenses. Use the Quantity field spinner to select a number of licenses to be added. Enter a short description in the Comment field, if needed, and click OK to add them. Read and accept the license agreement to place the new licenses into effect.

To delete client access licenses in per-server mode, click the Products View tab to display the Products View page. Click the product name for which you want to remove licenses to highlight it. From the License menu, click Delete to display the Select Certificate to Remove Licenses dialog. Use the Number of Licenses to remove spinner to specify the number of licenses to be removed and click Remove to remove them.

Using Network Client Administrator

Network Client Administrator is a convenience utility. It allows you to install the client software and tools that are bundled with Windows NT Server 4.0. The distribution CD contains the following client installation files:

- Microsoft Windows 95
- Microsoft Network Client for MS-DOS (v 3.0)
- Microsoft LAN Manager for MS-DOS (v 2.2c)
- Microsoft LAN Manager for OS/2 (v 2.2c)

The Windows NT Server 4.0 distribution CD also contains the following client utilities and tools:

- Client-based network administration tools
- Microsoft Remote Access Service (RAS) Client for MS-DOS (v 1.1a)
- Microsoft TCP/IP-32 for Windows 3.11 for Workgroups

Start Network Client Administrator, from the Start button by choosing **Programs ➤ Administrative Tools (Common) ➤ Network Client Administrator**. Choose one of the following option buttons to specify the action to be taken by Network Client Administrator.

Make Network Installation Startup Disk
: Choose this option button to create a disk that automatically starts the client computer, connects to the server where the installation files reside, and initiates the installation. Network Client Administrator supports only this type of disk set for the following clients: Windows NT Server, Windows NT Workstation, Windows 95, and Windows for Workgroups. You may use this type of disk set for the Network Client for MS-DOS.

Make Installation Disk Set
: Choose this option button to create a set of floppy disks that contains all files needed to install the client software. You can use this set of floppies to install the client manually at each client workstation. Network Client Administrator supports only this type of disk set for the following clients: TCP/IP-32 for Windows Workgroups, LAN Manager for MS-DOS, LAN Manager for OS/2, and RAS for MS-DOS. You may use this type of disk set for the Network Client for MS-DOS.

Copy Client-Based Network Administration Tools
: Choose this option button to install network administration tools to a client running Windows NT, Windows 95, or Windows for Workgroups.

View Remoteboot Client Information
: Choose this option button to view information about remoteboot clients. Note that you cannot install remoteboot support from this application, but only view the status of existing remoteboot clients.

Creating a Network Installation Startup Disk

To create a network installation startup disk, mark the Make Network Installation Startup Disk option button and click Continue. Windows NT scans your CD-ROM drive to locate the distribution files, and then displays the Share Network Client Installation Files dialog. If Windows NT locates the distribution files, it inserts the

Path where they are located automatically, and selects the Share Files option, using Clients as the default Share Name. Choose among the following options:

Path
: Enter the drive and directory where the distribution files are located.

Use Existing Path
: Mark this option button if you have previously used Network Client Administrator and want to use files in the same location you used previously.

Share Files
: Mark this option button if you want to use the files directly from the distribution CD, rather than copying them to the hard drive. Enter a Share Name for the share, or accept the default value if present.

Copy Files to a New Directory, and then Share
: Mark this option button if you want to copy the distribution files to your hard drive and create a new share. Enter values for the Destination Path and the new Share Name.

Use Existing Shared Directory
: Mark this option button if you have already copied the distribution files to a shared directory and want to use those files. Enter the Server Name and the Share Name of the existing share where the files are located.

When you have completed the Share Network Client Installation Files dialog, click OK to display the Target Workstation Configuration dialog, as shown in Figure 17-2.

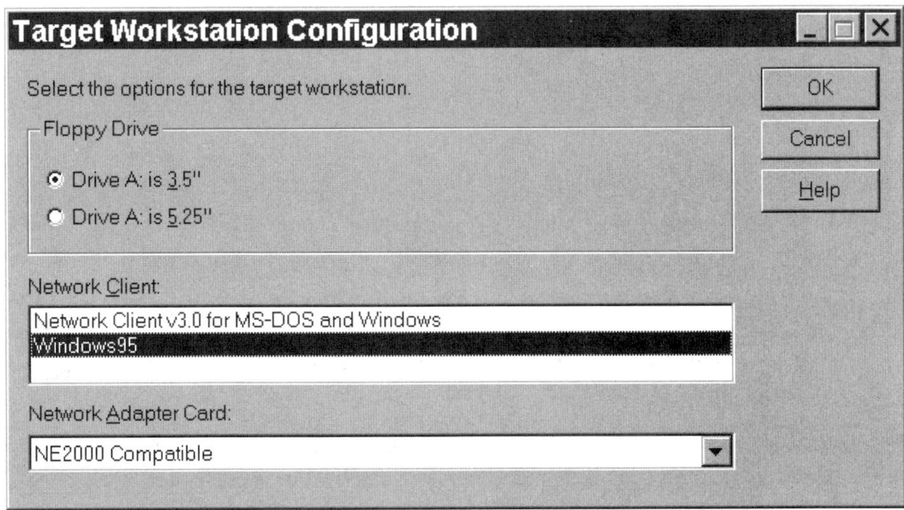

Figure 17-2. Use the Target Workstation Configuration dialog to specify the client software to be installed, the disk size, and the type of network adapter

Note that this procedure does not create a generic network installation diskette, but one specific to a particular workstation. Mark the appropriate option button for the type of floppy drive installed in the target system. Network Client Administrator creates only high-density (1.2 MB or 1.44 MB) floppy disks. Choose the type of network client software you want to install and the type of network adapter installed in that workstation. Click OK to continue. Network Client Administrator may display a warning message to notify you that you must have a valid license for that operating system and client before proceeding.

Click OK to display the Network Startup Disk Configuration dialog, as shown in Figure 17-3, with the default options selected by Network Client Administrator. Modify the following options as appropriate for the workstation you will be installing:

Computer Name
: Enter the unique NetBIOS computer name (Windows name) by which this workstation will be identified. No default value is entered for this field.

User Name
: Enter a user account name. By default, Network Client Administrator inserts the username of the account that creates the installation disk.

Domain
: Enter the domain of which this workstation is to be a member. By default, Network Client Administrator inserts the domain to which the computer that is creating the installation disk belongs.

Network Protocol
: Select the network protocol to be used for the over-the-wire installation. Only protocols that are installed on the server and suitable for over-the-wire installation are listed.

TCP/IP Settings
: If you select TCP/IP, the TCP/IP Settings pane becomes active. If your network includes a DHCP server, and if you want this client to receive its TCP/IP configuration from that server, mark the Enable Automatic DHCP Configuration check box. If your network does not include a DHCP server, or if it does, but for some reason you want to configure the TCP/IP configuration for this client manually, clear the check box and enter appropriate values for IP Address, Subnet Mask, and Default Gateway.

Destination Path
: Enter the location that you want to copy the distribution files to—by default, drive *A:*.

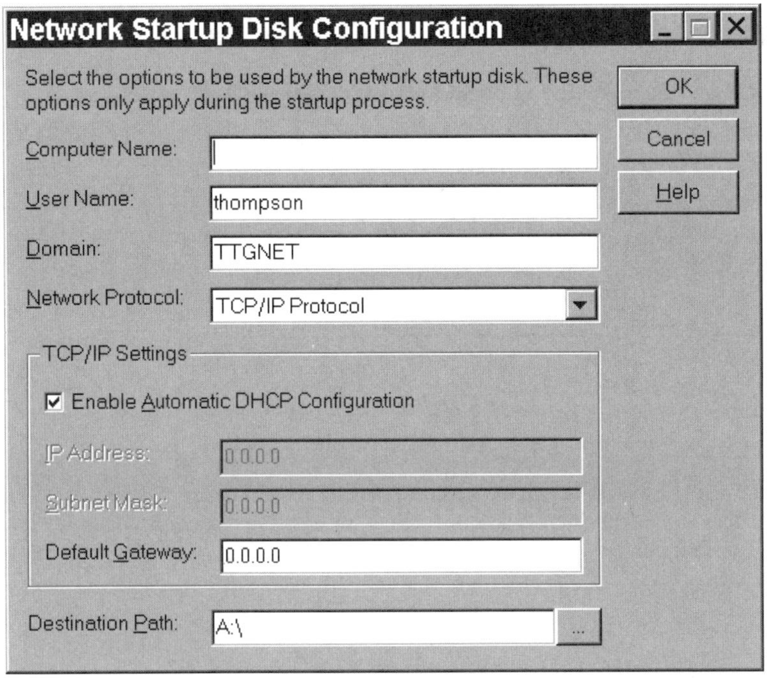

Figure 17-3. Use the Network Startup Disk Configuration dialog to specify the initial configuration options that will be used during the over-the-wire installation

When you have completed the Network Startup Disk Configuration dialog, click OK to continue. Network Client Administrator prompts you for a formatted high-density disk, to which it copies the files.

Creating an Installation Disk Set

To create an installation disk set, mark the Make Installation Disk Set option button and click Continue. Windows NT displays the Share Network Client Installation Files dialog. Specify the appropriate locations and shares, as described in the preceding section, and then click OK to display the Make Installation Disk Set dialog, as shown in Figure 17-4. Use the Network Client or Service scrolling pick list to specify the client software for which you wish to create the disk set, and select the Destination Drive. Network Client Administrator displays the number of diskettes that will be needed at the bottom. Mark the Format Disks check box, if desired, and click OK to create the disk set. Network Client Administrator displays the Copying Files dialog as the files are copied to the diskette, and then displays a final dialog to inform you that the files were copied successfully.

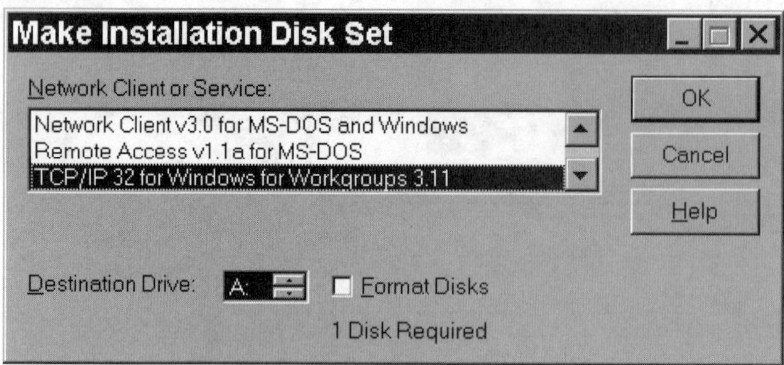

Figure 17-4. Use the Make Installation Disk Set dialog to specify which client software will be copied to the floppy diskette installation set

---

NOTE Unlike the Network Installation Startup Disk, which creates a diskette that is specific to a particular client workstation, the Installation Disk Set can be used for any number of clients.

Copying Client-Based Network Administration Tools

To copy the Client-based Network Administration Tools to your server, mark the Copy Client-based Network Administration Tools option button and click Continue. Windows NT scans your hard disk and CD-ROM drive to locate the distribution files, and then displays the Share Client-based Administration Tools dialog. This dialog is very similar to the Share Network Client Installation Files dialog, differing only in that it does not offer the Use Existing Path option button.

Specify the locations and shares as described in the preceding sections, and click OK to install the distribution files. Network Client Administrator installs distribution files for Windows 95 and for Windows NT. For Windows 95, this procedure installs versions of Event Viewer, Server Manager, and User Manager for Domains that allow Windows 95 to manage Windows NT Server components.

The inclusion of administration tools for Windows NT might seem puzzling at first. After all, why should Windows NT need special tools to manage Windows NT? The answer has to do with how Microsoft markets the server and workstation versions of Windows NT.

Essentially, the server and workstation versions are identical with two exceptions. First, a couple of Registry entries cause the workstation version to configure itself to optimize local interactive performance at the expense of degrading performance when servicing network requests. These Registry entries also cause the workstation version to place arbitrary limitations on itself regarding number of client connections, number of RAS ports, and so on—all changes meant to ensure that no one who pays only for Windows NT Workstation can turn around and use it as Windows NT Server. Second, the server version comes bundled with various utilities—e.g., the DHCP server and the WINS server—that are useful primarily in a server environment.

The Windows NT administrative tools that are installed by this procedure are the management utilities for the additional services that are bundled with Windows NT Server, e.g., WINS Manager and DHCP Manager. They are intended to be installed on Windows NT Workstation to allow it to manage Windows NT Server services. You don't need to install them on Windows NT Server—it already has them installed.

NOTE There is also a limited selection of client-based administration tools available to run under Windows 3.1x and Windows 3.1x for Workgroups. Unlike the Windows 95 and Windows NT Workstation 4.0 32-bit tools, these 16-bit client-based administration tools are not included on the Windows NT Server 4.0 distribution CD.

If you want to run the 16-bit client-based administration tools on a client running Windows 3.1x or Windows 3.1x for Workgroups, Microsoft recommends that you install the tools from the distribution files located on the Windows NT Server version 3.51 CD. Easy enough, if you happen to have a 3.51 CD. Pretty tough if you don't. I was unable to locate the 16-bit tools on the Microsoft web site.

While the 32-bit tools provide exactly the same functionality as the native Windows NT Server 4.0 tools, the 16-bit tools are limited both in scope and in functionality. The 16-bit toolkit includes only Event Viewer, Print Manager for Windows NT Server, Server Manager, and User Manager for Domains. It also includes a File Manager Security menu. Missing are the 32-bit-only tools, DHCP Manager, Remote Access Administrator, Remoteboot Manager, User Profile Editor, and WINS Manager. In addition, many of the 16-bit tools provide only a subset of the functions available with the 32-bit tools.

The 16-bit tools require Win32s to run. Installing the 16-bit tools automatically creates a Win32s subdirectory under the Windows *SYSTEM* directory and installs the necessary drivers.

I'm ignoring Remoteboot, because I can count on one finger the number of administrators I know who use diskless workstations and remoteboot. If you really want to do in your server and network that badly, it's easier just to shoot the server.

Building Universal Clients

In the context of this book, a "universal client" obviously must incorporate access to both NetWare servers and Windows NT servers. Beyond that, the explosive growth of the Internet and of TCP/IP-based corporate intranets during the last few years implicitly demands that—although we could build such a client using only IPX/SPX transport—a real universal client must include all the hooks needed for Internet access. In other words, it must run TCP/IP transport in addition to IPX/SPX. Accordingly, for our purposes, I'll define a universal client as one that supports both the NCP and SMB core protocols, and simultaneously supports both TCP/IP transport and IPX/SPX transport.

NOTE Some might wonder about the absence of NetBEUI support in these "universal" clients. In fact, it's easy enough to incorporate NetBEUI in any of them. However, there are good reasons for not using NetBEUI. It's an obsolete protocol, suited only to the smallest environments, and entirely inappropriate for an enterprise network. The only time NetBEUI is needed is if your network includes Microsoft peer networking clients, e.g., Windows 3.11 for Workgroups, that do not have IP or IPX installed. Because this situation is diametrically opposed to the universal clients discussed in this section, I have elected to ignore NetBEUI.

Two common operating environments are completely inappropriate platforms for building a universal client. The architectures of MS-DOS and Windows 3.0/3.1 (the non-"for Workgroups" versions) are deficient in their support for multiple protocol stacks and the other pieces needed to build a universal client. If you have clients running either of these products, chances are that they are now running Novell NETx client software, probably with the monolithic *IPX.COM* drivers. You'd probably prefer not to touch them, and that's a wise decision.

Instead, let Windows NT Server take up the slack. Install File and Print Services for NetWare (FPNW), described in Chapter 19, *Using File and Print Services for NetWare*. FPNW allows Windows NT Server to emulate a NetWare 3.12 server, allowing NetWare clients to access Windows NT Server resources. It's a quick fix, but, unlike most such solutions, it's actually viable as a long-term solution.

NOTE Two much less common environments—the Apple Macintosh and IBM OS/2—are somewhat more suited to building a universal client, but I have elected not to spend time or space covering them. Accurate numbers are difficult to come by, but most numbers I have seen indicate that fewer than one in one thousand clients on Windows NT Server networks are either Macintoshes or running OS/2, and that fewer than 1% of all Windows NT Server networks have either type of client connected.

I'm sure that both of these environments have their advantages, so please don't send me flame mail, but both of these types of clients tend to be concentrated on relatively very few networks. Then again, I don't own a Macintosh and haven't run OS/2 since Version 2.1, so perhaps I'm missing something good.

Three common operating environments are appropriate platforms for building a universal client. Ironically, the suitability to the task of each is about inversely proportional to the likelihood that it will be in use as a client on your network. In order of desirability, these operating systems are:

Windows NT Workstation
: Although it still has only a tiny share of the workstation operating system market, this is beginning to change as more administrators begin to appreciate the advantages that this operating system offers in comparison to the alternatives. Windows NT Workstation is a natural as a client for Windows NT Server. It is easier to install, configure, and use as a client for Windows NT Server than any of the alternatives. This is true for any recent release of Windows NT Workstation. Although Windows NT Workstation 4.0 has a prettier interface, version 3.51 makes just about as good a client. However, if you're running Windows NT Workstation 3.5 (usually called 3.50 for clarity) or earlier, you need to upgrade.

Windows 95
: If Windows NT Workstation is the best Windows NT Server client, Windows 95 isn't far behind. Windows 95 is less robust and less secure than Windows NT Workstation, but has some advantages of its own. Many administrators who would prefer to use Windows NT Workstation exclusively find themselves also supporting Windows 95 clients, particularly on portable systems, where Windows 95 support for Plug-n-Play and power management are important concerns.

Windows 3.11 for Workgroups
: This obsolete operating environment brings up the rear in terms of suitability as a network client for Windows NT Server networks. However, the limited penetration of both Windows 95 and Windows NT Workstation into corporate

networks makes it likely that you will have at least some clients running WfWG 3.11.

The following sections treat each of these three operating systems in turn.

Configuring Windows NT Workstation 4.0 as a Universal Client

As you might expect, Windows NT Workstation 4.0 is the ideal client to use on a Windows NT Server 4.0 network. Because they are essentially the same operating system, Windows NT Workstation 4.0 provides seamless support for Windows NT Server network services. In addition, Windows NT Workstation integrates the transport protocol support and client software needed to access NetWare resources into the operating system itself. Finally, Windows NT Workstation provides full support for the TCP/IP protocol and TCP/IP services needed to access the Internet and corporate intranets.

Installing the NWLink IPX/SPX compatible transport protocol

Depending on your network configuration, Windows NT Workstation setup may install only the TCP/IP protocol by default, although you may always elect also to install the NWLink IPX/SPX compatible transport protocol and/or NetBEUI during setup. Configuring the default TCP/IP protocol is described in Chapter 3, *Configuring Windows NT Server Networking*.

For full NetWare interoperability, the NWLink IPX/SPX compatible transport protocol must also be present. If the NWLink IPX/SPX compatible transport protocol was not installed during setup, take the following steps to install it now:

1. On the desktop, right-click the Network Neighborhood icon and choose Properties to display the Network dialog. Click the Protocols tab to display the Protocols page.
2. Click Add to display the Select Network Protocol dialog. Highlight the NWLink IPX/SPX Compatible Transport protocol and click OK.
3. Windows NT prompts you for the location of the distribution files, defaulting to the location from which you installed Windows NT. Accept the default location or provide another location, and click OK to continue. Windows NT copies the necessary files from the distribution media. When all files have been copied, Windows NT displays the Network dialog, showing the NWLink IPX/SPX Compatible Transport protocol and the NWLink NetBIOS protocol as installed.
4. Click Close to complete the installation. Windows NT configures, stores, and reviews the bindings, and displays the Network Settings Change dialog to notify you that the system must be restarted before your changes will take effect. Click Yes to restart the system immediately, or click No to defer availability of NWLink until the next routine system restart.

NOTE By default, Windows NT Workstation installs the NWLink protocol for the first adapter it locates, configures Frame Type to Auto Detect, and automatically determines the appropriate Network Number. If necessary, you can change the properties for NWLink by choosing Properties from the Protocols page of the Network dialog and assigning Frame Type and Network Number manually. Do not do so unless this client has problems connecting to IPX/SPX resources.

Installing the Client Service for NetWare

With Windows NT Workstation, Microsoft supplies the Client Service for NetWare, a NetWare-compatible redirector. Client Service for NetWare is similar to the Gateway Service for NetWare supplied with Windows NT Server, but provides redirection services only for the local machine upon which it is running. To install the Client Service for NetWare, take the following steps:

1. On the desktop, right-click the Network Neighborhood icon to display the Network dialog. Click the Services tab to display the Services page.
2. Click Add to display the Select Network Service dialog. Highlight Client Service for NetWare and click OK.
3. Windows NT prompts you for the location of the distribution files, defaulting to the location from which you installed Windows NT. Accept the default location or provide another location, and click OK to continue. Windows NT copies the necessary files from the distribution media. When all files have been copied, Windows NT displays the Network dialog, showing the Client Service for NetWare as installed.
4. Click Close to complete the installation. Windows NT configures, stores, and reviews the bindings, and displays the Network Settings Change dialog to notify you that the system must be restarted before your changes will take effect. Click Yes to restart the system immediately, or click No to defer availability of the Client Service for NetWare until the next routine system restart.

NOTE The first time you restart the computer after installing the Client Service for NetWare, the Select NetWare Logon dialog appears. Use this dialog to specify a Preferred Server or a Default Tree and Context. Mark the Run Login Script check box if you want the login script to run each time you log on.

Using Novell client software

The Microsoft Client Service for NetWare is a perfectly adequate NetWare client in a 3.1x NetWare environment. If you have one or more NetWare 4.x servers on your network, you might reasonably consider installing native Novell client software for Windows NT Workstation to gain several advantages touted by Novell, primarily more complete support for NDS. It has been my experience, however, that installing the Novell client creates more problems than it solves, particularly in an environment that has no NetWare 4.x servers present. In particular, the Novell client does not play nice with File and Print Services for NetWare.

Some of these problems may, as Novell states, be due to deficiencies in Windows NT rather than problems with the Novell client. Be that as it may, I recommend that you use the Microsoft Services for NetWare if at all possible. To find out more about the Novell client for Windows NT, set your web browser to:

http://support.novell.com/home/client/winnt/whatsnew.htm

For more information—from the Novell perspective—about the problems with FPNW, set your web browser to:

http://support.novell.com/cgi-bin/search/tidfinder.cgi?2907903

Connecting to network resources

One of the best measures of the suitability of a desktop operating system for use as a network client is how easily it allows you to connect to and use shared network disk and printer resources. Windows NT Workstation comes up a winner by this measure. Connecting to either shared Windows NT Server resources or shared NetWare resources is done in similar fashion, and is so easy as to be almost trivial.

Connecting to shared disk resources. Using Windows NT Workstation to connect to a shared volume on either a Windows NT server or a NetWare server is as simple as mapping a local Windows NT Workstation drive either to a Windows NT Server share or a NetWare volume. To do so, take the following steps:

1. From the desktop, right-click My Computer to display the context-sensitive menu. Click Map Network Drive to display the Map Network Drive dialog.
2. Use the Drive drop-down list to specify the local drive letter you want to assign. Only unassigned drive letters are available for selection.
3. In the Path field, type the location of the share to be assigned to the specified drive letter, or use the drop-down list to select from a list of available previously used shares. Alternatively, to connect to a Windows NT Server share, in the lower pane, double-click the Microsoft Windows Network icon to display

a list of available domains. Double-click a domain name to display the computers available within that domain. Double-click a computer name to display the shares available on that computer and highlight one of the shares to insert it in the Path field. Or, to connect to a NetWare volume, double-click NetWare or Compatible Network in the lower pane to display a list of NetWare servers, double-click a server name to display a list of volumes on that server, and then double-click the volume to insert it in the Path field.

4. By default, Windows NT Workstation connects to the share using the username you are currently logged in as. If you want to connect using a different username, enter that username in the Connect As field. If you do so, you will be prompted for a password before the connection to the share is established.
5. The Reconnect at Logon check box is marked by default, which causes the connection to be persistent. In other words, the connection to this share will be reestablished each time you log on. Clear this check box if you do not want to be reconnected to the share automatically.
6. Figure 17-5 shows the completed Map Network Drive dialog. Once you have completed the dialog, click OK to establish the connection to the share.

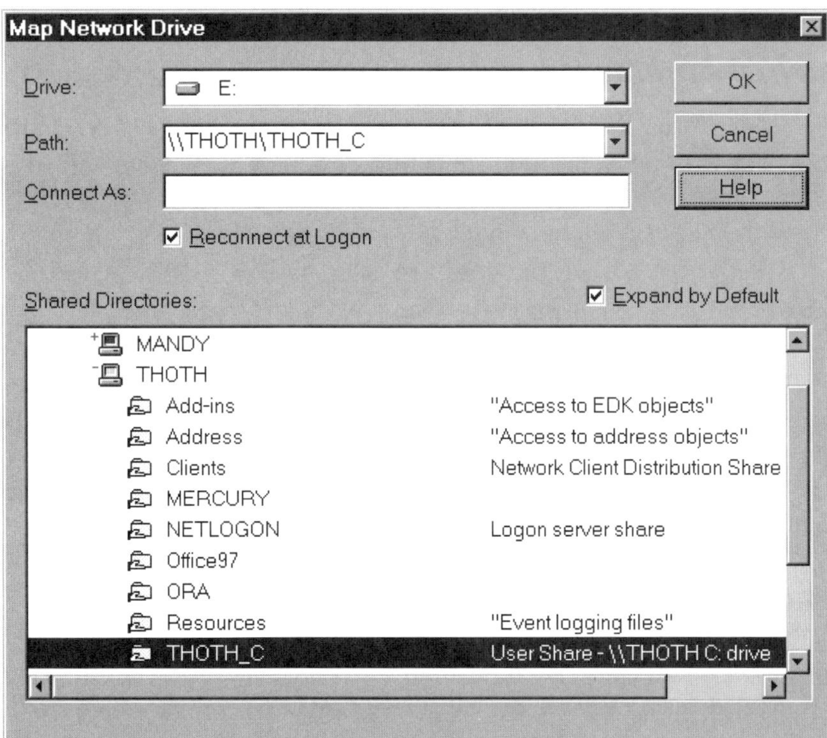

Figure 17-5. Use the Map Network Drive dialog to establish a connection to a Windows NT Server share

7. Click OK to establish the connection to the share. Windows NT Explorer displays the contents of the newly connected share.

Connecting to shared printers. Using Windows NT Workstation to connect to a shared printer on a Windows NT or NetWare server is no more difficult than connecting to a shared volume. To create a connection to a shared printer, take the following steps:

1. From the desktop, double-click My Computer to display the My Computer folder. Double-click Printers to display the Printers folder. Double-click Add Printer to invoke the Add Printer Wizard.
2. Mark the Network printer server option button and click Next to display the Connect to Printer dialog. Expand the display, as described in the preceding section, and select an available printer on a Windows NT server or an available print queue on a NetWare server.
3. Click OK to install the printer. The Add Printer Wizard displays a window to notify you that the printer has been installed successfully. Click Finish to complete the installation. The new printer now appears in the Printers folder and is available for use.

Configuring Windows 95 as a Universal Client

If Windows NT Workstation 4.0 is the ideal client to use on a Windows NT Server 4.0 network, Windows 95 is a close runner-up. Configuring Windows 95 as a universal client may take a few more steps than configuring Windows NT Workstation for the same purpose. The time required for these additional steps is usually counterbalanced by the availability of various Windows 95 ease-of-use features, notably Plug-n-Play.

Like Windows NT Workstation, Windows 95 provides seamless support for Windows NT Server network services. Windows 95 also integrates the transport protocol support and client software needed to access NetWare resources into the operating system itself. Finally, like Windows NT Workstation, Windows 95 provides full support for the TCP/IP protocol and TCP/IP services needed to access the Internet and corporate intranets.

Configuring the Network Properties Identification page

The Identification page of Network Properties contains the information needed to identify the Windows 95 client to other computers on the network and to define the workgroup or domain to which the client is assigned. To complete the Identification page, from the desktop, right-click Network Neighborhood to display the

Network property sheet. Click the Identification tab to display the Identification page, and complete the fields as follows:

Computer name
: Enter a name to identify this computer. This name will be the NetBIOS computer name, also called the Windows Networking computer name, and must be unique on the network. During installation, Windows 95 generates a default computer name using the first eight characters of the username. The computer name may be as long as 15 characters, and can include spaces. It cannot contain the following characters:

    ! @ # $ % ^ & * ( ) _ { } ' ~ `

Workgroup
: Enter the name of the workgroup or domain to which this computer is assigned. The Workgroup name has the same length and character restrictions as the computer name. If you are upgrading to Windows 95 from Windows 3.11 for Workgroups, this value defaults to the previous Workgroup name. If you are installing Windows 95 to a clean hard disk, it generates a default Workgroup name using the first 15 characters of the organization name. In either case, normally override the default value with the name of the domain to which you are assigning this workstation.

Computer description
: Optionally, enter a brief description of this workstation. This field is used primarily in peer networking environments to aid other computers in identifying the workstation. During installation, Windows 95 assigns the username as the default value for this field.

Configuring the Network Properties Access Control page

The Access Control page of Network Properties allows you to specify how access to resources shared by this computer will be controlled. Note that the settings you make on this page are effective only if the workstation is sharing its resources in a peer environment, using either File and Printer Sharing for Microsoft Networks or File and Printer Sharing for NetWare networks. To complete the Identification page, from the Network property sheet, click the Access Control tab to display the Access Control page, and select one of the following option buttons:

Share-level access control
: Selecting this option allows access to each shared resource on the workstation to be controlled by a workgroup password. For shared folders, you may specify Read Only Access, Full Access, or Depends on Password. Access to shared printers is controlled in similar fashion. Share-level access control is available for File and Printer Sharing for Microsoft Networks, but cannot be used with File and Printer Sharing for NetWare Networks.

User-level access control

Selecting this option requires that users seeking access to local shared resources be first validated by a Windows NT server or a NetWare server. If you are using File and Printer Sharing for Microsoft Networks, enter the name of the Windows NT domain in the Obtain list of users and groups from list box. If you are using File and Printer Sharing for NetWare Networks, enter the name of a NetWare 3.1x server (or a NetWare 4.x server running bindery emulation) in this list box.

When a network user attempts to access shared resources on this workstation, that user is first validated by the server or domain listed. If that user has no account on the validating server or domain, access is refused. If the user does have an account, he or she is granted access rights to the shared resource based on his or her account privileges on the validating server or domain.

In essence, using user-level access control adds an Access Control List (ACL) aspect to the broad-brush access limitations enforced by share-level access control. User-level access control allows you to refine access limits by granting or refusing access to specific resources on the basis of username or group memberships. User-level access control can be used with either File and Printer Sharing for Microsoft Networks or File and Printer Sharing for NetWare Networks.

Installing and configuring the Client for NetWare Networks

The Client for NetWare Networks uses the IPX/SPX-compatible protocol exclusively, and does not normally require any special configuration steps. In the NetWare 3.12 environment, the Microsoft Client for NetWare Networks essentially duplicates all of the services provided by native Novell client software, with one exception. The Client for NetWare Networks does not support the *NWPOPUP* utility, and provides only a partial replacement for it. The *WINPOPUP* utility, like *NWPOPUP*, allows users to exchange messages. However, *WINPOPUP* does not respond to NetWare system messages by popping up a message box over the foreground application. This means, for example, that users who are used to receiving notification of new email messages via *NWPOPUP* will no longer receive such notifications.

To install the Client for NetWare Networks, take the following steps:

1. On the desktop, right-click the Network Neighborhood icon and choose Properties to display the Network dialog. In the example, the Client for Microsoft Networks, the Client for NetWare Networks, the NE2000 compatible network

adapter card, the IPX/SPX-compatible protocol, the TCP/IP transport protocol, and the File and printer sharing for Microsoft Networks service have already been installed.

2. Click Add to display the Select Network Component Type dialog.
3. Highlight Client and click Add to display the Select Network Client dialog. Highlight Microsoft in the Manufacturers pane to display a list of available clients in the Network Clients pane.
4. Highlight Client for NetWare Networks and click OK to install the client software. The Network property sheet is redisplayed, showing Client for NetWare Networks as installed. Highlight it in the installed components list and click Properties to display the Client for NetWare Networks Properties property sheet. Use the Preferred server drop-down list to specify a preferred NetWare server. Use the First network drive drop-down list to choose the first drive letter to be assigned to network drives. Mark the Enable logon script processing check box if you want Windows 95 to process your NetWare login script.
5. When you have completed configuring the Client for NetWare Networks, click OK to return to the Network property sheet. Click OK again to complete installing the Client for NetWare Networks. Windows 95 prompts you for the location of the distribution files. Accept the default location or specify a new location. After the files are copied, Windows 95 configures the bindings and displays the System Settings Change dialog to inform you that your changes will not take effect until you reboot the workstation.

Installing and configuring the Client for Microsoft Networks

Install the Client for Microsoft Networks using the same procedure described in the preceding section for installing the Client for NetWare Networks. To configure the Client for Microsoft Networks, highlight it in the Network property sheet and click Properties to display the Client for Microsoft Networks Properties property sheet, as shown in Figure 17-6.

The Logon validation pane allows you to specify whether or not logons will be authenticated by a Windows NT Server domain. To authenticate logons, mark the Log on to Windows NT domain check box and enter the name of the domain that is to validate logons in the Windows NT domain field.

The Network logon options pane controls how the availability of network resources is determined at logon. Mark the Quick Logon option button if you want the availability of mapped network drives to be verified only when the client attempts to access them. Mark the Logon and restore network connections option button if you want the availability of each mapped network drive to be verified at logon.

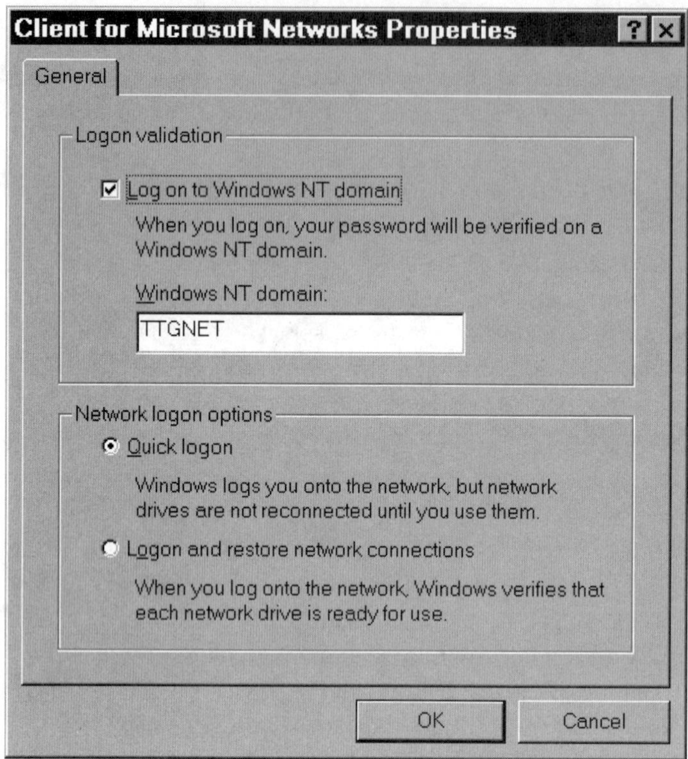

Figure 17-6. Use the Client for Microsoft Networks Properties property sheet to specify how logons will be validated and drive mappings verified

Setting the Primary Network Logon

The setting for Primary Network Logon determines which client software handles the initial actions that occur at login—user validation, running login scripts, and so on. Windows 95 sets the Client for Microsoft Networks as the default Primary Network Logon. If you install the Client for NetWare Networks, you can specify that it be used instead to perform initial startup functions. If you prefer that the workstation not connect to the network automatically each time it is started, select Windows Logon.

Use the Primary Network Logon drop-down list in the Network property sheet to specify which client to use as the Primary Network Logon. When you have done so, click OK to effect the change. Windows 95 displays the System Settings Change dialog to notify you that the change will not take effect until the next time the system is started (see Figure 17-7).

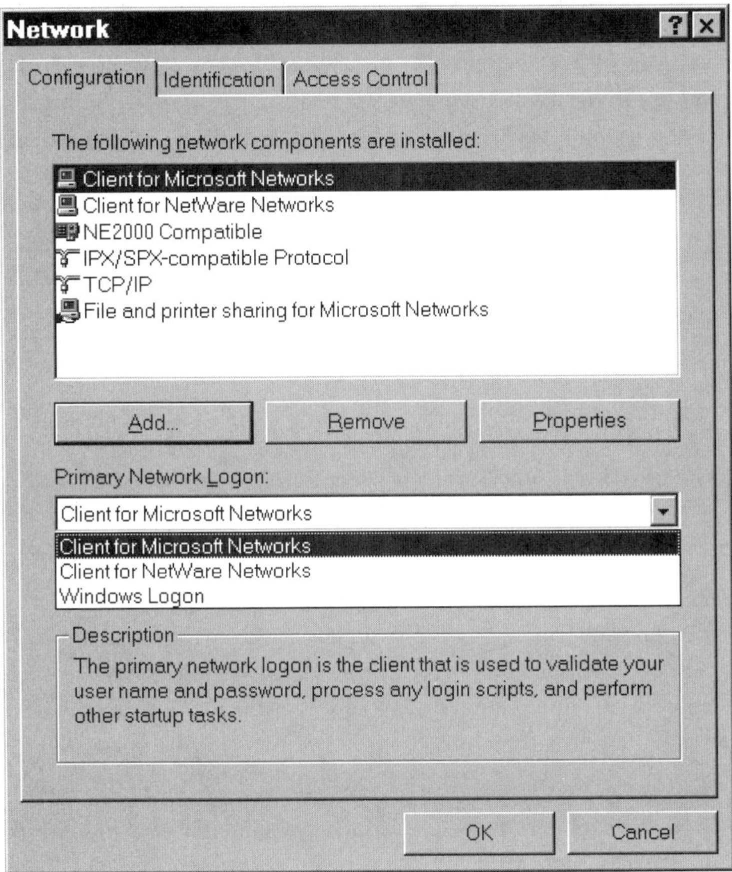

Figure 17-7. Use the Primary Network Logon to specify which network client will perform user validation and process login scripts each time the Windows 95 client boots

Using file and printer sharing

Windows NT Workstation 4.0 has the built-in ability to share its local disk and printer resources with other Microsoft Networking clients, and to secure them by using either share-level permissions or NTFS permissions. Windows 95 has similar, if more limited, abilities to share and control access to its local disk and printer resources with other Microsoft Networking clients, and can also share its resources with NetWare clients.

Windows 95 provides two sharing mechanisms. If the Windows 95 client is running the Client for NetWare Networks, you can install the NetWare Core Protocol (NCP) based file and printer sharing for NetWare Networks service. If the Windows 95 client is running the Client for Microsoft Networks, you can install the Server Message Block (SMB) based file and printer sharing for Microsoft Networks service. Only one of these services may be installed on a client.

File and Printer sharing for NetWare Networks. The File and Printer sharing for NetWare Networks service allows you to share the local disk and printer resources of the Windows 95 workstation with other network clients that connect via NCP, including DOS and Windows clients that are running native Novell client software, Windows 95 clients that are running the Client for NetWare Networks, and Windows NT computers that are running the Client Service for NetWare. Share-level security is not an option when you use this service. If you enable user-level security, a NetWare server provides authentication.

NOTE The workstation that is running File and Printer sharing for NetWare Networks must be using the Microsoft Client for NetWare Networks rather than native Novell client software.

A client running File and Printer sharing for NetWare Networks advertises its services using Workgroup Advertising or the Novell Service Advertising Protocol (SAP). Whether or not these services are visible to a client browsing the network depends on the client software it is using and the advertising method used by the Windows 95 workstation, as follows:

- Shared resources on the Windows 95 workstation are visible to clients running the Novell NETx shell or the VLM redirector only if the Windows 95 workstation uses SAP to broadcast the availability of its services. A shared folder appears as a server volume, and a shared printer appears as a Novell print queue.
- Shared resources on the Windows 95 workstation are visible to other Windows 95 clients running the Client for NetWare Networks and to Windows NT computers running the Client Service for NetWare no matter which advertising method the Windows 95 workstation is using, but with some differences. If the Windows 95 workstation is using Workgroup Advertising, it appears as a member of a workgroup. If it is using SAP, it does not appear as a member of a workgroup, but is visible to other clients only if they browse the entire network.

WARNING Both the File and Printer sharing for NetWare Networks service and the File and Printer sharing for Microsoft Networks service contained in the initial release of Windows 95 had serious security flaws that might allow unauthorized users to gain a dangerous level of access to the workstation. These problems have since been fixed, and the Windows 95 release that is currently shipping (OSR2) does not exhibit the problem. If you are using an earlier release of Windows 95, make sure before using either File and Printer sharing service to download and install the Windows 95 Service Pack 1 from *http://www.microsoft.com/windows95/default.asp*.

File and Printer sharing for Microsoft Networks. The File and Printer sharing for Microsoft Networks service allows you to share the local disk and printer resources of the Windows 95 workstation with other network clients that connect via SMB, including clients that are running the Client Service for NetWare on Windows NT Server or Workstation; the Client for Microsoft Networks on Windows 95; Windows 3.11 for Workgroups; LAN Manager; or DEC Pathworks. Access to shared resources on the Windows 95 workstation can be controlled by share-level security, or by user-level security with a Windows NT domain controller providing user authentication. Using File and Printer sharing for Microsoft Networks requires that the Windows 95 workstation be running the Client for Microsoft Networks.

Installing and enabling file and printer sharing. Install the File and Printer sharing for Microsoft Networks service or the File and Printer sharing for NetWare Networks service using the same steps described in the preceding sections for installing clients, but substituting "Service" for "Client" in the Select Network Component Type dialog. As usual, you must reboot the system before the changes take effect. You can configure the service by highlighting its name in the Network property sheet and choosing Properties, but either service works properly using the default values in nearly any environment.

After you have installed the service, you must enable it before other network users will be able to access shared resources on the Windows 95 client. To enable the service, in the Network property sheet, click File and Print Sharing to display the File and Print Sharing dialog. Mark one or both check boxes to enable File and/or Printer sharing on this workstation.

Installing and configuring the IPX/SPX-compatible transport protocol

The transport protocols installed automatically during Windows 95 setup depend on your network configuration. Windows 95 setup installs NetBEUI automatically if it detects NetBEUI frames on the wire. Windows 95 setup never installs TCP/IP automatically. Windows 95 setup automatically installs the IPX-SPX-compatible protocol when you install the Client for NetWare Networks or when you upgrade a Windows 3.1x workstation that is running Novell client software. For full NetWare interoperability, the IPX/SPX-compatible protocol must be present. If Windows 95 does not install IPX/SPX-compatible protocol during setup, take the following steps to install it now:

1. On the desktop, right-click the Network Neighborhood icon and choose Properties to display the Network dialog, shown in the preceding section as Figure 17-7.
2. Click Add to display the Select Network Component Type dialog.
3. Highlight Protocol and click Add to display the Select Network Protocol dialog. Highlight Microsoft in the left pane to display the list of available Microsoft protocols. Highlight IPX/SPX-compatible Protocol in the right pane and click OK to install the IPX/SPX-compatible Protocol and return to the Network property sheet, which now shows the IPX/SPX-compatible Protocol as installed.
4. Highlight the IPX/SPX-compatible Protocol in the installed components list, and click Properties to display the Bindings page of the IPX/SPX-compatible Protocol Properties property sheet, as shown in Figure 17-8. By default, Windows 95 binds the IPX/SPX-compatible Protocol to installed clients and services. To remove the bindings for clients and services that do not require this protocol, clear the associated check boxes. For example, if your Windows NT server is running TCP/IP transport, it would make sense to clear the IPX/SPX bindings for the Client for Microsoft Networks and the File and Printer sharing for Microsoft Networks service. Removing unneeded bindings frees system resources and increases performance.
5. Click the Advanced tab to display the Advanced page of the IPX/SPX-compatible Protocol Properties property sheet. It's somewhat surprising that Microsoft even provides this page, because (with one exception) none of these items needs to be modified in any typical network. Similarly obscure parameters are ordinarily changed by modifying Registry value entries. The one exception on this page is the Frame Type, changes to which are described earlier in this chapter, and in Chapter 3, *Configuring Windows NT Server Networking*.
6. Click the NetBIOS tab to display the NetBIOS page of the IPX/SPX-compatible Protocol Properties property sheet. Mark the check box if you need to enable NetBIOS over IPX/SPX. Windows 95 workstations can communicate with each other—and with Windows NT servers and NetWare servers—using only NWLink. Some network applications, however, notably IBM Notes,

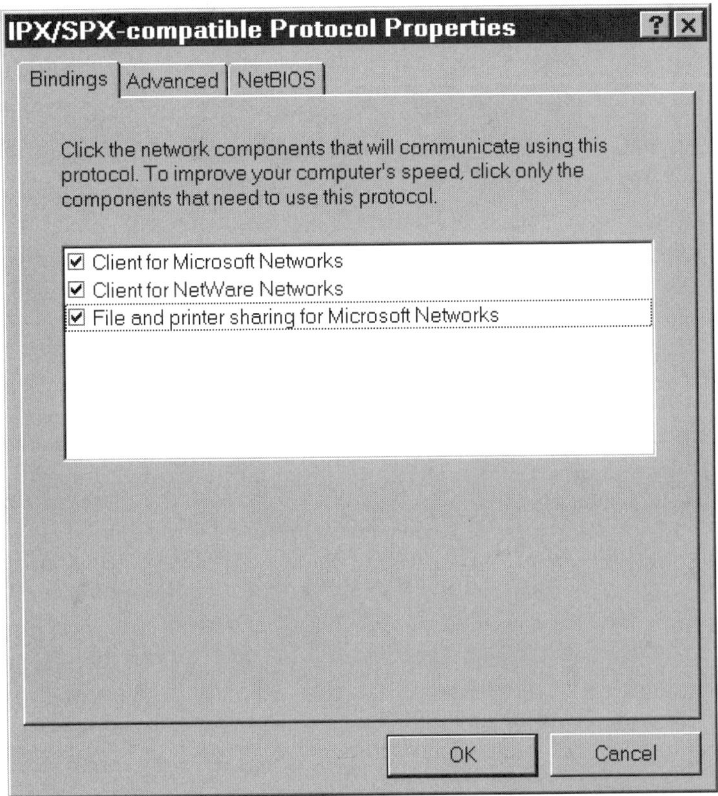

Figure 17-8. Use the Bindings page of the IPX/SPX-compatible Protocol Properties property sheet to remove unnecessary bindings to reduce resource consumption and increase performance

require NetBIOS. This check box is disabled by default. Leave it that way unless you have network applications that require NetBIOS over IPX/SPX to function.

7. When you have finished configuring IPX/SPX-compatible Protocol options, click OK to return to the Network property sheet. Click OK again to complete installing the IPX/SPX-compatible Protocol. Windows 95 prompts you for the location of the distribution files. Accept the default location or specify a new location. After the files are copied, Windows 95 configures the bindings and displays the System Settings Change dialog to inform you that your changes will not take effect until you reboot the workstation.

Installing and configuring the TCP/IP protocol

The TCP/IP protocol is essential for accessing the Internet and TCP/IP-based corporate intranets. Windows 95 setup does not install the TCP/IP protocol by default. Install the TCP/IP protocol using the steps described in the preceding section to install the IPX/SPX-compatible protocol. To configure TCP/IP, take the following steps:

1. Highlight the TCP/IP protocol in the Network property sheet installed components list, and click Properties to display the IP Address page of the TCP/IP Properties property sheet. By default, Windows 95 selects the Obtain an IP address automatically option button, which causes Windows 95 to obtain an IP address and other TCP/IP configuration information from a DHCP server on the network.

   If you are running DHCP server on your Windows NT server, the default value is normally the best choice. If you are not running a DHCP server, or if for some reason you don't want this workstation to use dynamic IP addressing, mark the Specify an IP address option button and complete the fields for IP Address and Subnet Mask. DHCP is described fully in Chapter 12, *Using Dynamic Host Configuration Protocol.*

2. Click the WINS Configuration tab to display the WINS Configuration page. By default, Windows 95 marks the Disable WINS Resolution option button. If you have one or more WINS servers on your network and want this workstation to use WINS for name resolution, mark the Enable WINS Resolution option button and enter the IP addresses of your primary and secondary WINS servers and the Scope ID. If this client is running DHCP, mark the Use DHCP for WINS Resolution option button. WINS is described fully in Chapter 12, *Using Dynamic Host Configuration Protocol.*

3. Click the Gateway tab to display the Gateway page. Enter the IP address of the border router for this network, if present, in the New gateway field, and click Add to move it to the Installed gateways list. You may add the IP addresses of additional routers the same way, but Windows 95 always uses the router that appears first on the list, if it is available. If this client is running DHCP, and the DHCP server is configured to provide the default router, these values will already be filled in. Routers are described in more detail in Chapter 11, *Understanding TCP/IP.*

NOTE In networking, the term *gateway* is used to mean two different things. In the OSI Model sense, a gateway is a device that translates incompatible protocols, e.g., cc:Mail to and from SMTP mail. The Internet community uses the term *gateway* to mean a router. In this case, Microsoft is using the word in its Internet sense, to mean a border router.

---

4. Click the DNS Configuration tab to display the DNS Configuration page, as shown in Figure 17-9. By default, Windows 95 marks the Disable DNS option button. If you have one or more DNS servers on your network and want this workstation to use DNS for name resolution, mark the Enable DNS option button and enter the following items:

   Host

   Enter the Internet name of this computer. Note that the Internet name of the computer need not be the same as the NetBIOS computer name (Windows machine name), although it usually is set to the same name to avoid confusion..

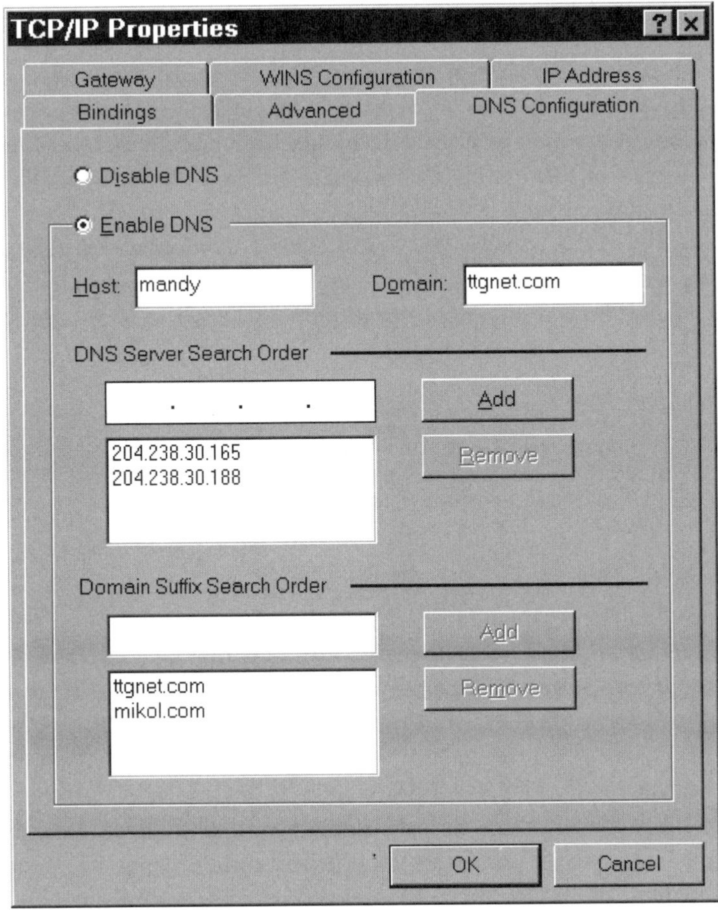

Figure 17-9. Use the DNS Configuration page of the TCP/IP Properties property sheet to specify DNS configuration items

Domain

Enter the Internet domain name. Note that this is the **Internet** domain name, **not** the Windows NT Server domain name.

DNS Server Search Order

Enter the IP addresses for your primary DNS server and click Add to move it to the installed DNS servers pane immediately below. Repeat the process for your secondary DNS server. The first IP address that appears in this list is designated the primary DNS server, and is used if available. Secondary and subsequent DNS servers are used only if the primary is unavailable.

Domain Suffix Search Order

You may optionally enter one or more Internet domain names in this list. Windows 95 uses the domain names that appear in the list to attempt to resolve partially qualified domain names. For example, my Internet domain is *ttgnet.com*, but I frequently access computers in the Internet domain *mikol.com*. Because *mikol.com* appears in the Domain Suffix Search order list, I can refer to the machine *adrian.mikol.com* simply as *adrian*. When it receives the partial name *adrian*, Windows 95 first attempts to locate the machine *adrian.ttgnet.com*. When it is unable to resolve that name, it continues down the list and attempts *adrian.mikol.com*, which it is able to resolve.

NOTE If this client is running DHCP, and the DHCP server is configured to provide IP addresses for the DNS servers, these values will be filled in automatically. DNS is described fully in Chapter 14, *Using Domain Name Service*

---

5. Click the Advanced tab to display the Advanced page. Depending on the TCP/IP environment of your network, some or no items may appear here. If configurable items do appear, it's generally a good idea not to touch them unless you have at least a shodan—and perhaps a sandan—in TCP/IP-kan. In this case, only TCP/IP was installed, so it is selected as the default protocol automatically. If you have more than one transport protocol installed, the Set this protocol to be the default protocol check box is enabled. Mark this check box if you want TCP/IP to be the default protocol, or clear it if you want to assign another installed protocol as the default.
6. Click the Bindings tab to display the Bindings page. The bindings page allows you to specify which clients and services should use the TCP/IP protocol. Clear the check box next to clients and services that do not need to use TCP/IP to reduce resource consumption and to increase system performance. You should

normally leave the Client for Microsoft Networks bound to TCP/IP. Clear the binding for File and printer sharing for Microsoft Networks unless you need to use this service in an internetworked TCP/IP environment.

7. When you have finished configuring TCP/IP options, click OK to return to the Network property sheet. Click OK again to complete installing TCP/IP. Windows 95 prompts you for the location of the distribution files. Accept the default location or specify a new location. After the files are copied, Windows 95 configures the bindings and displays the System Settings Change dialog to inform you that your changes will not take effect until you reboot the workstation.

Retrofitting Windows 3.11 for Workgroups for TCP/IP

Windows 3.11 for Workgroups is by far the least capable of the operating systems examined in this chapter, and is also the least well suited for use as a universal client. Out of the box, Windows 3.11 for Workgroups supports only NetBEUI transport and the SMB core protocol, leaving it to you to provide the IPX/SPX and NCP support needed to access NetWare, and the TCP/IP, Winsock, and packet driver support required for access to the Internet. In outline, enabling Windows 3.11 for Workgroups as a universal client requires the following steps:

- Install the Novell ODI drivers and VLM requester to support NetWare connectivity.
- Enable NetWare support within Windows 3.11 for Workgroups.
- Enable Windows 3.11 for Workgroups support for Windows Networking.
- Install a Winsock-compliant TCP/IP protocol stack.
- Install Windows packet driver support.

Because a Windows 3.11 for Workgroups client on your network is almost certain to have NetWare support already installed, and because most administrators will be familiar with the procedures for enabling network support in Windows 3.11 for Workgroups, this section concentrates on the final two steps in this process.

Installing a TCP/IP protocol stack

Unlike Windows NT Workstation 4.0 and Windows 95, Windows 3.11 for Workgroups does not bundle a native TCP/IP protocol stack. Using TCP/IP with Windows 3.11 for Workgroups requires adding a TCP/IP stack that is compliant with the Windows Sockets Specification, commonly called Winsock. There are many Winsock implementations available for Windows 3.11 for Workgroups, ranging in price from free to quite expensive. Fortunately, Microsoft has released a Winsock for Windows 3.11 for Workgroups, distributed as *TCPIP32B.EXE*, that is both free and sufficient to do the job.

The Microsoft TCP/IP stack provides all of the functionality that most administrators will need, and has the advantages of being free and of minimizing the likelihood that compatibility or configuration problems will occur. If you require dialer support or other advanced options, consider one of the alternative shareware or commercial products.

The Microsoft TCP/IP stack includes a standard *WINSOCK.DLL*. It provides partial, but adequate, support for the Microsoft DHCP Server, DHCP protocol options, and DHCP information options, including Subnet Mask (Option 1), Default Router (3), DNS server (6), NetBIOS Name (WINS) Server (44), NetBIOS Node Type (46), NetBIOS Scope ID (47), Lease Time (51), DHCP Message Type (53), Renewal Time (58), and Rebind Time (59). It also bundles various standard TCP/IP utilities, including *ARP.EXE*, *FTP.EXE*, *IPCONFIG.EXE*, *NBSTAT.EXE*, *NETSTAT.EXE*, *PING.EXE*, *ROUTE.EXE*, *TELNET.EXE*, and *TRACERT.EXE*.

To install the Microsoft TCP/IP stack, take the following steps:

1. Create a disk set for the TCP/IP stack by using the procedure described in the section "Creating an Installation Disk Set" earlier in this chapter.
2. From the Network program group, click Network Setup to display the Network Setup dialog, and then click Networks to display the Networks dialog.
3. Mark the Install Microsoft Windows Network option button and then click OK to return to the Network Setup dialog.
4. Click Drivers to display the Drivers dialog and then Add Adapter to display the Add Network Adapter dialog. Highlight the installed adapter and click OK to return to the Network Drivers dialog.
5. Click Add Protocol to display the Add Network Protocol dialog. Select Add Protocol, and double-click Unlisted or Updated Protocol. Windows prompts you to insert a disk containing the protocol.
6. Insert the diskette you created in step 1, and click OK to begin installing the protocol. Windows displays a message box to notify you that you are installing the Microsoft TCP/IP protocol. Click OK to begin copying the files.
7. When all files have been copied, Windows returns you to the Network Drivers dialog. Click Close to return to the Network Setup dialog. Click OK to return to the Microsoft Windows Network dialog.
8. Complete the Microsoft Windows Network dialog. Computer Name is the NetBIOS computer name (Windows machine name) of this workstation. Workgroup is the workgroup to which this computer is assigned. Note that this

value must be unique on the network, and is **not** the name of the Windows NT domain. Comment allows you to enter a description for the computer, which will be visible to Microsoft Networking clients browsing the network. Default Logon Name is the username of the Windows NT Server account. When you have completed this information, click OK to continue. Windows may prompt you for diskettes containing network adapter drivers or the Windows 3.11 for Workgroups distribution files.

9. After copying the necessary files, Windows 3.11 for Workgroups displays the Microsoft TCP/IP Configuration dialog. Enter the required information as described in the preceding section on configuring TCP/IP for Windows 95. Click DNS and Advanced in turn, and supply the required information. Click OK to complete TCP/IP configuration and exit Network Setup.
10. Exit to DOS and restart the computer.

Installing packet driver support

Packet drivers allow the ODI network adapter drivers and Windows itself to handle and route TCP/IP packets properly. Two free programs are used in nearly all Windows 3.11 for Workgroups environments to provide this support. `ODIPKT` provides packet driver support to the Novell ODI driver. `WINPKT` is a shim that provides packet support to Windows itself. These two programs can be downloaded from almost any web site, FTP site, or bulletin board system that has a Winsock files area.

ODIPKT allows a single network adapter running ODI drivers to support multiple packet driver protocol stacks. In the environment we are considering, *ODIPKT* is required to allow the network adapter to service IPX and IP packets simultaneously. Because the frame types that NetWare uses to transport IPX (e.g., 802.3 on a NetWare 3.11 network or 802.2 on a NetWare 3.12 network) are not appropriate for transporting IP, a single network adapter in a NetWare client is often bound to a second frame type (Ethernet II) for TCP/IP. Each of these frame types is bound to the adapter in *NET.CFG*, which causes ODI to treat each frame type as a separate logical network adapter. The following *NET.CFG* fragment illustrates a typical configuration:

```
Link Driver ne2000
port 300
int 10
frame ETHERNET_802.3
frame ETHERNET_802.2
frame Ethernet_II
```

The first three lines specify that the NE2000 link driver is to be used, at port 300 hex and interrupt 10. The following three lines bind three separate frame types to that link driver, in sequence as logical adapters 0, 1, and 2. This allows the client to access, respectively, NetWare 3.11 servers, NetWare 3.12 and 4.x servers, and UNIX hosts.

ODI uses buffers supplied by the ODI Link Support Layer, so make sure that `NET.CFG` specifies enough buffers, and that each is of sufficient size to handle the protocol in use. For example, if you are using standard Ethernet 1,514 byte frames, specify `BUFFERS 2 1600` in *NET.CFG*. Or, if you are using 4,202 byte Token Ring frames, specify `BUFFERS 2 4300`.

ODIPKT is normally invoked in *STARTNET.BAT*. It requires two command-line arguments, one to specify the logical adapter to which it is bound, and the second to specify the software interrupt vector to be used. Note that the interrupt vector is specified in decimal notation. Load *ODIPKT* **after** `LSL` and the `MLID` (which it requires) and **before** *WINPKT*. The following *STARTNET.BAT* fragment is typical:

```
lsl
ne2000
odipkt 2 96
winpkt 0x60
ipxodi
vlm /mx
```

The first line loads the Link Support Layer (LSL), that provides the low-level support needed to link the hardware to the protocol stack. The second line loads the Multiple Link Interface Driver (MLID), in this case *NE2000.COM*, that comprises the hardware driver specific to the network adapter card being used. The third line loads *ODIPKT*, binds it to virtual network adapter card 2 (the one running Ethernet II frames), and assigns it the software interrupt 96 decimal. The fourth line loads the *WINPKT* packet driver and assigns it the software interrupt 60 hex. Note that *WINPKT* uses hexadecimal notation, as opposed to the decimal notation used by *ODIPKT*, and that the software interrupts assigned to these two drivers must have the same value. In this case, 60 hex corresponds to 96 decimal. The fifth line loads the Novell `IPXODI` IPX support for ODI, and the final line loads the Novell requester.

18

Using Gateway Service for NetWare

This chapter explains how to install, configure, and use the Gateway Service for NetWare (GSNW), a utility that is bundled with Windows NT Server 4.0. When GSNW is installed on a server running Windows NT Server, it allows that server to access shared disk and printer resources on NetWare servers. With GSNW, the network administrator can also create gateways to allow clients that are running only Microsoft Networking client software to access these shared NetWare resources. However, GSNW is not a perfect solution. It creates a single channel between the GSNW gateway and the NetWare server, and shares that channel among all of the clients that are using the gateway. Although this sharing minimizes the need for licensing additional NetWare concurrent users, it also introduces performance, access control, and security issues.

Years ago, when GSNW was first announced, some people saw it as a dark plot to damage the then overwhelmingly dominant position of Novell in the NOS marketplace. You could, they said, buy a cheap five-user copy of NetWare, and use a Windows NT server running GSNW to allow hundreds of clients to access the resources on that five-user NetWare server. Well, that's not really what GSNW is about, and it never really has been.

GSNW is fundamentally a convenience product. You don't use it because it's the best way to get the job done. You use it because it is a cheap, quick, and easy solution to the problem of allowing Microsoft Networking clients to access shared NetWare resources. When something seems too good to be true, there's always a problem that someone forgot to mention. In the case of GSNW, the fly in the ointment is performance, or rather the lack thereof.

It's true that you could allow hundreds of Microsoft Networking clients to access shared NetWare resources through a single GSNW gateway. As a matter of fact, for reasons known only to God and Bill Gates, GSNW allows you to explicitly set the largest allowable number of simultaneous users for a single share to a number greater than four billion. It also allows you to set the number to "unlimited," presumably for those with networks that operate on a truly cosmic scale.

The reality, however, is that every concurrent user is contending for the bandwidth available on a single NetWare NCP session. In practical terms, you can allow perhaps as many as 20 or 25 users to share a connection for casual occasional use—checking email and so on. If the users will be performing work on the NetWare server that is moderately resource intensive, e.g., typical office automation tasks, you may get away with allowing five or eight users before performance becomes completely unacceptable. If users will need heavy disk access, even sharing the connection between two users may noticeably degrade performance.

With all of that said, GSNW can be a lifesaver if you have many workstations that run only Microsoft Networking client software. You probably don't have this problem. Chances are you're running NetWare client software on most or all of your workstations already. However, funny things happen when you bring Windows NT Server into a NetWare shop. For example, you might have a Windows for Workgroups peer-to-peer LAN that has never been connected to your NetWare network. The presence of Windows NT Server all of a sudden makes the idea of connecting that peer network to your main network a lot more palatable. Using GSNW lets you make this connection as a single easy step, rather than requiring you to modify the client software configuration for each workstation on the peer network.

Treat GSNW as an interim, stopgap solution, rather than as a permanent fixture on your network. Use it to allow yourself some breathing space while you install NetWare client software on Microsoft clients at your own pace, instead of being forced to upgrade all of your clients overnight. Used in this way, GSNW is an excellent product. Used any other way, it's liable to cause a lot of user complaints.

Gateway Service for NetWare Overview

GSNW is a superset of the Client Service for NetWare (CSN) supplied with Windows NT Workstation 4.0. Like CSN, GSNW serves as a NetWare redirector for the local machine it is running on, which allows that server to access shared disk and printer resources on NetWare servers connected to the network. In addition to these ordinary redirection functions, GSNW can also serve as a proxy redirector for Microsoft Networking clients that are connected to the server running GSNW. This means that these clients can access shared resources on a NetWare server without themselves having a local NetWare redirector installed.

GSNW uses two other NetWare interoperability features of Windows NT Server. The NWLink IPX/SPX Compatible Transport protocol allows Windows NT Server and NetWare to interoperate at the packet level. Without NWLink, the Windows NT server and the NetWare server cannot see or talk to each other. The NWLink NetBIOS protocol is the Microsoft implementation of Novell NetBIOS, and is used to communicate NetBIOS frames between Windows NT server and the NetWare server. If you install GSNW on a Windows NT server that does not already have both NWLink and NWLink NetBIOS installed, Windows NT Server installs them for you automatically.

Although NWLink provides interoperability between Windows NT Server and NetWare at the lower levels of the OSI model, a problem still remains. Windows NT Server and NetWare use fundamentally incompatible protocols at the upper layers. Windows NT Server uses the Server Message Block (SMB) protocol to communicate with Microsoft Networking clients, whereas NetWare uses the NetWare Core Protocol (NCP) to accomplish the same task. GSNW addresses this problem by serving as a bidirectional gateway that translates SMB calls to NCP calls, and *vice versa*. This allows the NetWare server and the Microsoft Networking clients to communicate freely, with each continuing to use its native protocols. As you might expect with any complex gateway, throughput is considerably lower than it would be on a connection that used exclusively native protocols.

To share NetWare disk resources with Microsoft Networking clients, the GSNW server first establishes an ordinary session with the NetWare server by logging on to it, redirects a local drive letter to a NetWare volume, and then shares that redirected drive with its clients. For example, the Windows NT server *kerby* might log on to the NetWare server *theodore* and map the directory *\\theodore\sys\users* to the local drive *H:* on *kerby*, and then assign that resource the share name *home*. Windows Networking clients that connect to *kerby* can then access the NetWare directory *\\theodore\sys\users* as *\\kerby\home*, using the same procedure they would use to access any other Windows NT share. The fact that this shared disk resource happens to be located on a NetWare server is transparent to the Microsoft Networking clients.

NOTE Once a disk or printer share is established with GSNW, it remains in effect and available to clients until the server is powered down, or until the administrator manually disables the share. Because GSNW runs as a Windows NT Server service, the gateway is available to the clients of the GSNW server even if no one has logged on to the console of that server.

Sharing NetWare printers with Microsoft Networking clients is done in a similar fashion. Using the shared logon to the NetWare server, you create a local Windows NT printer that maps to a NetWare printer. You then share this new Windows NT printer, which becomes visible to Microsoft Networking clients as just another Windows printer.

Configuring NetWare to Use Gateway Service for NetWare

GSNW is unique among Windows NT services because it requires you to make changes to your NetWare servers before the gateway services will function. You must make these changes on each NetWare server that will be accessed by gateway users. To prepare your NetWare servers to support GSNW, take the following steps:

1. Log in to the NetWare server as Supervisor or as a supervisor equivalent. Use *SYSCON.EXE* to create a new group named *NTGATEWAY*, as shown in Figure 18-1. This group name is hard-coded into GSNW. You cannot use an alternative group name. Grant the NTGATEWAY group the trustee rights and printer permissions that you want available to gateway users.

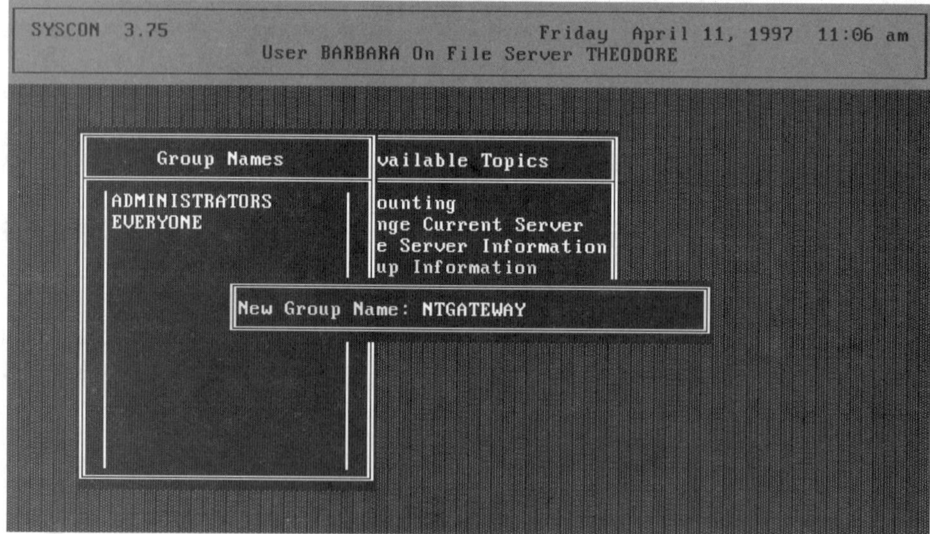

Figure 18-1. Use SYSCON.EXE to create the NTGATEWAY group and grant it the common trustee rights to be shared by GSNW users

2. Using *SYSCON.EXE*, create a new user, as shown in Figure 18-2, and grant that user supervisor equivalency. You can name this user as you wish. This

account will be used to administer GSNW, and may also be used by the Migration Tool for NetWare, which requires full administrative access to the NetWare server. The Migration Tool for NetWare is described fully in Chapter 21, *Migrating to a Pure Windows NT Server Environment.*

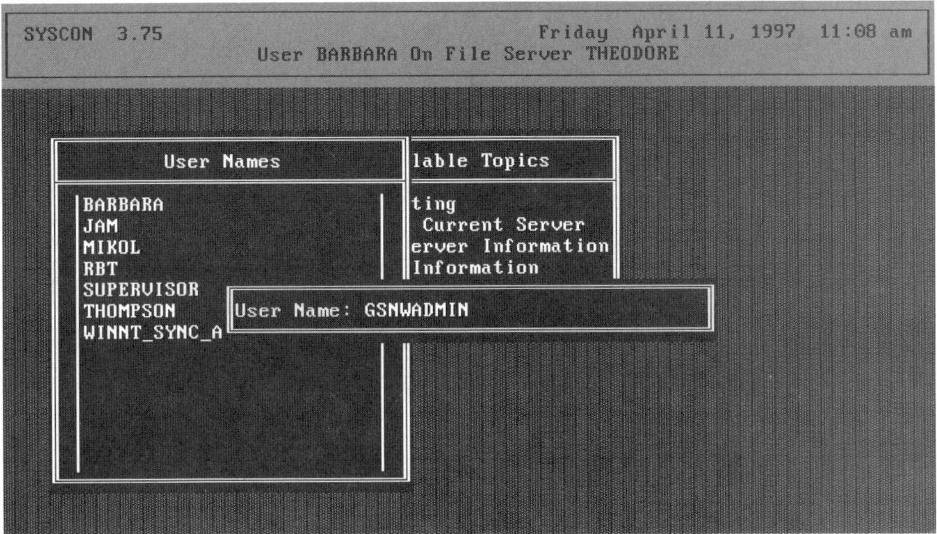

Figure 18-2. Create a GSNW administrative account, grant it supervisor equivalency, and assign it to the group NTGATEWAY

3. Using *SYSCON.EXE*, create another new user, as shown in Figure 18-3, and make this user a member of the NTGATEWAY group. You can name this user as you wish. This account will be shared by users who connect to the gateway to access resources on the NetWare server.

Installing Gateway Service for NetWare

The Gateway Service for NetWare is essentially a redirector, and provides services similar to those provided by the Novell NETx and VLM redirectors, or by the Client Service for NetWare running on Windows NT Workstation. There is one major difference, however, between ordinary redirectors and GSNW. An ordinary redirector provides redirection services only for the computer upon which it is running. GSNW provides redirection services both for the server on which it is running and for Microsoft Networking clients that are connected to that server. In other words, GSNW serves simultaneously as an ordinary redirector and as a proxy redirector.

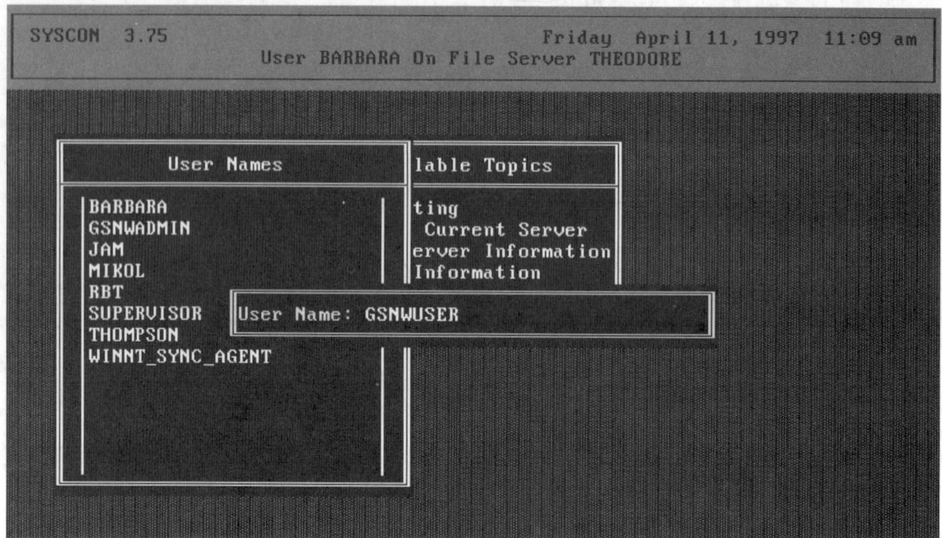

Figure 18-3. Create one or more ordinary user accounts for shared access, and assign them to the group NTGATEWAY

WARNING Because GSNW is fundamentally a NetWare redirector, it cannot co-exist with other redirectors that perform a similar service on the same computer. Therefore, before you install GSNW, remove any other NetWare redirectors, e.g., the Novell client for Windows NT.

Install the Gateway Service for NetWare, from the Network Services page of the Network property sheet (**Control Panel ➤ Network ➤ Services** tab). Select Add to display the Select Network Service dialog, where you can highlight Gateway (and Client) Service for NetWare for installation.

Windows NT displays the Windows NT Setup dialog to prompt for the location of the distribution files; accept the default or specify a new location as appropriate. If the NWLink IPX/SPX Compatible Transport protocol and the NWLink NetBIOS protocol are not already installed, Windows NT Server installs them before continuing. Windows NT copies the distribution files and returns to the Network property sheet, which now shows Gateway Service for NetWare as an installed service. When you close the installation dialog, Windows NT configures, stores, and reviews the bindings, and then asks if you want to restart your computer to activate the Gateway Service for NetWare.

Specifying a Preferred NetWare Server

When the server restarts, log on as an administrator. The GSNW service starts and the Select NetWare Logon dialog appears to prompt you for NetWare server options, as follows:

Preferred Server
: Mark this option button, which is selected by default, if you have a NetWare 3.1x server, or a NetWare 4.x server that is running bindery emulation. Use the Preferred Server drop-down list to choose a preferred server from the list of available bindery-based NetWare servers.

Default Tree and Context
: Mark this option button if you have a NetWare 4.x server running NDS. Fill in the appropriate values for Tree and Context.

Run Login Script
: Mark this check box, which is cleared by default, if you want the NetWare system login script to run migrate.

If you do not respond to this dialog within a minute or so, it times out and logs you on without configuring the NetWare server options. You must then complete these options by running the GSNW applet from Control Panel, to display the Gateway Service for NetWare dialog.

The Gateway Service for NetWare dialog includes all of the options available in the Select NetWare Logon dialog, and adds a Print Options section. Accept or modify these settings, as appropriate, as follows:

Add Form Feed
: Mark this check box, which is cleared by default, if you want gatewayed NetWare printers to eject a blank page following each print job.

Notify When Printed
: Mark this check box, which is enabled by default, if you want GSNW to notify users when the print jobs they send to a gatewayed NetWare printer have finished printing.

Print Banner
: Mark this check box, which is enabled by default, if you want gatewayed NetWare printers to separate print jobs by printing a banner page before each document.

When you have finished making changes to the Gateway Service for NetWare dialog, click OK to accept and save your changes.

WARNING Here's an odd problem that you need to be aware of if your network includes both NetWare 3.1x servers and NetWare 4.x servers. If you specify Default Tree and Context for the NetWare 4.x server, and then subsequently add shares to NetWare 3.1x servers, those shares may not be visible if the NetWare 4.x server is turned off or otherwise unavailable. Using the Gateway Service for NetWare dialog to respecify a NetWare 3.1x server as the preferred server does not fix the problem. Uninstalling and then reinstalling GSNW does not fix the problem. In searching the Microsoft web site and other resources, I was unable to find any solution for this problem. However, initially specifying the NetWare 3.1x server as the Preferred Server and then establishing gateway shares to the 4.x NetWare server appears to work.

WARNING Another problem that you need to be aware of if your network includes NetWare 4.x servers is related to the length of the context and tree. If you specify more than 32 characters, severe problems can occur, including heap corruption, failure of the GSNW Control Panel applet to load, access violations in *Services.exe*, and server crashes.

This problem can be resolved in several ways: install the updated *Nwwks.dll* that Microsoft posted explicitly to solve this problem; install Service Pack 2 or later; or modify Registry parameters as detailed in Article ID article Q156091. All of these files are available on *www.microsoft.com*.

Enabling and Configuring a GSNW Gateway

By default, GSNW provides only client redirection services to the server upon which it is installed. To enable proxy redirection services for Microsoft Networking clients connected to that server, you must enable and configure a gateway.

To do so, from the Gateway Service for NetWare dialog, click Gateway to display the Configure Gateway dialog. Mark the Enable Gateway check box to activate the rest of the dialog. Marking this check box enables both the disk and printer gateway services.

Type the name of the gateway user account in the Gateway Account box. This account must exist, and must be a member of the group NTGATEWAY on every NetWare server to which GSNW will establish gateways. Enter the password for that user in the Password and Confirm Password boxes. Note that this is the ordinary gateway user you created when preparing the NetWare server, **not** the supervisor equivalent user. Click Add to display the New Share dialog.

Provide the following information needed to define the new share:

Share Name
: Enter the name that Microsoft Networking clients will use to access the share. Share name can be as large as 12 characters, but don't use more than 8 characters if you want MS-DOS clients to be able to access the share.

Network Path
: Enter the path for the NetWare volume that is to be mapped to this share name. Use the UNC naming convention, i.e., *\\servername\volume.*

Comment
: Optionally, enter a description of the share.

Use Drive
: Use this drop-down list to set the local drive letter that is to be mapped to the share. GSNW uses the last available drive letter by default. This is the drive letter that is mapped to the share on the local server that GSNW is running on. In other words, if you log on to the console of this Windows NT server, you use this assigned drive letter to access the share. Conversely, Microsoft Networking clients who are connected to this server see this share just as they would a local volume on the server, e.g., *\\kerby\sys.* They may connect to the share by mapping their own choice of drive letter to it.

Choose one of the option buttons in the User Limit pane. By default, GSNW sets the number of allowable users to Unlimited, which can result in unacceptably slow performance because all GSNW users connected to this resource must share a single session to the NetWare server. If you want to limit the number of concurrent users allowed, use the Allow spinner to set an upper limit on simultaneous user count. When you select the Allow option button, GSNW defaults to 32 users. This value may be set in the range of 1 through 4,294,967,294 users. Click OK to define the gateway and return to the Configure Gateway dialog.

Define additional shares as necessary on the same or another NetWare server. After you have defined all of your shares, change the permissions for each of them, as necessary. By default, GSNW defines each share to provide the Full Control permission to the Everyone group. To change this setting, highlight the share name in the bottom pane of the Configure Gateway dialog and click Permissions to display the Access Through Share Permissions dialog. Setting share-level permissions is described fully in Chapter 6, *Controlling Access to Volumes, Folders, and Files.*

When you have finished setting permissions, click OK to return to the Gateway Service for NetWare dialog. Click OK again to save and activate the share.

Accessing NetWare Files Through the Gateway

In general, once the gateway has been established and configured, Windows Networking clients may access shared disk resources located on NetWare servers transparently. Because all Windows Networking clients share the single connection to the NetWare server established when you set up the NetWare GSNW user account, those clients also share the security restrictions of that account. These restrictions comprise the NetWare effective rights for the GSNW user account, less any rights removed by the share-level permissions in effect.

If some Microsoft Networking clients require different levels of access to the shared NetWare resource, you can simply modify the share to define additional users and groups with differing share-level permissions. For example, if a shared accounting database is stored on a NetWare volume, you might assign the group Everyone the Read Only permission, the group Accounting the Change permission, and the group Administrators the Full Control permission.

Also, GSNW does not support many of the file attributes available with NetWare. GSNW has no equivalent for the NetWare Copy Inhibit (CI), Purge (P), Read Audit (Ra), Read-Write (RW), Shareable (S), Transactional (T), and Write Audit (Wa) attributes. When a Microsoft Networking client writes a file to a NetWare server using GSNW, GSNW does, however, preserve the Archive (A), Hidden (H), System (S), and Read Only (R) attributes. There are minor differences in the way that NetWare and Windows NT Server handle file attributes for those that are supported. When GSNW opens a NetWare file, the file attribute mappings shown in Table 18-1 are applied.

Table 18-1. How GSNW Maps Windows NT File Attributes to NetWare File Attributes

Windows NT Attribute	NetWare Attribute
Archive (A)	Archive Needed (A)
Hidden (H)	Hidden (H)
System (S)	System (Sy)
Read Only (R)	Read Only (RO), Delete Inhibit (DI), Rename Inhibit (RI)

You can use the standard NetWare utilities, e.g., *FILER.EXE*, to modify the rights and attributes for a file saved by a GSNW client. Any such changes you make to the security of a file are subsequently respected by GSNW.

Running NetWare Utilities and NetWare-Aware Applications

GSNW allows you to run some, but not all, of the standard NetWare utilities and NetWare-aware applications from the command prompt of a Microsoft Networking client, including the following:

CHKVOL.EXE	*COLORPAL.EXE*	*DSPACE.EXE*	*FLAG.EXE*
FLAGDIR.EXE	*FCONSOLE.EXE*	*FILER.EXE*	*GRANT.EXE*
HELP.EXE	*LISTDIR.EXE*	*MAP.EXE*	*NCOPY.EXE*
NDIR.EXE	*PCONSOLE.EXE*	*PSC.EXE*	*PSTAT.EXE*
RCONSOLE.EXE	*REMOVE.EXE*	*REVOKE.EXE*	*RIGHTS.EXE*
SECURITY.EXE	*SEND.EXE*	*SESSION.EXE*	*SETPASS.EXE*
SETTTS.EXE	*SLIST.EXE*	*SYSCON.EXE*	*TLIST.EXE*
USERLIST.EXE	*VOLINFO.EXE*	*WHOAMI.EXE*	

It may, however, not be immediately obvious that you can run these NetWare utilities. It is not enough simply to have GSNW (or CSNW) installed. Installing either of these products copies the redirector program files to your hard drive, but does not load them. Enabling the GSNW gateway and mapping a shared drive causes the redirector to be loaded when the server is restarted. If you have not enabled a GSNW gateway (or otherwise loaded the redirector), attempting to run a NetWare utility will generate an error message.

For example, the Windows NT server that I am using to write this chapter has GSNW installed, but it is being used only to provide Client Service for NetWare services—that is, no gateway is enabled. Drive N: on this computer is mapped to the *sys:* volume of the NetWare server *theodore.* When I opened a command prompt, logged to drive *N:*, changed to *\public,* and attempted to run *SYSCON.EXE,* an error message resulted.

This might easily confuse a novice GSNW administrator. After all, you may well be logged in to a NetWare server under a privileged account name, so it's not immediately evident what the problem is. Your first thought might be to verify that you are logged in as a privileged user, which you can do by right-clicking Network Neighborhood and selecting Who Am I. Because this verifies that you are in fact logged on as a supervisor equivalent user, you may easily conclude that the *SYSCON.EXE* NetWare utility is simply not compatible with Windows NT.

This isn't true. The problem is due solely to the fact that you are trying to run a NetWare utility without first loading the redirector. To verify this, I loaded the redirector manually by opening a command prompt, changing to the *C:\WINNT\System32* folder, and running the two programs *nw16.exe* and *Vwipxspx.dll* one after the other. After doing so, I ran *SYSCON.EXE. SYSCON.EXE* (and the other supported NetWare utilities) now runs normally. Note that if I close and then reopen the command prompt and attempt to run *SYSCON.EXE* again without reloading the redirector, I again receive the error message.

To verify that enabling a GSNW gateway causes the redirector to be loaded automatically, I next enabled the GSNW gateway, created a share, mapped that share to local drive Z:, and restarted the server to activate the gateway. Once the server had restarted, I opened a command prompt window, logged to drive *Z:*, and again ran *SYSCON.EXE*. As expected, it ran normally.

Installing and Configuring a GSNW Print Gateway

To allow Microsoft Networking clients connected to the GSNW server to share NetWare printers, you must enable and configure a GSNW print gateway. To do so, from the desktop, double-click My Computer, then Printers, then Add Printer to display the Add Printer wizard. Choose the Network printer server option button, and click Next to display the Connect to Printer dialog.

Double-click the NetWare NDS Tree or server name in the Shared Printers pane to expand the display and show the printers available for that NDS tree or server. Select the desired printer, and then click OK to continue. Windows NT may display a message box to inform you that no suitable printer driver is installed on the NetWare server, and offer to install one on the GSNW server. Click OK to install the printer driver and continue.

The Add Printer Wizard dialog prompts you for the manufacturer and model of the printer on the NetWare server. Choosing a manufacturer in the Manufacturers pane displays a list of models made by that manufacturer in the Printers pane. Highlight a printer model, and click OK to install the driver for it. Alternatively, if you have a new or updated printer driver, click Have Disk and follow the prompts to install that driver.

Windows NT next prompts you to specify whether this printer should be the default printer. Select the Yes or No option button, and click Next to continue. The final Add Printer Wizard dialog appears to notify you that the printer has been installed successfully. Click Finish to complete the installation and return to the Printers folder, which now shows the new shared NetWare printer as installed.

Right-click the newly installed printer to display the context-sensitive menu, and click Properties to display the <*Printername* on *Servername*> Properties dialog. Click the Sharing tab to display the Sharing page. Click the Shared option button, and enter a name for the shared printer. Complete the other pages as described in Chapter 7, *Printing with Windows NT Server*. Click OK to save the changes to the shared printer and return to the Printers folder. Close the Printers folder. The NetWare printer shared by GSNW is now visible to any Windows Networking client with the necessary permissions, and appears as just another Windows printer.

NOTE You can install direct printing support for a client that runs another operating system by installing a local alternative printer driver on the GSNW server. To do so, make sure to have the distribution CD for that operating system handy, select it in the Alternate Drivers pane before closing the dialog, and follow the prompts.

19

Using File and Print Services for NetWare

In this chapter:

- *Installing File and Print Services for NetWare*
- *Configuring File and Print Services for NetWare*
- *Managing NetWare-Enabled User Accounts*
- *Managing Volumes, Folders, and Files*
- *Creating and Managing Shared Printers*
- *Managing File and Print Services for NetWare*

If you are running a mixed NetWare and Windows NT Server environment, do yourself a big favor and buy a copy of File and Print Services for NetWare (FPNW) immediately. Prior to Version 4.0, FPNW was available separately as a $99 utility. With the release of Version 4.0, FPNW is now bundled with Directory Service Manager for NetWare (DSMN) in a $149 package called Microsoft Services for NetWare (MSN), which is described in the following chapter. Microsoft Services for NetWare is almost a must-have for any administrator who is managing a network that includes both types of server.

FPNW is an optional utility that allows Windows NT Server 4.0 to emulate a NetWare 3.12 server. Once FPNW is installed, NetWare clients can access a Windows NT Server machine as just another NetWare 3.12 server—without requiring that any changes whatsoever be made to the NetWare clients. Shared Windows NT Server disk and printer resources are accessible to the NetWare clients as virtual NetWare shared resources. For all intents and purposes, the Windows NT Server host running FPNW might just as well **be** a NetWare server.

NOTE Many people seem to confuse Gateway Service for NetWare (GSN) and FPNW. Their purposes are exactly complementary. GSN lets Microsoft clients access shared resources on a NetWare server. FPNW lets NetWare clients access shared resources on Windows NT Server. GSN is bundled with Windows NT Server, whereas FPNW is an optional product. Given the obvious desire of Microsoft to replace NetWare with Windows NT Server, it is difficult to understand why they did not simply bundle MSN with Windows NT Server.

FPNW is useful both in an environment where Windows NT Server and NetWare will continue to coexist indefinitely and in an environment where the goal is eventually to migrate from NetWare to Windows NT Server. In the first case, FPNW provides almost complete interoperability between NetWare clients and Windows NT Server and between Windows clients and NetWare servers, obviating changes to a large installed client base. In the second case, FPNW provides convenient staging for the migration, avoiding the need for a sudden cut-over. You can migrate NetWare users and data to an FPNW server, replicating all or most of the contents and services of the NetWare server to Windows NT Server. One night, you simply turn off your NetWare server and rename the FPNW server to the same name as the old NetWare server, allowing the NetWare clients to continue to access the same NetWare resources using the same names. You can then update the client workstations gradually to Microsoft client software, rather than being forced to do it all at once.

FPNW provides an excellent—but not perfect—emulation of a NetWare 3.12 server. FPNW emulates the following NetWare functions:

User account management

FPNW uses User Manager for Domains to maintain user accounts for Windows NT Server and FPNW simultaneously. You can use Windows NT Server groups and User Rights to reproduce a similar level of privileges and rights for each user account on the FPNW server that exists on the NetWare server.

If you have many NetWare clients, you can use the Migration Tool for NetWare utility to import large numbers of user accounts from your NetWare servers in a single step, automatically creating corresponding Windows NT Server user accounts. Using the Migration Tool for NetWare for this purpose is described in Chapter 21, *Migrating to a Pure Windows NT Server Environment.*

Shared file access

Installing FPNW creates a virtual *SYS* volume with the same default directory structure as a real NetWare *SYS* volume. You can create additional virtual NetWare volumes to share any directory on the Windows NT Server disk. Directories can be shared only for NetWare clients, only for Windows clients, or for both. Access by NetWare clients to shared disk resources is controlled first at the share level, next by standard NTFS file permissions and NTFS directory permissions, and finally by attribute permissions.

You can use the Migration Tool for NetWare to replicate the entire directory and file structure of a NetWare volume to the FPNW server. When you perform such a migration, you can migrate not just the data, but the file and directory permissions that were in effect on the original volume.

Shared print services

Windows NT Server by itself allows Windows clients to access shared print resources on both Windows NT Server and NetWare servers. Installing FPNW allows you also to share Windows NT Server print resources with NetWare clients. FPNW also allows you to manage NetWare print resources directly from FPNW, rather than at each individual NetWare print server.

Script support

FPNW supports a system login script that executes when any user logs in to the FPNW server. FPNW also supports user login scripts specific to a particular user that execute when that user logs in.

NetWare utility emulators

FPNW provides several native utilities to substitute for commonly used NetWare utilities. These utilities include *attach, capture, chgpass, endcap, login, logout, map, setpass,* and *slist.* NetWare clients that connect to an FPNW server can continue to use familiar, identically named utilities to accomplish the same tasks they are used to performing with NetWare.

OS/2 name space support

FPNW provides long filename support compatible with the OS/2 LFN support used by NetWare.

In addition, FPNW provides numerous fundamental NetWare emulation functions, including secured logins, packet burst, large Internet packets, and various low-level NetWare synchronization and locking functions.

FPNW does not support the following NetWare functions:

Inherited Rights Masks

Because Windows NT Server does not use the concept of the Inherited Rights Mask, you must instead use NTFS file access permissions and NTFS directory access permissions to specify which shared disk resources can be accessed by a NetWare client that connects to an FPNW server using a NetWare-enabled user account. For all practical purposes, the level of control provided by NTFS permissions is entirely comparable to that provided by using IRMs, but you must constantly be aware of the differences between these two methods if you are to prevent users from having an unintended level of access to files.

Volume/Disk Restrictions

Windows NT Server provides no means to assign disk usage quotas at the user or group level, although this functionality is available from third-party add-ins. This lack of control—along with the lack of tools in Windows NT Server to determine which users are hogging disk space—is one of the more annoying failings of Windows NT Server relative to NetWare.

I once spoke to a Microsoft engineer about this problem. He told me that Microsoft could easily have added this function at the design stage, but simply failed to do so on the assumption that disks were getting larger and less expensive every day. Maybe so, but the fact is that the administrator who several years ago had to guard his 500 MB disk farm jealously must be just as careful with his 50 GB disk farm today.

If you do install a third-party utility to add this functionality, it will almost certainly function properly with FPNW, because a NetWare-enabled user account for FPNW is simply a standard Windows NT Server user account with a few options added. It is, however, worth asking the vendor beforehand to make sure before buying the product.

Accounting

For some companies, another major failing of Windows NT Server relative to NetWare is the absence of accounting. Because Windows NT Server itself makes no provision for charging out network services to users, FPNW has no mechanism for such charge-backs.

User Type Differences

Like NetWare, Windows NT Server has several predefined user types, each of which has a differing level of rights to perform system operations and to access system objects. A NetWare user who is Supervisor or Supervisor Equivalent has all privileges, as does a Windows NT Server user assigned to the Administrators group. Unfortunately, beyond these superuser types there are no direct matches.

In particular, there are no close equivalents in Windows NT Server for NetWare Workgroup Managers and User Account Managers. The closest match to either of these NetWare user types in Windows NT Server is the Account Operator, who has more power by far than even a Workgroup Manager.

In addition, as an emulation, FPNW, of course does not support specific native NetWare functions like NetWare Loadable Modules and the Transaction Tracking System. On balance, however, FPNW is probably the closest thing you'll ever see to native NetWare that doesn't come in a red box. For all practical purposes in the workaday world, to NetWare clients an FPNW server looks just like a NetWare 3.12 server, and that's what really counts.

Installing File and Print Services for NetWare

FPNW is installed as a Windows NT service. To install it, you must be logged on as a member of the Administrators group, and the Spooler service must be running. Install File and Print Services for NetWare from the Network Services page of the Network property sheet (**Control Panel ➤ Network ➤ Services** tab). Select Add to display the Select Network Service dialog. Because FPNW is not a bundled service, select Have Disk to display the Insert Disk dialog.

WARNING If an older version of FPNW is present on the server, File and Print Services for NetWare may already appear as a selectable item in the Network Service pane. If it does, **do not** select it. Instead, choose Have Disk, just as you would if FPNW was not already present.

Microsoft explicitly warns against using any existing occurrence of FPNW in the Network Service pane, although I have never seen the specific reasons for this warning. I can, however, say that while writing another book based on Windows NT Server Beta 1 (Build 1234), I violated this advice unintentionally and ended up trashing my NetWare server thoroughly. Fortunately, it was just a test server, and was easily recovered. I can't even say for certain that this was the cause of the problem. Still, just to be safe, make sure to always overwrite any earlier occurrence of FPNW.

FPNW is distributed on a CD-ROM disk that includes both 3.51 and 4.0 versions of File and Print Services for NetWare and Directory Service Manager for NetWare, as well as other files. These products are provided as separate executables for Intel, Alpha, MIPS, and PowerPC. For example, if your CD-ROM drive is *D:* and you are installing the Intel version, the distribution files are located in *D:\FPNW\NT40\I386*. By default, Windows NT Server attempts to retrieve files from the *A:* floppy drive. Enter the correct location of the FPNW distribution files, and click OK to display the Select OEM Option dialog. Specify whether you want to install the full FPNW product, or just the Administrative Tools.

The Install File and Print Services for NetWare dialog appears. Use this dialog to specify the name of the virtual NetWare SYS volume, to set the password for the supervisor account that will be used to administer FPNW, and to specify what level of resources should be allocated to FPNW.

Set the following items:

Directory for SYS Volume

Enter the name of the directory that will contain the virtual NetWare *SYS* volume for the FPNW server. The installation procedure uses *C:\SYSVOL* as the default. This directory will appear to NetWare users as the *SYS* volume for this FPNW server, and contains the standard NetWare top-level directories *\login, \mail, \public, and \system,* which are created automatically. Make sure that this directory is located on an NTFS volume. Otherwise, you will not be able to control access to the directories and files on that volume.

Server Name

Enter the name that NetWare clients will use to access this server. By default, the installation procedure uses the Windows computer name followed by an underscore and FPNW. For example, on the Windows NT Server machine, *thoth*, the FPNW server, is named *thoth_fpnw*. You cannot use the Windows computer name in this field.

Supervisor Account

Enter and confirm the password to be used for the administrator's account for the FPNW server. Any minimum password length restriction in effect for Windows NT Server is enforced in this field.

Choose one of the following Tuning option buttons to specify what level of server resources will be allocated to running FPNW and servicing user requests from NetWare clients:

Minimize Memory Usage

Choose this option button if this server is supporting only a small number of NetWare clients, or if the server is primarily an application server. This option uses minimal memory and places small demands on system resources, but provides slower file and print sharing performance.

Balance Between Memory Usage and Performance

Choose this option button if the server is a general-purpose server, providing both application server functions and file and print sharing functions. As you might expect, when configured this way, FPNW consumes an intermediate amount of memory and other resources and provides a moderate level of performance.

Maximize Performance

Choose this option button to give FPNW all of the memory and other resources it needs to offer the highest possible level of file and print sharing performance. This option button is most appropriate if the server is a dedicated file and print server, and has more than sufficient processor and memory resources to do its job.

On a slow or heavily loaded server, the option button you choose can make a very noticeable difference in FPNW performance. On a fast or lightly loaded server, you may be unable to tell any difference in performance no matter which option button you choose. For example, on my 486/66 test server (with 40 MB RAM), FPNW runs at noticeably different performance levels at each of these settings. This is evident even in something as simple as how long it takes to copy a file with only one user connected. Conversely, on a 133 MHz Pentium server with 64 MB of RAM and five users, no difference is apparent no matter what the setting and no matter what the other users are doing.

When you have completed the Install File and Print Services for NetWare dialog, click OK to display the File and Print Services for NetWare dialog. This dialog box is used to set the password for the service account to be used by FPNW. Enter and confirm the password and then click OK to continue.

NOTE FPNW requires its own service account. The installation procedure creates this service account automatically and assigns it to the Administrators group. Do not delete or disable this account, or reduce its level of privileges, or FPNW will not be able to start. If you plan to install FPNW on two or more domain controllers within a single domain, use the same password on each server.

The FPNW installation procedure is now complete, and returns you to the Network dialog. Click Close to finish installing FPNW. Windows NT Server configures, stores, and reviews the bindings, and then prompts you to restart the server to load FPNW.

NOTE FPNW is configured by default to start automatically when the server is booted. To modify this behavior, run the Services applet from the Control Panel, select File and Print Services for NetWare, click Startup, and change the Startup Type to Manual or Disabled. Do not under any circumstances change the settings in the Log On As pane, or FPNW will not function properly.

Configuring File and Print Services for NetWare

FPNW requires minimal configuration, particularly in a simple environment. If you need to change the FPNW tuning, if you are using multiple network adapter cards or multiple frame types, or if you need to specify the frame type manually, you must take a few additional steps to configure FPNW. From the Services page of the Network property sheet, highlight File and Print Services for NetWare and select Properties to display the File and Print Services for NetWare Configuration dialog.

To change the FPNW tuning, select one of the option buttons to specify a different level of resources to be allocated to FPNW, as described in the preceding section. Otherwise, click Advanced to display the Advanced IPX/SPX Configuration for File and Print Services for NetWare dialog, as shown in Figure 19-1.

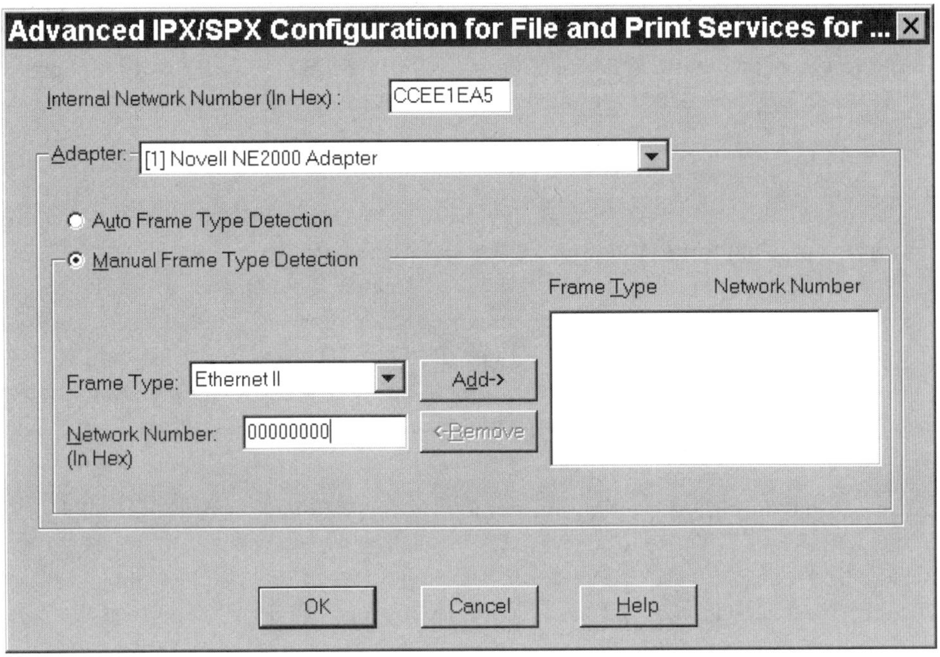

Figure 19-1. The Advanced IPX/SPX Configuration for File and Print Services for NetWare dialog

Set values for the following items:

Internal Network Number (In Hex)
: This 8-byte hexadecimal number identifies the server internal network. This value can range from 1 through FFFFFFFE, and must be unique within your network. By default, FPNW uses *00000000* for this value. You must provide a value for internal network number if you have more than one network adapter installed, if you are binding multiple frame types to a single adapter, or if FPNW will operate on a routed internetwork.

Adapter
: If you have more than one network adapter installed in the server, use this drop-down list to choose the adapter for which you want to set frame types. Each network adapter can be configured individually to automatically detect frame types or to use one or more frame types that you specify explicitly. Each combination of adapter and frame type must be assigned a unique network number.

Auto Frame Type Detection
: Choose this option button if you want FPNW to automatically detect and configure the appropriate frame type. Do not choose this option unless only one frame type is in use on the network and you have explicitly assigned

static network numbers. In particular, do not choose Auto Frame Type Detection if you have different network segments using different frame types, e.g., one segment with a NetWare 3.11 server running 802.3 and a second segment with a NetWare 3.12 server running 802.2.

Manual Frame Type Detection

Choose this option button if you want to explicitly assign one or more frame types to the selected network adapter. If you assign more than one frame type to a single adapter, each frame type assigned must have a different network number. This network number must correspond to the network number for the network segment and frame type used elsewhere on your network. To assign a frame type, use the Frame Type drop-down list to select from the available frame types, enter a value for the Network Number (In Hex) field, and click Add. Repeat this process as necessary until you have added all required frame types for all adapters.

After you have finished configuring frame types, click OK to return to the File and Print Services for NetWare Configuration dialog. Click OK again to close the dialog and complete the procedure. Windows NT Server displays the Network Settings Change dialog to inform you that you must restart the server before the changes you have made will take effect. Click Yes to restart the server immediately, or click No to defer effecting the changes until the next routine server restart.

TIP In a TCP/IP network environment, I find it useful to assign an Internal Network Number that corresponds to the IP address of the server. For example, in Figure 19-1, the Internal Network Number *CCEE1EA5* is the hexadecimal form of *204.238.30.165*, which is the IP address of the server running FPNW. Because IP addresses cannot be duplicated, using this method ensures that the Internal Network Numbers you assign are also unique.

Managing NetWare-Enabled User Accounts

A *NetWare-enabled user account* is simply an ordinary Windows NT Server user account that has a NetWare password associated with it. You create and maintain NetWare-enabled user accounts with User Manager for Domains in the same way that you create and maintain ordinary Windows NT user accounts. A NetWare-enabled user account allows a workstation that is running only NetWare client software to access the shared file and print resources that are available on a Windows NT Server host that has FPNW installed and running.

You can create new Windows NT Server NetWare-enabled user accounts for existing NetWare clients, or you can modify existing Windows NT Server user accounts to make them NetWare-enabled. If you have many existing NetWare clients that do not already have Windows NT Server user accounts, you can import client information from NetWare servers by using the Migration Tool for NetWare, rather than creating each new account separately. Using the Migration Tool for NetWare is described in Chapter 21, *Migrating to a Pure Windows NT Server Environment.*

NOTE You can use either the Migration Tool for NetWare (MTNW) or the Directory Service Manager for NetWare (DSMN) to migrate user accounts from NetWare servers to Windows NT Server. However, if you create NetWare-enabled users with FPNW before installing and configuring DSMN, DSMN will not recognize these existing accounts.

You can make a NetWare-enabled user account a member of one or more Windows NT Server groups, conferring the rights and privileges assigned to that group to that user account. For example, assigning a NetWare-enabled user account to the Administrators group makes that user account the Windows NT Server equivalent of a NetWare Supervisor Equivalent user.

Privileged Accounts

Like NetWare, Windows NT Server makes provision for administrative user accounts that have a higher level of privileges and rights than an ordinary user account. NetWare uses the three concepts of equivalencies, system-defined user types, and user-defined group memberships to confer these additional powers.

In the first case, for example, an ordinary NetWare user may be assigned equivalence with the user *Supervisor*, making that ordinary user a *Supervisor Equivalent.* In the second case, a user granted membership in the *Accounting* group, which is defined by a Supervisor to have specific rights and privileges, automatically inherits the rights and privileges granted to that group. In the third case, a user might be assigned as a Workgroup Manager, a system-defined user type that grants certain standard, unchangeable rights and privileges.

Windows NT Server, conversely, depends solely on group memberships to extend the rights and privileges of a user account. You grant extended rights and privileges to a user account by granting that account membership in one or more groups. For example, to accomplish the same assignments made in the paragraph above, you would grant the "supervisor equivalent" right to an ordinary Windows NT user account by making that account a member of the group Administrators.

You would grant a user membership in the group Accounting for exactly the same reasons noted above, and with exactly the same effect. To make a user account the rough equivalent of a NetWare Workgroup Manager, you would assign that user account membership in the group Account Operators.

NOTE User rights are cumulative. A user account that is a member of two or more groups has **all** of the user rights that are granted to **any** group of which it is a member.

Windows NT Server includes several standard, or built-in, groups, each of which possesses a standard, predefined group of user rights. You can also create new groups, and assign them any rights you wish. For that matter, you can alter the user rights assigned to a built-in group, although doing so is generally a bad idea. Groups and user rights are covered fully in Chapter 5, *Managing Users and Groups.*

Windows NT Server offers, in some respects, more flexibility than NetWare, and in other respects, less. NetWare offers only a few predefined user types from which to select. Windows NT Server, on the other hand, has dozens of specific User Rights, which allows you to finely tune the rights of groups you create. One difference you will notice quickly is that privileged Windows NT user accounts are, in general, considerably more powerful than privileged NetWare accounts. In essence, Windows NT Server "trusts" privileged users more than NetWare does. Table 19-1 lists the NetWare user types and their rough equivalents in Windows NT Server.

User Accounts

An ordinary NetWare user account and an ordinary Windows NT Server user account are very similar. Each contains pretty much the same information, and each serves pretty much the same purposes—to identify a user on the network and to control which shared resources that user may access, and at what level.

Both operating systems offer the ability to restrict the behavior of users, although NetWare has a twofold advantage in this regard. First, although both allow many restrictions to be made at the user level, several Windows NT Server restrictions are global in nature, whereas the corresponding NetWare restrictions can be set on a per-user basis. Second, NetWare offers one restriction that has no equivalent in Windows NT Server—the ability to set and enforce disk usage quotas on users. Table 19-2 compares the user restrictions available with NetWare and Windows NT Server.

Table 19-1. NetWare 3.1x Administrative User Types Versus FPNW Administrative Groups

NetWare 3.1x User Type	Windows NT Group	Description
Supervisor	Administrators	The Windows NT Server built-in account *Administrator* is fully equivalent to the NetWare *Supervisor*. Making an ordinary Windows NT user account a member of the *Administrators* group corresponds with making a NetWare user a *Supervisor Equivalent*.
Workgroup Manager / User Account Manager	Account Operators	Assigning membership in the *Account Operators* group is the nearest Windows NT equivalent to assigning a NetWare user as a *Workgroup Manager* or as a *User Account Manager*. The Account Operator, however, has more power than either of these NetWare user types. It can create, delete, and manage any user account or group except other administrative users and groups.
File Server Console Operator	Server Operators	Membership in the *Server Operators* group is the nearest Windows NT equivalent to the NetWare *File Server Console Operator* user type, but confers considerably more power than either of these NetWare user types. *Server Operators* can lock, unlock, and down the server; create and delete shares; and back up and restore files. A user account assigned to the *Server Operators* group has these powers for all servers in the domain, rather than being limited to a single server as a *File Server Console Operator* account may be.
Print Server Operator / Print Queue Operator	Print Operators	Windows NT Server integrates the server and queue elements used by NetWare. Membership in the *Print Operators* group confers the combined powers of the NetWare *Print Server Operator* and *Print Queue Operator* user types. You can restrict a Windows NT user account to rough equivalency with the NetWare user type *Print Queue Operator* by removing that user account from the *Print Operators* group and assigning it *Manage Documents* permission for one or more specific printers.

Table 19-2. NetWare 3.1x Versus FPNW Account Restrictions

NetWare Restriction	FPNW Restriction	Description
Account Disabled	Account Disabled	Prevents user from logging in.
Allow User to Change Password	User Cannot Change Password	Specifies whether users can change their passwords.
Expiration Date	Expiration Date	Sets the date when an account becomes invalid.
Force Periodic Password Changes	Maximum Password Age	Specifies the number of days for which a password may continue to be used. FPNW defaults to 42 days.
Grace Logins	Grace Logins	Specifies the number of times a user can log in after the password has expired.
Intruder Detection/ Lockout	Account Lockout	Specifies the number of failed login attempts that may occur. When this count is exceeded, the account is locked out for a specified period. FPNW defaults to 5 failed attempts and a 30-minute lockout period.
Limit Concurrent Connections	Limit Concurrent Connections	Specifies the maximum number of connections that a NetWare-enabled account can make to the FPNW server. When this count is exceeded, the user can no longer access additional shared resources on the server.
Minimum Password Length	Minimum Password Length	Specifies the minimum number of characters that are required for a password. FPNW defaults to six.
Require Password	Permit Blank Password	Specifies whether or not a password is required. In NetWare, this option may be set individually for each account. In Windows NT, this option is set globally for all users in User Manager for Domains Account Policy.
Require Unique Passwords	Password Uniqueness	Specifies the number of passwords that a user is required to use before reusing an earlier password. Again, NetWare allows this option to be set individually for each account, whereas Windows NT requires that it be set globally for all users in the Account Policy. For FPNW, this value may range from one through eight, and is set to five by default.
Station Restrictions	Logon Workstations	Specifies that a user may log in from all workstations versus only those explicitly listed.

Table 19-2. NetWare 3.1x Versus FPNW Account Restrictions (continued)

NetWare Restriction	FPNW Restriction	Description
Time Restrictions	Logon Hours	Specifies the earliest and latest times that a user may log in.
Volume/Disk Restrictions	No equivalent	Windows NT Server in general, and FPNW in particular, do not support the NetWare concept of setting quotas to limit disk space available to a user.

Creating and Enabling Accounts for NetWare Clients

You create user accounts for NetWare clients with User Manager for Domains in the same fashion that you create ordinary Windows NT Server user accounts. This process is fully described in Chapter 5, *Managing Users and Groups.* Installing FPNW makes minor additions and changes to some User Manager for Domains dialogs to allow you to configure NetWare-specific options for user accounts.

WARNING You must have a Windows NT Server user license for each NetWare client that will access the server running FPNW.

You can modify an existing Windows NT Server user account to enable NetWare-compatible functions using the steps described in this section. You can also create a new NetWare-enabled user account using the process described in Chapter 5, with the addition of these NetWare-specific steps. Accordingly, this section describes only the differences between NetWare-enabled user accounts and ordinary Windows NT Server user accounts.

To enable NetWare-specific functions for an existing user account, or for a newly created account, in User Manager for Domains, double-click a Username to display the User Properties dialog. If you examine this dialog closely, you will note two additions to the standard User Properties dialog. A new check box named Maintain NetWare Compatible Login appears, which allows you to enable NetWare functions for the selected user account. Also, a new icon appears, named NW Compat, which allows you to configure NetWare Compatible Properties for the selected user.

The Maintain NetWare Compatible Login check box is cleared by default, both for current users and in the dialog used to create a new user. Mark this check box to enable NetWare-compatible functions for the selected user. Doing so also activates the NW Compat icon.

After entering or modifying any necessary information for the account in the User Properties dialog, click the Groups icon to display the Group Memberships dialog. NetWare-enabled user accounts are added to Windows NT Server groups just as any other user is added. Remember when adding NetWare-enabled user accounts to groups that NetWare clients cannot access resources on Windows NT Server hosts unless FPNW is installed on that host.

Select Profile to display the User Environment Profile dialog. All values in this dialog are optional. A NetWare-enabled user account can have both a Windows Logon Script and a NetWare Login Script. The information in the User Profiles pane and in the Home Directory pane applies only when the user logs in from a Windows client. The NetWare Login Script for this user on the FPNW server is created and maintained in the NW Compatible Properties dialog, described later.

The NetWare Compatible Home Directory Relative Path text box appears only when FPNW is installed. Enter the relative path name for the NetWare home directory of the user. For example, on this server, the Home Directory Root Path is *C:\SYSVOL*. To specify that the NetWare home directory for a user be located in the directory *C:\SYSVOL\HOME\<username>*, specify only the portion *HOME\<username>*, which will be appended to the Home Directory Root Path. Do not use an initial backslash. Note that the directory you specify is not created automatically. You must create it manually.

Select Hours to display the Logon Hours dialog. These settings are identical to those for ordinary Windows NT user accounts, with one minor exception. Windows NT Server allows you to restrict logon hours in full-hour increments, whereas NetWare allows half-hour increments. For NetWare restrictions that do not fall on a whole hour, Windows NT rounds to the nearest full hour, giving the user the benefit of the doubt. For example, if the NetWare restriction allows logon at 0730, Windows NT Server rounds to 0700. Similarly, if NetWare requires logoff at 1730, Windows NT Server rounds to 1800.

Select Logon To to display the Logon Workstations dialog. On a server with FPNW installed, the NetWare-specific bottom pane is displayed. By default, the User May Log On To All NetWare Compatible Workstations option button is selected. If you want to limit logons to specific workstations, first select the User May Log On To These NetWare Compatible Workstations. Then click Add and enter the network address and, optionally, the node address, of a NetWare client computer from which the user should be permitted to log on. Repeat this process as necessary to add other workstations.

If you need to change account information for the user, select Account to display the Account Information dialog. If you need to change dial in information for the user, select Dialin to display the Dialin Information dialog. These dialogs are the same for NetWare-enabled user accounts as for regular Windows NT user accounts.

Select NW Compat to display the NetWare Compatible Properties dialog, as shown in Figure 19-2. When you mark the Maintain NetWare Compatible Login check box for a user, User Manager for Domains creates an Object ID to identify the user. This Object ID corresponds to the NetWare User ID. Just as NetWare creates a subdirectory for each user in *SYS:MAIL* named with the User ID, FPNW creates a subdirectory for each user in *SYSVOL\MAIL* named with the Object ID.

Set the following options in the NetWare Compatible Properties dialog:

NetWare Compatible Password Expired
: Mark this check box to force a password change the next time the user logs in from a NetWare client.

Grace Logins
: Mark the Unlimited Grace Logins option box (the default) to allow the user to continue indefinitely to log in with an expired password; or, mark the Limit Grace Logins option button and specify the number of Grace Logins to Allow. Once this number is reached, the user will no longer be permitted to log in. The Remaining Grace Logins text box specifies how many times the user may log in using a Grace Login before that user is locked out.

Concurrent Connections
: Mark the Unlimited option button (the default) to allow the user to establish any number of simultaneous connections to resources on the server; or, mark the Allow option button and specify a number of Concurrent Connections if you want to limit the number of sessions that this user can have active simultaneously.

FPNW supports both a system login script, which is executed when any user logs in to the FPNW server, and user login scripts, which are specific to the individual user, and execute when that user logs in. Click Edit Login Script to display the Edit Login Script dialog and to create or edit a personal login script for the user. As you might expect, login scripts are stored as *SYSVOL\MAIL\<Object-ID>\LOGIN* and *SYSVOL\MAIL\<Object-ID>\LOGIN.OS2*.

NOTE The system login script for the FPNW server is stored as *SYSVOL\PUBLIC\NET$LOG.DAT*. Use Notepad or a similar ASCII text editor to create or edit this file.

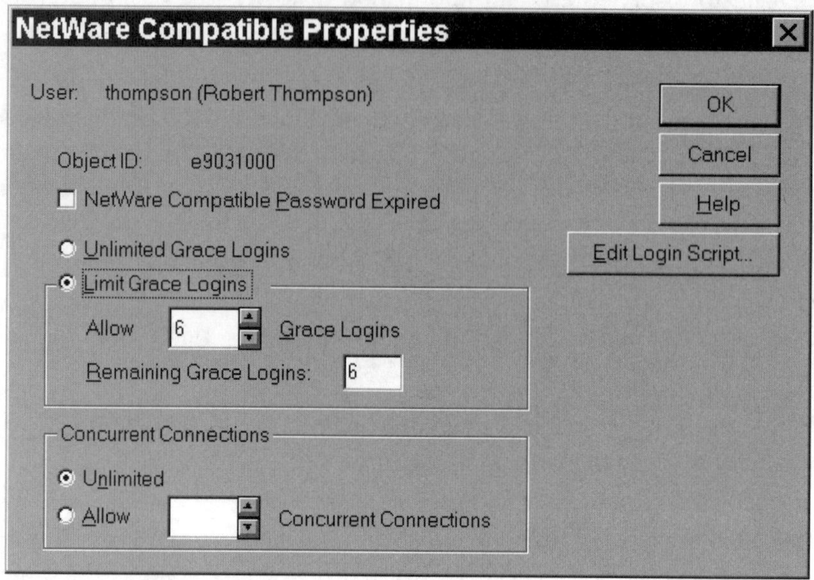

Figure 19-2. The NetWare Compatible Properties dialog allows you to set values for grace logins and concurrent connections, and to edit the user login script file

Keeping User Account Passwords in Sync

When you create a new NetWare-enabled user account, you assign a password to the account. This password serves as both the Windows NT Server password and as the FPNW password for that account. When you NetWare-enable a current Windows NT Server user account, the existing Windows NT Server password is also used as the FPNW password.

When the user logs in from a Windows client, the Windows NT Server password is used, and when the client logs in from a NetWare client, the FPNW password is used. Because these passwords are identical, at least initially, no problems arise. If an administrator uses User Manager for Domains to change the password for the account, both the Windows NT Server password and the FPNW password are changed simultaneously.

Password synchronization problems may occur, however, when users change their own passwords, depending on the type of client from which the user has logged in, as follows:

Windows NT 3.51/4.0 clients

Users change passwords by pressing Ctrl-Alt-Del to invoke the Windows NT Security dialog and then clicking Change Password to invoke the Change Password dialog. Using this procedure changes both the Windows NT Server password and the FPNW password at the same time.

NetWare clients

Users change passwords by running the *chgpass.exe* or *setpass.exe* utility. These programs are identical, and are provided as differently named files to accommodate NetWare filename conventions. Using either of these programs changes both the Windows NT Server password and the FPNW password at the same time, under most circumstances.

Other Microsoft clients

Users running Windows 95, Windows 3.x, the MS-DOS Microsoft Networking client, or Windows NT 3.5 or earlier may change their passwords using the standard means provided by the operating system in question. This change, however, affects only the Windows NT Server password. To keep his passwords synchronized, the user must also run the *chgpass.exe* or *setpass.exe* utility to change the FPNW password.

The *chgpass.exe* and *setpass.exe* utilities work as described above only if the following conditions are all true:

- The Primary Domain Controller (PDC) upon which the user account resides must have Gateway Service for NetWare installed and running.
- The PDC upon which the user account resides must have File and Print Service for NetWare installed.
- The client computer must be able to access the PDC with IPX/SPX transport.
- The files *rpc16c1.rpc, rpc16c6.rpc*, and *security.rpc* must exist in the same directory as the *chgpass.exe* and *setpass.exe* utilities. These *.rpc* support files are installed automatically in the *SYSVOL\PUBLIC* directory when FPNW is installed.

If any of the first three conditions are false, running *chgpass.exe* and *setpass.exe* changes only the FPNW password. If the final condition is false, neither *chgpass.exe* nor *setpass.exe* will run.

Managing Volumes, Folders, and Files

NetWare uses only its native filesystem, which may be extended by adding name space support, e.g., OS/2 or NFS. Windows NT Server, on the other hand, supports two native filesystems—FAT and NTFS. Although either type of volume may be shared, the extent to which you can control user access to shared disk resources is determined by the filesystem in use for that volume.

Access control on FAT volumes is at the share level. When you share a FAT volume, you specify who can access the volume, and at what level. Access control is limited to only four choices: No Access, Read, Change, and Full Control.

Whatever access level you specify applies equally to all files and folders on that volume. Also, share-level access control is effective only for users who connect across the network. A user logged in locally to the console is not prevented from accessing a volume that is protected only by share-level permissions.

Access control on NTFS volumes is determined by NTFS directory permissions and NTFS file permissions. Using NTFS permissions allows you to control very finely which users and groups are permitted to access which shared resources, and at what level. NTFS permissions can be used to further restrict share-level permissions, but cannot grant permissions greater than those in effect at the share level. For example, if a volume is shared as Read Only, no user, regardless of the NTFS permissions in effect, can have greater than Read Only access.

NTFS permissions are effective both for users who connect across the network, and for those who are logged in locally at the server console. Because a NetWare-enabled user account is really simply an ordinary Windows NT Server user account with some added NetWare-specific features, NTFS file permissions and NTFS directory permissions control these users' access to shared resources in the FPNW environment.

Chapter 6, *Controlling Access to Volumes, Folders, and Files*, provides complete information about share-level access control and NTFS permissions in the Windows NT Server environment. This section describes how share-level access control and NTFS permissions relate to the equivalent NetWare controls in the FPNW environment.

NTFS Permissions Versus NetWare Trustee Assignments

NTFS file permissions are closely analogous in purpose and effect to NetWare Trustee File Assignments. Similarly, NTFS directory permissions closely match NetWare Trustee Directory Assignments. In both cases, NetWare offers somewhat finer control than does Windows NT Server. However, for all practical purposes, you can accomplish nearly anything with NTFS permissions that you can with NetWare Trustee Assignments.

One significant difference is that the NetWare concept of the *Inherited Rights Mask (IRM)* is not supported by Windows NT Server. In NetWare, *Effective Rights* are the sum of the rights explicitly granted to the user **plus** the implicit rights inherited by the user from group memberships **minus** any rights revoked by the IRM. In Windows NT Server, the rights enjoyed by a user to a particular file or folder are the rights explicitly granted to that user **plus** the rights inherited from group memberships. Rights granted globally to a user in a particular folder by the

NTFS directory permissions in effect can be revoked by NTFS file permissions explicitly set for a file within that directory.

Table 19-3 details the standard NetWare trustee file rights and how they map to the closest corresponding NTFS file permissions. NTFS does not support the Create (C) and Filescan (F) rights at the file level, but allows you to create similar restrictions at the directory level.

Table 19-3. NetWare Trustee File Rights Versus Windows NT NTFS File Permissions

NetWare Trustee File Right	Windows NT NTFS File Permission
Read (R)	Read (RX)
Write (W)	Write (W)
Create (C)	Write (W)
Erase (E)	Delete (D)
Access Control (A)	Change Permissions + Take Ownership (PO)
Modify (M)	Write (W)
Supervisory (S)	Full Control (All)

Table 19-4 details the standard predefined NTFS file permission masks, and how these map to the closest corresponding group of NetWare trustee file rights. Note that NTFS permissions may be assigned individually (rather than in predefined groups) by using the Special File Access option.

Table 19-4. NTFS File Permission Masks and the Corresponding NetWare Trustee File Rights

Windows NT NTFS File Permission	NetWare Trustee File Right
Read (RX)	Read, Filescan (RF)
Change (RWXD)	Read, Write, Create, Erase, Modify, Filescan (RWCEMF)
Full Control (All)	Supervisor (S)

Table 19-5 details the standard NetWare trustee directory rights and how they map to the closest corresponding NTFS directory permissions. In the second column, the first item within parentheses lists the NTFS permissions in effect for the directory itself. The second lists the NTFS permissions that are applied to newly created files within that directory.

Table 19-5. NetWare Trustee Directory Rights Versus Windows NT NTFS Directory Permissions

NetWare Trustee Directory Right	Windows NT NTFS Directory Permission
Read (R)	Read (RX) (RX)
Filescan (F)	Read (R) (R)

Table 19-5. NetWare Trustee Directory Rights Versus Windows NT NTFS Directory Permissions (continued)

NetWare Trustee Directory Right	Windows NT NTFS Directory Permission
Write (W)	Write (W) (W)
Create (C)	Write (W) (W)
Erase (E)	Delete (D) (D)
Access Control (A)	Change Permissions + Take Ownership (PO) (PO)
Modify (M)	Write (W) (W)
Supervisory (S)	Full Control (All) (All)

Table 19-6 details the standard predefined NTFS directory permission masks, and how these map to the closest corresponding group of NetWare trustee directory rights. Again, the first parenthetical grouping in the first column lists the NTFS rights that apply to the directory itself, and the second lists the NTFS rights that apply to newly created files within that directory. Note that NTFS permissions may be assigned individually (rather than in predefined groups) by using the Special Directory Access option.

Table 19-6. NTFS Directory Permission Masks and the Corresponding NetWare Trustee Directory Rights

Windows NT NTFS Directory Permission	NetWare Trustee Directory Right
List (RX) (Not Specified)	Read, Filescan (RF)
Read (RX) (RX)	Read, Filescan (RF)
Add (WX) (Not Specified)	Write, Create, Modify (WCM)
Add & Read (RWX) (RX)	Read, Write, Create, Modify, Filescan (RWCMF)
Change (RWXD) (RWXD)	Read, Write, Create, Erase, Modify, Filescan (RWCEMF)
Full Control (All) (All)	Supervisor (S)
File Scan (F)	Read (R) (R)
Access Control (A)	Change Permissions + Take Ownership (PO) (PO)

Attribute Security

In NetWare, the first level of security is *Login Security*. The second is *Trustee Assignments*. The third, and final, level of security is *Attribute Security*. Attribute security is often the final determiner of whether a user is or is not able to accomplish a particular task. Even if that user has all of the necessary directory and file trustee assignments, attribute security can prevent him or her from performing the task.

Windows NT Server also uses attribute security. Windows NT offers a closely corresponding file attribute for each the most important file attributes supported by NetWare. However, NetWare has some file attributes that are not present in Windows NT Server. Some of these—e.g., *Indexed (I)* and *Transactional (T)*—are missing from Windows NT Server simply because the NetWare attributes are specific to the low-level design and functioning of NetWare, and are therefore not needed for Windows NT Server.

Other file attributes that are present in NetWare but missing in Windows NT Server—e.g., Copy Inhibit (CI)—are of little practical importance to most administrators. One NetWare file attribute—*Execute (X)*—that many administrators *wish* was missing from NetWare is present in Windows NT Server, but in a safe form. The one NetWare file attribute that is missing from Windows NT Server that is on everyone's wish list for the next release of Windows NT Server is *Purge (P)*—not so much for the file attribute itself as for what it implies—the ability to salvage deleted files.

Table 19-7 details the standard NetWare file attributes and the closest corresponding Windows NT Server file attributes.

Table 19-7. NetWare File Attributes Versus Windows NT NTFS File Attributes

NetWare File Attribute	Windows NT NTFS File Attribute
Archive Needed (A)	Archive (A)
Copy Inhibit (CI)	NetWare allows you to set the CI file attribute to grant a user the right to read a file, but not to copy it. NTFS has no equivalent file attribute. In NTFS, granting a user the right to read a file implies the right also to copy it.
Delete Inhibit (DI)	Read Only (R) or remove delete permission for that user for that file
Hidden (H)	Hidden (H)
Indexed (I)	NetWare automatically assigns this file attribute when a file exceeds 64 regular FAT entries. NTFS has no equivalent file attribute (nor does it need one).
Purge (P)	NTFS has no equivalent of the NetWare Purge and Salvage functions. Files deleted from the console may be retrieved from the local Recycling Bin, but files deleted by users who connect across the network may not.
Read Audit (Ra)	No directly equivalent file attribute exists. However, in the File Auditing dialog, you can set Read and Execute as audit events (for Success and/or Failure) to accomplish the same thing.
Read Only (Ro)	Read Only (R)
Rename Inhibit (RI)	No direct equivalent. You can approximate this attribute at the directory level by removing Write permission for that user for that directory.

Table 19-7. NetWare File Attributes Versus Windows NT NTFS File Attributes (continued)

NetWare File Attribute	Windows NT NTFS File Attribute
Shareable (S)	NTFS has no equivalent file attribute. Sharing can be set in Windows NT Server globally per server, but not per file.
System (Sy)	System (S)
Transactional (T)	Windows NT Server has no equivalent of the NetWare Transaction Tracking System, and therefore provides no equivalent file attribute.
Write Audit (Wa)	No directly equivalent file attribute exists. However, in the File Auditing dialog, you can set Write and Delete as audit events (for Success and/or Failure) to accomplish the same thing.
Execute Only (X)	Execute (X). Once this attribute is set in NetWare, it cannot subsequently be changed. Windows NT administrators can toggle this attribute on and off.

Creating FPNW Volumes

You create NetWare shares by sharing one or more folders on the server running FPNW. These shares appear to NetWare clients as ordinary NetWare volumes. You can modify an existing share to make it available to NetWare clients, or you can create a new share. You can make any share accessible only to Microsoft Networking clients, only to NetWare clients, or to both types of clients.

If you are using FPNW to replace an existing NetWare server, you can use the Migration Tool for NetWare to replicate all of the directories and files from the volumes on the NetWare server being replaced to NetWare shares on the FPNW server. This process also replicates the existing NetWare rights and attributes to the FPNW volume. Chapter 21, *Migrating to a Pure Windows NT Server Environment*, describes using the Migration Tool for NetWare.

Installing File and Print Services for NetWare adds an FPNW selection to the Server Manager main menu, as shown in Figure 19-3. Options within this menu allow you to view Properties for the FPNW server, to create and manage shared volumes and printers, and to send messages to NetWare clients. This extra Server Manager menu selection appears only on the server where FPNW is installed. It appears on other servers in the domain only if you install the FPNW remote administration tools on them.

To create a NetWare volume, from the Server Manager FPNW menu, select Shared Volumes to display the Volumes on <Servername> dialog. The Volumes pane displays the default *SYS* volume that was created when you installed FPNW.

Select Create Volume to display the Create Volume on <Servername> dialog. Enter a name for the volume in the Volume Name field. This is the volume name

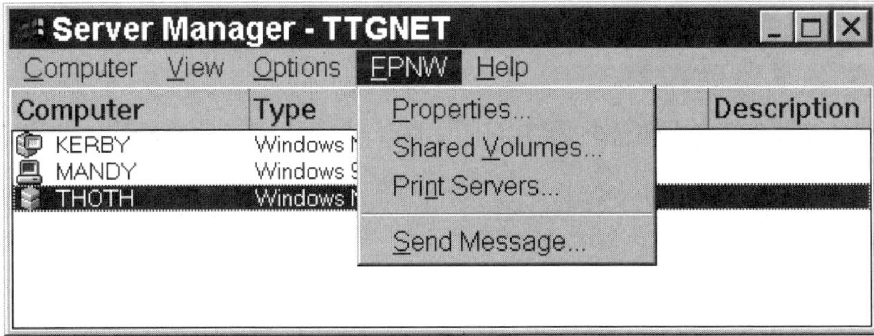

Figure 19-3. Installing File and Print Services for NetWare adds an FPNW selection to the Server Manager menu

by which NetWare clients will access the volume, in this case *HOME*. Do not enter the final colon. In the Path field, enter the location of the shared directory that will map to this volume. This directory need not have a share already in effect. If necessary, FPNW will create the new share. Finally, if necessary, set a User Limit. By default, the Unlimited option button is marked, allowing any number of clients to access this volume simultaneously. Under most circumstances, you should leave this setting at the default. If, however, you find that so many clients are using this resource at the same time that performance is beginning to degrade, you may mark the Allow option button and set a maximum limit for simultaneous users.

Select Permissions to display the Access Through Share Permissions dialog. Set share permissions as necessary. Setting share permissions is fully described in Chapter 6, *Controlling Access to Volumes, Folders, and Files*. After you have set share permissions for the volume, click OK to return to the Create Volume on <Servername> dialog. Click OK again to return to the Volumes on <Servername> dialog. Click Close to finish creating the NetWare volume.

After you create the NetWare volume, you can use the procedures described in Chapter 6, *Controlling Access to Volumes, Folders, and Files*, to set NTFS file permissions and NTFS directory permissions to further control access to the volume. You can also use Server Manager to stop sharing the volume or to modify the characteristics of an existing NetWare volume.

To stop sharing a volume, from Server Manager, click FPNW and then Shared Volumes to display the Volumes on <Servername> dialog. Click a volume name to highlight it, and then click Remove Volume. To modify the characteristics for a volume, from Server Manager, click FPNW and then Shared Volumes to display the Volumes on <Servername> dialog. Click a volume name to highlight it, and then click Properties to display the Volume Properties on <Servername> dialog.

Modify the User Limit or Permissions as needed and then click OK to place the changes into effect.

Creating and Managing Shared Printers

FPNW allows you to share NetWare and Microsoft Networking printers in both directions. You can make shared Microsoft Networking printers available to NetWare clients. You can also make shared NetWare printers available to Microsoft Networking clients by allowing FPNW to manage the NetWare printers. This bidirectional capability and single point of management makes it much easier to optimize printer sharing in a mixed NetWare and Windows NT Server environment. This section examines how to create both types of shared printers and how to manage them with FPNW.

Sharing Windows NT Server Printers with NetWare Clients

Allowing NetWare clients to access a shared Windows NT Server printer is almost trivially easy. Any shared Windows printer is visible to NetWare clients as just another NetWare print queue. Clients connect to this virtual NetWare print queue in the same way they would to any other.

NOTE To access a shared Microsoft printer, Microsoft clients use the **share** name of the printer, but NetWare clients use the **actual** name of the printer by specifying the printer name in the queue option of the capture utility.

Sharing NetWare Printers with Microsoft Networking Clients

Making a shared NetWare printer available to Microsoft Networking clients is a bit more complicated than allowing NetWare clients to share Microsoft printers. In broad brush, you must first create a logical local printer on the server running FPNW and assign it to a NetWare compatible port. You must then create a print server, add one or more printers to the print server, and, finally, add a print queue. The remainder of this section details the steps needed to share a NetWare printer with Microsoft clients.

NOTE This gets pretty confusing. Windows NT Server allows Microsoft clients to use NetWare printers, even if FPNW is not installed. However, in the absence of FPNW, you use the Add Printer Wizard to install a NetWare printer as a Network printer server, rather than as a locally connected printer on My Computer. Although Microsoft clients can then access the NetWare printer, it must still be managed from NetWare. The advantage to using FPNW to install a NetWare printer as a local printer is that you can then use FPNW to *manage* the NetWare printer.

To begin installing the printer, on the FPNW server, double-click My Computer, then Printers, then Add Printer, to display the Add Printer Wizard dialog. Accept the default My Computer option, and then click Next. Mark the check box associated with an available NetWareCompatiblePServerX port, and then click Next to continue.

If a suitable printer driver is not already installed, Windows NT Server offers to install the printer driver and prompts you for the location of the distribution files. If a suitable printer driver is already installed, Windows NT Server asks you whether you want to use the existing driver or replace it. Once the appropriate driver files are installed, Windows NT Server displays a dialog. Accept the default Printer name or type a new name for the printer. Specify whether you want this printer to be the default Windows printer and then click Next.

NOTE The printer name you specify in this step is the actual printer name rather than the share name. This is the printer name that will be used by NetWare clients to access the printer. To ensure compatibility with all applications, use a legal DOS name for the printer. In the example, I have changed the suggested printer name, *HP LaserJet 5*, to *NW-LJ5* for this reason.

Windows NT next displays a dialog. By default, the Not shared option button is marked. To share the printer, mark the Shared option button. Windows NT fills in the Share Name field with the printer name you specified in the preceding dialog. Accept this name, or enter a new share name. The share name you specify here is the name that will be used by Microsoft clients to access the printer. If you want to install native printing support for other operating systems, highlight them in the lower pane and be prepared to provide the distribution CD for each operating system you select. Click Next to continue. You are given the opportunity to print a test page. Specify Yes or No, and then click Finish to complete the installation.

After you create the printer, the next step is to create a printer server. To begin, from Server Manager, choose FPNW and then Print Servers to display the Print Servers for <Servername> dialog. Click Add to display the Add Print Server to <Servername> dialog.

In the Print Server field, type the name of the actual NetWare print server that services the printer, in this case the NetWare server *theodore*. Enter descriptive information in the Full Name field to further identify the server. Enter and confirm the password, and then click OK. Windows redisplays the Print Servers for <Servername> dialog with the new print server and its associated object ID shown.

After you have added the print server, the next step is to add one or more printers to the print server. To do so, click Printers to display the Printers on Print Server <Servername> dialog. Click Add to display the Add Printer to <Servername> dialog. Complete the information required in this dialog exactly as you would when using *PCONSOLE.EXE* in NetWare to configure a NetWare printer. In particular, note that the Printer field must use the name of the printer as it is known by the NetWare print server. In this case, for example, although when creating the printer I used *NW-LJ5* for both the printer name and the share name, I must instead use *LaserJet 5* in this field, because that is the name that this printer is known to by NetWare.

Once you have completed the Add Printer to <Servername> dialog, click OK to redisplay the Printers on Print Server <Servername> dialog, with the newly added printer displayed.

After you have added the printer, the final step is to add a print queue. To do so, click Queues to display the Queues Serviced by <Printername> dialog. Highlight a queue in the Available Queues pane, and use the Priority drop-down list to specify a priority for that queue. Click Add to install the queue and move it to the right pane. Click OK to complete the installation.

Managing File and Print Services for NetWare

FPNW provides a single integrated graphical utility to manage user connections, volumes, and files on your FPNW server. Command-central for FPNW is the File and Print Service for NetWare on <Servername> dialog, as shown in Figure 19-4. You can invoke this dialog in one of two ways. First, from Control Panel, double-click the FPNW applet. Alternatively, from Server Manager, choose FPNW and then Properties. Either method accomplishes exactly the same thing.

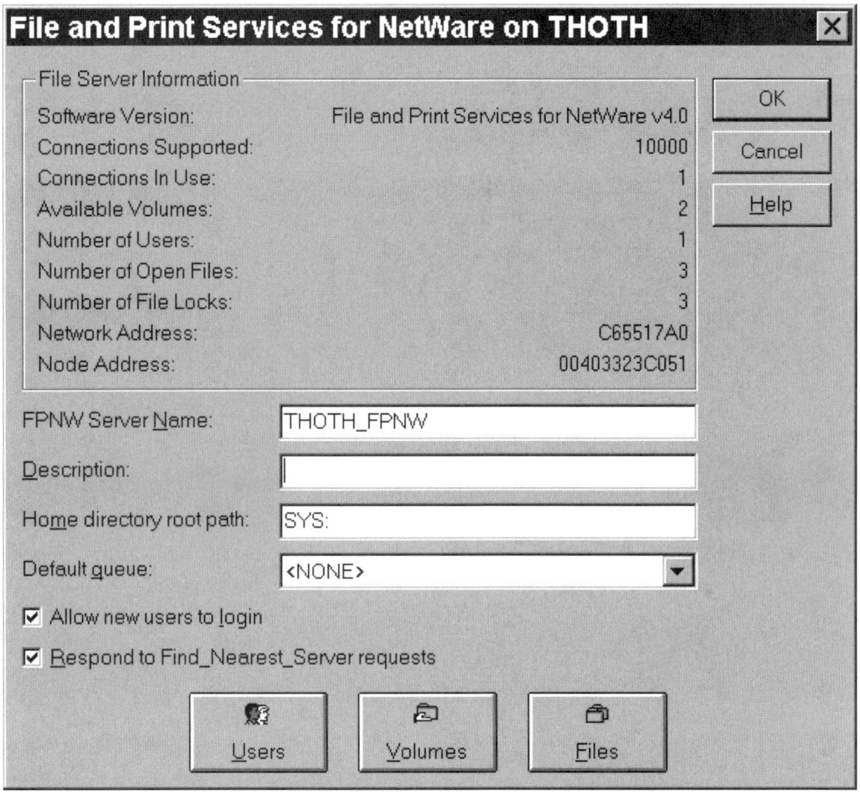

Figure 19-4. The File and Print Services for NetWare on <Servername> dialog is used to configure the FPNW server and to manage FPNW users, volumes and files

The File Server Information pane displays various items of information about the status and characteristics of the FPNW server. The fields below this pane allow you to specify or to change various properties of the FPNW server, as follows:

FPNW Server Name
: This is the name that NetWare clients use to access the server. You may change the name of an existing FPNW server, but, if you do so, you must stop and restart the FPNW service before the change will take effect. The name you use must not be identical to the Windows machine name of the server that is running the FPNW service.

Description
: This is a free text field that you can use to provide more information about the FPNW server, e.g., the physical location of the server or contact information for the administrator.

Home directory root path

This is the path, relative to the virtual NetWare *SYS* volume, that is the root location for user directories. FPNW does not create this directory automatically.

Default queue

This field specifies the default print queue for NetWare clients that connect to this FPNW server. Use the drop-down list to select among the available queues. If the only item that appears is <NONE>, you must create one or more queues before you will be able to assign a default queue.

Allow new users to login

Mark this check box, which is enabled by default, if you want NetWare-enabled user accounts to be able to log in to the FPNW server and access shared resources. Clear this check box to prevent new logins, perhaps while you are modifying the FPNW server.

Respond to Find_Nearest_Server requests

Mark this check box, which is enabled by default, if you want this FPNW server to respond to the Find_Nearest_Server request that is sent by a NetWare client when it starts. Clear this check box if you want to prevent the FPNW server from responding to such requests, perhaps because you do not want the FPNW server to behave as a primary NetWare server.

Managing FPNW User Connections

To manage FPNW user connections, from the File and Print Service for NetWare on <Servername> dialog, click Users to display the Users on <Servername> dialog. The Connected Users pane displays one line for each user connected to the FPNW server.

In the example, user BARBARA is the only one connected. The pane displays the user name, the Network Address, the Node Address (in this case, the Ethernet MAC address of the workstation), and the elapsed time in hours and minutes that the user has been logged in, in this case, 24 hours and 6 minutes. The Resources pane lists the resources being used by the highlighted user, the drive that is mapped to each shared resource, and the number of opens in effect against that resource.

NOTE Interestingly, Microsoft incorrectly states that the Login Time displays the time of day when the user connected to the FPNW server, rather than the elapsed duration of the connection.

Use the buttons at the bottom of the display to manage user connections. Click Disconnect to disconnect only the highlighted user. Click Disconnect All to disconnect all users. Disconnecting a user unceremoniously may cause that user to lose data. Accordingly, use Send Message to notify the user before disconnecting her. When you click Send Message, you are given the choice of sending the message to only the highlighted user or to all users on the FPNW server.

Managing Shared Volumes

To manage FPNW volumes, from the File and Print Service for NetWare on <Servername> dialog, click Volumes to display the Volumes Usage on <Servername> dialog. The Volume pane displays one line for each volume that has been defined on the FPNW server. For each volume, the dialog displays the volume name, the number of users currently connected, the maximum number of concurrent users permitted, and the path to which the volume is mapped.

Highlight one of the listed volumes to display the connected users for that volume. In the example, user BARBARA is the only one connected to the volume *HOME*. The Connected Users pane shows that BARBARA has been connected for seven minutes and has files open on the volume.

Use the buttons at the bottom of the display to manage user connections. Click Disconnect to disconnect only the highlighted user. Click Disconnect All to disconnect all users. As mentioned in the preceding section, you should always notify users before disconnecting them. Although Microsoft recommends that you use Send Message to notify users before disconnecting them, they forgot to put that option into this dialog. Use the Send Message option from Users to do so.

Managing Open Files

To manage files opened on FPNW volumes, from the File and Print Service for NetWare on <Servername> dialog, click Files to display the Files Opened by Users on <Servername> dialog. The Opened by column shows the user name of the user who opened the file; For shows the permission granted when the file was opened, in this case, Read/Write; Locks shows the number of locks on the file; Volume shows the name of the volume where the open file is located; and Path shows the path and filename of the opened file.

Use the buttons at the bottom of the display to manage open files. Click Refresh to update the display; click Close File to close the highlighted file, or Close All Files to close all open files on the FPNW server. Once again, notify users before closing any files they have open. Again, although Microsoft recommends that you use Send Message to notify users before closing a file, they forgot to put that option into this dialog. Use the Send Message option from Users to do so.

20

In this chapter:
- *Using Server Manager*
- *Using Directory Service Manager for NetWare (DSMN)*

Managing Servers in a Mixed NetWare and Windows NT Server Environment

For an administrator used to maintaining NetWare 3.1x servers, Windows NT Server administration comes as a breath of fresh air. Windows NT Server substitutes a few comprehensive graphical administration utilities for the grab-bag assortment of character-based utilities needed to maintain NetWare. If you administer multiple NetWare servers—and in particular if you have NetWare servers sited at remote offices—you're familiar with the quirks and annoyances of using *RCONSOLE* and *ACONSOLE* for remote administration. Windows NT Server provides comprehensive remote management capabilities, both across the network and via dial-up connections, making it just as easy to manage remote servers as it is to manage a local server.

Microsoft didn't stop with making Windows NT Server easy to manage. They also, via the optional Directory Service Manager for NetWare (DSMN), provide the tools to allow Windows NT Server to manage NetWare servers centrally.

This chapter examines two aspects of managing servers in a multiple server environment. The first part of this chapter examines the process of managing Windows NT Server with Server Manager, the general-purpose server administration utility provided with Windows NT Server. The second part of this chapter examines using DSMN to manage NetWare servers from Windows NT Server.

Running on Windows NT Server, DSMN allows the Windows NT Server administrator to use Windows NT Directory Services to manage the binderies on multiple NetWare 3.12 servers. The NetWare 3.12 bindery is a local object-oriented database, and Novell has never released much in the way of utilities for the 3.12 environment to allow centralized management of multiple NetWare 3.12 servers. Making a change to a NetWare 3.12 network with multiple servers means making that same change individually to each server. For example, adding a user to a

NetWare 3.12 network with eight servers requires that the administrator log on to each of the servers in turn and add the user manually. DSMN allows the administrator to manage user accounts and similar information on the Windows NT server running DSMN. These changes are then propagated to the multiple NetWare 3.12 servers, easing the burden of managing multiple servers significantly.

Using Server Manager

Server Manager is the main utility used to manage computers and domains in the Windows Networking environment. The name is somewhat of a misnomer, because Server Manager can also be used to manage workstations. Server Manager can manage computers running Windows NT Server and Windows NT Workstation without requiring any special configuration. If you want to use Server Manager to manage workstations running other operating systems, e.g., Windows 95, you must install the remote administration tools on the workstation to be managed.

Server Manager allows you to manage a domain or an individual computer. When you use Server Manager to manage a domain, you can add and remove computers from the domain, synchronize other servers with the primary domain controller, and promote a backup domain controller to be the primary domain controller. When you use Server Manager to manage an individual computer, you can display connected users, show defined shares, list open resources, manage directory replication, and configure alerts to specify which users and which computers should be notified of significant events that occur on the server in question. You can also use Server Manager to manage shared directories, control services, and send messages to users.

Server Manager duplicates the functions of the **Control Panel ➤ Server** applet and the **Control Panel ➤ Services** applet that are available locally on each server. However, while these applets are limited to managing the server that they are running on, Server Manager can be used to manage these functions both on the local server and on remote computers, thereby providing a central management function for your network.

To run Server Manager, from the Start button, select **Programs ➤ Administrative Tools (Common) ➤ Server Manager** to display the main Server Manager screen.

NOTE By default, Server Manager displays computers from the domain of which the computer you run it on is a member. You can display computers from a different domain by selecting **Computer ➤ Select Domain** to display the Select Domain dialog. Type the name of the domain you want to manage in the Domain list box, or select one of the domain names displayed in the Select Domain pane.

Filtering the Server Manager Display

By default, Server Manager displays all servers and workstations in the domain. If your network includes many servers and workstations, this default display may include so many computers that it is difficult to locate the computer that you want to manage. Use the Server Manager View menu to specify that only a subset of these computers be displayed, as follows:

Servers
: Checking this menu option, which is unchecked by default, causes Server Manager to display only servers—those computers that are members of the selected domain and participate in domain security. Workstations are filtered from the display.

Workstations
: Checking this menu option, which is unchecked by default, causes Server Manager to display only Windows Networking client computers that have been located by the Computer Browser service. Servers—those computers that participate in domain security—are filtered from the display.

FPNW
: Checking this menu option, which is unchecked by default, causes Server Manager to display only servers that are running FPNW. Workstations, and servers that are not running FPNW, are filtered from the display. This menu option appears only if File and Print Services for NetWare is installed on at least one server in the domain.

All
: Checking this menu option, which is checked by default, causes Server Manager to display all Windows machines, both clients and servers, that are members of the domain or that have been located by the Computer Browser service.

Show Domain Members Only
: Checking this menu option, which is unchecked by default, causes Server Manager to display only those computers that are members of the domain, i.e., computers running Windows NT and LAN Manager. If this option is unchecked, Server Manager displays both computers that are members of the domain and those reported by the Computer Browser service as active in the domain. This menu option toggles on and off.

Refresh
: Each time you start Server Manager, or choose a different domain to manage, Server Manager updates its main window to display the computers currently active in the domain, subject to any filters you have placed into effect. During operation, Server Manager does not update its display routinely. Performing

certain activities, e.g., changing properties or viewing services, causes the display to be updated, unless you are using the Low Speed Connection option, in which case the display is never updated automatically. Click Refresh to force a manual update.

With the exception of Refresh, each of these menu options is a toggle. When it is active, a check mark appears next to that option in the View menu to indicate which filter is in effect.

Managing Computer Properties

To manage properties for a computer, highlight that computer in the main Server Manager window and then select **Computer ➤ Properties** to display the Properties for <Servername> dialog. You may also simply double-click the computer name to display this dialog.

The Properties for <Servername> dialog displays current statistics for the selected server in the Usage Summary pane. You can optionally enter text in the Description box to further describe the server. However, the core of this dialog is the row of buttons along the bottom of the display. These buttons provide the following functions:

Users
: Displays a list of connected users by session, and allows you to disconnect one user or all users.

Shares
: Displays a list of defined shares on the selected computer. For each share, displays a list of Connected Users who are accessing that share, and allows you to disconnect one user or all users.

In Use
: Displays a list of open resources on the select computer, and allows you to close a selected resource or to close all resources.

Replication
: Displays the current directory replication configuration on the selected computer, and allows you to configure and manage directory replication for that computer.

Alerts
: Displays, and allows you to modify, a list of users and computers that will receive administrative alert messages generated when a significant event occurs on the selected computer.

The following sections examine each of these functions.

Managing user sessions

To manage user sessions, select Users from the Properties for <Servername> dialog to display the User Sessions on <Servername> dialog.

The top, Connected Users, pane displays one line for each user session, with a user icon; the name of the connected user; the computer to which that user is connected; the number of open resources for this user on this computer; the duration (in hours and minutes) that the session has been active; the amount of time (in hours and minutes) that has elapsed since the user last initiated an action; and, finally, whether or not that user connected as user Guest.

Highlighting a session in the upper pane displays in the lower pane the resources in use by the selected session. The lower, Resource, pane displays one line for each resource in use. This line lists the name of the resource; the number of current opens against it by the selected user session; and the duration (in hours and minutes) that has elapsed since the user opened the resource.

You can disconnect one user by highlighting the user name and clicking Disconnecting. You can disconnect all users by clicking Disconnect All. Before taking either of these actions, notify the user or users to be disconnected by using the **Computer ➤ Send Message** option on the main menu.

Managing shared resources

To manage shared resources, select Shares from the Properties for <Servername> dialog to display the Shared Resources on <Servername> dialog. This dialog allows you to view a list of shared resources on the selected computer. For each shared resource, you can view a list of the users connected to that resource.

The top, Sharename, pane displays one line for each shared resource. The far left column displays an icon specific to the type of share. The icon associated with the *IPC$* share name represents a named pipe; the icons associated with the *MERCURY* and *NETLOGON* share names represent shared folders; and the icon associated with the *NW-LJ5* share name represents a shared printer. The Uses column lists the current number of active connections to the shared resource. The Path column lists, if applicable, the path that maps to the share name.

Highlighting a Sharename in the upper pane displays in the lower pane the users connected to that shared resource. The Time column lists the elapsed duration (in hours and minutes) since the user first connected to the shared resource. The In Use column indicates whether the connected user currently has a file open on that shared resource.

You can disconnect one user from all shared resources by highlighting the user name in the lower pane and clicking Disconnect. You can disconnect all users from all shared resources by clicking Disconnect All. Before taking either of these actions, notify the user or users to be disconnected by using the **Computer ➤ Send Message** option on the main menu.

Displaying resources in use

To manage open shared resources, select In Use from the Properties for <Server-name> dialog to display the Open Resources on <Servername> dialog. This dialog displays the total number of open shared resources, the total number of locks in effect, and a list of open shared resources on the selected computer. Each open shared resource is displayed on a separate line that lists the user or computer that opened the resource; the permission level granted when the resource was opened; the number of locks in effect for the open resource; and the path associated with the resource.

The Open Resources on <Servername> dialog is static. It displays a snapshot of the resources that were open when the dialog was invoked. Click Refresh to update the display to reflect the current status of open resources. You can close one open shared resource by highlighting that resource and clicking Close Resource. You can close all open shared resources on the selected computer by clicking Close All Resources. Before taking either of these actions, notify the users that will be disconnected by using the **Computer ➤ Send Message** option on the main menu.

Managing replication

To manage directory replication on the selected computer, select Replication from the Properties for <Servername> dialog to display the Directory Replication on <Servername> dialog. This dialog allows you to configure directory replication for the selected computer. Directory replication is described fully in Chapter 6, *Controlling Access to Volumes, Folders, and Files.*

Setting alerts

To set administrative alerts, select Alerts from the Properties for <Servername> dialog to display the Alerts on <Servername> dialog. Alerts are notifications of significant events that occur on the selected computer.

In the Send Administrative Alerts To pane, this dialog displays the users and computers that are currently selected to receive administrative alerts for the selected computer. To add a user or computer to the alert list, type the name of the user or computer in the New Computer or Username box and click Add. To remove a user or computer from the alert list, highlight the name in the right pane and click Remove.

In order for a user or computer to receive administrative alerts, two conditions must be true. First, both the Alerter service and the Messenger service must be running on the computer that is to generate the alerts. Second, the Messenger service must be running on the computer that is to receive the alerts.

Managing Shared Directories

You can use Server Manager to create new shared directories, modify the properties of existing shared directories, and stop sharing directories. To manage shared directories, select **Computer ➤ Shared Directories** to display the Shared Directories dialog. This dialog displays existing shares, including the share name and the physical directory that is mapped to the share name.

Creating a new share

To create a new directory share, from the Shared Directories dialog, select New Share to display the New Share dialog. Enter the name for the new share in the Share Name box, the physical directory to which the share is to be mapped in the Path box, and, optionally, a descriptive comment in the Comment box. By default, Server Manager places no limit on the number of users who can access the new share simultaneously. If you want to limit the number of concurrent users, in the User Limit pane; mark the Allow option button and use the spinner to specify the maximum number of users. Next, click Permissions to display the Access Through Shared Permissions dialog and set the appropriate share permissions for the new share. The process of setting share permissions is described in Chapter 6, *Controlling Access to Volumes, Folders, and Files.* Once you have finished configuring the new share, click OK to place the share into effect and return to the Shared Directories dialog.

Modifying share properties

To modify the properties for an existing directory share, highlight that share in the Shared Directories dialog and click Properties to display the Share Properties dialog. You can modify the User Limit for the share by selecting the appropriate option button and, if necessary, specifying an allowable maximum number of users for the share. Modify share permissions for the share by clicking Permissions and modifying the Access Through Share Permissions dialog as appropriate.

Discontinuing a share

To discontinue a share, highlight the share name in the Shared Directories dialog, and click Stop Sharing. The directory itself is not removed, but users will no longer be able to access it as a shared directory. When you choose Stop Sharing, the share is discontinued unconditionally, rather than simply disabling further share opens.

If no users are currently using the share, the share will be discontinued immediately. If one or more users are currently active on the share, a Windows NT dialog is displayed to warn you that discontinuing the share may cause these users to lose data.

Managing Services

Server Manager allows you to start, stop, and configure services on both the local computer and on remote computers within the domain. Select **Computer ➤ Services** to display the Services on <Servername> dialog. This is the same dialog that is invoked by the **Control Panel ➤ Services** applet on an individual computer, and is used the same way. Server Manager, however, allows you to configure services on any server within the domain rather than just the computer upon which the applet is being run.

Managing FPNW Servers

If at least one of the computers within the domain is running FPNW, Server Manager adds an FPNW option to the main menu. You can use the FPNW menu option to view and modify the properties for FPNW servers, to manage shared FPNW volumes, and to manage FPNW print servers.

NOTE The FPNW menu option is active only when you have highlighted a computer that is running FPNW. Attempting to access the FPNW menu for a computer that is not running FPNW generates an error message.

Managing FPNW server properties

To manage FPNW server properties, first highlight a computer upon which FPNW is running. From the Server Manager main menu select **FPNW ➤ Properties** to display the File and Print Services for NetWare on <Servername> dialog, as shown in Figure 20-1. This dialog is identical to, and used in the same manner as, the dialog described in Chapter 19, *Using File and Print Services for NetWare.*

Managing FPNW shared volumes

To manage FPNW shared volumes, first highlight a computer upon which FPNW is running. From the Server Manager main menu, select **FPNW ➤ Shared Volumes** to display the Volumes on <Servername> dialog. This dialog is identical to, and

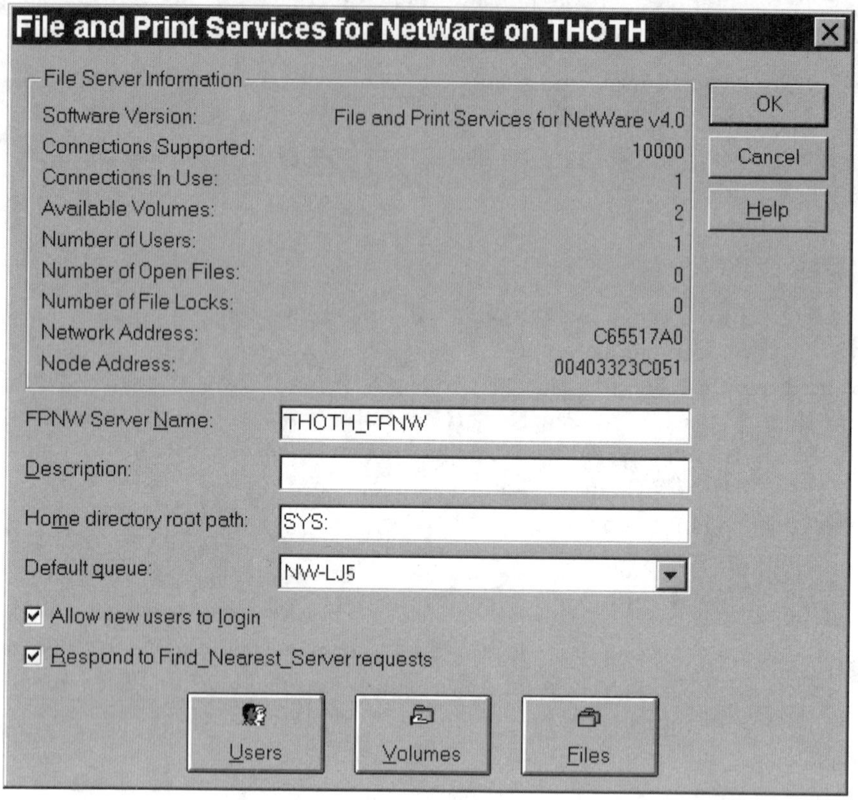

Figure 20-1. The File and Print Services for NetWare on <Servername> dialog allows you to manage an FPNW server from Server Manager

used in the same manner as, the dialog described in Chapter 19, *Using File and Print Services for NetWare.*

Managing FPNW print servers

To manage FPNW print servers, first highlight a computer upon which FPNW is running. From the Server Manager main menu, select **FPNW ➤ Print Servers** to display the Print Servers for <Servername> dialog. This dialog is identical to, and used in the same manner as, the dialog described in Chapter 19.

Using Directory Service Manager for NetWare (DSMN)

Directory Service Manager for NetWare (DSMN) is an optional Windows NT Server utility that allows you to synchronize user and group account information between a Windows NT Server domain and the binderies of one or more servers running NetWare 2.x or 3.x. DSMN is a part of the $149 Microsoft Services for NetWare package, which also includes File and Print Services for NetWare.

NOTE Directory Service Manager for NetWare is a particularly Machiavellian choice of product name, because Windows NT Server has no true directory service. Apparently because the absence of a directory service is widely perceived as a major shortcoming of Windows NT Server, Microsoft chose to rename what was formerly known as *Domain Services* to *Windows NT Server Directory Services.* Perhaps they thought using a good name would cause people not to notice the absence of the function itself.

Regardless of the machinations of the Microsoft marketing department, DSMN is an extremely useful product for administrators who manage a mixed NetWare and Windows NT environment. If you manage multiple NetWare servers, and particularly if those servers are at different sites, you know just how time consuming it can be to visit and update multiple servers each time you need to add a user or make a change. By using DSMN, you can centrally manage all user accounts from a single Windows NT server and proliferate additions and changes to remote NetWare servers automatically. I know of more than one NetWare administrator who has installed Windows NT Server for no other reason than easing the burden of managing multiple NetWare servers.

Installing Directory Service Manager for NetWare

DSMN is installed as a Windows NT service. To install it, you must be logged on as a member of the group Administrators. Install Directory Service Manager for NetWare from the Network Services page of the Network property sheet (**Control Panel ➤ Network ➤ Services** tab). Select Add to display the Select Network Service dialog. Because DSMN is not a bundled service, select Have Disk to display the Insert Disk dialog.

DSMN is distributed on a CD-ROM disk that includes both 3.51 and 4.0 versions of File and Print Services for NetWare and Directory Service Manager for NetWare, as well as other files. These products are provided as separate executables for Intel, Alpha, MIPS, and PowerPC. For example, if your CD-ROM drive is *D:* and you are installing the Intel version, the distribution files are located in *D:\DSMN\NT40\I386.* By default, Windows NT Server attempts to retrieve files from the A: floppy drive. Enter the correct location of the DSMN distribution files, and click OK to display the Select OEM Option dialog. Specify whether you want to install the full DSMN product, or just the Administrative Tools.

The Install Directory Service Manager for NetWare dialog appears. Enter and confirm the password for the account that will be used to run DSMN. If the service account to be used to run DSMN already exists, a warning dialog appears. Verify that you have entered the password correctly, and then click Yes.

NOTE DSMN requires its own service account, named the Sync Agent Account. The installation procedure creates this service account automatically, if necessary, and assigns it to the Administrators group. Do not delete or disable this account, or reduce its level of privileges, or DSMN will not be able to start. If you plan to install DSMN on multiple domain controllers within a single domain, use the same password for DSMN on each domain controller.

If you have installed File and Print Services for NetWare before you install DSMN, a message appears to warn you that previously configured NetWare-compatible accounts may not be propagated because DSMN does not know the passwords of these accounts. Click OK to allow DSMN to scan the user accounts. On a fast server with relatively few user accounts, this process occurs almost instantaneously. On a slower server, or one with many user accounts, this process may require several minutes.

The DSMN installation procedure is now complete, and returns you to the Network dialog. When you Close the dialog, Windows NT Server configures, stores, and reviews the bindings, and then displays the Network Settings Change dialog to notify you that you must restart the server before DSMN will be available.

NOTE DSMN is configured by default to start automatically when the server is booted. To modify this behavior, run the Services applet from the Control Panel, select Directory Service Manager for NetWare, click Startup, and change the Startup Type to Manual or Disabled. Do not under any circumstances change the settings in the Log On As pane, or DSMN will not function properly.

Configuring Directory Service Manager for NetWare

DSMN allows you to manage user and group accounts on one or more NetWare servers by importing some or all of the account information from the NetWare server to the Windows NT server, where it is subsequently administered. All changes to managed user and group accounts for the managed NetWare server are made on the Windows NT server.

Changed account information is periodically exported back to the NetWare server being managed. This process allows user and group account information to be managed centrally on the Windows NT server and replicated to the managed NetWare servers, obviating visiting each NetWare server and making the same changes repeatedly to different NetWare servers. The process of importing information to Windows NT Server and exporting it to the NetWare servers is called *propagating* account information.

The first step in configuring DSMN is to add a NetWare server to be managed. Once you have done so, you propagate some or all of the account information from that NetWare server to DSMN, which translates the NetWare user and group account information into the corresponding Windows NT Server form, and stores the NetWare user and group accounts as Windows NT Server user and group accounts. You then propagate user and group account information—which may include both accounts that originated on the NetWare server and accounts that originated on Windows NT Server—back to the NetWare server.

NOTE For DSMN centralized administration to work properly, all changes to account information must be made to the central DSMN database, rather than directly to the binderies of the slave NetWare servers. To prevent NetWare users from using NetWare utilities to change account information directly on the NetWare server—which would cause the servers to become unsynchronized—DSMN installs replacement versions of the NetWare utilities, which are DSMN-aware.

Understanding how account information is propagated

Although NetWare users and groups correspond closely to Windows NT Server users and groups, there are some differences. NetWare stores some information and supports some restrictions that Windows NT Server does not, just as Windows NT Server stores some information and supports some restrictions that NetWare does not. It is important to understand how these differences are accounted for when propagating NetWare account information to Windows NT Server and vice versa. The following sections examine these differences.

How NetWare user accounts are propagated to Windows NT Server. NetWare user accounts and Windows NT Server user accounts contain similar information and serve similar purposes. Although both offer the ability to restrict the behavior of users, they do so somewhat differently. NetWare allows you to set most account restrictions on a per-user basis, whereas Windows NT Server uses a combination of per-user and global controls. Some account restrictions that you can set individually for each user account in NetWare are set globally in Account Policy in Windows NT Server.

When you use DSMN to propagate NetWare user accounts to Windows NT Server user accounts, these differences must be accommodated. On the whole, DSMN does a remarkably good job of mapping NetWare restrictions to Windows NT account restrictions. However, inevitably, some of the NetWare per-user account restriction information is lost during the propagation, which means that it will not be available subsequently when those accounts are propagated back to the NetWare server. Stated simply, you lose some of the per-user account restriction flexibility offered by NetWare when you use DSMN to manage NetWare servers. Table 20-1 lists the NetWare account restrictions, and how these account restrictions are mapped to Windows NT account restrictions when NetWare accounts are propagated to Windows NT Server.

Table 20-1. How Account Restrictions Are Transferred When Propagating NetWare Users Accounts to Windows NT Server User Accounts

NetWare Restriction	Windows NT Restriction	Controlling Restriction and Exceptions
Account Disabled	Account Disabled	NetWare user account setting.
Allow User to Change Password	User Cannot Change Password	NetWare user account setting.
Expiration Date	Expiration Date	NetWare user account setting. But SYSCON shows the first date the account is expired, whereas User Manager for Domains shows the last date the account remains valid.
Force Periodic Password Changes	Maximum Password Age	NetWare user account setting. But SYSCON allows the NetWare administrator to set values for *Days Between Forced Changes and Date Password Expires* on a per-account basis, whereas Windows NT Server substitutes the domain Account Policy value for *Maximum Password Age*, which causes these two NetWare account restriction values to be lost.
Grace Logins	Grace Logins	NetWare user account setting.
Intruder Detection/ Lockout	Account Lockout	Windows NT Account Policy.
Limit Concurrent Connections	Limit Concurrent Connections	NetWare user account setting. But this restriction has no effect in Windows NT. It is maintained to prevent losing data when Windows NT user accounts are propagated back to a NetWare server.
Minimum Password Length	Minimum Password Length	Windows NT Account Policy.

Table 20-1. How Account Restrictions Are Transferred When Propagating NetWare Users Accounts to Windows NT Server User Accounts (continued)

NetWare Restriction	Windows NT Restriction	Controlling Restriction and Exceptions
Require Password	Permit Blank Password	Windows NT Account Policy.
Require Unique Passwords	Password Uniqueness	Windows NT Account Policy.
Station Restrictions	Logon Workstations	NetWare user account setting.
Time Restrictions	Logon Hours	NetWare user account setting. But NetWare uses half-hour settings, whereas Windows NT Server uses full-hour settings, rounding to the nearest hour that gives the account at least as much time as NetWare.
Volume/Disk Restrictions	No equivalent	Does not transfer. No Windows NT equivalent.

How Windows NT Server user accounts are propagated to NetWare. Of course, the real reason for using DSMN is to maintain centralized current account information on Windows NT Server so that you can propagate changes periodically to the managed NetWare servers. Just as some information is lost or abbreviated when you propagate from NetWare to Windows NT Server, the same occurs when you propagate in the opposite direction. Table 20-2 describes how Windows NT Server account data and restrictions are propagated back to a managed NetWare server.

Table 20-2. How Data Fields and Account Restrictions Are Transferred When Propagating Windows NT Server User Accounts to NetWare User Accounts

Windows NT Field or Restriction	NetWare Field or Restriction	Action Taken
User Properties Dialog		
Username	Username	Propagated
Full Name	Full Name	Propagated
Description	None	Not propagated
Password	Password	Propagated
User Must Change Password at Next Logon	Date Password Expires	If enabled, sets NetWare field to current date
User Cannot Change Password	Allow User To Change Password	Propagated
Password Never Expires	Date Password Expires	Propagated
Account Disabled	Account Disabled	Propagated
Account Locked Out	Intruder Detection/Lockout	Not propagated

Table 20-2. How Data Fields and Account Restrictions Are Transferred When Propagating Windows NT Server User Accounts to NetWare User Accounts (continued)

Windows NT Field or Restriction	NetWare Field or Restriction	Action Taken
Maintain NetWare Compatible Login	None	Must be enabled if account is to be propagated to the NetWare server
User Properties Dialog—Groups Icon		
Member of	Groups Belonged To	Propagated
Primary Group	None	Not propagated
User Properties Dialog—Profile Icon		
User Profiles pane	None	Not propagated
Home Directory pane	None	Not propagated
NetWare Compatible Home Directory Relative Path	Home Directory	Propagated
User Properties Dialog—Hours Icon		
Logon Hours	Time Restrictions	Propagated
User Properties Dialog—Logon To Icon		
User May Log On to All/These Workstations	None	Not propagated
User May Log On to All/These NetWare Workstations	Station Restrictions	Propagated
User Properties Dialog—Account Icon		
Account Expires pane	Account has expiration date/Date account expires	Propagated
Account Type pane	None	Not propagated
User Properties Dialog—Dialin Icon		
Dialin Information	None	Not propagated
User Properties Dialog—NW Compat Icon		
NetWare Compatible Password Expired	None	Not propagated
Grace Logins pane	Grace Logins	Propagated
Concurrent Connections pane	Limit Concurrent Connections/Maximum Connections	Propagated
Account Policies		
Maximum Password Age	Days Between Forced Changes	Propagated
Minimum Password Age	None	Not propagated
Minimum Password Length	Minimum Password Length	Propagated

Table 20-2. How Data Fields and Account Restrictions Are Transferred When Propagating Windows NT Server User Accounts to NetWare User Accounts (continued)

Windows NT Field or Restriction	NetWare Field or Restriction	Action Taken
Password Uniqueness	Require Unique Passwords	Propagated, but has no effect unless set between 8 and 24
Account Lockout	Intruder Detection/Lockout	Propagated
Forcibly disconnect remote users from server when logon hours expire	None	Not propagated
Users must log on in order to change password	None	Not propagated

How groups, user types, and security equivalences are propagated between NetWare and Windows NT Server. In NetWare, you assign extended privileges to a user by making that user a member of a group, by making that user a special user type (e.g., Workgroup Manager), or by assigning that user a security equivalence (e.g., Supervisor Equivalent). Windows NT Server uses only group memberships to accomplish the same things. Group memberships, privileged users, and special user types are propagated as follows:

Supervisor

The NetWare Supervisor account corresponds to the Windows NT Server Administrator account. Just as a NetWare user may be granted supervisor privileges by being assigned as a Supervisor Equivalent, a Windows NT Server user can be assigned administrative privileges by being assigned to the Administrators group. When you propagate NetWare information to Windows NT Server, you specify whether to add the Supervisor Equivalents to the Windows NT Server Administrators group. The Supervisor account itself is never propagated, and must be managed locally on the NetWare server. When you propagate Windows NT Server account information to a NetWare server, members of the Windows NT Server Administrators group are propagated as NetWare Supervisor Equivalents.

Workgroup Managers and User Account Managers

Windows NT Server provides no direct equivalent for either of these NetWare user types, which exist primarily to facilitate the decentralized management of NetWare servers. The closest Windows NT equivalent is membership in the Account Operators group, which provides more power than either of these NetWare user types. However, because DSMN centralizes account management, there is no need for either of these user types in a DSMN environment, and such users are therefore not added automatically to the Account Operators group. As a result, when a NetWare user assigned as a Workgroup

Manager or as a User Account Manager is propagated to Windows NT Server, these extra privileges are lost. When these accounts are subsequently propagated back to the NetWare server, they become ordinary user accounts.

File Server Console Operators

When you install DSMN or FPNW, Windows NT Server creates the Console Operators group to correspond to the NetWare user type File Server Console Operators. Membership in the Console Operators group confers no special privileges under Windows NT Server, but is available simply for compatibility with NetWare. When you add a NetWare server to the Windows NT Server domain, you are given the option to add NetWare users who have been assigned as File Server Console Operators to the Windows NT Console Operators group.

If you have assigned one or more NetWare groups as File Server Console Operators, the members of these groups are assigned individually to the Windows NT Console Operators group, rather than the NetWare group itself being assigned to the Windows NT Console Operators group. When you propagate Windows NT Server account information back to a NetWare server, members of the Windows NT Console Operators group are propagated as NetWare File Server Console Operators.

Print Server Operators and Print Queue Operators

Windows NT Server provides no direct equivalent for either of these NetWare user types. Although the Windows NT Print Operators group has a similar name, it provides different capabilities. When you propagate NetWare account information to Windows NT Server, users assigned to these user types lose their special privileges. When you propagate Windows NT Server account information back to a NetWare server, these users are propagated as ordinary users.

Everyone Group

Although both NetWare and Windows NT Server have a group named Everyone, these groups differ conceptually. The NetWare group Everyone is an actual group, to which individual users may be added and from which they may be removed. The Windows NT group Everyone is a default virtual group, to which all users are added automatically, and from which they may not be removed. The Windows NT group Everyone is simply a mechanism by which default global rights and permissions may be assigned to all users simultaneously. When you propagate NetWare account information to Windows NT Server, the Windows NT group Everyone is retained, and membership in the NetWare group Everyone is ignored. When you propagate account information from Windows NT Server to NetWare, you may choose to propagate all groups or selected groups. If you choose the latter, you cannot select the Windows NT group Everyone or Domain Users. If you want to propagate everyone, instead choose the All Accounts option.

Other Groups

When you add a NetWare server to a Windows NT domain, you specify which NetWare groups are to be propagated to the Windows NT domain. Each of these groups is propagated to the Windows NT server with its rights and permissions intact. When you propagate from Windows NT Server to NetWare, you specify which groups are to be propagated back to NetWare. The corresponding group information is propagated normally.

Preparing to propagate accounts

To prepare to propagate accounts, you must specify the name of the NetWare server from which the accounts are to be propagated, and a valid supervisor equivalent account name and password on that NetWare server. You then specify whether propagated users will be required to change their passwords, whether supervisors will be added to the Administrators group, and whether File Server Console Operators will be added to the Console Operators group.

WARNING The procedures described in this and the following sections make changes to the bindery on the NetWare server. Back up your bindery before proceeding. To do so, log on to the NetWare server as Supervisor or Supervisor Equivalent and notify all clients to log off. After they have done so, run *BINDFIX.EXE* to generate a backup of the bindery database. *NET$OBJ.OLD*, *NET$PROP.OLD*, and *NET$VAL.OLD* will be created in the *SYS:SYSTEM* directory. Make at least one copy of these three files to a diskette before proceeding. If worse comes to horrible and you somehow manage to trash the bindery, you can restore it by running *BINDFIX.EXE* against these three files.

You have been warned. If you don't back up your bindery before proceeding, don't blame me if you lose it. While writing an earlier book based on beta versions of Windows NT Server 4.0 and DSMN, I managed to mangle the bindery on my test-bed NetWare 3.12 server irretrievably. I still don't know whether it was a bug in the beta software, a problem due to the unstable nature of a server used for writing and testing, or simply ham-handedness on my part.

Of course, although I'd just written a horrifying warning like this one, I hadn't bothered to actually do what I was so strongly recommending. I ended up restoring from a month-old bindery backup. Don't find yourself in the same position. This time, I actually did what I suggested. The peace of mind is worth the few minutes it takes to back up the bindery.

To prepare to propagate accounts, run the Synchronization Manager (**Start button ➤ Programs ➤ Administrative Tools (Common) ➤ Directory Service Manager** for NetWare). The title bar displays the name of the domain being managed. When Synchronization Manager is first run, it displays an empty pane.

Select **NetWare Server ➤ Add Server to Manage** to display the Select NetWare Server dialog. Type the name of the NetWare server to be managed in the NetWare Server box, or select an available NetWare server from the Select NetWare Server pane.

Click OK to display the Connect to NetWare Server dialog, and type the Username and Password in the appropriate fields. The account information you enter here must correspond to a valid account on the NetWare server, and that account must be Supervisor or Supervisor Equivalent. Click OK to display the Propagate NetWare Accounts to Windows NT Domain dialog, as shown in Figure 20-2.

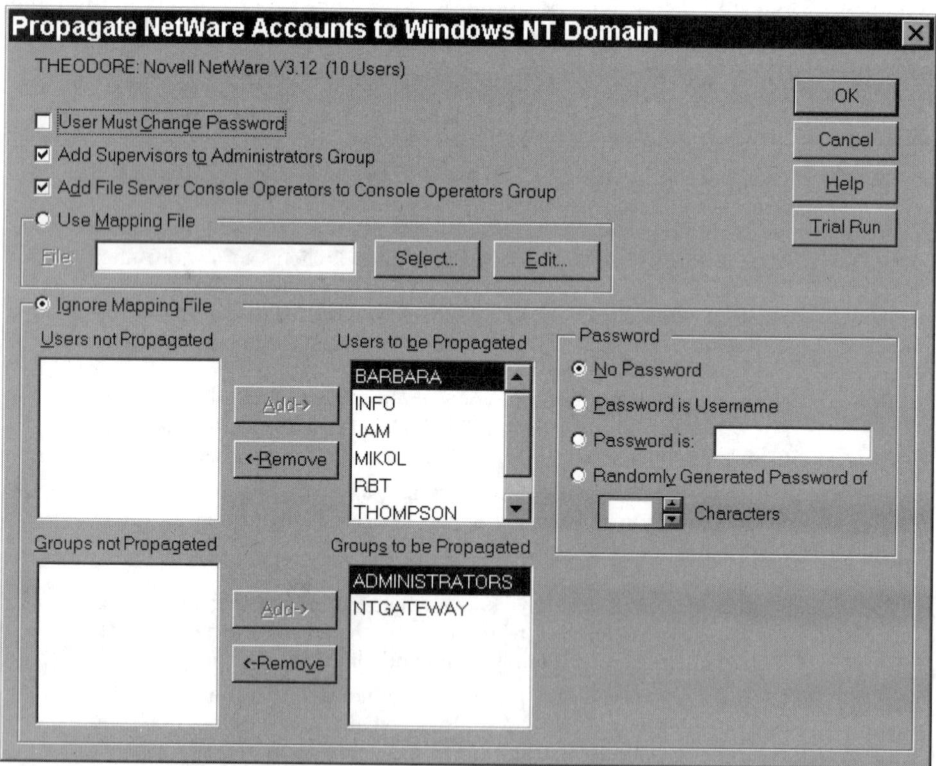

Figure 20-2. Specify the NetWare Supervisor or Supervisor Equivalent account to be used to connect to the NetWare server

Begin the propagation process by marking the appropriate check boxes to specify NetWare account propagation options, as follows:

User Must Change Password
: Mark this check box, which is cleared by default, to force each propagated user account to change password at the next logon.

Add Supervisors to Administrators Group
: Mark this check box, which is marked by default, to propagate NetWare Supervisor and Supervisor Equivalent user accounts to the Windows NT Domain Administrators group.

Add File Server Console Operators to Console Operators Group
: Mark this check box, which is marked by default, to propagate NetWare user accounts that are designated as File Console Operators to the Windows NT Console Operators group.

Once you have specified these NetWare account propagation options, decide whether you prefer to use a mapping file to specify individual user and group propagation options, or if you prefer to specify these options interactively. The main advantage to using a mapping file is that it offers more individual control over each user being propagated. For example, with a mapping file, you can migrate a user account name on NetWare to a different user account name on Windows NT, or select specific passwords for each user being propagated. The drawback to using a mapping file is that it requires a bit more work. The main advantage of not using a mapping file is that, by avoiding per-user customization, it allows you to migrate many users quickly and with minimum fuss. The drawback to not using a mapping file is that it results in a one-size-fits-all propagation. Using these two alternatives are described in the following sections.

Using a mapping file to specify users and groups to be propagated

You can use the following procedure if you prefer to use a mapping file to specify user and group propagation options. In the Propagate NetWare Accounts to Windows NT Domain dialog, mark the Use Mapping File option button to activate the File box. Type the name of a mapping file, or click Select to choose an existing mapping file or to create a new file. Click Edit to display the Create Mapping File dialog.

Mark the Do Not Include Users option button if you want to propagate only groups. Mark the Include Users option button if you want to propagate user accounts. If you choose to include users, choose one of the option buttons to specify how passwords will be assigned to the propagated user accounts, as follows:

No Password
: Mark this option button if you want propagated user accounts to have no initial password.

Password Is Username
: Mark this option button if you want the initial password for each propagated user account to be set equal to the account name.

Password Is: X
: Mark this option button and enter a value in the box if you want to set the initial password for all propagated users to the value you specify. This is the default option.

Randomly Generated Password of X Characters
: Mark this option button and use the spinner to select a password length if you want Synchronization Manager to assign a random initial password for each propagated user.

NOTE Choosing any of the first three options obviously introduces at least a potential security problem. Choosing the final option also introduces a problem, because most users don't get along well with assigned passwords, let alone randomly generated ones. If you choose the final option, keep the value of X reasonably low unless you're willing to field numerous user complaints.

Life would be much simpler for both the administrator and the users if the propagation procedure could simply use the existing NetWare password. Unfortunately, Synchronization Manager has no way to determine what the NetWare password is. Even if it could do so, incorporating this capability would introduce a gaping security hole for this (or any) NetWare server.

In most environments, the most workable choice is to set the password equal to the username. Notify your users before you propagate them of what is about to happen, and ask them to log on immediately and change their passwords.

Mark the Include Groups check box if you want to propagate NetWare groups as well as users. Once you have completed the Create Mapping File dialog, click OK. Synchronization Manager creates the Mapping file, using the options you have specified, and displays the mapping file in Notepad. Example 20-1 shows a mapping file generated by specifying that both users and groups are to be propagated and that the password is to be set equal to the username.

Example 20-1. The Mapping File Generated by Synchronization Manager

```
;SyncAgentV1.0
;From NetWare Server: THEODORE

[USERS]
;
; Format of each line:
;
; UserName [, New UserName] [, Password]
;    UserName- The user that is to be migrated from the NetWare server.
;    New UserName-The corresponding user name on Windows NT.
;    If this is blank, then the user name remains the same.
;    Password-The password of the user.
;

BARBARA, , BARBARA
INFO, , INFO
JAM, , JAM
MIKOL, , MIKOL
RBT, , RBT
THOMPSON, , THOMPSON

[GROUPS]
;
; Format of each line:
;
; GroupName
;      GroupName - The group that is to be migrated from the NetWare server
;

ADMINISTRATORS
NTGATEWAY
```

Edit the mapping file as necessary, using the formats specified within the file itself. Once you have completed any modifications, save the changes and exit Notepad to return to the Propagate NetWare Accounts to Windows NT Domain dialog.

Specifying interactively the users and groups to be propagated

As an alternative to using a mapping file, you may interactively select the users and groups to be propagated, and the options that will be used when performing the propagation. To do so, in the Propagate NetWare Accounts to Windows NT Domain dialog, mark the Ignore Mapping File option button. By default, all NetWare users and groups are selected to be propagated. Use Add and Remove to move users between the Users not Propagated pane and the Users to be Propagated pane. Similarly, use Add and Remove to move groups between the Groups not Propagated pane and the Groups to be Propagated pane.

Doing a trial run

There are enough potential snags involved in propagating users and groups that Synchronization Manager gives you the option of doing a trial run before doing the actual propagation. The trial run is simply a practice propagation that does not actually write the changes to the servers involved. Once you have configured the users and groups to be propagated and chosen propagation options, click Trial Run to see the results of your selections. Each time you use trial run, it checks for possible problems, displays warning messages when it finds one, and generates a log file that describes the actions that would have been taken if this were an actual propagation.

You can use trial run repeatedly, correcting any errors it finds at each pass. Each time a warning message is displayed, click No to stop the trial run, correct the problem described by the warning message, and restart the trial run. When trial run finally runs to completion without errors, the Synchronization Manager displays a message to inform you that the actual propagation will run without errors.

The next step is to view the log file. Although you are sure at this point that the propagation will take place without errors, you have not yet verified that it will accomplish exactly what you intend. To view a detailed description of the actions that will be taken by Synchronization Manager during the actual propagation, click Yes to view the log file. Synchronization Manager invokes Notepad to display the log file. An example log file is shown in Example 20-2.

Example 20-2. The Log File Generated During the Trial Run Propagation

```
Directory Service Manager for NetWare: Account Propagation Log File

    From NetWare server: THEODORE
    To Windows NT server: \\THOTH

    Summary:
        6 users were propagated.
        0 users failed to be propagated.
        3 existing Windows NT users' properties were changed.
        2 Windows NT users were added.
        0 users on the NetWare server were renamed.
        0 users were chosen not to be propagated.
        4 users' password were padded to the minimum password length.

        2 groups were propagated.
        0 groups failed to be propagated.
        1 groups added.
        0 groups were chosen not to be propagated.
```

Example 20-2. The Log File Generated During the Trial Run Propagation (continued)

```
[USERS]

BARBARA
    Already exists.
    Using existing NetWare compatible properties and password.
INFO
    Added.
    New Password: INFO00
    The password chosen is too short. It is padded with zeros to the domain's
    minimum password length.
JAM
    Added.
    New Password: JAM000
    The password chosen is too short. It is padded with zeros to the domain's
    minimum password length.
MIKOL
    Already exists.
    New Password: MIKOL0
    The password chosen is too short. It is padded with zeros to the domain's
    minimum password length.
RBT
    Already exists.
    New Password: RBT000
    The password chosen is too short. It is padded with zeros to the domain's
    minimum password length.
THOMPSON
    Already exists.
    New Password: THOMPSON

[GROUPS]

ADMINISTRATORS
    Already exists.
NTGATEWAY
    Added.
```

Performing the actual propagation

Before proceeding, verify that each propagation action described in the log file is what you intend to occur. Once you are satisfied that all actions to be taken are correct, and that all desired actions will be taken, close Notepad to return to the Propagate NetWare Accounts to Windows NT Domain dialog. Click OK to begin the actual propagation. Synchronization Manager displays a warning message to inform you that you should back up your NetWare bindery if you have not already done so. If you have not backed up your bindery, stop what you are doing immediately and back up the bindery before proceeding.

After you are satisfied that your NetWare bindery is safely backed up, click Yes to continue with the propagation. Synchronization Manager may display informational messages during the propagation to inform you of actions that it is taking. These actions are also recorded in the file *\%SystemRoot%\system32\SyncAgnt\Mssync.log.*

Synchronization Manager next displays the Set Propagated Accounts on <NetWare Servername> dialog, shown in Figure 20-3, to allow you to specify which user and group accounts should be propagated from the Windows NT Server domain to the NetWare server. By default, Synchronization Manager propagates only user accounts that are members of the Administrators group and the Console Operators group.

The "Users may only change their passwords via Directory Service Manager for NetWare" check box is marked by default. Before proceeding, ensure that this check box is marked to prohibit users in the groups you choose to propagate from using NetWare utilities to change their passwords. This ensures that the Windows NT and NetWare passwords remain synchronized.

If you want to propagate all groups and all NetWare-enabled user accounts to the NetWare server, mark the All Accounts option button. If you mark this option button, all groups that contain NetWare-enabled user accounts are propagated regardless of the contents of the Not Propagated pane and the Propagated pane.

If you want to propagate only user accounts from selected groups, mark the Accounts in Selected Groups option button, and use Add and Remove to relocate group names to and from the Not Propagated pane and the Propagated pane. All NetWare-enabled user accounts that are members of any Propagated group are also propagated. User accounts that are members of a Propagated group, but that are not NetWare-enabled, are not propagated.

When you have completed the Set Propagated Accounts on <NetWare Servername> dialog, click OK to propagate the accounts. Synchronization Manager propagates the accounts and then displays a Synchronization Manager dialog. If you want to remove the NetWare users and groups that you chose not to propagate from the NetWare server, click Yes. Otherwise, click No.

Managing Servers with DSMN

Once you have added one or more NetWare servers to be managed by DSMN, you use the Synchronization Manager utility to administer them. Synchronization Manager allows you to add and remove servers from the list of servers being managed by DSMN, to synchronize managed servers, and to back up the synchronization database. To manage servers with DSMN, from the Start button, choose **Programs ➤ Administrative Tools (Common) ➤ Directory Service Manager for NetWare**.

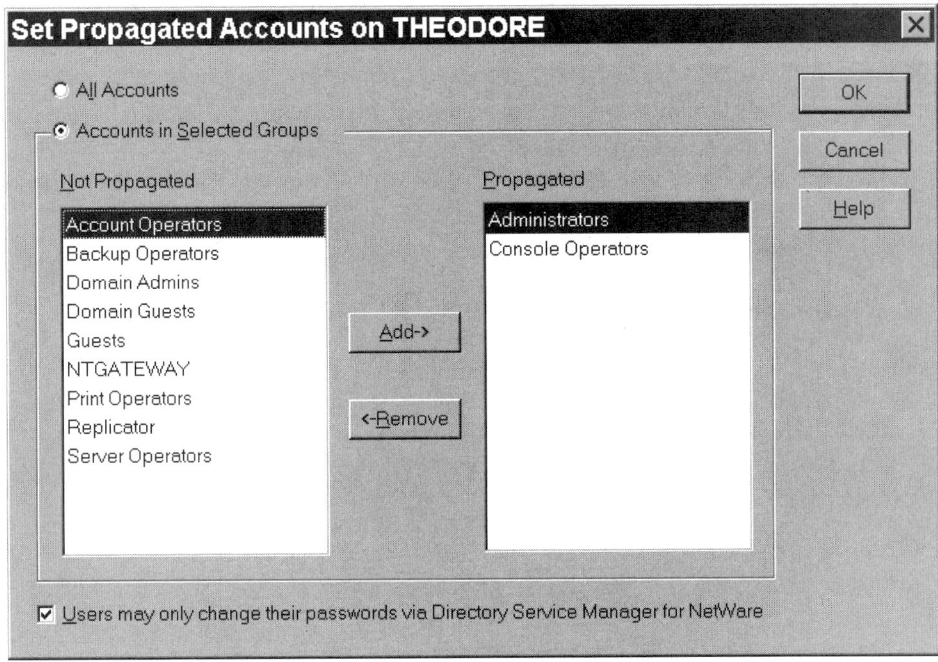

Figure 20-3. The Set Propagated Accounts on <NetWare Servername> dialog allows you to specify which user and group accounts should be propagated from the Windows NT Server domain to the NetWare server

Adding managed servers

To add an additional NetWare server to be managed as part of the selected domain, select **NetWare Server ➤ Add Server to Manage**. Synchronization Manager displays the Select NetWare Server dialog. Type the name of the server to be managed in the NetWare Server box, or choose one of the available NetWare servers listed in the Select NetWare Server pane. Complete the process of adding the NetWare server using the steps described in the preceding section.

Removing managed servers

To remove a managed NetWare server from the selected domain, select **NetWare Server ➤ Remove Managed Server**. Synchronization Manager prompts you to confirm that you want to remove the server. Once removed, that server no longer receives account information updates from Synchronization Manager. You must manage the server manually using NetWare utilities, or add the server to another domain.

Setting propagated accounts

When you add a NetWare server to a domain, you are given the opportunity to specify which accounts should be propagated to the NetWare server. If you subsequently need to change this list of propagated accounts for a particular server, first highlight that server name in the main Synchronization Manager pane. Then select **NetWare Server ➤ Set Propagated Accounts** to display the Set Propagated Accounts on <NetWare Servername> dialog. Make the necessary changes, using the steps described in the preceding section and click OK to save your changes.

Synchronizing servers

DSMN maintains an *Account Synchronization Database* that stores the update status of each user account and each group on each NetWare server that is managed by DSMN. As you add new Windows NT user accounts and groups and modify existing ones, the static account information on the NetWare server becomes dated.

Synchronize Selected Server
: Immediately sends updated account information to the selected NetWare server. Only the most recent account updates are sent to the NetWare server. Directory Service Manager for NetWare tracks which account updates have been sent to which NetWare servers, so when you use this command, the NetWare server receives only the updates it needs.

Fully Synchronize Selected Server
: Immediately sends complete information about all propagated user and group accounts to the selected NetWare server, replacing the information about those accounts. This command transfers all information about all propagated user accounts to all NetWare servers in the domain. This command is rarely necessary. Use it only when the NetWare server is extremely unsynchronized with the domain's Directory. To send a regular account update to a NetWare server, click Synchronize Selected Server on the NetWare Server menu.

Synchronize All Servers
: Immediately sends updated account information to all NetWare servers in the domain. Only the most recent account updates are sent to the NetWare servers. Directory Service Manager for NetWare tracks which account updates have been sent to which NetWare servers, so when you use this command, each NetWare server receives only the updates it needs.

Fully Synchronize All Servers
: Immediately sends complete information about all propagated user and group accounts to all NetWare servers in the domain, replacing the information about those accounts. This command transfers all information about all propagated user accounts to all NetWare servers in the domain. This command is

rarely necessary. Use it only when all or most NetWare servers in the domain are extremely unsynchronized with the domain's Directory. To send a regular account update to one or more NetWare servers, use the Synchronize Selected Server command or the Fully Synchronize Selected Server command. If only one NetWare server in the domain is extremely unsynchronized, click Fully Synchronize Selected Server on the NetWare Server menu.

Backing up the database

Set Database Backup Options

Specifies where the domain's account synchronization database is to be backed up. You can back up the database to one or more locations, on any network computer. It is strongly recommended that you back up the database to at least one location on a different computer. By default, the database is backed up daily, at a time you specify. To immediately back up the database, click Backup Database Now on the NetWare Server menu.

Backup Database Now

Immediately backs up the account synchronization database to all current backup locations. The backup locations include the locations specified using Set Database Backup Options on the NetWare Server menu, as well as the *SYNCAGNT\BACKUP* directory on the primary domain controller.

21

Migrating to a Pure Windows NT Server Environment

In this chapter:

From Microsoft's point of view, coexistence between NetWare and Windows NT Server is just fine in the short run, as the abundance of tools described in the preceding chapters makes clear. What Microsoft really wants, however, is for you to migrate completely to Windows NT Server and abandon NetWare entirely. The smart people at Microsoft realize that this just isn't going to happen unless they make the process as quick, easy, and automatic as possible. Their primary strategic weapon in this battle for your servers is a utility called the Migration Tool for NetWare. It should come as no surprise that the Migration Tool for NetWare utility is bundled as a standard feature of Windows NT Server.

The Migration Tool for NetWare utility can automatically transfer the following items from a NetWare 2.x server or a NetWare 3.1x server to a Windows NT server:

User and group accounts
: Migrate all or selected user accounts and group accounts, while maintaining the rights and other security information associated with the user or group, excepting only security information that has no direct equivalent in Windows NT Server.

Volumes, folders, and files
: Migrate all or selected parts of NetWare volumes and directories to corresponding Windows NT volumes and directories, while maintaining the associated file and directory attributes and rights.

Login scripts
: Migrate NetWare login scripts to a Windows NT server that is running File and Print Services for NetWare.

The Migration Tool for NetWare offers considerable flexibility in determining what information is transferred from which NetWare server or servers, and how it is stored on the destination server. These options include:

One-to-one migration
: Migrate users and data from a single NetWare server directly to a single Windows NT server.

Many-to-one migration
: Migrate users and data from two or more NetWare servers to a single Windows NT server, while reconciling duplicate user names and similar conflicts. If you have many NetWare servers running on older, slower computers with small disks, you can use Migration Tool for NetWare to consolidate all of these older servers onto a single, more capable computer running Windows NT Server, cutting your administrative burdens significantly while doing so.

Many-to-many migration
: Migrate information from two or more NetWare servers to two or more Windows NT servers, redistributing information as necessary.

Because the process of migration is potentially very complex, the Migration Tool for NetWare allows you to do one or more trial run migrations before you perform the actual migration. You can use these trial run migrations to identify and resolve problems, making sure that the actual migration proceeds exactly as you intend it to. Detailed log files can be generated during both trial run migrations and actual migrations.

Here's an amazing fact. According to Microsoft, you can perform both trial run migrations and actual migrations without affecting the NetWare server in any way, and while maintaining availability to users of all NetWare services and Windows NT services. Although this is true during trial migrations, it turns out not to be the case for an actual migration, during which all users must be logged off and all files closed.

Understanding the Migration Process

In outline, migrating the contents of a NetWare server to a Windows NT server requires the following steps:

1. Make sure that all of the computers that will be involved in the migration are configured correctly. The computer you are using to run the Migration Tool for NetWare must have the NWLink IPX/SPX compatible transport protocol installed, as must the Windows NT server computer to which you are migrating. If you are running the Migration Tool for NetWare on a computer

running Windows NT Workstation, the Client Service for NetWare must be installed and configured. If you are running the Migration Tool for NetWare on a computer running Windows NT Server, the Gateway Service for NetWare must be installed and configured. The Gateway Service for NetWare must also be installed and configured on the Windows NT server to which you are migrating.

2. Run the Migration Tool for NetWare.
3. Select the NetWare server that you want to migrate from. This is called the *source server*. You may select one or several source servers. You must have the account name and password for the Supervisor account or a Supervisor Equivalent account on the source NetWare server(s). Make sure that the computer you are running the Migration Tool for NetWare on does not have any drives mapped to the source NetWare server(s).
4. Select the Windows NT server that you want to migrate to. This is called the *target server*. You may select one or several target servers. You must be logged on to this computer with a user account that is a member of the Administrators group.
5. Select User Options to specify which users and groups, if any, will be migrated, and how they will be migrated.
6. Select File Options to specify which folders and files, if any, will be migrated, and how they will be migrated.
7. Select Trial Migration to do a test run. Without making any actual changes to either the source server or the target server, the trial migration generates a log file that specifies exactly what changes would have occurred during a real migration that used the settings you specified.
8. View the log file generated by the trial migration to verify that, during the actual migration, the Migration Tool for NetWare will take the actions you expect.
9. If necessary, make changes to User Options, File Options, and the other settings to correct problems you found when reviewing the trial migration log file. Run the trial migration again as needed until you have verified that all of the problems have been corrected and that the actual migration will proceed as intended.
10. Select Start Migration to perform the actual migration.
11. Verify that the users, groups, folders, and files you specified were migrated successfully, with the rights and permissions intended.

You do not have to perform all of these steps in one session. Each time you exit the Migration Tool for NetWare, all current settings are automatically saved in the file *NWConv.DAT* in the home directory of the user who is running the program. You may also select **File ➤ Save Configuration** to store Migration Tool for NetWare settings in a *.CNF* file in a location of your choice.

Migration Issues for User Accounts

NetWare user accounts correspond quite closely to Windows NT Server user accounts both in the information they contain and in the purpose they serve. There are, however, some differences that must be taken into consideration during a migration. Chapter 19, *Using File and Print Services for NetWare*, examines these issues from the viewpoint of using FPNW to emulate a NetWare server on a Windows NT server. Chapter 20, *Managing Servers in a Mixed NetWare and Windows NT Server Environment*, examines them from the perspective of using DSMN to manage NetWare servers from Windows NT Server. The following sections examine account migration issues for both ordinary user accounts and privileged accounts in the Migration Tool for NetWare environment, which has some minor variations from the similar issues described earlier in this book.

Migrating User Account Restrictions

As I mentioned in the two preceding chapters, minor differences exist in the way that NetWare and Windows NT Server restrict user accounts. Primarily, NetWare allows you to set most user account restrictions on a per-user basis with only a few restrictions that must be set globally. Conversely, Windows NT Server requires you to set most user account restrictions globally in Account Policy, while permitting a few user account restrictions to be set on a per-user basis. Also, some account restrictions that are available in NetWare are not available in Windows NT Server, and *vice versa*.

When you use the Migration Tool for NetWare to transfer user accounts and their associated restrictions, NetWare per-user restrictions that correspond to Windows NT per-user restrictions are transferred by individual account. NetWare per-user restrictions that map to Windows NT Account Policy global restrictions are migrated globally for all users. You may specify these global Account Policy settings in either of the following ways:

- By default, the Migration Tool for NetWare uses the global settings from the Supervisor account on the source NetWare server.
- You may specify that the Supervisor settings on the source NetWare server should be ignored and that the current Windows NT Server Account Policy settings be used instead.

Exactly how the Migration Tool for NetWare migrates account restrictions is determined by the configuration of the target server, specifically, whether File and Print Services for NetWare is installed. Table 21-1 lists NetWare user account restrictions, and how these account restrictions are mapped to Windows NT account restrictions when NetWare accounts are migrated to a Windows NT server that is not running FPNW. Table 21-2 lists the changes to this mapping that occur if FPNW is installed on the target server.

Table 21-1. How User Account Restrictions Are Migrated to a Windows NT Server That Is Not Running FPNW

NetWare Restriction	Windows NT Restriction	Migration Tool for NetWare Action
Account Disabled	Account Disabled	Uses individual NetWare user account setting.
Allow User to Change Password	User Cannot Change Password	Uses individual NetWare user account setting.
Days Between Forced Changes	Maximum Password Age	Uses global Account Policy.
Expiration Date	Expiration Date	Uses individual NetWare user account setting.
Force Periodic Password Changes	Password Never Expires	Uses individual NetWare user account setting.
Grace Logins	N/A	Does not migrate setting.
Intruder Detection/Lockout	Account Lockout	Uses global Account Policy.
Limit Concurrent Connections	N/A	Does not migrate setting.
Minimum Password Length	Minimum Password Length	Uses global Account Policy.
Require Password	Permit Blank Password	Uses global Account Policy.
Require Unique Passwords	Password Uniqueness	Uses global Account Policy.
Station Restrictions	N/A	Does not migrate setting.
Time Restrictions	Logon Hours	Uses individual NetWare user account setting.
Volume/Disk Restrictions	No Windows NT equivalent	Does not migrate setting.

NOTE With regard to the Expiration Date user account restriction, NetWare displays the first day the account is expired, whereas Windows NT displays the last day that the account is valid. NetWare accounts with any expiration date of 1/1/2000 or later are assigned a Windows NT expiration date of 2/6/2006. NetWare accounts with expiration dates of 12/31/99 or earlier are mapped normally to Windows NT.

Table 21-2. Changes in How User Account Restrictions Are Migrated to a Windows NT Server if That Server Is Running FPNW

NetWare Restriction	Windows NT Restriction	Migration Tool for NetWare Action
Grace Logins	Grace Logins	Uses individual NetWare user account setting.
Limit Concurrent Connections	Limit Concurrent Connections	Uses individual NetWare user account setting.
Station Restrictions	Logon Workstations	Does not migrate setting. Although FPNW provides a mechanism to set station restrictions, existing NetWare restrictions are not migrated.

Migrating Privileged Accounts

Like NetWare, Windows NT Server supports administrative user accounts that have a higher level of privileges than ordinary user accounts. The NetWare Supervisor account can assign limited administrative privileges to other user accounts by granting them equivalencies—e.g., supervisor equivalent—or by assigning them a special user type—e.g., Workgroup Manager or Print Queue Operator. The Windows NT Server Administrator account can similarly grant extended privileges to other user accounts by making those accounts members of one or more administrative groups—e.g., the Account Operators group or the Administrators group. Table 21-3 lists privileged NetWare user types and their rough equivalents in Windows NT Server.

Migration Issues for Folders and Files

The Migration Tool for NetWare enables you to migrate files, folders, and entire volumes from a NetWare server to a Windows NT Server volume. So long as the Windows NT Server volume is using the NTFS filesystem, most of the NetWare effective rights are transferred intact as the equivalent Windows NT Server permissions. The following sections examine how NetWare trustee directory rights, trustee file rights, and file attributes are translated to the corresponding Windows NT Server NTFS directory permissions, NTFS file permissions, and file attributes.

NetWare Trustee Assignments Versus NTFS Permissions

NTFS directory permissions are similar in purpose and effect to NetWare Trustee Directory Assignments, just as NTFS file permissions closely match NetWare Trustee File Assignments. In each case, NetWare trustee rights offer a little more control than do the corresponding Windows NT Server NTFS permissions. For all intents and purposes, however, you can accomplish almost anything by using NTFS permissions that you can by using NetWare Trustee Assignments.

Table 21-3. NetWare 3.1x Administrative User Types Versus Windows NT Administrative Groups

NetWare 3.1x User Type	Windows NT Group	Description
Supervisor	Administrators	The Windows NT Server built-in account *Administrator* is fully equivalent to the NetWare *Supervisor*. Making a Windows NT user account a member of the *Administrators* group corresponds with making a NetWare user a *Supervisor Equivalent*. When migrating supervisor equivalent NetWare user accounts, the Migration Tool for NetWare does not by default add these accounts to the group Administrators. Override the default to migrate NetWare Supervisor Equivalents as Windows NT Administrators.
Workgroup Manager/User Account Manager	Account Operators	Assigning membership in the *Account Operators* group is the nearest Windows NT equivalent to assigning a NetWare user as a *Workgroup Manager* or as a *User Account Manager*. The Account Operator, however, has more power than either of these NetWare user types. It can create, delete, and manage any user account or group except other administrative users and groups. Because Windows NT Server has no need of the decentralized administration for which these user types were designed, the Migration Tool for NetWare migrates users assigned to either of these NetWare user types as ordinary Windows NT users, and does not grant any special administrative privileges.
File Server Console Operator	Server Operators	Membership in the *Server Operators* group is the nearest Windows NT equivalent to the NetWare *File Server Console Operator* user type, but confers considerably more power. Because a Server Operator both has more power over an individual server and has these powers throughout the domain, the Migration Tool for NetWare migrates a File Server Console Operator as an ordinary Windows NT user rather than as a Server Operator.

Table 21-3. NetWare 3.1x Administrative User Types Versus Windows NT Administrative Groups (continued)

NetWare 3.1x User Type	Windows NT Group	Description
Print Server Operator	Print Operators	Windows NT Server integrates the server and queue elements used by NetWare. Membership in the *Print Operators* group confers the combined powers of the NetWare *Print Server Operator* and *Print Queue Operator* user types. Although membership in the Windows NT Print Operators group confers somewhat more power than the NetWare Print Server Operator user type, the Migration Tool for NetWare nevertheless migrates users and groups assigned as NetWare Print Server Operators to the Windows NT Print Operators group.
Print Queue Operator	Print Operators	Because membership in the Windows NT Print Operators group confers considerably more power than that enjoyed by a NetWare Print Queue Operator, such user accounts are migrated as ordinary Windows NT user accounts. You can grant an ordinary Windows NT user account approximate equivalency with the NetWare user type *Print Queue Operator* by assigning that user account the *Manage Documents* permission for one or more specific printers.

One thing you'll notice right away is that Windows NT Server provides no equivalent for the NetWare *Inherited Rights Mask* (*IRM*). NetWare *Effective Rights* are the sum of the rights granted explicitly to the user and the implicit rights inherited by the user from group memberships less rights revoked by the IRM. With Windows NT Server, the user rights to a file or folder are the sum of the rights explicitly granted to that user and the rights inherited from any groups of which that user is a member. Rights granted to a user by the NTFS directory permissions in effect for a folder can be revoked by NTFS file permissions explicitly set for a file within that folder.

Table 21-4 details how the Migration Tool for NetWare maps the NetWare trustee file rights on the source server to the closest corresponding NTFS file permissions on the target server. Note that NTFS does not support the Create (C) and Filescan (F) rights at the file level, but allows you to enforce similar restrictions at the directory level. The NetWare Create (C) trustee right is implied by the NTFS Write (W) file permission. The NetWare Filescan (F) trustee right is implied by the NTFS Read (R) file permission.

Table 21-4. NetWare Trustee File Rights and Corresponding Windows NT NTFS File Permissions

NetWare Trustee File Right	Windows NT NTFS File Permission
Read (R)	Read (RX)
Write (W)	Write (W)
Erase (E)	Delete (D)
Access Control (A)	Change Permissions + Take Ownership (PO)
Modify (M)	Write (W)
Supervisory (S)	Full Control (All)

Table 21-5 details how the Migration Tool for NetWare maps NetWare trustee directory rights on the source server to NTFS directory permissions on the target server. Note that, in some cases, the Migration Tool for NetWare does not use the most direct possible mapping when migrating the directory. For example, it assigns identical NTFS permissions (RWXD) to the NetWare trustee directory assignments Write (W), Erase (E), and Modify (M), rather than mapping these assignments more finely. In the second column, the first item within parentheses lists the NTFS permissions in effect for the directory itself. The second lists the NTFS permissions that are applied to newly created files within that directory.

Table 21-5. NetWare Trustee Directory Rights and Corresponding Windows NT NTFS Directory Permissions

NetWare Trustee Directory Right	Windows NT NTFS Directory Permission
Read (R)	Read (RX) (RX)
Filescan (F)	Read, Execute (RX) (Not Specified)
Write (W)	Read, Write, Execute, Delete (RWXD) (RWXD)
Create (C)	Write, Execute (WX) (Not Specified)
Erase (E)	Read, Write, Execute, Delete (RWXD) (RWXD)
Access Control (A)	Change Permissions (P) (P)
Modify (M)	Read, Write, Execute, Delete (RWXD) (RWXD)
Supervisory (S)	Full Control (All) (All)

WARNING The differences between the ways that NetWare and Windows NT Server handle security can cause problems in at least one common situation, as follows.

Assume that you have created a shared user folder on an FPNW volume, e.g., *\SYSVOL\USER*, that will contain individual user directories, e.g., *\SYSVOL\USER\JOHN*, *\SYSVOL\USER\BOB*, and so forth. You would like each NetWare client to have full control within his or her own directory, but no access rights in other user directories. Removing Everyone from the permissions list for these user directories and then granting each user explicit permissions to his or her own directory appears to do this. A NetWare client can use File Manager or Explorer to view and manipulate files in his or her own directory normally, but cannot access other user directories.

However, if the client is running DOS, or is shelled to DOS in Windows 3.1x or Windows 95, he cannot access his own directory. This presents a conundrum for DOS-based NetWare clients at login time. You want to map a drive to the user directory, but that directory is not visible if the group Everyone has no permissions in the directory. The alternative is to provide some level of access to the group Everyone. Doing so allows the user to see his own directory when logging in, but it also compromises security because every user has at least some access to every other user directory.

Microsoft is aware of this problem, and has updated FPNW to solve it. However, at the time this was written, they do not appear to have posted the fix to their web site, but instead supply it only to those who explicitly request it. Thanks go to Scott Johnson and Anthony Rollins at TransQuest for discovering this problem and bringing it to my attention.

NetWare Attribute Security Versus NTFS File Attributes

Like NetWare, Windows NT Server uses file attribute security. Windows NT provides a closely matching file attribute for each of the primary file attributes supported by NetWare. NetWare, however, supports some attributes that have no corresponding NTFS file attribute. Some of these, e.g., the *Indexed* (*I*) and *Purge* (*P*) attributes, are not supported by NTFS simply because Windows NT Server has no function that corresponds to the NetWare function supported by that attribute. Table 21-6 lists how the Migration Tool for NetWare maps supported NetWare file attributes to the Windows NT Server file attributes that correspond most closely to them.

Table 21-6. How Migration Tool for NetWare Migrates NetWare File Attributes to Corresponding Windows NT NTFS File Attributes

NetWare File Attribute	Windows NT NTFS File Attribute
Archive needed (A)	Archive (A)
Copy Inhibit (CI)	Not migrated
Delete Inhibit (DI)	Not migrated
Hidden (H)	Hidden (H)
Indexed (I)	Not migrated
Purge (P)	Not migrated
Read Audit (Ra)	Not migrated
Read Only (Ro)	Read Only (R)
Rename Inhibit (RI)	Not migrated
Shareable (S)	Not migrated
System (Sy)	System (S)
Transactional (T)	Not migrated
Write Audit (Wa)	Not migrated
Execute Only (X)	Not migrated

Using the Migration Tool for NetWare

All migration functions are done using the Migration Tool for NetWare. The following sections examine step by step the process of migrating from NetWare to Windows NT Server.

Starting the Migration Tool for NetWare and Selecting Servers

To run the Migration Tool for NetWare, from the Start button, select **Programs ➤ Administrative Tools (Common) ➤ Migration Tool for NetWare**. When you run it for the first time—i.e., if the file *NWConv.DAT* does not exist—the Select Servers for Migration dialog is displayed. When you run the Migration Tool for NetWare subsequently, your last configuration is restored automatically, until you perform an actual migration.

If you want to use a previously saved Migration Tool for NetWare configuration that is stored as a *.CNF* file, click Cancel to close the Select Servers for Migration dialog and display the main Migration Tool for NetWare screen. You may then select **File ➤ Restore Configuration** to load that file. Otherwise, use the following procedure to specify the source and target servers.

Type the name of the source NetWare server in the From NetWare Server box. Alternatively, click the ellipsis to display the Select NetWare Server dialog. Click the desired NetWare server in the Select Server pane to display it in the Server box, and then click OK to return to the Select Servers for Migration dialog. If you are not already logged in to that NetWare server, or if the account you are currently logged in with does not have supervisor privileges, the Migration Tool for NetWare prompts you for the name and password of an account with supervisor privileges before proceeding.

Type the name of the target Windows NT server in the To Windows NT Server box. Alternatively, click the ellipsis to display the Select Windows NT Server dialog. The Select Server pane displays the available domains. Double-click a domain name to expand the display to include the servers that are members of that domain. Click the desired Windows NT server in the Select Server pane to display it in the Server box. If the account you are currently logged in with is not a member of the Administrators group, the Migration Tool for NetWare prompts you for the name and password of an account with Administrator privileges before proceeding. Click OK to display the Select Servers for Migration dialog with the server pair filled in.

Click OK to return to the Migration Tool for NetWare main display, as shown in Figure 21-1. If you need to add additional server pairs, click Add to display the Select Servers for Migration dialog and repeat the preceding steps. Each server pair appears as a single row in the Migration Tool for NetWare main screen, and may be modified individually.

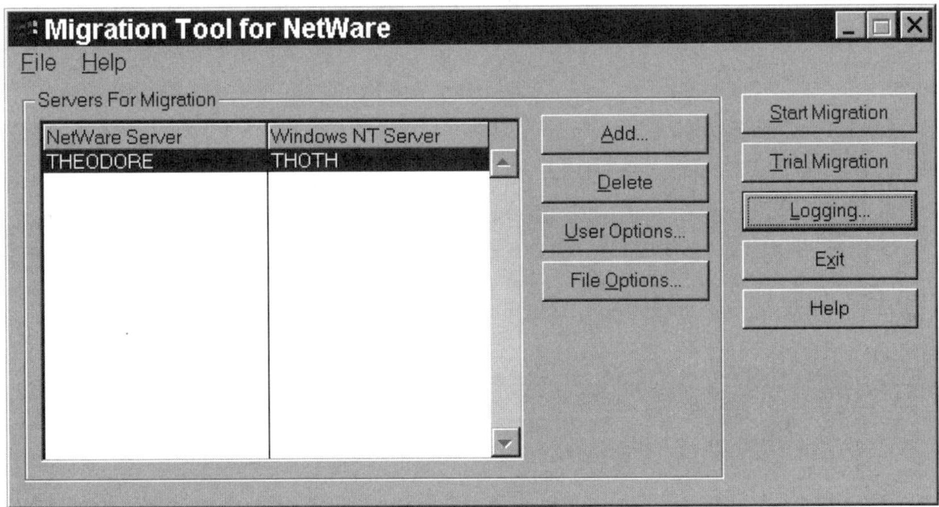

Figure 21-1. The Migration Tool for NetWare displays the source and target servers and allows you to configure migration options

Selecting Users and Groups to Be Migrated

After you configure the source and target servers, click User Options to display the User and Group Options dialog. This dialog allows you to specify whether users and groups will be migrated and whether a mapping file is to be used. It also includes four tabs—Passwords, Usernames, Group Names, and Defaults—that allow you to set options for migrating users and groups. Begin by marking one or both of the check boxes at the top of the dialog, as follows:

Transfer Users and Groups
: If marked, this check box, which is enabled by default, causes the Migration Tool for NetWare to migrate users and groups from the selected NetWare source server to the selected Windows NT target server. Clear this check box if you do not want to migrate users and groups, i.e., if you want to migrate only folders and files.

Use Mappings in File
: If marked, this check box, which is disabled by default, causes the Migration Tool for NetWare to use the mapping file you specify to determine user and group migration options. Using a mapping file allows you to migrate only selected users and groups, to set individual passwords, to change usernames and group names during the migration, and otherwise to customize the migration. Mapping files are described later in this section.

NOTE If your Windows NT domain is organized as a master domain, you can transfer accounts to the domain controller of the master domain. To do so, click Advanced, mark the Transfer Users to Trusted Domain check box, and then select a domain from the scrolling list.

Because NetWare passwords are stored in encrypted form in the NetWare bindery, the Migration Tool for NetWare cannot retrieve the plain-text passwords for the NetWare user accounts that are to be migrated. Therefore, each migrated user account must be assigned a new password, either by the administrator or by the Migration Tool for NetWare itself. You can use a mapping file to specify an individual password for each user account that is migrated. If you are not using a mapping file, use the Passwords page to tell the Migration Tool for NetWare how to assign new passwords to the migrated user accounts, as follows:

No Password
: Choose this option button if you want the Migration Tool for NetWare to create the new user accounts without assigning passwords to them.

Password is Username

Choose this option button if you want the Migration Tool for NetWare to create new user accounts with the password set equal to the username. Note that Windows NT Server passwords are case sensitive, and the password for each user account will be set to the username for that account, but in uppercase.

Password is

Choose this option button and enter a password if you want the Migration Tool for NetWare to assign the password you specify to all new user accounts.

Because any of these system-assigned passwords is insecure, the User Must Change Password check box is marked by default. Leave this check box marked if you want to force users to change their passwords the first time they log on. Clear this check box if you want users to be able to continue to use the password assigned to them by the Migration Tool for NetWare.

It is possible that one or more of the user accounts to be migrated will duplicate an existing username on the target Windows NT server, either because the same user has accounts on both servers or because different users have been assigned the same username on different servers. The Usernames page allows you to specify how these duplicate username conflicts will be resolved, as follows:

Log Error

Choose this option button, which is enabled by default, if you want the Migration Tool for NetWare to log username conflicts to the file *ERROR.LOG*. When this option is in effect, NetWare user accounts whose username conflicts with an existing Windows NT user account username are not migrated.

Ignore

Choose this option button if you want the Migration Tool for NetWare simply to ignore conflicts. When this option is in effect and a conflict occurs, the NetWare account information is not migrated, and this failure is not logged.

Overwrite with new Info

Choose this option button if you want the Migration Tool for NetWare to replace existing Windows NT user account information with NetWare account information. Conflicts are logged to the file *ERROR.LOG* for subsequent review.

Add prefix

Choose this option button and enter a prefix if you want the Migration Tool for NetWare to create a new, nonconflicting username automatically by adding the prefix you specify. Conflicts are logged to the file *ERROR.LOG* for subsequent review.

It is also possible that one or more of the group accounts to be migrated will duplicate an existing group name on the target Windows NT server. The Group Names page allows you to specify how these duplicate group name conflicts will be resolved, as follows:

Log Error
: Choose this option button if you want the Migration Tool for NetWare to log group name conflicts to the file *ERROR.LOG*. When this option is in effect, NetWare group accounts whose group name conflicts with an existing Windows NT group name are not migrated.

Ignore
: Choose this option button, which is enabled by default, if you want the Migration Tool for NetWare simply to ignore conflicts. When this option is in effect and a conflict occurs, the NetWare group account is not migrated, and this failure is not logged.

Add prefix
: Choose this option button and enter a prefix if you want the Migration Tool for NetWare to create a new, nonconflicting group name automatically by adding the prefix you specify. Conflicts are logged to the file *ERROR.LOG* for subsequent review.

WARNING The Migration Tool for NetWare has a minor bug related to NetWare group names. If a NetWare user account exists that has the same name as a NetWare group, the user account will be migrated, but the group account will not. No error message is generated to notify you of this failure. To make sure that this problem does not occur, compare group names with usernames to verify that no duplication exists. If duplicates do exist, rename the NetWare user or the NetWare group before migrating.

The Defaults page allows you to specify which default account restrictions will be used, how privileged NetWare accounts will be migrated, and whether account information that is specific to the NetWare account will be migrated, as follows:

Use Supervisor Defaults
: Mark this check box, which is enabled by default, if you want the migration to use the NetWare default account restrictions found in Supervisor Options. Clear the check box if you do not want to transfer the default NetWare account restrictions, but instead prefer to use the existing Windows NT Server Account Policy settings.

Add Supervisors to the Administrators Group

Mark this check box, which is cleared by default, if you want the migrated NetWare supervisor equivalent accounts to be added to the Windows NT Administrators group. Leave the check box cleared if you want NetWare supervisor equivalent accounts to be migrated as ordinary users without administrative privileges.

Migrate NetWare Specific Account Information

Mark this check box, which is enabled by default, to migrate NetWare account information that is stored, but not used, by Windows NT Server. Clear the check box if you want to migrate only account information that is common to both operating systems.

Creating and Using Mapping Files

Using the Users and Groups dialog from User Options is the easiest and fastest way to set the migration options for users and groups, but it has the drawback of not allowing you to individually manage the accounts to be migrated. For example, each user account on the selected NetWare server must be migrated to a Windows NT account of the same name. Even worse, none of the standard methods available in User Options for handling passwords for the new accounts is particularly desirable. Your only choices are to use no password at all; to use the username as the password; or to assign identical passwords to all migrated accounts.

As an alternative to this one-size-fits-all method of selecting the users and groups to be migrated, Migration Tool for NetWare allows you to use a *mapping file* to specify options on a per-user and per-group basis. By using a mapping file, you can:

- Migrate only selected users from the source NetWare server, rather than being limited to choosing all or none.
- Migrate a NetWare account to a different, individually specified username on the target Windows NT server.
- Specify a different, individual password for each user account being migrated.
- Migrate only selected groups from the source NetWare server, rather than accepting forced migration of all groups when you need to migrate users.
- Migrate a NetWare group to a different, individually specified group name on the target Windows NT server.

The syntax of a mapping file is pretty simple. You can create the mapping file manually using Notepad or any other ASCII editor. However, the Migration Tool for NetWare can create a mapping file for you automatically, which not only avoids possible syntax errors, but automatically imports all of the user and group information from the source NetWare server. To have Migration Tool for NetWare create a mapping file for you, from the User and Group Options dialog, click Create to display the Create Mapping File dialog.

Choose the desired options. By default, the Create Mapping File dialog imports both usernames and group names from the source NetWare server, and sets the password for each username to null. Clear one or the other check boxes if you want to import only usernames or only group names to the mapping file. If the Include User Names check box is marked, choose one of the option buttons to specify how the password will be set in the mapping file.

Type a name for the new mapping file in the Use Mappings in File box. Alternatively, click the ellipsis to display the Open dialog and select an existing mapping file. Click OK to import the usernames and group names from the source NetWare server and create the mapping file. Migration Tool for NetWare displays a NWConv message box to notify you that the mapping file was created successfully. If you want to edit the mapping file immediately, click Yes to invoke Notepad. Otherwise, click No to save the mapping file and exit.

Example 21-1 shows the mapping file that was created when I allowed the Migration Tool for NetWare to create the mapping file automatically from the bindery of my test-bed NetWare server, using the default options. The syntax is simplicity itself. Any line that begins with a semicolon is treated as a comment.

Example 21-1. An Automatically Generated Mapping File Lists All of the Users and Groups on the Source NetWare Server

```
[USERS]
BARBARA, BARBARA,
JAM, JAM,
MIKOL, MIKOL,
RBT, RBT,
WINNT_SYNC_AGENT, WINNT_SYNC_AGENT,

[GROUPS]
ADMINISTRATORS, ADMINISTRATORS
```

The first section, delimited by `[USERS]` on an otherwise empty line, lists the users to be migrated. Each line in this section contains the record for a single user, with each field delimited by commas and the record itself delimited by a CR/LF. The first field is the NetWare username; the second field is the username to be created on the target Windows NT server. Both of these fields are required. The third, optional, field contains the password to be assigned to that username.

The second section, delimited by `[GROUPS]` on an otherwise empty line, lists the groups to be migrated. Each line in this section contains the record for a single group, with exactly two fields delimited by commas, and the record itself delimited by a CR/LF. The first field is the NetWare group name; the second field is the group name to be created on the target Windows NT server.

NOTE Unfortunately, the Migration Tool for NetWare doesn't check for username and group name conflicts when it generates the mapping file, leaving it up to you to verify that no such conflicts exist. For example, the NetWare group Administrators shown in the example will obviously conflict with the Windows NT group of the same name.

Example 21-2 shows the automatically generated mapping file after several changes have been made, as follows:

- The NetWare username *BARBARA* will now be migrated to the Windows NT Server username *THOMPSBF*. Usernames may contain as many as 20 characters, and may include any mixture of upper-case and lower-case characters, except the following symbols: plus sign, equals sign, comma, less than, greater than, question mark, forward slash, backslash, double quotes, colon, semicolon, right square bracket, left square bracket, and pipe (split vertical bar).
- The newly created Windows NT username *THOMPSBF* will be assigned the password *WOM2bat*. Passwords may be as long as 14 characters, and are case sensitive.
- The NetWare username *MIKOL* will be migrated to a Windows NT account with the same username, but with the password *52Page52* assigned.
- The NetWare usernames *JAM*, *RBT*, and *WINNT_SYNC_AGENT* will not be migrated. To remove a NetWare username from the list of those to be migrated, simply delete the line that represents that username.
- The NetWare group *ADMINISTRATORS* will be migrated, but to avoid conflict with the existing Windows NT Server group of the same name, the NetWare group will be migrated to the new group name *ADMINS*.

Example 21-2. Edit the Automatically Generated Mapping File to Set User and Group Migration Options on an Individual Basis

```
[USERS]
BARBARA, THOMPSBF, WOM2bat
MIKOL, MIKOL,52Page52

[GROUPS]
ADMINISTRATORS, ADMINS
```

TIP It is possible to exert even finer control over user migration by using a combination of batch files and command-line utilities. Microsoft has developed a procedure that allows you to control nearly every aspect of user migration. For more information, see the article entitled, *How to Manage Migrated NetWare Users Accounts.* You can retrieve this article, numbered Q130017, by pointing your web browser to *http://www.microsoft.com/kb/articles/q130/0/17.htm*.

Selecting Directories and Files to Be Migrated

After you configure the users and groups to be migrated, click File Options to display the File Options dialog. This dialog allows you to specify whether volumes and files will be migrated at all, and, if so, which volumes and files will be migrated to which destinations.

The Migration Tool for NetWare by default configures every volume on the source NetWare servers to be migrated to a shared folder of the same name on the target Windows NT server. You may instead specify a different target folder for each NetWare volume. If the target folder does not exist, the Migration Tool for NetWare creates it.

WARNING The Migration Tool for NetWare has a minor bug that prevents it from accessing a NetWare server properly if the server name has only two characters. Although you can select the server initially, when you display the File Options dialog, the Source Files pane is blank and you cannot add volumes for that server manually. The only workaround for this problem is to rename the NetWare server temporarily, using a server name of three or more characters. After you migrate the server, you can rename it to the original name.

Begin configuring File Options by marking or clearing the check box at the top of the dialog, as follows:

Transfer Files

If marked, this check box, which is enabled by default, causes the Migration Tool for NetWare to migrate volumes and files from the selected NetWare source server to the selected Windows NT target server. Clear this check box if you do not want to migrate volumes and files, i.e., if you want to migrate only users and groups.

Adding and deleting source volumes

The first time you select File Options, the Migration Tool for NetWare scans the selected source NetWare servers to locate all available volumes on those servers before it displays the File Options dialog. Each volume found is listed in the Source Files pane of the File Options dialog, which indicates that that volume is selected for migration. Once created, the Source Files list is saved each time you exit the Migration Tool for NetWare, and is not automatically updated to reflect subsequent changes in the volume structure of the source NetWare server. You can, however, modify the Source Files list manually by adding and deleting volumes before performing the migration.

Ordinarily, the Add button is grayed out and inactive, because the Migration Tool for NetWare has automatically located and selected all available volumes. However, if, after running File Options for the first time, you create a new volume on a source NetWare server, that new volume will not be added to the Source Files list automatically. If you want to migrate the contents of the new volume, you must add it to the Source Files list manually. To do so, click Add to display the Add Volume to Copy dialog, select the source volume and the destination share from the scrolling lists, and click OK.

If the Source Files list displays one or more volumes that you do not want to migrate, simply highlight the volume name and click Delete to remove it. The volume is deleted immediately from the Source Files list. If you delete the wrong volume, you can simply return it to the Source Files list by using Add.

Selecting files to be migrated

The Migration Tool for NetWare by default selects all directories and all files on the selected NetWare volume to be migrated, with the following exceptions:

- The standard NetWare directories *SYS:ETC*, *SYS:LOGIN*, *SYS:MAIL*, and *SYS:SYSTEM* are not by default selected for migration. The *SYS:PUBLIC* directory, however, is selected.
- Files that have the Hidden or System file attribute set are not selected for migration, regardless of the directory in which they reside.

You can override these default selections by choosing Files from the File Options dialog to display the Files To Transfer dialog. Initially, this dialog displays only a single line in the left pane to represent the selected volume. You can expand and contract the tree display either by using the options in the Tree menu or by double-clicking the volume name or a directory name to expand and collapse branches. When a directory name is highlighted, files contained within that directory are listed in the right pane.

The tree display includes a check box to the immediate left of each branch, which indicates the status of file selections within that branch, as follows:

- If the check box is empty, no files and no directories within that branch are selected for migration. For example, the *ETC, LOGIN, MAIL,* and *SYSTEM* directories will not be migrated.
- If the check box is marked on a white background, all files and all directories within that branch are selected for migration. For example, the *PUBLIC, tmp,* and *usr* directories will be migrated, along with all of the files and subdirectories that they contain.
- If the check box is marked on a gray background, only some files and/or directories within that branch are selected for migration. For example, the *THEODORE**SYS*\ volume will have some, but not all, of its directories and files migrated.

Mark and clear check boxes as necessary to specify exactly which directories and files you want to be transferred. When you have completed your selections, click OK to return to the File Options dialog. Repeat this process as necessary for the other volumes to be migrated. When you have completed selecting directories and files to be migrated on all selected volumes, click OK to return to main Migration Tool for NetWare screen.

NOTE By default, the Migration Tool for NetWare does not migrate any file that has the Hidden or the System file attribute set. If you need to migrate such files, you have two choices. To migrate only selected Hidden or System files, mark the individual files to be migrated in the tree display. To migrate all Hidden files on the selected volume, from the Files To Transfer dialog, select **Transfer ➤ Hidden**. To migrate all System files on the selected volume, select **Transfer ➤ System Files**. Both of these menu options are toggles, and each applies to the entire selected volume. You cannot, for example, migrate only Hidden files from a specified directory. When using these menu options, you choose all or none.

Specifying destination shares

The Migration Tool for NetWare by default migrates each selected NetWare volume to a shared folder of the same name on the target Windows NT server. If the folder does not exist on the target server, it is automatically created and shared when you do the migration.

You can override the default destination share by choosing Modify from the File Options dialog to display the Modify Destination dialog. The From Server section displays the selected volume. Use the To Server section to modify the destination folder. You may use the Share drop-down list to select an existing share on the target server, or click New Share to create a new share and specify it as the destination.

By default, the Migration Tool for NetWare migrates the selected NetWare volume to the root level of the selected destination share. You can modify this behavior by entering the name of a Subdirectory within that share, which will cause the Migration Tool for NetWare to treat that subdirectory as the root when it migrates directories and files from the selected NetWare volume.

Be careful if you are migrating volumes from several source NetWare servers to a single target Windows NT server. Identically named directories from the different NetWare volumes will be migrated to the same folder on the target server. For example, the directory *SYS:PUBLIC* exists on all NetWare servers, and is migrated by default. If your migration includes more than one source NetWare server, the contents of the *SYS:PUBLIC* directories on all source servers will be migrated to the *SYS\PUBLIC* folder on the target server, thereby combining files from multiple source directories to a single target folder, which may not be what you want to do.

You can avoid this and similar problems in either of two ways. First, you may override the default destination share to transfer each volume to a different share. Alternatively, you may transfer all volumes to the same share, but to different subdirectories within that share.

TIP

Whatever you do, make sure that the share-level permissions for the destination share are set correctly before you perform the migration. These share permissions will be in effect for every folder and every subfolder that is created during the migration. Remember that NTFS permissions can only further restrict the rights granted by the share permission in effect.

For example, if the destination folder has the Read Only share-level permission set, all migrated directories and files will be limited to read-only access. It is best to set the Full Control share-level permission on the destination folder, and use NTFS permissions to further restrict access.

If the folder to which you are migrating currently exists, set the share permissions for that folder manually before doing the actual migration. If the folder will be created automatically during the migration, set the share permissions at the root level of the Windows NT Server volume upon which the share will be created.

Migrating Login Scripts

If the target Windows NT server is running File and Print Services for NetWare, you may optionally migrate NetWare user login scripts. To do so, for the source NetWare server in question, simply migrate the *SYS:MAIL* directory. When a user subsequently logs in from a NetWare client, that migrated login script executes as that user's personal login script. Remember that the *SYS:MAIL* directory is not migrated by default, so you must select this directory manually for each source NetWare volume that you want to migrate login scripts for.

Note that simply migrating the *SYS:MAIL* directory is insufficient unless the target server is also running FPNW. Although the directory itself and the login script files it contains may be migrated regardless, the login script will not run on a target server that is not running FPNW because the user accounts on that server do not contain the NetWare-specific account information necessary.

Setting Logging Options

The Migration Tool for NetWare automatically logs the actions it takes to various log files contained in the folder where the Migration Tool for NetWare resides. These log files include:

LogFile.LOG
: Contains a comprehensive listing of the users, groups, volumes, and files migrated, including their original status and their status after migration.

Summary.LOG
: Contains a summary overview of the migration process, including the source and target servers migrated, and the number of users, groups, and files migrated.

Error.LOG
: Contains an exception report that lists intended actions that could not be completed for one reason or another, e.g., username conflicts.

To set logging options or to view log files, from the main Migration Tool for NetWare screen, click Logging to display the Logging dialog. Set logging options by marking or clearing check boxes, as follows:

Popup on errors
: If marked, this check box, which is cleared by default, displays a warning message and pauses the migration each time an error occurs. This setting is effective for both trial migrations and actual migrations. If you use Trial Migration to eliminate errors before doing an actual migration—as you should—no errors should occur during the actual migration. However, it's a good idea to

mark this check box during the actual migration to catch errors, e.g., limited disk space, that did not become apparent during the trial migration.

Verbose User/Group Logging

If marked, this check box, which is enabled by default, causes detailed user and group information to be written to *LogFile.LOG*. If this check box is cleared, only summary user and group information is written to the log file. Even if your server has many users and groups, the information written to the log file when this option is enabled, though large, is still manageable. In general, it is a good idea to enable this option when doing an actual migration.

Verbose File Logging

If marked, this check box, which is cleared by default, causes detailed file and directory information to be written to *LogFile.LOG*. If this check box is cleared, only summary information is written to the log file, including the volumes migrated and the number of files transferred. On a typical production server, enabling this option causes an overwhelming number of log entries to be generated. However, during an actual migration, it is worthwhile to enable this option and save the resulting log file, if only to have it available for resolving problems after the migration.

The View Log Files button remains grayed out until you have performed a trial migration or an actual migration. Once you have data to be displayed, click View Log Files to display the LogView application, as shown in Figure 21-2. Use LogView to view, search, and print the various log files as needed.

Performing a Trial Migration

When you have finished configuring the Migration Tool for NetWare, the next step is to perform a trial migration. A trial migration differs from an actual migration only in that the proposed changes are not actually made to the target server. Running a Trial Migration allows you to verify that the options and settings you have specified will have the expected results before you do something that may be difficult to undo.

The trial migration process is intended to be used iteratively. You run it, check the log files for problems, correct the configuration to resolve the problems, and run the trial migration again. You continue this process until the trial migration runs without error. The time-consuming part is finding the errors and fixing the configuration. Even on a slow NetWare server with many users and files, the trial migration itself typically runs in a few seconds to at most a few minutes.

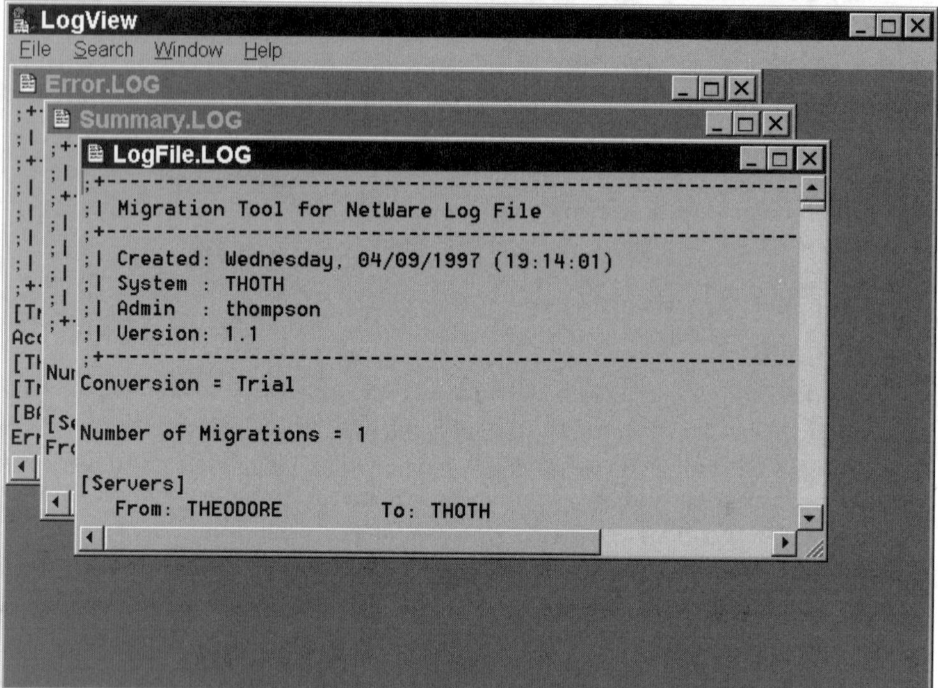

Figure 21-2. Use LogView to view, search, and print the log files that are generated during a migration

Completing the Actual Migration

After you have used trial migrations to verify that the Migration Tool for NetWare is configured properly, the final step is to run the actual migration. An actual migration is identical to a trial migration with two exceptions. First, you can run trial migrations to your heart's content while both servers continue to function normally. During the actual migration, all files should be closed and all users should be logged off both the source NetWare server(s) and the target Windows NT server(s). Second, depending on the aggregate size of the files to be transferred, the speed of the servers involved, and the network itself, the actual migration may require anything from several minutes to several hours to complete.

You should schedule the actual migration to be done after hours. Ideally, do the actual migration over a weekend to give you as much time as possible to verify that the migration completed as expected, and to recover if, despite all precautions, a disaster occurs. It should go without saying—but I'll say it anyway: do at least one full back up and compare on each affected server. If you're a belt and suspenders type of guy, do two or three.

I know that, in theory at least, no changes whatsoever are made to the NetWare server during the migration, so it shouldn't be necessary to do a special backup of your NetWare server just because you happen to be doing a migration. Still, while writing an earlier book, my test NetWare server was fine before an attempted migration and ended up irretrievably trashed afterwards. To this day, I don't know what caused the problem. It may have been caused by bugs in the beta version of the operating system, or the beta version of the Migration Tool for NetWare, by an interaction between the two, by the phase of the moon, or by something else entirely. I've done many subsequent migrations without any problems, but that doesn't mean the problem won't recur the next time I do a migration—or the next time you do one. Back up both servers.

When you're satisfied that the configuration is correct, that all servers are backed up properly, and that everything is otherwise ready for the actual migration, simply click Start Migration. The Migration Tool for NetWare displays status messages to keep you informed of the progress. When the migration completes, reboot both servers. Examine the log files to verify that the migration completed as expected, and without errors. Although I have no rational basis for doing so, I always spend some time verifying that all users and groups were transferred, that the aggregate number and size of the files matches on source and destination, and so forth. I also usually choose a few files at random to make sure that the security on the destination matches my expectations.

A Final Note

This chapter makes one very large simplifying assumption—that the NetWare server you are migrating from is used primarily to provide file and print services. If this is indeed the case, the Migration Tool for NetWare is a more than adequate tool for migrating to Windows NT Server. It migrates users, groups, and user data files perfectly well, with only the minor exceptions noted earlier in the chapter. Even shared server-based applications programs usually don't cause many problems. Most of them don't much care whether they happen to reside on a NetWare volume or on a Windows NT volume. At worst, you may need to spend a few minutes reinstalling the application on Windows NT Server or resetting a few permissions in the program folder.

If, however, your NetWare server is also functioning as an applications server, that opens a whole new can of wax. Client/server applications, back-end database server programs, and similar products are what cause the real migration problems. As a rule of thumb, assume that anything that runs as a NetWare *.NLM* just isn't going to port, at least not easily, no matter what the vendor tells you. If you're lucky, the vendor may have a Windows NT version of the program. If you're really lucky, it may even work. If you're unbelievably lucky, it may actually recognize and use the data that you transfer from your NetWare server.

Chances are, you won't be that lucky, so assume that each function you want to port from running as a NetWare *.NLM* to running as a Windows NT service will need to be treated as a separate project. By far the easiest solution is often simply to continue to run the application on the NetWare server. Even if you decide to port it to Windows NT, plan on having it continue to run on NetWare for at least weeks, if not several months. It will take you at least that long to port the application and to verify that it works as expected.

Client/server applications that were written in-house are often the thorniest problems. I have seen such applications written with hard-coded references to specific NetWare servers by name, which makes porting them to Windows NT problematic, to say the least. However, with these in-house applications you at least have the source code, which gives you some chance of porting them successfully. In another common situation, this isn't the case. Some commercial vertical market client/server applications have such limited distribution and are tied so tightly to NetWare that you might just as well consider them to be custom applications for which you don't have the source code. If your business depends on such an application, and if that application is not available in a version for Windows NT, you have no realistic alternative but to continue to run it on NetWare.

All of this said, with the Migration Tool for NetWare, Microsoft has done an amazingly good job of making square pegs fit into round holes. Although the Migration Tool for NetWare isn't perfect, it does do most of what needs to be done by most of the people who need to do it. Few other real-world software products can say as much.

Windows NT Server Resources

No one book can hope to cover the entire breadth of a product as comprehensive as Windows NT Server. This book attempts to provide a "fast start" for experienced Novell NetWare 3.1x administrators, but makes no pretensions to covering Windows NT Server exhaustively. While writing it, I often found myself completing a section that could easily have been expanded into a chapter, and a chapter that really deserved an entire book of its own. In some cases, other authors have written such books. This appendix lists some of these books, along with other Windows NT–related resources that I have found useful.

Books and Periodicals

A few years ago, characterizing a book was pretty straightforward. An author either knew the subject and wrote well or didn't. Things have changed over the last few years. Today, the press of day-and-date publication deadlines has resulted in the proliferation of gigantic, putatively comprehensive books that are written by many authors.

The theory espoused by some publishers is that a single author can have neither the breadth of knowledge nor the time required to write an entire book in time to get that book into print and onto bookstore shelves before the software ship date. A book that results from one of these collaborative efforts is often a hodge-podge of chapters that vary greatly in style, information density, and overall accuracy and completeness. As a result, some of the books listed here include some chapters that are absolute gems and others that are truly awful. It has, unfortunately, become the responsibility of the individual reader to sort the wheat from the chaff.

I have read nearly all of the books in this list. Those few that I have not read were recommended to me by friends and colleagues whose opinions I respect.

These, then, are books that I believe you may find useful, at least in part. That doesn't mean that any one of them is necessarily the best single representative of a particular topic. Because I do not have the time to read every book on each topic (or the money to buy them), there may well be one or more better books available for any given topic than those I have listed. In short, your mileage may vary.

NOTE Here's a blatant plug, but it comes directly from the author, and was in no way motivated by the fact that O'Reilly and Associates happens to have published this book. Take it for what it's worth.

O'Reilly and Associates is one of the very few publishers that has largely avoided the problem described above. Although they publish a few multiauthor books, they do so not to meet artificial deadlines, but to ensure that the topic is covered thoroughly.

You will probably find, as have I and many others, that an O'Reilly title is likely to be the most authoritative and comprehensive book available on any particular topic. In many cases, it will be the only book available that focuses narrowly on that topic. Who else, for example, would publish an entire book devoted to DNS & BIND or to Sendmail?

Each of the O'Reilly and Associates books listed has my unqualified endorsement. If you have any interest at all in the subject matter covered by one or more of them, do yourself a favor and buy the book.

Microsoft Windows NT

These are some of the books that I have found helpful in understanding various aspects of the Windows NT operating system. Some of them are based on the workstation version rather than the server version. This is of little concern, because the two versions of the operating system are nearly identical, differing essentially only in licensing terms, bundled utilities, and, of course, price. Both the server version and the workstation version run the same kernel, and the operating system configures itself as one or the other version at boot time based on Registry settings.

Also, you will find that many books written for Windows NT 3.51 continue to be useful. The core architecture and functionality does not differ greatly between versions 3.51 and 4.0 of Windows NT. The major differences are found in the updated Windows 95–like user interface and in the bundled applications. In fact, early test releases of V 4.0 were referred to by Microsoft as the Shell Update Release, or SUR. Many people thought that V 4.0 should have been labeled V 3.52, but that would have generated neither upgrade revenue for Microsoft nor new books sales for publishers. Such is life.

Custer, Helen, *Inside Windows NT*, Microsoft Press, Redmond, WA, 1995.

If you're interested in Windows NT internals, this is the place to start. Ms. Custer was a member of the Windows NT development team. This book covers the design philosophy, development history, and architecture of Windows NT from a developer's perspective.

Custer, Helen, *Inside the Windows NT File System*, Microsoft Press, Redmond, WA, 1994.

This 100-page, $10 book is not a quick read, but it's a nice introduction to learn about the details of the NTFS filesystem.

Honeycutt, Jerry, *Windows 95 and Windows NT 4.0 Registry and Customization Handbook*, Que, Indianapolis, IN, 1996.

One of the two books currently available that focuses on the Registry. This book compares the Windows 95 and Windows NT 4.0 Registries. It is an updated version of the author's earlier *Special Edition Using the Windows 95 Registry*, with new material added to cover the Windows NT Registry.

Jennings, Roger *et alia, Special Edition Using Windows NT Server 4,* Que, Indianapolis, IN, 1996.

This is a comprehensive guide to Windows NT Server, and one of the three or four general Windows NT Server titles that are worth having. It focuses on breadth of topics covered rather than on the depth with which any one is treated, but Mr. Jennings has done an excellent job of fitting a lot of information into a single volume of manageable size. Note that I wrote a significant portion of this book, so my opinion is no doubt biased.

Microsoft Corporation, *Microsoft Windows NT Server 4.0 Resource Kit,* Microsoft Press, Redmond, WA, 1996.

This $150 kit includes three volumes—a Resource Guide, a Networking Guide, and an Internet Guide—which together cover material specific to the server version of the operating system. The bundled CD includes various utilities as well as online versions of the printed material. It also includes an online version of the Windows NT Workstation Resource Guide, which covers most of the material common to both versions of the operating system. Microsoft releases periodic supplements to this kit, each of which you should also purchase.

Microsoft Corporation, *Microsoft Windows NT Workstation 4.0 Resource Kit*, Microsoft Press, Redmond, WA, 1996.

This $70 package includes a 1,400-page printed version of the Windows NT Workstation Resource Guide and a bundled CD. The Resource Guide covers material common to both the Workstation and Server versions of the operating system. Although the server version of the Resource Kit contains this material on the CD, this kit is probably worth buying for the convenience of having the printed version.

Microsoft Corporation, *TechNet*.

This inexpensive subscription service delivers two CDs each month, which are crammed full of technical support documents, updates and patches, case studies, and so forth. It is available in a single-user version for $299/year, an unlimited single-server version for $699/year, and various international versions. TechNet covers all Microsoft software products, including Windows NT and BackOffice. Although some of the information included is also available on the Microsoft web site and elsewhere, you probably want this subscription if you support Microsoft software. For more information about TechNet, set your web browser to *www.microsoft.com/technet*.

Nagar, Rajeev, *Windows NT File System Internals: A Developer's Guide*, Sebastopol, CA, O'Reilly & Associates, Inc., 1997.

This is a complete explication of the NT file I/O subsystems. It covers the I/O Manager, Virtual Memory Manager, and Cache Manager, and it provides the nuts and bolts of implementing an NT filesystem or filter driver.

Russel, Charlie and Crawford, Sharon, *Running Microsoft Windows NT Server 4.0: The Essential Guide for Administrators, Systems Engineers, and IS Professionals*, Microsoft Press, Redmond, WA, 1997.

I have nearly 100 Windows NT titles on my bookshelves. This book—along with the Jennings title—has found a permanent home on my desk. This book is a practical roadmap for anyone who is developing a Windows NT network from scratch or upgrading an existing one. It focuses on planning, strategy, and organizational needs, and is intended to be an everyday handbook and reference that fits between the Windows NT Resource Kit and the official multivolume Microsoft training materials.

Thompson, Robert Bruce, *et alia, Windows NT Workstation 4.0 Internet & Networking Handbook*, Que, Indianapolis, IN, 1996.

This is another of my books. Although it focuses on Windows NT Workstation, much of what is here is equally applicable to Windows NT

Server. In particular, you may find the chapters on Understanding TCP/IP and the Internet and on Building a Network Infrastructure useful when building your Windows NT Server network.

Tidrow, Rob, *Windows NT Registry Troubleshooting*, New Riders Publishing, Indianapolis, IN, 1996.

The other of the two books available on the Registry. Again, this book is an updated version of the author's earlier *Windows 95 Registry Troubleshooting*, with new material added to cover the Windows NT Registry.

Microsoft BackOffice

Microsoft BackOffice is an integrated suite of components designed to function with and extend the capabilities of Windows NT Server. The components of Version 2 of the BackOffice suite include Windows NT Server 4.0 itself, Internet Information Server, Exchange Server, SQL Server, SNA Server, and Systems Management Server. Since the release of V 2.0, various other components have been added (e.g., Index Server and Proxy Server) and upgraded. (e.g., Internet Information Server 3.0 and Exchange Server 5.0). Some of the better books on various BackOffice components are listed below:

Benage, Don, *Special Edition Using Microsoft BackOffice*, Que, Indianapolis, IN, 1997.

This two-volume set covers Microsoft BackOffice thoroughly. Although many books are available that are dedicated to the individual components of BackOffice, this set attempts—and largely succeeds—to cover the BackOffice suite as a whole. Written by many authors, many of whom are consultants for the G.A. Sullivan company, this set is less fragmented than you might expect of a multiauthor book.

Kapczynski, Mark, *et alia, Special Edition Using Microsoft Exchange Server*, Que, Indianapolis, IN, 1996.

A comprehensive guide to installing and implementing Microsoft Exchange Server v 4.0. Provides limited coverage of programming and development issues.

Knowles, Arthur, *et alia, Microsoft Internet Information Server 2 Unleashed*, sams.net, Indianapolis, IN, 1996.

This is the best title I've yet seen on implementing a web server using Microsoft Internet Information Server. It is reasonably comprehensive, although coverage of some topics (e.g., ISAPI and IDC) is limited or missing. This book covers IIS 2.0.

Networking, TCP/IP, and the Internet

Until the release of IntraNetWare 4.11, Novell had largely ignored the Internet and TCP/IP, depending instead on IPX/SPX transport and server-based solutions for Internet access. If, like many NetWare 3.1x administrators, you need to get up to speed on TCP/IP and the Internet, the following books will provide a solid grounding.

Albitz, Paul and Cricket Liu, *DNS and BIND, 2nd* ed., O'Reilly & Associates, Inc., Sebastopol, CA, 1996.

> Everything you always wanted to know about the Internet Domain Name System (DNS) and the Berkeley Internet Name Domain (BIND) software, the UNIX implementation of DNS. If you're responsible for maintaining your company DNS servers, you need this book.

Hunt, Craig, *Networking Personal Computers with TCP/IP*, O'Reilly & Associates, Inc., Sebastopol, CA, 1995.

> Covers TCP/IP networking from the client side. Includes both practical foundation knowledge and detailed instructions for setting up TCP/IP network clients.

Hunt, Craig, *TCP/IP Network Administration*, O'Reilly & Associates, Inc., Sebastopol, CA, 1992.

> A system administrators' guide to installing and managing a TCP/IP network. Although this book has some age on it, and focuses on the BSD and System V UNIX host environment rather than the PC LAN environment, there is still a wealth of information here for anyone who plans to run a TCP/IP-based network.

Liu, Cricket *et alia, Managing Internet Information Services*, O'Reilly & Associates, Inc., Sebastopol, CA, 1994.

> An excellent overview of information services available on the Internet, including mail-based services, ftp, gopher, telnet, WAIS, and the World Wide Web. This book focuses more on concepts and design goals than on product-specific information, although some products are covered. This book is currently an O'Reilly sale item, indicating that a new edition is in the works.

Zacker, Craig, *et alia, Upgrading and Repairing Networks*, Que, Indianapolis, IN, 1996.

> This massive book attempts to cover the entire spectrum of PC-based local area networking, including hardware, software, and a fair amount of theory. Mr. Zacker and his many coauthors do a generally credible job of covering an

extremely broad subject. As you might expect in such a large collaborative effort, many topics receive less attention than they should, and there are more than a few errors. Still, if you're looking for a single book as a general networking reference, this is the best I've seen. Incidentally, I wrote Appendix C on RAID subsystems for *Upgrading and Repairing Networks.*

Internet Sites and Newsgroups

These are the Internet sites and newsgroups that I have found most useful in working with and maintaining Windows NT. I use some of them on an almost daily basis. All of them are well worth adding to your browser's bookmark list or your newsreader's subscribed groups list.

www.microsoft.com is the main Microsoft web site. Slow at times despite using multiple T-3 connections, this site is indispensable to any Windows NT administrator. It contains news announcements, patch files, technical articles, and numerous other items you'll need to access routinely. I have a shortcut to this site on my desktop, and so should you. To avoid unnecessary loading of top-level screens, you may also want to bookmark the Windows NT Server home page at *www.microsoft.com/ntserver/default.asp* and perhaps the technical support home page at *www.microsoft.com/support/.*

ftp.microsoft.com is the main Microsoft ftp server. If you know exactly what file you're looking for, you can often get it much faster from this site than from the web site, which sometimes provides throughput of only a few KB per second even when using a direct T1 Internet connection. I set the initial directory in my ftp client software to *ftp.microsoft.com/bussys/winnt* to take me directly to the Windows NT area.

www.bhs.com gets you to the Beverly Hills Software Windows NT Resource Center. This site includes a plethora of Windows NT resources. Most useful is a well-organized and frequently updated file download area, which includes both Microsoft patches and third-party programs and utilities. There are also numerous links to Windows NT consultants and programmers and to other resources.

www.stroud.com takes you to the Stroud's Consummate Winsock Applications home page. The CWSApps List covers numerous commercial and shareware Winsock applications, for both client and server. The site is updated frequently. It rates each product, and includes an in-depth review and links to the vendor's site.

http://www.entmag.com/ describes itself as "The Independent Newspaper for Windows NT Enterprise Computing" and is well worth bookmarking. This site includes a searchable archive of articles, product reviews, white papers, and resource guides. It also provides a file download section and subscription information for those who wish to receive the printed version. This is a controlled circulation publication, so a subscription is free if you qualify.

www.winntmag.com is the online home of *Windows NT Magazine.* This site includes searchable online articles, software, a vendor directory, and subscription information for the printed version of the magazine.

USENET Newsgroups. If you can put up with the low signal-to-noise ratio, the spamming, and the huge daily volume of messages, you might find one or more of the dozen or so newsgroups in the *comp.os.ms-windows.nt.** hierarchy to be useful. When you have a technical question, you will often find that posting it to one of these groups is the fastest way to get an answer. Even if you don't read a particular newsgroup routinely, you can mention that fact in your post and politely request that responses be directed to your email address. Most responders will honor your request, and post both to the newsgroup and via email to you.

Microsoft Newsgroups. In addition to the general USENET newsgroups devoted to Windows NT, a second collection of about 450 newsgroups is maintained directly by Microsoft. A dozen or so of these are devoted to Windows NT–related issues, including some (e.g., File & Print Service for NetWare) that have no direct equivalent on the USENET newsgroups. You can read the Microsoft newsgroups by pointing your web browser to the page *www.microsoft.com/support.* You can also retrieve them with your newsreader by pointing it to the NNTP server *msnews.microsoft.com.* Most of these newsgroups have moderate to high volume, and a relatively high signal-to-noise ratio.

B

Using Norton Utilities 2.0 for Windows NT

Ever since manufacturers began installing hard drives in personal computers in the early 1980s, Norton Utilities has been an essential part of any well-equipped PC toolkit. Data recovery tools like Norton Undelete have saved millions of wasted hours that would otherwise have been spent recreating accidentally deleted files. Performance tuning tools like Norton Speed Disk have kept computers humming along at optimum levels. Monitoring tools like Norton System Information have made it easy to organize, view, and understand the hardware and software configuration of a computer. Over the years, Norton Utilities has made administrators' lives easier and has also saved more than a few people's jobs.

Although competitors like PC Tools and the Mace Utilities have popped up from time to time, Norton Utilities has remained the premier computer utility toolkit. As the computing world has shifted from the DOS command-line interface to the Windows GUI, Norton Utilities has kept pace. These utilities are a lot prettier now than they used to be, but they still do the same essential jobs that they always did.

Until recently, those running Windows NT had little choice but to make do with the limited set of tools bundled with the operating system, because Norton and its competitors had not released versions of their tools for Windows NT. This was true for two reasons. First, the Windows NT market was so small that most utilities vendors focused their attentions elsewhere, primarily on Windows 95. Second, the architecture of Windows NT isolates applications—including utility programs—from the underlying hardware, making it much more difficult to accomplish the low-level editing and repair tasks that utility programs have traditionally performed.

With the release of Windows NT 4.0, Symantec recognized that Windows NT was poised to become a major player in the operating system market, and set out to port the flagship Norton Utilities to Windows NT. Their first effort, Norton NT Tools, was released in mid-1996, and was apparently intended as a stopgap solution to fill the hole until they could bring the necessary resources to bear to produce a full-blown version of Norton Utilities for Windows NT. Norton NT Tools, as indicated by its low $49 retail price, was very limited in scope and functionality. It was, however, the first general utilities package shipped for Windows NT, and indicated Symantec's interest in the Windows NT market.

The other shoe dropped in early 1997, when Symantec released the $99 Norton Utilities 2.0 for Windows NT, which for simplicity I'll just call Norton Utilities in the remainder of this chapter. Norton Utilities can be used on either Windows NT Workstation or Windows NT Server. This release closely resembles the current versions of Norton Utilities for DOS and Windows 95 in functionality.

With Norton Utilities, Windows NT administrators finally have a safety net. The rest of this appendix describes how to install and configure the Norton Utilities and use them to:

Monitor your server with Norton System Doctor
: System Doctor runs in the background, finding and reporting small problems before they become large ones.

Keep Norton Utilities current using Norton LiveUpdate
: LiveUpdate automatically checks for newer versions of Norton Utilities programs and data files, and allows you to download and install them automatically.

Fix disk problems with Norton Disk Doctor
: Disk Doctor automatically detects and corrects most types of hard disk problems on NTFS and FAT volumes.

Recover deleted files with UnErase/Norton Protection
: UnErase/Norton Protection extends the functionality of the Recycle Bin to protect all deleted files, including those deleted by network users.

Optimize disk performance with Norton Speed Disk
: Speed Disk provides the defragmenting utility that Microsoft left out, and improves system performance by defragmenting files and consolidating free space.

View server configuration with Norton System Information
: System Information collects and organizes data about every aspect of your server, and can print or mail reports to you based on this data.

Installing Norton Utilities for Windows NT

Norton Utilities will install and run on any computer that is likely to be running Windows NT Server. Symantec states minimum system requirements to be an IBM PC or 100% compatible; Windows NT 4.0; a 486 processor with 16 MB RAM; 25 MB disk space required for full installation; a double-speed or better CD-ROM drive; and 256 color VGA video.

To install Norton Utilities, insert Norton Utilities distribution CD in your CD-ROM drive. On most servers, *Setup.exe* runs automatically. If it doesn't on yours, run *Setup.exe* manually from the *\Nunt* folder on the CD-ROM disk. Setup displays a message box to notify you that Norton Utilities has not yet been installed on this machine.

If you choose to continue installing the product, setup displays the first screen of the Norton Utilities for Windows NT Setup Wizard. Enter your Full name and, optionally, the Company name. Setup next displays the Setup Type screen, which allows you to specify whether to install all or only part of Norton Utilities. By default, the Complete option button is selected, which copies all Norton Utilities programs to your hard drive, and requires about 20 MB of disk space.

If you want to install only part of the product, select the Custom option button. Setup displays the Norton Utilities for Windows NT Main Selection dialog. Specify the components you want to install, and click OK to continue. The Program Location screen allows you to specify where Norton Utilities will be installed. By default, setup installs Norton Utilities in the *C:\Program Files\Norton Utilities NT* folder. If you want to install it elsewhere, use the New location text box to specify an alternative folder.

Setup displays the Group Location screen, which allows you to specify which users should have access to Norton Utilities—only the current user or all users of this machine. The Install Norton Utilities for all users of this machine option button is selected by default. Select the Install Norton Utilities into your profile only option button if you want Norton Utilities group and startup items to be installed only for the account you are using to install Norton Utilities.

NOTE Selecting the Install Norton Utilities for all users of this machine option button allows any user logged in to the console of the local machine to use Norton Utilities, but does not make them available to users who connect across the network. Each client workstation that needs Norton Utilities must have a local copy installed.

Setup next displays the System Doctor screen. The Run Norton System Doctor when Windows starts check box is marked by default, which causes System Doctor to load each time you start the server. Clear this check box if you prefer to start System Doctor only manually. Setup confirms your selections and then copies the distribution files to your hard drive and processes Registry entries. After all files have been copied, Setup displays a series of screens that list support options, contact information, and online registration options.

Finally, Setup displays the Check for Updates screen. If the server has a modem or is connected to the Internet, Setup can use Norton Utilities LiveUpdate feature to connect to the Symantec BBS or FTP server, download the most recent versions of the program and data files, and automatically update the program. If you choose to update your files, Setup prompts you to choose between connecting via modem or the Internet, makes the connection, downloads the updated files, installs them automatically, and finally displays the Setup Complete screen. If you choose not to update your files, Setup instead displays the Setup Complete screen immediately. In either case, select the Reboot my computer now option button to restart the server and make Norton Utilities available immediately. Select the Continue my Windows session option button to defer availability of Norton Utilities until the next routine server restart.

NOTE If you chose not to update your program and data files during installation, the next time you restart your server, the Norton System Doctor Notification dialog appears to notify you that your virus definitions are out of date. This occurs any time those definitions are 35 days or more older than the current system date.

Monitoring Your Server with System Doctor

System Doctor, as shown in Figure B-1, is the core of Norton Utilities. It runs in the background, monitoring the system and reporting problems before they become serious. System Doctor also serves as a central control panel for the other applications included with Norton Utilities, notifies you when each of them should be run, and can even run them automatically as needed.

By default, setup configures System Doctor to load automatically each time the server is started. You can also run System Doctor from Norton Utilities NT program group of the Programs menu. The following sections examine System Doctor in more detail.

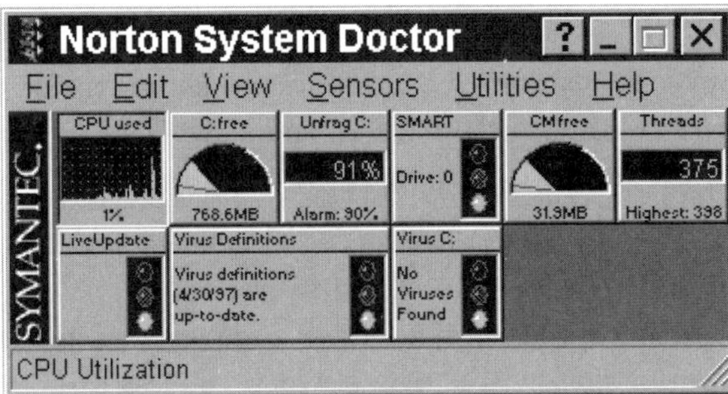

Figure B-1. System Doctor is the central control panel for Norton Utilities

Configuring Sensors

A sensor is an agent that monitors a particular aspect of the server and, when a problem occurs, generates an alert or takes corrective action. System Doctor uses sensors to monitor most aspects of your server, including the CPU and memory, the disks, and the network. By default, each active sensor is represented as an icon in the main System Doctor screen. System Doctor sensors are one of the following types:

Disk Sensors
: These sensors monitor disk drives and attempt to fix problems. Sensors are available to monitor Disk Fragmentation, Disk Slack Space, Disk Smart Status, and Disk Space.

Information Sensors
: These sensors gather information about the system. Sensors are available for Current Date and Time, Norton Protected Files, Norton Utilities LiveUpdate, and Windows Up Time.

Internet/Network Sensors
: These sensors monitor the server network connections. Sensors are available for Internet Packet Turnaround, Internet Speedometer, Network Reads Throughput, and Network Writes Throughput.

Memory Sensors
: These sensors monitor memory usage. Sensors are available for Commit Memory, Paging File Size, Paging File Utilization, and Physical Memory.

Performance Sensors
: These sensors monitor disk cache performance and various other Windows performance parameters. Sensors are available for Cache Hits, Cache Memory Utilization, Cache Throughput, and Performance Data. Individual Performance Data sensors are available for any of the performance parameters provided by Windows NT.

System Sensors

These sensors monitor general system performance and miscellaneous factors that are of interest to system administrators. Sensors are available for CPU Utilization, Threads, Users Connected, Virus Definitions, and Virus Scan.

With the exception of the sensors for Current Date and Time, Windows Up Time, and Performance Data, you can define an alarm for each System Doctor sensor. An alarm is triggered when the condition being monitored by the sensor reaches a specified maximum or minimum acceptable value. For example, you might define an alarm for the CPU Utilization sensor that triggers when processor usage exceeds 95%, or an alarm for the Disk Space sensor that triggers when free disk space falls below 100 MB.

When an alarm is triggered, it can notify you by displaying a message that suggests the appropriate corrective action, or by playing a sound that you specify. Also, if the sensor is visible in the System Doctor screen, its color can change to indicate that an alarm has been triggered. Some sensors can automatically take corrective action when an alarm is triggered, such as running Speed Disk to defragment the disk when the level of disk fragmentation reaches the threshold level you set.

NOTE If you want to generate an alarm based on a sensor, but do not want that sensor displayed in the main System Doctor screen continually, you can specify that the sensor be hidden.

Adding and removing sensors

By default, System Doctor displays a set of sensors that monitor what Symantec apparently believes are the most important system parameters. You can modify System Doctor to fit your own needs by adding sensors to monitor additional functions and by removing sensors that you don't need.

To add a sensor, select the Sensor menu to display a list of sensor types. Select Memory, Disks, System, Internet/Network, Performance, or Information to display a list of individual sensors of that type. Click the sensor name to activate it and add it to the main System Doctor screen. The main System Doctor screen automatically resizes itself as needed to accommodate additional sensors.

NOTE You can also add, remove, and configure sensors as described in the later section, "Configuring active sensors."

To remove a sensor, right-click the icon for that sensor to display the context-sensitive menu, and then click Remove. Note that removing a sensor not only deletes its icon from the display, but also deactivates the sensor itself. If what you really want to do is remove the sensor from the display, but leave it active so that it can generate alarms, you should hide the sensor instead of removing it. Hiding a sensor is described in the following section.

Modifying sensor properties

To modify the properties for a sensor, right-click the icon for that sensor to display the context-sensitive menu, and then choose Properties to display its property sheet. Which pages are available in a property sheet, and what is contained on those pages, depends on the sensor selected.

All sensors include the Style page; nearly all sensors include the Alarm page; most sensors include the Measurement page. Sensor types may include a page used only by sensors belonging to that group of sensors. For example, Disks sensors include a Drive page. Also, some individual sensors include special pages that apply only to that sensor. For example, the Virus Scan sensor includes a Files to Scan page. The remainder of this section uses the Disk Space sensor, which is fairly representative, for illustrative purposes.

Configuring sensor style properties. The Style page of the Disk Space sensor property sheet displays the current icon in the upper left. The Sensor Display pane allows you to specify the type of icon to be used for this sensor. Use the Type drop-down list to select among the available icon types, including Analog, Bar, Digital Counter, Histogram, and Stoplight. Not all icon types are available for all sensors.

Use the Sensor Size pane to select a Large or Small icon for the sensor. System Doctor uses small icons by default. For most sensors using most sensor display types, choosing a large icon simply occupies more screen real estate without making the sensor display more readable. However, some sensors, particularly those using bar chart icons, are more readable when displayed as large icons.

The Sensor Size pane also includes the Hidden check box. Mark this check box if you want the sensor to remain active, but not to be displayed in the main System Doctor screen. Marking this check box and setting an alarm for the sensor causes System Doctor to hide the sensor, but to notify you when a problem occurs.

The Sensor Scale pane allows you to control how sensor data is displayed by specifying the units of scaling or measurement and the "direction" to be used. For example, the Disk Space sensor can be set to display megabytes, kilobytes, bytes, or percentage, and can also be configured to display Amount Free or Amount

Used. The options available in this pane vary greatly between sensors. Some sensors provide no user selectable options here.

Configuring sensor alarm properties. The Alarm page of the Disk Space sensor property sheet, as shown in Figure B-2, allows you to configure an alarm for the sensor by specifying a threshold value, and the action to be taken when that value is reached. Most, but not all, sensors allow an alarm to be set.

The Alarm Settings pane allows you to enable or disable the alarm for the sensor, to set a threshold value that triggers the alarm, and to specify whether the threshold value will be displayed on the sensor icon. Mark or clear the Enabled check box to activate or deactivate the alarm for the sensor.

If you activate the alarm, use the slider bar to set the trigger level for that alarm, or enter a value directly in the list box immediately below the slider bar. Use the drop-down list to choose the units of measurement. If you want an indicator for trigger level to appear on the icon, mark the Show Trigger Level check box.

Use the Action pane to specify what action will be taken when the alarm triggers, by selecting one of the following option buttons:

No Action
: Do nothing when an alarm triggers.

Display Recommendation
: Display a message on the console to indicate that an alarm has been triggered, and suggest the recommended corrective action. If you choose this option, enter a value in the Repeat Every list box to specify how often the message should be redisplayed.

Repair Immediately
: This option is not available for all sensors, and appears only if the problem that triggers the alarm can be fixed by one of Norton Utilities. For example, setting this option for the Disk Fragmentation sensor causes Speed Disk to be invoked automatically when the amount of disk fragmentation exceeds the trigger level.

Repair At
: Similar to the Repair Immediately option, but defers automatic repair until the time specified.

Mark the Play Sound check box and specify a sound file to be used if you want an alarm that triggers to generate audible feedback. This option is grayed out and unavailable unless you have a sound card installed in the server.

Configuring sensor measurement properties. Use the Measurement page of the Disk Space sensor property sheet, shown in Figure B-3, to specify how frequently

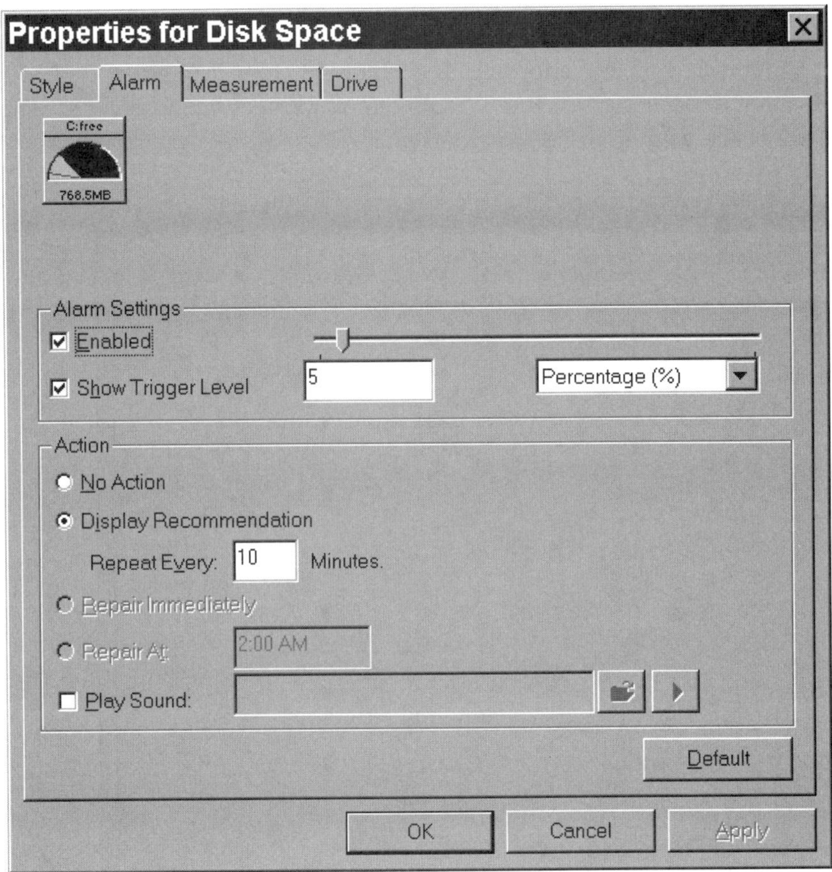

Figure B-2. The Alarm page of the sensor property sheet allows you to specify alarm settings, and the action to be taken when an alarm is triggered

the sensor is updated, whether measurements are instantaneous or averaged, and what maximum reading should be displayed.

The Time between Sensor Readings slider allows you to specify how often the sensor data should be refreshed. This value may be set within the range of one second and one week. The default value assigned to it depends upon the sensor, and is appropriate for the type of sensor. For example, the Disk Space sensor is updated every 30 seconds, whereas the Committed Memory sensor is updated every three seconds.

The Measurement Type pane allows you to specify how values are presented. Choose the Actual Value option button if you want to see the instantaneous value of the sensor. Choose the Decaying Average option button if you want to see an average over time for the sensor, with more recent values being given more weight.

The Sensor Maximum Reading pane allows you to specify what value should be used for the top of the scale. Choose the Let System Doctor Control option button to allow System Doctor to automatically determine and use an appropriate maximum value. Choose the Use Fixed Maximum option button and enter a value for Maximum if you want to decide for yourself.

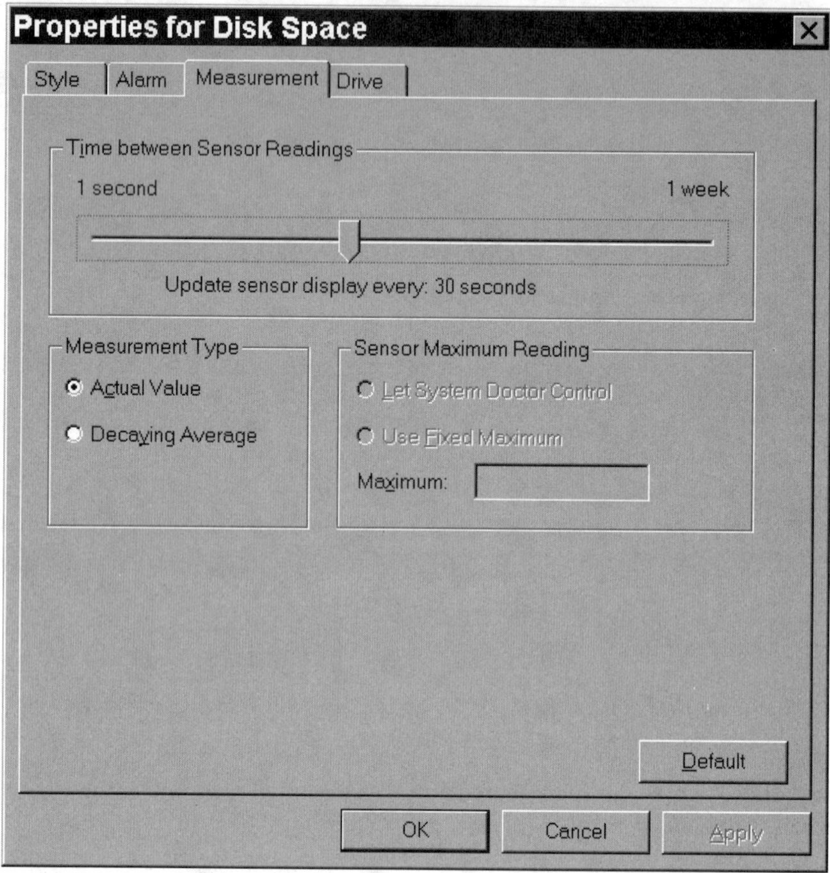

Figure B-3. The Measurement page of the sensor property sheet allows you to specify how frequently the sensor is updated, whether measurements are instantaneous or averaged, and what maximum reading should be displayed

Customizing System Doctor

System Doctor allows you a great deal of freedom in customizing its display and functioning. To configure System Doctor options, choose the View menu and then Options to display the Norton System Doctor Options property sheet. The following sections describe how to use this property sheet.

Configuring sensor appearance

Use the Sensor Appearance page of the Norton System Doctor Options property sheet to control the size and appearance of icons and other display elements, and to store alternative configurations for System Doctor, as follows:

- Use the Scheme drop-down list to save additional System Doctor configurations. Each scheme can contain its own group of sensors, and can be configured independently. For example, you might have one scheme that you run routinely to monitor server operation, and a second scheme that you run when you need to troubleshoot problems. To save a custom configuration as a named scheme, simply click Save As and follow the dialog.
- Elsewhere, System Doctor allows you to choose between small and large icons. If you prefer not to use this two-sizes-fits-all approach, use the slider bars in the Settings pane to set the exact icon size you want.
- Use the Item drop-down list to select a display element to be customized. You can select from Text, Graph Normal, Graph Warning, Graph Background, Graph Markers, Calendar, or Calendar Text. Click Color or Font to change the default value for the selected display element.
- Use the Bitmap Background field to browse for and select a bitmap graphics file (*.BMP*) to be used as the background.

You can cancel your changes for the selected scheme and revert to the default settings at any time by clicking Default.

Configuring window settings

Use the Windows Settings page of the Norton System Doctor Options property sheet to specify System Doctor startup options, to control how System Doctor is displayed, and to specify in what order the sensors are listed, as follows:

- In the Window Display pane, choose the Docked option button (and optionally mark the Auto Hide check box) if you want to display System Doctor as a taskbar. Note that the Windows NT Taskbar and the System Doctor taskbar must be located on different sides of the screen. Choose the Normal option button and mark the appropriate check boxes to display System Doctor as a normal windowed application.
- Use the Sensor Order pane to modify the order in which sensors appear in the main System Doctor screen. To reposition a sensor, highlight it in the scrolling list box and use Up and Down to alter its position. Sensors are displayed in the order they appear in this list, first from right to left and then from top to bottom.

- In the Startup Options pane, mark the Start Automatically with Windows check box if you want System Doctor to be run each time you boot the server. Mark the Start Minimized check box if you want System Doctor to start minimized in the System Tray.

You can cancel your changes and revert to the default settings at any time by clicking Default.

Configuring active sensors

Use the Active Sensors page of the Norton System Doctor Options property sheet to specify which sensors are to be active in the current scheme, and to configure properties for those sensors, as follows:

- Active sensors are listed in the Current Sensors pane. To add a sensor, highlight it in the Available Sensors pane and click Add.
- To remove a sensor, highlight it in the Current Sensors pane and click Remove.
- To configure properties for an active sensor, highlight it in the Current Sensors pane and click Properties to display the Properties for <sensor name> property sheet described in the preceding section, "Modifying sensor properties."

You can cancel your changes and revert to the default settings at any time by clicking Default.

Using System Doctor as a Control Panel

Installing Norton Utilities creates Norton Utilities NT program group on the Start button Programs menu. As a convenience for those who run it at all times, System Doctor also allows you to invoke other Norton Utilities components directly from its menu. To do so, display the Utilities menu and select a submenu or application.

Keeping Current with LiveUpdate

If your server is connected to a modem or directly to the Internet, you can use Symantec LiveUpdate to keep your Norton Utilities programs and data files updated. The LiveUpdate sensor periodically checks the Symantec web site or BBS, locates more recent versions of the Symantec programs you have installed, downloads these patches and updates, and installs them for you. How and when this process occurs, and whether the updates are installed automatically or only after you approve them is completely under your control.

You can run LiveUpdate from the System Doctor Utilities menu, or from Norton Utilities NT program group. The first time you run it, LiveUpdate displays the Configure LiveUpdate dialog. Mark the Preview phone number when connecting by modem check box if you want LiveUpdate to display the phone number (and allow you to change it) before it dials the Symantec BBS. This dialog is not displayed subsequently. Click OK to display Norton Utilities Update screen of the LiveUpdate wizard.

Use the How do you want to connect to Symantec drop-down list to select a connection method. The first time you run LiveUpdate, this value is set to Find device automatically, which attempts to detect a modem or an Internet connection. You may also specify Internet or Modem manually. After the first time, LiveUpdate defaults to the last connection method used.

NOTE If the LiveUpdate wizard determines that only one of these connection types is available on the server, it automatically configures LiveUpdate to use that connection. If it determines that both types of connection are available, it prompts you to choose the connection type. The default action is to use the Internet connection.

The LiveUpdate wizard displays the In Progress screen. A similar screen appears if you are using a modem connection to download updates from the Symantec BBS. After LiveUpdate establishes the connection, it compares the current versions of your files against the latest version available from Symantec. If it finds no differences, LiveUpdate notifies you accordingly and finishes immediately without making changes.

If LiveUpdate finds later versions of the files, it downloads them automatically, displaying the Retrieving Data status box to inform you of the Approximate Time Remaining, the Bytes Transferred, and the Total Bytes to Transfer. When the transfer is complete, LiveUpdate displays a message box to inform you that the updated files are being installed and that this process may take some time, typically 30 seconds or so at most. Depending on the exact files that are updated, LiveUpdate may or may not prompt you to restart your server to place the changes into effect. When the process is complete, LiveUpdate displays the final screen of the Wizard to notify you that the update occurred successfully. Click Finish to complete the update, and restart your server if necessary.

WARNING You might reasonably expect that running LiveUpdate would update all of your Norton Utilities files at the same time. This isn't the case. You must update your virus definitions as a separate step. To do so, right-click the Virus Definitions sensor to display the context-sensitive menu, and choose the Launch LiveUpdate menu option.

Repairing Your Disk with Norton Disk Doctor

Norton Disk Doctor is familiar to anyone who has used a recent version of Norton Utilities for DOS or Windows 95. Disk Doctor can diagnose and repair disk problems on FAT and NTFS volumes. You can run Disk Doctor from the System Doctor Utilities menu, or from Norton Utilities NT program group. You must log on with an account that is a member of the Administrators group to run Disk Doctor.

Configuring Norton Disk Doctor Options

Choose Options to display the Options for Norton Disk Doctor property sheet. The General page allows you to specify startup and surface test options.

Mark the Start automatically with Windows check box and select one or more drives in the Drives to Diagnose at Startup pane if you want Norton Disk Doctor to test the selected drives each time you start your server. Consider carefully before choosing this option. Enabling it can significantly increase the time it takes your server to boot. Mark the Enable Free Space Testing check box if you want Norton Disk Doctor to check only unused space on the drive.

The Appearance page allows you to specify appearance, sound, and custom message options. If you have a hi-color video driver installed, you can mark the Enable Animation check box, although doing so slows down the program, and accomplishes little else. Similarly, if you have a sound card and speakers installed on your server, you can mark the Play Music check box to add sound notifications to the text prompts.

The only really useful option on this page is the Show custom message check box, and even this option is helpful mainly for systems running Windows NT Workstation. You can use this option to display a custom message when a problem occurs, such as "Your hard disk may have a problem. Please contact MIS at extension 3012 immediately." To enter a custom message, mark this check box and click Edit to create or edit the message.

Using Norton Disk Doctor to Diagnose Disk Problems

To use Norton Disk Doctor to diagnose and repair disk problems, specify one or more drives to be diagnosed in the Select drive(s) to diagnose pane. Selected drives are indicated by a check mark in the box to the left of the drive icon. To both diagnose the disk and repair any problems detected, mark the Fix errors check box. If you want only to diagnose problems, and defer repairs until later, clear the check box.

By default, Norton Disk Doctor diagnoses disk volumes and reports any problems it finds. To have Norton Disk Doctor automatically repair problems, check Fix Errors on the main Norton Disk Doctor window.

NOTE Relative to Disk Doctor for DOS and Windows 95, Disk Doctor for Windows NT has a very limited ability to repair disk problems. This is not the fault of Disk Doctor, but is due to the fact that Windows NT isolates applications, including Disk Doctor, from the underlying hardware.

In order to make repairs, Disk Doctor must be able to reserve the volume for its own exclusive use. This is not possible if the Windows NT system files are installed on that volume; if a paging file exists on that volume; if any files are open on that volume; or if a command prompt is open and logged to that volume.

If you mark the Fix errors check box and Disk Doctor is unable to repair the volume for one of the reasons listed, it displays a message box to inform you of the problem, and offers to schedule a repair during boot the next time the system is started.

Click Diagnose to begin analyzing the selected disk drive(s). Disk Doctor displays progress as it checks the partition table, file structures, indexes, security descriptors, and optionally, the file data and free space. When the check is complete, the Test Results for Drive message box displays a summary of the test results. Click Details to view a more detailed description of the results, or if you want to print a report. Click OK to close the message box and return to the main Disk Doctor window.

Recovering Lost Files with Unerase/ Norton Protection

When experienced NetWare administrators first use Windows NT Server, they are invariably shocked to learn that Windows NT Server has no equivalent for the NetWare *SALVAGE* utility. Although Windows NT Server provides a minimalist undelete capability with the Recycle Bin, it is limited to recovering only files that were deleted using Explorer from the local console. Files deleted from a command prompt, or those deleted by users connected by the network to the server, are gone forever.

Clearly, something better is needed for a network file server. Unerase/Norton Protection is that something. Most Windows NT Server administrators will quickly find that this single function of Norton Utilities for Windows NT is worth the purchase price many times over.

NOTE Installing Norton Utilities modifies the Recycle Bin on your desktop, renaming it the Norton Protected Recycle Bin, and adding the Norton UnErase and Empty Norton Protected Files options to the context-sensitive menu. Although Norton Unerase works in conjunction with the Recycle Bin, it does not toggle the icon between the full and empty versions. If you have not deleted any files from the Windows NT Explorer since the last time the Recycle Bin was emptied, the empty icon will continue to be displayed, even if deleted files protected by Norton are available to be unerased.

Configuring the Norton Protected Recycle Bin

To configure the Norton Protected Recycle Bin, right-click the icon to display the context-sensitive menu and choose Properties to display the Norton Protected Recycle Bin Properties property sheet. The Desktop Item page allows you to specify the action that will be taken when you double-click the Norton Protected Recycle Bin icon. Choose one of the option buttons, as follows:

Norton UnErase Wizard
: Invokes the Norton UnErase Wizard in query/response format. You can instead display a list of files contained in the Recycle Bin by right-clicking the Norton Protected Recycle Bin icon and choosing Open.

All protected files
: Invokes the Norton UnErase Wizard in file list format, showing both Norton Protected files and Recycle Bin files.

Standard Recycle Bin
: Displays the Norton Protected Recycle Bin in folder view.

You can also modify the description associated with the Recycle Bin icon by changing the text contained in the Title box.

The Norton Protection page allows you to specify which drives will be protected by Norton, how long protected files will be saved, which file types will be excluded from Norton Protection, and how much of the disk drive will be allocated to storing protected files, as follows:

- Use the Drive drop-down list to select the disk drive for which you want to configure Norton Protection. Mark the Enable protection check box to use Norton Protection for the drive. Mark the Purge protected files after check box and use the spinner to specify a number of days if you want to purge older protected files based on their age.
- Click Exclusions to display the Exclusions dialog, where you can specify file types and folders that will not be protected by Norton. For example, you might exclude **.tmp* and **.bak* file types and the *c:\recycler* folder. If you exclude a folder, all subfolders are also excluded.
- Click Drive Usage to display the Norton Protection Drive Usage dialog, where you can use the slider to specify the maximum percentage of space on each protected drive that will be used to store Norton Protected files.

The Global page, shown in Figure B-4, allows you to specify whether Norton Protection will be configured globally for all drives, or individually for each drive. Choose among the following options:

Configure drives independently
: Choose this option button if you want to specify individual settings for each drive.

Use one setting for all drives
: Choose this option button if you want the setting that appears on this page to apply to all drives protected by Norton. Use the slider bar to set the percentage of disk space that will be allocated on each drive to storing Norton Protected files.

: Clear the Display delete confirmation dialog check box, which is marked by default, if you want to delete files without confirming each deletion. If you are using Norton Protection, this dialog is of very limited benefit, and should probably be disabled.

TIP Mark the Do not move files to the Recycle Bin. Remove files immediately on delete check box to disable Norton Protection temporarily on all drives. You might do this, for example, if you have a large number of files to be moved from one location to another or to be deleted permanently. Ordinarily, these files would be moved to the Norton Protected Recycle Bin, possibly flushing files that you would prefer to keep. Marking the check box allows you to do wholesale moves or deletes without swamping the Recycle Bin.

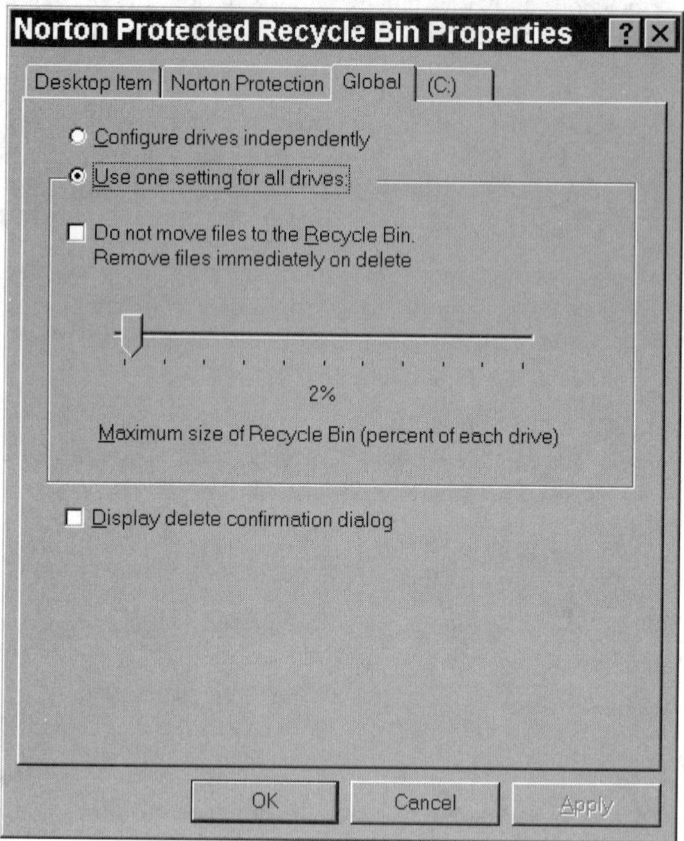

Figure B-4. The Global page of the Norton Protected Recycle Bin Properties property sheet allows you to configure Norton Protection globally for all drives or individually for each drive

The Norton Protected Recycle Bin Properties property sheet also includes a tab for each drive present on the server. You can use these tabs to configure properties individually for each drive if you have selected the Configure drives independently option button on the Global page. The options are the same as those that appear in the Use one setting for all drives section of the Global page, but apply only to the selected drive.

UnErasing Norton Protected Files

To retrieve deleted files, double-click the Norton Protected Recycle Bin icon to invoke the UnErase Wizard. The sequence of screens presented by the UnErase Wizard varies, depending upon how you have configured the Norton Protected Recycle Bin properties.

NOTE The first time you run the UnErase Wizard, it displays an introductory screen to explain Norton Protection. Clear the Show this screen next time you start the UnErase Wizard check box to prevent this screen from being displayed in the future.

If you specified the Norton UnErase Wizard option button in the property sheet for the Norton Protected Recycle Bin, select one of the following option buttons:

Find all protected files on local drives
: List every file that can be retrieved by Norton UnErase.

Find any recoverable files matching your criteria
: Display a dialog that allows you to enter a partial filename using wildcards, prompts you for the location of the deleted file, if known, and then displays all deleted files that match the partial filename.

After you have selected an option button (or if you specified the All protected files option button in the property sheet for the Norton Protected Recycle Bin), the UnErase Wizard displays a list of deleted files. Highlight one or more deleted files. You can use the standard Windows Shift-Click and Ctrl-Click conventions to select multiple files simultaneously. You can also click a column header to sort the files in ascending or descending order by that column. When you have highlighted all of the files you want to retrieve, click Recover to UnErase the file(s).

If UnErase is unable for one reason or another to recover the file, it displays a message to notify you of the problem. Otherwise, it notifies you that the file(s) have been recovered successfully and increments the Recovered counter at the lower right of the file list. The file list remains visible, allowing you to select more files for recovery. When you have finished recovering files, click Finish to save the recovered file(s) and exit the UnErase Wizard. You may instead click Next, but doing so merely displays a screen to notify you that the files were recovered.

Increasing Disk Performance with Speed Disk

The concept behind Norton Utilities Speed Disk is familiar to anyone who has used a disk defragmenting utility under DOS or earlier versions of Windows. As files are written to and deleted from a hard drive, those files may become fragmented. A fragmented file is one that is not stored in a single area of the disk, but is instead stored in multiple, noncontiguous areas of the disk.

Fragmented files are bad for three reasons. First, because the disk drive head must move further to read or write a fragmented file, fragmentation slows performance. Second, recovering deleted files from a fragmented drive is harder because the files are in many pieces. Finally, a heavily fragmented disk drive has to work much harder, making it more likely to die young.

A disk defragmenting utility like Speed Disk reorganizes fragmented files so that they are stored contiguously on the disk. It also reduces the severity of ongoing fragmentation by consolidating the many small areas of free disk space that typically exist on a fragmented drive into one or a few larger areas. The presence of larger areas of contiguous free space makes it much more likely that a file being written to disk can be written to a single block of disk space.

In the past, Microsoft claimed that the NTFS filesystem was not subject to fragmentation. Everyone pretty much had to take them at their word, since they did not supply a disk defragmenting utility with Windows NT, and there were no third-party disk defragmenting utilities available. Although it is true that NTFS minimizes the problems caused by fragmentation, NTFS is still subject to fragmentation. Speed Disk allows you to fix the problem.

TIP Speed Disk is just one part of Norton Utilities. If, however, a disk defragmenting utility is all you need, you don't have to buy Norton Utilities to get a good one. Download the free software DisKeeper Lite from the Executive Software web site at *http://www.execsoft.com*.

You can run Speed Disk interactively from the System Doctor Utilities menu, or from Norton Utilities NT program group. Click Start to begin the optimization process using the current options, or to restart it if it is paused. Click Stop to pause optimization, or Close to exit Speed Disk.

NOTE The initial display does not include the disk space map. You can click Show Map to display the map, or if the map is showing, click Hide Map to conceal it. You can also click Properties and then choose Legend to display an explanation of what each color in the map is used to represent.

You can also run Speed Disk as a scheduled task, or set it to run continuously in the background. Because, like the Norton UnErase Protection service, the Norton Speed Disk service installs and runs as a Windows NT service, it is always available.

This means that you do not need to leave Speed Disk minimized if you have scheduled optimization tasks or have chosen continuous optimization.

NOTE Server administrators always have two concerns about running a utility like Speed Disk on a production server—will it adversely impact performance, and, most important, is it safe? When set to its lowest priority, Speed Disk uses only idle time, and does not noticeably impact performance, even on a heavily loaded server. To test safety, I ran Speed Disk on a test server and pulled the power cord while it was operating. When the server rebooted, no data had been lost. It appears that Speed Disk fails safely.

Setting Speed Disk Options

Before you begin defragmenting your disk, verify that the Speed Disk options are set to your satisfaction. To do so, click Properties and then Options to display the Options for Speed Disk property sheet. This property sheet contains three pages, as follows:

Optimization Page
: Use this page to specify the drive to be optimized; whether Files Only, Free Space Only, or Both Files and Free Space are to be optimized; and whether Speed Disk should perform a Normal optimization, which does not pack the files, or a Thorough optimization, which packs the files to consolidate free space, but may require significantly more time.

Logging Page
: Use this page to globally enable or disable logging for Speed Disk, to specify individual logging options for events, and to enable or disable administrative alerts.

Resources Page
: Use this page to specify when and how Speed Disk should run. Choose Continuously if you want Speed Disk to run constantly in the background, defragmenting files in real time. Choose Number of Passes and use the spinner to specify a value if you want Speed Disk to run only when you explicitly invoke it. Use the Optimization Priority slider bar to assign a priority to the Speed Disk process, from low (Only When Idle) to high (Normal Priority).

Scheduling Speed Disk Operations

Speed Disk allows you to schedule optimization runs for times when your server is lightly loaded. To do so, click Properties and then Schedule to display the

Schedule dialog. Each scheduled task is displayed, along with when it is scheduled to run. You can modify the list of scheduled tasks as follows:

New
: To add a scheduled task, click this button to display the Schedule Task dialog. Select the drive to be optimized, and assign a unique Task Name. Click Options to configure the parameters to be used for this task, as described in the preceding section. Specify how often the task should be run—At Startup, Once, Hourly, Daily, Weekly, or Monthly. If you select Daily, you may click Select Days to specify the days of the week that the task will run. Specify a start time and, optionally, a stop time. Click OK to save the task.

Change
: Highlight a Task Name and click Change to display the Schedule Task dialog for the selected task. Make the required changes and click OK to save the modified task.

Disable
: Highlight a Task Name and click Disable if you want to temporarily suspend execution of that task, but not to delete it entirely. To reactivate the task, highlight its name and click Enable.

Remove
: Highlight a Task Name and click Remove if you want to delete it entirely from the list of scheduled tasks.

Viewing the Server Configuration with System Information

Norton System Information, shown in Figure B-5, presents information about various aspects of Windows NT and the hardware it is running on. System Information is the least useful of Norton Utilities, because it does little that Windows NT doesn't already do. Still, unlike Windows NT, System Information organizes the data in one place and presents it clearly as a property sheet, using tabs to group related information into pages. On each page, you can print Reports describing the information collected on that page. On the System, Memory, and Drive pages, you can click Details to drill down for more detailed data. Run System Information from the System Doctor Utilities menu, or from Norton Utilities NT program group.

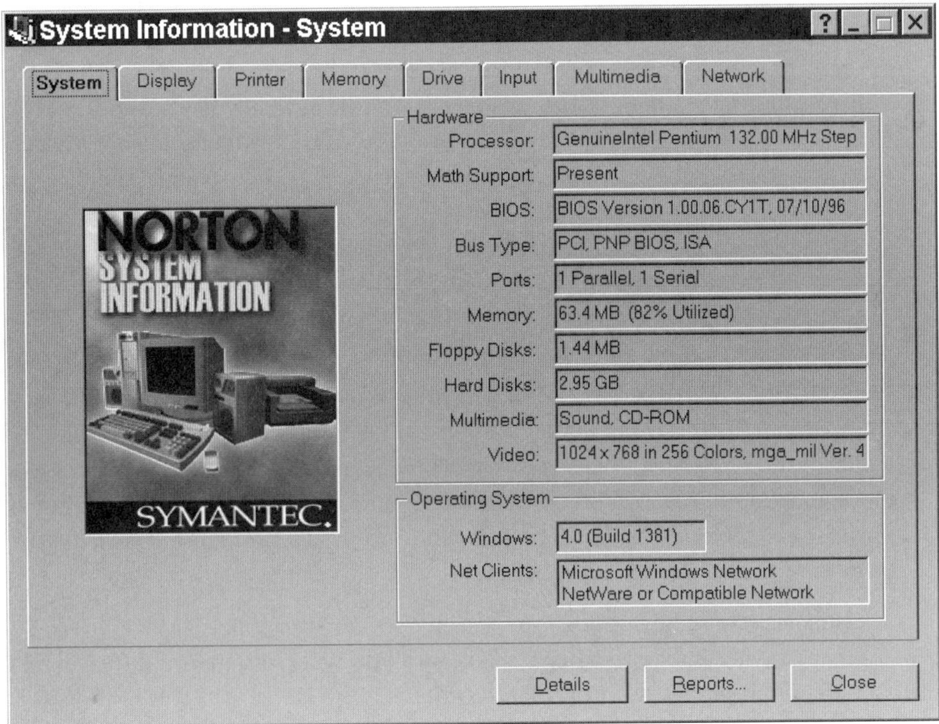

Figure B-5. Norton System Information organizes and presents information about Windows NT and the hardware it is running on

Adding the Functions That Symantec Left Out

Norton Utilities is an essential part of any Windows NT Server administrator's tool kit, but is nonetheless an incomplete product. Some of the utilities that were present in earlier versions of Norton Utilities for other operating systems are missing in Norton Utilities for Windows NT.

Anti-virus

Norton Utilities scans for viruses, but does not remove them. If System Doctor locates a virus on your system, you need a full anti-virus package to remove the virus. Two of the most popular anti-virus packages are Norton AntiVirus for Windows NT (*www.symantec.com/nav/fs_nav20nt.html*) and McAfee's Anti-Virus product line (*www.mcafee.com/prod/av/av.html*).

Sector Editor

Although few Windows NT Server administrators are brave (or foolish) enough to routinely use a low-level sector editor on a Windows NT Server volume, there are times when this is the only tool that will do the job. The Microsoft Windows NT Server 4.0 Resource Kit, available in bookstores, includes a usable sector editor and dozens of other useful utilities for managing Windows NT. Every Windows NT administrator should purchase a copy of the Server Kit, and keep it updated by buying the periodic updates. Note that the Server Kit is a supplement to rather than a superset of the Workstation Kit. Although the Workstation documents are included on the CD in the Server Kit, if you want a complete printed set of the Resource Kit, you must also buy the Workstation Kit.

Partition Editor

Unlike earlier releases, the Windows NT version of Norton Utilities does not include a partition table editor. The best third-party utility available for this purpose is PartitionMagic 3.0, available from PowerQuest (*www.powerquest.com/partitionmagic/30new.html*).

Norton Utilities forms the foundation of a general utility toolkit for Windows NT Server. Combine it with these other utilities, and you will have the right tool immediately at hand no matter what problem occurs.

Index

Symbols

A

B

C

D

G

H

K

L

M

N

O

Q

R

T

U

X

Y, Z

About the Author

With 25 years of industry experience, **Robert Bruce Thompson** was one of the first Novell Master CNEs, and has been immersed in Windows NT Server 4.0 since it was in alpha. Bob has written or contributed to several computer networking books, including *Special Edition Using Windows NT Server 4*, *Special Edition Using Microsoft BackOffice*, *Windows Magazine Windows NT Workstation 4.0 Internet and Networking Handbook*, and *Upgrading and Repairing Networking*, all published by Que Corporation. Bob is the president of Triad Technology Group, Inc., a Winston-Salem, N.C. network consulting practice.

Colophon

Our look is the result of reader comments, our own experimentation, and feedback from distribution channels. Distinctive covers complement our distinctive approach to technical topics, breathing personality and life into potentially dry subjects.

The animal featured on the cover of *Windows NT Server 4.0 for NetWare Administrators* is a lioness. The lion, *Panthera leo*, is a muscular, brownish-yellow cat that lives in social groups called prides, unique among wild cats. The pride consists of 5–35 members: 2–4 related males, 3–12 related females, and their young.

Female lions stand about 3.5 feet tall, and weigh 260–380 pounds. During the cool evening or morning hours, the pride's lionesses fan out and hunt together, but the dominant males eat first, after a successful kill by the females. Lions make the kill in about a quarter of their total attempts, and scavenged food accounts for 10–15 percent of their diet. When hunting, lionesses charge directly at their prey, and if they miss, will often quit and try elsewhere. Approaching zebra, wildebeests, and other potential victims at speeds of up to 35 miles per hour, lionesses use their weight, claws, and large paws to knock over and pin down prey before killing it with a strong bite. Lions can consume up to 15 pounds of meat in one sitting. They are asleep or inactive for most of the day. As lions are extremely social, they sleep in close contact with their fellow pride members.

Lionesses give birth to 2–4 cubs, after finding a safe, secluded birthing place away from the pride. The lioness rarely leaves her young offspring. They return to the pride after a few months, and the lionesses then share the responsibilities of raising and nursing their young. Cubs begin to hunt with their mother when they are a few months old, though they will not kill for themselves until they are about 2 years old.

Edie Freedman designed the cover of this book, using a 19th-century engraving from the Dover Pictorial Archive. The cover layout was produced with Quark XPress 3.32 using the ITC Garamond font.

The inside layout was designed by Nancy Priest and implemented in FrameMaker 5.0 by Mike Sierra. The text and heading fonts are ITC Garamond Light and Garamond Book. The illustrations that appear in the book were created in Adobe Photoshop 4.0 and Macromedia FreeHand 7.0 by Robert Romano.

Whenever possible, our books use a durable and flexible lay-flat binding. If the page count exceeds the limit for this type of binding, perfect binding is used.

Annoyances

Windows Annoyances

By David A. Karp
1st Edition June 1997
300 pages, ISBN: 1-56592-266-2

Windows Annoyances, a comprehensive resource for intermediate to advanced users of Windows 95 and NT 4.0, details step-by-step how to customize your Win95/NT operating system through an extensive collection of tips, tricks, and workarounds. You'll learn how to customize every aspect of these systems, far beyond the intentions of Microsoft. This book shows you how to customize your PC through methods of backing up, repairing, compressing, and transferring portions of the Registry. Win95 users will discover how Plug and Play, the technology that makes Win95 so compatible, can save time and improve the way you interact with your computer. You'll also learn how to benefit from the new 32-bit software and hardware drivers that support such features as improved multitasking and long filenames.

Word 97 Annoyances

By Woody Leonhard, Lee Hudspeth & T.J. Lee
1st Edition August 1997
356 pages, ISBN: 1-56592-308-1

Word 97 contains hundreds of annoying idiosyncrasies that can be either eliminated or worked around. Whether it's the Find Fast feature that takes over your machine every once in awhile, or the way Word automatically selects an entire word as you struggle to highlight only a portion of it, *Word 97 Annoyances* will show you how to solve the problem. It's filled with tips and customizations, and takes an in-depth look at what makes Word 97 tick—mainly character and paragraph formatting, styles, and templates.

This informative, yet humorous, book shows you how to use and modify Word 97 to meet your needs, transforming the software into a powerful tool customized to the way *you* use Word. You'll learn how to:

- Customize the toolbar so it works the way you want it to
- Reduce your stress level by understanding how Word defines sections or formats paragraphs and accepting some apparent annoyances that are built into Word
- Write simple VBA programs to eliminate your own personal annoyances

Excel 97 Annoyances

By Woody Leonhard, Lee Hudspeth & T.J. Lee
1st Edition September 1997
336 pages
ISBN: 1-56592-309-X

Learn how to shape Excel 97 in a way that will not only make it most effective, but will give you a sense of enjoyment as you analyze data with ease. Excel 97, which ships with Office 97, has many new features that may be overwhelming. All of the various toolbars, packed with what seems to be an unending array of buttons, might seem a bit intimidating, not to mention annoying, to the average user. *Excel 97 Annoyances* is a guide that will help create some order to the plethora of available options by providing many customizations that require only a few simple clicks of the mouse button.

This book uncovers Excel 97's hard-to-find features and tells how to eliminate the annoyances of data analysis. It shows how to easily retrieve data from the Web, details step-by-step construction of a perfect toolbar, includes tips for working around the most annoying gotchas of auditing, and shows how to use VBA to control Excel in powerful ways.

Office 97 Annoyances

By Woody Leonhard, Lee Hudspeth & T.J. Lee
1st Edition October 1997 (est.)
408 pages (est.)
ISBN: 1-56592-310-3

Despite marked improvements from version to version, much in Office 97 remains annoying. Two dozen shortcuts are scattered on the Start menu in no apparent order; the Shortcut Bar is filled with an overwhelming number of applications; and many hidden gems are tucked away in various places on the Office 97 CD. *Office 97 Annoyances* illustrates step-by-step how to get control over the chaotic settings of Office 97 and shows how to turn the vast array of applications into a simplified list of customized tools ready to execute whatever task they've been designed for.

This book shows you how to:

- Configure the Office Shortcut Bar to provide an effective tool for accessing Office applications and documents
- Use Visual Basic for Applications (VBA) as a macro language to control the behavior of the individual Office components
- Control pan-Office "sticky" settings

How to stay in touch with O'Reilly

1. Visit Our Award-Winning Web Site

http://www.oreilly.com/

★"Top 100 Sites on the Web" —*PC Magazine*
★"Top 5% Web sites" —*Point Communications*
★"3-Star site" —*The McKinley Group*

Our web site contains a library of comprehensiveproduct information (including book excerpts and tables of contents), downloadable software, background articles, interviews with technology leaders, links to relevant sites, book cover art, and more. File us in your Bookmarks or Hotlist!

2. Join Our Email Mailing Lists

New Product Releases

To receive automatic email with brief descriptions of all new O'Reilly products as they are released, send email to: **listproc@online.oreilly.com**
Put the following information in the first line of your message (*not* in the Subject field):
subscribe oreilly-news "Your Name" of "Your Organization" (for example: subscribe oreilly-news Kris Webber of Fine Enterprises)

O'Reilly Events

If you'd also like us to send information about trade show events, special promotions, and other O'Reilly events, send email to: **listproc@online.oreilly.com**
Put the following information in the first line of your message (*not* in the Subject field):
subscribe oreilly-events "Your Name" of "Your Organization"

3. Get Examples from Our Books via FTP

There are two ways to access an archive of example files from our books:

Regular FTP

- ftp to:
  ftp.oreilly.com
  (login: anonymous
  password: your email address)
- Point your web browser to:
  ftp://ftp.oreilly.com/

FTPMAIL

- Send an email message to:
  ftpmail@online.oreilly.com
  (Write "help" in the message body)

4. Visit Our Gopher Site

- Connect your gopher to:
  gopher.oreilly.com
- Point your web browser to:
  gopher://gopher.oreilly.com/
- Telnet to:
  gopher.oreilly.com
  login: gopher

5. Contact Us via Email

order@oreilly.com
To place a book or software order online. Good for North American and international customers.

subscriptions@oreilly.com
To place an order for any of our newsletters or periodicals.

books@oreilly.com
General questions about any of our books.

software@oreilly.com
For general questions and product information about our software. Check out O'Reilly Software Online at **http://software.oreilly.com/** for software and technical support information. Registered O'Reilly software users send your questions to: **website-support@oreilly.com**

cs@oreilly.com
For answers to problems regarding your order or our products.

booktech@oreilly.com
For book content technical questions or corrections.

proposals@oreilly.com
To submit new book or software proposals to our editors and product managers.

international@oreilly.com
For information about our international distributors or translation queries. For a list of our distributors outside of North America check out:
http://www.oreilly.com/www/order/country.html

O'Reilly & Associates, Inc.
101 Morris Street, Sebastopol, CA 95472 USA
TEL 707-829-0515 or 800-998-9938
(6am to 5pm PST)
FAX 707-829-0104

International Distributors

UK, Europe, Middle East and Northern Africa *(except France, Germany, Switzerland, & Austria)*

INQUIRIES
International Thomson Publishing Europe
Berkshire House
168-173 High Holborn
London WC1V 7AA, United Kingdom
Telephone: 44-171-497-1422
Fax: 44-171-497-1426
Email: itpint@itps.co.uk

ORDERS
International Thomson Publishing Services, Ltd.
Cheriton House, North Way
Andover, Hampshire SP10 5BE, United Kingdom
Telephone: 44-264-342-832 (UK orders)
Telephone: 44-264-342-806 (outside UK)
Fax: 44-264-364418 (UK orders)
Fax: 44-264-342761 (outside UK)
UK & Eire orders: itpuk@itps.co.uk
International orders: itpint@itps.co.uk

France

Editions Eyrolles
61 bd Saint-Germain
75240 Paris Cedex 05
France
Fax: 33-01-44-41-11-44

FRENCH LANGUAGE BOOKS
All countries except Canada
Phone: 33-01-44-41-46-16
Email: geodif@eyrolles.com

ENGLISH LANGUAGE BOOKS
Phone: 33-01-44-41-11-87
Email: distribution@eyrolles.com

Australia

WoodsLane Pty. Ltd.
7/5 Vuko Place, Warriewood NSW 2102
P.O. Box 935, Mona Vale NSW 2103
Australia
Telephone: 61-2-9970-5111
Fax: 61-2-9970-5002
Email: info@woodslane.com.au

Germany, Switzerland, and Austria

INQUIRIES
O'Reilly Verlag
Balthasarstr. 81
D-50670 Köln
Germany
Telephone: 49-221-97-31-60-0
Fax: 49-221-97-31-60-8
Email: anfragen@oreilly.de

ORDERS
International Thomson Publishing
Königswinterer Straße 418
53227 Bonn, Germany
Telephone: 49-228-97024 0
Fax: 49-228-441342
Email: order@oreilly.de

Asia *(except Japan & India)*

INQUIRIES
International Thomson Publishing Asia
60 Albert Street #15-01
Albert Complex
Singapore 189969
Telephone: 65-336-6411
Fax: 65-336-7411

ORDERS
Telephone: 65-336-6411
Fax: 65-334-1617
thomson@signet.com.sg

New Zealand

WoodsLane New Zealand Ltd.
21 Cooks Street (P.O. Box 575)
Wanganui, New Zealand
Telephone: 64-6-347-6543
Fax: 64-6-345-4840
Email: info@woodslane.com.au

Japan

O'Reilly Japan, Inc.
Kiyoshige Building 2F
12-Banchi, Sanei-cho
Shinjuku-ku
Tokyo 160 Japan
Telephone: 81-3-3356-5227
Fax: 81-3-3356-5261
Email: kenji@oreilly.com

India

Computer Bookshop (India) PVT. LTD.
190 Dr. D.N. Road, Fort
Bombay 400 001
India
Telephone: 91-22-207-0989
Fax: 91-22-262-3551
Email: cbsbom@giasbm01.vsnl.net.in

The Americas

O'Reilly & Associates, Inc.
101 Morris Street
Sebastopol, CA 95472 U.S.A.
Telephone: 707-829-0515
Telephone: 800-998-9938 (U.S. & Canada)
Fax: 707-829-0104
Email: order@oreilly.com

Southern Africa

International Thomson Publishing Southern Africa
Building 18, Constantia Park
138 Sixteenth Road
P.O. Box 2459
Halfway House, 1685 South Africa
Telephone: 27-11-805-4819
Fax: 27-11-805-3648